The Broadview Guide to Writing

A Handbook for Students

seventh Canadian edition

A Note on the Cover

For thousands of years humans have been likening the process of writing to the ways in which we interact with the land—ploughing and digging, sowing and reaping. In the early seventh century CE Isadore of Seville tells of how the Romans for their writing used styluses that were at first made of iron, later of bone, and quotes from a now-lost Roman play by the now-unknown playwright Atta: "we shall turn the ploughshare upon wax, and plough with a bone point." Around 1400 the German poet Johannes von Tepl begins his long poem *The Ploughman of Bohemia* with a reference to what he refers to as a well-known maxim of scribes: "the quill is my plough." In some sense the quill or pen is of course like a plough in that it digs into the writing surface. But the digging can also be likened more broadly to what writing does—as Seamus Heaney famously likens it in a 1964 poem about his father's digging and what Heaney himself will do with his "squat pen."

An image of ploughing, then, connects with the substance of this book as a metaphorical image of writing. But this particular image of ploughing connects in a more specific fashion to this particular writing guide: an extended discussion of *Landscape with the Fall of Icarus* features prominently in one section of this book, "Seeing and Meaning: How to Read (and Write About) Visual Images." The cover image is in this case also a reminder that writing is a matter of content as well as process.

The Broadview Guide to Writing

A Handbook for Students

seventh Canadian edition

Doug Babington, Corey Frost, Don LePan,
Maureen Okun, Nora Ruddock, and Karen Weingarten

Contributing Editor: Laura Buzzard

broadview press

Founded in 1985, Broadview Press remains a wholly independent publishing house. Broadview's focus is on academic publishing; our titles are accessible to university and college students as well as scholars and general readers. With over 800 titles in print, Broadview has become a leading international publisher in the humanities, with world-wide distribution. Broadview is committed to environmentally responsible publishing and fair business practices.

Library and Archives Canada Cataloguing in Publication

Title: The Broadview guide to writing : a handbook for students / Doug Babington, Corey Frost, Don LePan, Maureen Okun, Nora Ruddock, and Karen Weingarten ; contributing editor: Laura Buzzard.
Names: Babington, Doug, author. | Frost, Corey, author. | LePan, Don, 1954- author. | Okun, Maureen, 1961- author. | Ruddock, Nora, 1978- editor. | Weingarten, Karen, 1980- author. | Buzzard, Laura, editor.
Description: Seventh Canadian edition. | Includes bibliographical references and index.
Identifiers: Canadiana (print) 20220426309 | Canadiana (ebook) 20220426325 | ISBN 9781554815401 (softcover) | ISBN 9781770488120 (PDF) | ISBN 9781460407615 (EPUB)
Subjects: LCSH: English language—Rhetoric—Handbooks, manuals, etc. | LCSH: English language—Grammar—Handbooks, manuals, etc. | LCSH: Report writing—Handbooks, manuals, etc. | LCSH: Bibliographical citations—Standards—Handbooks, manuals, etc. | LCGFT: Handbooks and manuals.
Classification: LCC LB2369 .B23 2022 | DDC 808/.042—dc23

Broadview Press handles its own distribution in North America:
PO Box 1243, Peterborough, Ontario K9J 7H5, Canada
555 Riverwalk Parkway, Tonawanda, NY 14150, USA
Tel: (705) 743-8990; Fax: (705) 743-8353
email: customerservice@broadviewpress.com

For all territories outside North America, distribution is handled by the Eurospan Group.

Broadview Press Ltd. gratefully acknowledges the financial support of the Government of Canada for our publishing activities.

Canada

Cover Design: Lisa Brawn
Managing Editor: Tara Lowes
Design and Typesetting: Eileen Eckert

PRINTED IN CANADA

CONTENTS

HOW TO USE THIS BOOK AND ITS COMPANION WEBSITE

The goal of *The Broadview Guide* has always been to provide a comprehensive yet reasonably priced writing reference that is easy to use in every respect. For this edition we have made several changes in format that are designed to make the book better serve these goals. Many students and instructors have let us know over the years that they find ring or spiral bound books with cardboard dividers "clunky," and that books without a spine are hard to identify on the shelf. That may be a matter of opinion; beyond dispute is the fact that printing costs for special format bindings (such as the spiral binding with cardboard dividers that we have used for the past few editions of this book) have increased drastically in recent years. For the new edition we've chosen a format much closer to that of a traditional paperback (in appearance, and also in cost)—but bound using a recently developed type of binding called Otabind, which allows the pages to more easily lie open.

We've built in a number of features that we hope will make the book easy for you to find your way around in:

- Page headers: Book sections are indicated throughout in the headers for each page.
- Marginal tabs: For convenience, sections are also indicated with coloured tabs in the margin of each page—tabs that 'bleed' to the edge of the page to enhance visibility.
- Index: Go to the index at the back of the book to find the location within the body of the book for any topic, large or small.
- Table of contents: The detailed table of contents at the beginning of the book sets out sections, chapters, and topics within chapters.
- Section dividers: As well as being listed in the table of contents at the front of the book, the detailed contents for each section are listed on the section divider at the beginning of the section.

Companion website: The purchase price of *The Broadview Guide* includes free access to the companion website, where you will find various sorts of material related to this book. (If you have purchased a used rather than a new copy, you may purchase a passcode online through the main Broadview Press website.) Included on the companion site are the following:

- a wide range of exercises relating to almost every aspect of grammar and usage. Many of these are interactive; you can check immediately if you have answered correctly and—if you haven't—find an explanation. (Instructors may ask you to complete particular exercises and hand in your score sheet to them; but even if your instructor does not assign exercises for you to do, we encourage you to try them on your own—especially in areas that the Diagnostic and Review Exercises suggest may not be areas of strength for you
- information on the CSE Style of citation and reference
- additional sample essays
- a selection of expository essays, ranging historically from Montaigne to the present day; each is accompanied by questions and topics for discussion
- a selection of sample student essays
- sample business memos and business reports
- additional "Seeing and Meaning" materials
- National Variants: variants in English vocabulary and usage that are common in Australia, Britain, Canada, and the United States

This book does *not* provide certain features that you will find in most other writing guides and handbooks: glossy paper that is both expensive and environmentally unfriendly, and highlighting in many different colours throughout the book. We have added one accent colour, but we have no desire to add more—or to move away from our long-standing policy of using plain (and, as much as possible, recycled) paper stock. That's a choice that's good for the environment—and also one that helps us keep the price of this book at little more than half that of most other writing guides or handbooks.

If you have questions or comments about *The Broadview Guide* (or suggestions as to what else we should consider including for future editions, whether on the companion website or in the book itself), we'd like to hear from you. Just email <customerservice@broadviewpress.com>. Thank you!

PREFACE TO THE SEVENTH CANADIAN EDITION

As with every new edition, the seventh edition of *The Broadview Guide to Writing* has been fully updated throughout, with many small changes made. But there are also large changes; indeed, this edition has been revised and rewritten more fully than has been the case for any previous new edition. These are some of the changes:

- The book has been reorganized into three broad sections: writing processes, writing mechanics, and writing contexts.
- The material on researching and writing academic essays has been fully rewritten.
- A new sample essay in MLA style has been provided (on the topic of how to deal with public monuments honouring controversial figures).
- Coverage of personal and informal writing is included for the first time; the substantial new section includes a range of sample essays.
- The material on argument has been expanded and revised.
- Coverage of how to cite sources and how to integrate quotations into a research paper has been expanded.
- The "How to Be Good with Words" section (providing coverage of language and usage issues relating to gender, race, religion, sexual orientation, and so on) has been substantially revised and expanded.
- Throughout the book, material has been revised and updated.

As with every edition, the authors are indebted to many academics who have used *The Broadview Guide* with their students and who have taken the time to comment and to offer suggestions. We wish in particular to acknowledge the assistance provided by the following: Terri Baker, Mount Royal University; Ruth Bradley-St.-Cyr, University of Ottawa; Maria DiCenzo, Wilfrid Laurier University; Eileen Eckert; Dorrita Fong, Douglas College; Stephen Latta; Jonathan Lavery, University of Guelph; Kathryn MacLennan, University of Regina; Micaela Maftei, Camosun College; Robert M. Martin, Dalhousie University; Emily McGiffin, University of British Columbia; Sarah Waisvisz, Carleton University; Kevin Whetter, Acadia University. Warm thanks to all of you!

INTRODUCTION

When the second edition of this book was published in 2001, Diana Hacker's *A Writer's Reference* had established itself as the bestselling writing handbook in both Canada and the United States. "The Hacker," as it was almost universally referred to among academics and publishers, was a little dry, but it offered more comprehensive and more reliable information on the nuts and bolts of grammar and usage than did most of its competitors. And its sales were boosted immeasurably by its innovative format. Other writing handbooks were published as traditional hardcover or paperback books; "the Hacker" appeared in an innovative plastic ring binding, with stiff, tabbed dividers separating the sections of the book from one another.

Times have changed. Full-length writing handbooks that are *only* handbooks have become far less popular. Instructors who do choose a full-length book on writing increasingly look for one that provides *both* a handbook on the mechanics of grammar and usage *and* a wide-ranging guide to academic writing, as well as to a wide range of other "rhetorical situations"—as the publisher's description of today's most popular writing textbook, *The Norton Field Guide to Writing, with Handbook*, puts it. These instructors look, too, for writing guides that feature a considerable amount of material that students will find engaging to *read*—not just to consult for reference purposes.

The Broadview has a long tradition of offering a good deal more than "the Hacker" and other conventional handbooks by way of material on rhetorical matters. The long discussion of the writing process that opens the book has been widely welcomed, as have the chapters on "How to Be Good with Words" and on "Seeing and Meaning." With this edition, a substantial new section on "Informal and Personal Writing" continues that tradition. And, as befits a book that's designed to be read as well as referred to, we have changed the format of *The Broadview Guide*. Gone is the spiral binding; gone are the stiff, tabbed dividers. A paperback binding signals that this is a book for reading as well as for reference.

We know, of course, that no matter how fully it is read, the Broadview will also continue to be frequently consulted for reference purposes. With that in mind, we have chosen the distinctive

Otabind paperback format for this new edition. The Otabind process, developed in Finland, is designed to allow a book to lie flat rather more easily than does a book with a traditional paperback binding. As a paperback, it's in a more readable format than that of a handbook cluttered with heavy dividers between the sections. But if you are consulting rather than reading the Broadview—referring to it for details of MLA style, for example, as you work on an essay—the new *Broadview Guide* should remain open for you much more reliably than would a traditional paperback.

One other feature of the Broadview that has *not* changed deserves mention—our approach to price. Recent years have seen very considerable increases in printing costs. Had we retained a spiral binding with cardboard dividers format for this edition, we would have been forced to substantially increase the price of *The Broadview Guide*. The Otabind process, while slightly more expensive than a traditional paperback binding, is far less expensive than any spiral or ring binding with stiff dividers separating the sections. By choosing Otabind, we have been able to hold the line on price—indeed, to reduce the price of the book slightly. We have always striven to make the Broadview a text that gives full value to students for the lowest possible price; that tradition continues with the seventh edition.

WRITING PROCESSES

WRITING PROCESSES

P1 Getting Started

P1.1 Attitude and Voice

"The writing process" is a phrase often used, but most of us develop multiple writing processes—and the processes that work best will vary in different contexts. (The primary focus of this book is on academic writing contexts, though other forms of writing—including, in this edition, informal and personal writing—are also touched on.) Through practice, individual writers find the strategies that work best for them. Nevertheless, there are certain common assumptions and essential activities that most successful writers share; some generalizations are possible.

Much good writing results from a tension between two seemingly opposite impulses: innovation and convention. Innovation is fresh ideas, original insights, novel phrasing—it's what makes your writing new and interesting for people to read, and gives it a distinctive **voice**. But accepted conventions as to how the English language is used in various contexts pull in the other direction. Following these accepted conventions helps to make what you write accessible to your readers. Words work because people agree on their meaning. Similarly, conventions regarding **style** and **mechanics** allow readers to interpret your work and identify it as belonging to a particular context. Both innovation and convention are essential to most forms of writing.

> **Voice** can be thought of as the personality of your writing.
> **Style** refers in general to the way ideas are expressed. See P3.
> **Mechanics** refers to conventions such as grammar, usage, and punctuation. See M1–3.

When getting started on an academic writing project, it's helpful to keep a few things in mind. You are writing for a particular **audience**—members of a community defined by their interest in and ability to understand what you have to say—who expect you to communicate using certain conventions, including an appropriate academic style. You have an obligation to meet their expectations, but you have an equally important obligation to yourself: to put forward *your* ideas and opinions with precision and integrity.

One key to successfully putting forward your own ideas in writing is a mental **attitude** of self-confidence. The more confidence you can muster, the better able you will be to achieve a high level of control over the assignment at hand, the resources at hand, and the deadline that looms ahead. If no real confidence is felt to exist, then it's worth trying to manufacture it:

> "Three-thousand words in five days? Not a problem."
>
> "There are definitely ways in which Milton's verse disappoints me."
>
> "This professor of mine is about to really learn something."

Of course, establishing full control at the outset of the writing process is impossible. "How do I know what I think," wrote E.M. Forster, "until I see what I have to say?" The point is that writers see what they have to say—they start writing—only by believing in themselves. Some manufactured confidence at the outset will eventually lead to the real thing.

Weak writing can often be traced to attitudinal issues. Writers who lack all confidence often feel overwhelmed with trepidation as they view their blank screen. Writers who lack faith in their ability to develop their own perspective often worry too much about what the essay *should say*, and try to figure out what the instructor wants to hear. That sort of thinking leads to insincere and stilted writing. The fact is that university instructors usually want to hear *your* perspective, not a predetermined formulaic response. As one sociology professor advises her students,

How do I know what I think until I see what I have to say?
— E.M. Forster

> In writing the work, do not be afraid to give your own views. It is of considerable interest to the tutor to know what students think about the material, and especially what they think they have learned from the exercise. If you find material obscure or unconvincing say so, but always give the reasons.

Active and honest confrontation with an assignment, however tough that assignment may first appear, allows one's confidence, and one's voice, to grow.

P 1.2 Academic Style

Just as there are many academic disciplines, so too are there many academic styles. Here are a few examples:

> The reason toymakers have entered into the movie-making business is clear: the potential to create highly lucrative ancillary markets using product tie-ins, resulting in an "unprecedented synergy" between movie producers and merchandisers (Townsend, 2011, p. 56).
>
> Ellen Elizabeth Moore, "Green Screen or Smokescreen?: Hollywood's Messages about the Environment"

> People who complain about the homogeneity produced by globalization often fail to notice that globalization is, equally, a threat to homogeneity.
>
> Kwame Anthony Appiah, *Cosmopolitanism: Ethics in a World of Strangers*

> Why has Ophelia been such a potent and obsessive figure in our cultural mythology?
>
> Elaine Showalter, "Representing Ophelia"

> Rates of violence correlate with an abundance of young males within population groups. At least two large studies have suggested that countries with a larger population of young men are more likely to fight interstate and civil wars.
>
> Steven Pinker, "Why the World Is More Peaceful"

> When our civilization formed the views on the species barrier which it still largely holds, all the most highly developed nonhuman animals were simply unknown.
>
> Mary Midgley, "Is a Dolphin a Person"

> This paper presents new evidence on the effect of minimum wages on employment outcomes. We analyze the experiences of 410 fast-food restaurants in New Jersey and Pennsylvania following an increase in New Jersey's minimum wage.
>
> David Card and Alan B. Krueger, "A Case Study of the Fast-Food Industry in New Jersey and Pennsylvania"

Though these writers are addressing very different topics and writing within the conventions of quite different academic disciplines, we can notice points of similarity. In each of these passages of academic writing we can find words or phrases that do not occur frequently in most sorts of everyday conversation (*ancillary*, *homogeneity*, *cultural mythology*, *correlate*, *the species barrier*, *employment outcomes*), many of them abstract nouns. We may notice too the formality of the phrasing; contractions are not used, and neither are exclamation marks or emojis. Nor are there any slang or informal words. And, even in these brief excerpts, we can sense that each writer is in the process of making a case—of putting forward some form of structured argument.

Finally, we may notice that the claims being made in these academic arguments are typically evidence-based, and that—unlike many claims made in journalistic or popular writing—they are generally supported by sources. These may be primary sources (as, for example, when a historian cites a centuries-old document to support a claim being made about life in medieval Florence, or when a literary scholar cites a passage from a literary text to support a claim being made about the meaning of that text). They may be secondary sources—as is the case in the above examples. Moore cites Townsend, while Pinker alludes to "at least two large studies." Card and Kreuger, for their part, present the results of their own original empirical research. Even in more theoretical academic writing, the citation of sources is common practice. In a piece of journalism, one might generalize about the difference between Jacques Derrida's notion of *différance* and Homi K. Bhabha's notion of *cultural difference* without citing specific passages in works by either author. In a piece of academic writing on the same topic, one would be expected to provide specific references.

In all these ways, academic writing is at a very considerable remove from conversational English; a speaking voice has little in common with the voice of a piece of academic writing. As Louis Menand explains,

> speech is characterized by all the things writing teachers tell students to eliminate from their prose in the interest of clarity: repetition, contradiction, exaggeration, run-ons, fragments, and

> clichés, plus an array of tonal and physical inflections—drawls, grunts, shrugs, winks, hand gestures—unreproducible in written form. People talk for hours without uttering a single topic sentence. (94)

By contrast, writers of academic essays must deal with the necessity of topic sentences—and have no way of grunting or making gestures in the middle of a paragraph.

P 1.3 Audience

A strong and confident voice is the driving force behind any piece of writing, but it must be controlled and tempered by attention to audience. Competent writers realize the danger of locking themselves in to any set formulas of style or organization—because these things often change, depending upon the demands or expectations of a given audience. Different academic disciplines have different conventions for writing and for structuring academic work—as described later in this book. Beyond that, different instructors within a single academic discipline may favour quite different approaches to writing. What's a writer to do? Listen carefully, for one thing, and ask questions. Look over past essays written for similar audiences. Conformity to reasonable audience expectations does not mean slavish imitation. Ideas can be strong and original, and evidence can be compelling, even as a writer writes to please, say, the grammatical or bibliographical preferences of their reader-to-be.

Two examples from the world of academic publishing illustrate the sort of concessions good writers make to their audiences—and point out something important about essay introductions. Here are introductory passages from two articles, both of which appeared in publications aimed at general academic audiences. The first appeared in the science journal *Nature,* the second in *The New York Review of Books*. First, from "The Angelina Effect" by Dina L.G. Borzekowski and four co-authors:

> In May 2013, Angelina Jolie revealed in a *New York Times* opinion piece that she had undergone a preventive double mastectomy because she had a family history of cancer and carried a rare mutation of the *BRCA1* gene. Media coverage has been extensive, but it is not obvious what messages the public took from this personal

> health story. When celebrities reveal health narratives, their stories have the potential to stimulate public interest and awareness of illness or medical procedures, inspire others to face similar medical issues, and promote public health policy. Media coverage of celebrity cancer experiences has been shown to impact health service utilization and adherence to preventive health guidelines. [...] Given the intense media attention, this study was designed to examine immediate recall and public reaction to the story.

Second, from Garry Wills's "The Negro President" (an article summarizing for a wider readership the argument of his own book on the same topic):

> I have admired Jefferson all my life, and still do. [...] But I have now devoted an entire book to one deadly part of his legacy—the protection and extension of slavery through the three-fifths clause in the Constitution. That work depends on the general and growing labor of modern historians to grasp the pervasiveness of slavery's effects on early American history. I don't mean to join an unfortunate recent trend toward Jefferson-bashing. I disagree with those who would diminish his great achievement, the Declaration of Independence (Maier 1997). Or those who call him more a friend to despotism than to freedom (Cruise O'Brien 1996). Or those who would reduce his whole life to an affair with a slave. My Jefferson is a giant, but a giant trammeled in a net, and obliged, he thought, to keep repairing and strengthening the coils of that net. (45)

The authors of "The Angelina Effect" study public health and are used to writing for other scientists, while Wills is a historian, used to writing for other humanists. Not surprisingly, given this background, their approaches to writing introductory paragraphs differ. After clearly announcing their topic, the scientists explain the context of their research in neutral terms, avoiding subjective judgments. They use cautious language to limit their assertions ("it is not obvious," "have the potential to"). And they would be in trouble with the English professor who warns students against using the passive voice ("has been shown," "was designed"). The humanist also begins with a clear announcement of his topic, but that is where the similarity ends. He uses a first-person point of view and active verbs ("I have admired," "I disagree"). He immediately carves out the argumentative territory of his essay, stating his topic in his second sentence, and then summarizing a range of opposing views before presenting his own thesis. Wills would find more favour with the English professor who looks for a thesis statement in the last sentence of paragraph one.

Like most scientific writers, the public health scientists save their argumentative assertions—the answers to questions posed in the introduction—for the "Results" and "Discussion" sections of their article. Again, this bottom-heavy approach, which contrasts with the top-heavy approach of Wills, is related to the discipline the writers work in. Yet neither the public health scientists nor the historian ignores the wider profile of *Nature* and *New York Review of Books* readership; both publications have readers who may not be specialists in the topics discussed, and the writers strive to make their writing broadly accessible.

Certainly, the more diverse the audience, the more freedom a writer may enjoy in decisions of organization and style. Many college essay-writers tend to err, however, in the other direction: they envision an audience of one—namely, the instructor responsible for the assignment—and make assumptions about what that reader requires. For many students this can be very inhibiting: how do you write for a reader who knows the subject better than you do? Even if the professor may, in fact, be the only one who will read the paper, it is better to write for a broader audience—one's peers, but also other potentially interested readers—to avoid making the wrong assumptions or being inhibited in expressing your ideas.

P1.4 Purpose

Each writer requires a **purpose**—one that is more than the mere desire to earn a B+ from the instructor.

The stated assignment is an obvious place to begin. "Discuss the rise to power of fascist dictator Francisco Franco." Or "Thoroughly explain the advances in medical imaging since the beginning of this century." Or "Analyze the connections between Maya Angelou's poetry and her memoirs." Some writers may be limited only by the whims and dictates of their own consciences, but most receive orders or commands—Discuss, Explain, Analyze—from some external figure of authority—a professor or an editor or a boss. Such commands are usually quite vague and open-ended, though. It's enough to make an honest writer quiver and squirm:

> How am I supposed to discuss the rise to power of Francisco Franco? That could take years! And what is "Discuss" supposed to mean? Do I tell the story of the Spanish Civil War? Do I try to ascertain Franco's psychological makeup, or to analyze socio-economic influences at work at the time? What exactly does my professor expect from this paper, anyway?

If your instructor really cares about writing, she's probably hoping that her students will locate and try to resolve some tension. Purpose in writing typically comes from tension—from some conflict or uncertainty within the writer's mind, some clash that, as Janice Lauer puts it,

Purpose in writing typically comes from tension.

> ... engenders puzzlement, curiosity, a sense of enigma, sometimes of wonder, a pressure to restore equilibrium. While some people suppress such tension, the inquirer ... strives to resolve it by searching for new understanding, by going beyond the known. (90)

The "inquirer," then (to use Lauer's term), is interested in finding and exploring points at which there is tension. But how to locate such points if they are not obvious in an essay assignment? How to find something on which to build an argument that you will find engaging—and that can engage your reader? In this case, how might you give shape to your essay if you are asked to "discuss the rise to power of fascist dictator Francisco Franco"?

You could give such an essay a sort of shape, of course, simply by narrating a string of events from the 1930s. But that would be simply to recount Franco's rise to power, not to discuss it. To *discuss* something in an academic context means to deal with its shape. Going into the assignment, you might perhaps have little knowledge of Spanish history or of Franco. But you might well have some interest in the idea of power, or the ways in which political power is gained and the ways in which political power is wielded. And you might have some ideas about fascism and power. Is power an innately good or bad thing? Can it be both? Do fascists have a characteristic approach to power? Grappling with the tensions that surround the concept of power might lead the writer to a tentative statement of a main thesis for the essay: "Like most fascists, Franco saw power as an end in itself, not merely as a means to achieving other ends."

All of the above rests on the important assumption that the writing assignment is clear to the student. What if you are uncertain not only about what the professor wants, but also about what she means? After all, the language of assignments, like academic language generally, is often difficult. Here, for example, is how one sociology professor explained an assignment:

> The assignment involves learning to think sociologically and to present a sociological argument. The process involved is analogous to "inductive" reasoning (or what some sociologists refer to as "grounded theory") in that the object is to start from where you are and refine your thinking such that you develop general statements that represent the character of human social activity and that are capable of being treated with reference to empirical reality.

No student should be ashamed of asking for clarification here. In fact, it would be far worse to plunge blindly ahead, hoping against hope that your sentences live up to this description. Grappling independently with difficult concepts is central to anyone's higher education. Nevertheless, uncertainty and confusion may strike even the most experienced of writers. So always keep your lines of communication open. Talk over the assignment with fellow students, writing tutors, and teaching assistants, as well as with your instructor.

P 1.5 Focus

When student Robin Lee first received an "Effective Writing" essay assignment, they didn't know exactly what to write about. "Discuss and examine a case that raises issues of social or cultural importance in North America," the assignment read. "Include in your essay references to both popular and scholarly discussions of the issue." Robin knew that within the broad category of "issues of social or cultural importance in North America," there was a lot to choose from. Selecting a general topic came easily enough; Robin had always been fascinated by censorship and freedom of expression. From there, Robin needed to select a specific case, and not just because the assignment asked for it. They knew that their short essay might end up lacking depth if the **focus** was too broad. But what case should be the focus?

Robin had been very interested in several high-profile controversies concerning public monuments—including the 2017 removal in New Orleans of several monuments honouring Confederate leaders and the 2018 removal of a statue of Sir John A. Macdonald in Victoria, British Columbia. With regard to some of the issues involved, Robin felt genuinely torn. As a great believer in freedom of expression, they were reluctant to endorse the removal from public view (or the outright destruction) of works of art. But they were uncomfortable too with society honouring figures who embodied ideas that they thought of as morally repugnant.

They began, then, with a desire to sort out their own gut reaction. In other words, Robin Lee found a purpose by finding a focus. Exactly how Robin would sort out either their own feelings or the various arguments was initially far from clear.

P 1.6 Discovery

The final draft of Robin's essay, "Monumental Problems: Setting the Criteria for Decisions in Political Aesthetics," which you'll find on pages 658–92, is exactly that: the *final* residue of an intense thinking process, during which their original interest became focused on a specific topic, found a purpose, and eventually found articulate expression in a thesis and in the material supporting it. The sort of **discovery** process by which ideas are developed inevitably involves a good deal of thought; it also involves a good deal of reading.

The question of *what* to read is discussed later in Section P1.8 on research; just as important is *how* to read. It is essential to be able to read actively rather than passively—to make connections, to extend the ideas you are presented with, and to question those ideas. In the case of Robin Lee's research, it was important to look at the arguments presented by all sides and to weigh them against the evidence. And that, in turn, involves **taking notes**. Note-taking is a research tool, of course; paraphrasing key ideas from a text and copying useful quotations are essential activities. But note-taking can also help to transform reading into a catalyst for discovering one's own ideas.

Perhaps the most important principle in note-taking is to take great care to clearly label the words and ideas that come from your sources, so that you don't later confuse them with your own ideas and run the risk of inadvertently committing plagiarism. If you jot down a quotation, make sure you note carefully what book or article you are quoting (including page number as well as author and title)—and be sure to put quotation marks around the quoted passage so that you know when you look at it later that it *is* a quotation. Even if you are paraphrasing rather than quoting as you take notes, be sure to indicate clearly the author and title of the source you are working with. It's all too easy, for example, to just write "Foner" beside a note you make about slavery as you are working on an essay about the Underground Railroad, and then be completely unclear as to where it comes from when you look at it a week later. Is it from Eric Foner's *Gateway to Freedom: The Hidden History of the Underground Railroad*? From one of Eric Foner's many other books and articles on related topics? Or perhaps from the discussion of slavery in Philip Foner's *American Labor Songs of the Nineteenth Century*?

Another important principle is to read strategically. Rather than reading assigned pages straight through, first skim over the introduction, the lead sentences of paragraphs, and the conclusion. In other words, conduct a reconnaissance mission, based on your knowledge of the terrain found in most essays. The likely result will be an accurate sense of the essay's thesis, key terminology, range of evidence, and logical organization. You can then select passages for sustained and thorough surveillance, according to your purposes.

Reading as a reconnaissance mission.

Ideally, ideas will start to take shape in your mind as you read and take notes.

When it comes to shaping an essay of your own, though—even after you have begun to read extensively on the topic—you may well find yourself staring at a blank page and wondering how to fill it. Especially in the beginning, when the task at hand is choosing a topic or developing material for a thesis, an essay-writer's thinking may be quite unstructured. At this point, it's beneficial to play with ideas, to think freely, and to take rough notes based on whatever comes to mind. Rather than sit for hours mulling over an assignment sheet, better to put pen to paper or fingers to keyboard. This is where active brainstorming techniques come into play: simply listing ideas, for example, or writing random thoughts with no goal in mind.

Brainstorming Techniques

- **Free-writing** means writing whatever comes into one's head, without stopping, for a certain number of minutes, words, or pages. In this context, no idea is unworthy; the point is simply to write. A variation is "invisible writing": writing with one's eyes closed or the monitor switched off. The result might be mostly unusable—or it might point in intriguing directions.
- **Listing** can generate ideas in many different ways. Your list could contain examples, relevant questions on the topic, synonyms and antonyms, pros and cons, or simply any ideas that might be useful.
- **Visualizing** comes in many forms: doodles, maps, graphs, clusters, or webs of ideas. Ideas might be represented as branches on a tree or nodes in a network.
- **Seeing both sides** of a debate generates arguments and counter-arguments. You may begin with a strong opinion of your own, but playing devil's advocate will ultimately make your argument stronger.
- **Asking questions** is key to exploring the dimensions of an issue, even if you already have answers. One way to begin is with the journalist's six *W*s: Who? What? When? Where? Why? How? (That last one has the *w* at the end.)
- **Shifting perspective** can be important when topics are too familiar. Think about how you would address the topic differently in another discipline (as a scientist, say, or as a filmmaker). Or think about the issue from the point of view of a time, nation, race, or gender other than your own.

As your topic comes into focus, a bit more structure is needed; the writer begins working on the details of his argument. Of course, those very details may change as the writing process moves forward, but a solid foundation can still be achieved through the essential activity of **mapping**. Let's return to the example of Robin Lee. As their "Works Cited" list shows (pages 686–92), Robin read numerous articles, consulted several books, searched the Internet, and sought out images of a considerable number of statues in order to sort out their reaction to the issues raised in the various controversies over public monuments. With notes from this research, Robin was able to map out an essay yet to be written (see below).

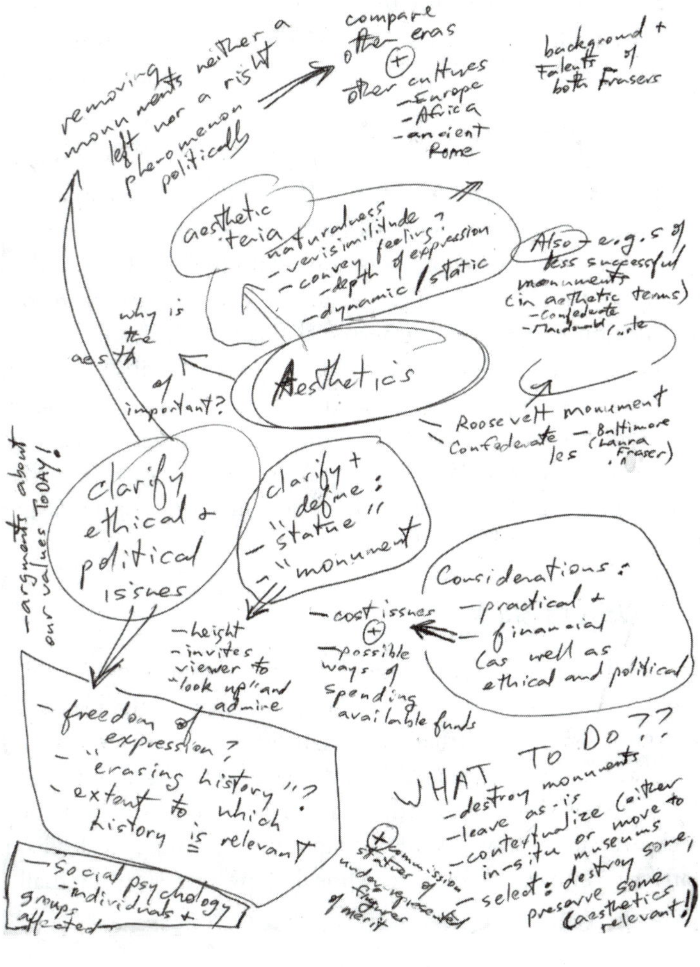

As Robin's work demonstrates, mapping allows the many threads of an argumentative essay to appear together for the first time on paper. They may take the form of a question ("What to do?", "'erasing history'?"), a key example ("Roosevelt monument"), or a sub-topic ("considerations: practical and financial"). All of them, however, connect ultimately to the biggest idea of all—Robin's thesis that aesthetic criteria should be taken into consideration in these controversies. Its importance on the map carries over to the final draft, as Robin signals at the end of paragraph one:

> This essay will examine issues of relevance from several angles, and will argue that one criterion in particular deserves to be considered more frequently—the aesthetic value of a work of art. Debates of these issues rightly include considerable discussion of historical, political, and ethical issues, but too often entirely neglect the aesthetic.

Reading, brainstorming, and mapping are essential activities that the essay writer can do individually. But writing rarely happens in a social vacuum, and **dialogue** with others can be a vitally important part of discovery. Talk about your topic with the people around you: classmates, friends, or family. You may also find it useful to start a conversation on your favourite social media website. For a major project, it's often helpful to make an appointment with your professor to review your plan and get advice. Another source for feedback and support is your university's writing or learning centre, if you have access to one. When your essay is still in its early, inchoate form, talking with a tutor can help focus your ideas or provide guidance to your research.

P 1.7 Writer's Block

Almost all of us know at first hand the frustrations of writer's block. One sits down to write, notes and map or outline at the ready. Then uncertainty strikes: "Perhaps my plan needs a bit more tinkering. What was it again that Smith and Sapsucker said about all this? Maybe I should go back and reread that passage. Maybe I should check over all my notes again—or take a few minutes to find some motivating music to listen to while I write this essay. Actually, a coffee might help."

Students aren't the only ones susceptible to writer's block. Often a professor will say, "I'm working on a paper dealing with such and such. It's pretty much done; all I have to do is write it up." The professor knows as well as the student that this is a convenient fiction—that the writing is the main business, not merely an afterthought. Sometimes, though, the task just seems too daunting.

How can the affliction of writer's block be avoided? The discovery tactics detailed above provide one antidote. Just force those keyboard keys to start clicking (or, for those with an appreciation of retro style, force that pen to move across the paper), quite literally writing anything that comes to mind, whether coherent or not, whether on or off topic. After ten or fifteen minutes, usable material will have turned up. The writing won't, of course, display perfect grammar, spelling, or punctuation—nor will it be organized into coherent paragraphs. But at this stage, none of that matters.

Once a writer has begun writing fluidly on the topic, it does *not* pay to pause when one hits a point in the argument that requires an example or a reference that's not handy. Instead, you should jot down a note in the margin ("find example—Taylor's book?" or "support this with quotation—gravediggers' scene?") and keep on going. There will be plenty of time later to check for the required item, and chances are that doing so now will mean losing the flow of the argument.

Eventually the moment comes to set down the pen for a few minutes and take stock of the words on the page or the screen: to decide how much fits in, and where, what needs fleshing out, what should be scrapped. It may be the time to start revising the map in the light of what's been discovered while writing. For, as every experienced writer knows, writing is *not* simply a process of putting down on paper what is already known in the writer's mind. The very act of writing forces the writer, inevitably (but often quite unexpectedly), to see things differently, to combine ideas in unanticipated ways.

P 1.8 Research

Regrettably, some university students approach research as an endeavour entailing nothing more than the finding and collating of old material on their assigned subject. The more imaginative and independent, however, will look to use others' work as a stepping-stone to new insights, seeking to arrange and examine what exists in order to present that which has never existed. Their essays' arguments are thereby strengthened through collaborative exposure to the work of others.

Consider the various ways in which Robin Lee draws on others' work. In paragraph 12, Robin takes issue with the arguments of Sathnam Sanghera, noting the inherent difficulties in "levelling the playing field" anytime soon in the way that Sanghera suggests. In paragraph 16, Robin draws straightforwardly on the work of Sinclaire Devereux Marber and of A.L. Freundlich in order to fill in the history relating to the Theodore Roosevelt Museum of Natural History monument. In paragraph 18, Robin draws on the comments of art history scholar Harriet F. Senie (and, in a supportive footnote, of Marber) in building an argument for the aesthetic merit of the Roosevelt statue; given the degree to which judgements as to artistic merit are subjective, it's particularly helpful for Robin's argument to be buttressed at this point by the scholarly authorities who can provide strong, collaborative support.

How do you locate strong, collaborative voices of this sort—voices that you can be confident are responsible ones, regardless of whether or not you may in the end agree with their conclusions? Search engines such as Google will turn up vast amounts of material on almost any topic—more than could possibly be taken account of in a single essay, perhaps more than could be read in an entire academic year. How do you choose? And how do you judge what is likely to be reliable, and what isn't? Below is some advice for finding sources, and then for sorting through the deluge.

P 1.9 Finding Sources

Let's follow some of the details of Robin's research process. An initial search for "monuments controversies" on Google returned over 12 million results. The first hit was a Wikipedia article. Though Wikipedia has often been disparaged by academics, it can be a very useful starting point for information on a topic that is new to you. Anyone can edit Wikipedia, which means it is susceptible to wayward opinions and misconceptions. It also means, however, that it is subject to intense collaborative scrutiny, and on many topics, especially in history and the sciences, its entries are likely to be as accurate as those in a traditional encyclopedia. In this case as in many others, Wikipedia served as a good source for commonly agreed-on facts. But after Robin scanned the article briefly, it didn't point her in any directions that she found particularly interesting.

Many of the other results from Robin's initial Google search were for newspaper reports on the various controversies. Several articles from *The New York Times*, *The Guardian*, and other reputable newspapers showed up on the first few pages of results. Robin found a long article in *The Guardian*—"Statue wars: what should we do with troublesome monuments?" by Tyler Stiem—particularly helpful in providing an overview of the topic. The article was not very up-to-date, and it didn't go into a lot of detail on any specific controversy; as a result, the article ended up not being included in Robin's eventual "Works Cited" list in the final essay. But it pointed Robin towards what seemed to be several of the most interesting controversies—including a number concerning Confederate monuments, several concerning monuments in honour of Canadian Prime Minister John A. Macdonald, and one concerning a monument to American President Theodore Roosevelt.

The monument to Roosevelt that formerly stood outside the Museum of Natural History in New York is one that Robin found particularly striking aesthetically. There seemed to be many articles on the topic—quite a number of them from *The New York Times*. Given that the controversy concerned a monument in New York and that *The New York Times* has the reputation of being among the most reliable of the world's newspapers, Robin naturally wanted to check out the numerous articles in that paper on the controversy. All those articles were listed on Google and easily findable—but Robin was only able to access half a dozen on the *New York Times* website before its paywall took effect (preventing non-subscribers from seeing further articles, and inviting them to become subscribers on a trial basis). Fortunately, Robin knew that there's another way; unlimited access to *The New York Times* (and many other newspapers and magazines) is available through almost any university library, once one has logged in using one's passcode.

By reading Wikipedia and various newspaper and magazine articles—and by consulting websites such as that of the American Museum of Natural History, which provided a good deal of background on the Roosevelt monument—Robin was able to get a decent picture of the facts of the case. But what about scholarly articles? Especially, what about recent scholarly articles?

You should be aware that most scholarly journals (and the electronic copies of most academic monographs) are not publicly accessible online. An article might be listed by your search engine but protected by a paywall, with only a brief abstract (or the first page of the article) publicly accessible. (A significant exception is JSTOR, which allows anyone to access at no charge a limited number of articles per month.) Besides, academic material is often given such a low score by the search engine's algorithm that you are unlikely to ever see it; most search engines put frequently consulted material at the head of the results—which means that popular astrologers or political cranks may rank far ahead of less flamboyant but far more reputable writers. For academic research, Google Scholar is an extremely useful supplement to the main Google search engine. But like Google, Google Scholar often gives you no more than an abstract or the first page of a scholarly article—just as Google Books (or Amazon's "Look Inside" feature) will typically provide only selected pages of monographs. It's worth making a note of anything that looks interesting and relevant in your initial search results—but to fully explore those articles and books, you'll need to gain access.

The best way to do that is through your institution's library. You can of course visit the library online from anywhere, using your identification number or passcode. Almost all university libraries today include a vast array of electronic material: newspapers, magazines, scholarly journals, and academic monographs that cannot be accessed without a passcode. And importantly, the library will have access to databases that let you search thousands of archived scholarly journals at once. These databases—there may be dozens available on your library website—provide more focused and comprehensive search capabilities than Google Scholar because they usually concentrate on certain fields. If you're not sure which one to use, ask your professors or a librarian about which databases are best for the research you want to do.

When Robin turned to Google Scholar as a search engine, and restricted their search to material from 2010 onwards, several promising articles popped up. Among them was an interesting-looking article entitled "Negotiating Strategies in New Orleans's

Memory-Work: White Fragility in the Politics of Removing Four Confederate-Inspired Monuments." When Robin tried to access the article directly, though, it turned out to be protected by a paywall; *Journal of Cultural Geography* is made available electronically through Taylor & Francis Online, a publishing group that sells access to a wide range of scholarly journals. The Taylor & Francis Online "Get Access" button leads to a page offering Robin several choices, including purchasing access to the article (for a fee of US $45.00). Another choice, though, is "Access through your institution." That seemed promising, and Robin typed in the name of their institution, "Vancouver Island University." What popped up then surprised Robin: "We could not find any result for Vancouver Island University." But maybe it shouldn't be surprising; VIU is a smaller university, and Robin was aware that its library wasn't able to subscribe to as many scholarly journals as large research universities routinely subscribe to. Maybe one really would have to pay a large fee in order to access the article. Just to be sure, though, Robin logged in to the VIU library in order to check if the article could be accessed there.

What to do when you're blocked by a paywall?

It was lucky for Robin that they did so; through the VIU library they were easily able to obtain access to the full article, at no cost. (Interestingly, there seem to be a great many universities in North America that the Taylor & Francis Online site says it cannot "find any result for," but which nevertheless do subscribe to many of its scholarly journals.)

Robin was also able through the university library to access a number of other scholarly works of interest—among them "The Original Plan for the Theodore Roosevelt Monument" (an article published in *Sculpture Review*) and *No Common Ground: Confederate Monuments and the Ongoing Fight for Racial Justice* (a monograph published by the University of North Carolina Press). One very useful long article turned out to be available through open access—"Bloody Foundation? Ethical and Legal Foundations of (Not) Removing the Equestrian Statue of Theodore Roosevelt at the American Museum of Natural History," published in the *Columbia Journal of Law and the Arts.*

For good reason, instructors usually advise students to focus on more recent material. But sometimes recent books or articles just don't provide all the information you want. Such was the case, for example, with the sculpture of James Earle Fraser; Wikipedia was helpful, but Robin wanted to know more about his work and couldn't find enough information in any recent books or articles—not even in two recently published books on the monuments controversies, Alex von Tunzelmann's *Fallen Idols: Twelve Statues That Made History* and Erin L. Thompson's *Smashing Statues: The Rise and Fall of America's Public Monuments*. When Robin removed any time filter in Google Scholar, though, they found that a 2001 book from an obscure publisher was prominently listed—*The Sculpture of James Earle Fraser*, by August L. Freundlich. It turned out to be a source of a good deal of information that didn't seem to be readily available elsewhere.

What if there seems to be little or nothing published on the subject? Perhaps it's an area on the border with one or more other territories; in that case, surveying those territories may be necessary. Perhaps it's a relatively new subject. It's always helpful to check the relevant scholarly indices as well, which aim to give a comprehensive list of scholarly articles in a discipline. Some of the most important of these for work in the arts and social sciences are:

- *Humanities Index*: covers articles published from 1974 onwards in such disciplines as English, history, and philosophy.
- *MLA Bibliography*: offers articles on the English language and literature as well as on French, German, Italian, Spanish, and so on.
- *Philosopher's Index*: the most comprehensive listing of articles on philosophy.
- *Social Sciences Index*: covers articles published from 1974 onwards in such areas as anthropology, economics, political science, psychology, and sociology.

These days, virtually all indices appear in electronic form. Keyword searches are indispensable for researchers: use a single word as your search term—or a combination of words—that you consider to be the "key" or main focus of your topic. The results will include sources that contain the keywords, usually in author, title, and subject heading fields.

Searching through Old Newspapers

Here's one small example of how difficult it can be for a novice to navigate the world of electronic research. Imagine you are doing an essay on some aspect of nineteenth-century British history and you would like to check out what the newspapers of that era had to say about a particular figure—the activist and inventor Lewis Gompertz, say. You might think of *The Times* of London and try to Google their archives. You would quickly find that, as with most newspaper archives nowadays, they are protected by a paywall. Luckily for you, a university library will often have a subscription to the *Times* archive. As long as you have your university ID and passcode you'll be able to access it easily—and utilize its very good search engine to quickly find electronic facsimiles of all articles mentioning Gompertz.

But what about other British newspapers of the nineteenth century? Chances are you won't find nineteenth-century archives for any other British newspapers listed in the periodicals section of your library's website. Don't give up! Do a little investigating. A Google search for "Victorian newspapers" or "British Newspapers 1800–1900" will point to the existence of "19th Century British Library Newspapers," a database that brings together dozens of different British newspapers covering the years 1800 to 1913. Back on your university's library site, you might find it under "databases." Like the *Times* site, it has an excellent search engine; once you are on the site you will quickly and easily be able to search those newspapers and check out all the articles in any of them that mentioned Gompertz at any time during the nineteenth century. And if your library doesn't subscribe to that database, it might well provide access to several other similar ones with a relevant focus—or to larger databases such as newspapers.com and newspaperarchives.com, both of which offer coverage of North America and some other areas as well as Britain.

If Google fails you in such situations, you still shouldn't give up. Ask your instructor or your university librarian. Chances are they will either be able to point you in the direction of what you want—or, at the very least, save you from hours of fruitless searching by letting you know that there is no convenient way to find what you'd like to find!

Basic Search Tips

Title or journal article

Omit initial article (*a*, *the*, *le*)

Type just the first few words

Use journal title for magazines, journals, newspapers

Author

Type last name first: *einstein, a*

Add first initial if known

For organizations use normal word order

Keyword

Results can include any of your words

Use "+" to indicate essential terms

Use "?" to truncate; use quotes for phrases: "*camp david*"

One further note about academic research: it's worth remembering that your academic library doesn't exist only in electronic form. It still has a physical location, where you will be sure to find a number of helpful librarians. Their job is to help you understand how to do research and do it well; they really can help. And most academic libraries also provide a great deal of material that you can touch and turn the pages of. It's worth doing that for at least two reasons. One is that the process of browsing in the stacks of the library can lead you to make connections and generate ideas in ways that don't always happen when you are searching and reading online. The second may surprise you: some important material is simply not available electronically.

Remember that your academic library doesn't exist only in electronic form.

That's not only true of certain books and articles from decades or centuries ago; it's also true of some very recent material. In a number of cases, academic journals are available on databases only after they have existed in print for several months or years (this is called a "moving wall," and it's a copyright measure). Before that, you may be able to access recent issues in electronic form if you subscribe to the journal—or you can visit a library that subscribes and has the journal in bound volumes. If it had turned out that their library did not have online access to needed journals, Robin would have asked a librarian for other options—such as which nearby libraries might be able to help. Ultimately, a researcher needs to calculate how much effort is warranted to obtain a single source.

P1.10 Evaluating Sources

Whatever combination of search engines you are using, chances are high that you will find far more material than you can easily deal with. How can you avoid spending a large amount of time merely amassing a large quantity of material, much of which may be unreliable or not relevant for your purposes? In evaluating which sources to use, the most important thing to consider—in a sense the only thing—is what the content of the source contributes to your argument. However, this is complicated by the necessity of sifting through sources before you've had a chance to read them, and by the fact that some citations will add to, while others will detract from, the credibility of your writing.

You should therefore consider several other factors. Some have to do with process: as your focus narrows and your argument develops, you will be better able to determine what material is relevant to your goals. You might want to start writing even before you have completed your research, allowing the writing process to reveal to you what sort of information you still need. Your research will also teach you which sources are reliable and relevant. Many researchers start by making a very brief list of materials to consult, working purely on the basis of what they know and what seems most relevant to the topic. Then, as they are scanning those materials, they will pay attention to which other books or articles are referred to most often by the authors; a work frequently cited by others is likely to be one you should be aware of. And, as you start to find articles and book chapters that are clearly relevant to the approach you wish to take, it makes good sense to consult the works that are cited in those articles and book chapters.

Consider, too, how timely the material is. For some research there is an obvious premium on more recent material, though this is truer in the sciences than in the humanities, and you should bear in mind that most recent is not necessarily best.

Also important is the reputation of the author. Is he or she an academic at a respected institution, and has he or she published widely on the topic? Big names in a given field often find their way into others' work, both because of the value of the research they have done and because their opinions carry weight. As you become more familiar with your subject you will recognize these names, and in some cases it will be obvious whom you should cite—it would be strange to write a paper on gender performativity without citing Judith Butler, or one on transformational grammar that doesn't mention Noam Chomsky, just as a paper on Marxism could hardly avoid referring to Karl Marx.

For certain sorts of research, another factor is point of view. If your topic is controversial, you will probably want to consult a range of different viewpoints. You are not, however, obliged to give equal weight to all points of view. Particularly online, implausible or downright irresponsible points of view are sometimes more widely available than are more measured opinions, even in matters of science. By the early years of this century, for example, the vast majority of reputable scientific opinion was in broad agreement about the dangers of global climate change. Dissenting scientific voices comprised only a small minority—but for years their views received disproportionate attention online, where numerous sites were largely devoted to casting doubt on the science of climate change. Citing both sides of a debate (or more often, multiple sides) is important when the debate is the point of the essay—but not when the debate is considered by almost everyone to be settled.

Implausible or downright irresponsible points of view are sometimes more widely available than are more measured opinions.

Whether a source is credible depends in part on whether it is scholarly. Does the work provide sources to back up its arguments, and is it possible to readily check the accuracy of those sources? Does it adhere to the conventions of academic discourse? Do other scholars recognize it as credible? It is usually easy to answer this last question, because scholarly publications have a built-in mechanism that certifies a source's credibility: peer review. The term "peer-reviewed journal" (or "peer-reviewed monograph," where a book-length academic study is concerned) refers to the publishers' practice of sending the submitted work of one researcher to respected academic authorities—the researcher's peers—to be vetted before the material is published. (The term "refereed" is often used in place of "peer-reviewed.") The process of peer review is far from foolproof, and often peer-reviewed journal articles or monographs will come to very different conclusions. But it is one important filtering device that can help separate responsible sources from irresponsible ones.

Most scholarly journals that are peer-reviewed will say so clearly in the masthead or on the website.

Where newspapers are concerned, it is better to cite "newspapers of record"—major papers with reputations for accuracy and integrity. In the US these include *The Washington Post, Los Angeles Times, The Wall Street Journal,* and *The New York Times* (for which the phrase "newspaper of record" was invented). In other countries where English is spoken the equivalents are newspapers such as *The Times, The Telegraph, The Independent, The Guardian,* and *The Economist* (UK); *The Globe and Mail, The Toronto Star,* and *The National Post* (Canada); *The Age* and *The Sydney Morning Herald* (Australia); *The Times of India* (India, naturally); and *Haaretz* (Israel). Though all these are reputable publications, it is also helpful to know that some (e.g., *The Wall Street Journal, The Telegraph, The National Post*) tend to be ideologically conservative, while others (e.g., *The New York Times, The Washington Post, The Guardian*) tend to be further to the left ideologically. Papers with smaller circulations may still provide accurate and important news, but they will be less universally recognized as credible sources.

The situation is similar if you are citing other sorts of news media; networks such as the British Broadcasting Corporation (BBC), the Canadian Broadcasting Corporation (CBC), the Australian Broadcasting Corporation (ABC), and Al Jazeera, for example, all maintain extensive and respected websites—while, in the other direction, Fox News is widely considered to be the least trustworthy of North America's major media outlets.

If you are uncertain about how reputable an academic source may be, consult your instructor. She will be able to tell you, for example, that *The American Historical Review* and *The Journal of American History* are both highly reputable, that *The Journal of Philosophy* is a much more reputable publication than is *Animus: A Philosophical Journal for Our Time,* and so on. That should not lead you to agree with everything you find in *The Journal of Philosophy,* of course—but it should save you some time in sorting out which articles are worth consulting.

You should also take account of the publisher of any book or article. From a scholarly point of view, publishers can be ranked by reputation. The most reputable are university academic presses, which are generally non-profit and have a stake in the accuracy of what they publish; some university presses are more prestigious than others. Academic trade publishers such as W.W. Norton or Routledge are considered highly reputable in certain fields. Books published by non-academic trade presses are generally not subjected to peer review and are therefore considered less reliable. Whether in bound or electronic form, a book from one of the world's most prestigious university presses (among them Oxford and Cambridge in the UK; California, Chicago, Duke, Harvard, Princeton, Stanford, and Yale in the US; Toronto and McGill-Queen's in Canada) is more likely to provide authoritative information than one from Pelican Publishing (a non-academic Louisiana publisher of books on politics, cooking, and various other topics) or from Sentinel Press (an imprint within the Penguin Group that dedicates itself to the promotion of right-wing causes). But at the same time, one should never take the reputation of a book's publisher as a guarantee of reliability. The university presses of Oxford and Harvard may be highly reputable, but even the most prestigious presses have published some real duds in their time. And, because librarians often have standing orders for all books from such presses, the chances of a dud finding its way onto the library's shelves or databases are good, compared to books from lesser-known publishers. Although the reputation of the publisher is a clue to a book's reliability, you should still read it with a critical eye.

With the growth of the Open Access movement, it is becoming more and more common for leading scholars and other reputable writers to bypass the traditional "gatekeepers" and post material online without it having been vetted beforehand by any process of peer review or assessment by publishers. There may often be significant advantages to this approach for both authors and readers: open access publishing makes up-to-date research available more quickly, in larger quantities, and from a wider range of viewpoints. It also reduces the undue influence that a handful of academic journal publishers have for many years exerted over the dissemination of research. But when you are checking out material published through an open-access publisher, you should be aware that not every publisher is alike. Open-access publishers such as PLOS and SSRN were founded by academics and are highly reputable. Even where there may be no formal process of peer review for self-archived pieces, basic vetting has been carried out, so articles by cranks and crackpots are few and far between. Some other open-access publishers, on the other hand, operate primarily through unsupervised self-archiving, where authors of any sort post their own work. Outstanding work may certainly sometimes be found on such a site, but it is likely to constitute a much smaller percentage of the total than it does on PLOS or SSRN. Outstanding work may also be found on websites or blogs unaffiliated with any institution—but as a general principle, material on a site with the domain name of an accredited university is more likely to be scholarly. (In some countries, accredited institutions may be identified by their Web addresses; in the US, the domain names of accredited universities and colleges end in .edu, and in the UK they end in .ac.uk.)

In the end, experienced researchers are willing to trust their own judgement: to glance at the table of contents and skim quickly through two or three dozen works on a subject and in each case make a snap decision as to its likely usefulness. These decisions are not, of course, irreversible; they may well find that one of the books initially set aside with barely a moment's notice is generally regarded as among the most important works in the field (in which case they will, of course, return to it with more care). Continued practice will make those snap judgements more reliable too, as one becomes more and more immersed in a rich intertextual collaboration with other scholars and writers.

The next step is to make sense of it all, and to make sense of it for others through writing.

P 2 Making Sense

P 2.1 Argument

Undergraduates are asked for many kinds of writing—a description of a lab experiment in one course, an autobiographical narrative in another. But most college essay writing is persuasive—writing that aims to present an **argument**. When people use the word *argument* in everyday speech, they tend to mean *a heated exchange of opposing views*—a type of argument that tends to be angry and loud and not very well reasoned. To speak of the argument of an essay, however, or of an argument made in a debate, is to use the word in a different sense: *a reason or set of reasons presented in order to persuade others.*

Here is the beginning of an argument in the first sense:

> A: I can't believe marijuana is still illegal in most of the world; how dumb is that?
>
> B: Said the stoner. You just want everyone to be as stupid as you are.
>
> A: You're the stupid one if you think marijuana makes you stupid.
>
> B: So go ahead, smoke your brains out. See if I care.

Neither person here is advancing arguments in the second sense of the word. They are making assertions, hurling insults, and ascribing motivations for the other person's views. But they are not providing reasons for what they believe—let alone putting a series of reasons together into a coherent whole.

For the argument of a persuasive essay, it is not enough simply to assert what you feel. An argument in this sense may be passionately advanced, or even scathing, but it is not angry; it aims to bring light, not heat. It explains what is involved and what is at stake. It draws distinctions and considers exceptions. It is alert for ambiguities and contradictions. It considers a range of different possibilities—often including hypotheticals that help to clarify the issues. It asks questions and suggests answers—and most importantly, it takes a position. It provides evidence, responds to objections, and draws a conclusion. In other words, it tries to convince the audience that its **thesis**—sometimes called the main point or even the main argument—is correct. This section explains how to craft an effective argument for your essay.

Argument: a reason or set of reasons presented in order to persuade others.

Thesis: the main point that an argument is designed to support. See P2.4.

First, though, let's take a closer look at how arguments work. Thousands of books have been written on this subject, so what we offer here is only a brief overview. The art of persuading someone with words—**rhetoric**—has been studied since ancient times (the word itself is derived from the Greek word *rhetor*, which means public speaker). Today, we often perceive rhetoric as somehow suspect, believing that mere words can hide the truth of a situation. But ancient Greek philosophers didn't see it that way: rhetoric was highly valued not just because of its power to persuade, but because they believed it helped develop, organize, and clarify thought. In academic writing, rhetoric has a similar role: constructing arguments helps writers home in on the truth as they see it. Awareness of rhetoric—recognizing when it's effective and when it's not, as well as when it's being used in the service of truth and when it's not—is an essential part of critical thinking. Successful arguments depend on this skill, and problems with student essays are often attributable to a lack of training in thinking critically.

Logos, pathos, and ethos

Aristotle, whose treatise *The Art of Rhetoric* is one of the foundational texts of the study of rhetoric, identified three kinds of persuasive appeals: *logos*, *pathos*, and *ethos*, or appeals based on reason, emotion, and character.[1] Emotional appeals alter the frame of mind of your audience through powerful, evocative language—like using patriotic slogans in a political debate. Character-based appeals attempt to convince your audience of your credibility and good will—essentially, you're asking the audience to trust you. There is a place for each of these in effective argument, but appeals based on reason have a special power: as long as we agree on the facts of a situation (which is never guaranteed, of course) and we apply valid

1 These different sorts of appeal are discussed at greater length in C2.9.6 below, in the section on Informal and Personal Writing.

logic, then reasonable people will agree that the conclusion must be true—which makes it pretty convincing. On the other hand, nothing sinks an essay more quickly than an illogical argument.

Rhetoric: the art of persuasion using words.

Logic: (derived from *logos*, which originally meant "the word") a system of thought that uses inferences to prove or disprove an assertion.

P 2.2 Logic

Logic helps us to understand which arguments make sense and which don't. In evaluating them, it helps to think of arguments as having formal parts—**premises** and **conclusions**. The premises are statements that are made in order to provide logical support for another statement—the argument's conclusion. In the following example, the first two statements are the premises; the third is the conclusion.

> When the economy is strong the ruling party always wins elections in this country. The economy as we approach the next election is extremely strong. Therefore the ruling party will win.

Notice here that if each of the premises is true, the conclusion follows logically—it *must* also be true. Arguments such as these, in which the truth of the conclusion is guaranteed by the truth of the argument's premises, are known as **deductive** arguments. In the example above, a conclusion is drawn from two premises—a form often referred to as a syllogism. Here is another classic example:

> Socrates is a human. All humans are mortal. Therefore Socrates is mortal.

Since most of us are more likely to put forward arguments about matters other than whether or not a particular human is mortal, it may be helpful to provide a further example:

First premise: *A successful baseball team must have good starting pitchers.*

Second premise: *This year's White Sox team does not have good starting pitchers.*

Conclusion: *This year's White Sox team will not be successful.*

Note that a deductive argument may be **valid** even if one or more of its premises is actually false. For example, you might believe that a baseball team can be successful without good starting pitchers. Regardless of whether you're right, the logic of the above syllogism is valid. However, if you can demonstrate that at least one of the premises isn't true, then you've shown that the argument isn't **sound**. To be sound, an argument must have valid logic *and* true premises. If it has both, we can be certain that the conclusion is also true.

The conclusion of an **inductive** argument, on the other hand, is not guaranteed by the truth of the argument's premises, but it is still convincing because it seems *likely* to be true—it provides not certainty but probability. Inductive arguments often generalize from particular instances to a general conclusion. Here is an example:

> Since the creation of the National League, every World Series winner has had at least three outstanding starting pitchers on its roster. It seems reasonable to conclude from this that a team with fewer than three outstanding starting pitchers has an extremely slight chance of winning the World Series.

In practice, arguments very frequently combine inductive and deductive elements; let's look at a couple of examples.

> Every poodle I've met has been friendly, so I suppose that all poodles must be friendly. Since all poodles are friendly, Maggie the poodle must be friendly.

The initial inference here is inductive; the general friendliness of poodles is inferred from particular observations of friendly poodles. We can't be certain about this general claim (in fact, some poodles might be unfriendly), but that doesn't necessarily mean that the inductive inference is unreasonable. If the general claim *is* true (all poodles are friendly), then we can be certain that Maggie is friendly, given that she is a poodle. This second inference is deductive because the conclusion must be true if the premises are true.

> I looked at the stats beforehand. Almost no one ever dies from this sort of operation, so there seemed to be no chance Frank would die. And yet he *did die* during the operation. It must be a case of malpractice on the part of the surgeons!

This is an argument that draws on both inductive and deductive reasoning—and that has multiple problems. The fact that very few people die during a particular procedure, of course, creates a probability for anyone about to undergo that procedure themselves—but not a certainty. A further problem is that the argument relies on a questionable unstated premise: that the few patients who did not survive were all victims of malpractice. This is not necessarily true—they might have died from factors beyond the doctors' control.

The preceding examples remind us of the importance, in logic, of the distinction between **some** and **all**. If you meet a few friendly poodles, you can be sure that "some poodles are friendly." If you meet many, many such poodles, you might even make the reasonable inductive inference that "all poodles are friendly." But it only takes one snooty poodle to disprove the generalization. This may seem an obvious point, but it is easy to lose track of in the twists and turns of an argument—or, indeed, in making offhand observations about things that seem self-evident:

> I asked some female hockey players if they wanted to play in the men's league and they said 'no.' Why should we open up the league to women if they don't even want to play?

The fact that *some* women don't want to play in the men's league doesn't imply that *no* women want to play in the men's league. The inductive inference in this case is based on insufficient evidence.

Similarly, illogical arguments can sometimes obscure the truth with a focus on just one side of the picture, or one sort of evidence. Especially in complex matters involving **numbers** and trends, it is easy to lose sight of the full picture. Here is an example:

> Even many of those who support the proposed climate change treaty say that it will cost jobs in industries ranging from oil and gas to mining to automobile manufacturing—perhaps hundreds of thousands of jobs. We cannot afford to let our economy shrink; it is essential that we oppose ratification of this treaty.

An unstated premise in this argument is that if jobs are lost in the stated sectors, the economy shrinks. But no estimate is given of the number of jobs that would be *created* if strong action were taken against climate change (in industries such as solar and wind power) or of industries that would be lost through *inaction* (because of the effects of climate change on agriculture, tourism, etc.). In reality, some experts estimate that the economy would grow just as fast if such action were taken, while others estimate it would grow more slowly, but few have suggested it would actually shrink. Here, as in many other cases, it is important to understand what exactly a trend signifies: the difference, for example, between a decline in the economy and a decline in the rate of growth of the economy. A saying popularized by Mark Twain goes, "There are three kinds of lies: lies, damned lies, and statistics." Another way of saying this is that the use of numbers as evidence can be misleading unless the context and meaning are clear.

One more type of logical pitfall is relying on irrelevant assertions—and it is often more difficult than one would think to judge what is relevant or irrelevant to a given argument. Here is an example:

> I don't agree with spending money on foreign aid. Before we worry about the troubles of people halfway round the world, we should take care of the problems people have here at home.

At first glance, the concluding statement here may seem to be a quite powerful argument against foreign aid. But the argument relies on the assumption that foreign aid precludes domestic aid, that we can't do both at the same time. In reality, no supporter of foreign aid would argue that we should help abroad *instead* of helping at home. What this writer actually seems to take issue with is the idea that we should pay *any* attention to the plight of those far away. In effect, the passage argues that we should *never* provide help to other countries as long as there are *any* problems in this country. Suddenly the argument seems a lot weaker. It seems to want to distract us from the question (Should we provide foreign aid?) by bringing up an unrelated question (Should we take care of domestic problems?). There are a variety of important issues that could be debated about a foreign aid program—whether it is necessary, whether it is effective, whether we have a moral obligation to help. Instead, our attention is redirected to an issue that is essentially a *non sequitur*.

These examples—in which *some* and *all* are confused, numbers are used misleadingly, and irrelevant points are made—demonstrate just some of the ways that arguments go bad. In the next section we'll look at a few of the classic bad arguments known as logical fallacies.

"We Are Omnivores": A Case Study in Argument

Here's a little case study in argument, on the topic of human and non-human animals. It starts with a letter to *The New York Review of Books* from reader Christof Koch, complaining that, in a December 19, 2013 article discussing extreme eating ("Food Tips for Christmas"), writer Jason Epstein makes no mention of the suffering of the non-human animals. Koch put it in this way in his letter ("The Pain of Animals," 6 February 2014):

> the penises, brains, hearts, and whole embryos that are now *de rigueur* to consume by our *haute cuisine* establishment derive from sentient creatures. These animals are all capable of sophisticated behaviors that, when they occur in people, are associated with empathy, attachment, curiosity, metacognition, and conscious awareness. Maybe even food writers and their critics can acknowledge this.

The New York Review of Books also printed a response from Epstein. He *might* have responded to Koch's letter simply by saying that food writers reviewing steakhouses or sushi restaurants are not expected to discuss the fact that much of the food consumed in such establishments comes from sentient creatures. Why should an article discussing the human consumption of less-frequently eaten parts of the same animals be any different? Would that have been a fair response, focused on questions of relevance?

Instead, Epstein responded in this way:

> We are omnivores. We eat anything edible, including ourselves. I deeply regret the suffering of animals but there are not enough vegetarians to solve the problem. Even Adolf Hitler, a vegetarian himself according to his intimates, with absolute power over those in his net, could do nothing to prevent this pain. I wish it were different but we are what we are.

There are several questions that may fairly be asked about the lines of argument Epstein uses here. For example, are humans *necessarily* omnivores? Cows are necessarily herbivores and cats are necessarily carnivores, but do humans have to eat meat?

Epstein is making an appeal to nature by suggesting that our diet is an innate behaviour, something we can't change about ourselves. The good health of most vegans suggests otherwise, as does the fact that in a great deal of the world (most of India, for example) most people are vegetarian. Also, how relevant is it that humans are capable of eating other humans? Does it strengthen Epstein's case or weaken it? What about the mention of Hitler? Hitler did not in fact make any effort to impose his own vegetarianism on others. Is it relevant? What effect is it supposed to have?

How many different ways does Epstein use rhetoric in these five sentences? Does he use *logos*? *Pathos*? *Ethos*? Does his argument fall into any logical fallacies?

P 2.3 Fallacies

A fallacious argument is one that suffers from faulty reasoning. Many forms of faulty reasoning have been identified and categorized in great detail; what follows is a short list of some of the most common ones. You may have heard some of these terms before, and it's worth knowing what they mean, but it's even more important to understand why these aren't sound arguments.

Ad hominem fallacy. The Latin *ad hominem* means *directed at the person*—this type of argument attacks the person making the claim rather than the claim itself. In both the following examples, the information supplied may be of interest, but it has no bearing on whether the positions being critiqued have merit:

> Nothing that George W. Bush has ever said about energy policy should be trusted. Remember, he made a fortune in the oil industry.

> John Kerry criticizes companies that send jobs overseas, but his own wife's fortune comes from the Heinz company, which has factories overseas.

Straw figure fallacy. A common practice in argument is to ascribe to one's opponent an exaggerated, extreme view that is easy to knock down (a "straw figure"), rather than addressing the more moderate view that the opponent actually holds. Here are two examples:

> I support capital punishment. How can anyone claim that the life of a convicted murderer is more valuable than the life of the innocent person he has killed?

> I oppose capital punishment. How can anyone claim that there is no chance of a criminal reforming, and no intrinsic value in human life itself?

Of course, neither the supporters nor the opponents of capital punishment make the suggested claims—but often people are able to get away with this sort of sleight of hand in the midst of an argument.

Begging the question. Many people use the phrase "it begs the question" when what they mean is "it prompts the question." But scholars of rhetoric use it very differently: begging the question means using a premise that is only true if the conclusion is true, a kind of circular reasoning. Originally, the phrase was a poor translation of the Latin *petitio principii*, which means, roughly, assuming the initial point. Here is an example:

> The Bible is the Word of God, and God doesn't make mistakes. The Bible tells us that God exists. Therefore, God exists.

If the premises of this argument are all true, then it seems that the conclusion must be true. But the initial premise *can't* be true unless the conclusion is true. The problem is that the argument assumes what it sets out to prove.

Formally invalid arguments. If the formal structure of a deductive argument is not valid, then the argument is fallacious, as in these examples:

> If water drips from the ceiling during a rainstorm, then there's a problem with the roof. No water drips from the ceiling during rainstorms. Therefore, there is no problem with the roof.

In this case it is certainly true that water dripping from the ceiling would likely indicate a problem with the roof. But we can't assume that no drip means no problem: the roof might leak but not produce any drips, only saturating the rafters and walls. As is often the case in logic, the distinction between *some* and *all* is important here;

some roof leaks result in dripping ceilings, but not all. The *if* part of the *if-then* clause above is known as the *antecedent*, and this kind of invalid argument is sometimes called *denying the antecedent*, because it simply inverts the *if*: "If drip, then leak; no drip, therefore no leak." But as we've shown, this inversion is not logically valid.

> If a lake is poisoned by acid rain, then no fish can live in it. This lake has no fish living in it whatsoever. Therefore, this lake must be poisoned by acid rain.

It is entirely true that lakes seriously affected by acid rain cannot support any aquatic life. But that is not the only possible cause for the disappearance of fish from a lake. There may be some other kind of pollution, or maybe the fish have all been caught. Again, the distinction between *some* and *all* is crucial; some lifeless lakes got that way because of acid rain, but not all. The *then* part of an *if-then* clause is called the *consequent*, so here the fallacy lies in *affirming the consequent*: "If acid rain, no fish; no fish, therefore acid rain." And the example shows us that this is not a valid logical move.

Slippery slope fallacy. The fallacy of the slippery slope is the suggestion that one development in a certain direction will inevitably lead to further developments in the same direction or *down the same slope*. Here is an example:

> Requiring people to carry ID may seem innocuous enough, but it should be resolutely opposed. If we are forced by the government to carry identity cards, pretty soon all our movements will be tracked, and all sorts of restrictions will be placed on our privacy. We have to stop these government intrusions into our lives!

This argument avoids making a case about identity cards *per se*, shifting the topic to something more alarming. It is entirely based on the premise that one move by the government will be followed by other, more drastic moves. Sometimes, of course, developments are part of long-term trends, but sometimes they are not—or they may represent the furthest extent of a particular trend. Slippery slope arguments may be suggestive, but they are too often based on faulty assumptions.

False dichotomy. A *dichotomy* occurs when things or ideas are split into two distinct alternatives. An argument that tries to insist on two and only two alternatives when in fact three or more possibilities exist (or gradations among possibilities exist) is one that poses a false dichotomy. You can see it in this conversation:

A. There should be laws prohibiting people from inciting hate against those of other races or religions.

B. So you're against freedom of speech? Without freedom of speech we wouldn't have a democracy!

Here, person B is oversimplifying the debate by suggesting that one must be either entirely for or entirely against freedom of speech.

A. No, I support freedom of speech—but within limits. It sounds to me as if you don't care about combatting bigotry and racism.

B. I do—but I believe that speaking out against bigoted or racist opinions is more effective than government attempts to prohibit them.

This time it's person A who is oversimplifying, by suggesting that anyone who disagrees with hate-speech laws must be indifferent to bigotry and racism. In fact, both sides hold nuanced views.

False and unconscious premises. Even a formally valid argument may be flawed if it depends on premises that are not true. Often, it is the unstated premises of an argument that are false or inadequately supported.

> Many have suggested that international terrorism is motivated by extreme poverty and oppression, but that doesn't square with the facts: few of the 9/11 attackers or the al-Qaeda leadership came from backgrounds of extreme hardship. Some, like Osama bin Laden, were highly privileged members of their society.

A missing or unacknowledged premise in this argument is that people will only take extreme action on behalf of their own social class. In fact, however, history is filled with examples of individuals from one nation or social class who became so involved with the plight of another that they devoted all their energies to fighting for change.

An example like this illustrates just how readily our perceptions of an argument are influenced by emotion and ideology. In this case, an entirely appropriate sense of anger and revulsion at terrorist acts makes it difficult for us to imagine that the terrorists might see themselves as acting altruistically on behalf of the poor and the oppressed. Regardless of whom the terrorists actually thought they were fighting for, the point is that one's economic background does not entirely define one's beliefs and actions, as this argument assumes.

Our perceptions of an argument are readily influenced by emotion and ideology.

An important first step towards logical conclusions is to be aware of the premises that guide your thought process. Most writing starts with certain conscious premises—and consciously held premises are surely useful (and indeed necessary) steps in building an argument. Watch out, though, for the power of unconscious premises—general beliefs and automatic assumptions that may covertly direct your critical thinking. *I cannot possibly have anything worthwhile to say on this topic* is an example; if allowed to lurk in the back of the mind, this premise—this crisis of attitude—will paralyze an essay's development. *Children over five years of age are just miniature adults* is a premise that could lead an editorialist to call for a return to corporal punishment in our schools. *Capitalism is in all circumstances the best system* is a premise that would certainly cloud a writer's judgement and reduce her capacity for understanding if she were writing an essay on the economic system of medieval Europe, or that of traditional Inuit society. *Something I find offensive could never be a work of art* is perhaps another premise capable of clouding a writer's judgement. Premises, be they strong or weak, do not always appear in the text of an essay. All the more reason, then, for all writers to examine theirs attentively, so that the essay's logic will be intentional, not inadvertent.

Appeals to nature. Many arguments implicitly or explicitly make an appeal to nature—the assumption being that if something is "natural" it is good, and if it is "unnatural" it is bad. But such arguments are complicated, first of all, by the difficulty of defining "natural," especially in the context of human culture. If people are a part of nature, then anything we do is natural—but if we consider ourselves separate from nature, then nothing we do is natural. Let us reflect, as well, on some of the things that have in the past been widely accepted as good on the basis that they represented the natural state for humans. Slavery was until the late eighteenth century presumed to be natural. So too (until well into the twentieth century in our society, and in many societies even today) has the subjection of women by men been taken to be natural, and therefore right. Looking further back, anthropologists tell us that unrestricted warfare came naturally to many early members of our species; perhaps we would find it came naturally to us as well were it not for all the "unnatural" restrictions our society places on our behaviour.

Post hoc fallacy. The Latin *post hoc, ergo propter hoc* translates as "after this, therefore because of this," and it refers to the mistake of imagining that if one thing happens after something else, then it must have happened because of that something else. Here is an example:

> The decline of frog populations throughout the world started to happen just after the thinning of the ozone layer; there has to be a connection!

But there doesn't have to be a connection—as becomes plain if we substitute a different event in the same logical structure:

> The decline of frog populations throughout the world started to happen just after the New York Yankees stopped winning the World Series with any degree of frequency; there has to be a connection!

In the first case damage from ultraviolet radiation is indeed one possible cause for the decline of frog populations—but scientists are still weighing the evidence, and are far from certain if it is one of several contributing causes, the primary cause, or simply an unrelated event. In other words, although the decline in frog populations and the thinning of the ozone layer may be *correlated* (the two trends are roughly in synch), one does not necessarily cause the other; *correlation* does not imply *causation.*

P 2.4 Thesis

In Section P1, we discussed the importance, when you set out to write, of having a *purpose* (P1.4) and a sufficiently narrow *focus* (P1.5), which is sometimes determined through the process of *discovery* (P1.6). After those early steps in the writing process, you'll be able to say what your essay is about—you'll have a *topic*. For some kinds of writing, that is enough to keep a reader's interest. When writing a persuasive essay, though, it's important to have not just a clear topic but also a clear *thesis*, which explains what the essay is designed to prove. Start with a tentative thesis, but feel free to go back and refine it as your argument takes shape. In the finished product, the thesis will state a clear position on a significant but specific topic of debate and will typically be expressed in a sentence or two—the *thesis statement*. You'll likely want to put it in the first paragraph of a short essay, though for longer essays or when complex arguments are being made, it may be helpful to postpone the thesis statement for several paragraphs or to extend it over a full paragraph, setting out a series of claims. Either way, letting readers know up front what your conclusion will be makes it easier for them to follow the rest of your argument.

A thesis statement need not declare anything earth-shattering, but it should not be trivial to the point that no one will care, or self-evident to the point that no one will disagree. Just imagine trying to sustain an argument around the thesis "my fingernails need to be cut" (too trivial) or "humans need to breathe air to live" (too self-evident). Of course, as with any examples we might give, you might be able to subvert these with thrilling results: an essay that argues that cutting fingernails is an unnecessary cultural convention, or that humans will evolve to breathe water rather than air, might very well be compelling. Ultimately you need to ask yourself, "Is my thesis interesting, both to me and to my imagined audience?"

Effective thesis statements are also molded to fit both the length of the essay and the expertise of the writer. There is no sense in asserting, at the outset of a 3,000-word history paper, that "every military leader since Attila the Hun has repeated his mistakes." The vocabulary of absolutes (*every*, *all*, *best*, *only*, etc.) commits a writer to universal coverage—and authoritative knowledge—of the topic. Strength in argumentative writing often comes from a willingness to qualify assertions. Words such as *often*, *usually*, and *largely*, and phrases such as *for the most part* and *to a great extent* are not necessarily signs that the writer lacks conviction; more frequently they are indications that she is careful and discerning. "Great military leaders have often repeated their mistakes" is a more manageable, though still compelling, thesis, suitable for a longer research paper. A shorter paper might discuss Attila the Hun's repeated mistakes—or even just one example.

Finally, a thesis must stake out a position that the writer is able to defend convincingly with the evidence available. It would be obviously inadvisable to make bold assertions about the nature of sub-atomic particles unless you have studied advanced particle physics. However, even if you are a relative expert on the topic—let's say you want to argue that "Minneapolis is America's most livable city," based on your many years of living in Minneapolis—you will need to deploy actual evidence rather than just subjective opinion. An opinion that can only be justified by the fallback defence "well, that's just my opinion" is one that should probably be re-evaluated.

P 2.5 Organization

As important as a clear thesis is, the success or failure of an argumentative essay depends on whether it makes its case. To do so, your essay needs sound arguments and solid evidence, as discussed in the sections above—but successful rhetoric requires more than that. You may have logic and the facts on your side, but if your argument is not presented in a clear and effective manner, your reader may not be convinced.

For ancient Roman orators there were five "canons" of rhetoric (you can think of them as parts of a process): invention, arrangement, style, memory, and delivery.[1] (The last two apply more to oral rhetoric than they do to writing, though they are very much worth thinking about.) If invention is how one comes up with arguments, and style is how one chooses to phrase them, arrangement is how they are organized or structured. It makes sense to refer to *structure* in this context, because it reminds us that although we read in a linear fashion, from beginning to end, we almost never write that way. The process is more like putting up a building: rather than planning and finishing one room at a time, a builder plans how all the rooms will fit together, and then erects a frame. The walls, windows, and details—what people see—are not usually added until the end. The difference with writing an essay, of course, is that the structure can easily be revised even after the essay draft is complete—working with words means that you can pick up a whole room and move it to a different wing if you think it's better that way.

1 Cicero, *De Inventione*.

Thesis Statements: Some Examples

needs checking *In this paper I will examine various reasons for launching the war in Kosovo in 1999.* [This is a statement of topic rather than a thesis.]

revised *The moral case for the US and its allies to wage a bombing-only war against Yugoslavia in 1999 was stronger than the strategic one; air attacks alone had never before been enough to win a war.* [This is the same topic, but now a position has been taken.]

needs checking *Art is important to society in many ways, and I will talk about them in this essay. One of the artists I will focus on is Robert Mapplethorpe.* [This is too general and too vague to have significance.]

revised *The controversial art of Robert Mapplethorpe deserves to be exhibited—and at public expense—even if most people find it abhorrent.* [This is more limited, more precise, more interesting.]

needs checking *The purpose of this essay is to explore the interplay between poetry and prose. I will demonstrate that good poets don't usually write good prose and vice versa.* [This might be the subject for a book, not an essay. Also, the generalization would be hard to defend: "What about Thomas Hardy or Boris Pasternak?" the professor will ask.]

revised *Though Maya Angelou's memoirs are more acclaimed, her best work is her poetry, because it has an elliptical quality that allows for more active readerly engagement than do her memoirs.* [A narrower but still controversial thesis on a similar topic.]

needs checking *Chocolate is the best flavor of ice cream.* [This runs the risk of being too trivial, and is also difficult to defend with evidence.]

revised *Chocolate's rise in popularity compared to vanilla is directly related to economic globalization.* [This is a more interesting thesis because it connects a seemingly trivial subject to significant underlying trends that can be demonstrated through evidence.]

In argumentative essay writing, the "rooms" or structural units are paragraphs. Each one has its own function or makes a separate point; taken together, the paragraphs should add up to a coherent argument that supports the thesis of the entire essay. The first paragraph (or paragraphs, in a longer essay) will be introductory, drawing the reader's attention to the topic and providing an overview of the argument. The last paragraph will usually be a conclusion, summarizing the argument and ending the essay with a note of finality or at least a sense of coherence. In between will be a number of body paragraphs, which comprise the bulk of the essay and serve various functions: providing background, describing circumstances, making logical points, and so on. These functions require different modes of writing, which we'll address in the next section. It's a good idea to have a working blueprint for your essay—an outline—that shows how it will all fit together. As you write, the outline will likely need to be revised—you may find yourself rewriting, expanding, splitting, combining, or omitting paragraphs—but the outline will help you keep the big picture in sight.

In order to keep things clear, both in the mind of the writer (as the essay is being composed) and in the mind of the reader (as the essay is being read), each of the paper's significant points should have its own body paragraph. But how many significant points should an essay include? In practice, that depends less on the subject of the essay than on the length of the essay. Let's say you have been asked to write a paper of 1,000 to 1,500 words arguing either for or against the legalization of marijuana. Was Canada right to do so? It would be possible to make an argument on this topic of 10,000 words or 100,000 words, but in a short essay, you might be able to make four or five good points—which means four or five body paragraphs, plus introductory and concluding paragraphs.

How long should a paragraph be? In the interest of variety it's good to vary the lengths, as it is to vary the lengths of sentences, but extremely long or extremely short paragraphs should generally be avoided in academic essay writing. It's all too easy for writers to lose their focus in writing an extremely long paragraph—and for readers to lose their focus as they try to wade through it. At the other extreme, the one-sentence paragraph is only rarely appropriate to academic writing. It is a punchy form that may have the force of an exclamation mark in certain styles of journalistic writing; like the exclamation mark, though, it very rarely serves to further the flow of an argument. The *average* length of a paragraph tends to be in the range of 150 to 250 words. Some significant points can be made in a couple of sentences, and some may require a full page or more to elaborate properly, but in most cases 150–250 words will be an appropriate amount of space to devote to introducing and explaining a significant point.

There is a degree of flexibility when it comes to deciding where to begin and end paragraphs. In many cases, the break signals a shift from one idea to another. If you have made a point about the public cost of marijuana law enforcement and next you want to discuss the health benefits of marijuana use, a new paragraph is called for. When narrating events, you might start a new paragraph when the story changes direction or when there is a gap in the timeline. You'll also start a new paragraph when you switch from one mode (such as description or analysis) to another. Other times, there may be overlap between two ideas and the decision of how to split them into paragraphs will be more subjective. You might fit several examples into one paragraph, or, if you go into greater detail, put each in a separate paragraph. Contrasting points, such as the effects of marijuana versus the effects of alcohol, might be treated the same way. If your discussion of the public cost of illegal marijuana segues into a discussion of tax revenue after legalization, those topics might be dealt with separately or together—again, the deciding factor is how much detail you want to provide. Once the essay is finished, paragraph boundaries will be less about separating ideas than about linking them (we'll talk about using transitions to connect paragraphs in Section P2.7).

In order to make sure that the function of each paragraph is clear, you may find it helpful to compose a ***topic sentence*** for each paragraph—a sentence that sets out clearly what you intend the paragraph to do, much as a thesis statement sets out what an essay intends to prove. Including an explicit topic sentence at the beginning of a paragraph is helpful but not always required; sometimes the topic is implied. It's a useful exercise to look at each paragraph in an essay and to identify the topic sentence or compose the "missing" topic sentence. Many writers find it helpful to draft topic sentences when they make outlines for their papers. This takes a little bit more time up front, but often saves quite a lot of time later; when you go to write the first draft, you can use them as the first or second sentence of each paragraph, and they will help you—and, later, your reader—keep track of the structure of your argument.

Let's take the marijuana topic as an example. Say you decide to argue in favour of legalization. Here's what a simple outline for your 1,000–1,500-word essay might look like, with topic sentences for each paragraph:

> First paragraph (introduction): Sketch the contemporary context and provide this thesis statement: *In both financial and social terms, the costs to society of enforcing laws prohibiting marijuana far outweigh the benefits.*
>
> Second paragraph: Laws prohibiting marijuana use encourage more serious crime; organized crime is often financed through the illegal sale of marijuana.
>
> Third paragraph: Enforcing marijuana laws incurs huge unnecessary costs on police resources, the courts, and the correctional system.
>
> Fourth paragraph: On the other hand, legalizing marijuana and taxing it provides a public revenue source: Canada's experience.
>
> Fifth paragraph: The harm caused by smoking marijuana is far, far less than that caused by other legal substances—notably alcohol.
>
> Sixth paragraph: The claim that legalizing marijuana leads to greater hard drug use commits the slippery slope fallacy.
>
> Seventh paragraph (conclusion): Summarize and reiterate thesis.

As everyone knows, there is more than one side to every argument. Let's say you'd prefer to argue against legalization. Then your plan might look like this:

> First paragraph (introduction): Sketch the contemporary context and provide this thesis statement: *The risks to society of legalizing marijuana far outweigh the benefits.*
>
> Second paragraph: It is often argued that marijuana isn't *very* harmful, but no one suggests that marijuana is not to some degree a harmful drug.

Third paragraph: Smoking marijuana causes harm to the lungs in addition to chemical changes in the brain; eating it creates a severe danger of overdose.

Fourth paragraph: When marijuana is legalized, this harmful drug becomes more widely used: cite Canada's experience.

Fifth paragraph: There is abundant evidence that many users of marijuana move on to other, more dangerous, "hard" drugs.

Sixth paragraph: Some argue that marijuana is less dangerous than alcohol (legal since the 1920s). But when we see the harm done by alcohol, why would we make another dangerous drug legally available?

Seventh paragraph (conclusion): Summarize and reiterate thesis.

Notice, first, that although these two essays argue two directly opposing viewpoints, they don't deal with exactly the same topics. The first outline emphasizes financial costs and benefits; the second outline focuses on the dangers and harms associated with the drug. These decisions about what to put in and what to leave out are also rhetorical: each essay uses arguments that best support its thesis. Notice, also, that some topics described in the outline are more closely related than others; different decisions could be made about how to combine and arrange them. Finally, these examples are not meant to suggest that every argument boils down to two opposing views; two people might agree that marijuana should remain legal, but disagree as to how sales should be regulated, as to the degree to which the government should participate in the market, etc.

The paragraph structure of longer essays tends to be more complex than in the two examples provided above. Consider once again Robin Lee's essay, in which there is a clear relationship between the essay's main points and the reasons supporting them. When Robin progressed from planning and prewriting activities (like the map of ideas we saw earlier), they produced an informal outline, which helped to arrange the sequence of points in their argument. Notice the three-part skeleton (introduction/body/conclusion), with the essay's thesis as the focus of the introduction:

Introduction

1) - sketch the outline of the battlefield(s) where these issues have been disputed
   - mention Canada and Britain as well as US
   - frame as a series of questions
   thesis: historical and political and ethical all important BUT so too is the aesthetic side

Body

1) - clearing away misconceptions
   - replacing monuments not a practice invented recently
   - not a monopoly of the left
   - removing monuments poses no threat to freedom of speech
   - monuments are not historical records (and removing them is not "erasing history")
2) - central issues involved are *today's* political and ethical standards
   - race and oppression, economic systems
3) - the historical aspect: seeing historical figures in the context of their own time
   - "the standards of the past" never uniform (examples: use Woodrow Wilson, John A. Macdonald and other Canadian prime ministers)
4) - social psychology: the effect on members of oppressed groups of seeing their oppressors honoured (use Canadian examples, also African Americans—including New Orleans)
5) - what to do? Tear down monuments? Or
   i) "level the playing field" by erecting new monuments, leaving old ones
   ii) display all controversial monuments—but in a contextualized, museum context
6) - the aesthetic side
   - Roosevelt statue – Natural History Museum
   - historical background
   - arguments over the message(s) the monument sends
   - subtlety of the statue, quality of the statue
   - Lee and Jackson statue, Baltimore
   - historical background
   - examples in the other direction: monuments of little aesthetic merit

Conclusion

1) - summary of arguments, including the issue of cost of preservation underlines the importance of taking the aesthetic into consideration
2) - [returning to thesis] we need not commit to preservation of all monuments forever—and in making choices, we should take the aesthetic as well as the ethical and the political into account

The material that is most crucial to Robin's argument appears here as point 6 in the body of the essay; as the outline shows, Robin has decided that a good deal of space should be devoted to "clearing the ground"—touching on the main points of the multi-pronged controversies over public monuments honouring controversial figures of the past.

The outline above might seem to focus too little on the material most crucial to Robin's own argument—but an outline is of course just that; it does not set out how much space is to be devoted to each point. But Robin will eventually decide to devote eight paragraphs and (when illustrations are factored in) almost half the pages of the full essay to elaborating on what appears here as point 6 in the body of the argument—the "aesthetic side." Such decisions concerning an essay's structure, as well as the weight to be placed on its various points, are often as important as the essay's internal logic.

The paragraph-by-paragraph outline below (pages 50–51) follows exactly the paragraphs in Robin's paper. It's important to be aware, though, that any paragraph outline you develop during the planning and writing process should be regarded as subject to change as you move forward. It's an important step in the process—but even at later stages you may well find that you need to make structural adjustments. You may decide that a paragraph is really expressing two important ideas instead of one, and should be split in two. You may decide that a couple of paragraphs represent an unnecessary digression, and should simply be cut. Or you may decide that one or more paragraphs would be more effective if they were moved to a different position in the essay. Like so many other things, it's virtually impossible to get all this right in your first draft; paragraphing should be something you pay almost as much attention to in the revision process as you do during the planning process.

Paragraph-by-Paragraph Essay Outline

Introduction

1. introduction to the topic; thesis statement (thesis: historical and political and ethical all important BUT so too is the aesthetic side)

Arguments Concerning Historical Monuments: The Background

Misconceptions

2. clearing away misconceptions (i) replacing monuments not a practice invented recently
3. clearing away misconceptions (ii): idea of replacing monuments not peculiar to the political left
4. clearing away misconceptions (iii): removing monuments poses no threat to freedom of speech
5. clearing away misconceptions (iv): purpose of monuments is to honour those represented (not to preserve the historical record)
6. clearing away misconceptions (v): removing monuments is *not* "erasing history"

Our values today

7. arguments about monuments are arguments about our values *today*—examples of John A. Macdonald and of Robert E. Lee/Jefferson Davis
8. another aspect of arguments over our values today: ideas about capitalism
9. the historical side: seeing historical figures in the light of the standards of their own time; history's nuances
10. issues of social psychology relevant to the issues: examples from Atlantic Canada and from New Orleans
11. [transition paragraph] Confederate statues in New Orleans

Options

12. options for dealing with controversial monuments (i): leave monuments where they are and level the playing field by erecting new monuments beside them to present other sides of the story
13. options for dealing with controversial monuments (ii): continue to display all controversial monuments, but in a museum context where they can be contextualized. The problem of cost

The Aesthetic Side of Monuments Controversies

14. statues and monuments: introduce topic of the aesthetic side

The Roosevelt monument

15. the Roosevelt monument (i): introduce example of Theodore Roosevelt monument
16. the Roosevelt monument (ii): background—the Roosevelt monument
17. the Roosevelt monument (iii): changing the status of the object (Roosevelt monument becomes statue)
18. the Roosevelt monument (iv): discussion of the aesthetic qualities of the statue

The Lee and Jackson monument

19. the Baltimore Robert E. Lee and Stonewall Jackson monument (i): background
20. the Baltimore Robert E. Lee and Stonewall Jackson monument (ii): discussion of the aesthetic qualities of the statue
21. the Baltimore Robert E. Lee and Stonewall Jackson monument (iii): short paragraph wrapping up discussion of the Baltimore statue
22. the aesthetic qualities of other, less attractive monuments: give 3 examples

Conclusion

23. summary of arguments, including the issue of cost of preservation—cost issue underlines the importance of taking the aesthetic into consideration
24. return to thesis: we need not commit to preservation of all monuments forever. In making choices, we should take the aesthetic as well as the ethical and the political into account

It is often helpful to think of the structure of a complex essay in terms of ***paragraph clusters*** as well as individual paragraphs. The structure of Robin Lee's essay, for example, can be broken down into the paragraph clusters you see in the paragraph-by-paragraph outline. Notice that not all the paragraphs directly advance the argument. Paragraphs 16 and 19, for example, provide background information; the writing here is primarily narrative and descriptive rather than argumentative.

Just as a table of contents (like the one in this book) is structured according to a hierarchy, with headings, sub-headings, and sub-sub-headings, in the outline on pp. 50–51 paragraph clusters form the large units in a long essay; individual paragraphs may be seen as subordinate categories within the clusters.

Robin Lee's careful organization makes their argument quite clear to the reader. As a result, they are able to get away without an expressly stated topic sentence for each paragraph—but the main idea is usually implied and not hard to recognize. You might find it helpful to reread the essay and identify or construct topic sentences for each paragraph.

For more on using paragraphs to structure arguments, we recommend Ian Johnston's *Essays and Arguments: A Handbook on Writing* (3rd edition 2015). It's a text that has a proven track record of improving students' skills in formulating written arguments.

P 2.6 Modes of Thought/Patterns of Writing

Traditionally, essays tend to be grouped into categories such as descriptive, narrative, expository, or argumentative. As discussed more fully in this book's section on "Informal and Personal Writing," such distinctions are overly simplistic; very few papers are written *purely* as narration, or description, or in any other pattern. College and university essays are usually organized around thesis statements, and tend to be primarily argumentative; the writer's paramount concern is the presentation of an informed point of view on her topic. Along the way, however, most argumentative essays employ several distinct modes of thought, manifested in distinct patterns of writing.

Robin Lee's essay "Monumental Problems," for example, is typical of university essays in the Humanities or Social Sciences in that it is primarily argumentative. But paragraph 16 employs narration a good deal, and several paragraphs (18, 20, and 22) employ description extensively in the course of discussing the aesthetic qualities of the statues under consideration.

Narration and description are the first of several modes of thought discussed in this section; they are discussed again from a diferent perspective in C2.9 (Informal and Personal Writing).

Narration

The basic mode of thought involved in narration is a very simple one: one thing happens, and then another thing happens, and then another thing happens. The words *and* and *then* are natural connectives, as are time-related adverbs—words such as *later*, *subsequently*, *simultaneously*, and *meanwhile*.

For most of us, narration is the most straightforward mode of thinking, and the most straightforward pattern in which to present written material. It is a mainstay of informal and personal writing (covered in a separate section of this book). And in a few academic contexts, narration plays a prominent role; the "Methods" section of a scientific lab report, for example, is usually organized around a narrative sequence of events:

> A sugar maple leaf was collected from an area close to the trunk. This leaf was cut so as to cover the surface area of a leaf chamber. Carbon dioxide was flushed into the chamber and the oxygen production per minute was measured. The average oxygen output per minute was then calculated, as was the standard deviation.

Students are well advised, however, to use narration quite sparingly in most academic writing contexts—and particularly in literature essays, where it may be tempting to rely extensively on narration. Professors of literature often warn students to "assume your reader has read the work"; if an argumentative essay merely retells the story of a novel or play, it's not much of an argumentative essay.

An essay about a literary work is an essay, not a story—it must not simply retell the narrative of the work being discussed.

An example may help to make this point clear. In the following passage from his monograph *Guilty Aesthetic Pleasures*, literary scholar Timothy Aubry recounts a succession of developments in the story line of Vladimir Nabokov's

Lolita. But Aubry is not presenting his readers with this material in order to familiarize them with the narrative thread of the novel; his purpose is to provide support for the contention he is putting forward concerning the character of Humbert:

> [An] important feature of Humbert's character...—one generally obscured by both his sexual predilections and his muscular rhetoric—is his weakness, his inability for much of the novel to produce any significant impact on the world around him. It is a feature he tends to underscore when addressing his scholarly and artistic endeavors. "I published tortuous essays in obscure literary journals," Humbert admits, adding "A paper of mine ... was chuckled over by the six or seven scholars who read it" (18). Unable to support himself through such work, Humbert lives off a moderate inheritance and the sinecure from a wealthy uncle perfume maker, before accepting a room in Charlotte Haze's suburban house ... (40). There, he sits around all day in his purple dressing gown, tracking the random movements of Charlotte's daughter Dolores (aka Lolita) through the house.... During the penultimate marital spat after she proposes a sojourn in England, Humbert blames Charlotte for dragging him daily to Hourglass Lake and thus interfering with the scholarly research he never considers doing when left alone (93). Unemployed, haughty, snobbish, endlessly distracted, filled with self-loathing..., Humbert is a portrait of the frustrated academic as a middle-aged man (146).

Any summary of story material that you include in your paper, then, must support a point—not substitute for one. That's just as true in other disciplines as it is in literary studies. If a professor of philosophy asks you to write an original essay on Plato's *Symposium* or a liberal studies professor asks you to write an original essay on Voltaire's *Candide*, she will *not* want you merely to recapitulate the narrative thread of those works.[1] If you are writing a history essay discussing the violence that broke out in the Sudanese region of Darfur in 2003, a nar-

1 Professors do sometimes assign short writing assignments in which students are asked, for example, to summarize or to restate in their own words the reasoning of a passage from Plato. Such assignments are to be distinguished from assignments that ask students to write original essays in which they develop and express views of their own.

rative pattern may well be the best one to adopt, at least for portions of the paper; the sequence of events is a complex one, and getting it straight is crucial to any argument as to the guilt or innocence of those involved. But in most academic arguments, narration should be introduced only in support of the writer's own argument; it should not be allowed to take the place of that argument.

Description

We often imagine that description is an objective process through which we convey information in a disinterested fashion. And in some cases it can indeed be very largely a process of this sort. But description is to some degree always subjective; when we describe something we will always be conveying our impressions of it, rather than the thing itself. Sometimes it is subjective to a very considerable degree; we should appreciate that description can be a means not only of conveying information but also of putting forward an argument. Compare these two 1855 descriptions of young women working in an American printing plant (one of which is accompanied by an illustration):

> The girl who stands at [the press] is called the feeder. She has a pile of damped paper on a stand over the press. The pile is inclined a little toward her, so as to make it easier for her to draw off the successive sheets.... The feeder has just placed a sheet to

THE POWER-PRESS.

> be printed on the inclined table before her.... The work goes regularly on, with no attendance whatever except the placing of each successive sheet within the reach of the iron fingers which are to draw it into the machine.... Every visitor who sees these girls at their work is struck with ... the healthy, and happy, and highly attractive appearance which they themselves and the scene of their labors exhibit. (Jacob Abbott, *The Harper Establishment; or, How the Story Books Are Made*)

> In one corner stood some huge frame of ponderous iron, with a vertical thing like a piston periodically rising and falling upon a heavy wooden block. Before it ... stood a tall girl, feeding the iron animal with half-quires of rose-hued notepaper, which, at every downward dab of the piston-like machine, received in the corner the impress of a wreath of roses. ... Not a syllable was breathed. Nothing was heard but the low, steady, overruling hum of the iron animals. The human voice was banished from the spot. ...The girls did not so much seem accessory wheels to the general machinery as mere cogs to the wheels. (Herman Melville, "The Paradise of Bachelors and the Tartarus of Maids")

Even without aid of the visual illustration, the first of these descriptions gives us the sense of a pleasant workplace and an undemanding occupation—while the second gives us a sense of demanding and deeply unpleasant work in a dehumanizing environment. It may be, of course, that some 1855 printing operations were perfectly pleasant workplaces and others were hellishly unpleasant, and that the two descriptions simply reflect that difference. But it seems more likely that the book issued by the Harper & Brothers publishing company to describe its manufacturing processes would naturally describe the operation of a printing press in glowing terms, while the description in a *Harper's* magazine article of such manufacturing processes by an author with a grudge against the company might be more inclined to accentuate the negative.[1] It is at any rate clear that Abbott is implicitly arguing that factories of this sort are to be wel-

1 Harper & Brothers book publishers had published *Moby-Dick* in 1851, but by 1855 were consistently rejecting Melville's novel-length manuscripts—even as the company's magazine division continued sporadically to publish his short fiction.

comed, while Melville is arguing the opposite; in neither case does the process of providing a description appear to be an inherently objective or disinterested one.

That description is a largely subjective process should not be taken to suggest that descriptions are inevitably put forward from a biased point of view or with suspect motives; far from it. Look, for example, at the ways in which Robin Lee describes the various statues discussed in "Monumental Problems" (in each case, including one or more photographs so that we can "see for ourselves"): "Jackson's expression conveys a rougher sort of determination," "arching backward but with one arm thrown forward, Davis is presumably meant to look heroic, but his pose seems awkward and ungainly." In describing the statues, Robin brings subjective impressions to bear in the service of the argument. The intent is to persuade, to be sure, but Robin at the same time acknowledges in various ways that these descriptions are subjective in nature. Assertions as to the appearance of the statues are often qualified with phrases such as "to me at least" (paragraph 18). Impressions that are suggested to Robin by the qualities of the statues (e.g., "and is there a hint, especially in the face of the African, of a strength and determination that could readily be refocused into resistance against the conqueror?" paragraph 18) are sometimes couched not as assertions but as questions—questions that suggest ways of seeing and interpreting what is before our eyes without insisting on that response. As they advance Robin's argument about the aesthetics of the statues being discussed, description, evaluation, and interpretation are not easily separated.

Definition

Closely related to classification as well as to description, definition is the process of making clear the meaning of a word—using other words to convey as precisely as possible the meaning(s) of the word you are defining. In an essay, the effort to clarify the meanings of key terms may well take you considerably beyond the sorts of definition commonly found in dictionaries, as you explore the relevant nuances of a given term. Sometimes definition may be the focus of an entire essay assignment:

- Discuss how definitions of "liberalism" have changed from the nineteenth to the twenty-first centuries.

- Discuss the ways in which the concept of metonymy in sixteenth-century Rhetoric differs from the concept of metonymy in modern critical theory.
- How and why did the term "making love" change its meaning in the 1950s and 1960s?
- How should we define "terrorist"—and "domestic terrorism"?
- Analyze Socrates' objections to Euthyphro's five attempts to define "piety" and "impiety" in Plato's dialogue, *Euthyphro*. Are these objections sound? How would you define these two terms?

In the first three of these examples, the student is asked to describe or analyze the ways in which a term or concept has been understood differently in different eras (a process that of course requires narration as well as description). How did the term *liberal*, which in the nineteenth century implied firm opposition to government intervention in the economy, come to imply the very opposite a hundred years later? How did *making love*, once understood to refer to acts of courtship that stopped short of overtly sexual acts, come in the 1960s to refer to nothing but such acts? And how do such changes in definition reflect or even cause broader changes in social attitudes? In the fourth and fifth examples, the student is asked to engage directly in argument over how particular terms should best be defined.

How did *making love*, once understood to refer to acts of courtship that stopped short of overtly sexual acts, come in the 1960s to refer to nothing but such acts?

Even where definition is not the primary focus of an essay, it can play an important role—as Robin Lee's essay illustrates. Of vital importance to Robin's argument is the implied definition of *monument* developed in paragraph 5 (and footnote 3); it is when a statue of a public figure is placed on a pedestal and raised above us—"to invite the public to look up to" the figure, "both literally and figuratively," that the statue becomes not *just* a statue, but a monument. A statue cannot properly be defined as a monument, Robin implies, unless it is raised above the viewer on a pedestal.

Notice that in setting out the difference between the two terms, *statue* and *monument*, Robin does not simply rely on a dictionary.

Dictionary definitions are often inadequate to the needs of academic writing; in this case, many dictionary definitions do not make entirely clear how a statue is to be distinguished from a monument (other than that a monument typically honours a public figure).

In a number of academic disciplines, indeed, dictionary definitions can occasionally be downright misleading; a term may have a meaning particular to an academic discipline—a meaning that may not appear in standard dictionaries. Such is the case, for example, with *emotive* when that word is used in meta-ethics discussions in the discipline of Philosophy; it is the case too with *critical animal studies* when that expression is used as a term identifying a sub-discipline with an implied set of shared attitudes in several humanities and social science disciplines.

Classification / Taxonomy

Clarifying the meanings of *statue* and *monument* is a matter of definition, but it is also a matter of classification. Classification is the process of sorting into groups, and taxonomy is the name we give to the study of how that sorting process works—and of how it *should* work. The mental act of classifying can be enormously complex, but it can also be enormously satisfying to our sense of order. And how well we learn to do it and to understand it can make a real difference to the logical fluency of our writing.

Classification has received particular attention in biology. Until the eighteenth century, biological classification was largely haphazard. With the publication of *Species Plantarum* in 1753 Swedish biologist Carl Linnaeus introduced a system according to which plants and animals were given two-part names, indicating their membership both in a large group—a genus—and a smaller group—a species. But what characteristics would be considered definitive for each genus or species? On such questions there was little agreement until Charles Darwin put forward with his 1859 *On the Origin of Species* a system organizing classification on the basis of evolution; species, genera—and the larger categories above them, families and orders—could be sorted according to the degree to which they could be shown to have shared ancestors. Darwin's approach still allowed for considerable uncertainty, however, and taxonomy itself has continued to evolve. (Chimpanzees, gorillas, and orangutans, for example, were classed in the early twentieth century as three species of great apes; they are now classed as seven—biologists identify two species of gorilla and three species of orangutan, and classify bonobos to be a species separate from chimpanzees.)

When we think of categories, we tend first of all to think of physical or empirically measurable entities—whether living beings, inanimate objects, or export totals. But taxonomy is also important (and also often contested ground) when it comes to purely abstract qualities. You might well be asked in some university courses, for example, to write an essay on the beautiful and the sublime—two aesthetic categories that were often the subject of discussion in the eighteenth century. Famously, Edmund Burke treated the two as entirely separate categories, and tried to identify the characteristics of each. But how distinct are they? Might it be the case, for example, that the sublime is a subset of the beautiful—that anything which is sublime has to it something of the beautiful? Or might it be that the two are overlapping categories—that some things are both beautiful and sublime, while others are sublime without being beautiful, and others still are beautiful without being sublime? (Taxonomic possibilities of this sort may sometimes be more easily conveyed through Venn diagrams than through prose.)

In still other cases, words naming categories may seem interchangeable but in fact refer to substantially different things; here we can see plainly how issues of classification can overlap with issues of definition. As Robin Lee discovered in writing the essay "Monumental Problems," for example, the words *statue* and *monument* are often used interchangeably in debates over what to do with statues/monuments of controversial figures. But (as is discussed more fully above, under "Definition"), the two words are not in fact synonymous; what makes a statue part of a monument is typically its placement on top of a pedestal or column, thereby raising it above its surroundings and, implicitly, suggesting that the figure portrayed in the statue is deserving of a special place of honour. The differences between the category *statues* (a category classifying a type of aesthetic object) and the category *monuments* (a category defined not by aesthetics but by the function of honouring something, whether it be a respected leader, those killed in a war or a calamitous event, or a group accomplishment) can in fact be profound. It was in large part an investigation into those differences that led Robin to an argumentative focus for the essay "Monumental Problems"—the importance of taking into account the aesthetic qualities of the statues that are displayed in these controversial monuments.

Classification is often important if an essayist is writing in a descriptive mode—telling what something looks like or how it works. If a writer is describing different skyscrapers, she might classify them by architectural style (*modernist, postmodern, art deco,* etc.); by structural system (*braced frame, rigid frame,* etc.); or simply by gradations of height (*tall, super-tall, mega-tall*). If a writer is attempting to describe inflation, he may decide to deal separately with different sorts of inflation (*cost-push inflation, demand-pull inflation, inflation caused by an expansion of the supply of money,* and so on), or he might deal in turn with categories based on the degree to which inflation is occurring (*hyperinflation, mild inflation, deflation,* etc.).

Not infrequently, the entire thrust of an essay will turn on issues of classification. This is obviously true with certain scientific topics (Should the domestic dog be classified as a type of wolf, as some have argued, or as a separate species?), but it can be true as well of essays in the humanities and social sciences. Philosophy essays argue the issue of whether non-human animals should be classified legally as property, or, in one sense or another, as persons. In other disciplines too, essays have often been written on the issues involved in classifying humans as persons, and on the long history of excluding certain categories of humans from personhood for certain purposes—as women, Indigenous people, blacks, and people of Asian background were long excluded from voting on the grounds that they were not possessed of full standing as "persons."

Essays continue to be written as well on the practice of classifying human beings according to skin colour. In the same way that it is impossible to identify a precise dividing line between blue and green on the colour spectrum, it is obviously impossible to identify a precise dividing line between black and white skin colour in humans. Should that be taken as evidence that categories such as *black* and *white* are almost meaningless where humans are concerned? Or even that such categories do not exist? Biologists have established that the concept of "race" as it was employed for many centuries is in fact so deeply flawed as to be in almost all circumstances of no practical use. Yet, people very often are categorized by race, on the basis of skin colour, ancestry, or in some cases self-identification. And there are social consequences to this categorization, including the long history of prejudice and racism that privileges some and disadvantages others. Should we continue to employ those categories—including for purposes of social justice and restitution—even if they've proved not to have a foundation in biology? Issues of taxonomy are central to all such discussions.

Classification is particularly important to argumentative essays that make comparisons or draw contrasts. If the writer is comparing the US economy with that of Canada, for example, she will sort the data or other evidence she has assembled into various classes: data pertaining to the sizes of the two economies; data pertaining to trade; banking and interest rates; geographical and climatic inputs; and so on. In doing so she will need to make a number of choices—choices that may have less to do with classification *per se* than they do with issues of how best to organize a piece of writing so as to maximize its rhetorical effect. What should be grouped with what? What will go in and what will be left out? And in what order should the material appear? Should an essay comparing types of economic activity in two countries deal with all aspects of one country's economy first, and then turn to the economy of the other country? Or deal with the various topics in turn, comparing the two countries under each heading?

Another such question is the matter of how much space should be accorded each topic. Should the discussion in Robin Lee's essay of the difference between the category *statues* and the category *monuments* be the subject of a sentence or two? Of a full paragraph or more? Or is it the sort of topic that would constitute a digression from the main argument, and would be better dealt with in a footnote? You'll want the answers to such questions to be dictated as much as possible by the thrust of your argument. It can be difficult, though, as you are in the midst of working through that argument, to see immediately what should receive the most emphasis, or how the material you want to present should best be arranged. You may well end up rearranging paragraphs or groups of paragraphs during the editing process.

Analogy

When we write poetically of an imagined likeness between two things, we are using metaphor and simile: that's what Shakespeare does when he likens his mental state while in love to "the lark, at break of day arising"; what Milton does when he describes time as the "thief of youth"; what Lorna Crozier does (in her poem "Sturgeon") when she writes of "their cold toothless mouths large as caves"; what Carol Ann Duffy does when she writes of the rain and her lover: "the endless northern rain between us / Like a veil." In a literary work, metaphor and simile may be particularly effective if they are vaguely suggestive of several points of likeness. In its literal meaning, Crozier's line likens only one aspect of these fishes' mouths to caves—their size—but the image of the cave is suggestive of various other qualities that hover in the background; such suggestiveness enriches the poetic meaning. In a literal sense, the rain between two people is like a veil in that it reduces visibility. But the word *veil* comes to us with a network of other associations—metaphorically, there is a long tradition of veils reducing understanding as well as visibility, and there is also a strong association between veils and grieving. Again, such layers of suggestiveness enrich poetic meaning.

Analogy can be likened to —and contrasted with— metaphor and simile.

When we draw likenesses of this sort in expository or persuasive prose, on the other hand—analogies, as they are usually termed—we generally aim for clarity and precision in drawing the likeness. Our aim is not to excite the poetic imagination but to employ a comparison in ways that will make the literal meaning of what we are saying more easily or more vividly understood, or more vividly felt. Analogy is often used to make a difficult concept feel more familiar; an analogy involving a stretched rubber sheet, a marble, and a bowling ball, for example, is often used to help explain gravity as Einstein first conceptualized it—as part of a space-time continuum rather than a physical force in three dimensions. But analogies can also be helpful if one is trying to show something familiar in a new light, or to make vivid a piece of information that is not conceptually difficult. There's nothing complicated about the G-force of a soccer header having been registered at between 50g and 100g, but some readers may understand that information much more readily and vividly if they are given an analogy: the level of force of a soccer header is similar to the impact of hard punches thrown by boxers.

As with metaphors and similes, the elements in an analogy have names. Whereas the subject in a metaphor is known as the *tenor*, the subject in an analogy is called just that—the *subject*. The thing (or quality, or process) that the subject is being compared to (in the case of a metaphor, known as the *vehicle*) is referred to as the *analog* in an analogy. In the above example, then, the soccer header is the subject, and the boxer's hard punch is the analog. One other term is important to a basic understanding of analogies: *target features*. In the case of many analogies, there is only one target feature; in this example, the G-force is the only point of comparison; a soccer header is not being likened to a boxer's punch in any other respect.

As this example may also illustrate, analogies can have considerable persuasive force. If you are arguing that restrictions should be placed on the use of headers in youth soccer leagues, employing an analogy such as that above is likely to help you to make your case. So too, if you are arguing against current poultry farming practices, your case will be helped if you compare the relative space allotted to laying hens to an equivalent amount of space allotted to a larger animal that your readers are likely to be more familiar with—the family dog, for instance:

> The poultry industry's guidelines for "humane practice" may make for soporific reading, but it's worth paying close attention to what they say. In "enriched cages," Canada's National Farm Animal Care Council advises, birds must be "provided with a minimum of 750.0 cm² (116.25 square inches) of total space," while in the United States, Humane Farm Animal Care's "Certified Humane 'Free Range'" requirement is 2 square feet per bird. Those figures may sound not too bad if we have no points of reference. But we should remember that these birds grow to at least twelve inches in height, that they are as long as they are tall, and that they like to roam around—and to fly. Having 1–2 square feet of available space for an animal the size of an average Leghorn bird is the rough equivalent of having 1–2 square metres of available space for a medium sized dog—an Irish terrier, say. We would think it ludicrous if someone were to suggest to us that 1–2 square metres of living space for an Irish terrier could fairly be described as an "enriched" or a "free range" environment. But unless we make these sorts of comparisons, we are likely to placidly accept that treating birds in this way constitutes "humane practice."

In this example, relative space is the key target feature; Leghorn hens and Irish terriers are not being likened to each other in a variety of different ways. With some analogies, though, there may be more target features than there are here—and, just as a metaphor may in some cases be extended through an entire poem, an analogy may sometimes be extended through an entire essay. Such is the case with the way in which Nicholas Van Damis of the School of Psychological Sciences at the University of Melbourne uses an analogy to make an argument regarding mindfulness meditation:

> Mindfulness meditation is routinely portrayed as a simple, happy, pleasant mind-hack that can help improve almost every aspect of our lives. ... If anyone feels hesitant, we're reminded that it's just like fitness for the mind—and who wouldn't benefit from a little mental exercise?
>
> Yet the way mindfulness meditation is commonly branded doesn't reflect the varieties of ways it's practised or its consequences. While it might be simple, at least in principle, it certainly isn't easy.... While it can lead to positive feelings or pleasant experiences, it can also cause discomfort. Sometimes meditation leads to new or worsened anxiety, depression or other mental illness. It's clear, then, that the answer to the question 'What's the worst that could happen?' is considerably more severe than most pundits would suggest. What's more, the ethics, values and assumptions behind the practice aren't always made clear. Thus, meditation is less like exercise in general than it is like mountain-climbing—something potentially strenuous that, depending on your objectives, you should approach with caution, training and an awareness of the risks....To return to the analogy, think carefully about mountaineering itself. There are numerous peaks of varying heights, which you might think about as different goals. There are paths of differing difficulty up those mountains, reflecting the challenges associated with different techniques. And there are precautions you should take, including finding a good guide and evaluating your own suitability—but some people still get hurt even when they do everything 'right.' And it's worth remembering that there are those who simply aren't interested in climbing mountains in the first place.

This is just a small part of Van Damis's overall argument; he continues to compare mindfulness meditation and mountaineering throughout his 1,700-word essay. He isn't of course suggesting that mindfulness meditation and mountaineering are alike in every respect. But he uses the analogy to draw attention to the numerous respects in which he feels that they are indeed very similar; in the analogy he draws between the subject (mindfulness meditation) and the analog (mountaineering), there are several target features.

In Robin Lee's "Monumental Problems" essay there are no extended analogies, but the thread of Robin's argument does several times make use of analogy. It is absurd, the essay suggests, to characterize the removal today of monuments such as those honouring Confederate leaders as an unprecedented effort by progressives to "erase the past"; by drawing numerous comparisons to monument removals in other eras and other parts of the world (by those on the political right as well as the political left), the essay makes the point that movements to remove monuments to past leaders are no more unique to our own era than they are the preserve of political progressives.[1]

Analogy, then, can be very useful when you are formulating an argument. One or two cautionary notes, though, should be sounded. One is that, much as drawing an analogy may help to make a point more vivid or make an argument more persuasive, it should not be expected to conclusively prove your argument. Likening mindfulness meditation to mountaineering may help to persuade the reader that mindfulness meditation is challenging in a variety of ways, and that it is not for everybody, but the analogy will not and cannot provide conclusive proof; even with analogies that are powerful, it is always possible to draw attention to *disanalogous* features. As with other argumentative tools, one should not expect too much from analogies.

One of the best-known examples of an analogy—and, some have suggested, one of the best examples of an analogy gone wrong—is William Paley's 1805 watchmaker analogy, in which the complexity

---

1 As some of the examples in Robin Lee's paper suggest, target features need not always be points of similarity; analogies may also draw attention to points of difference in otherwise similar subjects and analogs. One of the most famous analogies that calls attention to points of difference is an intentionally absurd analogy of relation: "A woman needs a man like a fish needs a bicycle" (an analogy coined by Australian Irina Dunn in 1970).

of nature is likened to the complexity of a watch—and the conclusion drawn that, just as the watch requires a watchmaker, so our world must have a creator:

> Let's say you're walking around and you find a watch on the ground. As you examine it, you marvel at the intricately complex interweaving of its parts, a means to an end. Surely you wouldn't think this marvel would have come about by itself. The watch must have a maker. Just as the watch has such complex means to an end, so does nature to a much greater extent. Just look at the complexity of the human eye. Thus we must conclude that nature has a maker too.

Paley takes the analogy as providing conclusive proof that nature "must have a maker." But surely we should not presume that if two things are alike in one respect, we may conclude with complete certainty that they are alike in others. Paley's argument identifies only one feature common to both nature and a watch—namely, their complexity. But doesn't complexity exist in some things that are formed through purely mechanical processes and without the intervention of an intelligent creator (snowflakes, for example, and fractals)? The analogy is at best a weak one, and seems insufficient to demonstrate the existence of an almighty creator.

Analogies are often used in discussions of ethical and political matters. As in other spheres, they may be useful in such contexts—but as in other spheres, they may go badly astray. Consider this example:

> For a modern nation to require all its citizens over a certain age to be vaccinated and to carry passports showing that they have been vaccinated is analogous to Nazi Germany requiring Jews to show their status by wearing a star-of-David badge.

In what way(s), we should ask, are these different sorts of action analogous? There is in fact only one analogous feature: they are both instances of a government requiring certain behaviour of certain of its citizens. But that analogous feature is shared by every government in the world; unless one were to suggest that the requiring by any government of anything is equivalent to the requiring by any other government of anything else, there is nothing whatsoever to be gleaned from the analogy.

Generalization and Abstraction

Generalization is the process of moving from an observation or conclusion about a single thing or a small number of things to a conclusion about all or most of that group. Most essays involve shifts not only from the particular to the general and back again, but also from one level of generalization to another:

- An art history essay on Chippendale chairs would probably refer to particular examples from the eighteenth-century studio of Thomas Chippendale himself, generalize about all chairs of that type, generalize further about the furniture of the period, and perhaps generalize at one higher level about how and why such designs suited the overall sensibilities of eighteenth-century England.
- An English literature essay might make a general claim about Jane Austen's use of irony. It might then descend one level of generality to discuss how the generalization applies in the various novels. It might then move to a more particular analysis, looking at scenes in *Northanger Abbey* that are suffused with Austen's sense of irony and those that are almost pure melodrama with no irony. Finally, the essay would doubtless give particular examples—sentences or paragraphs that exemplify an ironic tone.

Many people are a bit hazy on the difference between generalization and abstraction—not surprisingly, since the words have meanings that overlap to some degree. Abstraction, at its most basic level, is the isolation of some particular quality of a thing from the rest of its properties—the consideration of the colour of a particular object, for example. Most often, though, abstraction refers to the consideration of ideas instead of concrete objects or events. We often perform both abstraction and generalization simultaneously, when abstract words like "freedom" are used in a general sense, not in reference to the freedom of a particular person (as in the slogan "Freedom isn't free"). "While the opposite of *general* is *particular*," as C.R. Hallpike reminds us, "the opposite of *abstract* is *concrete*" (171). We can take a particular, con-

Many people are a bit hazy on the difference between generalization and abstraction.

crete thing—say, the stone lions in front of the New York Public Library—and make both generalizations ("Many Beaux-Arts public buildings feature statues of animals.") and abstractions ("Since the Great Depression, the NYPL lions have symbolized patience and fortitude.") or both at once ("Lion statues represent fortitude, among other qualities.").

Robin Lee's essay is continually involved both with the abstract (concepts such as *political left* in paragraph 3, *freedom of expression* in paragraph 4, and *erasing history* in paragraph 6) and with the concrete—the statues/monuments being discussed. The essay is intensely involved, as well, with issues involving generalization—the extent to which one can generalize about political leaders of the past, for example, or about the treatment accorded Indigenous people in Canada and the United States (paragraph 9). The thrust of the entire essay might fairly be couched as an argument that we should not attempt to generalize about all monuments to discredited public figures ("let us not commit to the preservation of all these works in perpetuity," as Robin puts it in the essay's concluding paragraph)—and that we should make distinctions among them, not least of all on aesthetic grounds.

Both abstraction and generalization are important mental processes for any writer; they help us, as Janet Giltrow puts it, to "name and manage otherwise unruly details" (141). But use them with care. As a rule, generalizations must be supported by evidence unless they are commonplace and uncontroversial ("Dogs have four legs," "War is a terrible thing")—just as any claim that is not generally accepted must be supported by evidence. Be careful, too, to show that you are aware that some generalizations may not apply in all cases. If you write that mammals give birth to live young while reptiles lay eggs, you should mention, even if only parenthetically, that there are exceptions: platypuses and echidnas are egg-laying mammals, while vipers and certain other snakes and lizards have live births. And you should be precise. *Canadians voted for a carbon tax in the 2021 federal election* is an imprecise generalization. *In the 2021 federal election a majority of Canadian voters cast their ballots for candidates who supported some form of carbon tax* is more accurate. Such concern for precision may seem like pedantry, but there is a big difference between the two statements. Important though it was, the issue of climate change (and how we should combat it) was certainly not the only contentious issue in the campaign; it was an election, not a referendum. Learning to be careful about such distinctions is an important aspect of becoming a better thinker, a better writer—and a better educated citizen.

Cause and Effect

Whereas the natural connectives in narration are *and* and *then*, the natural connectives when discussing causes and effects, or giving reasons, or providing explanations, are words such as *because* and *therefore*. A great deal of college writing involves discerning and analyzing causes and effects, first because it's essential to fully understanding issues and developing informed opinions, and second because doing it well requires practice.

Events often have more than one cause, and often claims must be justified by more than one reason. That sounds straightforward enough, but sorting out the relative importance of **multiple causes and effects** can be far from straightforward. What caused crime rates in the United States to decline so greatly between the late 1970s and the 2010s? Was it changes in demographics, as young people (who commit a high percentage of crimes) came to represent a much smaller percentage of the population? Was it new styles of policing (such as the "broken windows" approach)? Was it the elimination of lead in gasoline in the 1980s (due to lead's proven negative effect on impulse-control in young people exposed to it)? Or was it any one of at least a half dozen other possible causes? We are likely to mislead ourselves if we begin such inquiries with the question, "which *one*...?" Where complex phenomena are concerned, events are very likely to have multiple causes. In the case of declining crime rates, social scientists have struggled to sort out which causes were more or less important.

Events often have more than one cause, and often claims must be justified by more than one reason.

Determining cause is also closely tied to assigning responsibility, which is why it is at issue in so many court cases. Person A shoots a weapon at Person B, who dies. Obviously Person B's death was caused by Person A, right? Even in a seemingly clear-cut case, it is not always so simple. If Person B had attacked Person A, who then shot in self-defence, does our analysis change? Should we say that Person B caused the sequence of events? What if it turns out that Person A provoked Person B? Is Person A then to blame for the result after all? To take it to a further extreme, perhaps we should blame the parents of Person A (or Person B?) for failing to raise non-violent kids? Events often result from a **chain of causal factors**, and deciding how far back to trace them can be key to one's conclusions—and highly fraught, as well.

Sometimes, too, there may be contributing causes that can magnify an effect. What if Person A is a five-year-old who found a parent's gun and pointed it at a friend thinking it was a toy? In such a case, some part of the responsibility would surely be assigned to the gun owner who left a loaded gun where a child could access it. The situation illustrates the useful distinction between **sufficient** and **necessary causes**. That gun owner's negligence was not a sufficient cause, because leaving out the gun did not automatically cause the death, but it was a necessary cause, in that the death would not have happened without it.

Those sorts of complexities around individual cases might appear more often in courts of law than in college essays—but analogous complexities also arise when we look at broader issues, such as the cause of gun-related deaths generally. Supporters of the National Rifle Association have argued for decades (since the 1970s—before that, the NRA favoured strict gun control) that "Guns don't kill people; people kill people." Again, this seems obvious: except for improbable cases in which guns might accidentally go off without human agency, gun deaths can be said to be caused by people—the gun is simply the instrument. But instruments do matter, and the gun is an instrument designed to kill. If Person A attacks Person B and the only weapon at hand is an eggplant, a death is highly unlikely to result. And if the only weapon to hand is a knife, a death is still much less likely to result than if a gun is handy. So yes, it's true that most deaths caused by guns wouldn't occur if there weren't someone to pull the trigger. But it's also true that a great many of those deaths wouldn't occur if there were no guns present. Both the people and the guns are necessary conditions for a great many of those deaths, not just one or the other.

As is often the case when something has multiple causes, a narrow focus on an individual case may produce a simple explanation (Person A caused Person B's death by pulling a trigger), but we will arrive at a different kind of explanation—and often a more useful one—if we examine the broader context. The immediate cause of an individual gun-related fatality can be determined by an autopsy, but to answer larger questions, such as "Why do so many people die of gun violence in the United States?" we need to look at statistical data with large sample sizes. The United States has the highest rate of gun-related fatalities of any developed country. It also has more guns per capita than any country in the world. Doesn't it stand to reason that a society with more guns will suffer more gun-related deaths? What about the culture of fear that is created by and also justifies wide-scale gun ownership? Doesn't it stand to reason that if everyone has a gun, people nervous about being shot will be inclined to shoot first?

Of course, we don't all approach these issues from the same starting point. Our intuitions about cause-and-effect when it comes to morally heated issues such as gun control are often shaped by our upbringing and social context. For some, it stands to reason that restricting gun ownership will reduce the number of gun deaths; for others it stands to reason that the way to prevent gun deaths is for *more* people to carry guns. As with other controversial topics, gun control generates heated feelings. With such topics we all tend to have difficulty being objective; we tend not to see any flaws in our own reasoning even as we jump to point out others' flawed arguments. We tend to place too much importance on ***anecdotal evidence***—stories of individual cases that seem to support our point of view—or we seize on factoids that back us up while disregarding other relevant information. That's why it's so important to provide—and require—solid, verifiable evidence when making or assessing claims about cause and effect. When considering any controversial question, it can be useful to ask oneself, *what (if anything) would lead me to change my mind on this issue?*

On the question of how gun control affects the American death toll from guns, we could marshal various kinds of evidence. We've already mentioned that crime rates significantly declined beginning in the 1970s; for many decades that included the nation-wide homicide rate, which according to the FBI was 1 in 10,000 in 1980 and less than half that in 2016. Over the same period, the sheer number of guns in the US doubled. According to the Congressional Research Service, the number of guns per capita in 1968 was roughly one for every two people; by 2016 it was one for every man, woman, and child.

Those two trends taken together might seem to indicate that more guns = fewer homicides (and inversely, fewer guns = more homicides). But we should be careful how we interpret these statistics. For one thing, although it's true that the US has more guns than ever, there are fewer people who own them: gun ownership by household declined from 50% in 1980 to 36% in 2016, according to a CBS poll. Furthermore, although the rate of homicides by gun in the US decreased from the 1980s through to 2016, it remained roughly ten times as high as the rate in most other developed countries (as did the rate of suicides involving guns).[1] Meanwhile, compared to other developed countries, the US had fewer restrictions on gun acquisition and ownership. Those facts, taken together, would seem to lead to a different conclusion: fewer guns = fewer homicides.[2]

It is important to understand that any such conclusion should not be regarded as absolutely proven by the data. At best, the evidence can demonstrate a correlation, and as we've pointed out before, correlation is not causation. Even once you have assembled a large body of such evidence, your conclusions will still not be established with 100% certainty. They will rest instead on a strong weight of probability; rather than saying that something *seems* highly probable on the basis of your own intuition, you will now be able to say that it *is* highly probable, on the basis of empirical evidence.

---

1 Out of every 100,000 Americans, each year 3.55 are murdered with a gun, while 6.70 kill themselves with a gun. Comparable figures annually for some other countries include Australia: 0.16 gun homicides; 0.74 gun suicides; Canada: 0.38 gun homicides, 1.52 gun suicides; Germany: 0.07 gun homicides, 0.84 gun suicides; United Kingdom: 0.06 gun homicides, 0.15 gun suicides. (All figures are from the University of Sydney's www.gunpolicy.org website.)

2 The homicide rate in the United States since 2016, it should be noted, has not followed the pattern that held from the 1980s through to 2016; the US homicide rate went up considerably in both 2020 and 2021, even as overall crime rates stayed low. That *may* have had to do with more Americans who did not previously own guns having acquired firearms during this period; certainly many Americans rushed to purchase guns during the pandemic. But there remains considerable disagreement as to the causes of the spike in the American homicide rate. Interestingly, there has not been a parallel spike elsewhere; the homicide rate in Britain (where gun ownership remained low), for example, continued to decline from 2016 through 2021, and the homicide rate in Canada (where gun ownership remained low) increased only slightly.

Here are six other contentious issues that involve assessments of cause and effect:

- Resolved that pit bulls cause too many injuries and deaths: in highly populated areas, they should be banned.
- Resolved that there are no bad dogs—just bad owners: when dogs injure humans, whatever injuries there are have been caused by the dog owners, not their dogs, and the dogs should not be made to suffer for that.
- Resolved that we should hold the minimum wage steady, or even decrease it; increasing the minimum wage causes jobs to be lost.
- Resolved that the minimum wage should be set at no less than 50% of the median wage; a higher minimum wage causes economic growth and also decreases inequality—without increasing unemployment.
- Resolved that meat is a contributing cause of cancer, heart disease, and diabetes: it should be sold with a warning, just as tobacco products are.
- Resolved that meat eating necessarily entails cruelty to non-human animals and is harmful to human health; animal cruelty laws should be extended to cover farm animals, and meat consumption should be discouraged through taxation.

In each case, discuss some of the ways in which assessing causes and effects may be complicated. Which side of each issue would you find it easier to argue? What information would you want to look up in order to debate each question? If you have an opinion already on each issue, what facts (if any) might lead you to change that view?

P 2.7 Logical Fluency

Fluency in writing is often thought of as purely a matter of *style*. But the flow of one's writing is intimately connected to the flow of one's argument. Each point must connect smoothly and logically to the next point for your essay to be clear and convincing. One element of logical fluency is the organization of your paragraphs, as discussed in P2.5 above: your points need to be arranged in a logical order, both within each paragraph and from one paragraph to another. And, even when there is an inherent logic that you, the writer, can sense in the way your points are organized, that needs to be made abundantly clear to the reader as well. When moving from sentence to sentence and from paragraph to paragraph, it is all too easy to skip over steps in the argument that you, the writer, feel are obvious. The problem is that readers may not feel the same way. Deliberate writers always ask themselves one key question: "Am I making everything clear for someone who has not done the research I have and who does not know anything of my argument beyond what I've told him? Do I need to repeat anything for emphasis, or to remind the reader of the path the argument has been taking?" In Robin Lee's essay, for example, paragraph 14 includes a good deal of elaboration, as the writer recaps the essay's arguments to that point and points out the directions in which those arguments are about to turn. In conversation, it's easy to interrupt and say, "I can't quite follow your reasoning; where are you going with this?" Readers don't have the same luxury.

In conversation, it's easy to interrupt and say, "I can't quite follow your reasoning; where are you going with this?" Readers don't have the same luxury.

The amount of space that is devoted to the ideas that appear in your essay can be of as much importance as the order in which they appear. For this reason, it is important to avoid long discussions of matters you consider to be of less importance—or else to relegate them to a note outside the main body of the text. (Notice how Robin Lee has relegated several interesting points to the notes of "Monumental Problems.") Similarly, it is important to provide some elaboration of your main idea—whether through extending the argument itself or through providing numerous examples—in order to signal to the reader your sense of the relative importance of the various ideas you are presenting. You can of course signal your sense of the relative levels of importance of the ideas you are discussing through the use of words and phrases such as *most important*, *crucially*, and so on. But a good essay typically also signals relative importance by giving the most space to the ideas that the writer considers most important.

The amount of space devoted to an idea is one way of signalling its importance; another is to return more than once to an essay's most important points. Mere repetitiveness is obviously off-putting to the reader—but continually drawing attention to the way paragraphs connect to key points over the course of an essay can greatly enhance its argumentative focus. In Robin Lee's essay, for example, Paragraphs 12 and 13 return to questions first posed in Paragraph 1, reviewing the options for how to deal with controversial monuments. The aesthetic side of the argument is first introduced in paragraph 1, and the general issues are returned to both in paragraph 14 and at the essay's conclusion in Paragraphs 23 and 24.

On every level of essay structure—from the entire essay down to the individual sentence—it's helpful to supply guideposts to show your reader the way. Perhaps you've heard the following advice for creating a reader-friendly essay: first, you have to tell your readers what you're going to tell them. Then you have to tell them. Then you have to tell them that you've told them. It may sound redundant to the point of absurdity, and if taken literally it would be. But when guiding someone it does help to describe the path. In the interests of establishing logical fluency for the reader, an introductory paragraph should provide a sense of what is to come, and a conclusion should remind the reader of the essay's main points. Similarly, the topic of a paragraph can usefully be introduced with a topic sentence.

Logical fluency is important at the grammatical level too—particularly where transitions between one sentence and another (or one clause and another within the same sentence) are concerned. Transitions are often achieved with the help of *connectives*—words or phrases that provide useful signposts for the reader as to the direction a writer's argument is taking. The connectives in Robin Lee's essay include phrases such as *on the contrary*, *as well*, and *to begin with*, as well as words such as *however*, *moreover*, *further*, *but*, *conversely*, and *whereas*.

Let's look at an example of a paragraph without connectives such as *however* and *moreover*:

> Sathnam Sanghera is among those who have suggested that … it may be better to leave monuments where they are and to "level the playing field" not by destroying old monuments but by erecting new monuments alongside the old ones to present the other

> side of the story. As a purely practical matter, it would surely take many decades to "level the playing field" in this way. The approach Sanghera recommends would continue to invite the public to revere many figures who, most people now agree, do not deserve to be so honoured.

Without connectives, the reader is left to puzzle out how the ideas of these three sentences connect. Is the idea of the second sentence put forward by way of supporting Sanghera's proposal? Or does it constitute an objection to Sanghera's proposal? And similar questions arise with the third sentence. But in Robin Lee's Paragraph 12, connectives make the connections clear:

> Sathnam Sanghera is among those who have suggested that … it may be better to leave monuments where they are and to "level the playing field" not by destroying old monuments but by erecting new monuments alongside the old ones to present the other side of the story. As a purely practical matter, **however**, it would surely take many decades to "level the playing field" in this way. **Moreover**, the approach Sanghera recommends would continue to invite the public to revere many figures who, most people now agree, do not deserve to be so honoured.

Robin's use of *however* here conveys a clear message that the second sentence is raising an objection to Sanghera's proposal. And in the next sentence, the connective *moreover* indicates to the reader that what is coming will be a further objection to Sanghera's proposal. An essay's logical fluency often depends on choosing the right way to connect your ideas.

See Section M2.9 for a full treatment of the ways in which connectives can be used.

P 2.8 Your Arguments, Others' Arguments

Another way to look at the organization of arguments is in terms of one's own ideas and those of others. When the concepts of plagiarism and of "original work" are discussed, it is rightly emphasized that any essay (or article, or Web posting, or full-length book) should present one's own ideas, not simply regurgitate the ideas of others. But does that mean one's own work has to be written without reference to that of others? No—far from it. Nor does "original" in the context of academic writing mean that an essay or academic book has to present nothing but ideas that no one has thought of before. It simply means that the ideas put forward should be thought through and synthesized by you as an individual—that you should not simply borrow someone else's thinking.

The process of thinking-through, synthesizing, and developing an argument, then, cannot and should not be done in a vacuum. An essay in which Robin Lee tried to think through the possible arguments relating to controversial monuments entirely on their own, without reference to the arguments others had made with regard to this issue, would be far less interesting than the essay they produced—an essay that draws on some of what others have written for support, but also an essay that takes issue with the views that some other writers have expressed, and with their failure to address one significant aspect of the issue.

The importance of engaging in this way with the arguments of others is the central point of one of the past generation's most influential books about the nature of academic argument, Gerald Graff and Cathy Birkenstein's *They Say, I Say*. As Graff and Birkenstein point out,

> the underlying structure of effective academic writing—and of responsible public discourse—resides not just in stating your own ideas, but in listening closely to others around us, summarizing their views in a way they will recognize, and responding with our own ideas in kind.... [T]o argue well you need to do more than assert your own ideas. You need to enter a conversation, using what others say (or might say) as a launching pad or sounding board for your own ideas. (3)

Locating your argument in the context of what others have already written on the topic can be helpful in several ways. First and most obviously, it can help to buttress your argument if you can cite others who have put forward similar views; by citing the arguments others have made—and, where appropriate, by summarizing or quoting from those arguments in support of your own—you can often make the points in your argument more persuasive. Here's an example (adapted from Paragraph 22 in Robin Lee's essay), first of all showing the argument in its crudest form—as a mere assertion:

> **less persuasive:** To my mind, the Regina monument to John A. Macdonald is unimpressive from an aesthetic point of view.

Robin Lee goes beyond this bald statement of their own views in two ways. First of all, in support of their expressed view, Robin provides their own arguments—the perceived awkwardness of the way in which the left arm is extended, and the lack of verisimilitude, as attested by comparisons with photographs of the subject:

> **more persuasive:** To my mind, the Regina monument to John A. Macdonald is unimpressive from an aesthetic point of view. The pose is awkward, with the left arm extended awkwardly, and—as a comparison with photographs of Macdonald makes clear—the work bears very little resemblance to the person being portrayed.

Robin then goes further, buttressing the argument by citing the views of qualified others, quoted in support of Robin's claim that this statue is lacking in aesthetic merit:

> **still more persuasive:** To my mind, the Regina monument to John A. Macdonald is unimpressive from an aesthetic point of view. The pose is awkward, with the left arm extended awkwardly, and—as a comparison with photographs of Macdonald makes clear—the work bears very little resemblance to the person being portrayed. Others have held similar views of the quality of the statue; when it was first erected in 1966 one local gallery curator called it a "caricature" that "tells us absolutely nothing about the character of the man," while another (Ronald Bloore, who would soon become a nationally known artist) described it as a work that "totally lacks artistic merit" (qtd. in Martin).

In referencing arguments that others have made, however, you are not simply looking to find other views that agree with your own. Referencing views that you disagree with is also vitally important—not least of all in order to help your reader to understand the context in which you are making your argument. For this reason, too, you do not want to put forward your arguments in a vacuum. Imagine, for example, an essay that begins with a paragraph such as this:

> The ways in which Jefferson Davis and Robert E. Lee shaped American history, and the ways in which John A. Macdonald shaped Canadian history are entirely unaffected by whether or not their statues are displayed in places of honour in our cities.

Readers unfamiliar with the monuments controversies might well be puzzled by an opening of this sort—and might well wonder, *so what*? But when the argument is situated in the context of arguments that others have made, any reader can understand immediately where the writer is coming from:

> Politician Mike Huckabee and political commentator Tim Constantine are among the many who have suggested that removing a statue from a public place is tantamount to "erasing history" (Caplan, Constantine). But in itself the act of removing a monument from a public place has no effect whatsoever on the historical record. The ways in which Jefferson Davis and Robert E. Lee shaped American history, and the ways in which John A. Macdonald shaped Canadian history are entirely unaffected by whether or not their statues are displayed in places of honour in our cities. Regardless of whether or not a statue of Lee towers above a public space in New Orleans or a statue of Macdonald towers above a public space in Regina, the actions of these historical figures continue to be remembered, written about, and extensively discussed in schools and universities.

Graff and Birkenstein helpfully draw attention to the degree to which academic writers use formulaic constructions—*templates*, in their terminology—as they situate their arguments in the context of what others have already said. Templates for framing academic arguments are constructions such as these: *A traditional view of xxx is .... But, as I will argue in this paper...*; *Some commentators have suggested that yyy is unnecessary or wrongheaded. As I will argue, however, there are good reasons for supporting yyy*. Here are a few other examples:

> Many scholars have argued that.... Overall, their conclusions are surely well founded but, as I will argue in this paper, they deserve to be qualified in one important respect.

> It is often claimed that the members of Generation Z tend disproportionately to be xxx, yyy, and zzz. But, as this paper will show, those claims rest on a very flimsy foundation.

> Until recently, historians have tended to view xxx in terms of its political ramifications. But—as I will argue in this essay, xxx has important cultural ramifications as well.

Situating your argument in the context of what others have already written often entails pointing out weaknesses in the arguments of those who argue opposing positions. It may also entail—as is the case with Robin Lee's essay on monuments—pointing out omissions in the arguments others have put forward. Robin doesn't cite anyone who has argued *against* taking aesthetic considerations into account when trying to decide how best to proceed when controversies over monuments arise, for the very good reason that no one has put forward any such argument. As Robin details in footnotes 9 and 11, aesthetic considerations have rarely been mentioned at all when these issues are discussed; Robin's argument is in this respect genuinely original.

Let's look at how Robin Lee's essay does respond to the arguments of others. The essay doesn't devote a lot of space to arguing against ill thought-out positions such as the suggestion that removing monuments of controversial figures is an exclusive initiative of the political left, or the assertion that the removal of monuments is a censorship and freedom of speech issue; these misconceptions are dealt with in two short paragraphs (2 and 3).Considerably more space is devoted to arguing (in Paragraph 13) against the much more plausible position that "all such monuments should still be displayed publicly, but in a venue such as a museum where they can be accompanied by full contextualization."

In referencing others' arguments that you disagree with, it's important to address the strongest of such arguments, and, conversely, not to spend much time or effort on refuting the weakest or least plausible ones. If you're arguing in favour of legalized marijuana, for example, it would not be a good strategy to focus largely on refuting the argument put forward in the 1936 propaganda film *Reefer Madness* (that consumption of marijuana is likely to lead to insanity and suicide). Instead, you should look to refute the most credible arguments against legalization that have been put forward in our own time—the arguments advanced by the American Medical Association, for example—and focus on refuting those. And, of course, you should look for reputable authorities who can buttress the arguments you make; you might well want to refer to the 15 January 2022 *Globe and Mail* editorial, for instance ("Canada's legalization of cannabis is a success story, despite a shaky first act").

What if you aren't able to find strong arguments that challenge the points you wish to make? That may be a sign of several things. First of all, you should ask yourself if you have chosen a sufficiently interesting and challenging topic. If you are thinking of writing an essay arguing that men and women should receive equal pay for equal work, or that racism is bad, you're not likely to find strong and interesting opposing views to come to grips with.

But what if you are thinking of writing an essay about a newly published short story, or about a very recent political development, or about a philosophical position that has recently been advanced for the first time? You may not be able to find strong and interesting opposing views to come to grips with in those sorts of cases either—but in such cases you certainly shouldn't feel that you have chosen a poor topic. Often in such cases you can give substance to your own arguments by *inventing* as strong a set of opposing arguments as you can. You can try to anticipate the strongest possible argument you can imagine that *might* be made by someone taking an opposing position. If you can persuasively counter any such arguments, you will have surmounted an important test—and likely have written a first-rate essay.

In this connection it is worth drawing attention to the phrase in parentheses in the passage from Graff and Birkenstein quoted above: "You need to enter a conversation, using what others say (*or might say*) as a launching pad or sounding board for your own ideas." There are many ways in which writers introduce what others might say into their arguments. Sometimes these will merely be straw person arguments, but in many cases they represent a genuine effort on the part of the writer to imagine and to counter the strongest possible case that might be made against one's own position. Here are some ways in which ideas of this sort can be introduced:

> An opponent might argue that.... But that would be to....
>
> On the other side, it could be suggested that.... But in that case....
>
> We may well imagine the counter argument to this—that.... But this counter argument does not hold up to close scrutiny....

Whatever the reasons for incorporating the arguments of others into their essays, good writers are careful, in doing so, to document their sources accurately and completely. This is, first of all, a service to readers who would like to embark on a fuller investigation into the topic of a paper by looking up its sources themselves; every academic citation system gives readers all the information they need to access original source material. But it is also critical that there be complete clarity about which parts of an essay are the author's and which parts come from elsewhere.

Citing sources is fundamental to writing a good research paper, but no matter how diligent you are in making your acknowledgements, your paper will not be taken seriously unless its documentation is formatted according to an appropriate and accepted referencing style. For the sake of consistency, each academic discipline has adopted a particular system of referencing as its standard, which those writing in that discipline are expected to follow. Almost all of the humanities use the documentation guidelines developed by the Modern Language Association (MLA), a notable exception being History, which tends to prefer those of the *Chicago Manual of Style* (Chicago Style). The social and some health sciences typically follow the style rules of the American Psychological Association (APA), while the basic sciences most commonly use the referencing systems of the Council of Science Editors (CSE). Each of these styles is exacting and comprehensive in its formatting rules; following with precision the one recommended for a given paper's discipline is one of a responsible research writer's duties. Section C3 outlines the MLA, APA, and Chicago Style systems; details regarding the CSE system may be found on the *Broadview Guide to Writing* student resource website.

P 2.9 Incorporating Sources through Summary, Paraphrase, and Quotation

There are three main ways of working source material into a paper: summarizing, paraphrasing, and quoting directly. In order to avoid plagiarism, care must be taken with all three kinds of borrowing, both in the way they are handled and in their referencing. In what follows, a passage from page 102 of a book by Terrence W. Deacon (*The Symbolic Species: The Co-Evolution of Language and the Brain*, Norton, 1997) serves as the source for a sample summary, paraphrase, and quotation. The examples feature the MLA style of in-text parenthetical citations, but the requirements for presenting the source material are the same for all academic referencing systems.

For a similar discussion with a focus on APA style, see Incorporating Sources in APA Style (in Section C3.2).

original source Over the last few decades language researchers seem to have reached a consensus that language is an innate ability, and that only a significant contribution from innate knowledge can explain our ability to learn such a complex communication system. Without question, children enter the world predisposed to learn human languages. All normal children, raised in normal social environments, inevitably learn their local language, whereas other species, even when raised and taught in this same environment, do not. This demonstrates that human brains come into the world specially equipped for this function.

Summary

An honest and competent summary, whether of a passage or an entire book, must not only represent the source accurately but also use original wording and include a citation. It is a common misconception that only quotations need to be acknowledged as borrowings in the body of an essay. In fact, without a citation, even a fairly worded summary or paraphrase is an act of plagiarism. The first example below is faulty on two counts: it borrows wording (underlined) from the source, and it has no parenthetical reference.

needs checking Researchers agree that language learning is innate, and that only innate knowledge can explain how we are able to learn a system of communication that is so complex. Normal children raised in normal ways will always learn their local language, whereas other species do not, even when taught human language and exposed to the same environment.

The next example correctly avoids the wording of the source passage, and a signal phrase and parenthetical citation note the author and page number.

revised As Terrence W. Deacon notes, there is now wide agreement among linguists that the ease with which human children acquire their native tongues, under the conditions of a normal childhood, demonstrates an inborn capacity for language that is not shared by any other animals, not even those who are reared in comparable ways and given human language training (102).

Paraphrase

Whereas a summary is a shorter version of its original, a paraphrase tends to be about the same length. However, paraphrases, just like summaries, must reflect their sources accurately, must use original wording, and must include a citation. Even though it is properly cited, the paraphrase of the first sentence of the Deacon passage, below, falls short by being too close to the wording of the original (underlined).

needs checking Researchers in language have come to a consensus in the past few decades that the acquisition of language is innate; such contributions from knowledge contribute significantly to our ability to master such a complex system of communication (Deacon 102).

Simply substituting synonyms for the words and phrases of the source, however, is not enough to avoid plagiarism. Despite its original wording, the next example also fails but for a very different reason: it follows the original's sentence structure too closely, as illustrated in the interpolated copy below it.

needs checking Recently, linguists appear to have come to an agreement that speaking is an inborn skill, and that nothing but a substantial input from inborn cognition can account for the human capacity to acquire such a complicated means of expression (Deacon 102).

Recently (*over the last few decades*), linguists (*language researchers*) appear to have come to an agreement (*seem to have reached a consensus*) that speaking is an inborn skill (*that language is an innate ability*), and that nothing but a substantial input (*and that only a significant contribution*) from inborn cognition (*from innate knowledge*) can account for the human capacity (*can explain our ability*) to acquire such a complicated means of expression (*to learn such a complex communication system*) (Deacon 102).

What follows is a good paraphrase of the passage's opening sentence; this paraphrase captures the sense of the original without echoing the details and shape of its language.

revised Linguists now broadly agree that children are born with the ability to learn language; in fact, the human capacity to acquire such a difficult skill cannot easily be accounted for in any other way (Deacon 102).

Quoting Directly

Unlike paraphrases and summaries, direct quotations must use the exact wording of the original. Because they involve importing outside words, quotations pose unique challenges. Quote too frequently, and you risk making your readers wonder why they are not reading your sources instead of your paper. Your essay should present something you want to say—informed and supported by properly documented sources, but forming a contribution that is yours alone. To that end, use secondary material to help you build a strong framework for your work, not to replace it. Quote sparingly, therefore; use your sources' exact wording only when it is important or particularly memorable.

To avoid misrepresenting your sources, be sure to quote accurately, and to avoid plagiarism, take care to indicate quotations as quotations, and cite them properly. Below are two problematic quotations. The first does not show which words come directly from the source.

needs checking Terrence W. Deacon maintains that children enter the world predisposed to learn human languages (102).

The second quotation fails to identify the source at all.

needs checking Linguists believe that "children enter the world predisposed to learn human languages."

The next example corrects both problems by naming the source and indicating clearly which words come directly from it.

revised Terrence W. Deacon maintains that "children enter the world predisposed to learn human languages" (102).

P 2.10 Plagiarism

Most people understand that taking someone else's writing and passing it off as one's own is intellectual thievery. But it is important to be aware that you may commit plagiarism even if you do not use precisely the same words another person wrote in precisely the same order. For instance, here is an actual example of plagiarism. *Globe and Mail* newspaper columnist Margaret Wente borrowed material for one of her columns from a number of works, including an article by Dan Gardner that had appeared the previous year in another newspaper (the *Ottawa Citizen*) and a book by Robert Paarlberg called *Starved for Science* (which was the subject of Gardner's article). The similarities were brought to light by media commentator Carol Wainio, who presented a series of parallel passages, including the following, on her blog *Media Culpa* (the fonts are Wainio's—simple bold is for direct copying; the bold + italics is for "near copying"):

> Gardner: ***Many NGOs working in Africa in the area of development and the environment have been advocating against the modernization of traditional farming practices***, Paarlberg says. "**They believe that traditional farming in Africa incorporates indigenous knowledge that shouldn't be replaced by science-based knowledge introduced from the outside.** They encourage Africa to stay away from fertilizers, and be certified as organic instead. And in the case of genetic engineering, they warn African governments against making these technologies available to farmers."

> Wente: ***Yet, many NGOs working in Africa have tenaciously fought the modernization of traditional farming practices.*** **They believe traditional farming in Africa incorporates indigenous knowledge that shouldn't be replaced by science-based knowledge introduced from the outside.** As Prof. Paarlberg writes, "They encourage African farmers to stay away from fertilizers and be certified organic instead. And they warn African governments to stay away from genetic engineering."

Wente does not always use exactly the same words as her sources, but no one reading the passages can doubt that one writer is appropriating the phrasings of the others. Additionally, where Wente *does* quote Paarlberg directly, the quotation is lifted from Gardner's article and should be identified as such.

The penalties for such practices are not trivial; Wente was publicly reprimanded by her employer, and the CBC radio program *Q* removed her from its media panel. Other reporters have been, justifiably, fired under similar circumstances. At most colleges and universities, students are likely to receive a zero if they are caught plagiarizing—and they may be expelled from the institution. It's important to be aware, too, that penalties for plagiarism make no allowance for intent; it is no defence that a writer took someone else's words "by mistake" rather than intentionally.

How, then, can you be sure to avoid plagiarism? First of all, be extremely careful in your note-taking, so as to make it impossible to imagine, a few days later, that words you have jotted down from somewhere else are your own. Quotations from sources and summaries are best kept separate from the set of notes in which you are putting together your own ideas.[1] (In her *Globe and Mail* column responding to the plagiarism charges, Wente, in fact, claimed that she had accidentally mixed a quotation into her own ideas.) If your note-taking is reliable, then you will know which words need to be credited. One way to rewrite the passage above would simply be to remove the material taken from Gardner and to credit Paarlberg by quoting him directly, if you were able to access his book and could do so: "As Robert Paarlberg has argued in his book *Starved for Science*, many NGOs 'believe that traditional farming in Africa incorporates indigenous knowledge that shouldn't be replaced by science-based knowledge introduced from the outside.'" You would, of course, look up and provide the page number as well.

You may notice that the quoted material is a statement of opinion rather than fact—controversial views are being given, but without any evidence provided to back them up—so a careful reader would wonder whether NGOs are really as anti-science as the quotation suggests, or whether the writer hasn't done enough research on the debate. If you were to make an assertion like this in a paper of your own it would not be enough just to quote Paarlberg; you would need to do much more research and find information to support or

1 In putting together your own ideas, you can write "quote Paarlberg here" or "refer here to Gardner article."

deny your claim. If you are including quotations in an essay, the best sources to quote are not necessarily those which express opinions that mirror the ones you are putting forward. In a case such as this, for example, the argument would have been much more persuasive if Wente had quoted an official statement from one of the NGOs she was attacking. If her article had quoted a source making this specific case against "science-based knowledge" and then argued directly against that source's argument, Wente's own position would have been strengthened. Quoting many such sources would provide proof that the article's characterization of the position of NGOs was factually accurate.

Whenever you do quote someone else, it's important to cite the source. But do you need a citation for everything that did not come from your own knowledge? Not necessarily. Citations are usually unnecessary when you are touching on common knowledge (provided it is, in fact, common knowledge, and provided your instructor has not asked you to do otherwise). If you refer to the chemical composition of water, or the date when penicillin was discovered, you are unlikely to need to provide any citation, even if you used a source to find the information, since such facts are generally available and uncontroversial. (Make sure, however, to check any "common knowledge" with several reputable sources; if your information is incorrect, it reflects poorly on you, especially if you have not cited your source.) If you have any doubts about whether something is common knowledge or not, cite it; over-cautiousness is not a serious problem, but plagiarism always is.

P 3 Improving Style

P 3.1 Stylistic Fluency

What Northrop Frye has called "verbal cotton wool" (107) comes in at least two varieties. In one variety, the woolliness arises primarily from the words the writer has chosen. Here's an example:

> Critical curriculum theorists like Michael Apple have argued that what we teach and how we teach conveys something about what kinds of students and citizens we aim to shape within our English classrooms. Our selections are inherently political, they have told us: they are representative of our disciplinary and even ideological perspectives at the same time that they are constitutive of them. (Gatti 179)

The sentence structures here are relatively straightforward, but the passage's reliance on vague, abstract language makes the intended meaning difficult to discern. It's possible to puzzle through how one sort of thing may be representative of another sort of thing at the same time as it is "constitutive of" that other sort of thing, but it takes considerable effort. And what is the first sort of thing that is being referred to? "Our selections"—but selections of what? With a bit more effort we can infer that the writer must be referring to selections made for educational curricula—but again, it's not easy to unpack the meaning.

In the following passage, on the other hand (part of a circuitous disclaimer from Facebook), the woolliness arises from a sentence structure so convoluted as to make the passage's meaning almost impenetrable:

> Because Facebook provides a wide range of services, we may ask you to review and accept supplemental terms that apply to your interaction with a specific app, product, or service. To the extent those supplemental terms conflict with this statement of rights and responsibilities, the supplemental terms associated with the app, product, or service govern with respect to your use of such app, product or service to the extent of the conflict.

In the first of the above passages, then, the problem is a matter of **diction** (choice of words); in the second it's a matter of **syntax** (arrangement of words).

P 3.2 Diction

As George Orwell warned repeatedly, English can exert insidious power over human thought processes. Words group themselves together in familiar, formulaic packages that can leap from a writer's keyboard before she's had a chance to really think:

> Ready-made phrases come crowding in. They will construct your sentences for you—even think your thoughts for you, to a certain extent— … partially concealing your meaning even from yourself.... This invasion of one's mind by ready-made phrases ... can only be prevented if one is constantly on guard against them. (362)

It is easy even for a relatively inexperienced consumer of university writing to construct a lifeless sentence:

Certain	definite	elements	can be	identified
Several	key	components		illuminated
Numerous	crucial	factors		underlined
		aspects		isolated
		facets		
		areas		

... when discussing the monuments controversy.

Even the most attentive writers can dull their topics (and their minds!) with phrases such as *certain crucial facets* or *several key elements* or *numerous definite components* or (even worse) *certain crucial facets and several definite components*. Usually there is nothing at all "definite" or "certain" about such writing. Vague categories—factors, areas, components, and so on—are conjured up as empty vessels, without any specific material to fill them in.

If familiar words that lend themselves to vague and imprecise meanings are a temptation for many writers, so too are words that are a little less familiar, with meanings that we may be a little uncertain about. As Katherine Acheson sensibly advises, "if you want to write clearly, you have to choose the words that mean what you want to say." That may seem obvious, but as Acheson suggests, most of us often choose instead words that we think *might* mean what we want to say. And, as Acheson firmly advises, that's not good enough (9). An example may make this issue more clear. Let's say you're thinking of writing about movie star Jennifer Lawrence's performance in Debra Granik's film *Winter's Bone*. Which of these two sentences would be better?

> Jennifer Lawrence's performance in Debra Granik's 2010 film *Winter's Bone* was widely praised.

> Jennifer Lawrence's performance in Debra Granik's 2010 film *Winter's Bone* garnered considerable notoriety for the young thespian.

Many might imagine the words chosen for the second of these sentences to be more impressive—and more appropriate, because more "academic sounding." But they'd be wrong. The word *thespian* (in some contexts a synonym for *actor*) is generally used to refer to those who perform on the stage rather than on film. The word *notoriety* (in some contexts a near-synonym for *fame*) is used to refer to fame that comes as a result of doing something bad, not for something that brings praise. The word *garner* (in some contexts a synonym for *get* or *acquire* or *achieve*) is rather loose in its meaning, but is generally used when one has achieved something praiseworthy—not when one has become notorious. There would thus be nothing wrong with the following sentence:

> Jennifer Lawrence's performance in Debra Granik's 2010 film *Winter's Bone* garnered considerable praise for the young actor.

But the first sentence above would still be preferable as a matter of style; it's less wordy.

Because they are involved in intellectual discourse, academic and professional writers must of necessity use a good many abstract and conceptual nouns. But they should be continually wary of overdoing it. Too dense a concentration of abstractions or vague generalizations will frustrate the reader; readers can't put their hands on something that is too airy to grasp. They require, and deserve, a balance between abstraction and solidity.

Many who have written on style have advised against using too many adjectives or adverbs—though it is rare to find "too many" quantified. No doubt the widespread prejudice against adjectives and adverbs is in part a reaction against two unfortunate tendencies that many of us share. The first is to be repetitive in our use of adjectives; *tiny little* and *great big* are common conversational combinations that sometimes find their way onto the page as well. The second is to use adverbs as largely meaningless intensifiers; we don't usually need the *very* in *very important* or the *extremely* in *extremely tragic*. But in fact most good writers of non-fiction prose[1] use adjectives and adverbs freely, and to good effect. Look, for example, at the following passages by Ta-Nehisi Coates and Rebecca Solnit, both of whom are among the most widely admired prose stylists of the twenty-first century. Adjectives and adverbs have been underlined:

> We must imagine a new country. Reparations—by which I mean the full acceptance of our collective biography and its consequences—is the price we must pay to see ourselves squarely. The recovering alcoholic may well have to live with his illness for the rest of his life. But at least he is not living a drunken lie. Reparations beckons us to reject the intoxication of hubris and see America as it is—the work of fallible humans. (paragraph 140)

> While many question the motives of the childless, who are taken to be selfish for refusing the sacrifices that come with parenthood, they often neglect to note that those who love their children most intensely may have less love left for the rest of the world. [Things such as] writing and inventing and politics and activism—most of the things I value most, and from which I trust any improvements in the human condition will come, are violently incompatible with the actual and imaginative work of childcare. (paragraph 20)

Notice that, of the many adjectives and adverbs used here, none is at all rare, and none is used in a particularly striking or original fashion. *New, collective, drunken, fallible, selfish, intensely, human, violently*; these are everyday adjectives and adverbs, carefully chosen. Writers can certainly create an effect with references to the *elaborate casualness* of a politician's remark, or the *cerulean intensity* of an actor's blue eyes. But well-chosen adjectives and adverbs do not need

1 Overuse of adjectives and adverbs may be more of a live issue for those learning to write fiction and/or poetry.

P3 Improving Style

to be unusual or showy; they simply need to fit the context, and help the writer convey to the reader the desired sense.

Notice too that the above passages are both examples of argumentative rather than descriptive prose. It's sometimes imagined that adjectives and adverbs should be used freely only in descriptive prose, and not when one is making an argument; as the Coates and Solnit passages show, that's simply not the case.

Choosing words can be particularly perilous whenever a writer's topic involves technical or specialized language. "In order to ensure that a truly regional renal care delivery structure will be optimally functional, there must be patient accessibility to a number of interdigitated modalities of care," writes the medical essayist, forgetting simplicity in his pursuit of kidney doctors' respect. Chances are he has misconstrued his audience, anyway; even professionals at ease with the jargon of their own specialty would prefer *work well* to *be optimally functional*; and *several interconnected clinics* to *a number of interdigitated modalities of care*. Who really wants to read *the plan is more philosophical than operational in terms of framework*, rather than *the plan is still an idea; it has not been tested yet*?

As discussed in detail in Sections C1 and C2 of this book, academic writing depends upon the use of jargon in one sense of that word—namely, the specialized language of any scholarly field. In that sense, jargon is, quite simply, invaluable. But the word *jargon* also has a second meaning: unnecessarily vague and unfocused vocabulary. It's in this second sense that jargon is to be avoided. Jargon in this sense is as much a problem of psychology as it is a problem of grammar and usage—as, indeed, are many of the most pervasive writers' problems. As Virginia Woolf observed, "we write, not with the fingers, but with the whole person. The nerve which controls the pen winds itself about every fibre of our being…" (Ch. 5). In what sort of psychological state, then, are we most likely to use unnecessarily vague and unfocused language? When we become

Additional Material Online

Exercises on jargon and on word choice may be found at **sites.broadviewpress.com/writingcdn**. Click on **Exercises** and go to **"Style."**

more concerned with making ourselves sound knowledgeable than we are with acquiring knowledge. And when we become more concerned with making our ideas sound important than with thinking them through and expressing them clearly. Unfortunately, most of us are sufficiently impressionable to be taken in at least occasionally by jargon's allure. To resist it, we need to keep in mind not the impression we are trying to create, but what we are trying to convey to the reader.

P3.3 Syntax

Choosing words that mean what you say is of course only one of the elements of style. Just as important is the order in which the words appear—the structure of your sentences. The **syntax** of a sentence is the way in which the words and phrases are arranged. As the following sentence illustrates, poor syntax can significantly disrupt comprehension for your reader:

> In a 101-foot mine shaft, abandoned for almost fifty years, two injured men were rescued over the weekend after they lit a fire to attract the attention of passers-by.

Does this mean that the two men had been abandoned for almost fifty years? With a moment's reflection the reader is able to figure out that it's the mine shaft that's been abandoned for fifty years, not the men, but the phrasing of the sentence doesn't immediately make that clear. Fortunately, the problem is easily fixed by using verbs (*were trapped*, *had been abandoned*) in place of the past participle *abandoned*:

> Two injured men were trapped in a 101-foot mine shaft that had been abandoned for almost fifty years; they were rescued over the weekend after they lit a fire to attract the attention of passers-by.

Here is another example of a syntactical problem:

> Only a few facts are known about Smith's early life in the 1850s. Born in Halifax, Nova Scotia, in 1852, Smith's father was a navy officer.

Who was born in 1852? From the context the reader can figure out that it must be Smith—but according to the grammar of the

P3
Improving Style

sentence it's Smith's *father* who was born in 1852; grammatically, the past participle "Born" at the beginning of the second sentence can only refer to the subject of the sentence's main clause "Smith's father." Again, it's not difficult to fix the problem—and again, the easiest way to fix it entails replacing a past participle (*born*) with a subject/verb construction (*He was born*):

> Only a few facts are known about Smith's early life in the 1850s. He was born in Halifax, Nova Scotia, in 1852; his father was a navy officer.

When you start a sentence with a past participle, it would seem, you need to be always wary.

Even when garbled syntax doesn't create ambiguity, it can be very hard to read. The following two passages both express the same ideas. Which do you find easier to read?

> The subject matter of Gothic literature is typically dark and mysterious; night-time visions are often experienced, the supernatural is often suggested, and terror is often a powerful presence. "The Raven" and "The Haunted Palace," two of Poe's best-known Gothic poems, and "The Tell-Tale Heart" and "The Fall of the House of Usher," two of his best-known Gothic stories, display all these characteristics. When Poe wrote in the Gothic mode, he was influenced by earlier writers—British poets such as Samuel Taylor Coleridge and Lord Byron, and American writers such as Charles Brockden Brown. But Poe's Gothic writing is also highly original; his reputation as one the most important American writers of the mid-nineteenth century rests largely on these Gothic poems and tales.

> Both "The Raven" and "The Haunted Palace" demonstrate Poe's expression of several of the typical themes of Gothic literature, including the mysterious, supernatural occurrences, psychological terror, and hideous night-time visions. Writing in the wake both of British Gothic writing by poets of an earlier era, Samuel Taylor Coleridge and Lord Byron being two important examples, and of American Gothic writing by Charles Brockden Brown and other authors of note, Poe's Gothic works of poetry ("The Raven" and "The Haunted Palace," for example) as well as in the genre of prose fiction ("The Tell-Tale Heart" and "The Fall of the

> House of Usher" are both examples of the latter) are nevertheless in many ways highly original, and it is largely on the basis of these Gothic poems and tales that his reputation has become firmly positioned as one of the most important American writers of the mid-nineteenth century.

Almost every reader will find the second of these passages more difficult to read than the first. Part of the problem is simply unnecessary verbiage; the second passage takes 148 words to say what the first passage says in 123 words. But the problem is not only that the second passage is clogged with too many words; it's also that the words have been poorly chosen and awkwardly arranged. At one point, in fact, the second passage actually uses *fewer* words than does the first passage to say the same thing—but even at that point the second passage is more difficult to read:

> The subject matter of Gothic literature is typically dark and mysterious; hideous night-time visions are often experienced, the supernatural is often suggested, and terror is often a powerful presence. (29 words)

> ... the typical themes of Gothic literature, including the dark and mysterious, supernatural occurrences, psychological terror, and experiencing hideous night-time visions. (20 words)

Here the first passage is somewhat longer, but the parallelism of the sentence structure (*visions are often...*, *the supernatural is often...*, *terror is often...*) makes it easy for the reader to digest the meaning. In the second passage, in contrast, two participial phrases (*including the ... occurrences*, *experiencing ... visions*) point in different directions, while a simple noun and adjective combination is sandwiched between them.

It's common for students trying to learn the conventions of academic writing to overuse participial constructions—present participles (such as *including* or *experiencing*) just as much as past participles. Notice what happens in the second sentence of the second passage above, which starts off with the present participle *Writing*. What is the subject of the sentence? It's not until we are 40 words into the sentence that we reach the grammatical subject: *Poe's Gothic works*. But think about this for a moment: is it in fact *Poe's Gothic works* that were "writing in the wake of" the work of earlier writers? No; it was Poe himself who was doing that. By using a present participle at the beginning of the sentence and taking a long time to get to the subject, the writer has created an ungrammatical sentence structure. (See the section on Dangling Constructions in Section M2.1 of this book for more on this sort of error.) Good advice for undergraduates: stick for the most part to simple grammatical structures, with the subject near the beginning of each clause. And be very wary of participial constructions.

It's also common for writers at almost any level to feel instinctively that their academic writing will seem more impressive if they use long, unusual words and long, complicated sentences. But the fact is that, when we try to impress in this sort of way, we usually end up making more mistakes than we would have otherwise, and looking utterly unimpressive. It's difficult enough to put words together so as to convey straightforwardly to the reader what we genuinely mean to say. We make it more difficult both for our readers and for ourselves if we aim for complexity of expression—whether that's in the form of rarified words or convoluted syntax.

Not all syntactical problems stem from a desire to impress with long, convoluted sentences, of course. Another sort of problem is the tendency that many writers have to structure all their sentences in the same way. Some writers, for example, fall into the habit of prefacing every sentence with the same sort of phrase or subordinate clause. Others may develop a verbal tic of repeating the same strings of words in different contexts; many is the writer who has developed the habit of resorting to *in terms of xxx*, or *so far as zzz is concerned*, or *at the end of the day* far too often.

The goal in most writing should be a varied and flexible style, one that uses simple words wherever possible without becoming simplistic. But it is virtually impossible to achieve that sort of style on the first draft. To write prose that is straightforward, readily comprehensible, and engaging is always difficult, and always requires more than one draft. In part at least, the secret of learning good syntax is to allow yourself time between successive drafts of an essay. A day or three away from an essay will mean your eyes are fresh when you return to it. Even a single good night's sleep can enhance objectivity, so that the person who wrote the sentences can respond more as their eventual readers will respond.

P3.4 Rhythm

Style is not only a matter of conveying meaning; it is also a matter of aesthetics. That's obviously the case with prose fiction or poetry, but it's also true of non-fiction prose. Even in academic prose, the rhythm of your sentences can have a significant effect on the way in which your writing is received. One way to create resonant prose is of course through repetition. That's what Robin Lee does in this passage:

> When Indigenous Canadians such as Marie Knockwood testify that they feel "full of anger and bitterness" seeing Macdonald honoured with public monuments, it matters. When African Americans such as Nicole Moliere of New Orleans testify that walking or driving past statues of the likes of Lee and Davis feels like "a daily assault," it matters.

Rhythmic effects can also be created by varying the syntactical structures you use. The most predictable syntax in the grammar of English is SUBJECT-VERB-PREDICATE, as in sentences such as *The Board of Trustees commissioned James Earle Fraser to create the statue*, or *The financial implications should be considered*, or *The overall composition of the work is striking.* Upending that predictability occasionally can create variety in the rhythms of your prose, and can help to make your writing more readable. Notice how Robin Lee varies the structures of their sentences occasionally by putting the verb first (*Consider the financial implications*) or by putting what would normally be the predicate first (*Even more striking is the composition of the work*).

An important element in rhythmical distinctiveness is balance. Sometimes a pleasing balance is achieved simply by deliberately repeating phrases or grammatical forms:

> We may not wish to deny academics the right to publish such research. But nor can we deny the harm that it causes.

Sometimes balance may be achieved by placing words or phrases in apposition (where successive words or phrases fulfill the same grammatical function in a sentence, with the second helping to elaborate on or explain the first):

> Haldeman was Nixon's closest confidant, his most influential advisor.
>
> The generality of the images here has the effect of opening up the scene to the reader, of allowing her to graft her own archetypes of *river* and *hill* and *woods* onto the story.

Paired connectives (*if ... then, either ... or, not only ... but also*) can also help in achieving balance. But here, as always, the writer must be careful that the words are in the right places; otherwise the fragile element of balance is lost:

needs checking Hardy was not only a prolific novelist but wrote poetry too, and also several plays.

revised Hardy was not only a prolific novelist but also a distinguished poet and a dramatist.

(Here the noun *novelist* is balanced by the later nouns *poet* and *dramatist*.)

needs checking The experiment can either be performed with hydrogen or with oxygen.

revised The experiment can be performed with either hydrogen or oxygen.

(Here the choice is between the two gases, not between performing and some other thing.)

needs checking To subdue an aggressor through sanctions, the United Nations feels, is better than using military force.

revised To subdue an aggressor through sanctions, the United Nations feels, is better than to use military force.

or Subduing an aggressor through sanctions, the United Nations feels, is better than using military force.

(Here infinitive balances infinitive; participle balances participle.)

needs checking In 2008 there was a female Vice-Presidential candidate for a major American political party, and in 2020 too.

revised In both 2008 and 2020 a major American political party chose a female Vice-Presidential candidate.

Repetition of some grammatical phrase allows readers to sense a pattern in the writing. If parallel structure has been used to balance the parts of a sentence, even long sentences can be made easily comprehensible to the reader. In the following sentence from Robin Lee's "Monumental Problems" paper, for example, repetition and parallelism make the meaning easy to unpack.

> The ways in which Jefferson Davis and Robert E. Lee shaped American history, and in which John A. Macdonald shaped Canadian history, are entirely unaffected by whether or not their statues are displayed in places of honour in our cities; their actions continue to be remembered, written about, and extensively discussed in schools and universities.

But even careful balancing cannot make a steady diet of long clauses and long sentences palatable; varying the length of your sentences and clauses also makes a difference to the rhythm (and the readability) of your prose. It's worth noticing the way in which Robin Lee occasionally interjects very short sentences or clauses into their prose:

> Fraser spent twelve years working on the statue; it shows.

No writer naturally thinks, as she is drafting an essay, "Now I must remember to vary the length of my sentences." But when it comes time to revise your work—particularly if you have allowed a day or two to elapse after completing the rough draft—you will be better able to notice if and when your writing has become dominated either by very long sentences or by very short ones. You'll be able too to notice such things as a preponderance of *it is* ..., *there is* ..., and *there are* sentences:

needs checking It is important to remember that there are cultural as well as economic effects of free trade. There are many people who argue that over the long term these are just as significant.

revised Free trade has cultural as well as economic effects. Indeed, many argue that over the long term these are just as significant.

By making such changes as these, even when there are no actual errors in the rough draft, careful writers are able—with very little effort expended—to make their prose clearer, crisper, and more concise. And by doing so they make things considerably easier for the reader.

Additional Material Online
Exercises on balance and parallelism may be found at **sites.broadviewpress.com/writingcdn**. Click on **Exercises** and go to **"Style."**

P3.5 Figures of Speech

Another important element of style is figurative language: the use of images from beyond the realm of the essay's primary topic—most commonly in the form of metaphors or similes. By appealing to readers' senses, such images give life and clarity to abstract diction. An excellent example appears in George Orwell's famous essay on politics and language, where the writer complains about people who believe that "any struggle against the abuse of language is a sentimental archaism, like preferring candles to electric light or hansom cabs to airplanes" (353). His introduction of an abstract and difficult concept (*sentimental archaism*) is followed by two vivid figures of speech, which aid readers in understanding the point being made.

Orwell's use of the word *like* is enough to classify his figures of speech as similes, which are distinct from metaphors: *My love is a red, red rose* is a metaphor; *My love is like a red, red rose* is a simile. The difference is simply that similes make comparisons explicit through the use of words such as *like* or *as*, whereas metaphors fuse the objects of comparison.

Of course, as Orwell himself warns, dull or overly familiar figures of speech can undermine not only stylistic but also logical fluency. Most writers drink from the well of stale imagery more often than they realize. When they do, what ends up on the page has little life to it: *that will be the acid test*; *the United States is a melting pot*; *he's barking up the wrong tree*; *I threw caution to the wind*; *we were told that we would have to bite the bullet*; *put that on the back burner*.

For the most part these are what are known as dead metaphors—metaphors that have been used so frequently that they no longer conjure up any physical image in the minds of those who hear or read them. When we hear the phrase *miss the boat* we do not think of a boat, any more than we think of pavement when we hear the expression *paved the way for*. In similar fashion a phrase such as *the lifeblood of democratic society* has been used so often that the blood has been drained out of it. It is a moot point whether a dead metaphor is better than no metaphor at all, but certainly a fresh metaphor is far better than either. Instead of *paved the way*, for example, what about *opened a new channel*? Instead of *nipping something in the bud*, try *digging up the seedlings*. It may take a little longer, but the improvement in style will be worth it. Of course, so many people have been using metaphors for so long that it is extremely difficult to find a fresh one for every situation. One useful compromise is to try to bring dead metaphors to life by using them in new ways. For example, no one thinks of a wave in this sentence:

> The Prime Minister of Britain has been riding a wave of popular support since his election.

Mention the wave again in a slightly different way, however, and it becomes water again to the reader:

> The Prime Minister of Britain has been riding a wave of popular support since the election. The question now is when that wave will crest.

Similarly, few people think of plants when they read of something having been *nipped in the bud*—unless the writer has made an effort to bring the dead metaphor back to life:

> The company wanted to nip the spreading unrest among its employees in the bud.

> The company wanted to nip the spreading unrest among its employees in the bud before it became a tangled, snake-infested jungle.

Writers who use dead metaphors are also more likely to mix their metaphors. A mixed metaphor occurs when we are not really thinking of the meaning of the words we use:

> If we bite the bullet we have to be careful not to throw the baby out with the bath-water.

As soon as one really thinks about such sentences one realizes that the bullet is really better off out of the baby's bath-water:

needs checking The president is out on a limb and some of his colleagues are trying to pull the rug out from under him.

revised The president is out on a limb and some of his colleagues are preparing to saw it off.

Additional Material Online

Exercises on mixed metaphors may be found at **sites.broadviewpress.com/writingcdn**. Click on **Exercises** and go to **"Style."**

P3.6 Voice

As many authorities have pointed out, in most cases writers can make their sentences less wordy and more effective by using the active voice rather than the passive:

needs checking The election was lost by the governor. (Passive—7 words)

revised The governor lost the election. (Active—5 words)

needs checking Union power was seen by them to have constrained the possibilities for full investment, and for achieving full employment.

revised The shareholders thought that union power had constrained the possibilities for full investment, and for achieving full employment.

It is too extreme, however, to conclude that the passive should be avoided wherever possible. Writers often want—for perfectly good reasons—to keep the focus of their writing on the recipient of an action rather than its agent. In such cases they are quite right to use the passive voice:

passive John Paul Getty III was released in Italy after a 2.8-million-dollar ransom had been paid.

active His kidnappers released John Paul Getty III in Italy after they had been paid a 2.8-million-dollar ransom.

If John Paul Getty III is the focus, it may be more appropriate to keep him as the subject of the sentence than to shift the focus to his kidnappers.

The passive is also sometimes useful as a means of dealing with issues of gender and usage. Compare, for example, the following sentences:

> If a writer uses vivid adjectives, his or her descriptive writing will carry greater force.
>
> If vivid adjectives are used, descriptive writing will carry greater force.

The passive-voice version allows the wordy *his or her* to disappear. Altering syntax in this sort of way can also help writers to write inclusive prose without resorting to awkward phrasing. (See the section "How to Be Good with Words" for a full discussion of this issue.)

The vice associated with the use of passive voice, then, is not the passive *per se*, but the wordiness it sometimes gives rise to. (See Section M1.5 for further discussion of active and passive voice.)

Additional Material Online

Exercises on active and passive voice may be found at **sites.broadviewpress.com/writingcdn**. Click on **Exercises** and go to **"Verbs."**

P3.7 Tone

In academic writing, it's generally considered inappropriate to gush or to shout or to cajole or to insult. Most academic essays are formal pieces of writing, and should be approached as such. Your readers will typically expect a calm and disinterested tone, free of expressions of extreme emotion or conversational touches (for advice on avoiding slang expressions and contractions, turn to Section M2.7).

Avoiding extreme *expressions* of emotion, though, should not be taken to suggest that strong emotion is not sometimes *felt*. If you are writing about the history of racial segregation in the United States, for example, it may be hard not to feel emotions such as anger, outrage, and horror. But those emotions will likely be dulled for the reader if your focus is on direct expressions of outrage. Acclaimed essayist Nikole Hannah-Jones's 2015 article "School Segregation" is a good example of how a dispassionate relation of the facts can elicit a more powerful emotional response in the reader than would a passionate piece filled with adjectives such as "deplorable," "outrageous," or "unconscionable":

> It was in a St. Louis case in 1857 that the U.S. Supreme Court handed down one of its most infamous opinions. The court, in ruling against the enslaved Dred Scott, affirmed that black people were not citizens and "had no rights that the white man was bound to respect."
>
> The spirit of the ruling reverberated for generations in St. Louis, which in the years after the Civil War became the destination for large numbers of former slaves. Indeed, the Mississippi River town became a national leader in how to contain what white real estate agents called the "Negro invasion."
>
> In 1916, after a successful campaign that included placards urging, "Save Your Home! Vote for Segregation!," the city's residents passed a measure requiring that black and white residents live on separate, designated blocks. In doing so, St. Louis became the first city in the country to require housing segregation by popular ballot. The tactic eventually fell to a legal challenge, but white residents found other ways to keep themselves, and their schools, protected from black residents.
>
> One way was to write segregation into the sales contracts of houses. The clauses, known as real estate covenants, ensured the whiteness of neighborhoods by barring the sale of homes to black homebuyers—ever, and across entire sectors of the city. (paragraphs 27–30)

Hannah-Jones does not entirely eschew moral judgements in the piece; she makes her own views clear, for example, when she declares that her overarching theme is that the police shooting of Michael Brown in a suburb of St. Louis "reveals a subtle, ongoing racial injustice: the vast disparity in resources and expectations for black children in America's stubbornly segregated school system." But we may notice that it is through dispassionate prose and without any fanfare that Hannah-Jones conveys the appalling facts—and thereby conveys as well a powerful feeling of outrage.

Notice too how Hannah-Jones manages to make a strong argument and elicit powerful feeling without employing first-person pronouns: indeed, not once in the entire 5,000-word essay does she use *I* or *me* (or, for that matter, *we* or *us*). The objective of most formal essays is to present a clear argument; writers may often achieve that goal most effectively by letting the evidence speak for itself—and for that reason many instructors advise their students to avoid using first-person pronouns.[1]

P3.8 Revision and Proofreading

Perhaps the greatest failing among those learning to write well is a reluctance to spend sufficient time reworking and reorganizing their prose. Far too many writers assume that completing a first draft means, essentially, finishing the job. A very few writers are in fact capable of forging marvelous essays one exquisite and unbreakable link at a time. For almost all of us, exquisite first drafts are few and far between. As Ian Cameron puts it in *For All Practical Purposes*:

> A few students feel that they are as likely to make more mistakes in checking and correcting their work as they are to correct the mistakes they have already made, but in fact almost every student is able to improve his or her work at least 15% by checking it slowly and carefully. Remember, you are not checking simply for details such as spelling; you should be trying to replace words, to re-arrange paragraphs, to cut entire sections, to alter almost every sentence. (276)

By its very nature revising is likely to lead to more cuts than additions. Might this not cause damage? "Aren't I more likely to do well," some students may ask themselves, "if I've written more than the prof asked for?" If the instructor has asked for 1,000 words, they feel they should write 1,500; if 2,500 words are requested, they are sure

1 Even more than most stylistic guidelines, this one should not be regarded as written in stone. In the passage quoted earlier by the acclaimed historian Garry Wills, *I* and *me* appear frequently. So do they in equally acclaimed essays by writers such as George Orwell, Susan Sontag, and Rebecca Solnit. The degree to which it is considered appropriate in formal writing to employ the first-person remains a contentious topic, and one on which usage conventions in different disciplines differ considerably.

to top 3,000. Experienced writers have learnt that quantity matters much less than quality; unless an essay is well below the requested number of words, the only thing that matters is what it says, and how well it says it.

What, then, should you be looking for as you read over your first draft (or your second, or your third)? Are your points clear? Have you given appropriate emphasis to your most important points—and, conversely, signalled where you are providing supporting material or briefly digressing? More generally, do the ideas hang together? Does the argument make sense, and do the ideas of each paragraph seem to flow naturally from the preceding paragraph? Is the same true on a sentence-by-sentence basis; does each sentence flow naturally from the preceding sentence?

If not, what can you do to make the sentences and/or the paragraphs flow together better? Perhaps some paragraphs would work better at a different point in the essay. Perhaps some sentences would also work better if they appeared a little earlier or a little later in the argument. If you decide to move paragraphs or sentences, of course, you should be very careful about words and phrases that are designed to link them to the surrounding paragraphs; when you move a sentence from near the beginning to near the end of a paragraph, for example, you may need to introduce it with "Moreover, ..." rather than "To begin with, ..." And you may similarly need to change the connective tissue of adjacent sentences; the sentence that used to start "A second point here is that ..." may now need to begin, "For one thing, ..."

In revising your early draft(s), you should also be alert to what you *haven't* written. It may well be that you have omitted to mention one or more connections that seem to you to be obvious, but may well be anything but obvious to the reader. (This is one of the many areas in which having a friend read over what you have written may be immensely valuable.)

One other thing to watch for: have you made any overly broad generalizations or overly bold statements? Much as it is important to exhibit a strong point of view, it is also important to be careful in the observations you make and in the conclusions you draw. Here's an example:

> For all these reasons, then, the threat of climate change deserves to be seen as the most important issue of our time.

This is a perfectly well-constructed sentence, but it unnecessarily overstates the conclusion. Unless your essay really has compared the threat posed by climate change with that of every single other issue of our time (worldwide poverty, inequality, disease, all other threats to the environment, conventional war, nuclear war, etc.), you are making a claim far stronger than you need to when you describe it as "***the*** most important issue of our time." Happily, the matter is easily addressed through the addition of a word or two to qualify your conclusion:

> For all these reasons, then, the threat of climate change deserves to be seen as **among the most important issues** of our time.
>
> (or "... as one of the most important issues ..." or "... deserves to be rated high among the most important issues ...")

Students sometimes feel they will weaken their arguments if they use qualifying phrases in this sort of way. In fact, making sure the assertions you make in an essay are not overstated will always strengthen the essay's arguments, not weaken them.

Here's a slightly more complicated example of the same sort of thing:

> As I have demonstrated in this essay, it was Dorothy Richardson—not James Joyce or Virginia Woolf—who pioneered stream of consciousness techniques in English literature. Joyce and Woolf have received all the credit for the innovations of stream of consciousness fiction, when that credit should really go to Richardson.

Dorothy Richardson did indeed pioneer stream of consciousness techniques several years before Joyce or Woolf. But is *who came first* the only thing that matters? Should the pioneer receive all the credit for a literary innovation? Christopher Marlowe is responsible for certain innovations in dramatic writing that Shakespeare then took full advantage of and extended, but no one suggests that all the credit should go to Marlowe. And is it really true that Joyce and Woolf have received *all* the credit, and Richardson absolutely none? The writer here has engaged in a bit of hyperbole that spoils what would otherwise be an excellent conclusion. Again, the problem is easily remedied:

> As I have demonstrated in this essay, it was Dorothy Richardson—not James Joyce or Virginia Woolf—who pioneered stream

> of consciousness techniques in English literature. Joyce and Woolf have received virtually all the credit for the innovations of stream of consciousness fiction, when much of that credit should really go to Richardson.

Overstating your case, then, is one important thing to watch for when you are working on the second draft of your essay.

There are also some things you *shouldn't* be looking for at this stage of revision—among them typos or other spelling mistakes, mistakes in capitalization, errors in spacing, poor formatting of notes, and so on. If you happen to notice issues of this sort that you can easily address as you are working on the larger revisions, by all means do so. But for most of us, the work of checking all these sorts of things engages a different part of the brain; if you're preoccupied with checking formatting issues, you will be less likely to realize it if your argument does not flow well from one paragraph to the next. Our advice is to focus first on substantive revision—and to focus on proofreading only once you have a solid second draft in hand.

What, then, does proofreading entail? It's your last chance to notice issues of logical or stylistic fluency, of course, but at this stage that shouldn't be your primary focus. You should be looking for commas out of place—or places that need commas. You should be checking that every open quotation mark is followed a little further on by a closed quotation mark. You should be checking for words repeated—or missing words. You should be checking that all appropriate titles are italicized, that all appropriate words are capitalized, and that all the notes and references are formatted correctly. These and many other similar matters are often termed "mechanical," but if you are sloppy over them, that sloppiness will certainly take away from the effect of the essay as a whole. Proofreading is often thought of as a boring job, yet it can be one that brings real satisfaction: no writer is able to proofread an essay without finding things to fix, things to improve.

One final suggestion about proofing: try reading the essay aloud. Many writers feel silly reading aloud to themselves, but inevitably they find they catch things—a missing word, an extra letter—that even the most diligent silent proofing will have missed. For the few minutes it takes, it is always worth giving voice, in an entirely literal sense, to the written text.

P 3.9 Feedback and Criticism

Here are a few impressions from students, following one-to-one sessions with writing tutors:

> "I had a chance to explain what I wanted to convey. My tutor had a chance to look at my essay and then together we made progress based on her suggestions."

> "I liked the fact that I wasn't told what to do—it was more a discussion about possibilities. But I was also given excellent suggestions and advice on things that I was concerned about, such as my paragraph transitions."

> "I appreciate having someone new look over my work to give me a fresh perspective. Her helpful, clear comments will really aid me when I go back to revise my work."

Such dialogue is immediately encouraging for a serious essay writer, who can step away from the solitary turbulence and benefit from an attentive eye and sympathetic heart (writing centre tutors tend to be writers themselves!). As the students quoted above express, a conversation about your essay can be a truly collaborative exercise, one that places your work in a new light. Sometimes the simplest of gestures—such as hearing your paper read aloud by another person—will lead to revisions that might never have occurred otherwise.

Often, though, it may not be possible to see someone at a writing centre about each essay. One should also be ready and willing to show one's writing to friends, classmates—and of course instructors—at any stage. Too often we look at our work as sacrosanct; we want it to be perfect but, embarrassed by its weaknesses, we are shy of showing it to others. And if, when we do show it to others, they point to imperfections, we may be too easily hurt. The more confidence we are able to muster, the more we may be willing to seek out dialogue—and criticism—from others. An honestly critical stance towards our own work is worth striving for. We should accept that our writing is not and will never be perfect, and remember that dialogue with others will always present opportunities for improvement, and is in itself a stimulating and enjoyable activity.

P3.10 Online, On the Screen, On the Page

Proofreading may check some of the bad cognitive habits that computers breed in many writers who work only on screen; it certainly will not eliminate them all. For some of us, computers can be wonderful facilitators of flow; many people find it easier to get a lot of ideas out of their heads and "on paper" by using a computer than by using a pen and paper. But the same habits of scrolling that can facilitate flow in writing and in reading can distort our ability to arrange ideas in an ordered fashion so as to best present an argument. Though researchers are far from understanding why, they have now assembled a considerable body of evidence suggesting that seeing a succession of printed pages enables one to combine and connect ideas in ways that are not always evident if one restricts oneself to scrolling on the screen. This is why it is helpful for most writers to work with paper as well as on screen. Once you have a complete draft of a piece of writing, we recommend that you print it out and review the hard copy both with an eye for the big picture (Are the ideas presented in the best order? Should an extra paragraph be added anywhere to explain your ideas further?), and with an eye to the details (individual words and phrases, punctuation, typos). It's usually a good idea to treat these operations separately—to deal with matters of organization first, and not to worry about typos or small infelicities of style until the second or third draft.

We offer here several other pieces of advice—recognizing as we do so that a piece of advice which may be quite helpful to some students may seem so obvious to some others as to make them wonder why we would have devoted space to something any fool should know already.

- **Don't be all thumbs.** Many people nowadays do more typing with their thumbs on their smartphones than they do using all their fingers on a full-sized keyboard, and with voice recognition software becoming better and better all the time, it may seem as though touch typing is a skill that will soon be of little use. It is a skill that many high schools no longer teach; is it worth your while to learn it? For the foreseeable future, the answer is certainly yes. For academic writing, touch typing remains an invaluable skill. It can substantially reduce the time you spend compiling notes as you do your research, and it can significantly reduce the time you spend writing.

- **Try turning off your screen.** Many writers have an almost irresistible urge to start editing and revising their work even as they are in the preliminary stages of drafting and working out their ideas. For most of us, trying to edit at this stage doesn't make our writing any better; it simply causes us to lose our train of thought. If you are one of those who sometimes experiences this problem (and if you know how to touch-type!), we recommend that you try turning off your screen as you are generating your ideas—free writing or trying to shape a first draft.
- **Some things are best disabled.** Modern word processing software almost always has a number of built-in features that can turn out to be frustrating time wasters in many writing situations. If, for example, you are creating a numbered list of items, you may well find that the software you are using wants to format your list quite differently from the way you would prefer. If you are copying lines of poetry that all begin with words written in lower case, you are likely to find that your software will automatically insert capital letters. If you learn how to disable the automatic formatting functions in your software, it will save you a great deal of time in your writing career.
- **The art of saving.** Even if you have a reliable automatic saving mechanism that should provide you with a backup of anything you are writing, it is still a good idea to save frequently. But it's important as well to save in ways that will keep to an absolute minimum the chance of confusion arising later. If you are about to cut any significant amount of text from what you are working on, it's a good idea to save first and then save again under a new name, creating a new version. It's a good idea, though, not to leave windows open with more than one version at a time; it's all too easy to take a break and then return and start adding material to what you think is the latest version, discovering only later that you have muddled two versions. Saving different versions in a clear and consecutive fashion by using a simple numbering system, for instance, can help prevent confusion—as can the careful use of folders and subfolders.

- **Searching low and high.** Every program has its own search function, and every computer is also set up with a global search function. If you have misplaced a file, the search function within your word processing program or on your hard drive can be used to help track it down. Learn how to use these search functions, and you should be able to find almost anything you have lost or misplaced, using threads of words that you remember you have used in a document, even if you cannot remember the document's name.
- **Finding and replacing.** The *find* and the *replace* functions in your word processing software are tremendously valuable. The find function should allow you to go to exactly what you are looking for within seconds, so long as you can remember a relevant word, and the *find and replace* function can save you a great deal of time in the revision process. It's usually a good idea, though, to resist any urge you may have to instantly replace a particular word or phrase with what you have decided is a better version; if you take just a little more time to let the computer guide you to each instance where the word or phrase occurs and give your okay to the change in each case, that can save you a good deal of embarrassment.
- **Use track changes.** Some students imagine that the track changes function is used primarily when one is working collaboratively. In fact, it's tremendously useful when you are working independently as well, allowing you to keep a full record of what you have done in previous versions as part of a single document. It's sometimes assumed that the track changes function will always create a cluttered screen if it is activated. In fact, any good software program nowadays allows you to hide the tracked changes even when the function is activated.
- **Cutting and pasting from the Internet.** It can be a real time saver if, for example, you are quoting a long passage from a text that's available online to simply cut and paste rather than retyping. When you do that, though, be sure to "paste special" using "unformatted text," so you do not carry HTML formatting into your paper. Next, check the text you have imported carefully; look, for example, for any vertically straight quotation marks and change them to curved quotation marks, and be sure to put the material you have imported into the same

font that you are using for the rest of your essay. (Watch out as well for accidental plagiarism if you are cutting and pasting; all direct quotations must be attributed!)

For more advice on writing in a digital context, we recommend you consult the discussion of email in the "Writing in the Workplace" section of this book.

Spell-check and Grammar-check

Today's spell-checkers and grammar checkers have many virtues. If you confuse *its* and *it's* or *there* and *their*, such software will often draw your attention to your mistake. Some word processing software will even silently correct the mistake for you if you type, "Its a lovely day." But it will also often suggest there is something wrong with your writing when nothing whatsoever is wrong. (Not infrequently, for example, it will suggest you change from the subjunctive mood to the indicative when the subjunctive is in fact entirely correct.) And it will do nothing to alert you to any problem if you write either of the following sentences:

> The company's literary wing compliments its academic publishing program.
>
> The book includes a forward as well as a preface and an introduction.

No computer software, in short, can provide a reliable substitute for careful proofreading.

What is true for spelling and grammar is even more true for matters of style. Grammar checkers will offer advice on matters such as the length of sentences and the degree to which the passive voice is used. Such issues are by their nature not readily subject to precise formulations, and one should thus take advice of this sort from software programs with more than a grain of salt.

Additional Material Online

There are several good grammar sites on the Internet; one of the best is Purdue University's Online Writing Lab (OWL), which may be accessed at **https://owl.english.purdue.edu/.**

Observing Online Etiquette

The word *netiquette* is a clever little pun that neatly encapsulates the notion that standards of courtesy and consideration are as important in cyberspace as they are in other areas of human existence—and that the Internet is sufficiently different from other forms of communication as to make some special guidelines advisable.

Online means of communication lend themselves to a higher degree of informality (for both sender and recipient) than does the sending of a letter printed on corporate or departmental letterhead. The combination of distance, informality, and invisibility that electronic communication embodies seems to encourage the spontaneous expression of emotion in ways that might otherwise not feel appropriate. That's particularly the case with communication through various forms of social media, of course, but it's true to some extent even of email. Electronic communication often seems to foster a breeziness that is as friendly as it is efficient. But it also seems to lend itself to the venting of certain sorts of anger or irritation, in ways that other means of communication do not. And sometimes it leads people to divulge personal information that on reflection they might rather have kept to themselves. These tendencies—to foster sometimes unexpected degrees of intimacy, and to facilitate the unbridled expression of anger—argue for the wisdom of taking the time to edit and proof any electronic message, checking its tone quite as much as its grammar.

The ever-increasing use of electronic communication in a wide variety of contexts continues to raise issues of appropriate tone and of level of formality. For the most part, no one expects emails to conform to all the conventions of more formal communications; it would be foolish to worry about a typo or two in an email dashed off to a friend—let alone in a text message! But any email should be clear, unambiguous, and written in an appropriate tone; again, it is wise to edit and proofread carefully any message you send. And if you are using email as a convenient way to convey a more formal document, that document should indeed conform to the conventions of standard usage. A proposal submitted electronically or a memo circulated electronically should be phrased, proofread, and presented as carefully as you would the same document in hard copy form. As with all types of communication, the context and the expectations of your audience are always important.

Privacy issues are at least as important with electronic communications as they are with other forms of communication. As a recipient, consider the feelings of the sender; unless it is obviously appropriate to forward a message, for example, ask the permission of the sender before you pass it on. And as a sender, it is worth remembering that electronic communication can often end up being less private than regular mail, since recipients are not always as considerate as one might wish. And, particularly given that emails are often forwarded or copied by mistake to unintended recipients, it is wise to consider whether the potential recipients of a message may be a much larger group than intended—and word the message accordingly.

Point-form Online Etiquette

- Keep messages clear and brief.
- Edit/proof all messages before sending—for tone as well as form.
- Use clear subject headings.
- Make the text as easy to read as possible; leave a line between paragraphs (rather than indent); use italics—or place an underscore mark before and after the relevant word(s) as a substitute for italics; use only well-known abbreviations.
- When quoting from a previous message, quote only the necessary passage(s).
- Address the message carefully.
- Attachments: be aware that some recipients may have difficulty downloading attachments, and be prepared to use alternative means in such circumstances.
- In all communication, be sensitive to the demands you may be making on the time of others. If, for example, you are sending an "information-only" email to a department head who may deal with a hundred emails a day, make it clear in the heading or at the beginning of the message that this is for information only, and that no reply is required.
- The overriding principle: always show consideration for your reader(s).

Copyright

Copyright rules for written materials apply to the Internet just as they do to books or articles; written work is under copyright protection for many years after it is published. Indeed, copyright restrictions have been extended in recent decades in many jurisdictions. In the United States the 1998 Sonny Bono Copyright Amendment Act extended copyright protection by an additional twenty years; most written material remains in copyright for 95 years after publication. In the UK and other European countries, copyright restrictions were extended in the 1990s, such that work is now in copyright for seventy years after the death of the author (or translator); similar restrictions were imposed in 2005 in Australia, and Canada (where restrictions have long been somewhat less severe, with copyright extending for fifty years after the death of the author or translator) has agreed to adopt the same "seventy year rule."

There is now considerable feeling in many countries that, in extending copyright restrictions as far as they have been, governments have tilted the balance that such laws attempt to find (between the interests of authors and their heirs, and the interests of the general public) too much away from the public interest. Nevertheless, unless and until such laws are changed, a text such as Gwendolyn Brooks's *A Street in Bronzeville*, first published in 1945, will be in copyright in the United States through 2040, and in Canada, Europe (including Great Britain), and Australia through 2070 (Brooks died in 2000).

Online

The Canadian Intellectual Property Office posts "A Guide to Copyright" on its site.

Except for quoting brief passages (with the proper acknowledgement), you may not reproduce copyright material, whether you have found it in a written publication or on the Web, without the permission of the copyright holder. Nor may you post copyrighted materials online without permission from the copyright holders.

Works Cited

Acheson, Katherine. *Writing Essays about Literature: A Brief Guide for University and College Students*. 2nd ed., Broadview Press, 2021.

Aubry, Timothy. *Guilty Aesthetic Pleasures*. Harvard UP, 2018.

Borzekowski, Dina L.G., et al. "The Angelina Effect: Immediate Reach, Grasp, and Impact of Going Public." *Genetics in Medicine*, vol. 16, 2013, pp. 516–21. https://doi:10.1038/gim.2013.181.

Cameron, Ian. *For All Practical Purposes*. Broadview Press, 1988.

Coates, Ta-Nehisi. "The Case for Reparations." *The Atlantic*, June 2014, www.theatlantic.com/magazine/archive/2014/06/the-case-for-reparations/361631/.

Frye, Northrop. "Humanities in a New World." *Divisions on a Ground*, edited by James Polk, House of Anansi Press, 1982, pp. 102–17.

Gatti, Lauren. "Conversing with Longfellow: Democratizing the American Literature Curriculum." *Reconsidering Longfellow*, edited by Christopher Irmscher and Robert Arbour, Fairleigh Dickinson UP, 2014, pp. 177–92.

Giltrow, Janet. *Academic Writing*. 3rd ed., Broadview Press, 2002.

Graff, Gerald, and Cathy Birkenstein. *They Say / I Say: The Moves That Matter in Academic Writing*. 3rd ed., W.W. Norton, 2014.

Hallpike, C.R. *The Principles of Social Evolution*. Clarendon Press, 1984.

Hannah-Jones, Nikole. "School Segregation: The Continuing Tragedy of Ferguson." *Pro Publica*, 19 December 2014, www.propublica.org/article/ferguson-school-segregation.

Johnston, Ian. *Essays and Arguments: A Handbook for Writing Essays*. Rev. ed., Broadview Press, 2015.

Lauer, Janice. "Writing as Enquiry: Some Questions for Teachers." *College Composition and Communication*, vol. 33, no. 1, 1982, pp. 89–93.

Menand, Louis. "Comp Time." *New Yorker*, 11 September 2000, pp. 92–94.

Orwell, George. "Politics and the English Language." *Collected Essays*, Harvill Secker, 1961, pp. 353–67.

Solnit, Rebecca. "The Mother of All Questions," *Harper's Magazine*, October 2015, www.harpers.org/archive/2015/10/the-mother-of-all-questions/.

Wills, Garry. "The Negro President." *The New York Review of Books*, 6 November 2003, pp. 45–51.

Woolf, Virginia. *Orlando: A Biography*. The Hogarth Press, 1928.

Special Topic

HOW TO BE GOOD WITH WORDS

Styles of Writing When Considering Gender, Race and Ethnicity, Class, Religion, Sexual Orientation, Disability, and Human/Non-human Animal Issues

Special Topic

How to Be Good with Words

Styles of Writing When Considering Gender, Race and Ethnicity, Class, Religion, Sexual Orientation, Disability, and Human/Non-human Animal Issues

In at least one important respect the issues discussed in this section of *The Broadview Guide to Writing* differ from every other issue discussed in this book. Throughout, our focus is primarily on formal writing, and it has frequently been emphasized that many informal and colloquial usages that are inappropriate to formal writing may be fine to use in other forms of writing, or in speech. The same cannot be said of the difference between offensive language and considerate English usage. It is no less damaging to use sexist, racist, anti-Semitic, anti-Muslim, anti-gay, or anti-trans language in speech than it is in writing; such language is damaging in every context.

But should we really avoid *all* language that might cause offence? If so, George Orwell and Simone de Beauvoir and Martin Luther King Jr. and Nelson Mandela should certainly not have spoken out as plainly as they did. If so, we should never use a phrase such as "the cruelties of factory farming," for it is surely offensive to most managers of what they would prefer to call "intensive farming operations" or "concentrated animal feeding operations." If so, protesters should never say that "Black Lives Matter," since many white politicians have angrily condemned the phrase. The point about non-sexist language and culturally sensitive language, then, is not that you should never be willing to use language that might offend. It is that you should try never to use language that stereotypes particular groups, or that presumes other groups to be inferior.

The heading of this section in early editions of *The Broadview Guide to Writing* was "Bias-Free Language." That was a title we adopted in large part to get away from negatively focused headings such as "sexist language," "biased language," or "the language of prejudice." But "bias-free" is a term that can perhaps too easily take on a self-congratulatory ring. We should surely all keep trying to find and use bias-free language, but we should also always try to remember that none of us will ever be entirely free of bias or prejudice—and that the struggle against it is not only an ongoing one in society as a whole, but also a lifelong one within each of us.

Many writing guides and handbooks inform the reader that certain usages "are considered" inappropriate but do not devote much space to explaining why. Our intent in this section of *The Broadview Guide* is both to provide wider coverage of inappropriate usages than is the norm in guides of this sort, and to go into greater detail as to why they are considered inappropriate. We include substantial discussions of issues relating to gender, race, class, religion, sexual orientation, and disability—but of course it would be impossible to cover every ethical consideration that might come up in writing. Our hope is that this section will not just offer concrete advice about particular words and phrasings, but also demonstrate an approach to ethical writing that can be useful in all sorts of contexts.

Some General Principles

Expressions of outright bigotry in North American society diminished over the course of the late twentieth and early twenty-first centuries, and it became less common in some professional and public contexts to hear language that was overtly sexist, or racist, or contemptuous of "the lower classes." In the 2010s the use of hate speech and bigoted slurs was on the increase in certain segments of the population, as some political leaders and media figures tapped into racial and other biases as fuel for their campaigns and ratings; the sorts of crude slurs that for years had been on the wane made a resurgence in public discourse, targeting, among others, immigrants, Indigenous people, women, African Americans, and Asian people. The authors of this book join many others in their hope that the 2020s will be a very different decade.

Sexist and racist slurs are obviously harmful, but even when prejudice is not expressed openly, it can have devastating effects. American experiments in which large numbers of identical resumes are sent out, for example, indicate that a person with an Asian-American or an African American sounding name is far less likely to be granted an interview than is a person with a Euro-American-sounding name and exactly the same credentials.[1] Similar studies have found that a woman is far less

1 See, for example, Dina Gerdeman, "Minorities Who 'Whiten' Job Resumes Get More Interviews," Harvard Business School: Working Knowledge, 17 May 2017, https://hbswk.hbs.edu/item/minorities-who-whiten-job-resumes-get-more-interviews

likely to be considered for a science-related position at Yale University than is a man with identical credentials.[1]

Often, of course, prejudices are held in our subconscious rather than our conscious mind. Often, too, a style that is inclusive of others is not simply a matter of avoiding prejudiced words. It is always good to think about the first or third person pronouns one is using, and who they may include or exclude. In some cases it may be better to repeat a noun than to replace it with a pronoun. Consider these examples in which writers discuss a group they do not belong to, but which members of the audience they are addressing may well be a part of:

worth checking The twentieth century brought a revolution in the roles that women play in North American society; in 1900 they still were not allowed to vote in any North American jurisdiction.

(If the writer is not a woman, it is more inclusive to avoid using the third person *they*.)

revised The twentieth century brought a revolution in the roles that women play in North American society; in 1900 women still were not allowed to vote in any North American jurisdiction.

worth checking I would like to conclude my remarks with a prayer that has meant a great deal to me. We all know how God can bring light into our lives; certainly He has done so for me.

(This is appropriate if the speaker is addressing a crowd that is entirely made up of fellow believers—but inappropriate if the speaker is addressing people with a variety of spiritual beliefs.)

revised I would like to conclude my remarks with a prayer that has meant a great deal to me. Many of you may have experienced the feeling of God bringing light into your life; certainly He has done that for me.

(This is appropriate if the speaker is addressing people with a variety of spiritual beliefs.)

When you are writing about people from a group you do not belong to, it is helpful to imagine that a member of that group

1 See Corinne A. Moss-Racusin et al., "Science Faculty's Subtle Biases Favor Male Students," *PNAS*, vol. 109, no. 41, 9 October 2012. Moss-Racusin et al. also found that women were offered lower starting salaries than men with the same credentials.

is reading your work—will they feel included and respected by the language you are using? It is best to use language recommended by the groups or individuals in question. If you are referring to an individual and know or can find out what terms they use to describe themselves, use those. Advocacy groups also provide resources on preferred language that writers can and should consult. (For example, autisticadvocacy.org is a good resource to consult for language regarding autism, while GLAAD is a good resource for language principles regarding LGBTQ+ people.)

A related issue often arises in writing dealing with political and cultural issues. It is all too easy to slip into language that presumes the norm in one's own area to be the norm throughout the entire country, or the norm in one's own society to be the norm worldwide. In such situations it is worth taking the time to find wording that is more precise.

worth checking In the world we live in today, most people learn to drive before they reach their late twenties.

(This is no doubt true in North America and much of Europe—but it is certainly not true of "most people" in India, or Nigeria, or Papua New Guinea. Overall, far fewer than half the world's population learn to drive at any age.)

revised In the United States and Canada today, most people learn to drive before they reach their late twenties.

Another unconsciously biased habit to avoid is the use of unnecessary racial or religious identifiers. Mentioning a person's gender, race, religion, or sexual orientation in connection with occupation is a common habit, but one that reinforces stereotypes as to what sort of person one would naturally expect to be a lawyer or a doctor or a nurse. Unless race or gender or religion is in some way relevant to the conversation, it is inappropriate to refer to someone as a male nurse, or a Jewish doctor, or an Indigenous lawyer.

Similarly, the more we foreground a person's race when it is *not* a characteristic relevant to the discussion, the more we encourage people to emphasize race rather than focusing on other human attributes.

worth checking I was given a ticket for speeding last week; a Black police officer pulled me over just after I'd crossed the Port Mann bridge. So I had to pay the bridge toll *and* an eighty dollar fine!

revised I was given a ticket for speeding last week; a police officer pulled me over just after I'd crossed the Port Mann bridge. So I had to pay the bridge toll *and* an eighty dollar fine!

worth checking I've heard that Professor Andover's course in American literature is very interesting. She's of Asian background from the look of her; she just joined the department this year. Apparently she's an expert on Bob Dylan and the connections between literature and music.

revised I've heard that Professor Andover's course in American literature is very interesting. She just joined the department this year; apparently she's an expert on Bob Dylan and the connections between literature and music.

It's one thing to acknowledge this principle; it's quite another to put it into practice, since in many cases doing so goes against the habits of a lifetime. For many North Americans, the only thing that might be thought of as objectionable in the following passage from David Sedaris's highly amusing autobiographical essay "Guy Walks into a Bar Car" is the loud man's off-colour joke:

> When a couple of seats opened up, Johnny and I took them. Across the narrow carriage, a black man with a bushy mustache pounded on the Formica tabletop. "So a nun goes into town," he said, "and sees a sign reading, 'Quickies—Twenty-five Dollars.' Not sure what it means, she walks back to the convent and pulls aside the mother superior. 'Excuse me,' she asks, 'but what's a quickie?'
>
> "And the old lady goes, 'Twenty-five dollars. Just like in town.'"
>
> As the car filled with laughter, Johnny lit a fresh cigarette. "Some comedian," he said.

Sedaris's account of the train journey unfolds over several pages. The man with the mustache continues to tell crude jokes—and Sedaris continues to identify him not as *the man with the bushy mustache* or *the loud man*—but as *the black man*—even as other (presumably white) people are identified in other ways:

> "All right," called the black man on the other side of the carriage. "I've got another one." ... A red-nosed woman in a decorative sweatshirt started to talk, but the black fellow told her that he wasn't done yet.... As the black man settled down,...
>
> "Here's a clean one," the black man said....

Why should it matter, you may ask. Maybe his blackness is what the writer has noticed first about the man. Isn't that harmless enough? The short answer is no. If writers identify people first and foremost by their race and not by other, more individualized characteristics, they subtly colour perceptions—both their readers' and their own. And that is of course particularly harmful when the characterization is a negative one. Sedaris is a wonderful writer, but in this instance he would have been a better writer had he referred repeatedly to *the mustachioed man* (or *the loudmouth*) and not to *the black man*. If North American history included the mass enslavement of mustachioed men or loudmouthed men, the point might be argued rather differently. But it doesn't.

Our internalized prejudices can also cause us, when we describe individuals, to emphasize the characteristics that reinforce those prejudices while deemphasizing characteristics that don't match our expectations. Consider the following descriptions of political candidates of different genders who have essentially the same backgrounds:

- Carla Jenkins, a lawyer and a school board trustee, is also the mother of three lovely daughters.
- George Kaplan, a lawyer and a school board trustee, has a long record of public service in the region.
- George Kaplan, a lawyer and a school board trustee, is also the father of three lovely daughters.
- Carla Jenkins, a lawyer and a school board trustee, has a long record of public service in the region.

The impression left in many minds by such phrasings is that the person described as having a long record of public service is well suited to public office, while the person whose parenting is emphasized may be better suited to staying at home. Some may feel that parenthood is relevant in such cases; if you do, be sure to mention it for everyone, not just for women. The guideline here is that, when describing a person, you should mention only the qualities you feel are relevant. And be sure to describe everyone you discuss in the same context with the same lens: if you feel it necessary to refer to relationship status or physical appearance, do so for everyone; if you mention degree qualifications or career achievements, do so for everyone.

Nor is it generally appropriate to stereotype members of particular groups even in ways that one considers positive; by doing so, one may fail to give credit for individual achievement while leaving the harmful impression that the given group possesses innate qualities that are universal among members of the group.

needs checking Of course she gets straight As in all her subjects; she's from Hong Kong.

revised It's no wonder she gets straight As in all her subjects; her parents have given her a great deal of encouragement, and she works very hard.

It's clear, then, that we should not overemphasize a person's race, gender, or membership in any other group in ways that reinforce stereotypes about that group. But what about situations where a person's membership in a given group contradicts common stereotypes? Certainly, you would not want to call attention to the fact that a certain CEO is Black or a certain pastor is bisexual every time you mentioned that person. But it is also important to keep in mind that "CEO" and "pastor" are two of many descriptors that, for some people, carry with them a harmful set of default assumptions—in these cases, that, unless we are told otherwise, any given CEO or minister is a white, heterosexual man. If we try to ignore internalized assumptions by pretending that race, gender, and other differences do not exist, we risk perpetuating the "default" status of whiteness, maleness, and so on.

Some people may pride themselves on being "colourblind" when it comes to race, for example, or on thinking that gay and heterosexual people are "just the same." But just as it is a worthy goal not to overemphasize differences, it is important not to overlook them entirely, as though the vast differences between the life experiences of human beings were insignificant or embarrassing. Acknowledging difference is important, in large part, because many differences come with relative degrees of privilege and prejudice attached, and ignoring difference is often tantamount to ignoring discrimination. But recognizing difference is also important simply because human beings are not all the same, and all experiences ought to be acknowledged—not just the experiences of the "default" race, gender, sexual orientation, religion, class, size, and so on. Audre Lorde, an important Black lesbian feminist theorist of the twentieth century, suggested that the acknowledgement and even celebration of difference was central to combatting prejudice:

> [W]e have *all* been programmed to respond to the human differences between us with fear and loathing and to handle that difference in one of three ways: ignore it, and if that is not possible copy it if we think it is dominant, or destroy it if we think it is subordinate. But we have no patterns for relating across our human differences as equals....

> Certainly there are very real differences between us of race, age, and sex. But it is not those differences between us that are separating us. It is rather our refusal to recognize those differences.[1] …

In writing, one way to acknowledge significant differences is to describe them clearly and precisely. In general, if you are referring to a group of people, or to an individual's membership in a group, the best practice is to use the most specific term that describes that group. If, for example, you are writing about discrimination against Chinese Canadians specifically, use the term *Chinese Canadians* rather than *Asian Canadians* or *people of colour*; if you are writing about the disproportionately high suicide rates of trans youth, use the term *trans youth* rather than *queer youth* or *LGBTQ+ youth*.

political correctness: It is often claimed that "political correctness" goes to ridiculous lengths to avoid giving offence—and that does indeed sometimes happen. In most cases, though, the complaints that are made as to the supposed euphemistic excesses of political correctness turn out to be entirely spurious. Those who object to making linguistic changes for cultural reasons often present the situation as a binary: either we begin using an awkward new word or continue using a biased word. But most often there is a replacement word that is just as serviceable as the biased one. Think, for example, of the word *middleman*. If someone were to suggest we replace it with the phrase *distributional intermediary*,[2] most writers would cringe at the awkwardness and obscurity that would attend such usage. But let's approach the word *middleman* in a different frame of mind. To start with, the fair comparison is not between *distributional intermediary* and *middleman* but between *intermediary* and *middleman*. Perhaps the former is more awkward, but it is not obviously so:

- One of the reasons for high prices in this industry is that there are too many middlemen.
- One of the reasons for high prices in this industry is that there are too many intermediaries.

Alternatives in different circumstances may include *wholesalers*, *distributors*, *go-betweens*—none of them obscure, confusing, or laughable.

1 "Age, Race, Class, and Sex: Women Redefining Difference," *Sister Outsider*, 1984.

2 This phrase was in fact presented as an example of political correctness gone too far in the fourth edition of *The Rinehart Guide to Grammar and Style* (Bonnie Carter and Craig Skates, Rinehart, 1996).

Regrettably, the prevailing tack taken by those fighting against gender-neutral and other inclusive language has remained mockery rather than argument. Thus, for example, columnist Ron Haggart mocked efforts to replace the term *manhole cover* by suggesting as an alternative *circular utility access alternative facilitative infrastructure.*[1] Ha ha. The most commonly proposed alternative to *manhole*, of course, is nothing so awkward or absurd. Moreover, *sewer hole* more accurately describes the object in question; someone new to English would surely never be able to guess the meaning of *manhole* from its component parts. (Indeed, the word might lead to embarrassing misunderstandings.)

None of this should be taken to suggest that there are not awkwardnesses to struggle with in the search for appropriate means of expression. But the awkwardnesses are surprisingly few. *Chair* and *flight attendant* felt a little odd at first, but few are bothered by them now. And the process can and should continue.[2] One of the authors of this book had assumed that *sportship* would somehow make an awkward substitute for *sportsmanship*—until he heard former Olympian Abby Hoffman on the radio, speaking quite naturally of the sportship of certain athletes at the Rio Olympics.

linguistic appropriation: For hundreds of years, the dominant culture in North America has appropriated the languages and dialects of the peoples it has oppressed, and especially of the people of colour it has enslaved and colonized; Black Vernacular English (BVE), in particular, has had, and continues to have, a profound effect on American English. James Baldwin remarked eloquently on the history of white linguistic appropriation in his 1979 essay "If Black English Isn't a Language, Then Tell Me, What Is?":

> Now, I do not know what white Americans would sound like if there had never been any black people in the United States, but they would not sound the way they sound. *Jazz*, for example, is a very specific sexual term, as in *jazz me, baby*, but white people purified it into the Jazz Age. *Sock it to me,* which means, roughly, the same thing, has

1 Ron Haggart, "That Covers It," *The Globe and Mail*, 19 March 2004.

2 The process can be free-spirited and entertaining as well as serious. As a gender-neutral alternative to *snowman*, for example, we'd suggest that *snowbody* (rhymes with *nobody*) is worthy of consideration; perhaps that new coinage will never catch on, but it's worth noting that there are few things more gender-neutral than a body made up of three spheres of snow.

> been adopted by Nathaniel Hawthorne's descendants with no qualms or hesitations at all, along with *let it all hang out* and *right on! Beat to his socks* which was once the black's most total and despairing image of poverty, was transformed into a thing called the Beat Generation, which phenomenon was, largely, composed of *uptight*, middle-class white people, imitating poverty, trying to *get down*, to get *with it*, doing their *thing*, doing their despairing best to be *funky*, which we, the blacks, never dreamed of doing—we *were* funky, baby, like *funk* was going out of style.

Baldwin proceeds in this essay to explicate the origins of Black American language, which was developed by enslaved Americans who spoke different languages and dialects when they were brought to America; they crafted a new language with which to speak to each other, and also to speak without being entirely understood by their enslavers. Appropriation of this language by white people, who do not share this history and who continue to occupy a position of privilege, is thus highly problematic. Non-Black people should examine their motives when they appropriate BVE and use words such as *bae*, *woke*, *basic*, *hella*, *yas queen*, *lit*, *on fleek*, *throwing shade*, or *turn up*. Regardless of whether the adoption of such language is intended as an act of homage to Black culture or is simply an attempt to be *with it*, non-Black people should be cognizant of the historical and contemporary ramifications of appropriating Black language.

It is nonetheless true, as Baldwin points out, that many terms from BVE have become endemic in standard American usage; we cannot expect privileged groups to avoid using all terms borrowed from Black English. The same is true of various Indigenous languages, from which numerous words such as *hurricane* (originally Taíno), *sasquatch* (Halkomelem), and *raccoon* (Powhatan) are appropriated. It is important, however, to avoid the most harmful forms of linguistic appropriation, particularly if one's use of another group's language will bring commercial gain (i.e., you might profit from it), if it is tokenizing (i.e., it is merely a gesture, rather than a sincere attempt towards being inclusive), or if you are using it to bolster your image in some way. It is also particularly important to avoid appropriating terms in ways that disrespect the specific and complex practices of other cultures; when it comes to appropriation from Indigenous languages, non-Indigenous people should avoid, for example, calling anything their *spirit animal*, describing their family as their *tribe*, or referring to a regular meeting as a *powwow*.

neutrality and false neutrality: Awareness of the concept of *false neutrality* (also known as *false equivalency* and as *bothsidesism*) has been on the rise in recent years. It is of course good writing practice to treat fairly the different sides of any legitimate argument—and, among journalists, it is often good writing practice to remain neutral in reporting competing claims. (Opinion pieces are another matter—and the line between news reports and opinion pieces is, unfortunately, often blurred.) But neutrality is not always the recommended course; false neutrality is the insistence of the legitimacy of more than one side of an argument when in reality there is a firm set of facts that resolves the debate. If a viewpoint is based on false information, it does not deserve to be treated as one side of a legitimate debate.

To write the following in January of 2021, for example, would have been to practice false neutrality:

> Many Republicans continue to claim that there was widespread voter fraud in Georgia and in numerous other states in the 2020 American election. Democrats insist that no widespread voter fraud occurred.

In this case a comprehensive set of facts was well established. The following was thus by January 2021 a more responsible approach to adopt:

> Many Republicans continue to claim that there was widespread voter fraud in Georgia and in numerous other states in the 2020 American election. Democrats insist that no widespread voter fraud occurred—and independent authorities have overwhelmingly agreed. Trump's lawyers have lost every case they have filed; at least 96 judges, of all political stripes, have concluded that Republican claims of widespread voter fraud are baseless.

Once the facts have been established for a prolonged period, however, it has become accepted practice to indicate more briefly which side of the argument is in accord with the facts:

> Many Republicans have continued to claim, falsely, that there was widespread voter fraud in Georgia and in numerous other states in the 2020 American election.

> Fueled by the baseless claim that there was widespread fraud in the 2020 election, Republican lawmakers around the country have made an aggressive push to pass new voting regulations.

It is often the case, of course, that limited information is available; in that case, pure neutrality may be entirely appropriate. On the issue of the risk of outdoor transmission of COVID-19, for example, the following neutral tone would have been entirely appropriate in a news report in late March or early April of 2020:

> Ron DeSantis, the Republican Florida governor, has refused to issue a statewide order to close Florida beaches, claiming that there is little risk of the virus spreading outdoors. Many have disagreed, suggesting that the virus is likely to spread quickly on Florida's beaches.

A year later, much more information had become available; the following, much more detailed approach to reporting the same situation had by the spring of 2021 become a more appropriate approach to adopt:

> Florida Governor Ron DeSantis was widely criticized in 2020 when he refused to issue a statewide order to close Florida beaches. DeSantis said on 1 July that he was not very worried about the virus spreading at outdoor events held at places like parks or beaches: "It's the indoor events," he said, "that are a concern." Florida Representative Debbie Wasserman Schultz was among the many who condemned the governor's decision at the time: "he needs to close our beaches until this is really under control," she said. On this issue, however, DeSantis's view seems to have been proven largely correct. The science was certainly far from settled in the spring of 2020, but even at that time authoritative studies—notably a widely reported study released 16 April 2020, conducted by a team led by Hiroshi Nishiura of Hokkaido University—had already concluded that the risk of infection in an outdoor environment such as a beach was extraordinarily low; the odds of transmission in a closed environment, they reported, were "18.7 times greater, compared to an open-air environment." More recent studies have supported the view that (as an authoritative study by an Italian scientific team concluded) the probability of outdoor airborne transmission is "extremely low."

Most of us, of course, have our own political and ideological orientations, and it can be difficult to acknowledge that they can shape our assessments of an argument's validity almost as strongly as the facts themselves. It is easier for all of us to see, in a clear-eyed fashion, facts that support arguments we already agree with—and much more difficult for us to see in a clear-eyed fashion facts that may point in a different direction.

In your own writing, it's always worth striving to be fair minded—and part of being fair minded is to be direct and to say so if the preponderance of facts clearly supports one side of an argument.

Gender

The healthy revolution in attitudes towards gender roles in recent generations has created some awkwardness in English usage—though not nearly so much as some have claimed. *Chair* is a simple non-sexist replacement for *chairman*, as is *businesspeople* for *businessmen*. Nor does bias-free usage necessitate the use of *garbageperson* or *police-person*; *police officer* and *garbage collector* are entirely unobjectionable even to the linguistic purist.

The use of *mankind* to mean *humanity*, and of *man* to mean *human being*, have for some decades been rightly frowned upon. Ironically enough, *man* originally had *human being* as its only meaning; in Old English a *wērman* was a male adult human being, a *wifman* a female. It was not until after the Norman Conquest in 1066 that the word *man* began to do double duty—to be used both to mean *human being* and to mean *male human being*. No doubt inevitably, that lopsided pattern of usage fostered a bias towards the masculine in the word *man*. That male bias became powerfully reinforced over the centuries—until finally, in the twentieth century, the use of *man* to mean *human being* or *humankind* came to be broadly recognized as biased towards the male—sexist, in other words. Broadly recognized, but not universally: a remarkable number of adults still cling to these sexist usages. Professor James White of Alpha and Omega Ministries, for example, assured his readers on 13 March 2021 that "man has the capacity to direct his passions, to control his passions," with no suggestion that he intended to refer to only one half of the human race.

Well, why can't *man* be gender neutral? To start with, because of the historical baggage such usage carries with it. Here, for example, is what the best-selling novelist Grant Allen had to say on the topic in a magazine called *Forum* in 1889:

> In man, I would confidently assert, as biological fact, the males are the race; the females are merely the sex told off to recruit and reproduce it. All that is distinctly human is man—the field, the ship, the mine, the workshop; all that is truly woman is merely reproductive—the home, the nursery, the schoolroom.

But the baggage is not merely historical; much of the problem remains embedded in the language today. A useful litmus test is how sex and gender differences are approached. Look, for example, at this sentence from a 14 September 1996 issue of *The Economist*:

- One of the most basic distinctions in human experience—that between men and women—is getting blurrier and blurrier.

Now let's try the same sentence using *man's* instead of *human*:

- One of the most basic distinctions in man's experience—that between men and women—is getting blurrier and blurrier.

In this sort of context we are all forced to sense that something is amiss. We have to realize when we see such examples that *man* and *he* and even *mankind* inevitably carry with them some whiff of maleness; they can never fully and fairly represent all of humanity. Most contexts are of course more subtle than this, and it is thus often easy for humans—but especially for men—not to notice that the male terms always carry with them connotations that are not gender-neutral. *Humanity*, *humans*, *people*—these words are not in any way awkward or jargon-ridden; let's use them.

needs checking Mankind faces an uncertain future.
gender neutral Humanity faces an uncertain future.

What of *man*ual, or *man*ipulate, or *man*age? If we are to find substitutes for *policeman* and *salesman*, should we not also find replacements for these words? Should we not, as more than a few wags have sarcastically suggested, start saying *personipulate*? "But wait!" the satirist is likely to continue. "Look at the *-son* in *person*. We mustn't have male bias of that sort! Surely we had better say *peroffspringulate* instead. Shouldn't we?"

The short answer to that, of course, is no. And not only because of the awkwardness of such words. Constructions of this sort are "solutions" to a problem that never existed. In any meaningful sense, there is no maleness embedded in the noun *manipulate*, for *manipulate* does not mean "handle like a man" or anything of that sort. The words *manipulate*, *manual*, and *manage* stem from the Latin *manus*, meaning hand, rather than from any word having to do with gender—and there should thus be no suggestion of manual work being for males only. And the word *person*? It stems not from anything having to do with a male child but rather from the Latin *persona*, meaning *human being*. In any meaningful sense, there is not in fact a *son* in *person*.

The same sort of etymological confusion lies at the heart of any suggestion that we should regard it as problematic that there is a *-man* in *human*, and a *-man* in *woman*, and a *-male* in *female*. The word *human* derives from the Latin words *humanus* and *humana*, meaning "of or relating to the human." The word *female* comes to us not from anything to do with masculinity but from the Latin *femella*, meaning *girl*. The word *male*, on the other hand, comes from the Old French *masle*, which in turn comes from the Latin *masculus*—both meaning masculine. (Along the way we may as well point out that the word for *bad* in French is *mal*, but that there is no *mal* in *male*, any more than there is any *ale* in *male*—or in *female*, for that matter.)

• **guys**: The ubiquitous practice of using the term *guys* as an all-inclusive noun is another instance of having a male term represent everyone, including women and gender nonconforming people. As with *men*, some people think of *guys* as gender neutral, but others find it alienating to be referred to as a *guy*. If you are addressing an all-male group, *guys* is of course unproblematic, but in other contexts it's best to avoid the use of *guys* as a catch-all noun. "I'll see you all at the park" or "I'll see you folks later" are easily available, gender-neutral alternatives.

• **pronouns**: To replace *man* with *humanity* is not inherently awkward to even a slight degree. But the pronouns are more difficult. Clearly the consistent use of *he* to represent everyone is unacceptable. Yet *he/she*, *s/he*, and *he or she* are undeniably awkward, and such constructions are no longer recommended, primarily because they are not inclusive—they leave out nonbinary people. The use of *they* as a singular pronoun has long been commonplace in spoken language, and it is now widely accepted in formal writing as well, both as a pronoun for a nonbinary individual and as a gender-neutral replacement for *he/she*. Some instructors may still prefer students to adhere to older grammatical rules that insist pronouns should match their subjects in number (i.e., that a singular subject cannot use *they* as a singular pronoun). If that is the case for some of your instructors, you can still avoid biased language by revising your sentences to make pronouns such as *he/she* unnecessary. The following examples illustrate various ways to avoid using discriminatory gendered pronouns: using *they* instead of *he/she*, removing the pronoun entirely, and revising the sentence so that both the subject and the pronoun are plural. All of these methods are good ways to ensure your writing remains grammatical while avoiding discriminatory language.

worth checking	Every gardener should wait until the frost risk has passed to plant her seeds outdoors.
revised	Every gardener should wait until the frost risk has passed to plant their seeds outdoors.
or	Every gardener should wait until the frost risk has passed to plant seeds outdoors.
or	Gardeners should wait until the frost risk has passed to plant their seeds outdoors.

Many nonbinary or otherwise gender-nonconforming people use pronouns other than, or in addition to, *he* or *she*. The most common of these is the singular *they*, but many other pronouns exist, and some people use more than one set of pronouns (e.g., one person might be accurately described by *he* or *they*, while another might be accurately described by *she* or *he*). Regardless of the specifics, whenever someone tells you what pronouns should be used to refer to them, it is important to respect their wishes and use these pronouns. The pronouns *she* and *he* are fine to use if you know that the person you are discussing in your writing is a man or a woman; if you don't know, you are better off using the singular *they*. Because trans people often need to specify their pronouns in social and professional situations, it is a best practice for everyone to do so (e.g., by specifying your pronouns in your email signature, including them when you write your name on a name tag, or, in some contexts, stating them when you introduce yourself).

• **sex/gender/sexual orientation**: It is important to use these terms correctly in your writing. Many scholarly disciplines—and many people in everyday life—tend to treat *sex* and *gender* as different things. According to these definitions, the term *sex* or *biological sex* refers to the male, female, or intersex category assigned to a person at birth based on their physical attributes. *Gender*, by contrast, refers to the behaviours, roles, and psychological experiences attached to one's identity as a woman, man, nonbinary person, or other similar category. Our psychological experience of gender may or may not accord with the biological sex we are assigned at birth. People can be described as *cisgender* (meaning your gender accords with your sex assigned at birth) or *transgender* (meaning your gender does not accord with your sex assigned at birth). *Nonbinary* people have a gender experience that does not conform to the binary of "man" and "woman," or no gender experience at all; many people describe themselves simply as nonbinary, but "nonbinary" is also an umbrella term incorporating categories such as *genderfluid*, *genderqueer*, *gender nonconforming*, and *agender*. When describing the gender of an individual, always use the terms they use to describe themselves. Note as well that sex and gender are both different from sexual and romantic orientation, which express the nature of a person's sexual and romantic desires; for example, a transgender man who desires sexual relationships exclusively with women would quite likely describe himself as *straight*.

• **trans and nonbinary people and language**: Given the extent of the prejudice that trans and nonbinary people continue to face in the twenty-first century, it is important to choose words that don't reinforce that prejudice. The slang term *shemale* is broadly considered

If you and i were treated the same ...

In recent years some writers have begun to follow the practice of writing the pronoun "I" using lower case, like this: *As soon as i saw that painting, i loved it; If you and i agree on the outline, i suggest we meet to discuss next steps.* That may seem like a radical innovation, but it's the norm in the vast majority of languages (*je* in French, *yo* in Spanish, *ich* in German, and so on) to write the first-person singular subject pronoun in the same way that all the other pronouns are written—in lower case. It was the norm in English too until roughly the fourteenth century. No one seems to be entirely sure how English came to be such an outlier—and no one seems to have advanced any persuasive argument as to why we should remain so, other than the argument that it is conventional practice, and might thus be difficult to change.

In the other direction, it's been suggested that habitually capitalizing the first-person subject pronoun may be contributing to at least some small degree to whatever tendency we already possess towards exaggerating our own sense of self-importance. Is it time to challenge the convention of the capital I? It seems at the very least a topic worth discussing. (For two divergent views on this topic, see Caroline Winter's "Me, Myself, and I," *New York Times*, 3 August 2008, and Sara Boboltz's "Only English Speakers Capitalize 'I,' But That Doesn't Mean We're Obsessed with Ourselves," *HuffPost*, 9 June 2015.)

an offensive slur and should be avoided by cisgender (that is, non-transgender) people; *tranny*, another slang term, has a more complex history and should be used only with great care. It is also important not to confuse trans people with *transvestites* or *cross-dressers*, both terms used to describe people who wear the clothing of a gender different from their own; since a trans woman, for example, is a woman, if she dresses as a woman this is by definition not cross-dressing. (Trans people should also not be confused with *drag queens*, *drag kings*, or other *drag performers*, who experiment with gender as a form of art, usually by adopting the clothes and mannerisms of a gender not their own.) Other usage mistakes are more subtly disrespectful; common mistakes include referring to all transgender people as *transsexuals* (to some, *transsexual* has a medical connotation many transgender people don't identify with), using *transgender* as a noun (i.e., calling people *transgenders* instead of *transgender people*), and using quotation marks around terms relating to a transgender person's gender:

needs checking In her autobiographical essay, "Leanne" writes about "her" personal experience coming out as a "woman."

revised In her autobiographical essay, Leanne writes about her personal experience coming out as a woman.

The general rule is to use the pronouns and other language that match a person's gender, never to refer unnecessarily to biology, and never to imply through your language that anyone is not "really" their gender. It is also recommended practice not to draw attention to someone's previous name. Even if you are describing events that occurred before an individual's transition, you should still use their current name and pronouns.

needs checking Boyd Burton served in the US Navy before he became a woman named Fallon Fox.

revised Fallon Fox served in the US Navy before her gender transition.

When addressing or referring to specific individuals, it is essential to use their correct name, terminology, and pronouns. If you are unsure and it is important to identify someone in these respects, the best practice is to ask; if you are corrected regarding someone's appropriate name or pronouns, the best practice is to briefly express thanks for the correction and move on. In every case, it is important to refer to people as they have specified, but in general there is no need to mention someone's trans status unless you are certain they are publicly out *and* it is relevant to the subject being discussed. For further discussion of best practices surrounding pronouns, please see the above section entitled "Pronouns."

Acknowledging the existence of trans and nonbinary people in what we say and write is not just a matter of using respectful terminology; it also entails avoiding language that implies the existence of rigid gender categories. If you're addressing a crowd of people you don't know, it's better to begin by saying *Good evening, everyone* than by saying *Good evening, ladies and gentlemen* (or *good evening, men and women*). If you're describing a massacre in which the identity of the particular individuals is not known, it's better to write that *hundreds of people were killed* or that *hundreds of unarmed civilians—including many children—were killed* than to write that *hundreds of men, women, and children were killed.*

It's now widely advised that we avoid language that equates a given gender with a fixed biological category. If, for example, you're discussing pregnancy, expressions such as *those who are pregnant* acknowledge the fact that some trans men and nonbinary people can also become pregnant. It's important to note that using inclusive language such as this where appropriate in no way means that we should stop using the noun *women* in connection with pregnancy. The American Civil Liberties Union was rightly criticized (by many on the political left as well as many on the right) in 2021 when it published a list of groups affected by the threat to *Roe v. Wade* and did not include "women" anywhere on the list; it's of course appropriate to acknowledge that legislation regarding pregnancy and birth primarily affects women. And, in any case in which you are discussing a specific woman or group of women, it's of course appropriate to use the phrases *pregnant woman / pregnant women.* But where the most inclusive language is what is being sought, phrases such as *those who are pregnant* or *pregnant people* are entirely appropriate.

Race

When Joe Biden entered the race to become the Democratic Party's nominee for the American presidency in 2007, he put his foot in his mouth right away by praising fellow-candidate Barack Obama; for the first time in American history, he suggested, a presidential race included a "mainstream" African American who was "articulate and bright and clean and a nice-looking guy." Biden quickly apologized for the remark and was forgiven by Obama, who made an effort to minimize the significance of Biden's gaffe ("We have got more important things to worry about. We have got Iraq. We have got health care. We have got energy. This is low on the list."). But he and millions of others nevertheless recognized the inappropriateness of what Biden had said. To understand why such comments are inappropriate, one has to explore what is implied as well as what is stated. "Articulate" is a long way from "eloquent"; it's a weak term of praise used particularly in situations where one doesn't expect someone to be able to speak well at all. If someone who looks as if they are very drunk starts to speak in perfect sentences, one might describe them as "surprisingly articulate." If one praises a candidate as an "articulate African American," one is thus implying that, among African Americans, the norm is to be inarticulate. And if one praises an African American for being "clean and nice-looking," one is again implying that such is not the norm.

Biden clearly did not intend his unfortunate remark as a racist comment, and his gaffe demonstrates the difficulty of compensating for the prejudices embedded in one's thought and language—for everyone, but especially for people whose own privileges may make those prejudices more difficult to see. Obama appears to have recognized that mistakes of this sort can happen even among the well-intentioned, and he chose Biden to be his vice presidential running mate. The rest is history, so far as American presidential politics is concerned.

Unfortunately, vast and persistent inequality is also part of history—in Canada and the United States as elsewhere. Inequality in the world is of course not only a matter of racial inequality; overall, as of 2019, the richest 1% owned 44% of the world's wealth. Most billionaires are men; women regularly make up at most 10 or 12% of *Forbes*'s list of billionaires. Additionally, the great majority of billionaires are white: of the 614 American billionaires listed in *Forbes* in 2020, only 7 are Black. Extreme levels of inequality also persist, of course, in most other countries as well, and the gap between the top 1% and the rest of the population continues to grow worldwide.

Why is it important to know some of that background when you are thinking about language? Think of the case of a white student who is not accepted to Harvard Medical School, even though some Hispanic and African American applicants with somewhat lower marks were accepted; not infrequently you'll hear it claimed that this sort of result amounts to "racism" or "reverse racism" against whites and in favour of members of these or other underprivileged groups. Is that in fact the case? Emphatically not. Affirmative action of this sort attempts to redress the realities of systemic racism, acknowledging the fact that certain groups, particularly white people, have long held positions of privilege in society, while underprivileged groups have faced entrenched discrimination in all their interactions with the state, including, for example, their attempts to access education, healthcare, criminal justice, employment, and political representation. Whatever the rights or wrongs of policies followed by institutions such as the Harvard Medical School that do not base admission solely on marks, they are surely not policies founded on a belief that one race is superior to another. They may be intended to create a campus environment more representative of society as a whole; they may be intended to take account of systemic racism. Whether such policies are appropriate or not, whether they are effective or not—these are legitimate questions to debate. But they are surely not based on a belief that whites are inferior—and it is thus wrong to describe them as racist.

• **Aboriginal/First Nations/Indian/Indigenous**: In Canada the word *Indian* has become tainted by centuries of history in which those who had taken the land from the Indigenous peoples used the word *Indian* to denigrate those peoples. It's not uncommon for some First Nations people to refer to one another informally or ironically as Indians. If you hear an Indigenous person calling another Indigenous person "Indian," does that mean it's all right for every Canadian to do that? Emphatically not: given that many First Nations people consider the term offensive, other Canadians should avoid using it. (One exception is discussions of individuals or groups who embrace the term because of the political rights it connotes; the word Indian is still used by the Canadian government to indicate Indian status.) The most widely accepted terms used to refer to Indigenous Canadians are *Indigenous people* and, less often, *First Peoples*. Canada's Indigenous peoples can be divided into three large groups—*First Nations*, *Inuit*, and *Métis*—and these terms should be used when you are referring to one group specifically, but be careful not to make the common mistake of using "First Nations" when you really mean Indigenous people more generally:

needs checking In the past decade, government policies have reflected a change in attitude toward First Nations rights in Canada, from the Far North to the Great Lakes.

revised In the past decade, government policies have reflected a change in attitude toward Indigenous rights in Canada, from the Far North to the Great Lakes.

Whenever you can, the best thing to do is refer to a specific tribe[1] or nation:

worth checking Jeannette Armstrong is a First Nations writer, professor, and activist.

revised Jeannette Armstrong is a Syilx Okanagan writer, professor, and activist.

It is also important to avoid talking about Indigenous cultures as if they exist only in the past. To do so takes part in a centuries-old practice of romanticizing Indigenous cultures as tragically doomed by colonization and falsely declaring them to be dying or extinct. This practice contributes to the ongoing erasure of Indigenous lives and helps to conceal the ongoing impacts of colonization on Indigenous people.

needs checking The Teme-Augama Anishnabai lived in the Temagami area for thousands of years.

revised The Teme-Augama Anishnabai have lived in the Temagami area for thousands of years.

- **African American/African Canadian/Black/black**: For the past two or three generations *Black* (or *black*) and *African American* have been widely considered appropriate terms. The latter, of course, is only appropriate if one is referring to an American:

needs checking Nelson Mandela is widely considered to have been the greatest leader of his generation—not just the greatest African American leader, but the greatest leader, period.

revised Nelson Mandela is widely considered to have been the greatest leader of his generation—not just the greatest Black leader, or the greatest African leader, but the greatest leader, period.

In Canada *Black Canadians* is a much more widely used term than is *African Canadians.*

We know that it is correct to capitalize words that describe ethnicity or national origin, such as *Hispanic American*, *African American*, *Irish Canadian*, and so on. But what about *white* or *black*? According to some style guides, these should not be capitalized because they describe skin colour rather than nationality or ethnicity. According to this argument,

1 In Canada the term "band" remains a commonly used term in, for example, government documents, but "tribe" is now preferred by most Indigenous groups.

a given person's ethnicity would not be accurately described as *white* or *black* but as, say, *Somali* or *Danish*.

Many, however, argue that a large number of North Americans do in fact use *Black* as a term of ethnic identification—and for a very good reason. Whereas North Americans of, say, Italian or Irish background can readily explore their "pre-American" ethnic background, Black North Americans whose ancestors were enslaved find it more difficult to do so: they have fewer ways of knowing if their ancestors came from (to pick only three of many examples, each with cultures at least as different one from another as are those of France and Spain and Italy) the Khassonke-speaking Khasso Empire in what is now Mali, the Yoruba-speaking Oyo Empire in what is now Nigeria, or the Asante-speaking Ashanti Kingdom in what is now Ghana.

Given that the history of slavery has deprived most Black North Americans of the connection to specific national roots that most other North Americans have, many regard the identifier *Black* as a primary descriptor of ethnicity. When *Black* is used in this way, capitalization recognizes its legitimacy as an ethnicity—whereas not capitalizing it, some argue, may be taken to implicitly disparage Black people and culture.[1]

Should we capitalize *Black* at all times? Some argue that consistently capitalizing *Black* is a pragmatic approach, since it can sometimes be difficult to distinguish in practice between its use as a descriptor of skin colour and its use as the proper name of an ethnic group. Of writers who use this approach, some capitalize *White* as well, for the sake of symmetry. But *white* is often capitalized in the writings of white supremacists, and most writers rightly want to avoid any association with that ideology. Moreover, *white* simply doesn't serve as a primary ethnic identifier for any large group in the way that *Black* arguably does in North America—or indeed in any area where a history of slavery stripped large numbers of people of their original ethnic identity. (Conversely, in many parts of the world *black* is not capitalized because it implies nothing whatsoever as to culture or ethnicity; in Zambia virtually everyone has black skin, but the Bemba, Tonga, Kaonde, etc. all have different linguistic and cultural traditions.)

---

1 These issues of usage, it should be noted, remain controversial. The *New York Times*, for example, mandates use of capitalized "Black," but black *New York Times* language issues columnist John McWhorter prefers not to capitalize (see "Capitalizing 'Black' Isn't Wrong, But It Isn't That Helpful, Either," 4 March 2022).

• **n-word**: Almost everyone knows that the *n-word* is a highly derogatory term that was once very widely used in North America; that the term conveyed a presumption that Black people were inferior to whites; and that the term was frequently employed as an expression of blatant hatred and contempt. In the mid-twentieth century the *n-word* began to be acknowledged as racist and hence utterly unacceptable, and it disappeared from mainstream publications and from most conversation. But it never went away: the forbidden term continued to be used by individuals and hate groups as an expression of racism—and it still continues to be so used today.

In the late twentieth century, as a gesture of resistance in the face of the continuing oppression of Black people in the United States, some groups of young African Americans began to "reclaim" the *n-word* as their own, using it defiantly among themselves to refer to one another. That remains common practice today—and as a result, some young people of other backgrounds now sometimes wonder why they too shouldn't be allowed to use the "forbidden" term. The reason is simple: it remains tainted by the history of oppression with which it is associated. It is one thing for members of a group that has been on the receiving end of oppression to embrace such a term as an expression of solidarity among themselves. It is quite another for those belonging to other groups to presume to do the same.

In recent years greater emphasis has been placed on the importance of not using this offensive term, even when the term is mentioned or quoted rather than used in a way that endorses its meaning. In order to avoid controversy and to avoid subjecting others to a word that provokes strong reactions because of the extreme racial hatred it implies, it is recommended practice to avoid the word in writing or speech. If you feel it is essential to mention it, it is best to do so by alluding to the word (as "the n-word," for example) rather than by using it in full.

• **gyp/gypsy**: A few racial and cultural terms are so deeply encoded in the language that people may use them without being aware of their underlying meaning. One example of this is the word *gyp*, which originated in the stereotype that Roma people—often referred to as *gypsies*, though the term is now widely considered a slur—are congenital cheats. In North America, the "gypsy" stereotype is often imagined as a fictional or historical figure, but this stereotype does a great deal of harm to contemporary Romani people across North and South America, and especially in Europe. Both Amnesty International and the European

Commission have censured the European Union for institutionalized discrimination against the Roma.

needs checking I'm convinced that the shopkeeper tried to gyp me.
revised I'm convinced that the shopkeeper tried to cheat me.

• **Hispanic/Latino/Latina/Latinx**: Though the terms are often used interchangeably in practice, *Hispanic* and *Latinx* [pronounced *lah-TEE-neks*] have slightly different definitions. *Hispanic* describes people who are from or whose ancestors are from a predominantly Spanish-speaking culture or country—including Spain, as well as Mexico, parts of the Caribbean, and most Central American and South American countries (but not Brazil, where the dominant language is Portuguese). *Latino* (used for men and sometimes for groups of mixed or unknown gender), *Latina* (used for women), and *Latinx* (gender neutral) describe people who are from or whose ancestors are from any part of Latin America—meaning Mexico, parts of the Caribbean, and most Central American and South American countries, including Brazil.

A good deal of uncertainty surrounding the usage of *Hispanic* and *Latinx* is to be expected, given that these terms represent efforts to group together such a wide range of people from such a very large geographic area. In fact, many Latinx people are highly critical of the concept of *latinidad*, the idea that there is a shared geopolitical and cultural identity among those who have emigrated to Canada and the United States from Central and South America; critics point out, in particular, that Black and Indigenous groups from these areas often have their particular identities erased under the *Latinx* category. For this reason, many people who might be described as Hispanic or Latino prefer wherever possible to be identified more specifically and locally—as *Argentine Americans*, *Cuban Americans*, *Mazatecs*, *Afro-Colombians*, and so on. The broader markers *Latinx* or *Hispanic* can still be useful, however, because they acknowledge a shared history of colonialism, some shared cultural characteristics, and the existence of diverse, integrated Latino and Hispanic communities within the United States and Canada.

When it is appropriate to use *Hispanic* or *Latinx*, is it better to use one term than the other? There is no consensus on this, and practices vary by region; in Texas, the most extreme example, *Hispanic* is almost always used and *Latinx* rarely used. When a specific group's preference is unknown, it is fine to use either term, but if such a preference is known, it is of course best to use the preferred designation.

When using *Hispanic* and/or *Latinx*, it is important to keep a few things in mind. One is that, though both terms are sometimes treated as racial identifiers, neither refers to race; Hispanic people and Latinx people can be Amerindian, white, Black, a combination, or anything else. It is also important to note that, though *Hispanic* refers to the Spanish language, not all Hispanic people speak that language; many whose families have lived in the United States for multiple generations do not speak any Spanish. And, finally, *Hispanic* and *Latinx* are normally used in reference to populations in the United States; the general term typically used to describe people living in Latin America is *Latin Americans*. In Canada, *Latinx* and *Hispanic* are both commonly used, as is the term *Canadian Latin American*; but once again, if possible use a more specific, local designation, such as *Salvadorean-Canadian* or *Peruvian-Canadian*.

• **Orientalism and Occidentalism**: Readers will find *Oriental* on the list at the end of this chapter of terms to avoid. Why? *The Orient* was for centuries an acceptable short form combining geographical areas that are now referred to as *East Asia* and *the Middle East*—or by more specific names. Why the problem with the old name? In a now-famous book called *Orientalism* (1978), the literary and political scholar Edward Said set out to answer that question. As Said demonstrated conclusively, the term had come to embody a great many deeply rooted stereotypes. "Orientals" were regarded as exotic, inscrutable, less fully human than white Europeans, and mentally unsuited to the job of governing themselves; they were better off under the colonial rule of a Western power. Such views have underlain a great many of the actions of Western powers over several centuries—from the exertion of British colonial power in India and the Middle East in the nineteenth century to the approach taken by the American government of George W. Bush (and subsequent American administrations) to Iraq and Afghanistan. The term *Oriental* also had the effect of flattening difference. Use of the term reinforced the human tendency to see individuals from other groups as indistinguishable—and, in this case,[1] thereby reinforced racist views of those

1 "Don't they all look the same?" There is a seemingly universal human tendency to perceive the individual members of racial or ethnic groups one is unfamiliar with as all looking very similar. When I was working for some years as a teacher in rural Zimbabwe, I was for an extended period one of only two white men for miles around—the other being Bernard Uters, a German doctor. I was thirtyish, slight of build, dark haired and clean shaven; Bernard was fortyish, muscular, blond, and bearded. We could hardly have looked more different—to anyone used to looking

groups. If one uses a single patronizing umbrella term to group together a vast and diverse body of different cultures, one is spared the effort of learning about how those groups may differ one from another. It is best to be as specific as possible about the countries and cultures you are speaking about and to avoid blanket terms—but if you are referring to a large region as a whole, use terms such as *Asian*, *East Asian*, or *Middle Eastern* rather than *Oriental*.

Arguably *Africa* and *African* have taken on some of the same qualities that *the Orient* and *Oriental* once held for Westerners. Victorian writers such as the famous journalist and explorer Henry Morton Stanley (author of *In Darkest Africa*) helped to spread outrageous stereotypes about Africa, many of which still persist in Western countries—as does the tendency to flatten distinctions between the many different parts of the continent and its many different cultures, reducing the continent to one amorphous mass. In reality, how much do the peoples of Morocco and Nigeria and the Sudan and Botswana have in common with each other? Certainly far less than do the people of the United States and Canada, or the people of France and Belgium. But we do not flatten Europeans in the same way as we do Africans; North Americans might speak of a vacation in Amsterdam or in Italy, but if they go on a vacation to Kenya many are likely to say they are going "to Africa." In your writing, try to avoid this tendency and refer directly to the specific country and culture you are discussing, unless indeed you are writing about the continent as a whole.

• **people of colour**: This term is perfectly fine to use, but it is a blanket term and as such collapses differences among various groups (for example, in political discourse it is often assumed that "people of colour" vote a similar way and share similar goals and perspectives). It is preferable to be more specific in your writing (by referring for example to Indigenous people, Asian Canadians, or Black Canadians instead of Canadian people of

---

at white people and interacting with them. But many in the local community were not—and so it was that I would very frequently be accosted in the marketplace by people calling me "Doctor" and hoping I would be able to help them.

In itself, then, the tendency to perceive the members of unfamiliar groups as all appearing similar is not necessarily racist; those who called me "Doctor" clearly were not stereotyping all white people in any racist way. But it is nevertheless a tendency to be wary of (and to try actively to counteract as one becomes more familiar with members of other groups), for it can have truly pernicious effects if combined with various sorts of negative feeling. [DL]

colour), if that is possible. When you do use the term *people of colour*, give some thought as to whether there might be a more specific alternative.

Class

Another example of a widely used expression that is strongly coloured with bias is the expression *white trash*. This disparaging term (and similar terms such as *trailer trash*) are most often applied to working-class white people, often those living in rural areas or on the outskirts of towns. The implications of the expression are made clear in the following passage:

> The [Jerry Lee] Lewis and [Jimmy] Swaggart clans were, in the harsh modern parlance, white trash. They lived in the black part of town, and had close relations with blacks. Mr. Swaggart's preaching and Mr. Lewis's music were strongly influenced by black culture. "Jimmy Swaggart was as black as a white man can be," said black elders in Ferriday. (*The Economist*, 15 April 2000)

This passage brings out very clearly the racial implications of the expression; the "trashiness" that is the exception for white people is implicitly regarded as the norm for Black people. Yet, remarkably, mainstream white North America continues to use the expression as if it were ethically unproblematic. The September 2016 cover of *The Atlantic* magazine, for example, carried the heading *White Trash* on its cover—without quotation marks or any other acknowledgement that the phrase carries deep levels of bias within it. The piece mentioned on the magazine cover was a review article focused in large part on historian Nancy Isenberg's 2016 book *White Trash: The 400-Year Untold History of Class in America*—which again carries no quotation marks around the expression "White Trash" to indicate that it is being referenced as a historical artifact rather than an unexceptionable phrase that may be used without any qualms today.

The inappropriateness of expressions such as *white trash* is starting to be widely acknowledged. Less widely understood is the degree to which various expressions that are often used to describe wealthy people carry class baggage. Think, for example, of expressions such as these:

- She comes from a good family.
- He's making a good income now.
- By some definitions the couple may not be rich, but they are certainly well-off.

- As an investment counsellor, she deals primarily with people of high net worth.

A centuries-old tradition among the rich and the middle class in North American and European culture holds that it is vulgar to refer to oneself or to friends and acquaintances as rich. For generations it has been accepted among the wealthy (and among many who aspire to wealth) that in most situations one should use euphemisms when referring to wealth and income. Many euphemisms do no harm, of course. But when one uses phrases such as *good family* to mean *rich family*, one is subtly colouring the financial with the moral. So too if one refers to someone as *high net worth* rather than as *wealthy* or *rich*. By implication, such phrasings further disadvantage those already disadvantaged by poverty, lending it a taint of a moral as well as a financial shortfall. Of course a phrase such as *good family* can also be used in contexts where wealth is not implied; the phrase can be and is often applied to families that are not rich. All who believe that it's preferable to make one's meaning clear (and who believe that poverty is not evidence of any moral failing) should consider avoiding such euphemisms, and use more precise wording:

- She comes from a family that has long been regarded as wealthy and respectable.
  [if one means to convey that the family is wealthy]
- She comes from a family that is very well regarded in the community.
  [if one is using the phrase without any connotation of wealth]
- He's making a large amount of money now.
- By some definitions the couple may not be rich, but they own a summer place as well as a large house in town, and most years they manage a vacation in Europe.
- As an investment counsellor, she deals primarily with wealthy people.

worth checking The novel focuses on a woman who comes from a good family in New York; when the family falls on hard times, she faces difficult choices.

revised The novel focuses on a woman who has moved in high society in New York; when her family falls on hard times, she faces difficult choices.

Even when you are using accepted terminology to discuss class, it is good to keep in mind the effects your word choice might have. *Lower class*, for example, is a widely used term that suggests a negative value judgement; descriptors such as *working class* (where appropriate) and *low-income* may be preferable.

Religion

Given the generally high level of awareness in Western society of the evils of antisemitism, it is extraordinary that *Jew* is still sometimes used in casual conversation as a verb in the same way that *gyp* is used—and that *Jewish* can still sometimes be encountered as a synonym for *stingy*. These are usages that have their roots in a long tradition of anti-Jewish prejudice—in the many centuries during which most Christian societies prohibited Jews from entering most respectable occupations, leaving Jews little choice but to provide services such as moneylending that Christians needed but considered sinful. Moneylending then became part of the vicious stereotyping that surrounded Jews. Like other extremely offensive terms discussed in this book, terms that preserve longstanding antisemitic prejudices should never be allowed to go unchallenged. When they are challenged, speakers will often realize they have been unthinkingly using a coinage learnt in childhood—and will change.

A difficult issue is how to refer to extremists affiliated with a particular religion. Should those who profess faith in Islam but believe it is acceptable for them to kill and maim vast numbers of civilians who are associated with organizations they despise (Osama bin Laden's followers killing 2,996 people on 11 September 2001, followers of the Islamic State movement killing thousands in Iraq and Syria in 2014) be called Islamic fundamentalists, or Islamists, or jihadis, or terrorists, or simply mass killers? If someone claims to be following the Islamic faith and commits extreme acts of horrendous violence against unarmed civilians in the name of their faith, many argue that it's entirely fair to describe that person as an Islamic extremist. But fair to whom? When the two words are brought together, inevitably something of the one rubs off on the other, leaving some suggestion in the minds of those reading or hearing the term that extremism comes naturally to Muslims. Many North Americans of Christian background may appreciate this point more clearly if we think of the phrase *Christian extremist*. Would it seem appropriate to use that term to describe some of the insurrectionists who stormed the US Capitol in January 2021 (many of whom carried signs with Christian slogans and who gathered in Christian prayer in the Senate chamber)?[1] Probably not: a strong argument can be made that no religion deserves to be identified through the actions of its most violent and dogmatic adherents.

The best way to approach such questions may be to be as specific as possible—and to try to use language that cannot be taken to equate the beliefs of an entire religion with those of extremists on the fringes of that religion.

worth checking Hindu terrorists killed over a thousand Muslims in the violence in India's Gujarat state in 2002.

revised Extremists believed to be associated with the Vishva Hindu Parishad (VHP) killed over a thousand Muslims in the violence in India's Gujarat state in 2002.

Much as one should be careful in choosing one's words in such cases, one should also strive to be direct where the facts are plain, or where the weight of probability points clearly to a particular conclusion.

worth checking Extremists believed to be associated with the Vishva Hindu Parishad (VHP) killed over a thousand Muslims in the "communal violence" in India's Gujarat state in 2002. Some have claimed that the state police and the Gujarat state government were complicit in the violence; it has been alleged that the police and the Gujarat state government (led by Narendra Modi, now Prime Minister of all of India) did little or nothing to stop the massacres or to prosecute the perpetrators, and some have suggested that Modi's government helped to plan the targeted attacks on Muslims.

---

1 Tragically, further examples abound for virtually all religions. Timothy McVeigh professed his faith in Christianity but killed 168 innocent people in Oklahoma City in 1995, just as Anders Behring Breivik professed his faith in Christianity but killed 77 innocent people (many of them children) in Norway in 2011; should they be called Christian extremists, or right-wing extremists, or terrorists, or simply shooters and bombers? Baruch Kopel Goldstein professed his faith in Judaism but killed 29 innocent people at prayer in 1994; should he be called a Jewish extremist, or a Zionist extremist, or a terrorist, or simply a shooter? Various people professing faith in Hinduism killed more than 1,000 innocent Muslims in the Indian state of Gujarat in 2002; should they be called Hindu radicals, or Hindu extremists, or terrorists, or simply mass killers?

[Though Modi and others deny it, Human Rights Watch and other impartial organizations have all concluded that the police and Gujarat state government facilitated the killings. What remains to some degree uncertain is whether or not they helped plan the attacks. In such cases responsible writers give their readers a sense of the weight of probability, rather than retreat into *false equivalency* (see above).]

revised Extremists believed to be associated with the Vishva Hindu Parishad (VHP) killed over a thousand Muslims in the "communal violence" in India's Gujarat state in 2002. A strong body of evidence suggests that the state police and the Gujarat state government were complicit in the violence; the police and the Gujarat state government (led by Narendra Modi, now Prime Minister of all of India) did little or nothing to stop the massacres or to prosecute the perpetrators, and reputable sources have claimed that Modi's government helped to plan the targeted attacks on Muslims.

The term *radical Islam* was bandied about very freely during the 2016 American presidential campaign, with Republican candidate Donald Trump accusing Democratic candidate Hillary Clinton of being "afraid" to use the term. Groups such as ISIS/ISIL and al-Qaeda are indeed radical, and they do indeed represent certain strands of Islam. Why, then, should we not refer to them as representing radical Islam? Isn't that just being truthful?

No is the short answer. And the reason is simple: such phrases work to create an ambiguity that fosters the impression that the religion as a whole is radical, or that the actions of radicals in some way reflect the beliefs of moderate members of the religion. Imagine calling those Christians who call for gay people to be sentenced to death representatives of radical Christianity. Or those Buddhists who would like to exterminate Muslims in Burma and Sri Lanka representatives of radical Buddhism. Such phrases can readily suggest that Islam, or Christianity, or Buddhism, or whatever religion is being named, is by its very nature radical—and that any member of that religion is prone to extremism.

Sexual Orientation

The term *sexual orientation* has for the most part replaced *sexual preference* when it comes to describing gay, lesbian, bisexual, heterosexual, and other sexualities—and for a good reason. The word *preference* carries with it a connotation of choice—the notion that one *chooses* whether or not to be gay. It is on that sort of presumption that conversion therapists have tried to "cure" people of same-sex desires, and that bisexual people have been pressured to pretend heterosexuality. It's on that presumption too that some still refer to a *gay lifestyle*, as if sexual orientation were akin to deciding either to settle down in a quiet, leafy suburb or travel round the world as a backpacker. In fact, of course, gay, lesbian, bisexual, and asexual people choose from among just as many lifestyles as do heterosexual people. And, as a great many studies have shown, most people—whether they are gay, lesbian, heterosexual, bisexual, asexual, or anything else—do not "choose" the genders they are or are not attracted to.

• **gay/homosexual**: The term *gay* is now preferred to the term *homosexual*; why is that? Because of its history, is the short answer. The term *homosexual* was for so many generations used as a term of abuse—and, in the medical profession, as a term naming a form of mental illness—that it has now become tainted. Consequently, it is inappropriate to use phrases such as *homosexual sex* or *homosexual relationship* in most contexts; these phrases in particular are frequently used in anti-gay rhetoric to evoke the connotations of deviance and mental illness that *homosexual* can carry. That said, there are still a variety of contexts in which the word *homosexual* may (and should) still be used. In cases where one is speaking of the history of medical or legal conversations around same-sex love, using the language of that context may be appropriate; one may also in such cases choose to sidestep the issue with phrases such as *same-sex sexuality* that do not carry the same degree of cultural baggage.

• **"That's so gay"**: Soon after the word *gay* came to be recommended in the late twentieth century as the preferred non-pejorative term for same-sex sexual orientation, the expression *that's so gay* began to be widely used in conversation by young people. Its meaning? *That's really stupid*, or *That's weak and ineffectual*, or "..." But inevitably such usages connect at some level with other meanings; if you use such a term, it's impossible to avoid a broader association of what is gay with what is stupid, weak, and ineffectual. Much as many have protested that *that's so gay* is an "innocent expression," it's not. The cumulative repetition of this and similar colloquial expressions does a great deal to reinforce human prejudice against gays, lesbians, and bisexuals, and to make it more difficult for those who are gay to be open about it, and proud of it.

- **queer/LGBTQ+**: What of the term *queer*? For much of the twentieth century *queer* and *faggot* were the most common terms of abuse hurled at gay people and lesbians. In the last quarter of the last century, however, many gay, lesbian, bisexual, and trans people began to defiantly claim the term *queer* as their own—in the process declaring their difference from what was felt (with good reason) to be the straitjacket of straight society. "We're here, we're queer—get used to it" became a familiar chant at gay rallies and protests.

As with other terms of abuse that have been reclaimed by members of the group that has been on the receiving end of the abuse, use of the term *queer* should not be taken lightly by those who are not members of the victimized group. But while with cases such as the *n-word* the right approach is straightforward—those not part of the group the word is used to denigrate should simply not use the word—the case of *queer* is more complicated. While many gay, lesbian, bisexual, and transgender people feel that the word is inherently and extremely offensive, the word has also been taken up by others in ways that call upon people outside the community to use it. In the humanities, *queer theory* (a branch of critical theory) attaches specific meanings to the word *queer*, and the word can and should be used as an academic term in that context. Many activists also use phrases such as *queer community* to refer to all people whose sexual orientation or gender identity challenges cultural norms; the commonly used alternative, *LGBTQ+* (an acronym meaning *lesbian/gay/bisexual/transgender/queer/other nonconforming identities*), is seen by some as less inclusive because it does not—and could not possibly—name all of the incredibly diverse identity markers that fall under the umbrella of *queer* (though the addition of the + is an attempt to be inclusive of all sexual and gender minorities).[1] And some people with whom the radical tone or the open-ended meaning of

1 The awkwardness of this approach is continually lamented, and more inclusive possibilities are frequently proposed. One alternative umbrella term is "gender and sexual minorities" or GSM, though some critics express concern that this category may in fact be too broad (including, for example, swingers and pedophiles as well as people who would fall under the LGBTQ+ umbrella).

queer resonates prefer to identify themselves as *queer* in addition to—or even instead of—*gay*, *lesbian*, or anything else. The bottom line is that some audiences will find the use of *queer* alienating and offensive while others will find it inclusive and celebratory, so it is important to take care when deciding whether or not to use the word in a given context.

Ability, Disability, and Neurodivergence

The language we use when we talk about disability, health conditions, and neurodivergence has a profound impact on the individuals and communities of people who identify as disabled, autistic, blind, or Deaf (and many other designations). Confusingly, this language isn't always clearly agreed upon by all, and it is evolving quickly. While professionals and policy makers have historically been taught to use "person first" language (e.g., *girl with autism* or *woman with vision impairment*), many disabled self-advocates now express a preference for "disability first" language (e.g., *autistic girl* or *blind woman*). These preferences, they say, relate to individuals' perceptions of their state of being; autism or blindness aren't add-ons to their personality but intrinsic parts of who they are.

We recommend that you defer to an individual or community's preferred terms of reference where possible (in much the same way that we honour an individual's gender pronouns or ethnic self-identification terms). If that preference is unknown, try to employ specific terms for the physical, mental, or cognitive impairment and use them respectfully and with consideration for your audience or reader (who may well identify as disabled themselves). The care with which we choose language around impairment and disability reflects our willingness to not only be aware of, but to fully accept and include, those with a variety of support needs in our communities. As with gender and race or cultural background, there is no need to mention a disability unless it is relevant to the topic of discussion.

needs checking This classroom environment creates unnecessary obstacles for students with autism.

revised This classroom environment creates unnecessary obstacles for autistic students.

needs checking Professor Caswell joined the History Department in 2019. A distinguished scholar, he is the author of several books on early American society. He's confined to a wheelchair, though.

[If you are outlining Professor Caswell's credentials and accomplishments, his physical disability is not something you need to mention.]

revised Professor Caswell joined the History Department in 2019. A distinguished scholar, he is the author of several books on early American society.

Notice also how the reference to the wheelchair is worded in the above example. Phrases such as "confined to a wheelchair" can subtly colour people's judgements as to whether or not someone will be an asset to a community, or a burden on it.

needs checking The members of the interviewing committee noticed that Professor Caswell is confined to a wheelchair.

revised The members of the interviewing committee noticed that Professor Caswell uses a wheelchair.

Note also that many writers on the subject distinguish *disability* from *impairment*. The emerging discourse recognizes that individuals have impairments (physical, mental, or cognitive) but sees the notion of *disability* as a result of society's inability to simply accommodate everyone's needs. An impairment becomes disabling when an individual must function in a society that accommodates those with needs considered "typical" rather than all needs universally. Thus, an *impairment* is a state of body or mind while *disability* is a result of society's response to an impairment. The term *neurodivergence*, an umbrella category that includes autism, ADHD, and many other traits, is used to describe nonstandard ways of thinking and learning as normal variations in human brain function; the term does not necessarily imply any form of impairment. An individual may identify as *neurodivergent* if they possess any of the traits considered part of this category, or *neurotypical* if they do not.

Humans and Other Animals

In recent decades the ways in which humans treat other animals have become the subject of widespread discussion. But there has been scant attention paid to how changing attitudes should be reflected in English usage. In particular, the issue of what pronouns to use has until recently been little discussed.

• **he/she/it—pronoun issues**: No one nowadays thinks it odd to refer to a pet as *he* or *she*, but beyond that there is a great deal of inconsistency. At issue is not only *it* versus *he* or *she* (or *they*), but also *who* and *whom* versus *that* and *which*. Should we say *the dog that lives next door* or *the dog who lives next door*? Should we say *the pig that plays a central role in* Charlotte's Web? Or *the pig who plays a central role in* Charlotte's Web? Should we say *the pig that they ate for dinner* or *the pig who they ate for dinner*?

In contexts where non-human animals are portrayed as pets or as friendly and lovable, "who" seems to be quite accepted. "The cat who..." and "The dog who..." are commonly used, as are "the pig who..." and "the cow who" in contexts such as children's stories. With dogs and cats *who* seems a widely accepted alternative, even in negative contexts; Google N-Gram, for example, shows "dogs who bite" occurring almost as frequently as "dogs that bite" in 2018 (whereas as recently as 2000 "dogs that bite" occurred more than four times as frequently).[1] Wild animals too we seem comfortable referring to as living creatures rather than things. In the case of the non-human animals many humans make a practice of eating, though, *it*, *that*, and *which* are used far more frequently. Should they be? Is a cow any more a thing than is a tail-wagging Labrador? Is a calf or a piglet any more a thing than is a kitten or a puppy? What about a shrimp? Or a clam? Where does one draw a line? For many people there may be no easy answers to such questions, but they are surely worth asking; as has often been the case in human history, debates over appropriate linguistic usage provide some of the most interesting windows into large ethical, political, and epistemological issues.

What should you do if you are writing of non-human animals? Treat them grammatically as things? Or treat them in the way we do fellow beings? Is there any good reason to refer to any animal as *it* rather than *he* or *she* (or *they*)? Or to say *that* rather than *who*? Try as we might, we can't see any. We have to acknowledge that the state of our language is still some distance away from any point where it would be frowned upon to refer to non-human animals as things—calves or chimpanzees, bears or bonobos, dogs or ducklings, hens or hippopotamuses. But we'd like to try to bring all of us, as human beings—human animals—closer to that point.

---

1 Interestingly, Google N-Gram also indicates that "dogs who bite" was used at least as frequently as "dogs that bite" for much of the nineteenth century; not until the mid 1890s did "dogs that bite" start to be used with much greater frequency.

worth checking The cow that's pictured on that carton of milk looks a lot happier than a real cow looks when its children have been taken away from it so that humans can drink the milk it produces.

revised The cow who's pictured on that carton of milk looks a lot happier than a real cow looks when her children have been taken away from her so that humans can drink the milk she produces.

Much as it may seem forced or odd to refer to non-human animals in this way, English usage of this sort in fact represents a return to linguistic practice that was once well established. In 1865, for example, one Dr. Kidd recounted in the *Times* of London how he had saved a cow during the cattle plague of that year: "The men thought her dying…," "Determined not to give her up…" "little by little she revived." With "intensive" farming practices having become near universal in North America, most of us now have little or no contact with living cows and pigs and sheep and hens; no doubt it is not by coincidence that the growth of factory farming has been accompanied by a shift in the English language towards usages that encourage us to think of non-human animals as things rather than as living creatures.

• **other—and leaving the "other" out**: Whether to say *who* or *which* is far from the only issue when it comes to how we refer to non-human animals. Let's look at another example:

needs checking The way humans view animals determines how we treat them.

To be correct, such sentences as these should also include the word *other*:

revised The way humans view other animals determines how we treat them.

This sort of error is clear to us in sentences where humans are not one of the species being compared. Any editor who came across a sentence such as "The robin was flying higher than the birds" would think immediately *Wait—a robin is a bird—that's wrong*, and would correct it to "The robin was flying higher than the other birds." But the human tendency to exaggerate the degree to which humans are different from the members of other species is so ingrained that in these contexts we forget that we humans are in fact a species of animal.

At some level, of course, we all know that the human species is a form of animal life—we are neither vegetables nor blocks of stone. Is it needless carping to suggest that we should acknowledge our animality in our habits of speaking and writing? Is it merely pedantic to insist that it's better to refer to *the way humans view other animals* rather than *the way humans view animals*? As researchers long ago discovered, the way we use language both reflects and helps to shape our thinking. If we treated all non-human animals well, how we speak of them might fairly be considered a matter of less seriousness. But the fact is that we don't; throughout the world non-human animals are horrifically mistreated; here in North America, over 99% of the meat and dairy products we consume come from animals who spend their lives in conditions of extreme hardship in factory farms. The more we hang on to habits of speaking of (and thinking of) **other** animals as creatures entirely different from ourselves, the easier it is for us to rationalize the cruelty that we condone.

Ironically enough, the above example of the practice of writing *humans and animals* rather than *humans and other animals* is taken from an excellent book called *The Inner World of Farm Animals* (2009), which presents a wealth of research demonstrating that farm animals are far closer to humans in their intellectual and emotional capabilities than has commonly been assumed. Even those who are working to challenge the old stereotypes, in other words, sometimes use language that helps to reinforce them. It took the authors of this book a long time to learn the importance of being careful about how we use *man*; no doubt the same will be true of *animals*.

Other Issues

• **body language**: It was long considered acceptable in much of Western culture to give to anyone who carried a good deal of weight around their midriff a nickname that drew attention to their body shape—whether they liked it or not. In George Orwell's 1939 novel *Coming Up for Air*, for example, the protagonist describes himself as "the active, hearty kind of fat man, the athletic bouncing type that's nicknamed Fatty or Tubby and is always the life and soul of the party." To thoughtful English speakers in the twenty-first century it may seem self-evident that we should never use the word *fat* to describe another person. To many people, the word remains inherently insulting. But many activists advocating for the better treatment of fat people disagree: using euphemisms to skirt the issue of fat, such activists argue, implies that fatness is something other than a neutral fact about a person's body. In some areas of formal writing the terms *overweight* and *obese* are considered the preferred alternatives to *fat*, but some fat activists have also raised objections to these. The use of *overweight*, they argue, implies that a single weight standard should be applied to everyone despite individual variation (in muscularity or genetic predisposition, for example). *Obese*, they argue, captures an attitude towards fatness that classifies it as a public health issue—and is used to justify the public judgement and shaming of fat individuals—while also denying fat people the compassion normally offered to sick people, because western society does not generally recognize being fat as a disease. In fact, as medical professionals have been discovering, it's often not difficult to find alternatives, even if one is using the BMI categories as reference points; a doctor or nurse can say to a patient, for example, "I see that you score quite high on the BMI scale" (*not* "I see that you're quite overweight"). The relationship between weight and health is complex—as is the relationship between weight and poverty, and weight and personal choice—but regardless of one's views on these issues it is still imperative not to speak or write about fat people in a disparaging or dehumanizing way.

Accepting that *fat* may be an acceptable term does not mean that using the word *fat* is a good idea in every circumstance. Fat activists may have done much to reclaim the term *fat*, but if your friend asks *How do I look in this outfit?* you might want to consider the reception you'll get if you answer *Fat and fabulous*! Because *fat* has long been—and still is—used as a dehumanizing slur, it is possible that the use of *fat* with positive intention will still come across as an insult. *Fat* is also a vague term—how much body fat does a person have to have in order to qualify as fat?—so using it can put a writer in the position of describing other people as fat who would not describe themselves that way.

Despite the reasonable objections of fat activists, some writers find that words or phrases such as *plus size*, *heavy*, *larger*, or *people with a high BMI* can provide the best solution in situations where the positive use of *fat* might not come across to most readers. In some contexts, using the terms *obese* and *overweight* may be unavoidable; these remain standard terms in journalism, and they are used in medical and other scientific writing to define particular body types according to BMI (Body Mass Index) and other measurements. There are some basic rules, however, that can be universally applied: obviously, avoid using *fat* as a slur (*he's nothing but a fat slob*; *she's a fat pig*) and avoid using other slurs that disparage fat people. Similarly, avoid using *fat* as though it had an inherently negative meaning (*Ick, I feel so fat after all that pizza*; *Do I look fat in this shirt?*). Also avoid references to "normal" weight—a meaningless and misleading term (since not everyone has the same healthy weight). And, with body shape, as with characteristics such as gender, race, and sexual orientation, when one is describing an individual it is always a good idea to consider whether a characteristic is relevant to the context. Whether the individual is fat or extremely thin, if their body shape isn't relevant to the context, don't mention it.

• **diverse/diversity**: The word *diverse* is sometimes erroneously used to describe a person (e.g., *she is diverse*). While there is nothing wrong with using the words *diversity* and *diverse* correctly in your writing, their meanings are broad and it may often be appropriate to use narrower and more precise language. Those who have expressed frustration with these words point to their lack of emotional resonance and generalizing tendency; the journalist Anna Holmes, for example, has written in an article for the *New York Times* magazine that "the notion of diversity feels … fraught, positioning one group (white, male Americans) as the default, and everyone else as the Other." The best alternative to *diverse* is, wherever possible, to choose more specific, direct phrasing.

needs checking The production company was committed to hiring diverse actors.

still needs checking The production company was committed to greater diversity.

(This represents an improvement over the first sentence; it is correct in terms of its use of language. But it is needlessly vague. Does it mean that the company is committed to producing material on a broader range of subjects? Committed to new policies regarding hiring writers and directors?)

revised The production company was committed to hiring actors from underrepresented groups.

• **prostitution/sex work/commercial sex**: When it comes to the controversial issue of exchanging sex for money, one of the most fraught language issues is what to call people who engage in this practice. It should be obvious that—unless one works in the sex trade oneself—one should avoid using words such as *whore* and *hooker*, or any of the dozens of other overtly derogatory words English offers for this purpose.

It is one thing to be clear about the word *whore*. But what of the word *prostitute*? Activists generally agree that this word, too, ought to be avoided; it carries with it an enormous amount of prejudicial baggage regarding the gender, morality, and human value of the people it labels. Many activists suggest instead the phrase *sex worker*—a phrase that is gender neutral and relatively free of cultural baggage, and that treats sex work as a job much like any other. (In this, *sex work* contrasts with *sex trafficking*, in which the participants are coerced; many activists argue that forced participation in the sex trade must be distinguished from sex work as a chosen job.) The economic terminology of sex work is extended to people who hire sex workers—who have long been informally called *johns*, but who sex workers prefer to refer to as *clients* or *customers*. (It is worth noting that *sex worker* can have a broader meaning than *prostitute*, applying to anyone who works in the sex industry—including porn actors, strippers, and so on.)

Though *sex worker* is the most commonly preferred term, it is important to acknowledge that it is not accepted by all activists. In particular, those who believe that the sale of sex for money can never be a healthy or freely chosen career argue that *sex worker* should not be used precisely because it suggests that "sex work" should be thought of as a job like any other. (This is, of course, the reason why many other activists embrace the term so readily.) Those who wish to emphasize the damaging aspects of commercial sex use terms such as *prostituted people*, or *victims* or *survivors of commercial sexual exploitation*. Terms such as *client* or *customer* are, similarly, replaced by *offender* or *exploiter*. Unsurprisingly, the terms writers use tend to reflect their opinions regarding how commercial sex should be treated under the law; users of *sex worker* tend to support legalization, while users of *commercial sexual exploitation* tend to argue that paying for sex should be a criminal offence.

Regardless of what terminology you choose, be careful not to use language that unduly highlights someone's involvement in the sex trade.

needs checking I asked a sex worker on the corner for the time.
revised I asked a woman on the corner for the time.

• **slave/enslaved person**: When you are writing about slavery, it is best to refer to an individual who has suffered under that system as an *enslaved person* rather than as a *slave*. The term *enslaved person* foregrounds the fact that slavery is a condition imposed by some human beings on other human beings; to identify a person as a slave, on the other hand, may be taken to imply that their very identity is defined by their enslaved condition.

needs checking	Harriet Jacobs was a slave in North Carolina before she escaped to New York and eventually gained her freedom.
revised	Harriet Jacobs was enslaved in North Carolina before she escaped to New York and eventually gained her freedom.

Seriousness and Humour, Euphemism and Plain Speaking

It's often felt that all the issues we are asked to take account of in speaking and writing about gender, race, religion, sexual orientation, and disability create, in aggregate, something of an oppressive atmosphere—that we are forced to tread on our toes all the time in the name of "political correctness," that we can't speak plainly, and that we're being asked to give up our sense of humour. It's true that there are serious issues involved, and that trying not to denigrate people different from ourselves can take a fair bit of thought and a fair bit of effort. In that respect it's not a lot different from the rest of life. It can take a fair bit of thought and a fair bit of effort to be courteous and tactful to our relatives, or to people in our school or at our place of work who are from backgrounds quite similar to our own. And yet we manage—and we manage to express our sense of humour, too.

We do have to acknowledge that there are restrictions in what it's appropriate to say or do—just as we have to acknowledge that the conventions of acceptable behaviour impose restrictions when it comes to what we can say to our parents and grandparents, and how we refer to them. Not least of all, we are obliged to accept some restrictions on certain forms of humour. It's often suggested by well-meaning opponents of racism, sexism, and so on that racist and sexist jokes are never truly funny. But that's just not true; if it were not possible for humans to find humour in racist and sexist jokes and comments, no one would ever have laughed at them. One of the saddest things about the human species is that our sense of humour is far from an unqualified good; we are all too easily amused by jokes about those who are less powerful than we are, or who are simply different from us.

We should, then, be prepared *not* to make some jokes, even if they really are funny, and *not* to comment in certain ways, even if we know that the comment is sure to get a laugh. We should, as we grow up (and for some of us this takes longer than for others), be prepared to put other values ahead of *getting a laugh.* But does that mean we have to give up our sense of humour? Not at all. We don't even have to give up humour that's about gender or race or religion or sexual orientation. What we should be prepared to give up is humour that's based on contempt and superciliousness, humour that comes at the expense of those less privileged than ourselves, humour that comes at the expense of those who have done nothing to deserve it. Let's look at a comparative example:

> Three religious leaders are comparing notes on how they deal with the funds that have been donated to their institutions during services.
>
> "Well, I have a system that seems to work pretty well," says one. Of course my institution is a place of God, and when people donate money they expect that it will be for God's work. But I have various expenses, and I could not do God's work myself without receiving some recompense. This is the system that I have found works best: I draw a line on the floor, and from a point on that line I throw the entire amount donated that week into the air. What lands on one side of the line is for God's work; what lands on the other side of the line is my own compensation."
>
> "How funny!" says the second religious leader. "I have a very similar system. I draw a circle on the floor, and from any point on the circumference of that circle I throw the entire amount donated that week into the air. What lands inside the circle is for God; what lands outside is my own compensation."
>
> "This is truly extraordinary!" says the third religious leader. "We all three of us have very similar systems. The way I do things is almost precisely the same. Of course everyone takes a somewhat different approach when it comes to the specifics. My own approach this: I throw the entire amount donated that week into the air—and what God wants, he keeps."

This is a joke that has been told in slightly different ways for decades, almost always with the three leaders identified as belonging to a particular religious group—Catholics, Scottish Presbyterians, Muslims, Jews, whoever. Told that way, it becomes a joke that is in part at least against a particular religion; however funny it may be, it is surely an example of humour that is objectionable. Told in the way it is set out above, on the other hand, with no religions specified, it becomes a joke about selfishness and greed, and about how humans are all too often able to rationalize their selfishness and greed.

If humour is consistent with doing one's best to take ethical considerations into account in one's speaking and writing, so too is plain speaking. A great many people feel that striving to make the language we use free of bias is likely to result in euphemism and silliness—and that, for that reason, it's not worth the effort. Absurd examples such as "vertically challenged" are put forward again and again as if they were the typical products of any striving for bias-free language; in fact, such euphemisms are seriously recommended by almost no one. That's not to say that ongoing efforts to speak and write fairly about other groups have not resulted in some absurdity, and some euphemistic language. To be sure, they have—and in some of those cases the euphemisms may have been unfortunate. But anyone who wishes to take issue with the use of a euphemism such as *mentally challenged* should on the same grounds take issue with other forms of euphemism—most certainly including euphemisms of a truly horrific sort that are sometimes used by some who style themselves as opponents of "political correctness." Former American Vice President Dick Cheney, who oversaw the American government's use of interrogation techniques during the administration of George W. Bush, is an example of just such a person. Cheney was known to attack others for using euphemisms rather than speaking plainly. But how did he refer to the practice of repeatedly subjecting prisoners to extreme pain? He called it "enhanced interrogation of high-value detainees." A wide range of impartial authorities have concluded that the "waterboarding" and other techniques practised by the American military under Cheney's oversight were, quite simply, forms of torture, and ought to be articulated as such. Like many others, some politicians will doubtless never learn to be good with words.

With the arrival of Donald Trump on the political scene in 2016, political controversies surrounding language intensified, and the gulf grew wider and wider between what was considered to be acceptable linguistic practice in professional and academic life and what was considered acceptable practice in populist politics, in some news media, and on some social media sites. It is our hope that this gulf may grow narrower in the 2020s. We recognize the frustration many feel with the demands of changing linguistic practice. There are legitimate fears that certain segments of the university-educated population may in some social contexts exercise undue influence over linguistic usage—and may impose undue censure on those who do not conform thoroughly enough or quickly enough. Many on the political right have suggested that such trends constitute a threat to free speech, and we do not dismiss such suggestions out of hand.[1] It seems abundantly clear to us, though, that such threats are dwarfed by those posed by governments under the influence of industrial lobbyists. The threat posed by the "ag-gag" laws adopted in several Canadian provinces as well as in numerous American states—laws that make it a crime punishable by massive fines and long prison terms to reveal what goes on behind the walls of factory farms—is very real indeed. So too is the censure faced in Alberta and Saskatchewan by schoolteachers who encourage open debate on the practices of the oil industry. Such developments have received relatively little media coverage, but seem to us to pose a far, far greater threat to freedom of speech than do any the linguistic practices followed on North American university campuses. At the great majority of those campuses, indeed, vigorous debate on the sorts of issues discussed in this chapter continues to be encouraged. We encourage it too; we feel strongly that there should be ample room for lively and respectful debate on such issues. (We include a number of prompts to such debate on this book's companion website.) Our continuing belief is that it is always possible, while striving to use ethical language that avoids bias, to do so in a welcoming way that aims for clarity and steers clear of elitism.

One final thought: as thoughtful writers, we should strive to be ethical and accurate and open to change, but none of us will be successful all of the time. Just as continuing to learn (and being open to changing one's practices when there is good reason to do so) is an important part of being a good writer, so too is it important to cultivate self-compassion along with compassion for others as we learn to be good with words. That's true of individual writers, and it is also true of society as a whole.

1 It is of real concern, for example, that professors at Canadian universities have been censured not for using the "n-word," but merely for mentioning it (specifically, mentioning the title under which Pierre Vallières's famous 1968 book *Nègres blancs d'Amérique* was published in English).

Bias-free Vocabulary: A Short List

actress	actor
addict	person with an addiction
alderman	councillor
anchorman	anchor/news anchor
Anglo-Saxon	Early medieval, pre-conquest (Note: This term is also used as a pseudonym or dog-whistle by white supremacist groups to mean "white.")
Asiatic	Asian
bad guy	villain
bellboy	bellhop
bogeyman	bogey monster
brotherhood	fellowship, community (when not speaking of all-male situations)
businessman	businessperson, entrepreneur
caveman	cave-dweller
chairman	chair
cleaning lady	cleaner
clergyman	minister, clergy member
common man	common person, average person, ordinary person
congressman	representative, congressperson
con-man	con-artist
draftsman	drafter
Eskimo	Inuit (Note: Some Alaskan groups still prefer *Eskimo*. Note also that *Inuk* is the singular form of *Inuit*; because *Inuit* translates as *the people*, there is no need to refer to the group as the *Inuit people*.)
farmer's wife	farmer
fireman	firefighter
fisherman	fisher
forefathers	ancestors
foreman	manager, supervisor
freshman	first-year student
frontman	figurehead, front
garbageman	garbage collector

grandfather	grandparent (Note: As in "Under this clause of the contract, transactions that occurred on or before 31 December are grandparented.")
gunman	shooter
guys	you all, everyone, folks
gyp	cheat, con
Gypsies	Roma (Note: *Gypsy* may still be a useful term of self-description for some people of Roma background.)
handyman	handyperson
hearing impaired	deaf, Deaf (Note: This depends on context; in limited contexts, *hearing impaired* may be appropriate.)
homosexual	gay (unless *homosexual* is being used in historical contexts.)
homosexual couple	couple, gay couple (if sexual orientation is relevant)
Indians	Indigenous people, First Peoples (Note: First Nations, Inuit, and/or Métis may also be used. Wherever possible it is best to specify the relevant nation [e.g., Mississauga, Cayuga, Seneca]. The above references current Canadian usage; in the United States, American Indian and Native American remain commonly used.)
infantryman	footsoldier
insurance man	insurance agent
junkie	drug user, person with an addiction
layman	layperson
longshoreman	shiploader, stevedore
maid	housekeeper
mailman	letter carrier, mail carrier
male nurse	nurse
man	humanity
man (an exhibit)	staff

man (a barricade)	fortify, occupy
man (a ship)	crew
man enough	strong enough
manhandle	rough-up, attack
manhole	sewer hole, access hole
manhole cover	sewer cover, access hole cover, utility cover
man hours	staff time, work time
mankind	humankind, people, humanity, humans
manly	self-confident, courageous, straightforward
manmade	handmade, human-made, constructed
man of letters	intellectual
middleman	intermediary, go-between
midget	little person, dwarf, person of short stature
minority group	marginalized group, underrepresented group
mothering	parenting
mother tongue	native language, first language
Negro	Black, African American
niggardly	stingy (Note: The word *niggardly* has no etymological connection with the n-word. Since the one suggests the other to many minds, however, it is safer to avoid using it.)
opposite-sex relationship	mixed-gender relationship
Oriental	Asian, Middle Eastern
penmanship	handwriting
policeman	police officer
postman	letter carrier, mail carrier
preferred pronouns	pronouns (avoid use of "preferred")
pregnant women	pregnant people
Renaissance man	Renaissance person, polymath
salesman, saleslady	salesperson, sales clerk, sales representative
seaman	sailor, mariner
sex change operation	gender confirmation surgery
slave	enslaved person
slaveowner	enslaver
Siamese twins	conjoined twins
snowman	snowbody (rhymes with *nobody*), snow person

spokesman	representative, spokesperson, agent
sportsman	sportsperson
sportsmanship	sportship
statesman	politician, political figure
stewardess	flight attendant
unsportsmanlike	unsporting
waitress	server
weatherman	weather forecaster
widower	widow
womanly	warm, tender, nurturing, sympathetic (or other more specific adjective suited to the circumstance)
workman	worker, laborer, wage earner

WRITING MECHANICS

WRITING MECHANICS

M1 GRAMMAR

M1.1 Introduction: Right and Wrong in Writing

In what sense are errors in grammar and usage wrong? *Are* they in fact wrong in any meaningful sense? Should "wrong" in this context be read as always having quotation marks around it? For example, the rules prescribe "you" as the pronoun to use when addressing a group of people, but many people unconsciously pluralize it into the form "youse." *Would you like anything else? Would youse like anything else?* Is one form better than the other?

Too often this sort of question becomes so infused with assumed political content that it is not taken seriously. On the one hand, the conservative is likely to refuse to even debate the question of whether *you* or *youse* is the inherently superior form. Of course the form established as correct is superior; of course the colloquialism is debased. On the other side are those who regard it as an article of faith that rules of grammar and usage are changeable conventions, and that consequently there can be no rational justification for preferring *you* to *youse*.

Is *you* correct and *youse* incorrect in the same way that *12 x 3 = 36* is correct and *12 x 3 = 35* incorrect? Or in the same way that *The capital of Maharashtra is Mumbai* is correct and *The capital of Maharashtra is Delhi* is false? No. It is not wrong in either of those sorts of ways; one pointer is that it would seem distinctly odd to describe *Would youse like anything else?* as false. In what sense, then, is it wrong? The problem is not that it fails to map onto a structure of reality. In fact, as the cognitive scientist Steven Pinker points out, it makes such a connection with a greater degree of precision than does currently correct usage:

> The mavens lament the loss of conjugal distinction in *he don't* and *we was*. But this has been the trend in standard English for centuries. No one minds that we have abandoned the second-person singular form of verbs, as in *thou sayest*. And by this criterion it is the non-standard dialects that are superior, because they provide their speakers with second-person plural pronouns such as *y'all* and *youse*. (23)

Returning for a moment to Mumbai may help us to sense the way in which *youse* may fairly, if in a limited sense, be thought of as wrong. The sentence *The capital of Maharashtra is Bombay* is wrong in something like the same sense that *Would youse like anything else?* is wrong. Both use the symbolic system of language to correspond to an understood reality. But in both cases the signs used are not those used under currently accepted conventions; though a few may still cling to the old usage, almost everyone has now adopted the late 1995 change of name (from Bombay to Mumbai) for India's largest city. "Bombay" certainly still corresponds to reality; it is not false. But nor is it right.

But why stick to the conventional where the essay or the business report is concerned? Is there any legitimate argument in favour of the conventions of standard English? One such argument may fairly be grounded in pedagogy; the acquiring of a knowledge of English grammar and syntax is an enormously helpful way of strengthening habits of abstract thought. But that speaks to the value of a byproduct, not of the thing itself. There may be only two *essential* justifications for standard English: ease of communication, and elegance of expression. The first of these is to a large extent obvious, but it is worth stressing that the ease of communication which standard forms or conventions of usage make possible extends not only from individual to individual but also from

Online

Here are three fascinating discussions of the ways in which issues of correctness in writing are often confused with issues of style, tone, and voice:

Louis Menand, "Bad Comma: Lynne Truss's Strange Grammar," *The New Yorker*, 28 June 2004
www.newyorker.com/magazine/2004/06/28/bad-comma

Stephen Pinker, "10 'Grammar Rules' It's OK to Break (Sometimes)," *The Guardian*, 15 August 2014
www.theguardian.com/books/2014/aug/15/steven-pinker-10-grammar-rules-break

Nathan Heller, "Steven Pinker's Bad Grammar," *The New Yorker*, 3 November 2014
www.newyorker.com/culture/cultural-comment/steven-pinkers-bad-grammar

(For the record, the authors of this book are in entire agreement with Menand, side with Pinker on the first of his ten points [it's OK to begin sentences with *And* or *But*], but side with Heller's criticisms of Pinker regarding most of the other nine.)

one culture to another, and over very long periods of time. It has been often noted that the ordinarily literate person in our own time is able to respond to the language of Shakespeare in a way that the ordinarily literate person in Shakespeare's day was quite unable to respond to *Beowulf*, simply because the conventional codification of grammar and usage that print made possible has drastically slowed down the rate of linguistic change. (Cullen Murphy has interestingly suggested that the development beginning in the late nineteenth century of electric and then of electronic methods of reproducing sound has given the sloppy and unruly nature of the spoken word a much greater influence on the shaping of the language and on the speed of change than it had in the sixteenth through nineteenth centuries.)

The second legitimate argument in favour of standard English is by far the weaker, and it should be readily conceded that elegance of expression is often achievable outside the confines of standard English. But complex syntactical and grammatical pathways will inevitably tend to have been worn smoother in a greater variety of ways in long-established conventions of formal expression. Colloquial or non-standard usages may have a freshness to them or in other syntactical ways may appeal strongly in ways that standard English cannot compete with. But they are unlikely to consistently lend themselves to long and elegantly balanced combinations of clauses and phrases in the way that the mainstream of our culture has been training standard English to do for centuries.

If this book is prescriptive, then, it should be understood that it is prescriptive only in a context that recognizes correct English as a matter of convention, not as one in which one form is understood to be necessarily or absolutely better than another. If we suggest that you should use "aggravate" to mean "make worse," not to mean "annoy" or "irritate," that advice should be understood as a convenient short form for "in formal written English, if you wish to conform to the most commonly accepted conventions of usage, use...." And, to return to the example with which this chapter began, *youse* is an alternative form, arguably superior in terms of precision, which we may legitimately reject only on the grounds of convention.

On other specific issues, though, the case for standard usage is sometimes considerably stronger. Take the confusion of words that have related but different meanings, like *uninterested* (which means not feeling any interest) and *disinterested* (which means not demonstrating any bias). It has become common to use *disinterested* when the meaning intended is closer to the conventional meaning of *uninterested*. If *disinterested* loses its original meaning as a result, it will represent a measurable loss of the communicative capacity of the English language, and it will be more difficult and more cumbersome to express a variety of meanings. Yet there can be no question that many who are unperturbed by this use of *disinterested*—indeed, who may not even recognize the distinction—cringe at the supposed abomination of *youse*. What such cases drive home to us is the degree to which the ways in which we use standard English (and the assumptions we make about standard English) may be linked to irrational sentiments such as social snobbery, or class or gender-based prejudice. (How many there still are who ludicrously claim *fisher* and *chair* to be "more awkward" than the longer and cumbersome forms *fisherman* and *chairman*.) There are good reasons for not abandoning standard English—but good reasons as well to keep questioning our own assumptions about it.

One of the ways in which this book differs from many other guides to grammar and usage is in its approach to change in language, and in the degree to which it attempts to resist the assumption that where the English language is concerned, change implies debasement. Thus in the chapter on part-of-speech conversions such previous entries as *liaise* and *mandate* have been dropped. The back formation of a verb from the noun *liaison* might not be a pretty thing. But a bias against it might not reflect anything more than habit; certainly it can be difficult in many cases to choose more economical replacements. The prejudice against such words might not be any better grounded than was the bias a generation or two ago against using *contact* as a verb. *Finalize* still grates slightly on some ears, too. But sometimes *finish* just does not capture the sense, and *finalize* is more concise than *make final* or *put into final form*. A comparison of the current state of attitudes today towards the word *finalize* with attitudes of the mid-twentieth century may be instructive as to whether or not there are any good grounds today for objecting to *finalize*:

> *Finalize* is not standard: it is special, and it is a peculiarly fuzzy and silly word. Does it mean *terminate*, or does it mean *put into final form*? One can't be sure, really, what it means, and one gets the impression that the person using it doesn't know, either, and doesn't want to know. (Strunk and White, *The Elements of Style* [New York, Macmillan: 2/e, 1972], 75–76)

That may have been true in 1957, when the first edition of *The Elements of Style* appeared, or even in 1972, when the second edition was published. But no one today uses *finalize* to mean *terminate*; that denotation has dropped away, and the word's meaning has stabilized as *put into final form*.

If Strunk and White are out of date on the particulars, this remains a good example of the wisdom of their advice to writers that one danger of "adopting new coinages too quickly is that they will bedevil one by insinuating themselves where they do not belong" (75–76). What was a fuzzy coinage in the 1950s has found a clearly defined place in the language of today. And even conservative arbiters such as Strunk and White recognize that language must change, and that this is no bad thing. In the end guides such as this one should continually strive for a balance between the value of continuity in language and in usage, and the value of language as a living thing; without change there can be no life.

In one area in particular this guide is not only unresistant to change but embraces change: the move towards bias-free language. In this one area a different sort of *correctness* than the correctness spoken of elsewhere in these pages is involved. Call it political correctness if you will,[1] but however it is referred to, it concerns things that are right and wrong in a sense that goes far beyond questions of what is conventional or convenient. The point involved here is that language can have an important part to play in helping us to do the right thing. To treat men and women on an equal footing, to avoid discrimination on the basis of religion, or race, or class—language can be used to help accomplish all of these goals.

David Foster Wallace is not alone in claiming that the "central fallacy" of the so-called politically correct is "that a society's mode of expression is productive of its attitudes rather than a product of those attitudes" (55). In fact, the fallacy is to assume that it need be either/or; research has suggested *both* that changes in attitudes produce

---

1 When the pejorative term "political correctness" is fairly and carefully used—as it is, for example, by Pinker when he discusses taboos and dissent—it refers to a lamentable tendency to restrict free discussion of controversial topics. Sadly, it is more common to find the term used in shrill polemical discourse that itself seems more interested in closing down free discussion than opening it up. (See, for example, John Harmon McElroy's rant that, "since the 1960s, a 'correct' political language has been imposed on Americans." What evidence does McElroy provide that the terms he dislikes (among them *African American*, *environmentalism*, *Native American*, and *human being* as a substitute for *man*) are being "imposed"? Simply the fact that they are now listed in the dictionary.

changes in modes of expression *and* that modes of expression help shape attitudes. Of course it is not possible to eliminate elitism and unfairness simply by ceasing to use "vocabulary that is historically associated with elitism and unfairness" (55). But equally clear is that the perpetuation of such vocabulary can only help to perpetuate elitism and unfairness; precisely how much difference language makes may be open to dispute, but it *does* make a difference. As the distinguished linguist Sally McConnell-Ginet puts it in her *Words Matter: Meaning and Power*, "linguistic and social change go hand in hand because linguistic practices are fundamental to social practices more generally. Words are woven into the social fabric" (7).

A strong emphasis on the ways in which language can help or hinder social change of this sort is thus an important part of this book; the section "How to Be Good with Words" provides a much more thoroughgoing treatment of these issues than do most other guides to usage.

Works Cited

McConnell-Ginet, Sally. *Words Matter: Meaning and Power*. Cambridge UP, 2020t.

McElroy, John Harmon. "Leftists' Politically Correct Dictionary." *The Washington Times*, 15 Oct. 2012, www.washingtontimes.com/new/2012/oct/15/leftists-politically-correct-dictionary-activists-/.

Murphy, Cullen. "The Lay of the Language: The Decline of Semantic Distinction, and What It Suggests about Linguistic Evolution." *The Atlantic Monthly*, May 1995, pp.20–22.

Pinker, Steven. "Grammar Puss: The Fallacies of the Language Mavens." *New Republic*, 31 Jan. 1994, pp. 19–24.

—. "Steven Pinker on Taboos, Political Correctness, and Dissent." Interview by Greg Lukianoff. *Foundation for Individual Rights in Education (FIRE)*, 13 Sept. 2012, www.youtube.com/watch?v=hAMTPBspcfs.

Strunk, William Jr., and E.B. White. *The Elements of Style*. 2nd ed., Macmillan, 1972.

Wallace, David Foster. "Tense Present: Democracy, English, and the Wars over Usage." *Harper's Magazine*, Apr. 2001, pp. 39–58.

M 1.2 Parts of Speech

It's not strictly necessary to know the rules and terminology of English grammar in order to write well and according to convention. In learning the standard dialect, most English speakers learn, for example, to say and write the forms "I walk" and "he walks"—that is, they know that a third-person singular present tense verb takes an *s*, perhaps without ever knowing what "third-person" or "present tense" or "verb" even means. You don't need to understand what goes on in a car's engine in order to drive a car. But someone who aspires to be a professional race-car driver should have at least some basic mechanical knowledge. Similarly, if you want to improve your speaking and writing skills to the level required in professional life, if you want to recognize the difference between standard and non-standard forms, if you want to use the language with precision and eloquence and flexibility, then you should understand the basics of its structure and operation.

In this section, we'll begin with a quick overview of the parts of speech (nouns, verbs, adjectives, adverbs, pronouns, prepositions, and conjunctions are the categories we'll use). These labels designate the potential uses to which a word can be put, so in the dictionary you'll notice that each word has been given at least one of these labels. Sometimes a word can only belong to one category: *between*, for example, is always a preposition. Often, though, a word can have more than one meaning and be used as more than one part of speech. Take the word *down*, for example, which can be:

a noun ("The team scored on the first *down*."),
a verb ("I thirstily *downed* the whole bottle."),
an adjective ("He was feeling a little *down*."),
an adverb ("The airplane went *down*."), or
a preposition ("I walked *down* the street.").

Labeling a word as a part of speech tells us what kind of a word it is, but it doesn't tell us what function it might serve in a particular sentence—for that you need to understand the parts of a sentence. It's a bit hard, though, to define one without referring to the other, so if some of the terminology used below seems unfamiliar, the next section should provide clarity. As you read this intro to grammar basics, you should also keep something important in mind: although there is a science to studying language, the categories and labels we'll use here are not so much scientific fact as they are convenient fictions. "Verbs" and "nouns" are not naturally occurring phenomena with clearly defined characteristics like elements or species. Rather they are attempts to define certain features of language that usually act in certain ways, so that we can accurately describe the functioning of this infinitely complex and fascinating system we use to communicate.

The upshot of this is that there are often disputes among reasonable people about how best to categorize these features of language. Some grammar guides say that articles are a distinct part of speech; for others, they are a subset of adjectives. For some there are four categories of pronouns; others count more. Don't get too bogged down in these details; for non-linguists studying grammar is useful mostly in that it makes clear that there *is* a system, even if that system can be described in various ways.

Nouns

Nouns are words that name people, things, places, or qualities.

Some examples:
girl, Wilma, surgeon, grandparents, Admiral Byrd (people);
spaghetti, hippo, atmosphere, word, motion, English (things);
hospital, bedroom, Zambia, Mt. Rushmore, Venus (places);
silence, intelligence, anger, height, loveliness (qualities)

Nouns can be used to fill the gaps in sentences like these:

I saw ________ at the market yesterday.
He dropped the ________ into the soup.
That is not the right ________ for the occasion!
We live in a __________ in the middle of ___________.
Has learning Italian taken a lot of ________?

Nouns can be either **countable** (e.g., *hat, street, clown*) or **uncountable** (e.g., *air, milk, knowledge*) and this affects how they are pluralized and combined with articles. We say, for example, *he's wearing a hat* or *he's wearing many hats*—because *hat* is a countable noun and can therefore be **singular** or **plural**. But we never say, *he's breathing an air* or *he's breathing many airs*—because *air* is uncountable, and so can't be pluralized. The correct forms would be *he's breathing air* or *he's breathing a lot of air.*

Nouns can also be either **common** nouns (e.g., *city, whale, toy, president*), which are not capitalized, or **proper** nouns, which refer to specific individual things or people (e.g., *Syracuse, Shamu, Frisbee, Obama*) and are capitalized.

Many nouns are **compound nouns**—combinations in which two or more words have been brought together in a single grammatical unit that acts as a noun (e.g., *office tower, public speaking, animal rights, soap opera, business partner*). Long established compounds often become new words, either with a hyphen (e.g., *meeting-room*) or without (e.g., *lawnmower, skyscraper, haircut, rainfall, girlfriend, software*). Notice that the meaning of the compound exists unto itself; the meaning of *greenhouse* (compound noun) is different from that of *green house* (adjective *green* plus noun *house*), and many people would not automatically class a *boyfriend* or a *girlfriend* as a type of *friend*. In some cases (e.g., *cultural genocide*), the precise meanings of compounds can be difficult to pin down—and can be subject to vigorous debate.

Verbs

Verbs are words that express actions or states of affairs. Most verbs can be conveniently thought of as "doing" words (e.g., *do, think, make, say, get, receive, munch, plummet, contemplate*), but several verbs do not fit into this **action verb** category. Indeed, the most common verb of all—*be*—expresses not an action but a state of affairs. It belongs to another category called **linking verbs**, which tell us something about the subject of the sentence, not what the subject is doing.

Action verbs	Linking verbs
Tiger hit the ball.	The chances looked good.
Sara loves Silas.	Silas is her only love.
I felt the wind in my hair.	The wind felt cool.

Note that some verbs (like *feel*) can be either action or linking verbs.

Verbs sometimes change form depending on number, as nouns do: compare "the dog *barks*" (singular subject and verb) and "the dogs *bark*" (plural subject and verb). They can also change form depending on whether the subject is the speaker ("first person"), the addressee ("second person"), or someone else ("third person"): *I am* vs. *you are* vs. *he is*, all forms of the verb *to be*. One thing that makes verbs different from other parts of speech is that they also change form depending on time frame; in other words, they have **tenses**. *I am*, *you are*, and *he is*, for example, are all present tense forms. Past tense forms of the verb *to be* include *I was*, *you were*, and *he was*. Some verb forms require **auxiliary verbs** (or "helping verbs") to indicate a tense, and auxiliary verbs are also used to form negatives or interrogatives. **Modal** auxiliaries are a small set of specialized words that don't change form but change the meaning of the verb they are placed in front of.

Tiger *is hitting* the ball. (auxiliary verb: *is*)
Tiger *has won* many championships. (auxiliary verb: *has*)
Tiger *does* not *play* baseball. (auxiliary verb: *does*)
Do you *know* what he plays? (auxiliary verb: *do*)
Can you *guess*? (modal auxiliary: *can*)
It *should be* obvious. (modal auxiliary: *should*)

Finally, the form of **regular** verbs follows rules that apply to all regular verbs, but **irregular** verbs don't follow the same rules and may have their own unique forms. In the present tense, the only verbs that have irregular written forms are *to be* and *to have*. However there is a long list of verbs that are irregular in the past tense, such as *drive* (*drove*), *sing* (*sang*), or *speak* (*spoke*).

See section M1.4 (page 213) for a more complete discussion of verb tenses.

Adjectives

Adjectives describe or modify our perception of nouns. There are two classes: **descriptive adjectives**, like *yummy*, *huge*, *terrible*, or *purple*, are the most obvious kind; the other kind is **determiners**, which we'll address below. Here are some examples of descriptive adjectives:

The *small* boy lifted the *heavy* table.
A *revised* version will be sent to your *downtown* office.
Loud, *frenetic* music was emanating from the *open* window.

Notice that adjectives usually come before the nouns that they describe. This is not always the case, however; **predicate adjectives** come after the noun and after the verb *to be*:

That woman is particularly *careful* about money.
The exercise is too *difficult*.
My brothers and sisters are *dependable*.

Determiners appear before a noun and give us some information that modifies our perception of it without describing it, as in "*a* cookie" vs. "*the* cookie." If the noun is also modified by descriptive adjectives, the determiner comes first, as in "the *scrumptious* cookie."

A, *an*, and *the* are a sub-category of determiners known as **articles**. For native speakers, using articles is fairly intuitive—but explaining how to use them can be complicated, and they can cause problems for some non-native speakers. Generally speaking, the **indefinite article** (*a*, or *an* when used before a vowel) is used when the noun is a member of a general class, or its specificity has not yet been established. "Yesterday I met *a* poodle" doesn't tell us which poodle in particular. The **definite article** (*the*) most often indicates that the noun should be taken as specific, either because it is unique, or because its specificity has been previously established.

Yesterday I met *the* friendliest poodle ever.

(The noun is specific in that there can only be one friendliest poodle ever.)

Yesterday I met *the* poodle that Sara adopted.

(The noun is specific because of the extra information supplied after the noun.)

The choice of article is often context-dependent.

I looked out my window and saw *the* moon.
I looked up at the sky of the alien planet and saw *a* large reddish moon.

She had *a* conversation with *a* friend.
She had *the* conversation she needed to have with *the* friend she trusts the most.

Besides articles, the category of determiners includes **numbers** ("one cookie"), **quantifiers** ("some cookies"), **possessives** ("Sara's cookie"), and **demonstratives** ("that cookie").

Adverbs

These words are usually used to describe or modify our perceptions of verbs, although they can also be used to modify adjectives or other adverbs. Many adverbs are easily recognized because they consist of an adjective (like *easy*) with the letters *ly* appended (*easily*), but be careful: some adverbs look the same as their adjective counterparts (like *far*). And some words that end in *ly* are not adverbs at all (like *early*). Here are a few examples, alongside adjectives for comparison:

Adjective	Adverb
careful	carefully
beautiful	beautifully
slow	slowly
fast	fast
good	well

The adverbs above are all used to tell us *how* an action is done, but adverbs can also tell us *when*, *where* or *to what degree* something happens: *there*, *here*, *high*, *low*, *later*, *soon*, *often*, *occasionally*, and *entirely* are all adverbs. Words like *very*, *extremely*, or *somewhat* are adverbs that can be used to modify adjectives or other adverbs, and sometimes adverbs actually modify whole clauses or sentences.

> Joe walks *quickly*.
> (The adverb *quickly* tells us how he walks.)
>
> He *soon* arrives home.
> (The adverb *soon* tells us when he arrives.)
>
> He looks *up*.
> (The adverb *up* tells us where he looks.)
>
> He is *so* happy to see Rover.
> (The adverb *so* modifies the adjective *happy*.)
>
> Rover wags his tail *very* happily.
> (Here *very* modifies the adverb *happily*.)
>
> *Undoubtedly* they are both glad he's home.
> (*Undoubtedly* modifies the sentence.)

Pronouns

Pronouns replace or stand for nouns. Instead of saying, "I saw Sara when Sara arrived," we can say, "I saw Sara when *she* arrived." *Sara* is now the pronoun's *antecedent*—the noun the pronoun refers back to. There are several different classes of pronouns; here is a quick overview. Note that some pronouns can be used more than one way (e.g., *that* can be either a relative pronoun or a demonstrative pronoun). Help with common pronoun errors can be found on pages 291–95.

Personal pronouns refer to specific people or things, and they come in different forms depending on what role they play in a sentence (see M1.3 for more on parts of sentences) and whether they are singular or plural. **Subject pronouns** replace subjects—the doers of an action—and **object pronouns** replace objects—the recipients or targets of an action.

	singular	*plural*
Subject Pronouns:	I	we
	you	you
	he / she / it	they
Object Pronouns:	me	us
	you	you
	him / her / it	them

She loves Silas. (The pronoun is the subject.)

Silas loves *her*. (The pronoun is the object; *Silas* is the subject.)

There are also personal **interrogative pronouns**: *who* and *what* (subject) as well as *whom* and *what* (object).

Who loves Silas?	*What* is her name?
Whom does Silas love?	*What* do you think?

Personal pronouns also include the **possessive pronouns** *mine*, *ours*, *yours*, *his*, *hers*, and *theirs*, which generally stand for a noun phrase showing possession (*its* is only rarely used this way).

Is this cookie *yours*?
(The pronoun replaces "your cookie.")

He ate his cookie and Sara ate *hers*.
(The pronoun replaces "her cookie.")

Note the difference between *yours* and *your*. In the phrase "your book," *your* is a **possessive adjective** (as are *my*, *our*, *his*, *her*, *its*, *their*, and *whose*). Because these words are only used as modifiers for a noun (as in "your book"), they are technically adjectives, not pronouns.

Reflexive pronouns, which include *myself*, *yourself*, *himself*, *herself*, *itself*, *ourselves*, *yourselves*, and *themselves*, usually replace the object of some self-directed action.

Sara treated *herself* to a cookie.
(The pronoun replaces "Sara" as the object of a sentence in which Sara is also the subject.)

Whereas personal pronouns refer to a definite person, **indefinite pronouns**, such as *each*, *every*, *all*, *either*, *neither*, *one*, *another*, *much*, or *many* are used when the antecedent is indefinite (that is, it could be any or all of a number of possibilities).

Great cookies! Can I have *another*?
(The pronoun replaces "another cookie.")

These words may be used as pronouns or as adjectives.

All is good.	(*All* is a pronoun.)
All cookies are good.	(*All* is an adjective.)

There are four **demonstrative pronouns**: *this*, *that*, *these*, and *those*. They serve to point to something, and they can also be used as pronouns or adjectives (determiners).

This is Sara. *That* is Silas. She likes *these* cookies; he likes *those*.

Relative pronouns (*who*, *whom*, *whose*, *which*, and *that*) relate a clause to a noun that has been used earlier in the same sentence. Consider how repetitious these sentences sound: *I talked to a man. The man wore a red hat.* We could of course replace the second *man* with *he*. Even better, though, is to relate the second idea to the first by using a relative pronoun: *I talked to a man* who *wore a red hat*. This turns the second sentence into a **relative clause**. Relative clauses are usually placed near the part of the sentence they relate back to. Compare:

I found the cookie under the bed. I had lost the cookie a year ago.
I found the cookie that I had lost a year ago under the bed.

Try replacing the second noun in these pairs of sentences with a relative pronoun, so as to make only one sentence out of each pair:

I ate the cookies. Silas had made the cookies.

The Prime Minister is on a trip to Asia. The trip was originally slated for last year.

Rhetoric refers to the art of persuasion using words. *Rhetoric* is derived from a Greek word meaning "speaker."

Prepositions

Prepositions are joining words, normally used before nouns or pronouns to create prepositional phrases, which can function to modify nouns or verbs. Some of the most common prepositions are:

about	before	into	over
across	for	of	to
after	from	off	until
at	in	on	with

I will tell you *about* it *in* the morning.
Please try to arrive *before* eight o'clock.
He won't get *to* Edmonton *until* tomorrow.
I received a letter *from* my sister.

Conjunctions

Conjunctions and conjunctive adverbs are normally used to join words or groups of words together, and in particular to join clauses together. Conjunctions can be divided into three types: coordinating, subordinating, and correlative.

Coordinating conjunctions are words that indicate a connection between words or groups of words that form grammatical elements of the same type and rank. There are only seven such conjunctions in English: *and*, *but*, *for*, *nor*, *or*, *so*, *yet*. (Since there are so few of them, they can easily be memorized; some people use the acronym FANBOYS as a memory aid—For, And, Nor, But, Or, Yet, So). Coordinating conjunctions can indicate a connection between two or more nouns (*cars* ***or*** *trucks*); two or more verbs (*see, hear,* ***and*** *understand*); two or more adjectives (*sturdy* ***yet*** *flexible*); or two or more adverbs (*slowly* ***but*** *surely*). They can indicate a connection between phrases (*with patience* ***and*** *with understanding; in warm sunshine* ***or*** *in the midst of winter*). Perhaps most notably, coordinating conjunctions can be used to join two or more independent clauses within one sentence:

> They arrived quite late, **and** they left very early.
>
> The company wanted to increase its market share, **so** it lowered prices on all its products.
>
> Everyone agreed that the statue was beautifully sculpted, **but** many felt the monument honoured someone who did not deserve this sort of public commemoration.
>
> (Note that when coordinating conjunctions are used to join independent clauses in this way, they are typically preceded by a comma.)

It's less widely known that coordinating conjunctions can also be used to indicate a connection between two independent clauses that form separate sentences; it would be grammatically correct to begin a new sentence with the coordinating conjunction in any of the three examples above. But, as a matter of style rather than of grammatical correctness, it may be particularly appropriate to start a new sentence with a coordinating conjunction in cases where a sentence would otherwise become quite long or syntactically complex:

> In the face of growing competition, the company was nevertheless determined to increase its market share. **So** it lowered prices on all its products.
>
> Everyone agreed that the statue was beautifully sculpted and that it depicted its subject very realistically. **But** many felt the monument honoured someone who did not deserve this sort of public commemoration.

The above point deserves emphasis, particularly where the coordinating conjunctions *and* and *but* are concerned, since many students emerge from high school with the sense that it is wrong to start a new sentence with *and* or *but*. That's simply not the case; so long as they are used to begin a sentence that includes a subject and a verb, it is perfectly correct to use *and* or *but* to begin a sentence. The group of words *but not that way* cannot form a complete sentence; it lacks both a subject and a verb. The same is true of this group of words: *And now, the most anticipated film of the year.* But the following are both perfectly correct:

> Authorities claimed that the armed forces had been restrained in dealing with the protest. But the video evidence tells a different story.
>
> Dozens of films were postponed or cancelled last month as a result of the pandemic. And now, the most anticipated film of the year has also been indefinitely postponed.

Here are a few more examples of the ways in which coordinating conjunctions can be used:

> Carmen hated the movie, but we really liked it.
>> (The coordinating conjunction *but* joins two independent clauses. Note that it is preceded by a comma.)
>
> His anxiety made him uncomfortable yet improved his playing.
>> (The coordinating conjunction *yet* joins two verb phrases.)
>
> The action of the novel is fast-moving and intense.
>> (The coordinating conjunction *and* joins two adjectives that modify the same noun.)

Subordinating conjunctions are used to indicate a connection between dependent clauses and independent clauses; they indicate that the one is subordinate to the other (in other words, that it is of a lower grammatical rank). A dependent clause can provide information of various sorts about the action in an independent clause—when that action occurred, for example, or why it occurred, or where it occurred.

> She left Manitoba and moved to the west coast **when her marriage collapsed.**
>
> I will wash the floor **after I have done the dishes**.
>
> The administration has set this deadline **because it needs to make a decision soon**.

Dependent clauses introduced by subordinating conjunctions can also provide information as to concessions being made with regard to the statement contained in the independent clause, or as to conditions being attached to the statement in the independent clause, or as to comparisons being made with the action named in the independent clause:

> We are very confident of achieving success, **though we expect a struggle.**
>
> I will tell her the news **if I see her**.
>
> The Flames have had an excellent season this year, **whereas they missed the playoffs last year.**

Notice that a dependent clause need not be shorter in length than an independent clause, and notice as well that a dependent clause need not follow the independent clause to which it relates:

> **After I have done the dishes,** I will wash the floor.
>
> **Because the administration needs to make a decision soon,** it has set this deadline.
>
> **If I see her,** I will tell her the news.
>
> **Though we expect a struggle,** we are very confident of achieving success.

English has many subordinating conjunctions; below is a list of some commonly used ones. (Note that some subordinating conjunctions are groups of words rather than single words.)

> after, although, as, as a result of, as long as, as soon as, as though, because, before, even if, even though, if, in order that, just as, provided that, since, so that, though, unless, until, whenever, whereas, while

Correlative conjunctions come in pairs and can join single words or word groups. Here are some examples:

both ... and,	neither ... nor,	so ... that
either ... or,	not only ... but also,	such ... as

Whatever is joined by correlative conjunctions must have the same grammatical structure, as in the examples below:

> That dishcloth is *both* smelly *and* unsanitary.
>
> (Two adjectives are joined—*smelly* and *unsanitary.*)
>
> *Neither* the dollar *nor* the economy will fare well if oil prices drop any lower.
>
> (Two noun phrases are joined—*the dollar* and *the economy.*)

Not only is our candidate well educated *but* she is *also* personable.

(Two clauses are joined—*our candidate is well educated* and *she is personable*. Note that when joining clauses, *not only* requires that the usual order of subject and verb in the following clause be reversed—and *but also* is split by the following clause's subject and verb.)

Conjunctive adverbs, as their name suggests, are adverbs that join word groups as well as modifying them. Conjunctive adverbs can join main clauses together or join a stand-alone main clause to a previous sentence; either way, and unlike other types of conjunctions, conjunctive adverbs need not appear exactly at the beginning of the word groups they join—but they are usually set off by commas. Here are some common conjunctive adverbs:

accordingly	alternatively	certainly
finally	furthermore	hence
however	indeed	in fact
likewise	meanwhile	moreover
nonetheless	otherwise	similarly
subsequently	that is	therefore
thus	unfortunately	

Miss Polly was busy hiding the silverware. Meanwhile, the Foley brothers arrived at the ranch.

(*Meanwhile* links the two sentences by indicating the time relationship between them.)

That new tablet is fantastic. No one, however, will want to pay such a high price for it.

(*However* signals a contrast between the two points made by the two sentences, and so is a transition joining them. Because it is embedded in its sentence, *however* is set apart with commas.)

They must have felt confident that their house would weather the hurricane. Otherwise, they would have evacuated when they heard the storm warnings.

(*Otherwise* links the two sentences by indicating that the second sentence is presenting an alternative scenario.)

The storm became much less intense as it approached the coast. Therefore, most people saw no reason for concern.

(*Therefore* links the two sentences, indicating that the information provided in the first sentence offers an explanation for people's lack of concern.)

Certain groups of words can also act as conjunctive adverbs. Here are some of the most commonly used:

as a result	at the same time	even so
for example	for instance	in addition
in conclusion	in other words	on the other hand

The storm became much less intense as it approached the coast. As a result, most people saw no reason for concern.

(Here the phrase *as a result* functions as a conjunctive adverb—functioning in the same way as *therefore* does above.)

Distinctions between grammatical categories such as coordinating conjunctions, subordinating conjunctions, and conjunctive adverbs are sometimes seen as the sorts of detail that students at the undergraduate level need not be bothered with. But understanding the differences can be a real help in learning to avoid incomplete sentences and run-on sentences in your writing. (More on this below, pages 196–204.)

M 1.3 Parts of Sentences

Sentences are the basic units of prose writing. They tell us about something happening or something existing or something exhibiting some quality. But what is a **sentence**? It could be defined as a set of words that contains at least one independent clause and conveys a complete thought. The problem with this definition, though, is likely obvious: what is an independent clause? And what is a complete thought? As in the last section, many of the terms we'll use in this section need to be defined with reference to each other, so read on.

A **clause** is a distinct group of words, such as "my new phone died suddenly," that includes both a subject and a predicate. A **phrase**, by comparison, is a group of words that either lacks a subject, such as "died suddenly," or lacks a predicate, such as "my new phone." An independent clause is one that can stand on its own as a complete sentence; a dependent clause, on the other hand, while it still has a subject and predicate, is not a complete sentence.

Independent clause	my phone died
Dependent clause	which I bought yesterday

Every sentence has at least one **independent clause**. (Where there is only one, it may also be referred to as the **main clause**.) Other clauses in the sentence that wouldn't be a sentence on their own are called **subordinate clauses** or **dependent clauses**.

A clause tells us about or refers to the actions of—or the existence of or the qualities of—some entity. That entity—a thing, a person, an idea—is the **subject**. The action or state or quality is described by the **predicate**. The core subject can always be narrowed down to one word, which is always a noun or pronoun, but the complete subject may contain determiners and modifiers and other clauses and may even be a clause itself. The predicate always contains a verb, and may be as simple as that, but it can also contain verb modifiers, including other clauses.

My new phone died suddenly.

Phone is the core subject in this example. *My new phone* is the complete subject. The event described by the predicate is something that the phone did—it *died suddenly*. The predicate consists of a verb and an adverb that describe what the subject did and how.

My new phone, which I bought yesterday, died suddenly.

Here the complete subject includes a subordinate clause (*which I bought yesterday*)—which has its own subject (*I*) and predicate (*bought yesterday*).

My fantastic, expensive, next-gen, whip-smart smart phone is extinct.

Here the subject is a phrase consisting of a noun (*phone*) preceded by a string of modifiers (adjectives). The predicate is the linking verb *is* followed by a predicate adjective that describes the subject.

The next example is as simple as they come: a pronoun as subject and a predicate consisting of a one-word verb.

It died.

A sentence that has just one main clause is called a **simple sentence**, while one that contains additional subordinate clauses is called a **complex sentence**. A sentence may also contain more than one main clause, joined by a coordinating conjunction or a semicolon, in which case it is a **compound sentence**. Sentences can be both complex and compound at once, as well.

Simple sentence	My new phone died suddenly.
Complex sentence	My new phone, which I bought yesterday, died suddenly.
Compound sentence	My new phone died and I was bereft.
Compound-complex sentence	My phone died and I was bereft, so I wept.

Types of Predicate

If you were paying close attention to the examples so far, you may have noticed that while subjects are always essentially a pronoun or noun plus modifiers, predicates can operate in several fairly distinct ways and can include other important parts—objects or complements. The most familiar predicate is the **intransitive verb**, as in "I wept." Predicates like these describe an action taken by the subject, and they can also include adverbial modifiers, as in "I wept like a baby."

Verbs can also be **transitive**, meaning that they describe an action that is done *to* something or someone. That something or someone is the **direct object**. This second type of predicate describes an action that the subject does to the object, as in "I threw the phone to the ground." In this example the direct object is *phone*. Note that some verbs are always intransitive (such as *weep*), some are always or nearly always transitive (such as *throw*), and some can be either (such as *break*).

In addition to a direct object, some predicates include an **indirect object**—someone or something that the action is done *for*. In this case the predicate describes an action that the subject does to the direct object for the indirect object, as in "My mother bought me a new phone," where the subject is *mother*, the direct object is *phone*, and the indirect object is *me*. If a clause has an indirect object, it always has a direct object as well (and if there is only one object, it is always a direct object). Note, too, that instead of an indirect object, the same meaning can be conveyed with a prepositional phrase (a preposition, usually *to* or *for* in this case, plus a noun or pronoun), as in "My mother bought a new phone for me."

Those first three types of predicate all involve action verbs. In a clause like "my phone is extinct," however, the predicate is different in that it describes a state rather than an action. The verb here is *to be*, the most common of the **linking verbs**. Linking verbs don't describe actions, and they don't take objects; rather they describe states, and they take complements. Other linking verbs include *appear*, *become*, *feel*, *look*, *seem*, *sound*—if you can complete the predicate with an adjective, then the verb is a linking verb. There are three basic ways that a predicate with a linking verb can be completed:

- by an adjective (or adjectival phrase) that describes the subject, as in "my phone is extinct" (an **adjectival subject complement**);
- by a noun (or noun phrase) that describes the subject, as in "my phone was a dud" (a **nominal subject complement**); or
- by an adverb (or adverbial phrase), as in "my phone is there, on the ground" (an **adverbial complement**).

There is one more type of predicate that is a little bit rarer, though surely recognizable. Some transitive verbs take an **object complement** in addition to an object, as in "My mother called me irresponsible." In this example, *me* is the direct object, but the meaning is not complete without the adjective *irresponsible*, which is the object complement. Like subject complements, object complements can be adjectives (as in the above example) or nouns (as in "They elected her President"), but not adverbs. There are only a handful of verbs that work this way; other examples would be "Consider it done," or "It makes me happy."

Not every grammarian will agree with how this list is organized (one could argue that the three kinds of subject complement are three different types of predicate, for example), but they will all agree that it is comprehensive. To review, here are five example sentences illustrating the five predicate types we've outlined:

Intransitive	The professor reads in class.
Transitive with one object	The professor reads poems in class.
Transitive with two objects	The professor reads her students a poem in class.
Transitive with object complement	She declares the poem brilliant.
Linking with subject complement	The professor is an avid reader of poems.

Types of Clause

The two main types of clause—**independent** and **dependent** (also known as **main** and **subordinate**)—can be distinguished based on whether they form a complete sentence. There is a certain degree of circularity involved in this definition: a sentence contains an independent clause, while an independent clause is one that can form a sentence in itself. The difference is usually clear in practice, though. A complete sentence or independent clause—"My parrot has escaped again!"—should elicit a response of "oh, I see." An incomplete sentence or dependent clause, on the other hand—"The last time my parrot escaped"—will make one ask, "well, what about it?" Independent clauses are not introduced with conjunctions (though they may be joined by the coordinating conjunctions *and*, *but*, *or*, *nor*, *for*, *yet*, and *so*), so if a clause begins with a word such as *because*, *although*, or *if*, you can be confident it is a dependent clause. (See above under "Conjunctions" and below under "Complete and Incomplete Sentences" for much more on this subject.) Similarly, relative pronouns introduce dependent clauses—never main clauses.

> She lives near Vancouver.
>
> (One main clause forming a complete sentence.)
>
> He danced in the street because he was feeling happy.
>
> (Main clause: *He danced in the street*; subordinate clause: *because he was feeling happy.*)
>
> Mavis has a cat who likes to drink from the kitchen faucet.
>
> (Main clause: *Mavis has a cat*; subordinate clause: *who likes to drink from the kitchen faucet.*)

Dependent (or subordinate) clauses can also be classified into several different types, based on the function they serve in the sentence. **Adjectival clauses** (also called relative clauses) modify nouns or pronouns, as adjectives do. Adjectival clauses begin with relative pronouns such as *who*, *whom*, *whose*, *which*, and *that*.

> The parrot *who escaped yesterday* is sitting on my car.
>
> I don't really like the phone *that my mother bought for me.*

Adverbial clauses tell us more about the action of the verb—telling *how*, *when*, *why*, or *where* the action occurred.

> The parrot escaped because someone left the window open.
>
> When someone buys you a new phone, you can't complain.

Noun clauses act like a noun to form the subject or object of a sentence or the object of a preposition.

> I'll never forget what the parrot said as it left.
>
> My mother told me that she expected me to pay her back.

Subordinate clauses can also be divided into **finite** and **nonfinite** clauses, which is important when we look at the wide variety of clauses we commonly use. All of the clauses in the examples above are finite clauses, because they use verbs that match their subjects. Nonfinite clauses use verbs that don't change form to agree with their subjects—participles (*-ed* and *-ing* verb forms), infinitives (such as *to be, to go*), or gerunds (*-ing* forms used as nouns). Here are a few examples of nonfinite clauses:

My phone dying was the worst moment of my week.

The parrot flew into the sky, *its colourful plumage shining brightly.*

Would it be possible *to keep the window closed*?

Types of Phrase

Just as with clauses, phrases can serve different functions within a sentence. They can be labelled according to form or function.

A **noun phrase** contains a noun (or pronoun) and invariably functions in roles suited for nouns—as a subject or object or complement. It may also contain adjectives (determiners or modifiers) that tell us more about the noun.

a tan van — five cheese pizzas

my dearly-departed phone — everyone here

A **prepositional phrase** contains a preposition followed by a noun or pronoun or noun phrase, which is called the object of the preposition. It can function in various roles, modifying nouns or verbs.

My friend *with the poodle* came to visit.

The police called *during the night.*

He suggested that we go *to infinity and beyond*!

An **adjectival phrase** functions as an adjective (it modifies a noun or pronoun) and can have various forms—a string of adjectives, for example, or a prepositional phrase, or a non-finite verb phrase.

She is looking for someone who is *tall, dark, and handsome.*

This taco *from the truck on the corner* is excellent.

Have you seen a poodle *wearing a pink collar*?

An **adverbial phrase** functions as an adverb (it modifies a verb or adjective or adverb) and can also have various forms. There are two adverbial phrases in each of these example sentences.

On my thirteenth birthday my family went to an amusement park.

I can't see very well with my left eye.

The monster wandered down the street destroying buildings.

This is a fairly simplified explanation of how English sentences work, but it provides a glimpse of the complexity and flexibility of this—or any—language. You will have noticed that phrases can occur inside other phrases and clauses, and clauses can occur inside phrases too. Take the sentence "That's the driver of the car that hit my dog!" *My dog* is a noun phrase serving as the object of the verb *hit*, which is the predicate of a relative clause modifying *car*, which in turn is the object of a prepositional phrase modifying *driver*. Linguists call this recursion, and it's one of the properties of language that allow it to be infinite in scope and infinitesimal in precision.

Distinguishing Phrases and Clauses

They were late *because of the weather*.

[*Because of the weather* is an adverbial *phrase*—not a clause, because it has no predicate.]

They were late because the weather was bad.

[*Because the weather was bad* is an adverbial *clause*—it has a subject (*the weather*) and a predicate (*was bad*).]

The man *at the corner* appeared to be upset.

[Adjectival *phrase*]

The man *who stood at the corner* appeared to be upset.

[Adjectival *clause*]

Parts of Speech and Parts of the Sentence

As practice in recognizing the parts of speech, label each of the words and phrases in this example. Then identify the parts of the sentence.

After the generous man with the big ears has bought presents, he will give them quickly to his friends.

Parts of speech:

after: *conjunction*	the: *article*	generous: ________
man: ________	with: ________	the: ________
big: ________	ears: ________	has bought: ________
presents: ________	he: ________	will give: ________
them: ________	quickly: ________	to: ________
his: ________	friends: ________	

Parts of the sentence:

main clause: He will give them quickly to his friends.

subject: ________ verb: ________

direct object: ________ indirect object: ________

subordinate clause: After the generous man with the big ears has bought presents

core subject: ________ complete subject: ________

adjectival phrase: ____________ verb: ____________

direct object: __________

Additional Material

A discussion of run-on sentences ("comma splices") and sentence fragments ("incomplete sentences") follows below (M1.3).

For exercises on grammar go to **sites.broadviewpress.com/writingcdn**. Click on **Exercises** and **Writing Mechanics.**

M 1.3.1 Complete and Incomplete Sentences

What constitutes a complete or incomplete sentence? What constitutes a run-on sentence, or a sentence fragment?

An incomplete sentence (or sentence fragment) is a group of words that has been written as if it were a complete sentence, but that, as a matter of grammatical correctness, needs something else to make it complete. If you write "And in the morning" and put a period after what you have written, the sentence has been left incomplete. It's a sentence fragment, not a complete sentence. Your reader will be left wondering "And in the morning, what?" Similarly, the group of words "When the meeting ends" cannot form a complete sentence on its own; grammatically, it is structured as a dependent (or subordinate) clause. Like independent clauses, dependent clauses include both a subject and a verb. Unlike independent clauses, though, they begin with a subordinating word. Subordinating conjunctions such as *because*, *although*, and *when* may be used in this way, as can relative pronouns such as *that*, *which*, and *whose*. To turn a dependent clause into a complete sentence, one can either transform it into an independent clause ("The meeting will end tomorrow") or attach it to a separate, independent clause ("When the meeting ends tomorrow, we should have a comprehensive agreement").

Focusing on the word "fragment," some people imagine incomplete sentences to be always very short. That's not the case. The idea of a sentence fragment is a grammatical concept, unrelated to how many words there may be in a phrase or clause; whether a sentence is complete or not is a matter of grammatical correctness, not a matter of sentence length. The first (quite short) group of words below forms a complete sentence, while the much longer group of words that follows is a sentence fragment:

> Marina walked to the sea.
>
> While Marina was walking to the sea and thinking of her father.

To correct the mistake here, one can either remove the subordinating conjunction *while*—

> Marina was walking to the sea and thinking of her father.

Or add an independent clause—

> While Marina was walking to the sea and thinking of her father, she heard the sound of a wood thrush.

In similar fashion, the grammatical concept of a run-on sentence is just that—a grammatical concept. A run-on sentence need not be long. Here is a very short example of a comma splice (one form of run-on sentence):

> Night fell, the moon rose.

To correct it, one can divide it into two sentences—

> Night fell. The moon rose.

or connect the two parts with a coordinating conjunction—

> Night fell, and the moon rose.

or use a semicolon rather than a comma to separate the independent clauses—

> Night fell; the moon rose.

Let's look at four more examples:

> Protests were widespread, but the authorities refused to back down.
>
> [complete sentence—two independent clauses, joined by a coordinating conjunction (*but*)]
>
> Although protests were widespread, the authorities refused to back down.
>
> [complete sentence—subordinate clause (introduced by the subordinating conjunction *although*), followed by a main (or independent) clause]
>
> Protests were widespread, however the authorities refused to back down
>
> [comma splice (a form of run-on sentence). *However* is a conjunctive adverb; if it is used to join independent clauses, it must be preceded by a semicolon rather than a comma.]
>
> The authorities refused to back down. Although protests were widespread.
>
> [The second is an incomplete sentence—as a subordinating conjunction, *although* cannot introduce a clause that can stand independently as a complete sentence.]

Students often experience considerable frustration when faced with examples such as these. In all four cases the meaning is plain, yet—according to the conventional rules of English grammar and usage—only two of the four are correct. The distinctions among categories such as coordinating conjunctions, subordinating conjunctions, and coordinating adverbs—confusing enough in themselves—become understandably more confusing when the words involved mean more or less the same thing. It may seem hard not to feel that the definitions of *complete sentence* and *incomplete sentence* are, to the extent that they rely on such distinctions, purely arbitrary. Such feelings are not unreasonable. Yet those distinctions matter in the academic world and in the world of work; if you are able to understand and follow the conventions of English grammar and usage in your writing, it is sure to be noted and appreciated by many of your instructors and co-workers.

The question of what constitutes a complete sentence, then, is a highly complicated one. It involves the structures of English grammar (M1.2) and the conventions governing the use of various joining words (M2.9), as well as the rules governing the use of periods, commas, and semicolons (M3.1). For a full understanding, we recommend you read all these sections, in addition to the material below. We recommend as well that you complete all of the interactive exercises that are included in the M1.3 section of the companion website for this book.

• **run-on sentences**: A run-on sentence is a sentence that continues running on when, as a matter of grammatical correctness, it should be broken up into two or more sentences. Sometimes people use the expression *run-on sentence* loosely to refer to a sentence that is simply very long, regardless of whether or not it is grammatically correct. A well-constructed long sentence, though, can be an excellent means of expressing complex ideas; for the sake of clarity, then, it's important not to confuse the idea of a long sentence with the idea of a run-on sentence. The term *run-on sentence* should be used only when issues of grammatical correctness are involved.

One variety of run-on sentence (a **fused sentence**) occurs when independent clauses are not separated by any punctuation.

needs checking Early last Thursday we were walking in the woods it was a lovely morning.

revised Early last Thursday we were walking in the woods. It was a lovely morning.

A second (and more common) variety of run-on sentence occurs when a comma (rather than a period or a semicolon) is used between independent clauses, without the addition of any coordinating conjunction. This type of run-on sentence is called a **comma-splice**.

Online

If you have been under the impression that a run-on sentence is by definition a long sentence, a blog post entitled "The Long Sentence and the Freight Train" may be worth consulting. It provides an extended discussion of how the issues involved in writing run-on sentences differ from those involved in writing long sentences, and discusses long and run-on sentences not only in academic writing but also in fiction (a context in which it is quite acceptable to write long sentences that are grammatically incorrect). The post may be found online at **http://donlepan.blogspot.com/2015/08/the-long-sentence-and-freight-train.html**.

needs checking It was a lovely morning, we were walking in the woods.
revised It was a lovely morning. We were walking in the woods.
or It was a lovely morning, and we were walking in the woods.

In simple examples such as those above, the matter may seem straightforward. Sometimes, though, it is not so simple. The conventions of English dictate that only certain words may be used to join two independent clauses into one sentence. The seven coordinating conjunctions (*and, but, or, for, nor, so,* and *yet*) may be used to join independent clauses; other classes of joining words—notably, conjunctive adverbs—may not be used in the same way. Some of the words most commonly used as conjunctive adverbs are *also, besides, consequently, finally, hence, however, indeed, likewise, meanwhile, moreover, nevertheless, next, otherwise, still, then,* and *therefore.*[1]

When a coordinating conjunction is used to connect two independent clauses, then, you may combine them into a single sentence, with a comma separating the two clauses. But when a conjunctive adverb is used to indicate how the ideas of two independent clauses are connected to each other, you must use a period (or semicolon) to separate the ideas from each other. They should not be "spliced" together with a comma:

needs checking The temperature stayed below freezing, therefore the ice did not melt.
revised The temperature stayed below freezing. Therefore, the ice did not melt.
or The temperature stayed below freezing, so the ice did not melt.

[The word *therefore* is a conjunctive adverb, not a coordinating conjunction; it thus may not be

1 A cautionary note: Categorizing words by their part-of-speech function is not always easy, since some words can function in more than one way. Notably, several of the words listed here that can function as conjunctive adverbs can also act as ordinary adverbs or as adjectives. In the sentence *Finally, we must consider taking concrete action* the word "finally" functions as a conjunctive adverb, whereas in the sentence *He was finally ready* the word "finally" functions as an ordinary adverb modifying the adjective "ready." Similarly, in the sentence *Otherwise, thousands will die of starvation* the word "otherwise" functions as a conjunctive adverb, whereas in the sentence *She will respond quickly if she is not otherwise occupied* the word "otherwise" acts as an ordinary adverb modifying the adjective "occupied." Additional information on this topic (together with an interactive exercise) is included on the companion website.

used to join independent clauses. The word *so* is a coordinating conjunction, and may thus be used to join independent clauses—provided that a comma is used as well.]

needs checking You had better leave now, otherwise we'll call the police.
revised You had better leave now. Otherwise, we'll call the police.
or You had better leave now; otherwise, we'll call the police.
[The word *otherwise* is a conjunctive adverb, not a coordinating conjunction, and thus may not be used to join independent clauses.]

needs checking With the exception of identical twins no two people have exactly the same genetic makeup, hence it is impossible for two people to look exactly the same.
revised With the exception of identical twins no two people have exactly the same genetic makeup. Hence, it is impossible for two people to look exactly the same.
or With the exception of identical twins no two people have exactly the same genetic makeup; hence, it is impossible for two people to look exactly the same.

needs checking During the rainy season more water flows over Victoria Falls than over any other falls in the world, however several other falls are higher than Victoria.
revised During the rainy season more water flows over Victoria Falls than over any other falls in the world. However, several other falls are higher than Victoria.
or During the rainy season more water flows over Victoria Falls than over any other falls in the world; several other falls, however, are higher than Victoria.

needs checking Money was tight and jobs were scarce, therefore she decided to stay in a job she did not like.
revised Money was tight and jobs were scarce; therefore, she decided to stay in a job she did not like.

Notice in the above cases that one way to correct a comma splice is often to use a semicolon. Unlike a comma, a semicolon may be used as a connector between clauses. (The discussion of the semicolon below may be helpful in this connection.)

The most common culprit when it comes to run-on sentences may well be the word ***then***. The word *then* may act as an ordinary adverb or as a conjunctive adverb, but it can never act as a coordinating conjunction, and thus should not be used to join two clauses together into one sentence. *And then* may be used, or a semicolon, or a new sentence may be begun.

needs checking We applied the solution to the surface of the leaves then we made observations at half-hour intervals.

revised We applied the solution to the surface of the leaves. Then we made observations at half-hour intervals.

or We applied the solution to the surface of the leaves; then we made observations at half-hour intervals.

or We applied the solution to the surface of the leaves, and then we made observations at half-hour intervals.

needs checking Yugoslav troops began withdrawing, then the NATO bombing was suspended and the war in Kosovo ended.

revised Yugoslav troops began withdrawing. Then the NATO bombing was suspended and the war in Kosovo ended.

needs checking The pilot checked the speedometer and the altimeter, then she knew what to do.

revised The pilot checked the speedometer and the altimeter. Then she knew what to do.

or The pilot checked the speedometer and the altimeter; then she knew what to do.

or The pilot checked the speedometer and the altimeter, and then she knew what to do.

needs checking The Montreal Canadiens produced vital goals early in the game, then they wrapped their iron defence around the Calgary Flames.

revised The Montreal Canadiens produced vital goals early in the game, and then they wrapped their iron defence around the Calgary Flames.

or The Montreal Canadiens produced vital goals early in the game; then they wrapped their iron defence around the Calgary Flames.

and and ***but***: Almost every schoolchild is advised at some point that one should not begin a sentence with *and* or *but*. Many are taught to follow a more general rule—that one should not begin a sentence with any of the seven coordinating conjunctions (*and*, *but*, *for*, *nor*, *or*, *so*, *yet*). As we noted above in discussing coordinating conjunctions (pages 185 to 186), that advice is wrong, and that rule does not exist. It is perfectly correct to begin a sentence with *and* or *but* (or another of the coordinating conjunctions) so long as all the needed components of a complete sentence are present. Coordinating conjunctions may be used to join two independent clauses so as to make one sentence; they may also be used, however, as a pointer to the way in which the idea of one sentence connects to the idea of the previous one:

> Smith has written that Buckner's error led directly to Boston's World Series loss. **But that is not the way it happened.** Buckner's error was only one of several developments leading to Boston's loss in Game 6 of that series; the Red Sox still had to lose Game 7 to lose the series.

> Jones points out that the fact of the riot having broken out following the speech does not prove the speech caused the riot. **And he makes a fair point.** The order of events tells us nothing in itself; we have to look carefully at the content of the speech to understand the ways in which it was incendiary.

Notice that the bolded sentences above include both a subject ("that" in the "But" sentence, "he" in the "And" sentence) and a verb ("is" in the "But" sentence, "makes" in the "And" sentence). By way of contrast, consider the groups of words bolded below:

> Buckner's error occurred in the eighth inning. There was still the ninth inning to come. **And Game 7 the next day.**

> Ellis has said that he was willing to give Trump the benefit of the doubt before the assault on the Capitol. **But not now.**

The first group of bolded words does not include a verb; it cannot be a complete sentence. And the second group of bolded words includes neither a subject nor a verb; clearly it cannot be a complete sentence either. Whether or not a group of words forms a complete sentence, once again, depends simply on whether or not the elements needed to make a complete sentence are present; the fact that the group of words begins with *and* or *but* is not relevant.

The same is true of the other five coordinating conjunctions. Coordinating conjunctions can join independent clauses within a sentence—or they can start a new sentence:

> Real Madrid might certainly win the cup, as might Barcelona**, or** it might be won by a team that no one is now expecting to have a serious chance. [correct—the coordinating conjunction *or* has been used to join two independent clauses]

> Real Madrid might certainly win the cup, as might Barcelona. **Or** it might be won by a team that no one is now expecting to have a serious chance. [correct—the coordinating conjunction *or* has been used to begin a new sentence]
>
> In the 2019 Canadian election, the Conservatives won more votes than any of the other parties, **yet** the Liberals won the most seats. [correct—the coordinating conjunction *yet* has been used to join two independent clauses]
>
> In the 2019 Canadian election, the Conservatives won more votes than any of the other parties. **Yet** the Liberals won the most seats. [correct—the coordinating conjunction *yet* has been used to begin a new sentence]

If there is no prohibition on beginning a sentence with coordinating conjunctions such as *and* or *but*, neither is there any prohibition, as a matter of grammatical correctness, on including *and* or *but* several times within a single sentence. As a matter of style, however, the appearance of more than one *and* or more than one *but* in a single sentence is often a signal that the ideas might better be rephrased.

needs checking Beaverbrook mobilized the resources of the country to serve the war effort overseas, and he later was knighted, and he is also well-known for creating a media empire.

> [So far as the rules of grammar are concerned, this cannot be classed as a run-on sentence; it is perfectly correct grammatically. But as a matter of style, the repetitive structure leaves much to be desired.]

revised Beaverbrook mobilized the resources of the country to serve the war effort—an accomplishment for which he later was knighted. He is also well-known for creating a media empire.

or Beaverbrook, who had created a vast media empire before the war, then distinguished himself by mobilizing the resources of the country to serve the war effort. It was in recognition of this service that he was knighted.

or Beaverbrook, who had created a vast media empire before the war, then distinguished himself by mobilizing the resources of the country to serve the war effort; it was in recognition of this service that he was knighted.

• **sentence fragments (incomplete sentences)**: As we have seen, a grammatically complete sentence must include both a subject and a verb. A group of words such as *in a minute* or *from Toronto to Montreal* includes neither subject nor verb; such groups of words are simply phrases. But nor can groups of words such as *which I find very useful* or *if we finish in time* be complete sentences; such groups of words do include both a subject and a verb, but they are dependent clauses (discussed above, pages 186 and 190). A grammatically complete sentence must always include at least one independent clause.

Some sorts of sentence fragments might be classed as "afterthought fragments"; the writer completes a sentence, and then adds an afterthought:

needs checking Unemployment was a serious problem in Britain in the early 1990s. In fact, throughout the world.

revised Unemployment was a serious problem in Britain in the early 1990s. In fact, it was a serious problem throughout the world.

or Unemployment was a serious problem in the early 1990s—not just in Britain but throughout the world.

needs checking In Nathaniel Hawthorne's story "Young Goodman Brown," the main character chooses not to trust the members of his own community but instead to presume them to be corrupted by sin. Although he has no way of knowing if they are truly corrupted or not.

revised In Nathaniel Hawthorne's story "Young Goodman Brown," the main character chooses not to trust the members of his own community but instead to presume them to be corrupted by sin, although he has no way of knowing if they are truly corrupted or not.

or In Nathaniel Hawthorne's story "Young Goodman Brown," the main character chooses not to trust the members of his own community. Instead, he presumes them to be corrupted by sin, although he has no way of knowing if they are truly corrupted or not.

needs checking When asked to propose an appropriate punishment after having been convicted by an Athenian jury for having committed impious acts, Socrates suggests that he be provided with free meals at public expense. An award that was typically given to Olympic champions.

revised When asked to propose an appropriate punishment after having been convicted by an Athenian jury of having committed impious acts, Socrates suggests that he be provided with free meals at public expense, an award that was typically given to Olympic champions.

or When asked to propose an appropriate punishment after having been convicted by an Athenian jury of having committed impious acts, Socrates suggests that he be provided with free meals at public expense—an award that was typically given to Olympic champions.

or Socrates is asked to propose an appropriate punishment after he has been convicted by an Athenian jury of having committed impious acts. He suggests that he be provided with free meals at public expense—an award that was typically given to Olympic champions.

Notice that in the last two cases, the "afterthought fragment" is preceded by quite a long sentence. It's easy to imagine the writer of such sentences thinking "I've made this sentence pretty long already; I had better stop, and start a new sentence with my next thought." As a matter of style, it's certainly a good thing to pay attention to sentence length—and to vary the lengths of your sentences. But as the last example in each group above illustrates, there are many ways to vary sentence length while still writing entirely in grammatically correct sentences.

We have seen that a sentence fragment need not be short. Indeed, writers can often be led into writing grammatically incomplete sentences by becoming tangled in their thoughts when attempting to write a long sentence. While "afterthought fragments" tend to be short follow-ups after a long sentence, "tangle-thought fragments" are typically themselves quite long:

needs checking In the event that interest rates remain low and the exchange rate remains favourable, Canadian companies that are contemplating export markets, so long as those markets are stable and the distribution channels are relatively efficient.

[For all its length, this sentence lacks an independent clause.]

revised In the event that interest rates remain low and the exchange rate remains favourable, Canadian companies can contemplate export markets with confidence, so long as those markets are stable and the distribution channels are relatively efficient.

or Interest rates may well remain low and the exchange rate favourable. In that case, Canadian companies can contemplate export markets with confidence—so long as those markets are stable and the distribution channels are relatively efficient.

needs checking While it is important to acknowledge the important role that Indigenous peoples have played within Canada, no less important, as a matter of historical accuracy as well as of fairness, acknowledging that national borders such as those separating Canada and the United States are, particularly in the case of Indigenous peoples, artificial borders.

revised While it is important to acknowledge the important role that Indigenous peoples have played within Canada, it is no less important, as a matter of historical accuracy as well as of fairness, to acknowledge that national borders such as those separating Canada and the United States are, particularly in the case of Indigenous peoples, artificial borders.

or While it is important to acknowledge the important role that Indigenous peoples have played within Canada, it is no less important to acknowledge that national borders such as those separating Canada and the United States are artificial borders. To recognize such artificiality is vitally important where Indigenous peoples are concerned; it's a matter of historical accuracy, and also a matter of fairness.

Here again we may notice that one can vary the length of one's sentences—and the order in which one's thoughts are presented—while being careful to write entirely in grammatically correct sentences.

because: As discussed above, many schoolchildren are given the erroneous impression that one should never begin a sentence with *and* or with *so*. So too with *because*—and the impression is erroneous here, too. The case of *because* is different from that of *and* and *so*, however. Whereas *and* and *so* are both coordinating conjunctions (see above, page 185), *because* is a subordinating conjunction (see above, page 186). A subordinating conjunction cannot be used to introduce an independent clause; subordinating conjunctions introduce dependent clauses. And as we have seen, a sentence with a dependent clause must also include an independent clause if the sentence is to be complete.

needs checking The government decided to shut down virtually everything. Because of the pandemic.

[*Because of the pandemic* is a phrase; it lacks both a subject and a verb.]

revised The government decided to shut down virtually everything because of the pandemic.

or Because of the pandemic, the government decided to shut down virtually everything.

needs checking In the early 1980s, Sandinista leaders told their people to be ready for war. Because the United States had been trying to destabilize Nicaragua.

[*Because the United States had been trying to destabilize Nicaragua* is a dependent clause.]

revised In the early 1980s, Sandinista leaders told their people to be ready for war, because the United States had been trying to destabilize Nicaragua.

or In the early 1980s, Sandinista leaders told their people to be ready for war; the United States had been trying to destabilize Nicaragua.

needs checking Because of the cold and wet weather, which affected the whole area. Many people were desperately trying to find more firewood.

revised Because of the cold and wet weather, which affected the whole area, many people were desperately trying to find more firewood.

or The cold and wet weather affected the whole area; many people were desperately trying to find more firewood.

Notice in the above examples that it does not matter whether the word *because* comes at the beginning or in the middle of the sentence; what is important is that the sentence has two parts. And notice too that using a semicolon to link two clauses where the meaning of the one follows from the meaning of the other can be an attractive alternative. (See also pages 190 and 186 regarding subordinate clauses and subordinating conjunctions, and pages 199 and 202 regarding use of the semicolon.)

• **complete sentences and sentence style**: Noticing how semicolons can be used effectively both to separate and to link the groups of words with which you express yourself points to an important point about grammatical correctness. The goal of writing in a readable, engaging style and the goal of writing grammatically correct prose are two separate goals to strive for; while they may sometimes be interconnected, they may also sometimes exist in tension with each other. One of the reasons that schoolteachers have long advised students against beginning sentences with *and* or *so* or *because* is that doing so can have unfortunate consequences stylistically. This series of three sentences concerning *The Handmaid's Tale* is not incorrect grammatically—but nor does it constitute good writing:

needs checking Margaret Atwood's novel *The Handmaid's Tale* was first published in 1985. And it was made into a 1990 film. And in 2017 it became the basis for a successful television series.

revised Margaret Atwood's novel *The Handmaid's Tale*, which was first published in 1985, was made into a 1990 film, and in 2017 became the basis for a successful television series.

or Margaret Atwood's 1985 novel *The Handmaid's Tale* was made into a 1990 film; in 2017 the book became the basis for a successful television series.

Good writing, then, requires us to do more than make sure that all our sentences are grammatically correct. Here is a more extended example of a passage made up of grammatically correct complete sentences:

> The American Revolutionary War ended with the 1783 Treaty of Paris. Under its provisions, the "Northwest Territory" (much of modern-day Ohio and Indiana) was ceded by the British to the new American nation. The British were giving away what was not theirs to give. The British had previously agreed that most of this territory would be controlled by the Shawnee and other Indigenous groups. The 1783 treaty made no reference to these agreements. American settlers poured in to the Northwest Territory and started to farm and build homes on land that the Shawnee had long occupied. The Shawnee and other Indigenous groups tried to stop these encroachments. There were several battles. The Shawnee and their allies were defeated in 1794 at the Battle of Fallen Timbers by an American force led by "Mad Anthony" Wayne. Tecumseh, a Shawnee chief, became one of the most important figures in early nineteenth-century North American history. He was a young warrior when he participated in the Battle of Fallen Timbers. And then Tecumseh and the Shawnee ceded much of what is now Ohio to the Americans. In 1795 they signed the Treaty of Greenville. And then the Shawnee were forced to move west. They formed several new towns, the largest of them near the point where the Tippecanoe River meets the Wabash River. That is now

> part of western Indiana. By 1809 American settlers were encroaching on Shawnee settlements. Tecumseh formed a Confederation. He united various other Indigenous groups with the Shawnee. In 1811 he was away, trying to enlist more support. An American force led by William Henry Harrison defeated Shawnee forces near the mouth of the Tippecanoe River. It was called the Battle of Tippecanoe. Tecumseh then joined forces with the British (in what is now known as the War of 1812). And they won significant victories at Brownstown, Fort Detroit, and Fort Meigs. Tecumseh was defeated by Harrison and killed on October 5, 1813 (at Moraviantown, near present-day Chatham, Ontario) in the Battle of the Thames. Most of the Shawnee warriors surrendered. The dream of a Confederation of Indigenous peoples came to an end. The war ended. The Shawnee were forced to move farther west. The victories of the American army in battles such as Fallen Timbers and Tippecanoe were once seen as triumphs of the forces of civilization over those of savagery. Nowadays those battles are recognized as tragic episodes in a long narrative of aggression by settler colonial society against Indigenous peoples. The War of 1812 was once seen as a conflict between British and American forces that ended with no clear victor. Nowadays it is recognized as a three-way conflict. The Indigenous peoples of North America lost out.

This passage is written in grammatically correct English, but it lacks the sorts of links between clauses and sentences that help the reader to continually make connections. There are many ways in which such connections might be made. The rewrite below shows one way, with linking words (and/or semicolons) added, and with the material divided up into paragraphs.

> The American Revolutionary War ended with the 1783 Treaty of Paris. Under its provisions, the "Northwest Territory" (much of modern-day Ohio and Indiana) was ceded by the British to the new American nation. **But** the British were giving away what was not theirs to give**; they** had previously agreed that most of this territory would be controlled by the Shawnee and other Indigenous groups. The treaty**, however,** made no reference to these agreements.
>
> American settlers poured in to the Northwest Territory and started to farm and build homes on land that the Shawnee had long occupied. **As one might expect,** the Shawnee and other Indigenous groups tried to stop these encroachments**, and** there were several battles. The Shawnee and their allies were **finally** defeated in 1794 at the Battle of Fallen Timbers by an American force led by "Mad Anthony" Wayne.

> Tecumseh, a Shawnee chief who became one of the most important figures in early nineteenth-century North American history, was a young warrior when he participated in the Battle of Fallen Timbers. Tecumseh and the Shawnee were forced to cede much of what is now Ohio to the Americans **when** in 1795 they signed the treaty of Greenville.
>
> Forced to move west, the Shawnee **then** formed several new towns, the largest of them near the point where the Tippecanoe River meets the Wabash River in what is now western Indiana. By 1809, **however,** American settlers were **once more** encroaching on these new Shawnee settlements. Tecumseh formed a confederation**, uniting** various other Indigenous groups with the Shawnee. **But** in 1811, **while Tecumseh** was away trying to enlist more support, an American force led by William Henry Harrison defeated Shawnee forces near the mouth of the Tippecanoe River **in what became known as** the Battle of Tippecanoe. Tecumseh then joined forces with the British (in what is now known as the War of 1812). **Though** Tecumseh and his warriors won significant victories at Brownstown, Fort Detroit, and Fort Meigs, Tecumseh was **eventually** defeated by Harrison and killed on October 5, 1813 (at Moraviantown, near present-day Chatham, Ontario) in the Battle of the Thames. Most of the Shawnee warriors surrendered**, and** the dream of a Confederation of Indigenous peoples came to an end. **When** the war ended, the Shawnee were forced to move farther west.
>
> The battles of Fallen Timbers and Tippecanoe were once seen as triumphs of the forces of civilization over those of savagery. Nowadays**, however,** they are recognized as tragic episodes in a long narrative of aggression by settler colonial society against Indigenous peoples. The War of 1812 was once seen as a conflict between British and American forces that ended with no clear victor. Nowadays**, though,** it is recognized as a three-way conflict **in which** the Indigenous peoples of North America lost out.

Try rewriting the first passage in a different way yourself, breaking up and combining the material into complete sentences in different ways.

For more on how to make your writing clear and engaging in these sorts of ways, see M2.9 Joining Words and M1.6 Sentence Combining.

• **acceptable sentence fragments**: As the above example demonstrates, writing may be perfectly correct so far as the conventions of English grammar and usage are concerned, and nevertheless be in serious need of improvement: correctness is only one aspect of good writing. And sometimes, good writing may even include sentences that are grammatically incorrect. That is obviously the case with some works of fiction, in which an author may use stream-of-consciousness or other techniques in order to convey characters' thought processes to the reader. But it can also be true of essays and other forms of non-fiction. For skilled writers, the brevity of certain sorts of incomplete sentence may make for an effective means of emphasizing a point or of indicating a change of direction:

> In baseball, a lead of four runs going into the ninth inning is a safe lead. **Not this time.**
>
> Is the original film better than the re-make? **In every respect.**
>
> Ellis has said that he was willing to give Trump the benefit of the doubt before the assault on the Capitol. **But not now.**
>
> She wanted it to be a surprise. **A big surprise.**
>
> **A tumble on the basepaths by the Rays' best hitter, and two fielding errors by the Dodgers.** That was how Game 4 of the 2020 World Series ended.
>
> At the end of every day she felt tired. **Bone tired.**
>
> **Popular policies. A strong leader. An experienced staff.** All the ingredients for an election victory seemed to be in place.

Contexts in which such writing may be considered appropriate occur far more frequently in informal writing than in formal writing—and instructors at the post-secondary level often disagree as to when it is acceptable to deviate in this sort of way from grammatical conventions. For those reasons, students are well advised to consult their instructors before making a habit of intentionally writing sentence fragments in formal academic writing.

M 1.4 Verb Forms

The Infinitive

Although not properly speaking a verb tense, the infinitive is the starting point for building knowledge of verb tenses; the infinitive is the most basic form of the verb. Some examples of infinitives are *to go*, *to be*, *to do*, *to begin*, *to come*, *to investigate*. The infinitive form remains the same, of course,. whether the action happens in the past, the present, or the future.

> **EAL**
>
> For particular problems with verbs faced by those whose native language is not English, see the EAL section later in the book (pages 439–78).

split infinitives: The most common mistake involving infinitives is undoubtedly the slang substitution of *and* for *to*, especially in the expression *try and do it* for *try to do it* (see page 364 for a fuller treatment). The great issue in this area among grammarians, however, is the split infinitive—the infinitive which has another word or words inserted between *to* and the verb:

needs checking The time has come to once again go to the polls. Economic conditions are likely to greatly influence the outcome, and the prime minister has promised to forcefully speak out in defence of the government's fiscal record.

With re-united infinitives, the same passage looks like this:

revised The time has come to go once again to the polls. Economic conditions are likely to influence greatly the outcome, and the prime minister has promised to speak out forcefully in defence of the government's fiscal record.

On what grounds can the second passage be considered better? It comes down to a matter of sound and rhythm. To most ears *to go once again* and *to speak out forcefully* are preferable to the split alternatives, but *to influence greatly* seems more awkward than *to greatly influence*. Happily, most authorities are now agreed that it is not a grievous sin to split an infinitive; Philip Howard, former editor of *The Times* of London, calls the split infinitive "the great shibboleth of English syntax," and even the traditionalist H.W. Fowler allows that while "the split infinitive is an ugly thing, we must warn the novice against the curious superstition that splitting or not splitting makes the difference between a good and a bad writer."

This is not to say that the splitting of infinitives should be encouraged. In many cases a split infinitive is a sign of wordiness; in cases such as the following it is better to drop the adverb entirely:

poor The chair said it was important to really investigate the matter thoroughly.

better The chair said it was important to investigate the matter thoroughly.

Like all verb forms, most infinitives have both an *active* and a *passive* voice. The active, which is more common, is used when the subject of the verb is doing the action, whereas the passive is used when the subject of the verb is receiving the action, or being acted on. *To do, to hit, to write* are examples of infinitives in the active voice, while *to be done, to be hit, to be written* are examples of infinitives in the passive voice.

On the Companion Website

Exercises on split infinitives may be found at **sites.broadviewpress.com/writingcdn**. Click on **Exercises** and **Writing Mechanics** and go to **"Verbs."**

The Simple Present

	singular	*plural*
1st person	I say	we say
2nd person	you say	you say
3rd person	he, she, it says	they say

subject–verb agreement: The simple present tense seems entirely straightforward, and usually it is. Most of us have no difficulty with the first person or the second person. But almost all of us occasionally have problems in writing the third person correctly. All too often the letter *s* at the end of the third person singular is left out. The simple rule to remember is that whenever you use a verb in the third person singular of the simple present tense, it must end in *s*:

needs checking He go to Vancouver at least once a month.
revised He goes to Vancouver at least once a month.

needs checking The litmus paper change immediately when the solution is mixed.
revised The litmus paper changes immediately when the solution is mixed.

(*Paper*, which is the subject, is an *it* and therefore third person singular.)

It is not particularly difficult to ensure that the subject agrees with the verb in the above examples, but even professional writers often have trouble with more complex sentences. Here are two common causes of subject–verb agreement errors:

(a) The subject and verb are separated by a long phrase or clause, especially when an intervening noun could be mistaken for the subject.

needs checking The state of Afghanistan's roads reflect the chaotic situation.
revised The state of Afghanistan's roads reflects the chaotic situation.

Here the writer has made the mental error of thinking of *roads* as the subject of the verb *reflect*, whereas in fact the subject is the singular noun *state*. *The state reflect* ... would immediately strike most people as wrong, but the intervening words have in this case caused grammatical confusion.

needs checking As the statement by Belgium's prime minister about his country's deficit and unemployment problems indicate, many nations are in the same shape, or worse.
revised As the statement by Belgium's prime minister about his country's deficit and unemployment problems indicates, many nations are in the same shape, or worse.

(The subject is the singular noun *statement*, so the verb must be *indicates* rather than *indicate*.)

needs checking Courses offered range from the history of the Greek and Roman world to the twenty-first century, and covers Britain, Europe, North America, Africa, and the Far East.
revised Courses offered range from the history of the Greek and Roman world to the twenty-first century, and cover Britain, Europe, North America, Africa, and the Far East.

Sometimes a long sentence can in itself throw off a writer's sense of subject–verb agreement, even if subject and verb are close together. In the following example the close proximity of the subject *simplifications* to the verb has not prevented error:

needs checking	The decline in the quality of leadership is mirrored in the crude simplifications which characterizes the average person's view of the world.
revised	The decline in the quality of leadership is mirrored in the crude simplifications which characterize the average person's view of the world.

(b) The error of using *there is* instead of *there are* when the subject is plural has become more and more frequent in writing as well as in speech. When these two expressions are used, remember that the subject comes after the verb; use *is* or *are* depending on whether the subject is singular or plural:

needs checking	There's many more opportunities of that sort than there used to be.
revised	There are many more opportunities of that sort than there used to be.

On the Companion Website

Exercises on subject–verb agreement may be found at **sites.broadviewpress.com/writingcdn**. Click on **Exercises** and **Writing Mechanics** and go to **"Verbs."**

historical present: To use the "historical present" is to use the present tense in a narrative set in the past. In many medieval histories the narrative alternates frequently between the present tense and the past tense, but from the sixteenth century until the late twentieth century most narratives of past action were recounted using the past tense. The historical present was used on a very selective basis by some historians and journalists (and by a few writers of fiction), the purpose being to lend a sense of immediacy to particular scenes that the writer wanted to express with memorable vividness. Here is an example, from Pierre Berton's work of popular history, *The Invasion of Canada*:

> [The British] are encouraged to strengthen their defences in Canada against possible invasion. This is Isaac Brock's doing.... The young lieutenant-colonel ... goes on to press for a better trained and expanded militia and for repairs to the fortress of Quebec. He does not easily get his way, but from this time on the prospect of an American invasion is never far from that determined and agile mind. When and if the Americans come, Isaac Brock intends to be ready.

In the twenty-first century the historical present has become much more commonly used in a wide variety of contexts. Many works of fiction are now written entirely in the present tense. Many works of history shift back and forth continually between the past tense and the historical present. Even newscasts now use the historical present frequently. As in earlier eras, the aim is presumably to impart a greater sense of immediacy and interest to what is being recounted. It is all too easy in such circumstances, however, to create a sense of confusion rather than a sense of immediacy in the reader's mind—particularly given that the present tense is often also used idiomatically to refer to future events (e.g., *We arrive at 9:00 in the morning* rather than *We will arrive at 9:00 in the morning*). It is essential, then, to pay careful attention to what tenses are being used.

needs checking Throughout the day, shells fall on the city. Dozens are killed. The President, however, refused to authorize a ceasefire. The Cabinet holds an emergency meeting tonight.

(The passage begins in the historical present, but then switches to the past tense. The fourth sentence shifts back to present tense—but it is not clear what time is being referred to. Is the emergency meeting also in the past (and the report being filed late at night)? If so, what was the outcome of the meeting? Or is the report being filed before "tonight"—in which case the emergency meeting is still in the future.)

revised Throughout the day, shells fell on the city. Dozens were killed. The President, however, refused to authorize a ceasefire. The Cabinet will hold an emergency meeting tonight.

or Throughout the day, shells fall on the city. Dozens are killed. The President, however, refuses to authorize a ceasefire. The Cabinet will hold an emergency meeting tonight.

The Simple Past

	singular	*plural*
1st person	I finished	we finished
2nd person	you finished	you finished
3rd person	he, she, it finished	they finished

irregular verbs: The occasional problems that crop up with the simple past tense usually involve irregular verbs—that is to say, verbs that do not follow a regular pattern in the formation of the simple past and other tenses. (See pages 260–67 for a fuller discussion and list.) One lesser-known past tense form is *might,* which, in addition to being a modal verb with the same meaning as *may* in the present tense, is also the past tense of *may.* More simply put, use *might* with past tense verbs, never *may.*

needs checking Bands such as U2 and Barenaked Ladies gained a foothold in North America through campus radio; without it they may not have broken through.

revised Bands such as U2 and Barenaked Ladies gained a foothold in North America through campus radio; without it they might not have broken through.

Two other verbs that often cause problems in the simple past are *lie* and *lay* (see also page 264). The difficulty many people have in keeping these straight is often ascribed to other factors, but is in part also attributable simply to the forms of the tenses; the past tense of *lie* is the same as the present tense of *lay.* Also, the past participle of *lie* is *lain*, not *laid*:

needs checking Many in our party have just laid down and rolled over; they cannot get over the fact that we have lost control of the House of Commons.

revised Many in our party have just lain down and rolled over; they cannot get over the fact that we have lost control of the House of Commons.

Given the difficulty of getting one's tongue round *lain down* rather than *laid down*, and the fact that almost anyone will know what meaning is intended with these words, many now feel that the distinctions are not worth troubling over in informal contexts. They remain important, however, in formal, written English.

habitual action: The simple past tense is often mistakenly used to express what is called habitual action—the way an action ordinarily, or habitually, occurs. The simple present tense should be used to name such action even if the main verb of the sentence is in the past or future tense:

needs checking The professor told us that Jupiter was the largest planet.
revised The professor told us that Jupiter is the largest planet. (Jupiter has not stopped being the largest since he spoke.)

The Simple Future

	singular	*plural*
1st person	I will arrive	we will arrive
2nd person	you will arrive	you will arrive
3rd person	he, she, it will arrive	they will arrive

The Progressive (or Continuous) Aspect

The Present Progressive

	singular	*plural*
1st person	I am saying	we are saying
2nd person	you are saying	you are saying
3rd person	he, she, it are saying	they are saying

verbs not normally used in the continuous aspect: In English the continuous tenses are not normally used with many verbs which have to do with feelings, emotions, or senses. Some of these verbs are *to see, to hear, to understand, to believe, to hope, to know, to think* (meaning *believe*), *to trust, to comprehend, to mean, to doubt, to suppose, to wish, to want, to love, to desire, to prefer, to dislike, to hate.*

needs checking He is not understanding what I meant.
revised He does not understand what I meant.

The Past Progressive

	singular	*plural*
1st person	I was leaving	we were leaving
2nd person	you were leaving	you were leaving
3rd person	he, she, it were leaving	they were leaving

The problems that sometimes occur with the past continuous are the same as those that occur with the present continuous (see above). Remember to avoid these forms when using verbs having to do with feelings, emotions, or senses (e.g., *see*, *hear*, *understand*, *believe*, *hope*, *know*, *think*, *trust*, *comprehend*) and when using the verb *to have* to mean *own*, *possess*, or *suffer from*:

needs checking At that time he was believing that everything on earth was created within one week.

revised At that time he believed that everything on earth was created within one week.

The Future Progressive

	singular	*plural*
1st person	I will be finding	we will be finding
2nd person	you will be finding	you will be finding
3rd person	he, she, it will be finding	they will be finding

The Perfect Aspect

As used to refer to the perfect verb forms, the word *perfect* means *completed*; as you might expect, then, the perfect tenses are often (though not always) used to express actions that have been completed. They are formed by combining some form of the verb *to have* with a past participle (e.g., *opened*, *finished*, *believed*, *done*).

The Present Perfect

	singular	*plural*
1st person	I have worked	we have worked
2nd person	you have worked	you have worked
3rd person	he, she, it has worked	they have worked

continuing past actions: One way in which this tense is used is to speak of past actions which may continue into the present, or be repeated in the present or future. In the sentence *Anne Carson has written a number of books*, for example, the form of the verb shows that she will probably write more; she has neither died nor given up writing.

Understanding this sort of thing is a simple enough practice in normal usage, but in the long sentences that often occur in academic writing, it is easy to become confused:

needs checking Since it called the First World Food Congress in 1963, the Food and Agriculture Organization has said clearly that the world, with the science and technology then known, had enough knowledge to ensure man's freedom from hunger. Successive world congresses and conferences have repeated this contention. (from a paper given by a distinguished professor at an academic conference)

Here the writer has evidently chosen the present perfect, thinking that he is referring to a situation which has continued on into the present. But when he refers to the science and technology then known and to successive world congresses and conferences, he has cut off the 1963 conference from any grammatical connection with the present. This is the sort of mistake that most writers can catch only during the revision process.

revised When it called the First World Food Congress in 1963, the Food and Agriculture Organization said clearly that the world, with the science and technology then known, had enough knowledge to ensure man's freedom from hunger. Successive world congresses and conferences have repeated this contention.

The Past Perfect

	singular	*plural*
1st person	I had believed	we had believed
2nd person	you had believed	you had believed
3rd person	he, she, it had believed	they had believed

Since the verb remains unchanged in all these forms, the past perfect is one of the easiest tenses to remember. What is difficult is learning how and when to use it. In English, however, there are quite definite rules about when the past perfect tense should be used. Its chief use is to show that one action in the past was completed before another action in the past began. Here are some examples:

I told my parents what had happened.
(The happening occurred before the telling.)
By the time the group of tourists left Mozambique, they had formed a very favourable impression of the country.
(The forming occurred before the leaving.)

When he had gone I thought very seriously about what he had said.
(Both the going and the saying occurred before the thinking.)

The usefulness of the past perfect tense can be clearly seen in passages in which the writer wishes to flashback, or move backwards in time. If you compare the following passages, you will see that the use of the past perfect tense in the second passage removes any confusion about the order in which the events happened. In the example below, when only the simple past tense is used, it sounds as if the dead snake is able to crawl:

needs checking The tail was still moving, but the snake itself was quite dead. It crawled out from the sewer and slowly moved across the pavement as I was turning the corner.

revised The tail was still moving, but the snake itself was quite dead. It had crawled out from the sewer and had slowly moved across the pavement as I had been turning the corner.
(In the second passage it is clear that the snake emerged *before* it died, and not afterwards.)

Perhaps the most common occasions in which we use the past perfect tense are when we are using indirect speech:

She said that she had knocked on my door in the morning, but that there had been no answer.
(The knocking happened before the saying.)

The chair of the committee repeatedly asked the witness when the president had known of the diversion of funds.
(The knowing happened before the asking.)

In a few cases it is possible to speak correctly of two actions which happened one after the other in the past by using the simple past tense for both actions. The use of the word *after*, for example, often makes it clear that the first action was completed before the other began.

past actions at different times, or over a prolonged period: Writers often neglect to use the past perfect to name the earlier action when they are speaking of two (or more) actions that happened at different times in the past:

needs checking He asked me if I talked to his secretary before coming to him.

revised He asked me if I had talked to his secretary before coming to him.

needs checking By the time the Allies decided to resist Hitler, the Nazis built up a huge military machine.

revised By the time the Allies decided to resist Hitler, the Nazis had built up a huge military machine.

needs checking Johnson's girlfriend, Marsha Dianne Blaylock, said she knew Williams since October 2013, when she and Johnson began their relationship.

revised Johnson's girlfriend, Marsha Dianne Blaylock, said she had known Williams since October 2013, when she and Johnson began their relationship.

(Note that like the present perfect, the past perfect is very frequently required with *since* or *for*.)

The past perfect is also used to indicate that a past action occurred over a prolonged period:

In the early 1960s Sonny Bono was a disheveled pop singer and songwriter with hippie tendencies; by the time of his death in 1998 he had become a conservative Republican member of the House of Representatives.

needs checking In 1980, 10 per cent of Chile's families did not have sufficient income to satisfy the minimum food requirements recommended by international organizations; in 2000 the figure grew to 32 per cent.

revised In 1980, 10 per cent of Chile's families did not have sufficient income to satisfy the minimum food requirements recommended by international organizations; by 2000 the figure had grown to 32 per cent.

or … in 2000 the figure was 32 per cent.

(The original suggests that the figure had remained at 10 per cent in every year from 1980 to 2000, and then jumped in the course of one year to 32 per cent.)

The Future Perfect

	singular	*plural*
1st person	I will have gone	we will have gone
2nd person	you will have gone	you will have gone
3rd person	he, she, it will have gone	they will have gone

Conditional

	singular	*plural*
1st person	I would go	we would go
2nd person	you would go	you would go
3rd person	he, she, it would go	they would go

The above forms are used when we are speaking of actions that would or might happen if certain conditions were fulfilled. Here are some further examples:

> If I wanted to go to Australia, I would have to fly.
> If I drank a lot of gin, I would be very sick.
> I would lend Joe the money he wants if I trusted him.
> I might enjoy basketball more if I were taller.

Each of these sentences is made up of a main clause, in which a modal auxiliary verb (*would, might*) is used, and a subordinate clause beginning with *if*, with a verb in the same form as the simple past tense (*wanted, drank, trusted*, etc.). In all cases the action named in the *if* clause is considered by the speaker to be unlikely to happen, or quite impossible. The speaker does not really want to go to Australia; she is just speculating about what she would have to do if she did. Similarly the second speaker does not expect to drink a lot of gin; if he did, he would be sick, but he does not plan to. In the same way, the speaker of the third sentence does not trust Joe; he is speaking about what the situation would be if he did trust Joe. Situations like these which are not happening and which we do not expect to happen are called *hypothetical situations*: we speculate on what *would* or *might* happen *if* ... but we do not expect the *if* ... to come true.

If we think the *if* ... is likely to come true, then we use the future tense instead of the conditional in the main clause, and the present tense in the subordinate *if* clause, as in these examples:

> If I drink a lot of gin, I will be very sick.
> (Here the speaker thinks that it is very possible or likely that he will drink a lot of gin.)
> If I want to go to Australia, I will have to fly.
> (Here the speaker thinks that she may really want to go.)

Notice the difference between the following two sentences:

If a socialist government is re-elected in Venezuela, the American administration will not be pleased.

(Here the writer thinks that it is quite possible or likely that the socialists will be re-elected.)

If a socialist government were elected in Venezuela, the American administration would not be pleased.

(Here the writer is assuming that the socialists probably will not be re-elected.)

On the Companion Website

Exercises on conditional sentences may be found at **sites.broadviewpress.com/writingcdn**. Click on **Exercises** and **Writing Mechanics** and go to **"Conditional Constructions."**

choosing the right verb when writing about conditions: Some writers mistakenly use the auxiliary verb *would* in the *if*... clause when they are also using *would* in the main clause. Others use the present tense (instead of the past tense) in the *if*... clause when they are using *would* in the main clause. Both are incorrect.

needs checking If television networks would produce fewer series about violent crime, parents would allow their children to watch even more television than they do now.

revised If television networks produced fewer series about violent crime, parents would allow their children to watch even more television than they do now.

or If television networks were to produce fewer series about violent crime, parents would allow their children to watch even more television than they do now.

needs checking If I want to buy a car, I would look carefully at all the models available.

revised If I wanted to buy a car, I would look carefully at all the models available.

(The speaker does not want to buy a car.)

or If I want to buy a car, I will look carefully at all the models available.

(The speaker may really want to buy a car.)

Note that whenever one is referring to situations that are imagined, wished for, or in some other way contrary to fact, the subjunctive (typically, identical in form to that of the simple past tense) is used in the conditional *if...* clause. The subjunctive mood is explained in greater detail in the next section.

The Past Conditional

	singular	*plural*
1st person	I would have gone	we would have gone
2nd person	you would have gone	you would have gone
3rd person	he, she, it would have gone	they would have gone

This verb form is used in conditional sentences in which we are speaking of actions which never happened. It is used in the main clause, with the past tense in the subjunctive mood being used in the *if...* clause. Notice in the examples below that these past tense subjunctive forms are identical in form to the past perfect tense formations in the indicative mood.

If I had studied harder, I would have passed.
(meaning that in fact I did not study very hard, and did not pass)

If Kitchener had arrived at Khartoum a day earlier, he would have saved Gordon and the rest of the British garrison force.
(meaning that Kitchener did not come early enough, and was not able to prevent the 1885 massacre at Khartoum)

choosing the right verbs when writing about past conditions: Some people mistakenly use the past conditional in both clauses of sentences such as these; remember that the past conditional should be used only in the main clause:

needs checking If the *Titanic* would have carried more lifeboats, hundreds of lives would have been saved.

revised If the *Titanic* had carried more lifeboats, hundreds of lives would have been saved.

Other Verb Forms

The present perfect continuous tense—*I have been running, you have been working*, etc.

The past perfect continuous tense—*I had been looking, you had been following*, etc.

The future perfect continuous tense—*I will have been sleeping, they will have been studying*, etc.

The conditional continuous tense—*I would be bringing, she would be starting*, etc.

The past conditional continuous tense—*I would have been working, he would have been driving*, etc.

M 1.5 Mood and Voice

In grammatical terms, **mood** (sometimes called *mode* or *modality*) is not a measure of how grumpy or cheery a sentence is. Rather it reflects, essentially, how the speaker sees the relationship to reality of the states or events described by the verb: are they real, desired, or purely hypothetical? The tenses discussed in the previous section, and the vast majority of sentences we write, are all in the **indicative mood**; that is the way we express (or *indicate*) real—or really possible—actions.

It's easier to understand what the indicative mood is when we look at sentences that are not indicative. In English, there are two other moods that have distinct verb forms (though more moods may be expressed through the arrangement of the sentence). The **imperative mood** uses the simple form of a verb (e.g., *be, do, eat, come*) to express commands and instructions:

Follow the path to the right.
Come here immediately!

The mood that even many native English speakers find difficult to use correctly is the **subjunctive mood**. The subjunctive is used to denote actions or states that are wished for or imagined or otherwise not factual. It frequently appears in archaic expressions, such as "*Suffice* it to say…" or "*Be* that as it may…," where *suffice* and *be* are both in the subjunctive mood. In common English usage the indicative mood is now often employed where once the subjunctive was mandatory, but the subjunctive has by no means disappeared—and it is a frequent source of confusion for writers. Below are some example sentences that use the subjunctive:

The doctor advises that he *quit* smoking immediately.

(*Quit*, not the indicative form *quits*: here the doctor is not telling us that the patient is in fact stopping; he's conveying a strong suggestion.)

The judge insists that she *appear* in court for the trial.

(*Appear*, not *appears*: her presence in court is not a fact at this point but something expected to happen.)

In the above examples, the italicized verbs are both third person singular, which is the only form that differs between indicative and subjunctive in the present tense. If the verb were plural (or first or second person singular), the subjunctive form would be the same as the indicative:

The judge insists that we *appear* in court for the trial.

Since much of the time the subjunctive form is the same as the indicative form, we often use the subjunctive correctly without even thinking about it. This is true with unreal conditional sentences also, where the subjunctive form used is the same as the simple past form:

If I *had* a hammer, I'd hammer in the morning.
If we *went* to Iceland, would you go with us?

Until the second half of the twentieth century it was far more common than it is today to say *if we were to go* instead of *if we went.* Both forms are still acceptable, but the dominant form in formal writing as well as in conversation is the simple past tense. Where people used to say *If I were to send her something,* they would now typically say *If I sent her something.* Note that if the verb in the subjunctive is *to be* (which unlike other verbs has two simple past forms), the subjunctive form is always *were,* never *was.*

If the verb *were* plural, the subjunctive form would be the same.
If she *were* a man, she would have gotten the job.

It is perhaps tempting to say "if the verb *was* plural" or "if she *was* a man," but *was* is the simple past form: it indicates not a present hypothetical but a real situation in the past. "If she *was* a man, she would have gotten the job" suggests that she would be employed now if at some point in the past she actually *was* a man. As much as subjunctive forms play a smaller role in English than they used to, it is still important to use them correctly when called for. Given the difficulties involved, it may be worth spending some time on these.

Active and Passive Voice

As touched on above (P3.6), discussions of the active and passive in writing are often the site of considerable controversy—and considerable confusion. The most frequent reference point in such discussions is George Orwell's "Politics and the English Language," in which Orwell made "never use the passive where you can use the active" one of his six elementary rules of writing. In his essay Orwell persuasively suggests links between verbal subterfuge and political duplicity. Given this background, it is perhaps unsurprising that many have tended to conflate the use of a passive voice (in itself a matter purely of grammar and sentence construction) with the use in general of words to disguise agency—something that may be effected through a variety of verbal means. For example, the sentence *the police officer killed the protestor with a single baton blow to the head* is a simple sentence using the verb *to kill* in the active voice. One way to disguise agency here is to make *the protestor* the subject of the sentence and use the same verb in the passive voice. Such a construction readily allows for the omission of any mention of who wielded the baton: *the protestor was killed by a single baton blow to the head.* But one could also disguise agency with a sentence such as the following: *a blow to the head from a baton was the cause of the protestor's death.* In that case the change is not a matter of shifting from the active to the passive voice but of choosing a different verb.

As background here, it is essential to appreciate that the distinction between active and passive voice is not relevant to all verbs, but only to transitive verbs. You can hit someone or something, and someone or something can be hit by you; the active voice/passive voice distinction is certainly relevant to the verb *to hit.* But you cannot sleep someone or something, or be slept by someone or something; the active voice/passive voice distinction is not relevant to an intransitive verb such as *to sleep*. Nor is it relevant to that most common of verbs, the verb *to be*. In some cases, agency may be disguised by using either the active voice or the passive voice of a verb. Such, for example, is the case with the verb *to violate*, which may be used with the agent as the subject but may also be used with the action itself as the grammatical subject:

> The detention of the suspect without any charges violates her constitutional rights.

> The suspect's constitutional rights are violated by her detention without any charges.

> The prosecutor violated the defendant's constitutional rights by detaining her without laying any charges.

Agency is as much disguised in the first of these sentences as in the second, though the first is in the active voice, the second in the passive voice.

Let us look at another example of disguised agency. The sentence *I knocked that vase off the shelf* uses the past tense *knocked* in the active voice. Switching to the passive voice gives us *that vase was knocked off the shelf*, and of course allows for the option of omitting *by me*; this is one way of disguising agency. But if I wanted to disguise agency in such a situation I would be more likely to choose a different verb entirely, perhaps an intransitive verb such as *to fall* for which the active voice/passive voice distinction is not relevant: *that vase fell off the shelf*.

Many verbal stratagems that disguise agency use the pronoun *it* as the grammatical subject. If someone has just dumped a girlfriend or boyfriend, for example, the "dumper" is not always keen to say *I dumped her* or *I dumped him*. But nor is it likely that the speaker will shift to the passive voice and say *she was dumped by me/he was dumped by me*. Much more likely would be a shift to the use of *it* as the subject, together with intransitive verbs such as *to be* or *to work*: *it is over between us*, for example, or *it just didn't work out*.

It is important to recognize that there is nothing pernicious in itself in using the passive voice. In many cases, indeed, one may wish to use the passive voice in making political points of the sort that Orwell himself would approve of. Orwell himself does precisely this when he wishes to place appropriate emphasis on the recipient of an action—as in the following example, where he is emphasizing the experience of victims as well as the duplicity of language used to describe their suffering: "People are imprisoned for years without trial, or are shot in the back of the neck, or are sent to die of scurvy in Arctic lumber camps: this is called *elimination of unreliable elements*."

awkwardness or wordiness arising from inappropriate use of the passive voice: The passive voice, then, is one means that *may* be used to disguise agency, and it is also a verbal construction that *may* involve awkwardness or unnecessary wordiness. If either is the case, it is often better to rephrase by using the active voice:

needs checking The ceremonial first pitch was thrown by the president. (Passive—9 words) *revised* The president threw the ceremonial first pitch. (Active—7 words)

But again, the passive voice *per se* is not the problem. For more on this issue see the discussion of style in the first section of this text, and the section on writing in scientific disciplines such as biology (C1.4).

M 1.6 Sentence Combining: How to Build Sentences

As they become more and more skilled, writers become more adept at manipulating and varying the structures of their sentences. Such flexibility is a goal all serious writers should aspire to reach, and one of the best ways to achieve it is to engage in a process called sentence combining. As a means of helping students develop facility with more mature sentence structures, this technique goes back to the writing classrooms of the nineteenth century. But it wasn't until the 1960s that sentence combining gained a substantial following among writing teachers, largely because Noam Chomsky's new, highly influential linguistic theory, transformational-generative grammar, appeared to provide a theoretical rationale for this writing exercise. Subsequent research into the effectiveness of sentence combining in improving the fluency and maturity of developing writers' sentence structures gave the technique firm support (Connors 103–07). Since then, newer alternatives to and further development of Chomsky's grammar may also give some insight into the basis for the efficacy of sentence combining (Myers 611–12). But since it works, many are content to leave theoretical discussion to the specialists and simply take advantage of this useful practice.

In its most elementary practice, writers join two or more simple sentences, called "kernels," into a longer sentence or group of sentences. Kernels can be kept as they are and joined with conjunctions or conjunctive adverbs, or they can be embedded into other kernels, a process that often involves shortening the inserted structures. The corollary to combining short sentences is taking apart long sentences in order to examine how they were put together in the first place. Writers can analyze their own sentences in this way as well as those of other, admired authors, becoming conversant with the many options present whenever a writer considers how to express and even create a thought with words. Together, these combining and analyzing procedures are simple but effective. Mastering them confers an important component of the stylistic fluency described in the "Writing Process" chapter of this guide; writers gain greater conscious control over and facility with their sentence structures and sentence variety, become better able to avoid problems like wordiness and repetition, and find elegance and strategic emphasis easier to achieve. Research into writing practices has shown that when unskilled writers revise a draft, they tend to focus exclusively on deleting and changing single words and phrases (Sommers 381–82). What these basic writers often fail to do is reorder and add to their initial material (386); experienced writers, on the other hand, use all of these revision techniques, especially the latter two. Rewriting for them is an entire reworking and rethinking of their arguments (see section P3.8 for more advice in this regard). At the level of sentence style, then, inexperienced writers would do well to include in their studies practice in the reordering of sentences. The work of sentence combining, "de-combining," and recombining affords just such practice.

For many students, another plus of sentence combining and its offshoots is that they don't require an extensive knowledge of grammatical terminology. The exercises work on writers' intuitive understanding of language structures and help practitioners build an increased "feel" for them, which translates into yet another benefit: the ability to avoid certain kinds of grammatical sentence errors. For example, because some sentence combining exercises require kernels to be shortened and embedded as modifiers into other sentences, practice makes it easier to spot dangling constructions and other modifier errors (see as well the discussion on dangling constructions starting on page 254). Working with kernels, which are always short but full sentences, helps students internalize what constitutes a full sentence or main clause and so avoid sentence fragments, run-ons, and comma splices (see also section M3.1). Developing writers are also better able to recognize and write balanced, parallel structures (see pages 100–02 and 297–300 in *The Guide*) after gaining greater awareness of sentence constituents.

A key ability of more experienced writers is reading well. Writers who are also good readers are able to see their own work as a reader would see it and allow that crucial insight to guide their revisions. Combining kernels and reconfiguring the results a few times gives writers more practice in reading at the level of the sentence, and because the process generates a variety of arrangements of the same words, students have an opportunity to compare them and decide which of the structures are most effective and why. It's important to note, though, that sentence combining alone cannot confer the ability to judge such matters well. Enthusiastic combining sessions can produce all manner of unfortunate sentences; an important complementary exercise is analysis both of sentences that work well and of ones that work less well. Those that work well may of course be used as models. Practice in analyzing the work of others also yields another benefit: greater ease in reading more sophisticated and difficult texts. Along the way, students can also examine the elements that make up an individual author's style. All told, diligent sentence "de-combining" and recombining leads to better reading skills, and better reading leads to better writing.

These exercises in sentence manipulation and analysis have been shown to be particularly useful for students who are learning to write in English as an additional language. The kernels and guidelines for combining them in various ways contain both explicit and implicit instructions on how English sentences are structured and on which words can combine with others in which ways (Myers 615–17). All of this information provides EAL students with useful models for their own writing.

For a closer look at sentence combining in action, see the books by William Strong and the articles by Sharon A. Myers, Glenn J. Broadhead and James A. Berlin, and Charles R. Cooper listed in Works Cited at the end of this chapter; these works inform what follows.

Combining

Joining Kernels

One of the simplest ways to combine kernel sentences is to join them with a connecting word or phrase. Deciding on the best connector, of course, depends on the relationship among the kernels' ideas; see the section on joining words (pages 364–86) for advice on appropriate choices.

Consider the following kernels:

1) My ruse was sloppy.
2) My ruse deceived everyone.

Two noticeable features of a list of kernels are their choppiness of style and their tendency towards unnecessary repetition of words and phrases. Two of the tasks of sentence combining, consequently, are to create more fluent structures out of the kernel lists and to avoid wordiness. An obvious strategy in the case of the kernels above is to use a pronoun to replace one of the "my ruse" phrases. Joining the kernels will take care of the choppiness. Because the second kernel reverses the expectations raised by the first, a helpful joining word may be used to signal the contrast between the two. Here are some options for joining them.

A coordinating conjunction:

> My ruse was sloppy, but it deceived everyone.

A subordinating conjunction (note that this conjunction does join the kernels despite its position before one of the kernels rather than between the two):

> Even though my ruse was sloppy, it deceived everyone.

A conjunctive adverb:

> My ruse was sloppy; nevertheless, it deceived everyone.

In some cases, word order can be rearranged somewhat, as in the following example that joins the kernels with the subordinating conjunction "though":

> Sloppy though my ruse was, it deceived everyone.

If a pair of kernels consists of linked or supporting ideas, several connecting words would be suitable (see, for examples, those listed on pages 371–74), but it might also be stylistically effective to join the kernels with only a mark of punctuation. This option makes for a punchier sentence that emphasizes the closeness of relationship between the joined ideas. Consider the following kernels:

1) My ruse was brilliant.
2) My ruse deceived everyone.

Joined with a conjunction, the kernels make a sentence that is satisfactory:

> My ruse was brilliant, and it deceived everyone.

Using only a semicolon as a connector, however, makes a more dramatic alternative:

> My ruse was brilliant; it deceived everyone.

Using a dash instead heightens the drama even further:

> My ruse was brilliant—it deceived everyone.

If one kernel illustrates, specifies, or provides an explanation for the other, a colon is an appropriate connector:

1) She had only one thing to say.
2) Don't touch the chocolate.

She had only one thing to say: don't touch the chocolate.

Embedding Kernels

Structurally more complex sentences can be built by embedding one kernel within another. The embedded kernel can stay whole or substantially so, or parts of it can be deleted to create phrases and even single words for insertion into what then becomes the sentence's main kernel.

WHOLE CLAUSES EMBEDDED WITH PUNCTUATION

Certain marks of punctuation—paired dashes and parentheses, for example—allow for an entire kernel to be embedded in another unchanged.

1) The secret to Edith's success is her stubbornness.
2) The secret cannot be denied.

The secret to Edith's success—it cannot be denied—is her stubbornness.

1) She hung on to the bitter end.
2) She is so very stubborn.

She hung on (she is so very stubborn) to the bitter end.

RELATIVE CLAUSES

An embedded kernel left whole can also take the form of a relative clause, that is, an adjective clause introduced by a relative pronoun (see page 182). Like other pronouns, relative pronouns eliminate some repetition of words or phrases by substituting for them. Below are examples of embedded relative clauses using the relative pronouns *that*, *who*, *which*, *where*, and *when*.

1) The music is the best music of all.
2) The music plays only in Chester's head.

The music that plays only in Chester's head is the best music of all.

Note that in the next two examples, which involve the relative pronoun *who*, the kernel that will become the relative clause in the combined sentence indicates which form, *who* or *whom*, the pronoun should take. In the first example, the pronoun takes the place of the kernel's subject and so takes the subject form, *who*. In the second, the pronoun takes the place of the kernel's object and so takes the object form *whom*. Here is one instance of the ways in which sentence combining practice can help writers master some grammatical rules.

1) Lewis writes the best books.
2) Lewis is despicable.

Lewis, who is despicable, writes the best books.

1) Lewis writes the best books.
2) I despise Lewis.

Lewis, whom I despise, writes the best books.

1) Lewis is despised by all.
2) Lewis's books are the best.

Lewis, whose books are the best, is despised by all.

1) That book is everyone's favourite.
2) No one can understand that book.

That book, which no one can understand, is everyone's favourite.

1) Frieda's thoughts turned to evil at a precise moment.
2) No one knows the precise moment.

No one knows the precise moment when Frieda's thoughts turned to evil.

1) She left him in the attic.
2) No one ever goes to the attic.

She left him in the attic, where no one ever goes.

Abbreviated Kernels Joined as Absolute Phrases

Absolute phrases are shortened kernels that contain nouns and modifiers but no main verb (see page 179 for a definition of verbs). Absolutes often modify entire sentences and attach to them with commas.

1) Willard is an impatient man.
2) The experiment went badly.

Willard being an impatient man, the experiment went badly.

1) No one waited for the banana flambé.
2) The party was already wrecked by Shirley's antics.

The party already wrecked by Shirley's antics, no one waited for the banana flambé.

Abbreviated Kernels Embedded as Verb and Noun Phrases

Kernels can be abbreviated to phrases or even single words before being inserted into other kernels. When the ideas of paired kernels have an equal, independent status, they can be shortened to phrases and joined with coordinating conjunctions.

NOUN PHRASE

1) Dolores always cries while watching *Casablanca*.
2) Stan always cries while watching *Casablanca*.

Dolores and Stan always cry while watching *Casablanca*.

VERB PHRASE

1) Morton sang "Danny Boy."
2) Morton expected our applause.

Morton sang "Danny Boy" and expected our applause.

Abbreviated Kernels Embedded as Modifiers

Shortened kernels can also serve as various kinds of modifiers, including adjectives, adverbs, prepositional phrases, past and present participles, infinitive phrases, and appositives.

KERNELS EMBEDDED AS SINGLE-WORD ADJECTIVES

1) Herman's handshake was floppy.
2) Herman's handshake irritated his in-laws.

Herman's floppy handshake irritated his in-laws.

KERNELS EMBEDDED AS SINGLE-WORD ADVERBS

1) Estelle was doubtful.
2) Estelle frowned at the chocolate mousse bombe.

Estelle frowned doubtfully at the chocolate mousse bombe.

KERNELS EMBEDDED AS PREPOSITIONAL PHRASES

1) The glove looked suspiciously familiar.
2) The glove was in the hallway.

The glove in the hallway looked suspiciously familiar.

1) Terrence threw Mabel's letter.
2) Mabel's letter landed on the fire.

Terrence threw Mabel's letter on the fire.

KERNELS EMBEDDED AS PRESENT PARTICIPLES

1) Walter paddled doggedly.
2) Walter finished another lap of the pool.

Paddling doggedly, Walter finished another lap of the pool.

KERNELS EMBEDDED AS PAST PARTICIPLES

1) Rita's insight was wrapped in obscurity.
2) Rita's insight went unnoticed.

Rita's insight, wrapped in obscurity, went unnoticed.

KERNELS EMBEDDED AS INFINITIVE PHRASES

1) They went home.
2) They reflected on their bad behaviour.

They went home to reflect on their bad behaviour.

KERNELS EMBEDDED AS APPOSITIVES

1) Carl is a wily tactician.
2) Carl always wins at checkers.

A wily tactician, Carl always wins at checkers.

Combining and Recombining

For building effective revision practices, exercises in recombining kernels work very well. The idea is to combine the same list of kernels into several combinations and compare the results. An important decision in any combination is which kernel will form the main clause or clauses of the sentence. The rule of thumb is that the main idea should rest in the main clause. Varying the way the kernels are combined can change the emphasis or even the fundamental idea of a sentence. Consider the following kernels:

1) I love ice cream.
2) I don't eat ice cream often.

The two could be given equivalent status and joined by a coordinating conjunction or conjunctive adverb into a sentence with two main clauses:

> I love ice cream, but I don't eat it often.
>
> I love ice cream; however, I don't eat it often.

In combinations such as this, notice that *but* must stay where it is, while *however* is able to move to a variety of spots in the sentence:

> I love ice cream; I don't, however, eat it often.
>
> I love ice cream; I don't eat it often, however.

Each option is subtly different from the others. Placed at the beginning of its clause, *however* signals an upcoming contrast right away, so readers anticipate some sort of reversal of the first idea. Placed after *I don't*, the transition word interrupts its clause and so emphasizes the idea of not doing something; the shift from the first clause's affirmative statement to the second's negative one is thus immediately more specific than the first sentence's broader signal of contrast. The third sentence delays the transition word until the very end, confronting the readers with a starker contrast between the affirmative and negative statements as their expectations after reading the first clause are suddenly reversed without notice.

Coordinating main clauses is not the only option for these kernels; one clause can be subordinated to the other for still different effects.

> Although I love ice cream, I don't eat it often.
>
> Although I don't eat it often, I love ice cream.

Each kernel becomes the sole main clause in each of the variations above. In the first, the emphasis is on not eating ice cream, while in the second, the focus is on loving it.

Embedding each kernel as a relative clause achieves a similar effect, but again, there are subtle differences:

> I love ice cream, which I don't eat often.
>
> I don't often eat ice cream, which I love.

There, the relative clauses feel more like wistful afterthoughts and less like blunt statements of fact (as in the sentences using *although*).

Here are still more variations with still different effects:

> I love but don't often eat ice cream.
>
> I don't often eat my beloved ice cream.
>
> Despite loving ice cream, I don't often eat it.
>
> Despite not often eating it, I love ice cream.

Depending on a writer's rhetorical purposes, any of these sentences would work well in a larger context. Sentence recombining helps writers see what options are available to them so that they can consider which would be preferable.

Combining Several Kernels into a Single Sentence

The next step after the simple combining of pairs of kernels is to work on joining three, four, and even more kernels. Consider the following list of kernels:

1) Clutter is far from causing certain things.
2) Clutter does not make the mind disorganized.
3) Clutter does not make the mind distracted.
4) Clutter does not make the mind distressed.
5) Clutter can foster thinking.
6) The thinking is creative.
7) Clutter can contain order.
8) The order is of a high degree.
9) The order is not visible to observation.
10) The observation is initial.
11) The observation is casual.

The more kernels in a list, the more options there are for combining them, and the more choices a writer must make. Not all possibilities are equally felicitous, however. It is very possible for an excited sentence combiner to produce questionable sentences. Here is one example:

> You might say that clutter makes the mind disorganized, that it makes the mind distracted, and that it makes the mind distressed, but clutter is far from having these effects; instead, it can foster thinking in a creative manner, and it can also contain a kind of order that is of a high degree but that is not visible to the first glance of the casual observer.

The sentence above is grammatically correct and makes some interesting substitutions and additions to the original list of kernels, but it is unnecessarily wordy and needn't be so long. The goal of sentence combining is never to write the longest, most complex sentence possible. Good writers vary their sentence lengths and recognize the rhetorical value of short, simple sentences for emphasis. For combining exercises involving more than two kernels, leaving one or more kernels uncombined is always an option. Other stylistic choices that such exercises call for are whether kernels should be joined or embedded, where embedded kernels should be placed within the finished sentence, whether transitions or conjunctions would be effective and which ones would work best, and, importantly, which kernel should become the main clause of a combined sentence. The section on stylistic fluency in this book, starting on page 71, gives some guidance on how to make such choices well. Some writers also find reading sentences out loud helpful, and many solicit the opinions of other readers. But particularly beneficial is taking the time to configure and then reconfigure a list of kernels, and then compare the results. Here are two more arrangements of the kernel list above:

> Clutter, far from making the mind disorganized, distracted, and distressed, can foster creative thinking and, moreover, contain a high degree of order not at first visible to casual observation.

> Clutter seems sure to make the mind disorganized, distracted, and distressed. Not so, however—it can actually foster creative thinking. Even more surprising, it can contain a high degree of order, which casual observation may not at first reveal.

Both of the recombinations above are less wordy than the first try and seem better for that reason. Which of the last two you prefer, however, will likely depend on what context you imagine the passages belonging to. The final combination includes more transitional words and so directs readers more strongly toward conclusions to be drawn from the claims it makes. It is also more casual in tone, largely because of phrases like *seems sure to*, and *not so*, and the use of a dash rather than, say, a semicolon. The middle combination is leaner and gives the impression of a less familiar, perhaps more professional voice behind the words.

"De-Combining" and Recombining

While combining kernels improves a writer's understanding of sentence structure, analyzing a complete sentence into its possible constituent kernels yields even more insights. The practice can clarify certain grammar problems (as in the relative clause examples above that use *who* and *whom*), helping writers to avoid them, and in the process, become better readers of their own work, an important skill that sets experienced writers apart from the less skilled. "De-combining" sentences can also help students become better able to read even difficult texts and more adept at grasping the components that make up the styles of a variety of writers and types of writing.

Help with Some Grammatical Errors: Two More Examples

Dangling Modifiers

Inexperienced writers sometimes dangle modifiers (see the section beginning on page 254 for more information on dangling constructions). Sentence combining can help writers recognize and so better avoid this common problem. Consider the following sentence:

> While watching an abominable film, even the popcorn tasted vile.

Dividing the sentence into kernels gives the following result:

1) The popcorn tasted vile.
2) _____ watched a film.
3) The film was abominable.

There is an obvious problem with kernel 2; it has no subject. That's what causes it to dangle when combined with the others. Embedded as a modifier, it attaches to the closest noun, *popcorn*, and creates the unintentionally amusing image of popcorn watching a film. Once the problem is clearly laid out in a kernel list, it's easy to see and to fix:

1) The popcorn tasted vile.
2) We watched a film.
3) The film was abominable.

> Because we were watching an abominable film, even the popcorn tasted vile.
>
> We were watching an abominable film; even the popcorn tasted vile.

Syntactic Ambiguity

Sometimes, unwanted ambiguity in a sentence comes from its syntax, or the arrangement of its words. The following is the title of an anthology of key philosophical texts:

Enduring Issues in Philosophy

The title is not an entire sentence, but there are nonetheless abbreviated kernels underlying it. Analyzing the title shows that it has two possible underlying groups of kernels:

1) Philosophy has issues.
2) The issues have endured.

1) Philosophy has issues.
2) People can endure the issues.

It's doubtful that the publisher of that book intends us to read the second possible meaning of the title, but that reading is nonetheless available. An unambiguous title would combine one of the pairs of kernels above, presumably the first. Here are two possible reconfigurations:

Some Enduring Issues in Philosophy
Philosophy's Enduring Issues.

Help with Reading Challenging Texts

Often, students have difficulty reading the work of authors from earlier eras simply because the language has changed considerably in the interval. Some of the challenge comes from changes in vocabulary, of course, for which the best remedy is to consult a good dictionary or glossary of words from the period. But some confusion can result from unfamiliar sentence structure, too; careful analysis of some sample sentences into their constituent kernels will, with practice, help students raise their literacy skills to the point where such texts no longer pose a problem. Look, for example, at the following passage from Thomas Hobbes's *Leviathan* (16):

> A LAW OF NATURE (*lex naturalis*) is a precept or general rule, found out by reason, by which a man is forbidden to do that which is destructive of his life, or taketh away the means of preserving the same, and to omit that by which he thinketh it may be best preserved. (98)

Here is a possible division of this sentence into kernels:

1) The Latin for "law of nature" is *lex naturalis.*
2) A law of nature is a precept.
3) A law of nature is a general rule.
4) A law of nature is found out by reason.
5) A law of nature forbids a man to do certain things.
6) Some things are destructive of the man's life.
7) Some things take away means.
8) The means are for preserving his life.
9) A law of nature forbids the man to omit certain things.
10) Some things preserve the man's life.
11) The man thinks this.

Recombining these kernels into more contemporary language and, for better understanding, expanding them somewhat can help elucidate Hobbes's meaning.

> A law of nature, which in Latin is called a *lex naturalis,* is a precept or general rule. This kind of law can be discovered by reasoning; that is, the law does not need to be revealed to us by any other agent. A law of nature forbids a person[1] to do anything that would destroy his life or that would take away the means by which he preserves his life. A law of nature also obliges a person to follow any course of action that he thinks will help preserve his life.

The result is perhaps a little more cumbersome than it need be, but it is clear, and the point of this exercise in any case is to understand a challenging passage rather than offer a rewrite of it to a reader.

Here is another example, this time a passage from Sonnet 116 by William Shakespeare.

> Let me not to the marriage of true minds
> Admit impediments. Love is not love
> Which alters when it alteration finds,
> Or bends with the remover to remove.
> O, no, it is an ever-fixèd mark
> That looks on tempests and is never shaken;
> It is the star to every wandering bark,
> Whose worth's unknown, although his height be taken.

---

1 In working through the meaning of a passage such as this, we may also need to ask whether the writer intended words such as man to apply only to males, or to all humans. In this case context makes clear that Hobbes intended the latter.

Part of our potential puzzlement on reading this passage comes again from unfamiliar vocabulary (for example, *remove* means *leave*, not *take away*, and *bark* is a noun meaning *ship*), but the glosses that are now almost always published with Shakespeare's work can help with that. Beyond gaining experience with his words and terms, readers of Shakespeare must gain skill interpreting the structures of his lines of verse. An important first step is to realize that a line does not necessarily constitute a sentence; the periods in the passage above show that it consists of three sentences divided over eight lines. Here is a list of kernels generated from the passage above, with more modern expressions substituted as needed. For ease of analysis, the kernels are grouped according to the sentences they make up, and the kernel that underlies each sentence's main clause or clauses are underlined:

Sentence One

1) Do not let me allow certain things.
2) The things are impediments.
3) The impediments interfere with a marriage.
4) The marriage is between minds.
5) The minds are true.

Sentence Two

1) Certain things can seem like love.
2) These things are not love.
3) One thing changes under a certain circumstance.
4) This thing finds a change (in the one loved).
5) Another thing changes (*bends*) under a certain circumstance.
6) The loved one (*the remover*) goes away.
7) This thing departs (*removes*).

Sentence Three

1) Love is not this thing.
2) Love is a landmark that never moves or changes.
3) The landmark looks at tempests.
4) The landmark is not shaken.
5) Love is a star.
6) The star guides ships.
7) The ships are off course.
8) The star has a worth.
9) The worth is unknown.

10) The star has a height (above the horizon).
11) The height has been measured.

Note that some of the kernels include understood elements that don't appear in the original but that must nonetheless be included in the kernels in order to make them complete. Consider the clause *when it alteration finds*; in order to understand the point of this clause, we need to answer the question *alteration in what?* The line does not directly say what it is that alters, but the context of the rest of the poem, with its focus on the properties of true love, strongly suggests that this hypothetical alteration is in the object of such love.

Once the kernels are carefully written, recombining them yields a paraphrase of the passage. The meaning of much poetic language lies condensed in the structures of its words; the rendering below of the ideas of this sonnet includes an interpretive expansion of the metaphors used in the poem.

> Do not let me allow impediments to the marriage of minds that are true to one another. Some things can seem like love, but they are not love. For example, if a supposed lover changes his or her attitude when there is a change in the loved one, it is not love. Similarly, when a supposed lover stops loving if the beloved is gone, it is not love. Love is like an unchanging landmark at sea. Such a landmark is witness to tempests, but storms cannot move or change it. Likewise, love does not change or fall if there is any upheaval in its circumstances. Love is like a guiding star that helps every ship that's gone off course find its way. Such a star has a worth so great that it cannot be known, even if its physical height above the horizon has been measured. Likewise, the worth of love is too great to know, even if love's more mundane details can be described.

The process of analysis again helps to clarify the original meaning and points to the places where material must be added to or expanded on in order to facilitate this illumination. The subsequent recombination of the kernels is thus an exercise in careful interpretation of what rests within the poetic language. The paraphrase is again ungraceful, and because it provides a single reading with little possibility of variation in its own interpretation, it paints a unidimensional picture of a deeply textured original. But all that just serves to highlight the beauty and mastery of the sonnet, in which multiple meanings are folded into musical lines.

Gaining Awareness of Writing Style

A particular benefit of sentence "de-combining" comes from analyzing the work of admired writers. A close look at their sentences reveals sentence strategies that less experienced writers can use as models for their own writing. It may also serve to illuminate the characteristics of a given writer's style or the characteristics of a particular genre of writing.

Below is a passage by Lewis Thomas, a non-fiction writer justly praised for his prose style:

> I am a member of a fragile species, still new to the earth, the youngest creatures of any scale, here only a few moments as evolutionary time is measured, a juvenile species, a child of a species. We are only tentatively set in place, error-prone, at risk of fumbling, in real danger at the moment of leaving behind only a thin layer of our fossils, radioactive at that. (25)

Here is a list of kernels generated from the passage by Thomas. Again, the kernels are grouped according to the sentences they are part of, with the main clause kernels underlined:

Sentence One

1) <u>I am a member of a species</u>.
2) The species is fragile.
3) The species is new to the earth.
4) The species consists of creatures.
5) The creatures are the youngest.
6) All creatures are ranked on many scales.
7) The creatures are here over moments.
8) The moments are few.
9) The moments are measured.
10) The measurement is of evolutionary time.
11) The species is juvenile.
12) The species is a child.

Sentence Two

1) <u>We are set in place</u>.
2) The setting is temporary.
3) We are error-prone.
4) We are at risk.
5) The risk is of fumbling.

6) We are in danger.
7) The danger is real.
8) The danger is now.
9) The danger is of leaving a residue.
10) The residue is the only one.
11) The residue is a layer.
12) The layer is of fossils.
13) The layer is thin.
14) The fossils are radioactive.

The list of kernels makes some aspects of Thomas's style jump out. Both of the two sentences that make up the passage start with a main clause made up of a whole kernel without any kind of transition leading in to it. Each of the sentence-opening kernels has another kernel embedded in it as a single-word modifier: *fragile* and *tentatively*. A series of abbreviated kernels acting as modifiers then follows each main clause. In the first sentence, if we consider the first three phrases following the main clause, *still new to the earth*, *the youngest creatures of any scale*, and *here only a few moments as evolutionary time is measured*, we can see that they are progressively more complex—each contains more embedded kernels than the last. The final two phrases of sentence one, *a juvenile species* and *a child of a species*, are then again made up of simple abbreviated kernels.

The pattern of the second sentence is similar, though not exactly the same. Set off by commas after the main clause are three phrases that are again progressively more complex: *error-prone*, *at risk of fumbling*, and *in real danger at the moment of leaving behind only a thin layer of our fossils*. The sentence then ends with one simple abbreviated kernel: *radioactive*. The two sentences together, then, create a pleasing symmetry that is varied just enough to keep it from being rigid. Another graceful touch is the pairing of a whole kernel with a list of abbreviated kernels in each sentence. Within the lists themselves, the movement in the modifying phrases toward greater complexity gives each sentence a momentum that is softly slowed with the simple closing kernels. In all, these structural elements contribute to the elegance of the passage.

Here, from Ursula K. Le Guin's novel *Lavinia*, is a passage of fictional prose that reveals the author's skill in crafting language. The speaker is Lavinia, a young woman. Her future husband, Aeneas, is looking with his people for a new homeland and has just arrived in her country.

> And in the twilight of morning of the next day, alone, kneeling in the mud by Tiber, I saw the great ships turn from the sea and come into the river. I saw my husband stand on the high stern of the first ship, though he did not see me. He gazed up the dark river, praying, dreaming. He did not see the deaths that lay before him, all along the river, all the way to Rome. (95)

This passage can be "de-combined" into kernels as follows (the italicized kernel of sentence two is a full but subordinate clause):

Sentence One

1) It was twilight.
2) It was morning.
3) It was the next day.
4) I was alone.
5) I was kneeling in the mud.
6) The mud was by the Tiber.
7) I saw ships.
8) The ships were great.
9) The ships turned from the sea.
10) The ships came into the river.

Sentence Two

1) I saw my husband.
2) My husband stood on the stern.
3) The stern was of the first ship.
4) The stern was high.
5) *My husband did not see me.*

Sentence Three

1) My husband gazed up the river.
2) The river was dark.
3) My husband was praying.
4) My husband was dreaming.

Sentence Four

1) My husband did not see the deaths.
2) The deaths lay before him.
3) The deaths lay all along the river.
4) The deaths lay all the way to Rome.

Kernel analysis shows that Le Guin's passage also has an overall symmetry, though again it is not strict. The passage pulls the reader along from sentence to sentence with a pattern in which structures are mirrored by what follows next across sentence boundaries. After opening with six abbreviated kernels, the first sentence consists of one main clause, *I saw the great ships*, with three kernels embedded in it. The very next clause at the start of sentence two, *I saw my husband stand*, also contains three shortened kernels serving as modifiers. In structure (as well as wording), it closely repeats the pattern of the first sentence's main clause: *I saw the great ships turn* and *I saw my husband stand* echo one another substantially, and both are similarly followed by a short series of abbreviated kernels.

The next full clause is the second, subordinate clause of the second sentence, *he did not see me*. This clause, again a whole kernel, is itself echoed, though again not rigidly, by the next clause, which opens sentence three: *He gazed up the dark river*. This clause also consists of an unshortened kernel, though it has one embedded modifier. Attached to the end of this clause are two kernels abbreviated into a pair of present participles, *praying* and *dreaming*. That structure is loosely repeated in the next sentence, which features a whole kernel, *He did not see the deaths*, with one embedment (the relative clause *that lay before him*), to which are attached a pair of kernels shortened into two prepositional phrases, *all along the river* and *all the way to Rome*.

All of these echoed structures are contained within a whole that has its own mirror symmetry: the passage begins with six abbreviated kernels leading into a main clause, and ends with a main clause leading to three abbreviated kernels. These strings of shortened kernels slow the reader's progress, creating a heightened anticipation at the start of the passage and a sense of ending and inevitability at the close. In addition, the four kernels that are left whole are similar in wording and thematically linked; *I saw*, *I saw*, *He gazed*, and *He did not see* are all about seeing and not seeing, key themes in the novel as a whole. That these clauses have little or nothing embedded directly within them makes them stand out, startling and grave; the important themes they embody are thus highlighted and reinforced.

As the structure of such samples suggests, an almost but not quite exact symmetry is a common feature of powerful prose—both fictional and non-fictional.

Finally, consider the opening to the play *Glengarry Glen Ross* by David Mamet. The speaker is Shelly Levene, a real estate salesman in imminent danger of losing his job; he is addressing John Williamson, his supervisor:

> **Levene:** John ... John ... John. Okay. John. John. Look: *(Pause.)* The Glengarry Highland's leads, you're sending Roma out. Fine. He's a good man. We know what he is. He's fine. All I'm saying, you look at the *board*, he's throwing ... wait, wait, wait, he's throwing them *away*, he's throwing the leads away. All that I'm saying, that you're wasting leads. I don't want to tell you your *job*. All that I'm saying, things get *set*, I know they do, you get a certain *mindset*.... A guy gets a reputation. We know how this ... all I'm saying, put a *closer* on the job. There's more than one man for the ... Put a ... wait a second, put a *proven man out* ... (15)

A possible breakdown of the passage into kernels is as follows:

1) John, listen. (uttered four times)
2) John, look.
3) You are sending Roma out.
4) Roma (is to do something).
5) Roma (will close) the Glengarry Highland leads.
6) That is fine.
7) Roma is a good man.
8) We know Roma.
9) Roma is (a certain kind of salesman).
10) Roma is fine.
11) I am saying only one thing.
12) Look at the board.
13) Roma is throwing the leads away. (uttered three times)
14) John, wait. (uttered three times)
15) I am saying only one thing.
16) You are wasting leads.
17) I don't want to tell you something.
18) Your job (is a certain thing).
19) I am saying only one thing.
20) Things get set.
21) I know they do.
22) You get a mindset.
23) The mindset is a certain kind.
24) A guy gets a reputation.
25) We know something.

26) This happens (in a certain way).
27) I am only saying one thing.
28) Put a closer on the job.
29) More than one man is suitable.
30) The suitability is for the (job).
31) Put a (closer on the job).
32) John, wait a second.
33) Put a man out.
34) The man is proven.

The kernel list makes several remarkable features of the passage immediately apparent. Four kernels (1, 11, 13, and 14) are repeated several times, with three of the repetitions (all but kernel 11) occurring in sequence. Other kernels are close but not exact repetitions: *Roma is a good man* and *Roma is fine*, and *put a closer on the job* and *put a proven man out*, for example. Very few kernels are embedded into others; in fact, almost all of the passage's sentences either consist of single, unembellished kernels or are a string of simple kernels. Some of the kernels as represented in the passage are incomplete: for example, *John* for *John, listen to me*; *all I'm saying* for *I'm only saying one thing*; and *The Glengarry Highland's leads, you're sending Roma out*, with the connection between the two elements left unspoken. Several of the kernels are also conceptually incomplete: how do things get set, and what are those things? What sort of mindset does one get about what? What kind of reputation does a guy get, and how?

These arresting features create some important effects. With its many broken and repeated kernels, the passage closely mimics spontaneous speech and implies non-verbal responses by Williamson to which Levene subsequently reacts. Both stylistic effects are common to drama, particularly modern drama. The choppy strings of simple and incomplete kernels also help establish Levene's emotional agitation. But the structure of the passage has thematic significance, as well. Throughout the play, salesmen use words to manipulate one another and their clients ruthlessly; what is implied by and left out of the utterances creates a subtext that has a crucial importance to the circumstances of each man. Unspoken completions to fragmented kernels imply a shared understanding and friendly intimacy, neither of which may actually exist. But their apparent existence is all that matters. Levene is clearly trying hard to play this game well, to manoeuvre Williamson into giving him a break. The gradual deterioration of the speech graphically illustrates Levene's growing desperation as he feels his skill at closing a "sale" slip away.

With great skill, Mamet has built word structures that fulfill a writing purpose quite different from Le Guin's.

Works Cited

Broadhead, Glenn J., and James A. Berlin. "Twelve Steps to Using Generative Sentences and Sentence Combining in the Composition Classroom." *College Composition and Communication*, vol. 32, no. 3, 1981, pp. 295–307. *JSTOR*, www.jstor.org/stable/356192.

Connors, Robert J. "The Erasure of the Sentence." *College Composition and Communication*, vol. 52, no. 1, 2000, pp. 96–128. *JSTOR*, www.jstor.org/stable/358546.

Cooper, Charles R. "An Outline for Writing Sentence-Combining Problems." *The English Journal*, vol. 62, no. 1, 1973, pp. 96–108. *JSTOR*, www.jstor.org/stable/814087.

Eichhoefer, Gerald W., editor. *Enduring Issues in Philosophy*. Greenhaven, 1995.

Hobbes, Thomas. *Leviathan*. 1651. Edited by A.P. Martinich, Broadview Press, 2002.

Le Guin, Ursula K. *Lavinia*. Harcourt, 2008.

Mamet, David. *Glengarry Glen Ross*. Grove, 1982.

Myers, Sharon A. "ReMembering the Sentence." *College Composition and Communication*, vol.54, no.4, 2003, pp. 610–28. *JSTOR*, www.jstor.org/stable/3594187.

Shakespeare, William. "Sonnet 116." *The Longman Anthology of British Literature*, David Damrosch, general editor, vol. 1, Longman-Addison, 1999, pp. 1176.

Sommers, Nancy. "Revision Strategies of Student Writers and Experienced Adult Writers." *College Composition and Communication*, vol. 31, no. 4, 1980, pp. 378–88. *JSTOR*, www.jstor.org/stable/356588.

Strong, William. *Sentence Combining: A Composing Book*. 3rd ed., McGraw Hill, 1994.

—. *Writer's Toolbox: A Sentence-Combining Workshop*. McGraw Hill, 1996.

Thomas, Lewis. "The Art and Craft of Memoir." *The Fragile Species*, Touchstone, 1992, pp. 16–27.

M2 USAGE

M2.1 Verb Issues

Dangling Constructions

An error made frequently by writers at all levels of ability—including holders of graduate degrees in English—is allowing large chunks of sentences to "dangle," unrelated grammatically to the core of the sentence. For that reason several pages are devoted here to that problem.

> **On the Companion Website**
>
> In *The Broadview Guide* we group together under the heading **dangling constructions** types of error that in many other texts are treated as separate categories. Information on the complex taxonomy of *dangling modifers*, *misplaced modifiers*, and *squinting modifiers* is provided alongside a range of relevant exercises at **sites.broadviewpress.com/writingcdn**. Click on **Exercises** and go to **M2.1**.

Dangling Participles and Infinitives

A present participle is an *-ing* word (*going*, *thinking*, etc.). When combined with a form of the verb *to be*, participles form part of a finite verb. They can also be used in a number of ways on their own (as non-finite verbs), however:

The president felt that visiting China would be unwise at that time.
(Here *visiting China* acts as a noun phrase.)

Having taken into account the various reports, the committee decided to delay the project for a year.
(Here *having taken into account the various reports* acts as an adjectival phrase modifying the noun *committee*.)

Dangling present participles or participial phrases: The danger of dangling occurs with sentences such as the second example above. If the writer does not take care that the participial phrase refers to the subject of the main clause, some absurd sentences can result:

needs checking Waiting for a bus, a brick fell on my head.
(Bricks do not normally wait for buses.)

revised While I was waiting for a bus, a brick fell on my head.

needs checking Leaving the room, the lights must be turned off. (Lights do not normally leave the room.)

revised When you leave the room you must turn off the lights.

In sentences such as these the amusing error is relatively easy to notice; it can be much more difficult with longer and more complex sentences. Even seasoned writers and public speakers can easily find themselves using dangling constructions. Here, for example, is what one prominent politician said as he contemplated the prospect of resigning his position: "Although still hypothetical, I would be better able to devote myself to my family." What he meant to say, of course, was that the prospect of his resignation was hypothetical—not that *he* was hypothetical.

Experienced writers are especially alert to this pitfall if they begin a sentence with a participle or participial phrase that describes a mental operation; they are wary of beginning by *considering*, *believing*, *taking into account*, *remembering*, *turning for a moment*, or *regarding*:

needs checking Believing that he had done no wrong, the fact of being accused of dishonesty infuriated the company's CEO.

revised Believing that he had done no wrong, the company's CEO was infuriated at being accused of dishonesty.

or The company's CEO was infuriated at being accused of dishonesty; he believed he had done no wrong.

needs checking Considering all the above-mentioned studies, the evidence shows conclusively that smoking can cause cancer.

revised Considering all the above-mentioned studies, we conclude that smoking causes cancer.

better These studies show conclusively that smoking can cause cancer.

needs checking Turning for a moment to the thorny question of Joyce's style, the stream of consciousness technique realistically depicts the workings of the human mind.

revised Turning for a moment to the thorny question of Joyce's style, we may observe that his stream of consciousness technique realistically depicts the workings of the human mind.

better Joyce's style does not make *Ulysses* easy to read, but his stream of consciousness technique realistically depicts the workings of the human mind.

needs checking Taking into account the uncertainty as to the initial temperature of the beaker, the results are not conclusive.

revised Taking into account the uncertainty as to the initial temperature of the beaker necessitates that the results be deemed inconclusive.

better Since the initial temperature of the beaker was not recorded, the results are inconclusive.

Notice that in each case the best way to eliminate the problem is to dispense with the participial phrase entirely. More often than not one's writing is improved by using active verbs rather than participial phrases. Many people seem to feel that writing which is filled with participial phrases somehow sounds more important; in fact, such phrases tend to obscure the writer's meaning under unnecessary padding. This is true even when the participles are not dangling:

needs checking Another characteristic having a significant impact on animal populations is the extreme diurnal temperature range on the desert surface.

(Can a characteristic have an impact? A small point is here buried in a morass of meaningless abstraction.)

better The extreme diurnal temperature range on the desert surface also affects animal populations.

needs checking Referring generally to the social stratification systems of the city as a whole, we can see clearly that types of accommodation, varying throughout in accordance with income levels and other socio-economic factors, display an extraordinary diversity.

(Is there anything either clear or extraordinary about this?)

better In this city rich people and poor people live in different neighbourhoods, and rich people live in larger houses than poor people.

By cutting out the padding in this way the writer may occasionally find to his surprise that instead of saying something rather weighty and important as he had thought he was doing, he is in fact saying little or nothing. But he should not be discouraged if this happens; the same is true for all writers. The best response is simply to chuckle and scratch out the sentence!

dangling past participles (e.g., *considered*, *developed*, *regarded*): The same sorts of problems that occur with present participles occur frequently with past participles as well:

needs checking Considered from a cost point of view, Combarp Capital Corporation could not really afford to purchase Skinflint Securities.

(Combarp is not being considered; the purchase is.)

poor Considered from the point of view of cost, the purchase of Skinflint Securities was not a wise move by Combarp Capital Corporation.

better Combarp Capital Corporation could not really afford to buy Skinflint Securities.

needs checking Once regarded as daringly modern in its portrayal of fashionable *fin de siècle* decadence, Wilde draws on traditional patterns to create a powerful new Gothic tale. (*The Cambridge Guide to Literature in English*)

(The novel is an *it*; Oscar Wilde was a *he*.)

revised *The Picture of Dorian Gray* was once regarded as daringly modern in its portrayal of fashionable *fin de siècle* decadence. In the novel Wilde draws on traditional patterns to create a powerful new Gothic tale.

needs checking Used with frequency, a man will feel refreshed and rejuvenated. (aftershave advertisement)

revised Used with frequency, this product will help a man feel refreshed and rejuvenated.

dangling infinitive phrases:

needs checking To conclude this essay, the French Revolution was a product of many interacting causes.

(The French Revolution concluded no essays.)

poor To conclude this essay, I would like to say that the French Revolution was a product of many causes.

better The explanations given for the French Revolution, then, are not mutually exclusive; it was a product of many interacting causes.

(A good writer does not normally need to tell her readers that she is concluding an essay; they can see the space at the bottom of the page. A little word such as *then*, set off by commas, is more than enough to signal that this is a summing-up.)

needs checking To receive a complimentary copy, the business reply card should be returned before June 30.

(The card will not receive anything.)

revised To receive a complimentary copy, you should return the business reply card before June 30.

needs checking To appreciate the full significance of the Camp David Accords, a range of factors needs to be considered.

(A factor cannot appreciate.)

poor To appreciate the full significance of the Camp David Accords, we need to consider many things.

better The Camp David Accords were important in many ways.

dangling gerund or prepositional phrases:

needs checking In reviewing the evidence, one point stands out plainly.

(A point cannot review evidence.)

poor In reviewing the evidence, we can see one point standing out plainly.

better One point stands out plainly from this evidence.

needs checking When analyzing the figures, ways to achieve substantial savings can be discerned.

(The ways cannot analyze.)

poor When we analyze the figures we can see ways to achieve substantial savings.

better The figures suggest that we can greatly reduce our expenses.

Other sorts of phrases can be caught dangling too. But almost all writers are capable of attaching them properly if they re-read and revise their work carefully.

needs checking On behalf of city council and the people of Duluth, it gives me great pleasure to welcome you to our city. (from an announcement by the mayor)

(The mayor, not a faceless *it*, is acting on behalf of the others.)

revised On behalf of city council and the people of Duluth, I am pleased to welcome you to our city.

needs checking By adding more component parts to the prototype, this would cause an increase in the price of the product.

revised By adding more component parts to the prototype, we force an increase in the price of the product.

or Adding more component parts to the prototype makes it necessary to increase the price of the product.

A dangling modifier is not always cause for confusion, but don't assume that your intended meaning will be clear to your reader. "One morning I shot an elephant in my pajamas," said the comedian Groucho Marx. You might think the meaning is obvious, until he says the punch-line: "How he got into my pajamas I'll never know."

Sequence of Tenses

If the main verb of a sentence is in the past tense, other verbs must also express a past viewpoint (except when a general truth is being expressed). Some writers have trouble keeping the verb tenses they use in agreement, particularly when indirect speech is involved, or when a quotation is incorporated into a sentence.

agreement of tenses in indirect speech—past plus subjunctive:

needs checking He said that he will fix the engine before the end of the year.

revised He said that he would fix the engine before the end of the year.

(*He said that he will fix the engine* implies that the fixing has not yet occurred but may still occur.)

agreement of tenses in indirect speech—past plus past perfect:

needs checking He claimed that he smoked drugs many years earlier, but that he never inhaled.

revised He claimed that he had smoked drugs many years earlier, but that he had never inhaled.

agreement of tenses—quoted material:

needs checking Prime Minister Rudd admitted that "such a policy is not without its drawbacks."

(The past tense *admitted* and the present tense *is* do not agree.)

There are two ways of dealing with a difficulty such as this:

(a) Change the sentence so as to set off the quotation without using the connecting word *that*. Usually this can be done with a colon. In this case the tense you use does not have to agree with the tense used in the quotation. The words before the colon, though, must be able to act as a complete sentence in themselves.

(b) Use only that part of the quotation that can be used in agreement with the tense of the main verb:

revised Prime Minister Rudd did not claim perfection: "such a policy is not without its drawbacks," he admitted.

or Prime Minister Rudd admitted that such a policy was "not without its drawbacks."

Here are some other examples:

needs checking Churchill promised that "we shall fight on the beaches, ... we shall fight in the fields and in the streets, we shall fight in the hills; we shall never surrender."

(This suggests that you, the writer, will be among those fighting.)

revised Churchill made the following promise: "We shall fight on the beaches, ... we shall fight in the fields and in the streets, we shall fight in the hills; we shall never surrender."

(Notice that the word *that* is now removed.)

or Churchill promised that the British people would "fight on the beaches, ... in the fields and in the streets, ... in the hills," and that they would "never surrender."

On the Companion Website

Exercises on sequence of tenses may be found at **sites.broadviewpress.com/writingcdn**. Click on **Exercises** and **Writing Mechanics** and go to **"Verbs."**

Irregular or Difficult Verbs

The majority of verbs in English follow a regular pattern—*I open* in the simple present tense, *I opened* in the simple past tense, *I have opened* in the present perfect tense, and so forth. However, most of the more frequently used verbs are in some way or another irregular. To pick an obvious example, we say *I went* instead of *I goed*, and *I have gone* instead of *I have goed*. What follows is a list of the main irregular or difficult verbs in English. The past participle (column 3) is used in tenses such as the present perfect (e.g., *I have grown*, *he has found*) and the past perfect (*I had grown*, *I had found*).

The verbs that most frequently cause problems are given special treatment in the following list:

(Note: In both regular and irregular verbs, the present tense is formed by using the infinitive without the preposition *to*.)

Present & Infinitive	*Simple Past*	*Past Participle*
arise	arose	arisen

check A problem had arose even before the discussion began.
revised A problem had arisen even before the discussion began.

awake	awoke	awoken/woken
	(passive: *was awakened*)	
be	was/were	been
bear	bore	borne

check It was heartbreaking for her to lose the child after having bore it for so long.
revised It was heartbreaking for her to lose the child after having borne it for so long.

beat	beat	beaten

check The Yankees were badly beat by the Blue Jays.
revised The Yankees were badly beaten by the Blue Jays.

become	became	become
begin	began	begun

check He had already began treatment when I met him.
revised He had already begun treatment when I met him.

bend	bent	bent
bite	bit	bitten
bleed	bled	bled
blow	blew	blown
break	broke	broken
bring	brought	brought
build	built	built
burn	burned/burnt	burned/burnt
burst	burst	burst

check The pipes bursted while we were on holiday.
revised The pipes burst while we were on holiday.

buy	bought	bought
can	could	been able
catch	caught	caught

	Present & Infinitive	*Simple Past*	*Past Participle*
	choose	chose	chosen

check In 1999 East Timor choose to become a nation.
revised In 1999 East Timor chose to become a nation.

cling	clung	clung
come	came	come
cost	cost	cost
dig	dug	dug
dive	dived/dove	dived

less accepted He dove into the shallow water.
more formal He dived into the shallow water.

do	did	done
drag	dragged	dragged

check The newspapers drug up a lot of scandal about her.
revised The newspapers dragged up a lot of scandal about her.

draw	drew	drawn
dream	dreamed/dreamt	dreamed/dreamt
drink	drank	drunk

check He has drank more than is good for him.
revised He has drunk more than is good for him.

drive	drove	driven
eat	ate	eaten
fall	fell	fallen
feel	felt	felt
fight	fought	fought
find	found	found
fit	fit	fitted
flee	fled	fled
fling	flung	flung

check George flinged his plate across the room.
revised George flung his plate across the room.

fly	flew	flown
forbid	forbade	forbidden

check Yesterday he forbid us to climb the fence.
revised Yesterday he forbade us to climb the fence.

Present & Infinitive	*Simple Past*	*Past Participle*
forecast	forecast	forecast

check The weather office has forecasted more rain.
revised The weather office has forecast more rain.

forget	forgot	forgotten
forgive	forgave	forgiven
freeze	froze	frozen
get	got	got
give	gave	given
go	went	gone
grind	ground	ground
(e.g., *I have ground the coffee.*)		
grow	grew	grown
hang	hanged/hung	hanged/hung

Note: *Hanged* is used only when referring to a person being killed by hanging. Say *The criminal has been hanged*, but *We have hung the picture on the wall*:

check No one has been publicly hung in Canada since 1962.
revised No one has been publicly hanged in Canada since 1962.

have	had	had
hear	heard	heard
hide	hid	hidden
hit	hit	hit
hold	held	held
hurt	hurt	hurt
keep	kept	kept

On the Companion Website

Exercises on irregular or difficult verbs may be found at **sites.broadviewpress.com/writingcdn**. Click on **Exercises** and **Writing Mechanics** and go to **"Verbs."**

M2
Usage

Present & Infinitive	*Simple Past*	*Past Participle*
kneel	knelt	knelt
know	knew	known
lay	laid	laid

(Note: Although many authorities feel that the distinction is not worth troubling over in informal English, formal English still distinguishes between *lay* and *lie*; you *lay* something on a table, and a hen *lays* eggs, but you *lie* down to sleep. In other words, *lie* is an intransitive verb; it should not be followed by a direct object. *Lay*, by contrast, is transitive.)

check That old thing has been laying around for years.
revised That old thing has been lying around for years.

lead	led	led
lean	leaned/leant	leaned/leant
leap	leaped/leapt	leaped/leapt
learn	learned/learnt	learned/learnt
leave	left	left
lend	lent	lent
let	let	let
lie	lay	lain

check He asked if I would like to lay down and rest.
revised He asked if I would like to lie down and rest.

light	lighted/lit	lighted/lit
lose	lost	lost
make	made	made
may	might	
mean	meant	meant
meet	met	met
must	had to	had to
pay	paid	paid
plead	pleaded/pled	pleaded/pled

(Note: The growing use of *pled* rather than *pleaded* irks some traditionalists, but it is difficult to see why *pleaded* should not follow *leaded* to the grave where the latter was long ago led. If you are trying to please a traditionalist professor, it is probably still best to avoid *pled*. Otherwise, use consistently whichever of the two you prefer.)

accepted He had pled guilty to the same offence previously.
accepted He had pleaded guilty to the same offence previously.

Present & Infinitive	*Simple Past*	*Past Participle*
prove	proved	proven

check We have proved the hypothesis to be correct.
revised We have proven the hypothesis to be correct.

put	put	put
read	read	read
ride	rode	ridden

check The actor had never rode a horse before.
revised The actor had never ridden a horse before.

ring	rang	rung

check I rung the bell three times, but no one answered.
revised I rang the bell three times, but no one answered.

rise	rose	risen
run	ran	run
saw	sawed	sawed/sawn
say	said	said
see	saw	seen
seek	sought	sought
sell	sold	sold
sew	sewed	sewed/sewn
shake	shook	shaken
shall	should	
shine	shone	shone

check The moon shined almost as brightly as the sun.
revised The moon shone almost as brightly as the sun.

(Note: *Shined* is the accepted formation of the simple past tense where the verb is transitive. Thus we say *she shined her shoes*.)

shoot	shot	shot
show	showed	showed/shown
shrink	shrank	shrunk

check The government's majority shrunk in the election.
revised The government's majority shrank in the election.

M2 Usage

Present & Infinitive	*Simple Past*	*Past Participle*
shut	shut	shut
sing	sang	sung
sink	sank	sunk

check The *Edmund Fitzgerald* sunk on Lake Superior.
revised The *Edmund Fitzgerald* sank on Lake Superior.

sit	sat	sat
sleep	slept	slept
slide	slid	slid
smell	smelled/smelt	smelled/smelt
sow	sowed	sowed/sown
speak	spoke	spoken
speed	speeded/sped	speeded/sped
spell	spelled/spelt	spelled/spelt
spend	spent	spent
spill	spilled/spilt	spilled/spilt
spin	spun	spun
spit	spat	spat
split	split	split
spread	spread	spread
spring	sprang	sprung

check The soldiers hurriedly sprung to their feet.
revised The soldiers hurriedly sprang to their feet.

stand	stood	stood
steal	stole	stolen
stick	stuck	stuck
sting	stung	stung
strike	struck	struck
swear	swore	sworn
sweep	swept	swept
swim	swam	swum

check Pictures were taken while the royal couple swum in what they thought was a private cove.
revised Pictures were taken while the royal couple swam in what they had thought was a private cove.

Present & Infinitive	*Simple Past*	*Past Participle*
swing	swung	swung
take	took	taken
teach	taught	taught
tear	tore	torn
tell	told	told
think	thought	thought
throw	threw	thrown
tread	trod	trodden/trod
understand	understood	understood
wake	woke	woken
wear	wore	worn
weep	wept	wept
win	won	won
wind	wound	wound
wring	wrung	wrung
(e.g., *She wrings out her clothes if they are wet.*)		
write	wrote	written

Infinitives, Gerunds, Objects: "To Be or Not To Be?"

gerunds and prepositions: Gerunds have the form of verbs but act as nouns, and as such they do not necessarily require any preposition to introduce them. In particular, when a gerund does not relate to a preceding verb, it should not be accompanied by a preposition. Nor does it require a pronoun to stand in for it as the subject of a verb:

needs checking With using coal-fired generators, it is bad for the environment.

revised Using coal-fired generators is bad for the environment.

When a gerund follows a verb, however, it often must be introduced by a preposition—and unfortunately, there are no rules governing when this happens, or which preposition should be used. More broadly, there are no rules in English to explain why some words must be followed by an infinitive (*to go*, *to do*, *to be*, etc.), while others must be followed by a preposition plus a gerund (*of going*, *in doing*, etc.), and still others by a direct object. Following are some of the words with which difficulties of this sort most often arise:

• **accept something** (not *accept to do something*): It needs a direct object.

needs checking The committee accepted to try to improve the quality of the postal service.
revised The committee accepted the task of trying to improve the postal service.
or The committee agreed to try to improve the postal service.

• **accuse someone of doing something** (not *to do*)

needs checking Klaus Barbie was accused to have killed thousands of innocent civilians in WW II.
revised Klaus Barbie was accused of having killed thousands of innocent civilians in WW II.

• **appreciate something**: When used to mean *be grateful*, this verb requires a direct object.

needs checking I would appreciate if you could respond quickly.
revised I would appreciate it if you could respond quickly.
or I would appreciate a quick response.
(The verb *appreciate* without an object means *increase in value*.)

• **assist in doing something** (not *to do*)

needs checking He assisted me to solve the problem.
revised He assisted me in solving the problem.
or He helped me to solve the problem.

• **capable of doing something** (not *to do*)

needs checking He is capable to run 1500 metres in under four minutes.
revised He is capable of running 1500 metres in under four minutes.
or He is able to run 1500 metres in under four minutes.

• **confident of doing something** (not *to do*)

needs checking She is confident to be able to finish the job before dusk.
revised She is confident of being able to finish the job before dusk.
or She is confident that she will finish the job before dusk.

• **consider something or someone to be something** or **consider it something** (not *as something*)

needs checking According to a recent policy paper, the party now considers a guaranteed annual income as a good idea.

revised According to a recent policy paper, the party now considers a guaranteed annual income to be a good idea.

or According to a recent policy paper, the party now regards a guaranteed annual income as a good idea.

- **discourage someone from doing something** (not *to do*)

needs checking The new Immigration Act is intended to discourage people to enter the country illegally.

revised The new Immigration Act is intended to discourage people from entering the country illegally.

- **forbid someone to do something** (not *from doing*)

needs checking The witnesses were forbidden from leaving the scene of the crime until the police had completed their preliminary investigation.

revised The witnesses were forbidden to leave the scene of the crime until the police had completed their preliminary investigation.

EAL

For particular problems with infinitives, gerunds, and objects faced by those whose native language is not English, see Section M4.

- **insist on doing something** or **insist that something be done** (but not *insist to do*)

needs checking The customer has insisted to wait in the front office until she receives a refund.

revised The customer has insisted on waiting in the front office until she receives a refund.

- **intention**: *Have an intention of doing something* but *someone's intention is/was to do something*

needs checking Hitler had no intention to keep his word.

revised Hitler had no intention of keeping his word.

or Hitler did not intend to keep his word.

or Hitler's intention was to break the treaty.

- **justified in doing something** (not *to do something*)

needs checking He is not justified to make these allegations.
revised He is not justified in making these allegations.

- **look forward to doing something** (not *to do something*)

needs checking I am looking forward to receive your reply.
revised I am looking forward to receiving your reply.

- **opposed to doing something** (not *to do something*)

needs checking He was opposed to set up a dictatorship.
revised He was opposed to setting up a dictatorship.
or He was opposed to the idea of setting up a dictatorship.

- **organize something** (not *to do something*)

needs checking We organized to meet at ten the next morning.
revised We organized a meeting for ten the next morning.
or We arranged to meet at ten the next morning.

- **persist in doing something** (not *to do something*)

needs checking Despite international disapproval, the Reagan administration persisted to help the rebels in Nicaragua.
revised Despite international disapproval, the Reagan administration persisted in helping the rebels in Nicaragua.

- **plan to do** (not *on doing*)

needs checking They planned on closing the factory in Kingston.
revised They planned to close the factory in Kingston.

- **prohibit someone from doing something** (not *to do*)

needs checking Members of the public were prohibited to feed the animals.
revised Members of the public were prohibited from feeding the animals.

- **regarded as** (not *regarded to be*)

needs checking He is commonly regarded to be one of the country's best musicians.
revised He is commonly regarded as one of the country's best musicians.
or He is commonly thought to be one of the country's best musicians.

• **responsible for doing** (not *to do*)

needs checking Mr. Dumphy is responsible to market the full line of the company's pharmaceutical products.
revised Mr. Dumphy is responsible for marketing the full line of the company's pharmaceutical products.

• **sacrifice something** (not *to do*): The use of *sacrifice* without a direct object may have crept into the language through the use of the verb as a baseball term (*Tatis sacrificed in the ninth to bring home Machado*).

needs checking He sacrificed to work in an isolated community with no electricity or running water.
revised He sacrificed himself to work in an isolated community with no electricity or running water.
or He sacrificed a good deal; the isolated community he now works in has no electricity or running water.

• **seem to be** (not *as if*)

needs checking The patient seemed as if he was in shock.
revised The patient seemed to be in shock.

(Exception: When the subject is *it*, *seem* can be followed by *as* [e.g., *It seemed as if he was sick, so we called the doctor.*].)

• **suspect someone of doing something** (not *to do*)

needs checking She suspected him to have committed adultery.
revised She suspected him of committing adultery.
or She suspected that he had committed adultery.

• **tendency to do something** (not *of doing*)

needs checking Some Buick engines have a tendency of over-revving.
revised Some Buick engines have a tendency to over-rev.
or Some Buick engines have a habit of over-revving.

M2.2 Preposition Issues

The prepositions used in English often make little or no sense. What good reason is there for saying *inferior to* but *worse than*? None whatsoever, but over the centuries certain prepositions have come to be accepted as going together with certain verbs, nouns, etc. There are no rules to help one learn the combinations; here are some of the ones that most commonly cause difficulty:

M2
Usage

• agree with someone, with what someone says; agree to do something, to something; agree on a plan, proposal, etc.

needs checking	The union representatives did not agree with the proposed wage increase.
revised	The union representatives did not agree to the proposed wage increase.
or	The union representatives did not agree with management about the proposed wage increase.

• angry with someone; angry at or about something

needs checking	He was angry at me for failing to keep our appointment.
revised	He was angry with me for failing to keep our appointment.

• annoyed with someone; annoyed by something

needs checking	The professor is often annoyed with the attitude of the class.
revised	The professor is often annoyed by the attitude of the class.
or	The professor is often annoyed with the class.

• appeal to someone for something

needs checking	The governor appealed for the residents to help.
revised	The governor appealed to the residents for help.

• approve; approve of: When the verb *approve* is used with *of* (and without a direct object), it means *have a good opinion of*. In this sense the verb is frequently used where issues of right and wrong are concerned (e.g., *I don't approve of allowing children to run wild like that*). When the verb *approve* is used with a direct object (e.g., *approve a proposal, approve the application*), it typically refers to formal administrative or bureaucratic procedures.

needs checking	The issue of new shares was formally approved of by the Board of Directors at their August 28 meeting.
revised	The issue of new shares was formally approved by the Board of Directors at their August 28 meeting.

• argue with someone about something

needs checking	They argued against each other for half an hour.
revised	They argued with each other about the merit of exams.

• arrive in a place, at a place (not *arrive a place*, except *arrive home*). Airlines have led the way in using both *arrive* and *depart* without prepositions. In formal writing one should still say *arrive in* or *arrive at*, and *depart from*.

needs checking He won't join the team until tomorrow night when they arrive Winnipeg.
revised He won't join the team until tomorrow night when they arrive in Winnipeg.

• **attach two or more things** (not *attach together*)

needs checking The conjoined twins were attached together at the hip.
revised The conjoined twins were attached at the hip.

• **borrow something from someone**

needs checking I borrowed him a pair of trousers.
revised I borrowed a pair of trousers from him.

• **cancel something** (not *cancel out*, except when the verb is used to mean *counterbalance* or *neutralize*)

needs checking She cancelled out all her appointments.
revised She cancelled all her appointments.
or After playing hockey, he ate a huge snack that cancelled out the calorie loss of the exercise.

• **care about something** (meaning *to think it worthwhile or important to you*)

needs checking George does not care for what happens to his sister.
revised George does not care what happens to his sister.
or George does not care about what happens to his sister.

• **centre: centred on something** (not *around something*; for one thing to be centred around another is physically impossible)

needs checking The novel is centred around the conflict between British imperialism and Native aspirations.
revised The novel centres on the conflict between British imperialism and Native aspirations.

• **chase someone or something away for doing something**: Despite the way the word is used in baseball slang, in formal writing the verb *chase* with no preposition means *run after*, not *send away*.

On the Companion Website

Exercises on preposition problems may be found at **sites.broadviewpress.com/writingcdn**. Click on **Exercises** and **Writing Mechanics** and go to **"Parts of Speech."**

M2
Usage

informal Starting pitcher José Fernandez was chased in the fifth inning.

more formal Starting pitcher José Fernandez was pulled from the game in the fifth inning.

• **collide with something** (not *against something*)

needs checking The bus left the road and collided against a tree.

revised The bus left the road and collided with a tree.

• **compare to, compare with**: To compare something *to* something else is to liken it, especially when speaking metaphorically (e.g., *Shall I compare thee to a summer's day?*). To compare something *with* something else is to judge how the two are similar or different (*If you compare one brand with another you will notice little difference*). In informal writing it is now considered acceptable to use *compare to* and *compare with* interchangeably, but in formal academic writing it is best to use *compare with* when noting differences.

needs checking The First World War was a small conflict compared to the Second World War, but it changed humanity even more profoundly.

revised The First World War was a small conflict compared with the Second World War, but it changed humanity even more profoundly.

• **concerned with something** (meaning *having some connection with it, having something to do with it*) and **concerned about something** (meaning *being interested in it or worried about it*)

needs checking The inspector is very concerned with the level of pollution in this river.

revised The inspector is very concerned about the level of pollution in this river.

• **conform to** (not *with*)

needs checking The building does not conform with current standards.

revised The building does not conform to current standards.

or The contractors did not comply with current standards.

• **connect two things, connect one thing with another** (not *connect up with*)

needs checking As soon as he connects up these wires, the system should work.

revised As soon as he connects these wires, the system should work.

• **conscious of something** (not *that*)

needs checking He was not conscious that he had done anything wrong.
revised He was not conscious of having done anything wrong.
(Note: Unlike *conscious*, *aware* can be used with *of* or with a *that* clause.)

• **consist in/consist of**: *Consist in* means *to exist in, to have as the essential feature*; *consist of* means *to be made up of.*

needs checking Success consists of hard work.
(i.e., *The essence of success is hard work.*)
revised Success consists in hard work.
needs checking The US Congress consists in two houses—the House of Representatives and the Senate.
revised The US Congress consists of two houses—the House of Representatives and the Senate.

• **consult someone** (not *consult with someone*). Unlike the verbs *talk* and *speak*, the verb *consult* does not need *to* or *with*.

needs checking She will have to consult with a lawyer before giving us an answer.
revised She will have to consult a lawyer before giving us an answer.
or She will have to talk to a lawyer before giving us an answer.

• **continue something, with something, to a place** (not *continue on*)

needs checking We were told to continue on with our work.
revised We were told to continue with our work.

• **convenient for someone, for a purpose; convenient to a place**

needs checking This house is very convenient to me; it is only a short walk to work.
revised This house is very convenient for me; it is only a short walk to work.

• **cooperate with someone** (not *cooperate together*)

needs checking Countries should cooperate together to break down trade barriers.
revised Countries should cooperate with one another to break down trade barriers.

• **correspond to** (*be in agreement with*); correspond with (*exchange letters with*) *needs checking* The fingerprints at the scene of the crime corresponded with those of the suspect.

revised The fingerprints at the scene of the crime corresponded to those of the suspect.

• **couple of things, times, people, etc.**: In some informal contexts the omission of the word *of* in the expression *a couple of* is now considered acceptable, but in formal writing *of* should be included.

needs checking The body had been partially hidden under a pier on Lake Union, a couple hundred feet from the Aurora Avenue Bridge.

revised The body had been partially hidden under a pier on Lake Union, a couple of hundred feet from the Aurora Avenue Bridge.

or The body had been partially hidden under a pier on Lake Union, approximately two hundred feet from the Aurora Avenue Bridge.

(In formal writing it is better to use *two* than *a couple of*.)

• **criticism of something or somebody** (not *against*)

needs checking His criticisms against her were completely unfounded.

revised His criticisms of her were completely unfounded.

• **depart from a place**: See also **arrive** (above).

needs checking One woman was heard saying to a friend as they departed Wrigley Field....

revised One woman was heard saying to a friend as they departed from Wrigley Field....

or One woman was heard saying to a friend as they left Wrigley Field....

• **die of a disease, of old age; die from injuries, wounds**

needs checking My grandfather died from cancer when he was only forty-two years old.

revised My grandfather died of cancer when he was only forty-two years old.

• **different from, to, than**: *Different to* and *different from* are both accepted British usage; *different from* is the preferred form in Canada and the US. (*Different than* is a common alternative in certain contexts in the United States, but in formal writing *different from* is the more widely accepted of the two.)

UK These results are different to those we obtained when we did the same experiment yesterday.

North America These results are different from those we obtained when we did the same experiment yesterday.

• **discuss something** (not *discuss about something*; no preposition is needed)

needs checking They discussed about what to do to ease tensions in the Middle East.

revised They discussed what to do to ease tensions in the Middle East.

• **divide something** (no preposition necessary)

needs checking Lear wants to divide up his kingdom among his three daughters.

revised Lear wants to divide his kingdom among his three daughters.

• **do something for someone** (meaning *something that will help*); **do something to someone** (meaning *something that will hurt*)

needs checking Norman Bethune did a lot to the people of China.

revised Norman Bethune did a lot for the people of China.

• **end: at the end of something; in the end:** *In the end* is used when the writer does not say which end he means, but leaves this to be understood by the reader. *At the end of* is used when the writer mentions the end he is referring to.

needs checking In the end of *Things Fall Apart*, we both admire and pity Okonkwo.

revised At the end of *Things Fall Apart*, we both admire and pity Okonkwo.

or In the end, we both admire and pity Okonkwo.

• **end at a place** (not *end up at*)

needs checking We do not want to end up at the same place we started from.

revised We do not want to end at the same place we started from.

• **fight someone or with someone** (not *against*; *fight* means *struggle against*, so to add *against* is redundant)

needs checking They fought against each other for almost an hour.
revised They fought with each other for almost an hour.
or They fought each other for almost an hour.

• **frightened by something** (when it has just frightened you); **frightened of something** (when talking about a constant condition)

needs checking He was suddenly frightened of the sound of a door slamming.
revised He was suddenly frightened by the sound of a door slamming.

• **graduate from a school**: In informal usage some people drop the preposition, but in formal writing *graduate from* remains standard usage.

needs checking He graduated McGill in 2019.
revised He graduated from McGill in 2019.

• **help doing**, as in *be unable to refrain from doing* (not *help from doing*)

needs checking She could not help from agreeing to his suggestion.
revised She could not help agreeing to his suggestion.

• **hurry** (not *hurry up*)

needs checking She told me to hurry up if I didn't want to miss the train.
revised She told me to hurry if I didn't want to miss the train.

• **in/into/throughout/within**: Whereas *in* typically indicates a particular location, *into* implies motion, and *throughout* implies omnipresence. *Within* and *in* are not interchangeable; *within* should be used only in certain contexts involving extent, duration, or enclosure.

needs checking Within the prologue to the play, the chorus addresses the audience directly.
revised In the prologue to the play, the chorus addresses the audience directly.

Note as well that *in to* should not always be converted to *into*; often the word *in* goes together with a previous verb rather than with *to*.

needs checking The authorities keep giving into her demands.
revised The authorities keep giving in to her demands.

• **independent of something or someone** (not *from*)

needs checking I would like to live entirely independent from my parents.
revised I would like to live entirely independent of my parents.

- **inferior to someone or something** (not *than*)

needs checking Many people think that margarine is inferior than butter.
revised Many people think that margarine is inferior to butter.

(*Inferior* and *superior* are the only two comparative adjectives which are not followed by *than*.)

- **inside or outside something** (not *of something*)

needs checking Within thirty minutes a green scum had formed inside of the beaker.
revised Within thirty minutes a green scum had formed inside the beaker.

- **interested in something, in doing something** (not *to*)

needs checking She is very interested to find out more about plant genetics.
revised She is very interested in finding out more about plant genetics.

- **investigate something** (not *investigate about or into something*)

needs checking The police are investigating into the murder in London last week.
revised The police are investigating the murder in London last week.

- **join someone** (not *join up with*)

needs checking Conrad Black joined up with his brother Montagu in making the proposal to buy the company.
revised Conrad Black joined his brother Montagu in making the proposal to buy the company.

- **jump** (not *jump up*)

needs checking Unemployment has jumped up to record levels recently.
revised Unemployment has jumped to record levels recently.

- **lift something** (not *lift up*)

needs checking I twisted my back as I was lifting up the box.
revised I twisted my back as I was lifting the box.

- **lower something** (not *lower down something*)

needs checking They lowered the coffin down into the grave.
revised They lowered the coffin into the grave.

• **meet/meet with**: *Meet with* in the sense of *attend a meeting with* is a recent addition to the language. If one is referring to a less formal or less prolonged encounter, however, there is no need for the preposition.

needs checking Stanley finally met with Livingstone near the shores of Lake Tanganyika.

revised Stanley finally met Livingstone near the shores of Lake Tanganyika.

(The meaning here is *came face to face with for the first time.*)

• **mercy: have mercy on someone; show mercy to or towards someone**

needs checking We should all have mercy for anyone who is suffering.

revised We should all have mercy on anyone who is suffering.

• **near something** (not *near to something*)

needs checking The village of Battle is very near to the place where the Battle of Hastings was fought in 1066.

revised The village of Battle is very near the place where the Battle of Hastings was fought in 1066.

• **object to something** (not *against*)

needs checking Some people have objected against being required to wear a seat belt.

revised Some people have objected to being required to wear a seat belt.

• **off something** (not *off of*)

needs checking The man stepped off of the platform into the path of the moving train.

revised The man stepped off the platform into the path of the moving train.

• **opposite**: When used as a noun, *opposite* is followed by *of*; when used as an adjective, it is followed by *to* or *from*, or by no preposition.

needs checking His conclusion was the opposite to mine.

(Here, *opposite* is a noun.)

revised His conclusion was the opposite of mine.

or His conclusion was opposite to mine.

(Here, *opposite* is an adjective.)

- **partake of something; participate in something**

needs checking They have refused to partake in a new round of talks on the subject of free trade.
revised They have refused to participate in a new round of talks on the subject of free trade.
or They have refused to partake of a new round of talks on the subject of free trade.

- **pass away** (as a euphemism for *die*): When someone says "he passed," it can mean "he passed his examination," "he passed on the betting in a round of poker," or a number of other things. There are so many meanings of the verb *pass* that, in the interests of clarity as well as directness, it makes sense to choose *pass away* rather than *pass* if you want to use a euphemism for *die*. (See also the discussion of diction and tone in sections P3.2 and P3.7.)

needs checking I heard yesterday that his sister has passed.
revised I heard yesterday that his sister has passed away.
or I heard yesterday that his sister has died.

- **prefer one thing or person to another** (not *more than another*)

needs checking They both prefer tennis more than golf.
revised They both prefer tennis to golf.

- **protest something** (not *protest against*). *To protest* means *to argue against*; the preposition is redundant.

needs checking The demonstrators were protesting against the government's decision to allow missile testing.
revised The demonstrators were protesting the government's decision to allow missile testing.

- **refer to something** (not *refer back to something*)

needs checking If you are confused, refer back to the diagram on page 24.
revised If you are confused, refer to the diagram on page 24.

- **regard/regards: With regard to something; as regards something**

needs checking I am writing in regards to the balance owing on your account.
fair I am writing with regard to the balance owing on your account.
better I am writing about the balance owing on your account.

(Note that *in regard to*, *with regard to*, and *as regards* may often be used interchangeably [*in regard to the issue you have raised*, *with regard to the issue you have raised*, *as regards the issue you have raised*]. All tend towards wordiness, however; usually there is a better way.)

• **rejoice at something** (not *for something*)

needs checking He rejoiced for his good fortune when he won the lottery.
revised He rejoiced at his good fortune when he won the lottery.

• **repeat something** (not *repeat again*)

needs checking If you miss an answer you must repeat the whole exercise again.
revised If you miss an answer you must repeat the whole exercise.

• **request something** or **request that something be done** (but not *request for something* unless one is using the noun—*a request for something*)

needs checking He has requested for two more men to help him.
revised He has requested two more men to help him.
or He has put in a request for two more men to help him.

• **retroactive to a date** (not *from*)

needs checking The tax changes are retroactive from July 1.
revised The tax changes are retroactive to July 1.

• **return to a place** (not *return back*)

needs checking He wanted to return back to the city as soon as possible.
revised He wanted to return to the city as soon as possible.

• **seek something or someone** (not *seek for something*)

needs checking She suggested that we seek for help from the police.
revised She suggested that we seek help from the police.

• **sight: in sight** (*near enough to be seen*); **out of sight** (*too far away to be seen*); **on sight** (*immediately after being seen*)

needs checking The general ordered that deserters be shot in sight.
revised The general ordered that deserters be shot on sight.

• **speak to someone** (when one speaker is giving information to a listener); **speak with someone** (when the two are having a discussion)

needs checking She spoke harshly with the secretary about his spelling mistakes.

revised She spoke harshly to the secretary about his spelling mistakes.

• **suffer from something** (not *with*)

needs checking He told me that he was suffering with the flu.
revised He told me that he was suffering from the flu.

• **superior to someone or something** (not *than someone or something*)

needs checking The advertisements claim that this detergent is superior than the others.
revised The advertisements claim that this detergent is superior to the others.

• **type of person or thing**

needs checking This type carburetor is no longer produced.
revised This type of carburetor is no longer produced.

• **underneath something** (not *underneath of*)

needs checking When we looked underneath of the table, we found what we had been looking for.
revised When we looked underneath the table, we found what we had been looking for.

• **until a time or an event** (not *up until*)

needs checking From 1942 up until 1967 the National Hockey League was made up of only six teams.
revised From 1942 until 1967 the National Hockey League was made up of only six teams.

• **warn someone of a danger, against doing something** (*not about something or to do something*)

needs checking She warned me about the danger involved in the expedition.
revised She warned me of the danger involved in the expedition.

• **worry about something** (not *at something or for something*)

needs checking He is always worried at what will happen if he loses his job.
revised He is always worried about what will happen if he loses his job.

prepositions in pairs or lists: If a sentence includes two or more nouns or verbs that take different prepositions, make sure to include all the necessary words:

needs checking The fire was widely reported in the newspapers and television.

revised The fire was widely reported in the newspapers and on television.

ending a sentence with a preposition: It's true that in some cases ending with a preposition makes for awkward English—but in some cases the reverse is also true. It's more awkward to say *It's the first driveway on the right that you should turn at* (with the preposition at the end) than it is to say *You should turn at the first driveway on the right* (with the preposition coming earlier). But *That is the film of which I am thinking* (with the preposition in the middle of the sentence) is obviously more awkward than *That is the film I'm thinking of* (with the preposition at the end). So to those who still suggest that sentences should not end with prepositions, we say *Of what are you thinking?*

M 2.3 Noun and Pronoun Issues

unusual nouns: A number of nouns are unusual in the way that either the singular or the plural is formed. Here is a list of some that frequently cause mistakes. The most troublesome—as well as a few pronouns that cause similar difficulties—are also given individual entries below:

appendix	appendices
attorney general	attorneys general
bacterium	bacteria
basis	bases
court martial	courts martial
crisis	crises
criterion	criteria
curriculum	curricula
datum	data
daylight-saving time	[no plural]
ellipsis	ellipses
emphasis	emphases
erratum	errata
father-in-law	fathers-in-law
focus	foci
index	indexes or indices
matrix	matrixes or matrices
medium	media

millennium	millennia
nucleus	nuclei
parenthesis	parentheses
referendum	referenda or referendums
runner-up	runners-up
stratum	strata
symposium	symposia
synthesis	syntheses
thesis	theses

• **accommodation**: An accommodation is something provided to accommodate someone (to make them comfortable, in other words). The singular is used when discussing some specific arrangement, and the plural is used when discussing the practice more generally, or when discussing a set of provisions, like a hotel room (which includes bed, desk, toilet, shower, etc.).

> Prof. Rice was willing to provide extra time on the test for that student as an accommodation.
> The Office of Specialized Services provides accommodations for students with disabilities.
> Before I arrived in the city I booked accommodations downtown.

• **anyone/anybody/each/every/no one/nobody/someone/somebody**: All are singular. It is often difficult to find a way to get all the verbs and subjects to agree, and at the same time avoid awkwardness.

not in agreement	Anyone may visit when they like.
in agreement	Anyone may visit when he or she likes.
in agreement	Anyone may visit at any time.
not in agreement	No one likes to leave a place that they have grown fond of.
in agreement	No one likes to leave a place that he or she has grown fond of.
in agreement	No one likes to leave a place that has fond memories attached to it.
not in agreement	Each person applying for the job must fill out this form before they will be granted an interview.
in agreement	Each person applying for the job must fill out this form before he or she will be granted an interview.
in agreement	Each person applying for the job must fill out this form before being granted an interview.

In informal English it has long been common practice to depart from grammatical correctness in such situations, and use *they* rather than *he or she*; as discussed above (pages 135–36), the singular *they* has in this century gradually come to be accepted in formal English as well. Some traditionalists still insist that students use *he or she* in such situations, but most regard any of the following as acceptable:

> Someone has forgotten to turn off the stove; they should be more careful.
> Someone has forgotten to turn off the stove; he or she should be more careful.
> Some careless person has forgotten to turn off the stove.

Following is a list of common indefinite pronouns:

always plural: *both, many*

always singular: *another, anybody, anyone, anything, each, either, every, everybody, everyone, everything, neither, nobody, no one, nothing, one, somebody, someone, something*

singular or plural, depending on the context: *all, any, more, most, none, some*

• **bacteria**: A plural word; the singular is *bacterium*.

needs checking There were many bacterias in the moldy bread.
revised There were a lot of bacteria in the moldy bread.

• **behaviour**: Although social scientists speak of *a behaviour* or of *behaviours* in technical writing, in other disciplines and in conversational English the word is uncountable (i.e., it cannot form a plural or be used with the indefinite article). Say *types of behaviour*, not *behaviours*:

needs checking He has a good behaviour.
revised His behaviour is good.
or He behaves well.

• **between/among**: It is often supposed that *between* should always be used for two, *among* for more than two. As the *Oxford English Dictionary* points out, however, "in all senses *between* has been, from its earliest appearance, extended to more than two." Perhaps the most important difference is that *between* suggests a relationship of things or people to each other as individuals, whereas *among* suggests a relationship that is collective and vague. Thus we say *the ball fell among the hollyhocks* where we are expressing the relationship of the ball to many flowers collectively, and where the precise location of the ball is unspecified. But we should not say, as we watch a baseball game, *the ball fell among the three fielders*; here we know the precise location of the ball and are expressing the relationship between it and the three individuals.

• **both/all**: Use *both* to refer to two, and *all* to refer to more than two.

needs checking Harris and Waluchow were the chief speakers in the debate yesterday. They all spoke very well.

revised Harris and Waluchow were the chief speakers in the debate yesterday. They both spoke very well.

• **brain**: One person can have only one brain. The use of the plural to refer to the brain of one person (e.g., *He blew his brains out*) is slang, and should not be used in formal written work.

needs checking He used his brains to solve the problem.

revised He used his brain to solve the problem.

• **children**: Be careful when forming the possessive; the apostrophe should come before the *s*.

needs checking All the childrens' toys had been put away.

revised All the children's toys had been put away.

• **confusion**: Uncountable—we do not normally speak of *a confusion* or of *confusions*.

needs checking The misunderstanding about his time of arrival caused a confusion.

revised The misunderstanding about his time of arrival caused confusion.

• **criteria**: Plural; the singular is *criterion*.

needs checking The chief criteria on which an essay should be judged is whether or not it communicates clearly.

revised The chief criterion on which an essay should be judged is whether or not it communicates clearly.

EAL

For particular problems with nouns faced by those whose native language is not English, see Section M4.

• **damage**: In its usual meaning, this noun has no plural, since it is uncountable. We speak of *damage*, not *a damage*, and of *a lot of damage*, not *many damages*. The word *damages* means *money paid to cover the cost of any damage one has caused.*

needs checking	The crash caused many damages to his car, but he was unhurt.
revised	The crash caused a lot of damage to his car, but he was unhurt.

• **data**: Like *bacteria*, *media*, and *phenomena*, the noun *data* originated as a Latin plural (the rarely used singular form is *datum*). But usage is changing; even *The Economist* now accepts the singular data in most circumstances.

correct	These data prove that the lake is badly polluted.
also acceptable	This data proves that the lake is badly polluted.

• **each other/one another**: Use *each other* for two, *one another* for more than two.

needs checking	The three brothers often tell stories to each other.
revised	The three brothers often tell stories to one another.
needs checking	The two had begun to get on one another's nerves.
revised	The two had begun to get on each other's nerves.

• **either/neither**: *Either* and *neither* are both singular.

needs checking	So far neither the party rank and file nor the electorate seem satisfied with the leader's performance.
revised	So far neither the party rank and file nor the electorate seems satisfied with the leader's performance.

• **either/any; neither/none**: Use *either* and *neither* for two, *any* and *none* for more than two.

needs checking	Shirley has six sisters, but she hasn't seen either of them since Christmas.
revised	Shirley has six sisters, but she hasn't seen any of them since Christmas.

• **government**: A singular noun.

needs checking	The government are intending to build a new terminal at this airport before 2030.
revised	The government is intending to build a new terminal at this airport before 2030.

• **graffiti**: A plural noun; the singular form is *graffito*.

needs checking	Graffiti covers most of the subway cars in the city.
revised	Graffiti cover most of the subway cars in the city.

• **media**: In most cases this noun should be treated as plural; the singular is *medium*.

needs checking	The media usually assumes that the audience has a very short attention span.
revised	The media usually assume that the audience has a very short attention span.

Many authorities now regard it as acceptable in *some* contexts to use media as a collective noun—in other words, as a noun that can take a singular verb. That is particularly the case with the phrase *social media*. In some contexts, the phrase *social media* is clearly plural and countable:

needs checking	Social media such as Facebook, Instagram, Snapchat, and Twitter plays an important role in modern life.
revised	Social media such as Facebook, Instagram, Snapchat, and Twitter play an important role in modern life.

In other contexts, though, *social media* can function either as a plural noun or as a non-count, collective noun. Most authorities now consider both of the following to be correct:

Social media were what I relied on during the pandemic.
Social media was what I relied on during the pandemic.

• **money**: Some people seem to think that *monies* has a more official ring to it than *money* when they are talking of business affairs, but there is no sound reason for using this plural form in good English.

needs checking	The mayor has promised to provide some monies for this project.
revised	The mayor has promised to provide some money for this project.

• **news**: Despite the *s*, this is a singular collective noun. Make sure to use a singular verb with it.

needs checking	Today's news of troubles in the Middle East are very disturbing.
revised	Today's news of troubles in the Middle East is very disturbing.

• **none**: Although *no one* and *not one* are always singular, common usage allows *none* to be either singular or plural depending on the context. In a sentence such as *Of all European cities, none is more beautiful than Prague* the pronoun *none* is clearly singular—just as *not one* would be if used in its place. In the sentence *None of the field is dry* the pronoun *none* refers to the singular noun *field*—though here, we notice, it would not be possible to substitute *not one*. In the sentence *None of the girls want to leave* the word *none* refers to the plural noun *girls*, and may thus take a plural verb. In the same way the pronouns *all*, *any*, *more*, *most*, and *some* may be either singular or plural depending on whether they refer to a singular or a plural referent. *Most of the sugar is gone*, but *most of the people are happy*. Some argue, however, that *none* should be treated grammatically as *no one* and *not one* are treated, and should always take a singular verb (i.e., that we should say *none of the girls* **wants** *to leave*, *none of the things she wants* **is** *available*, and so on). If in doubt (or in fear of a grammatical traditionalist) treat *none* as always singular; otherwise, make it agree with its referent.

widely accepted	None of the issues concerning indefinite pronouns are of earth-shattering importance.
universally accepted	None of the issues concerning indefinite pronouns is of earth-shattering importance.

• **phenomena**: Plural; the singular is *phenomenon*.

needs checking	The great popularity of disco music was a short-lived phenomena.
revised	The great popularity of disco music was a short-lived phenomenon.

• **police**: A plural noun. Be sure to use a plural verb with it.

needs checking	The police is investigating the case, and hope to make an arrest soon.
revised	The police are investigating the case, and hope to make an arrest soon.

On the Companion Website

Exercises on singular and plural nouns and pronouns may be found at **sites.broadviewpress.com/writingcdn**. Click on **Exercises** and **Writing Mechanics** and go to **"Parts of Speech."**

Pronouns: *Who Cares about Whom?*

Those unfamiliar with the territory may wish to refer to the section on pronouns on pages 182–84 in Section M1. Readers may also wish to refer to the discussion of *y'all* and *youse* on pages 171–73 above.

• **extra pronoun**: It is easy to add an extra pronoun, particularly if the subject of the sentence is separated from the verb by a long adjectival clause:

needs checking The countries which Hitler wanted to conquer in the late 1930s they were too weak to resist him.

revised The countries which Hitler wanted to conquer in the late 1930s were too weak to resist him.

needs checking The line that is longest in a right-angled triangle it is called the hypotenuse.

revised The line that is longest in a right-angled triangle is called the hypotenuse.

• **first person**: In formal writing it is customary to use *I* and *me* infrequently or not at all. The object of a formal piece of writing is normally to present an argument, and writers realize that they can best argue their case by presenting evidence rather than by stating that such and such is what they think. Thus many teachers advise their students always to avoid using the first person singular (*I* and *me*) in their writing.

This guideline should not be regarded as a firm and fast rule. George Orwell, often praised as the finest essayist of the last century, uses *I* and *me* frequently. As the following example illustrates, however, he employs the first person to guide the reader through his argument, not to make the points in the argument:

> If one gets rid of these habits one can think more clearly, and to think more clearly is a necessary first step towards political regeneration: so that the fight against bad English is not frivolous and is not the exclusive concern of professional writers. I will come back to this presently, and I hope that by that time the meaning of what I have said will become clearer. ("Politics and the English Language")

Phrases such as *I think* and *I feel*, on the other hand, will not help you convince the reader of the strength of your main points.

needs checking Many authorities assume inflation to be a cause of high interest rates, but I think that high interest rates are a cause

M2
Usage

of inflation. This essay will prove my argument through numerous examples.

revised Many authorities assume inflation to be a cause of high interest rates; in fact, high interest rates are often a cause of inflation. Let us take the years 1978 to 1983 in the US as an example.

• **I/me/myself**: Perhaps as a result of slang use of *me* as a subject pronoun (*Me and him got together for a few beer last night*), the impression seems to have lodged in many minds that the distinction between *I* and *me* is one of degree of politeness or formality. It's not; the distinction is simply between subject pronoun (*I*) and object pronoun (*me*).

needs checking There is no disagreement between you and I.
revised There is no disagreement between you and me.

(Both *you* and *I* are here objects of a preposition—*between. Between you and I* is no more correct than is *I threw the ball at he.*)

Many are also sometimes uncertain as to how *myself* should be used. One way is as a reflexive pronoun used as a direct or indirect object (*I hurt myself*; *I talk to myself*). Another is as an intensifier, to point up a contrast or add emphasis (*Someone from our company will attend, but I won't be there myself*). Note that *myself* is used in conjunction with another first person pronoun, however, not in place of *I* or *me*.

needs checking There was no need to consult Carol and myself about this.
revised There was no need to consult Carol and me about this.

On the Companion Website

Exercises on pronoun problems may be found at **sites.broadviewpress.com/writingcdn**. Click on **Exercises** and **Writing Mechanics** and go to **"Parts of Speech."**

• **non-human and human animals**: Is a non-human animal an *it*? Or a *he* or *she*? To some extent the answer may be necessarily context-dependent. If you cannot tell whether the bird you see flashing by in the sky or the fish you see flashing by in the water is male or female, you are surely not likely to refer to the creature as *he* or *she*. But if you do know whether what you are looking at is male or female, there is no good reason not to refer to that animal as *he* or *she*, and to use the same pronouns we use for people as appropriate: *his*, *her*, *who*, *whose*, etc.

worth checking Our new puppy, which is six months old, chewed on my shoes.

revised Our new puppy, who is six months old, chewed on my shoes.

• **than**: Does *than* take a subject or an object pronoun? Purists argue that we should say *She's brighter than I* [*am*], and *He's louder than she* [*is*]—that the verb is always understood in such sentences, even when we do not say it or write it, and that the unspoken verb requires a subject. It's hard to argue, however, that the increasingly widespread use of object pronouns after *than* is either ugly or confusing.

less formal She always sleeps later than him.

more formal She always sleeps later than he [does].

• **unreferenced or wrongly referenced pronoun**: Normally a pronoun must refer to a noun in the previous sentence or clause. In the following sentence, for example, the pronoun *she* clearly refers to the noun *Charity*, which is the subject of the first clause in the sentence:

- Charity told Alfred that she would start work at nine.

Notice how confusing the sentence becomes, however, if there are two possible *shes* in the first part of the sentence:

- Charity told Mavis that she would start work at nine.

Does this mean that Charity will start work at nine, or that Mavis will? From the sentence it is impossible to tell. In cases like this, where it is not absolutely clear whom or what a pronoun refers to, use the noun again instead:

clear Charity told Mavis that she (Charity) would start work at nine.

In the following case the writer has gone astray by mentioning two things—one singular, one plural—and then matching only one of the two with a pronoun. In this instance the best remedy is to substitute a noun for the pronoun:

needs checking Shields's characters are so exquisitely crafted and her plot so artfully conceived that it keeps the reader riveted until the final page.

revised Shields's characters are so exquisitely crafted and her plot so artfully conceived that the book keeps the reader riveted until the final page.

Similar mistakes are often made in writing about a general class of people, such as police officers, or doctors, or football players. When writing in this way one can use either the third person singular (e.g., *A doctor helps patients. She ....*) or the third person plural (*Doctors help patients. They ....*). Mixing the two in such situations often leads people to write unreferenced pronouns:

needs checking A herbalist knows a lot about plants. They can often cure you by giving you medicine.

(Here the pronoun *they* is presumably meant to refer to the plural noun *herbalists*, but the writer has referred only to *a herbalist*.)

revised A herbalist knows a lot about plants. He can often cure you by giving you medicine.

or Herbalists know a lot about plants. They can often cure you by giving you medicine.

It may also not be clear what or whom a pronoun refers to if it is placed too far away from the noun:

needs checking The Board of Trustees increased tuition fees by an average of 43 per cent. Other measures taken included a $100 million cut in student assistance and the closing of the office of the ombudsman. They also introduced a variety of measures to help recruitment.

revised The Board of Trustees increased tuition fees by an average of 43 per cent. Other measures taken included a $100 million cut in student assistance and the closing of the office of the ombudsman. The Board also introduced a variety of measures to help recruitment.

Be particularly careful when using *this* as a pronoun; if the preceding sentence is a long one, it may not be at all clear what *this* refers to:

needs checking The deficit was forecast to be $800 million, but turned out to be over $6 billion. This reflected the government's failure to predict the increase in interest rates and the onset of a recession.

(*This what?*)

revised The deficit was forecast to be $800 million, but turned out to be over $6 billion. This vast discrepancy reflected the government's failure to predict the increase in interest rates and the onset of a recession.

Sometimes the meaning may be clear, but the omission of a pronoun may create unintended and humorous ambiguity:

needs checking She visited a doctor with a bad case of the flu. (Did the doctor have the flu?)

revised She visited a doctor when she had a bad case of the flu.

needs checking The Cougar was a sporty car aimed at the youthful-feeling who wanted luxury in their automobiles. Its buyers were similar to Mustangs, but more affluent.

revised The Cougar was a sporty car aimed at the youthful-feeling who wanted luxury in their automobiles. Its buyers were similar to those who bought Mustangs, but more affluent.

• **who/whom**: The subject pronoun and the object pronoun, but it's not as simple as that. Nor is the distinction merely a matter of stuffiness or pedantry on the part of grammar purists. Sound has a great deal to do with it. Even purists must sometimes find themselves saying, *I didn't know who I was talking to*, even though the rules say it should be *whom* (subject—*I*; object—*whom*). In similar fashion the enemies of *whom* must surely be tempted to sacrifice principle rather than attempt such an owlish mouthful as *To who was he talking*? They would do so not on the grammatical grounds of *whom*, the object pronoun, being correct since it is acting as the object of the preposition *to*, but on the grounds of *whom*, the word with an *m* on the end, being in that sentence a lot easier to say. In such circumstances convenience of pronunciation occasionally overrides arguments either for or against formality.

less formal Scott Fitzgerald never cared who he irritated.
more formal Scott Fitzgerald never cared whom he irritated.

M 2.4 Word Order

Word order problems are of many sorts. See also, for example, the discussions elsewhere in this book of syntax; of ambiguity; of split infinitives; of indefinite pronouns such as *each*, *every*, and *anyone*; and of *not only ... but also*.

• **ambiguity/confusion**: Inappropriate word order is one of the most common sources of ambiguity and confusion. Often a change in punctuation may also be required to correct the problem.

needs checking The liner tilted dramatically after fire broke out in the engine room, 50 miles south of Cyprus.

revised The liner tilted dramatically after fire broke out in the engine room. At the time the ship was 50 miles south of Cyprus.

needs checking He has not come under any pressure to make way for a new leader, despite the failure of any tangible benefits from his government's economic policies.

revised He has not come under any pressure to make way for a new leader, despite the failure of his government's economic policies to bring any tangible benefits.

needs checking Proportion of overweight people between 18 and 64 years trying to lose weight by sex in Alberta, 1990.

(Heading on chart, Alberta Heart Health Survey, reprinted in *The Calgary Herald*)

revised Proportion in Alberta, Canada, of overweight people between 18 and 64 years, by sex, who were trying to lose weight, 1990.

• **amounts**: For no good reason, adjectives having to do with amounts or quantities (e.g., *much*, *few*, *many*) normally precede the noun or pronoun to which they refer, even when the verb *to be* is used. In this way such adjectives differ from other adjectives. For example, we can talk about a happy man, putting the adjective *happy* before the noun *man*, or we can use the present tense of the verb *to be* and say, *The man is happy*, in which case the adjective *happy* comes after the noun *man*. In contrast, it is considered awkward to say, *We were many at the meeting*, or *The people here are few*. Instead the sentence should be changed around, and the adjectives put before the nouns. The easiest way to do this is by using *there* and the verb *to be*. The revised versions of the above sentences are as follows:

revised There were many of us at the meeting.
revised There are few people here.

A further example:

needs checking The students at the football game were many.
revised There were many students at the football game.

EAL

For particular problems with word order faced by those whose native language is not English, see Section M4.

• **balance and parallelism**: As discussed earlier (sections P3.3 and P3.4), paired connectives (*if... then*, *either ... or* [given a separate entry below], *not only ... but also*, *both ... and*) can help in achieving balance. But difficulties in getting all the words in the right order can easily arise.

needs checking As a critic she is both fully aware of the tricks used by popular novelists, as well as realizing that "serious" novelists sometimes resort to the same tricks.

revised As a critic she is fully aware both of the tricks used by popular novelists, and of the fact that "serious" novelists sometimes resort to the same tricks.

needs checking The argument that Hellman puts forward not only fails to rebut the strongest arguments of Singer and Regan, but he also does not even directly engage with those arguments.

revised Hellman not only fails to rebut the strongest arguments of Singer and Regan; he does not even directly engage with those arguments.

We tend to think of constructions involving words such as *both ... and* and *not only ... but also* when we think of balance and parallelism in written work. But the principles involved extend far more widely. Finding the right order for the words in a long sentence can be surprisingly challenging, even for experienced writers. Keeping words, phrases, and clauses grammatically balanced is less difficult where a pairing of two is concerned—though even here it is easy enough to go astray if you're not careful:

needs checking This holiday we plan on keeping healthy and we'll get lots of rest.

revised This holiday we plan on keeping healthy and getting lots of rest.

needs checking The new government aims to reduce conflict with its neighbours and increasing the rate of economic growth.

revised The new government aims to reduce conflict with its neighbours and to increase the rate of economic growth.

needs checking The study concludes that Facebook use is associated with declines in subjective measures of well-being, and the more people use Facebook, the worse they tend to feel.

revised The study concludes that Facebook use is associated with declines in subjective measures of well-being, and that the more people use Facebook, the worse they tend to feel.

[Repetition of the function word *that* makes clear to the reader how the second part of the sentence is connected to the first; the sentence's second part reports another of the same study's conclusions.]

When it is a matter of keeping three or more elements parallel or in balance, everything becomes more difficult.

needs checking His accomplishments included a succession of strategic successes during World War II, helping to revive Europe after the war, and he founded an important new international organization.

revised His accomplishments included a succession of strategic successes during World War II, a plan to revive Europe after the war, and the foundation of an important new international organization.

or He is remembered for his strategic successes during World War II, for his plan to revive Europe after the war, and for the foundation of an important new international organization.

[These are only two of many ways in which the sentence might be revised so as to make its three parts grammatically parallel.]

needs checking A plant-based, whole foods diet is associated with improvements in heart condition, greater life expectancy, diabetes is reduced, lowering of cancer rates, less chance of Alzheimer's, and also there are other health benefits.

revised A plant-based, whole foods diet is associated with improvements in heart condition, greater life expectancy, lower rates of diabetes, lower incidence of cancer, lower incidence of Alzheimer's, and many other health benefits.

or A plant-based, whole foods diet typically improves heart condition; increases one's life expectancy; significantly lowers one's chances of being afflicted with diabetes, heart disease, cancer, or Alzheimer's; and is associated with many other health benefits as well.

[Again, these are only two of many ways in which the problem of the sentence's faulty parallelism may be corrected.]

In the above examples parallelism is a matter of grammatical structure first and foremost. But (as discussed in sections P3.3 and P3.4 in the first section of this book) the importance of balance and parallelism to writing is not only a matter of grammar. Sentences that are balanced and that include parallel structures tend to be both more comprehensible and more pleasing to the reader. In the following examples the initial sentence is not grammatically incorrect; the revisions are a matter of style rather than of correctness. You may judge for yourself as to how they compare in terms of the reader's experience.

worth checking Teams with very low payrolls are unlikely to achieve much success, even in the regular season, and very unlikely to be able to win in the postseason against teams who are able to afford the best-paid stars. The Oakland As are often cited as an exception to the rule that low budget teams are unlikely to succeed in baseball, and it's true that they have enjoyed a surprising degree of success in the regular season. Perhaps inevitably, however, they have not enjoyed much success in the postseason.

revised Teams with very low payrolls are likely to struggle in the regular season, and to struggle even more if they reach the playoffs and face teams who can afford the best-paid stars. If the Oakland As's low payroll makes their regular season success seem surprising, it also makes their postseason failures seem inevitable.

worth checking What Marianne and her mother conjectured one moment as perhaps being possible, the next moment they believed to be probable. Anything they wished might happen they soon found themselves hoping for, and soon after that the hope would become an expectation.

revised What Marianne and her mother conjectured one moment, they believed the next; with them, to wish was to hope, and to hope was to expect.

(Jane Austen, *Sense and Sensibility*)

worth checking Our nation is made up of people of all sorts of religious beliefs. Many Americans are Christians but we also have Jews, Muslims, and Hindus among us, and there are also

M2
Usage

many American nonbelievers. America has also been shaped by many languages and cultures, from all over the world.

revised We are a nation of Christians and Muslims, Jews and Hindus, and nonbelievers. We are shaped by every language and culture, drawn from every end of this earth.

(Barack Obama, First Inaugural Address)

In most cases, revising to strengthen parallel structures in your writing will have the happy byproduct of making it more concise. But that's not always the case; the second sentence from the Obama passage quoted above is longer than it need be, but a pleasing instance of parallelism nonetheless.

• **direct object position**: The normal position for direct objects is after the verb. When the direct object is put at the beginning of a sentence it sounds awkward, and the word order may lead writers to include an extra, unwanted pronoun later in the sentence. It is usually best to keep the direct object after the verb.

needs checking Some of the money I put it in the bank.

(Notice the extra pronoun *it*.)

revised I put some of the money in the bank.

(*I* is the subject; *some of the money* is the direct object of *put*.)

• **either ... or**: These words should directly precede the pair of things to which they refer. The same applies to *neither ... nor*.

needs checking I will either pick an apple or a banana.

revised I will pick either an apple or a banana.

(*Either* and *or* refer to *apple* and *banana*. Therefore they must come immediately before those words.)

needs checking He will go either to New York for the holiday or remain here.

revised He will either go to New York for the holiday or remain here.

(The choice is between *going* and *remaining*.)

needs checking We will either buy a poodle or a spaniel.

revised We will buy either a poodle or a spaniel.

(The choice is between breeds of dogs, not between *buying* and a dog breed.)

• **except**: A phrase beginning with *except* should appear directly after the noun or pronoun to which *except* refers.

needs checking We all had to wait except for those who had bought tickets in advance.
revised All except those who had bought tickets in advance had to wait.

• **first person last**: When speaking about both yourself and another person (or other people), always mention the other person first. The first person pronoun (*I, me*) should come last.

needs checking I and my brother decided to go shopping.
revised My brother and I decided to go shopping.

On the Companion Website

Word order mistakes involving words such as *only* are often classed as one variety of misplaced modifier error; a full discussion of the category **misplaced modifier** (including how it relates to the category **dangling modifier**) is provided alongside a range of relevant exercises at **sites.broadviewpress.com/writingcdn**. Click on **Exercises** and go to **"Verbs, Subjects, Modifiers."**

• **only**: The adverb *only* should come directly before the word or words it refers to. *She could only see him* implies that she could not hear, smell, or touch him; *She could see only him* implies that she had eyes for no one else.

needs checking She only asked six people to the party.
revised She asked only six people to the party.

• **questions in indirect speech**: In a question we normally reverse the order of the subject and the verb. For example, to change the statement *She was sad* to a question, we reverse the order of *she* and *was* and ask, *Was she sad?* The same rule does not apply, however, to questions in indirect speech. These are considered to be part of a statement and, as in any other statement, the entire verb should come after the subject. For example, to turn the above sentence into indirect speech we would say, *I asked her if she was sad* (not *I asked her was she sad*).

needs checking I asked him how was he.
revised I asked him how he was.
needs checking She asked her brother where was he going.
revised She asked her brother where he was going.

Notice as well that these sentences are statements, not questions. They therefore do not end with a question mark.

• **relative pronouns**: Relative pronouns (*who*, *which*, *whom*, *whose*, etc.) normally refer to the word that has come immediately before them. This may sometimes turn out to be difficult, in which case the word order may have to be changed.

needs checking He purchased his friend's shop, whom he had known for many years.

(The relative pronoun *whom* refers to *friend*, not *shop*. Change the word order to put *whom* directly after *friend*.)

revised He purchased the shop from his friend, whom he had known for many years.

needs checking On Saturday I went to my brother's wedding, whose new wife is a senior government official.

revised On Saturday I went to the wedding of my brother, whose new wife is a senior government official.

On the Companion Website

Exercises on word order and on one-word/two-word problems may be found at **sites.broadviewpress.com/writingcdn**. Click on **Exercises** and **Writing Mechanics** and go to **"Words and Usage."**

M2.5 Word Meanings

• **accept/except**: These two words are often confused because of their similar sounds. *Accept* is a verb meaning *to receive something favourably* (or at least without complaining). Examples:

- We accepted the invitation to his party.
- We will have to accept the decision of the judge.

Except, on the other hand, is a conjunction (or sometimes a preposition) which means *not including* or *but*.

needs checking All the permanent members of the Security Council accept China voted to authorize the use of force.

revised All the permanent members of the Security Council except China voted to authorize the use of force.

• **adapt/adopt/adept**: *To adapt something* is *to alter or modify it*; *to adopt something* is *to approve it* or *accept responsibility for it*; *adept* is an adjective meaning *skillful*.

needs checking The board adapted the resolution unanimously.
revised The board adopted the resolution unanimously.

• **adverse/averse**: *Adverse* means *unfavourable*; *averse* means *reluctant* or *unwilling*.

needs checking The plane was forced to land because of averse weather conditions.
revised The plane was forced to land because of adverse weather conditions.
or The pilot was averse to the idea of landing in the fog.

• **afflict/inflict**: A person *inflicts* pain or hardship on someone else, who is *afflicted* by the pain and hardship.

needs checking The Mugabe government began as early as 1983 to afflict terrible suffering on large numbers of Zimbabweans living in Matabeleland.
revised The Mugabe government began as early as 1983 to inflict terrible suffering on large numbers of Zimbabweans living in Matabeleland.

• **aggravate/annoy/irritate**: *Aggravate* means *make worse*. Here is an example:

- The injury was aggravated by the bumpy ride in the ambulance.

In formal English *aggravate* should not be used to mean *annoy* or *irritate*.

needs checking She found his constant complaints very aggravating.
revised She found his constant complaints very irritating.

• **alliterate/illiterate**: *Alliterate* is a verb meaning *to use consecutively two or more words that begin with the same sound*.

- The big, burly brute was frighteningly fierce.

Illiterate is an adjective meaning either *unable to read* or *unable to read and write well*. Those who confuse the two are sometimes, if unfairly, accused of being illiterate.

needs checking Over forty per cent of the population of Zambia is functionally alliterate.

revised Over forty per cent of the population of Zambia is functionally illiterate.

• **alternately/alternatively**: *Alternately* means *happening in turn, first one and then the other*; alternatively means *instead of.* Be careful as well with the adjectives *alternate* and *alternative.*

needs checking An alternate method of arriving at this theoretical value would be to divide the difference between the two prices by the number of warrants.

revised An alternative method of arriving at this theoretical value would be to divide the difference between the two prices by the number of warrants. (or Another method of ...)

needs checking Professor Beit-Hallahmi seems to have trouble alternatively in reading his own book accurately and in reading my review of it correctly.

revised Professor Beit-Hallahmi seems to have trouble alternately in reading his own book accurately and in reading my review of it correctly.

• **ambiguity**: There are many types of ambiguity; for other references see pages 254–59, pages 293–95 on "Pronouns," page 296 on "Word Order Problems," and the entries below for such words as *flammable.*

• **amiable/amicable**: *Amiable* is used to describe someone's personality; *amicable* describes the state of relations between people.

needs checking Navratilova said that the split with her former tennis partner had been an amiable one.

revised Navratilova said that the split with her former tennis partner had been an amicable one.

• **amoral/immoral**: An *amoral* act is one to which moral standards do not apply; an *immoral* act, on the other hand, is one that goes against a moral standard.

needs checking The reader is unlikely to share Austen's views as to what constitutes amoral behaviour.

revised The reader is unlikely to share Austen's views as to what constitutes immoral behaviour.

• **amused/bemused**: If you are *bemused*, you are a bit puzzled about something—though not in any troubled fashion, and perhaps even in a somewhat amused one. From that slight point of connection (as well as the similarity in sound) has arisen the erroneous belief that the two words are synonymous.

• **anti/ante**: If you remember that *anti* means *against* and *ante* means *before* you are less likely to misspell the many words that have one or the other as a prefix.

needs checking	The UN had many anticedents—most notably the League of Nations formed after World War I.
revised	The UN had many antecedents—most notably the League of Nations formed after World War I.

• **antonym/homonym/synonym**: Antonyms are opposites—two words with opposite meanings (e.g., *hot* and *cold*, *good* and *bad*). Homonyms have different meanings but the same spelling or sound. There are thus two types of homonyms; homophones have the same sound but may have different spellings, like *sight* and *site*, while homographs have the same spelling but may be pronounced differently, like *bass* (the instrument, rhymes with "pace") and *bass* (the fish, rhymes with "pass"). *Pole* meaning *long stick* and *pole* meaning *extremity of a planet* are homonyms that are both homophones and homographs. Synonyms (e.g., the verbs *shut* and *close*) are words with the same meaning.

• **anxious/eager**: The adjective *anxious* means *uneasy*, *nervous*, *worried*; it should not be used in formal writing to mean *eager*.

needs checking	He was anxious to help in any way he could.
revised	He was eager to help in any way he could.

• **appraise/apprise**: *To appraise something* is *to estimate its value*; *to apprise someone of something* is *to inform him or her of it.*

needs checking	The house has been apprised at $660,000.
revised	The house has been appraised at $660,000.
or	He apprised her of the house's jump in value.

• **assure/ensure/insure**: To *assure* someone of something is to tell her with confidence or certainty; to *ensure* that something will happen is to make sure that it does; to *insure* something is to purchase insurance on it so as to protect yourself in case of loss. In American English especially, it is common—and acceptable to some—to use *insure* in the sense of *ensure*, but the difference in meaning is significant enough that the distinction should really be maintained.

Red Tape Holds Up New Bridge

The following are all examples of ambiguity in newspaper headlines. In some cases it may take several moments to decipher the intended meaning.

Two pedestrians struck by bridge
Man held over giant L.A. brush fire
Illegal aliens cut in half by new law
Passerby injured by post office
Red tape holds up new bridge
Village water holds up well
Jerk injures neck, wins award
Bishop thanks god for calling

(The above examples come courtesy of columnist Bob Swift of Knight-Ridder Newspapers, and Prof. A. Levey of the University of Calgary.)

Here are two gems provided by editor Beth Humphries:

The fossils were found by scientists embedded in red sandstone.
She walked into the bathroom tiled in sea-green marble.

And, from a Global News weather telecast, the following prediction:

"Out west tomorrow, they're going to see the sun, as well as Atlantic Canada."

needs checking Our inventory is ensured for $10,000,000.
revised Our inventory is insured for $10,000,000.
needs checking He ensured us that it would not happen again.
revised He assured us that it would not happen again.
less widely accepted Please insure that it does not happen again.
more widely accepted Please ensure that it does not happen again.

• **be/become**: The difference between the two is that *to be* simply indicates existence, while *to become* indicates a process of change. Whenever you are talking about a change, use *become* instead of *be*.

needs checking I had been quite contented, but as time went by I was unhappy.
revised I had been quite contented, but as time went by I became unhappy.
needs checking After years of struggle, East Timor finally was independent in 2002.
revised After years of struggle, East Timor finally became independent in 2002.

• **beg the question**: The original meaning of *beg the question* is *take for granted the very thing to be argued about*—not *invite the question*. In the words of philosopher Thomas Hurka, "'begging the question' is not what the host does on Jeopardy." The extension of the phrase to mean *invite the question* or *prompt the question* has become so widespread in recent years that it may be vain to think of the tide being reversed, but the original concept of question begging is a useful one, and we should be reluctant to allow it to disappear.

needs checking This sort of sexual abuse case begs the question as to how such behaviour could be hidden for so many years.
revised This sort of sexual abuse case makes us wonder how such behaviour could be hidden for so many years.

Note: For more on *begging the question* see P2.3 above (pages 36–7).

• **beside/besides**: *Besides* can mean *in addition to*, *moreover* (as in the sentence *Besides, he deserved to lose*), *other than*, or *except* (as in *no one was there besides me*). *Beside* may mean *at the side of* (as in *no one was there beside me*) or *irrelevant to* (as in the common phrase *beside the point*); in this latter meaning confusion with *besides* sometimes arises.

needs checking Much of Dawkins's argument is besides the point.
revised Much of Dawkins's argument is beside the point.

• **bored/boring**: *Bored* is the opposite of *interested* and *boring* is the opposite of *interesting*. In other words, one is quite likely to be bored when someone reads out what one has already read in the newspaper, or when one is watching a football game when the score is 38–0, or when one is doing an uninteresting job. To be bored, however, is not the same as to be sad, or depressed, or irritated, or angry.

needs checking She was so bored with her husband that she tried to kill him.

revised She was so angry with her husband that she tried to kill him.

• **breach/breech**: *To breach a wall or a contract* is *to break or break through it*, and *the breach* is *the breaking*. *Breech* refers to a part of a cannon or rifle—or to *the buttocks* (hence a *breech birth*, in which the buttocks or feet emerge before the head).

needs checking The lawyers claimed that her actions constituted a breech of contract.

revised The lawyers claimed that her actions constituted a breach of contract.

• **brusque/brisk**: *To be brusque* is *to be abrupt or slightly rude in speech or manner*; *brisk* means *quick* or *lively*.

needs checking He didn't say anything rude to me, but his manner was rather brisk.

revised He didn't say anything rude to me, but his manner was rather brusque.

• **can/may**: In formal writing *can* should be used to refer to *ability*, *may* to refer to *permission*.

needs checking Can I leave the room?

(This makes literal sense only if you are an injured person conversing with your doctor.)

revised May I leave the room?

• **capital/capitol**: As a noun, *capital* can refer to *wealth*, to *the city from which the government operates*, to *an upper case letter*, or to *the top of a pillar*. It can also be used as an adjective to mean *most important* or *principal*. *Capitol* is much more restricted in its meaning—*a specific American legislative building or Roman temple*.

needs checking The prosecution alleged that he had committed a capitol offence.

revised The prosecution alleged that he had committed a capital offence.

• **career/careen**: As a verb, *career* means *to swerve wildly*. *Careen* originally meant *tilt or lean*, but now is often treated as a synonym for *career*. Since *careen* has other specifically nautical meanings, some authorities resist the conflation of the two verbs—but the fact that *career* carries unintended echoes of the noun meaning *profession* leads many, not unreasonably, to prefer *careen*.

• **careless/uncaring**: *Careless* means *negligent* or *thoughtless*; you can be careless about your work, for example, or careless about your appearance. Do not use *careless*, however, when you want to talk about *not caring enough about other people*.

needs checking He acted in a very careless way towards his mother when she was sick.

revised He acted in an uncaring way towards his mother when she was sick.

• **censor/censure**: *To censor something* is *to prevent it, or those parts of it that are considered objectionable, from being available to the public*. *To censure someone* is *to express strong criticism or condemnation*.

needs checking The Senate censored the attorney general for his part in the scandal.

revised The Senate censured the attorney general for his part in the scandal.

• **childish/childlike**: The first is a term of abuse, the second a term of praise.

needs checking Her writing expresses a childish innocence.

revised Her writing expresses a childlike innocence.

• **classic/classical**: As an adjective *classic* means *of such a high quality that it has lasted or is likely to last for a very long time*. *Classical* is used to refer to *ancient Greece and Rome*, or, particularly when speaking of music, to refer to *a traditional style*.

needs checking Sophocles was one of the greatest classic authors; his plays are classical.

revised Sophocles was one of the greatest classical authors; his plays are acknowledged classics.

• **climatic/climactic**: Weather is not necessarily the high point of life.

needs checking Difficulties in predicting long-term trends are inherent in any climactic projections.

revised Difficulties in predicting long-term trends are inherent in any climatic projections.

• **collaborate/corroborate**: *To collaborate* is *to work together*, whereas *to corroborate* is *to give supporting evidence*.

needs checking He collaborated her claim that the Americans had corroborated with the Nazi colonel Klaus Barbie.

revised He corroborated her claim that the Americans had collaborated with the Nazi colonel Klaus Barbie.

• **compliment/complement**: *To compliment someone* is *to praise him*, and a *compliment* is the *praise*; *to complement something* is *to add to it to make it better or complete*, and a *complement* is *the number or amount needed to make it complete*.

needs checking None of the divisions had its full compliment of troops.

revised None of the divisions had its full complement of troops.

needs checking Prince Fielder's mission in Detroit was to compliment Miguel Cabrera, who was at that time the best hitter in baseball.

(Literally, this would mean that Fielder's job was to keep saying, "Nice work, Miguel," and so on.)

revised Prince Fielder's mission in Detroit was to complement Miguel Cabrera, who was at that time the best hitter in baseball.

On the Companion Website

Exercises on word meanings may be found at **sites.broadviewpress.com/writingcdn**. Click on **Exercises** and **Writing Mechanics** and go to **M2.5.**

• **comprise/compose/constitute**: The whole *comprises* or includes the various parts; the parts *compose* the whole. The verb *constitute*, similar in meaning to *compose*, is commonly used to refer to abstract concepts (e.g., *The point you make does not constitute an argument*, *The case you refer to constitutes a legal precedent*).

needs checking The British House of Commons is comprised of far fewer ministries than is the Canadian government.

revised The British House of Commons comprises far fewer ministries than does the Canadian government.

or The British House of Commons is composed of far fewer ministries than is the Canadian government.

• **conscience/conscious/consciousness**: *To be conscious* is *to be awake and aware of what is happening*, whereas *conscience* is *the part of our mind that tells us it is right to do some things and wrong to do other things (such as steal or murder). Conscience* and *consciousness* are both nouns; the adjectives are *conscientious (aware of what is right and wrong)* and *conscious (aware).*

needs checking She was tempted to steal the chocolate bar, but her conscious told her not to.

revised She was tempted to steal the chocolate bar, but her conscience told her not to.

• **contemptuous/contemptible**: We are *contemptuous* of anyone or anything we find *contemptible.*

needs checking The judge called the delinquent's behaviour utterly contemptuous.

revised The judge called the delinquent's behaviour utterly contemptible.

• **continual/continuous**: If something is *continuous* it *never stops*; something *continual* is *frequently repeated but not unceasing*. The same distinction holds for the adverbs *continually* and *continuously*.

needs checking He has been phoning me continuously for the past two weeks.

(Surely he stopped for a bite to eat or a short nap.)

• **decimate**: Most etymologists agree that originally this word meant *kill one of every ten*. It has come to be used more loosely to mean *destroy a considerable number of*, and sometimes *kill nine of every ten*, but many authorities advise against using the word in any way that expressly contradicts the original sense.

needs checking The regiment was decimated; fewer than 40 per cent of the troops survived.

revised The regiment suffered extreme losses; fewer than 40 per cent of the troops survived.

• **deduce/deduct**: *Deduction* is the noun stemming from both these verbs, which is perhaps why they are sometimes confused. *To deduce* is *to draw a conclusion*, whereas *to deduct* is *to subtract.*

needs checking	Sherlock Holmes deducted that Moriarty had committed the crime.
revised	Sherlock Holmes deduced that Moriarty had committed the crime.

• **definite/definitive**: If something is *definite* then there is *no uncertainty about it*; a *definitive* version of something *fixes it in its final or permanent form*—just as a dictionary definition attempts to fix the meaning of a word. Often a sentence is better with neither of these words.

needs checking	Glenn Gould's recording of Bach's Goldberg Variations is often thought of as the definite modern version.
revised	Glenn Gould's recording of Bach's Goldberg Variations is often thought of as the definitive modern version.
needs checking	Once we have completed our caucus discussion I will be making a very definitive statement.
revised	Once we have completed our caucus discussion I will be making a statement.
or	Once we have completed our caucus discussion I will have something definite to say.

• **degradation/decline**: *Degradation* carries the connotation of *shame and disgrace. To degrade something* is not *to reduce it*, or *downgrade it*, or *destroy it.*

needs checking	Among those units in which women played a combat role there was no degradation in operational effectiveness.
revised	Among those units in which women played a combat role there was no decline in operational effectiveness.
or	... there was no reduction in operational effectiveness.
needs checking	According to some authorities, the threat of war has now been significantly degraded.
revised	According to some authorities, the threat of war has now been significantly reduced.

• **demur/demure**: To *demur* is to raise an objection; to be *demure* is to be modest and shy in an appealing way.

• **deny/rebut/refute**: *To deny something* is *to assert that it is not true*; *to rebut an argument* is *to oppose it*; *to refute it* is *to prove conclusively that it is not true.*

needs checking During yesterday's press conference the president angrily refuted the allegations: "There has been no improper relationship," he said.

revised During yesterday's press conference, the president angrily denied the allegations: "There has been no improper relationship," he said.

• **deprecate/depreciate**: *To deprecate something* is *to suggest that it is not valuable or worthy of praise*; something that *depreciates* loses its value.

needs checking Leonard Cohen was very self-depreciating throughout the interview.

revised Leonard Cohen was very self-deprecating throughout the interview.

• **discrete/discreet**: *Discrete* means *separate* or *distinct*, whereas *discreet* means *prudent* and *tactful; unwilling to give away secrets.*

needs checking Anthony Weiner is not renowned for being discrete.

revised Anthony Weiner is not renowned for being discreet.

• **disinterested/uninterested**: A *disinterested* person is *unbiased; uninfluenced by self-interest, especially of a monetary sort.* It is thus quite possible for a person who is entirely disinterested in a particular matter to be completely fascinated by it. If one is *uninterested in* something, on the other hand, one is *bored by* it.

needs checking He was so disinterested in the game that he left after the fifth inning with the score at 2–2.

revised He was so uninterested in the game that he left after the fifth inning with the score at 2–2.

needs checking The controlling shareholders had grown tired of the CEO's futuristic strategies and disinterest in day-to-day operations.

revised The controlling shareholders had grown tired of the CEO's futuristic strategies and lack of interest in day-to-day operations.

• **disorient/disorientate**: Both are considered correct by many authorities, but the extra syllable of the second grates on the ear.

needs checking I was entirely disorientated in the darkness.

revised I was entirely disoriented in the darkness.

• **dissemble/disassemble**: *To dissemble* is *to disguise your feelings*—a mild form of lying. *To disassemble* is *to take apart.*

needs checking For the test we are required to first assemble and then dissemble a six-cylinder engine.

revised For the test we are required to first assemble and then disassemble a six-cylinder engine.

• **dissociate/disassociate**: There is no need for the extra syllable.

needs checking T.S. Eliot speaks of a disassociation of sensibility that began in the seventeenth century.

revised T.S. Eliot speaks of a dissociation of sensibility that began in the seventeenth century.

• **distinct/distinctive**: *Distinct* means *able to be seen or perceived clearly; easily distinguishable from those around it. Distinctive* means *unusual; not commonly found.* There is a similar contrast between the adverbs *distinctly* and *distinctively*, and the nouns *distinction* and *distinctiveness.*

needs checking I distinctively heard the sound of a car engine.

revised I distinctly heard the sound of a car engine.

• **ecology/environment**: *Ecology* is the study of some aspects of the environment; you cannot "harm the ecology."

• **economic/economical**: *Economic* means *pertaining to economics*, or *sufficient to allow a reasonable return for the amount of money or effort put in. Economical* is a word applied to people, which means *thrifty*. The difference applies as well to *uneconomic* and *uneconomical.*

needs checking Controversy over whether it would be economical to develop the vast Hibernia oilfield continued for many years.

revised Controversy over whether it would be economic to develop the vast Hibernia oilfield continued for many years.

• **effective/efficacious/effectual/efficient**: *Effective*, *efficacious*, and *effectual* all mean *sufficient to produce the desired effect. Efficacious*, however, applies only to *strategies* or *things* (though it strikes many as a rather pompous word in any application). A person, then, cannot be efficacious. *Effectual* was once applied only to actions, but is now sometimes applied to people as well. *Effective* can apply to actions or people. *Efficient* has an added connotation: *producing results with little waste of money or effort*. Thus a promotional campaign to persuade people to buy a product by giving away free samples to every man, woman, and child in the country might be effective, but it would certainly not be efficient; a good deal of waste would be involved. The same difference applies to the nouns *effectiveness* and *efficiency*. (*Efficacy* is a rather pretentious noun that is usually best avoided.)

needs checking	The board wants to increase the efficacy of the machinery we use.
revised	The board wants to increase the efficiency of the machinery we use.
needs checking	He is the most efficacious worker in the office.
revised	He is the most effective worker in the office.

• **e.g./i.e.**: The abbreviation *e.g.* is short for *exemplum gratia* ("example given"; or, in the plural *exempli gratia*, "examples given"). It is sometimes confused with the abbreviation *i.e.*, which is short for *id est* ("that is to say").

needs checking	Those citizens of India who speak Hindi (e.g., over 500 million people) are being encouraged to learn a second language.
revised	Those citizens of India who speak Hindi (i.e., over 500 million people) are being encouraged to learn a second language.

• **elemental/elementary**: A thing is *elemental* if it forms *an important or essential element of the whole*; it is *elementary* if it is *easy to understand*, or *at a relatively simple level.*

needs checking	He lacked even the most elemental understanding of the problem.
revised	He lacked even the most elementary understanding of the problem.

• **elicit/illicit**: *Elicit* is a verb; one elicits information about something. *Illicit* is an adjective meaning *illegal* or *not approved.*

needs checking	She has been dealing in elicit drugs for some time.
revised	She has been dealing in illicit drugs for some time.
or	The police elicited details about her drug use.

• **eligible/illegible**: One is *eligible* for a job or for membership in an organization if one *meets the standard* set for applicants. One of the requirements might be that one's handwriting not be *illegible.*

needs checking	He regretted that I was not illegible to join his club.
revised	He regretted that I was not eligible to join his club.

• **emigrant/immigrant**: *To migrate* is *to move from one place to another.* The prefix *ex*, shortened to *e*, means *out of*, so an *emigrant* from a country is *someone who is moving out of it.* The prefix *in* or *im* means *in* or *into*, so an *immigrant* to a country is *someone moving into it.* Similarly, *emigration* is *the movement of people out of a country*, while *immigration* is *the movement of people into a country*. Notice the spelling in both cases: *e-migrant* (one *m*), *im-migrant* (two *ms*).

needs checking	More than one million emigrants entered America last year.
revised	More than one million immigrants entered America last year.

• **eminent/imminent/immanent**: A person is *eminent* if she is *well-known and well-respected*; an event is *imminent* if it is *about to happen*; a quality (or a god) is *immanent* if it *pervades* everything.

needs checking	Even those working for the party in the campaign did not believe that a majority victory was immanent.
revised	Even those working for the party in the campaign did not believe that a majority victory was imminent.

• **empathy/sympathy**: To *sympathize* with another person is to feel for that person; to *empathize* is to do so in a way that identifies oneself with that person.

• **enervate/invigorate**: Because of the similarity in sound between *enervate* and *energy*, *enervate* is often thought to mean *make more energetic*. In fact *enervate* means just the opposite—*to lessen the strength of.* If something makes you more *energetic* it *invigorates* you.

needs checking	She found the fresh air quite enervating; I haven't seen her so lively in months.
revised	She found the fresh air quite invigorating; I haven't seen her so lively in months.

• **enormity/enormousness**: Originally the adjective *enormous* simply meant *deviating from the norm*, but by the early nineteenth century it had also come to mean *abnormal*, *monstrous*, or *extraordinarily wicked*. Today the only meaning is of course *vast in size or quantity*, but the connotation of wickedness is preserved in the noun *enormity*. We may speak of the enormity of a person's crime, but if we want a noun to express vast size we should use *enormousness* or *vastness*.

needs checking	What most impresses visitors to the Grand Canyon is its sheer enormity.
revised	What most impresses visitors to the Grand Canyon is its sheer enormousness.
better	What most impresses visitors to the Grand Canyon is its vastness.

• **envious/jealous**: One is envious of someone else's good fortune, jealous of one's own possessions. In common parlance *jealous* is often used as a synonym for *envious*, but arguably the distinction between the two words is worth preserving.

needs checking	He felt jealous whenever he thought of how much land his brother owned.
revised	He felt envious whenever he thought of how much land his brother owned.

• **epithet/epigraph/epitaph/epigram**: four words often confused. Here are their meanings:

- Epithet—an adjective or short phrase describing someone *("The Legion of Boom"—an epithet first used in 2012 to describe the secondary defence of the Seattle Seahawks—involves an allusion to another epithet, "Legion of Doom," which has been used by teams both in ice hockey and in professional wrestling).*
- Epigraph—an inscription, especially one placed upon a building, tomb, or statue to indicate its name or purpose; or a motto or quotation appearing at the beginning of a book (or the beginning of a chapter in a book).
- Epitaph—words describing a dead person, often the words inscribed on the tomb.
- Epigram—a short, witty, or pointed saying.

needs checking	His epigram will read, "A good man lies here."
revised	His epitaph will read, "A good man lies here."

• **equal/equitable/equable**: Things that are *equal* have the *same value*. Arrangements that are *equitable* are *fair and just*. An *equable* person is one who is *moderate and even-tempered*.

needs checking	The distribution of seats in the American Senate is not an equable one; Rhode Island, with its one million people, is allocated two senators, while California, with its forty million people, is also allocated two senators.
revised	The distribution of seats in the American Senate is not an equitable one; Rhode Island, with its one million people, is allocated two senators, while California, with its forty million people, is also allocated two senators.

• **explicit/implicit**: If something is *explicit* it is *unfolded—stated in precise terms, not merely suggested or implied.* Something that is *implicit* is *folded in—not stated overtly*. By extension *implicit* has also come to mean *complete or absolute* in expressions such as *implicit trust* (i.e., trust so complete that it does not have to be put into words).

needs checking I told you implicitly to have the report on my desk first thing this morning.

revised I told you explicitly to have the report on my desk first thing this morning.

• **financial/fiscal/monetary/economic**: The terms used in personal, business, and government finance are not always the same. Here are four that are often not clearly understood:

- Financial—having to do with finance or the handling of money.
- Fiscal—having to do with public revenue.
- Monetary—having to do with the currency of a country. (Only in very limited circumstances, such as the expression *monetary value*, can *monetary* have the more general meaning of *having to do with money*.)
- Economic—having to do with the economy. Thus a government's economic program embraces both fiscal and monetary policies.

needs checking My brother is a nice person, but he has no monetary ability.

revised My brother is a nice person, but he has no financial ability.

• **finish/be finished/have finished**: In informal usage *to be finished* means *to be at the end of one's life or career (If that player's knee is seriously injured again, he will be finished).* In formal writing, this special use should not be extended to the verb *finish* in its normal meaning.

needs checking When you are finished the experiment, tabulate the results carefully.

revised When you have finished the experiment, tabulate the results carefully.

• **flammable/inflammable**: The two words share the same meaning; *flammable* may have originated because of the possibility for confusion with the word *inflammable*, which looks like a negative but isn't. *Non-flammable* should be used to mean *difficult or impossible to burn.*

needs checking Asbestos is an inflammable material.

revised Asbestos is a non-flammable material.

• **fleshing/flushing**: The expression *flesh out* means add to—just as flesh is added to a growing animal. The similarity in sounds often leads people to write *flush* instead of *flesh*, but if you suggest someone *flush out* their argument, you are surely not suggesting they expand it.

• **flout/flaunt**: *To flout* is *to disobey or show disrespect for*; *to flaunt* is *to display very openly*.

needs checking Aggressive policing seems to have had no effect on the number of people flaunting the law.

revised Aggressive policing seems to have had no effect on the number of people flouting the law.

• **formerly/formally**: The similarity of sound often leads to confusion.

needs checking In August Mr. Laurel formerly broke with Mrs. Aquino.

revised In August Mr. Laurel formally broke with Mrs. Aquino.

• **fortunate/fortuitous**: *Fortunate* means *lucky* and can refer to people as well as occurrences; *fortuitous* means *happening by chance*, and can refer only to occurrences or situations, not people.

needs checking This combination of circumstances is not a fortuitous one for our company; we shall have to expect reduced sales in the coming year.

revised This combination of circumstances is not a fortunate one for our company; we shall have to expect reduced sales in the coming year.

• **forward/foreword**: You find a *foreword* before the other words in a book (and an *afterword* after the other words).

needs checking The author admits in the forward to her book that the research was not comprehensive.

revised The author admits in the foreword to her book that the research was not comprehensive.

• **founder/flounder**: As a verb, *founder* means *to get into difficulty*, *to stumble or fall*, *to sink* (when speaking of a ship), or *to fail* (when speaking of a plan). *To flounder* is *to move clumsily or with difficulty*, or *to become confused in an effort to do something*.

needs checking He foundered about in a hopeless attempt to solve the problem.

revised He floundered about in a hopeless attempt to solve the problem.

• **fulsome/effusive**: *Fulsome* means *insincere* or *excessively flattering*; fulsome praise is not the sort one wants to receive. But we all like to receive *effusive* (or *enthusiastic*) praise.

needs checking He was pleased to be showered with fulsome compliments.

revised He was pleased to be showered with effusive compliments.

• **further/farther**: *Farther* refers only to *physical distance*.

needs checking Eisenhower argued that the plan should receive farther study.

revised Eisenhower argued that the plan should receive further study.

• **gender/sex**: The word *gender* is used to refer to characteristics that are associated with one's sex but that have been formed through social influences. When we refer to the *female sex* or the *male sex*, on the other hand, we are speaking of biological difference.

• **herbs/spices**: The difference lies in the origin; *herbs* come from the stems, leaves, or flowers of plants, while *spices* come from the roots, the bark, the seeds, or the buds.

• **historic/historical**: *Historic* means *of sufficient importance that it is likely to become famous in history*; *historical* means *having to do with history* (*historical research, historical scholarship*, etc.).

needs checking We are gathered here for a historical occasion—the opening of the city's first sewage treatment plant.

revised We are gathered here for a historic occasion—the opening of the city's first sewage treatment plant.

• **hopefully**: one of the greatest causes of disagreement among grammarians. Traditionalists argue that the correct meaning of the adverb *hopefully* is *filled with hope*, and that the use of the word to mean *it is to be hoped that* is therefore incorrect. On the other side it is plausibly argued that many adverbs can function as independent comments at the beginning of a sentence. (*Finally, let me point out that ... ; Clearly, we have much to do if we are to ... ; Obviously, it will not be possible to ...*). Why should *hopefully* be treated differently? Why indeed? Using *hopefully* for this purpose might not make for beautiful English, but it should not be regarded as a grievous error.

needs checking Hopefully, it will be possible to finish before tomorrow.
(As usually happens, *hopefully* is here used with the passive, making for a wordy sentence.)

revised We hope we can finish before tomorrow.

needs checking Hopefully, we will arrive before dusk.
(This sentence should be rewritten in order to ensure that the sentence does not suggest the meaning, *we will arrive filled with hope before dusk*.)

revised I hope we will arrive before dusk.

• **human/humane**: Until the eighteenth century there was no distinction made between the two in either meaning or pronunciation; they were simply alternative ways of spelling the same word. In recent centuries *humane* has come to be used to refer exclusively to the more attractive human qualities—kindness, compassion, and so forth.

needs checking Their group is campaigning for the human treatment of whales and dolphins.
revised Their group is campaigning for the humane treatment of whales and dolphins.

• **idioms**: Similarity in sound and meaning between words often leads to the mixing-up of idioms.

needs checking Authorities termed it a democratic transition, but for all intensive purposes it was a coup d'état.
revised Authorities termed it a democratic transition, but for all intents and purposes it was a coup d'état.

needs checking The new recruits were reminded that they would have to tow the line.
revised The new recruits were reminded that they would have to toe the line.

• **illusion/allusion**: An *allusion* is *an indirect reference to something*; an *illusion* is *something falsely supposed to exist.*

needs checking Joyce is making an illusion in this passage to a Shakespearean sonnet.
revised Joyce is making an allusion in this passage to a Shakespearean sonnet.

• **imply/infer**: *To imply something* is *to suggest it without stating it directly*; the other person will have to *infer* your meaning.

needs checking I implied from his tone that he disliked our plan.
revised I inferred from his tone that he disliked our plan.

• **in to/into**: The difference is that *into* is used to indicate movement from outside to inside.

needs checking Many expressed sympathy for Rushdie's decision, although some said he was caving into pressure.
revised Many expressed sympathy for Rushdie's decision, although some said he was caving in to pressure.

For more on these words see pages 433–34.

• **incidents/incidence**: *Incidents* is the plural of *incident* (*happening*), whereas *incidence* is a singular noun meaning *the rate at which something occurs.*

needs checking The incidents of lung cancer is much lower in Zambia than it is in North America.

revised The incidence of lung cancer is much lower in Zambia than it is in North America.

• **ingenious/ingenuous**: *Ingenious* means *clever*; *ingenuous* means *pleasantly open and unsophisticated.*

needs checking Her manner was completely ingenious; I cannot imagine she was trying to deceive us.

revised Her manner was completely ingenuous; I cannot imagine she was trying to deceive us.

• **innumerable**: *so numerous that it is impossible to count*; do not use this word as a synonym for *many.*

needs checking Scholars have advanced innumerable explanations for the dinosaurs' disappearance.

revised Scholars have advanced many explanations for the dinosaurs' disappearance.

• **insist/persist**: To *insist* (that something be done, or on doing something) is to *express yourself very forcefully.* To *persist in doing something* is to *keep on doing it, usually despite some difficulty or opposition.*

needs checking Even after he had been convicted of the crime, he persisted that he was innocent.

revised Even after he had been convicted of the crime, he insisted that he was innocent.

• **instinctive/instinctual**: There is no difference in meaning; arguably, it is thus better to stay with the older (and more pleasant sounding) *instinctive.*

needs checking Biologists disagree as to what constitutes instinctual behaviour.

revised Biologists disagree as to what constitutes instinctive behaviour.

• **judicial/judicious**: *Judicial* means *having to do with law courts and the administration of justice. Judicious* means *having good judgement.*

needs checking He made one or two judicial comments about the quality of the production.

revised He made one or two judicious comments about the quality of the production.

• **know**: When one *knows* something, that piece of knowledge has been in one's mind for some time. The process of gathering or acquiring knowledge is called *discovering*.

needs checking Although I noticed the new employee on Monday, I did not know her name until today.

revised Although I noticed the new employee on Monday, I did not discover her name until today.

• **later/latter**: *Later* means *afterwards in time*, whereas the *latter* is the *last mentioned (of two things).*

needs checking I looked up the battle of Stalingrad in both the *Encyclopedia Britannica* and Wikipedia. The later provided much more information.

revised I looked up the battle of Stalingrad in both the *Encyclopedia Britannica* and Wikipedia. The latter provided much more information.

• **laudable/laudatory**: *Laudable* means *worthy of praise*; *laudatory* means *expressing praise*.

needs checking His efforts to combat poverty are very laudatory.

revised His efforts to combat poverty are very laudable.

• **liable/likely**: *Liable* means *obliged by law* or *responsible under the law (You will be liable for any damage caused when you are driving the vehicle)*; or *in danger of doing or suffering from something undesirable (That chimney is liable to fall)*. Since in the latter meaning *likely* can often be used in place of *liable*, it is often assumed that there is really no distinction between the two. Careful writers, however, do not use *liable* unless they are referring to possible consequences of an undesirable nature.

needs checking Last Sunday Singh won the Colonial Open. He's liable to win again before the end of the year.

revised Last Sunday Singh won the Colonial Open. He's likely to win again before the end of the year.

• **libel/slander**: *Libel* is written (and published); *slander* is oral.

needs checking He was careful in his speech to avoid making any libellous remarks.

revised He was careful in his speech to avoid making any slanderous remarks.

• **lightning/lightening**: One is not likely to see the sky *lightening* until after the thunder and *lightning* are over.

needs checking Three of the men were severely injured by the lightening.
revised Three of the men were severely injured by the lightning.

• **like/such as**: In formal writing, *like* is used to draw comparisons, while *such as* is used when you want to provide examples. *We need someone like LeBron James on this team* means *We need someone who resembles LeBron James*—a superb all-round basketball player. If you say *The Miami Heat teams of 2012 and 2013 featured stars like LeBron James and Dwyane Wade*, the literal meaning of the sentence is that those teams featured stars who *resembled* LeBron James and Dwyane Wade—which presumably is not what you mean to say, since these players didn't resemble the leading stars; they were the leading stars. In a case such as this the words you want are *such as*: *The Miami Heat teams of 2012 and 2013 featured stars such as LeBron James and Dwyane Wade.*

needs checking In the early twentieth century, writers like T.S. Eliot, Ezra Pound, and Virginia Woolf were leading figures in the movement we now call modernism.
revised In the early twentieth century, writers such as T.S. Eliot, Ezra Pound, and Virginia Woolf were leading figures in the movement we now call modernism.
or T.S. Eliot, Ezra Pound, and Virginia Woolf were leading figures in the early twentieth-century movement we now call modernism.

[It was not writers similar to Eliot, Pound, and Woolf who led the literary movement; it was Eliot, Pound and Woolf themselves.]

See also page 346 below—**like/as**.

• **literally**: *Literal* means *by the letter—in exact agreement with what is said or written*. A literal meaning is thus the opposite of a figurative or metaphorical meaning. Do not use the adverb *literally* simply to emphasize something.

needs checking As silviculturalists, we are—literally—babes in the woods. (Ken Drushka, *Stumped: The Forest Industry in Transition*)

(Silviculturalists may be literally in the woods, but they are not literally babes.)

revised As silviculturalists, we are babes in the woods.

• **make/allow/make possible**: *To make someone do something* is *to force them to do it (often against their wishes)*; *to allow someone to do something* is *to permit them or make it possible for them to do something that they want to do.*

needs checking A new hospital wing is being built; this will make many more people come for treatment.

revised A new hospital wing is being built; this will allow many more people to come for treatment.

or A new hospital wing is being built; this will make it possible for many more people to come for treatment.

• **masterful/masterly**: *Masterful* means *domineering*; *masterly* means *exhibiting mastery or great skill.*

needs checking Once again last night, Diana Krall gave the audience a masterful performance.

revised Once again last night, Diana Krall gave the audience a masterly performance.

• **mitigate/militate**: To *mitigate something* is to *make it less harsh or severe*; thus, mitigating circumstances are those that make a criminal offence less serious. *To militate against something* is *to act as a strong influence against it.*

needs checking The natural history orientation of early anthropology also mitigated against studies of change. (Bruce G. Trigger in *Natives and Newcomers*)

revised The natural history orientation of early anthropology also militated against studies of change.

• **momentarily**: *Momentarily* means *lasting only a moment (He was momentarily confused).* Common usage also allows the word to mean *in a moment* or *soon*; in formal writing it is best to avoid this use.

needs checking Ms. Billings has informed me that she will join us momentarily.

revised Ms. Billings told me that she will join us soon.

• **moot/mute**: A *moot court* discusses a hypothetical case; a *moot point* is one that may be argued from either side. *Mute* means *silent* or *incapable of speech.*

needs checking In her recent article Nussbaum suggests that Williams's point is mute.

revised In her recent article Nussbaum suggests that Williams's point is moot.

• **moral/morale**: The *morale* of a group is their level of confidence, optimism, shared positive feeling—not to be confused with the *moral* of a story, or with *moral* issues.

• **nauseous/nauseated**: Something that is *nauseous* makes you feel *nauseated.* Informally many people speak of feeling *nauseous*; in the context of formal writing they should feel *nauseated* instead.

• **need/want**: The verb *need* conveys the idea that it would be difficult or impossible for you to do without the needed thing. If you are talking about acquiring something that is not necessary or essential, use *want* instead; everyone *needs* water and food, but no one really *needs* a new smartphone. Be careful too not to commit to paper the slang use of *need to* for *should.*

needs checking I need to marry someone who is very beautiful, very intelligent, very kind, and very rich.

revised I want to marry someone who is very beautiful, very intelligent, very kind, and very rich.

needs checking The government needs to improve the roads in this area.

revised The government should improve the roads in this area.

• **non sequitur**: A *non sequitur* is a *statement that has no clear relationship with what has preceded it.* There may be some connection within the mind of the speaker or writer, but it has not been expressed in words.

needs checking It's time our government did more to help southern Africa. Besides, consumers appreciate inexpensive clothes.

revised It's time our government did more to help southern Africa. Lowering the current barriers against importing cheap food and textiles would be an important step in that direction. Such a move would benefit our own citizens too; consumers appreciate inexpensive food and clothing.

• **novel**: A novel is an extended work of prose fiction. Perhaps because students in high school are rarely asked to read extended works of prose *non*-fiction, the mistaken idea often takes root that any extended prose work can be called a novel. It can't. Extended works of non-fiction—of history or philosophy or political theory or science, for example—are not works of fiction, so they cannot be novels.

needs checking Darwin's *The Voyage of the Beagle* appeared twenty years before his greatest novel, *On the Origin of Species*, was published.

revised Darwin's *The Voyage of the Beagle* appeared twenty years before his greatest work, *On the Origin of Species*, was published.

needs checking In Chapter 25 of his novel, Machiavelli writes that it is "better to be adventurous than cautious."

revised In Chapter 25 of *The Prince*, Machiavelli writes that it is "better to be adventurous than cautious."

or In Chapter 25, Machiavelli writes that it is "better to be adventurous than cautious."

(if the context makes clear which text is being referred to)

• **numbers and things**: In any sentence about things and numbers associated with those things, it can be easy enough to become grammatically tangled up between the things and the measure of number. Always have this question in the back of your mind: what is the subject of the verb? Here's an example:

needs checking Delays in new product launches have hammered the company's share price, which started the year at about $60 and now trades at less than $30.

That may seem fine at first glance, but look again. What is the subject of the verb *trades*? It's the noun *price*. But is it in fact the price that trades at under $30? No; it's the shares that trade at less than $30.

revised Delays in new product launches have hammered the company's share price, which started the year at about $60 and is now less than $30.

or Delays in new product launches have hammered the company's shares, which started the year at about $60; now the stock trades at less than $30.

Here are other examples of the same sort of problem:

needs checking Many people have said that the price of the Tesla is too expensive.

revised Many people have said that the price of the Tesla is too high.

or Many people have said that the Tesla is too expensive.

needs checking The height of the Shanghai Tower rises more than 2,000 feet.

revised The Shanghai Tower rises more than 2,000 feet.

or The height of the Shanghai Tower is more than 2,000 feet.

needs checking The speed of the Sopwith Camel flew at just over 100 miles per hour during WWI.

revised The Sopwith Camel flew at just over 100 miles per hour during WWI.

or The maximum speed of the WWI Sopwith Camel was just over 100 miles per hour.

• **obsolescent/obsolete**: Something *obsolescent* is becoming out of date; something *obsolete* is completely outmoded.

• **obtuse/abstruse**: *Obtuse* means *rounded* or *blunt* (as opposed to sharp)—and by extension, when used about humans, *dull* or *dim-witted* (sometimes with the implication that the person is wilfully refusing to see the truth). *Abstruse* refers to ideas, not people, and means *obscure, difficult to understand* (sometimes with the implication that the material is of considerable weight or importance).

• **of/have**: The difference in meaning is obvious, but the similarity in sound consistently leads people to write sentences involving such meaningless expressions as *should of, would of, could of, may of, might of,* and *must of.*

needs checking The experiment would of succeeded if the solution had been prepared correctly.

revised The experiment would have succeeded if the solution had been prepared correctly.

needs checking Hitler believed that Rommel should of been able to defeat Montgomery at El Alamein.

revised Hitler believed that Rommel should have been able to defeat Montgomery at El Alamein.

• **other**: If one uses the words *the other* it suggests that the thing or person you are about to mention is the **only** other one you are going to write about. If there are several others to be mentioned, *another* is the word to choose.

On the Companion Website

Exercises on word meanings may be found at **sites.broadviewpress.com/writingcdn**. Click on **Exercises** and **Writing Mechanics** and go to **M2.5.**

needs checking One reason Germany lost the Second World War was that Hitler underestimated the importance of keeping the United States out of the conflict. The other reason was that the German intelligence network was inferior to that of the Allies. Moreover, Hitler's decision to invade Russia was a disastrous mistake.

(Here the use of *the other* in the second sentence leads the reader to believe this is the only other reason. When a third reason is mentioned in the next sentence, the reader is taken by surprise.)

revised One reason Germany lost the Second World War was that Hitler underestimated the importance of keeping the United States out of the conflict. Another reason was that the German intelligence network was inferior to that of the Allies. Moreover, Hitler's decision to invade Russia was a disastrous mistake.

• **our/are**: Like the substitution of *of* for *have*, the confusion of *our* and *are* should never survive the rough draft stage.

needs checking Almost all are time is spent together.

revised Almost all our time is spent together.

• **palate/palette/pallet**: Your *palate* is in your mouth. An artist uses a *palette* to mix paint on. (By extension, people often refer to the range of colours typically used by a painter as her *palette*.) Finally, a *pallet* (or skid) is a *wooden frame designed for transporting goods*.

needs checking In his later work Matisse's pallet was more limited; much of his work was in unmodulated, primary colours.

revised In his later work Matisse's palette was more limited; much of his work was in unmodulated, primary colours.

• **partake/participate**: *Partake* refers to *things* (especially food and drink), *participate* to *activities*.

needs checking The mayor made a brief appearance, but did not partake in the festivities.

revised The mayor made a brief appearance, but did not participate in the festivities.

• **penultimate/ultimate**: The *penultimate* one comes just before the last one; the *ultimate* one is the last one. A widespread misconception is that *penultimate* carries the implication of being higher than or better than or beyond the *ultimate*; not so.

• **persecute/prosecute**: To *persecute* someone is to treat them in a harsh and unfair manner, especially because of their political or religious beliefs. To *prosecute* someone is to take legal action against them in the belief that they have committed a crime.

needs checking Catholics began to be prosecuted in England in the sixteenth century.

revised Catholics began to be persecuted in England in the sixteenth century.

• **persuade**: To persuade someone *of* something is to make that person believe that it is true. To persuade someone *to do* something is to lead that person, through what one says, to do the desired thing. If one does not succeed in making people believe or do what one wants, then one has not persuaded or convinced them, but only tried to persuade them. (The confusion of *refute* with *deny* [pages 312–13] is a parallel mistake.)

needs checking After all Portia's persuasion, Shylock still refuses to change his mind.

revised After all Portia's attempts to persuade him, Shylock still refuses to change his mind.

• **pore/pour**: As *The Globe and Mail Style Book* puts it, one should "not write of someone pouring over a book unless the tome in question is getting wet."

needs checking After pouring over the evidence, the committee could find no evidence of wrongdoing.

revised After poring over the evidence, the committee could find no evidence of wrongdoing.

• **practical/practicable**: *Practical* means *suitable for use*, or *involving activity rather than theory*. *Practicable* means *able to be done*. Changing the railway system back to steam locomotives would be practicable but extremely impractical. In most cases *practical* is the word the writer wants; excessive use of *practicable* will make writing sound pretentious rather than important.

needs checking We do not feel that the construction of a new facility would be practicable at this time.

revised It would not be practical to construct a new facility now.

• **prescribe/proscribe**: To *prescribe* something is to recommend or order its use; to *proscribe* something is to forbid its use.

needs checking One local physician has already proscribed this new drug for a dozen of her patients, and in every case their condition has improved after they take it.

revised One local physician has already prescribed this new drug for a dozen of her patients, and in every case their condition has improved after they take it.

• **presently**: The subject of much disagreement among grammarians; should *presently* be restricted to its original meaning of *soon*, or should common usage of the word to mean *now* be allowed to spread unopposed? Traditionalists argue that the acceptance of both meanings encourages ambiguity, but in fact the verb tense usually makes clear whether the speaker means *soon* or *now* (*I will be there presently, I am presently working on a large project*, etc.). Perhaps the best solution is to avoid the rather pompous *presently* altogether, and stick to those fine simple words *soon* and *now*.

needs checking I am seeing Mr. Jones presently.

revised I am seeing Mr. Jones now.

or I will be seeing Mr. Jones soon.

• **proposition/proposal**: The only formally correct meaning of *proposition* is *a statement that expresses an idea*, as in *This country is dedicated to the proposition that all humans are created equal.* It is better not to use it to mean *proposal*.

needs checking The department has put forward a proposition for increasing sales.

revised The department has put forward a proposal for increasing sales.

• **prove**: *To prove something* is *to eliminate any doubt whatsoever as to its truth*. Outside of mathematical or philosophical logic, proof is rarely possible; what one is doing when writing about history or political science or literature is presenting an argument, not a proof. Be cautious in the claims you make in formal writing.

needs checking The following passage proves that T.S. Eliot was antisemitic.

revised The following passage strongly suggests that T.S. Eliot was antisemitic.

or Antisemitic feeling is clearly present in the following passage.

• **raise/rise**: As a verb, *raise* means *to lift*; *rise* means *to come up*.

needs checking They rose the curtain at 8 o'clock.
revised They raised the curtain at 8 o'clock.
or The curtain rose at 8 o'clock.

(Note: Both words are also used as nouns; in North America a *raise* is an *increase in salary*; the UK equivalent is a *rise* in salary.)

• **rational/rationale**: *Rational* is an adjective meaning *logical* or *sensible.* A *rationale* is an *explanation for something.*

needs checking The underlying rational for the proliferation of soaps and detergents is not to make our skin or clothes any cleaner, but to increase the profits of the manufacturers.
revised The underlying rationale for the proliferation of soaps and detergents is not to make our skin or clothes any cleaner, but to increase the profits of the manufacturers.

• **ravish/ravage**: *Ravish* has two quite unrelated meanings—*to rape*, or *to fill with delight. To ravage* is *to damage or destroy.*

needs checking The tree had been ravished by insects.
revised The tree had been ravaged by insects.

• **real/genuine**: The basic meaning of *real* is *existing*; the opposite of *fake* or *forged* is *genuine.*

needs checking The buyer had thought the painting was a Cézanne, but he soon discovered it was not real.
revised The buyer had thought the painting was a Cézanne, but he soon discovered it was not genuine.

• **regime/regimen/regiment**: A *regime* is either a *system of government* or a *period in which a particular government is in power* (e.g., *military regime, democratic regime*). A *regimen* is a *precisely fixed course of activity* (e.g., a *program of daily exercise and dieting*, a *schedule according to which medication must be taken*). A *regiment* is an *army unit.* Sometimes medical authorities use *regime* and *regimen* interchangeably; there is some benefit to keeping all three clearly separate.

needs checking A regiment of exercise and heavy medication kept Kennedy performing into his third year as president.
(*The National Post*, 7 June 2003)
revised A regimen of exercise and heavy medication kept Kennedy performing into his third year as president.

• **reign/rein**: A monarch *reigns* over a territory; to control a horse you *rein* it in (using the reins). A new manager takes up the *reins* of an organization.

needs checking The new leader has so far shown no signs of reigning in the armed forces.

revised The new leader has so far shown no signs of reining in the armed forces.

• **relatable**: Until relatively recently, most people were in the habit of using phrases such as *easy to relate to* where many now use *relatable*. Some traditionalists see *relatable* as an awkward or inappropriate coinage, arguing that the word does not follow the usual pattern of adjectives formed from transitive verbs (*catchable*, *hittable*, etc.). But, as Ben Zimmer and others have pointed out, many useful adjectives (*reliable*, *laughable*, etc.) have been formed from intransitive verbs, and are regarded as entirely acceptable. There is thus no good reason not to accept *relatable* as perfectly correct English; indeed, the argument may fairly be made that using *relatable* in some contexts reduces wordiness; compare *Most people will find the premise of Greta Gerwig's new film easy to relate to* (15 words) with *Most people will find the premise of Greta Gerwig's new film relatable* (12 words).

The problem with *relatable* is not that it shouldn't ever be used; it's that many people use it too often to mean too many different things. If you're going to write that something is *relatable*, it may be useful to ask yourself before you do so *who* is likely to find that thing easy to relate to, and *why* they may be likely to find it easy to relate to. It will sharpen what you write if you can be more specific:

> That's something that anyone under 30 can probably relate to.
>
> That's a feeling that any young woman in twenty-first-century North America is likely to be able to relate to.
>
> This is a book that young people of colour are particularly likely to find relatable—but it's also a book that may help whites to better understand the challenges that people of colour face.
>
> It's difficult for most modern readers to directly relate to the situation that Shylock finds himself in when Portia turns the tables on him in *The Merchant of Venice*, but the way in which Shakespeare structures the scene—and, in particular, the inclusion of Shylock's "Hath not a Jew eyes?" speech at this point in the play—makes it easy for us to feel some sympathy for his predicament.

The unfortunate habit that many students fall into when using *relatable* to describe a book or a film or an idea is using the word as a vague catch-all term that in the end means little more than *I can relate to this*; or *I like this*. The more you can train yourself to think in terms of specifics, the less likely you will be to use *relatable* to convey meanings that are vague and unhelpful—and it may be that you'll find yourself using *relatable* a good deal less frequently.

• **respectively/respectfully**: *Respectively* means *in the order mentioned*; *respectfully* means *done with respect*.

needs checking	Seattle, Denver, and New England were, respectfully, the three best teams in the NFL last season.
revised	Seattle, Denver, and New England were, respectively, the three best teams in the NFL last season.

• **reticent/reluctant**: *Reticent* means *reluctant to speak*; *reserved about speaking*. A country may be *reluctant* to go to war; it cannot be *reticent* to go to war. And to say *reticent to speak* is to repeat oneself.

needs checking	She was reticent to speak up, even when her family's reputation had been attacked.
revised	She was reluctant to speak up, even when her family's reputation had been attacked.
or	She remained reticent, even when her family's reputation had been attacked.

• **rite/right**: A *rite* is a *ceremonial or ritualistic act*; the word is most frequently used to denote formal acts, such as those of religious ceremonies (e.g., *marriage rites*). Many cultures have formal ceremonies to mark a new stage in a person's life—ceremonies referred to by social scientists as *rites of passage*. That phrase has come to be used informally to refer to any event marking a significant life change. Perhaps because rights and privileges are sometimes conferred during a ceremonial *rite*, the two words are sometimes confused and two *right*s end up making a wrong.

needs checking	For some students, political protests are a right of passage.
revised	For some students, political protests are a rite of passage.

• **sensory/sensuous/sensual**: Advertising and pornography have dulled the distinction among these three adjectives. The meanings of *sensory* and *sensuous* are similar—*sensual* is the sexy one:

- Sensory—having to do with the senses.
- Sensuous—having to do with the senses, or appealing to the senses.
- Sensual—offering physical pleasure, especially of a sexual sort.

needs checking Boswell suggested they go to a house of ill repute, but Johnson had no desire for sensuous pleasures.

revised Boswell suggested they go to a house of ill repute, but Johnson had no desire for sensual pleasures.

• **set/sit**: *To set* means *to place something somewhere.*

needs checking I could remember everything, but I had difficulty sitting it down on paper.

revised I could remember everything, but I had difficulty setting it down on paper.

needs checking He asked me to set down on the couch.

revised He asked me to sit down on the couch.

• **shall/will**: Historically *shall* was used primarily for simple statements or questions in the first person—both singular (*I*) and plural (*we*)—and *will* primarily for simple statements or questions in the second person and third person. When *shall* was used in the second or third person it implied control or authority, expressing promises, commands, or a sense of determination. The old "distinctions" are still maintained in questions (*shall I eat a peach?, will you have some tea?*) but in other respects the distinctions long ago weakened. A sense of control is expressed with just as much force in the second person using *will* (*you'll do as I say*) and expressions of determination in the first person often use *shall* (*we shall overcome*). At most, then, a slight difference in tone lingers. In legal documents, for example, *shall* is often used rather than *will*, but either wording carries with it the same meaning—and confers the same legal obligation.

correct The undersigned shall fulfill the said requirements on or before December 31, 2027.

also correct The undersigned will fulfill the said requirements on or before December 31, 2027.

• **simple/simplistic**: *Simplistic* is a derogatory word meaning *too simple* or *excessively simplified.*

needs checking The questions were so simplistic that I was able to answer all but one correctly.

revised The questions were so simple that I was able to answer all but one correctly.

• **somehow**: *Somehow* means *by some method (Somehow I must repair my car so that I can arrive in time for my appointment).* It does not mean *in some ways, to some extent,* or *somewhat.*

needs checking	His brother is somehow mentally disturbed.
revised	His brother is mentally disturbed in some way.
or	His brother is somewhat disturbed mentally.

• **specially/especially**: *Specially* means *for a particular purpose (These utensils are specially designed for left-handed people). Especially* means *particularly* or *more than in other cases.*

needs checking	The entire system pleased her, but she was specially happy to see that the computer program had been especially created for small business users.
revised	The entire system pleased her, but she was especially happy to see that the computer program had been specially created for small business users.

• **stationary/stationery**: *Stationary* means *not moving*; *stationery* is *what you write on.*

needs checking	As Mr. Blakeney remembered it, Lord Taylor "would always park his car in the no-parking zone outside the Bessborough Hotel, leaving House of Lords stationary on the windshield."
revised	As Mr. Blakeney remembered it, Lord Taylor "would always park his car in the no-parking zone outside the Bessborough Hotel, leaving House of Lords stationery on the windshield."

• **stimulant/stimulus**: *Stimulus* (plural *stimuli*) is the more general word for *anything that produces a reaction*; *stimulant* normally refers to *a drink or drug that has a stimulating effect.*

needs checking	The shocks were intended to act as stimulants to the rats that we used as subjects for the experiment.
revised	The shocks were intended to act as stimuli to the rats that we used as subjects for the experiment.

• **tack/tact**: *Tack* is a sailing term; *a different tack* means *a different direction relative to the wind. Tact* is *skill in saying or doing the right or polite thing.*

needs checking	We will have to exercise all our tack in the coming negotiations.
revised	We will have to exercise all our tact in the coming negotiations.

• **then/than/that**: The difference in meaning is obvious, but slips of the pen or keyboard too often allow the error to make it to the final draft. Spell-check won't help, of course.

needs checking It turns out that the company needs more money that we had expected.
revised It turns out that the company needs more money than we had expected.
needs checking There were fewer people in attendance then had been predicted.
revised There were fewer people in attendance than had been predicted.

• **they/their/there/they're**: Four words that are confused perhaps more frequently than any others. *They* is a pronoun used to replace any plural noun (e.g., books, people, numbers). *There* can be used to mean *in* (or *at*) *that place*, or can be used as an introductory word before various forms of the verb *to be* (*there is*, *there had been*, etc.). *Their* is a possessive adjective meaning *belonging to them*. *They're* is a contraction of *They are*. Beware in particular of substituting *they* for *there*:

needs checking They were many people in the crowd.
revised There were many people in the crowd.

The easiest way to check whether one is making this mistake is to ask if it would make sense to replace *they* with a noun. In the above sentence, for example, it would obviously be absurd to say, *The people were many people in the crowd.*

The confusion of *they*, *there*, and *their* is the sort of mistake that all writers are able to catch if they proofread carefully—particularly if they do so out loud.

needs checking Defenceman Zdeno Chára was considered to be there toughest player.
revised Defenceman Zdeno Chára was considered to be their toughest player.
needs checking There all going to the dance this Saturday.
revised They're all going to the dance this Saturday.
or They are all going to the dance this Saturday.

• **tiring/tiresome**: Something that is *tiring makes you feel tired*, though you may have enjoyed it very much. Something that is *tiresome* is *tedious and unpleasant*.

M2
Usage

needs checking Although it is tiresome for him, my father likes to play tennis at least twice a week.

revised Although it is tiring for him, my father likes to play tennis at least twice a week.

• **to/too/two**: Too can mean *also* or be used to indicate *excess* (*too many, too heavy*); *two* is of course the number.

needs checking She seemed to feel that there was to much to do.

revised She seemed to feel that there was too much to do.

• **to/towards**: *To* indicates *direction*; *towards* indicates *motion*.

(Note that *toward* and *towards* may be used interchangeably.)

needs checking The deer moved slowly to me through the tall grass.

revised The deer moved slowly towards me through the tall grass.

• **tortuous/torturous**: *Tortuous* means *full of twists and turns*; *torturous* means *having to do with torture*.

• **unexceptional/unexceptionable**: *Unexceptional* means *ordinary, not an exception*; *unexceptionable* is used when you do not object (or take exception) to the thing or person in question.

needs checking A great deal of confusion and controversy surrounded the unexceptional White House plan to reflag 11 Kuwaiti tankers with the Stars and Stripes. It was a modest proposal that in itself should not have caused the handwringing it did on Capitol Hill.

(The plan to reflag Kuwaiti tankers as American ships clearly was an exception; the US had not done anything similar for years. What the writer means to say is that the plan was unexceptionable—that no one should have any objection to it.)

revised A great deal of confusion and controversy surrounded the unexceptionable White House plan to reflag 11 Kuwaiti tankers with the Stars and Stripes. It was a modest proposal that in itself should not have caused the handwringing it did on Capitol Hill.

• **unique/universal/perfect/complete/correct**: Many authorities insist that none of these terms can be a matter of degree. According to this line of thought, something must be either *unique* or *not unique*, *perfect* or *imperfect*, and so on; it is thought to be wrong to speak of something as being *very unique* or *largely correct*, or as being *more complete* than something else. Instead, we are instructed to use phrases such as *almost unique* and *more nearly complete*. It's worth noting that not all authorities agree as to the importance of drawing a clear line in this way between adjectives and adverbs which admit of comparison and adjectives and adverbs which do not. Not a few have pointed out that the phrase "more perfect union" has been lent authority through its inclusion in the preamble to the American constitution. Nevertheless, students are well advised to pay attention to this issue in formal writing.

needs checking Frida Kahlo made a rather unique contribution to twentieth-century art.

revised Frida Kahlo made a unique contribution to twentieth-century art.

or It is arguable that Frida Kahlo made a unique contribution to twentieth-century art.

- **valid/true/accurate**: An *accurate* statement is one that is *factually correct*. (A combination of accurate facts may not always give a true picture, however.) *Valid* is often used carelessly and as a consequence might seem fuzzy in its meaning. Properly used it can mean *legally acceptable*, or *sound in reasoning*; do not use it to mean *accurate*, *reasonable*, *true*, or *well-founded*.

needs checking Churchill's fear that the Nazis would become a threat to all of Europe turned out to be valid.

revised Churchill's fear that the Nazis would become a threat to all of Europe turned out to be well-founded.

- **vein/vain**: *Veins* run through your body; *to be vain* is *to be conceited*; an effort that fails to bring any of the desired results has been *in vain*.

needs checking Shakespeare portrays Sir John Oldcastle—or Falstaff, as he is usually known—as vein and irresponsible but immensely amusing and likeable.

revised Shakespeare portrays Sir John Oldcastle—or Falstaff, as he is usually known—as vain and irresponsible but immensely amusing and likeable.

- **verbal/oral**: *Oral* means *spoken* rather than written, whereas *verbal* means *having to do with words*. A person who is unable to speak may have a high level of verbal skill.

needs checking I can write well enough, but I have difficulty in expressing ideas verbally.

revised I can write well enough, but I have difficulty in expressing ideas orally.

• **were/where**: *Were* is of course a past tense form of the verb *to be*, while *where* refers to a place. Spell-check will not tell you if you have used the correct word.

needs checking This is the place were Dante met Beatrice.

revised This is the place where Dante met Beatrice.

M2.6 Part-of-Speech Conversions

A well-known Calvin and Hobbes cartoon strip nicely conveys the amusement that part-of-speech conversions may engender:

Calvin: "I like to verb words."

Hobbes: "What?"

Calvin: "I take nouns and adjectives and use them as verbs. Remember when *access* was a thing? Now it's something you do. It got verbed.... Verbing weirds language."

Hobbes: "Maybe we can eventually make language a complete impediment to understanding."

In fact, however, there is no good reason why a word that has become established as one part of speech should not be used as another; the language has always been changing and growing in this way. As Tom Shippey asks:

> What can be the matter with using nouns as adjectives? Everyone does it; how about *stonewall*? It has been built into the language since before English settlers found Ireland, let alone America.... As for converting nouns to verbs, what about *water*? *Watering the horses* is recorded from before the Conquest. (*Times Literary Supplement*, 19–25 October 1990)

For that matter, what about *chair*, *table*, *paper*, *shelf*, *bottle*, *cup*, *knife*, *fork*, *eye*, *mouth*, *finger*? The list of nouns that have also become verbs or other parts of speech is a very long one, and it includes many of the most basic words in the language. (Ironically enough, the adjective *weird*, used humorously in the cartoon as a verb, began life as a noun;

in Old English a weird was the personification of a powerful but unpredictable natural force.) The point in being aware of the conversion of one part of speech to another, then, is not that the practice is always a bad one. Rather it is to keep oneself aware of whether or not one is saying something in the best possible way. If the new creation fills a need, saying something more clearly and concisely than it is possible to do otherwise, then it deserves to survive. But if it fulfills no useful purpose—if clearer and more concise ways of saying the same thing already exist—then it's better to avoid it.

• **access**: For many years authorities felt, except in the vocabulary of computers, *access* should be used as a noun, not a verb. The use of *access* as a verb is now much more widely accepted, but some purists still argue that alternatives such as *enter* and *reach* are usually more precise:

less widely accepted	The cafeteria may be accessed from the warehouse or the accounts department.
more widely accepted	The cafeteria may be reached through the warehouse or the accounts department.

• **adjective for adverb**: If a word is modifying a verb, it should as a general rule be an adverb rather than an adjective. This is normally the case when the descriptive word comes directly after the verb. We say *The boy laughed quietly*, for example (rather than *The boy laughed quiet*), because the descriptive word *quietly* refers to the verb *laughed*, not the noun *boy*. Similarly, in the sentence *The quiet boy laughed* we use the adjective *quiet* to refer to the noun *boy*.

In most cases a descriptive word following a verb will apply to that verb, and should take the form of an adverb:

needs checking	She asked us not to talk so loud.
revised	She asked us not to talk so loudly.
needs checking	According to Mr. Adams, "most books will go heavier into evolution, which is a good thing."
revised	According to Mr. Adams, "most books will go more heavily into evolution, which is a good thing."
needs checking	He performs bad whenever he is under pressure.
revised	He performs badly whenever he is under pressure.

In some cases, however, a descriptive word following a verb may refer not to the verb, but to the subject. This happens most frequently with the verb *to be*, which of course does not name an action in the way that other verbs do. Thus we say *The boy is quiet*, not *The boy is quietly*; we use the adjective rather than the adverb because we are describing the boy, not the action of being. Verbs such as *taste*, *smell*, and *feel* resemble *be* in this respect; it is correct to say *I feel good* rather than *I feel well*, since the descriptive word is clearly intended to describe your condition, and not the act of feeling. Similarly, we say *it tastes good*, not *it tastes well*, and *it smells sweet*, not *it smells sweetly*. In some other cases, too, an adjective rather than an adverb will be appropriate after a verb. It makes perfect sense, for example, to write that *someone sliced the bread thin* (rather than *sliced the bread thinly*), since the descriptive word is intended to refer to the resulting slices, and not to the action of slicing.

The principles outlined above also apply to the comparative and superlative forms of adjectives and adverbs:

needs checking They both ran quicker in the final than they had in the semi-final.

revised They both ran more quickly in the final than they had in the semi-final.

needs checking He performs worse under pressure than he does when he is relaxed.

revised He performs less well under pressure than he does when he is relaxed.

needs checking Of all the contestants, Hawkins ran the quickest.

revised Of all the contestants, Hawkins ran the most quickly.

Given that comparative and superlative adverbs are often more long-winded compound formations, it is not surprising that in everyday speech the shorter adjectival equivalents are often used in their stead. And such usages are becoming more and more common as well in written English. Should the *Financial Post* editor have corrected the headline that read "Northern Miners Breathe Easier"? Certainly it's easier to use the adjective here in place of the two-part adverb *more easily*. Whether or not it's better is less clear; certainly many purists are not pleased by the practice.

less widely accepted The purpose of desktop publishing is to do the same old thing cheaper, easier, and quicker.

more widely accepted The purpose of desktop publishing is to do the same old thing more cheaply, more easily, and more quickly.

• **advice/advise**: *Advice* is the noun; *advise* is the verb.

needs checking	They refused to take our advise.
revised	They refused to take our advice.

• **affect/effect**: *Effect* is normally used as a noun meaning *result.* (It can also be used as a verb meaning *put into effect,* as in *The changes were effected by the committee.*) *Affect* is a verb meaning *cause a result.* (It can also be used as a noun meaning *emotion* or *mental state,* as in *affect theory.*)

needs checking	When the acid is added to the solution, there is no visible affect.
revised	When the acid is added to the solution, there is no visible effect.

needs checking	"The issues that effect us here on the reserve are the same issues that effect the whole constituency," Mr. Littlechild said. (*The Globe and Mail*)
revised	"The issues that affect us here on the reserve are the same issues that affect the whole constituency," Mr. Littlechild said.

• **author**: The noun *author* seems to have been first used as a verb in the seventeenth century. That usage died out, but it reappeared in the twentieth century, and has become quite common in the twenty-first. Some authorities still regard the use of *author* as a verb to be an outright error, however, and others feel that it has a pretentious feel to it, and in most situations see no need to find substitutes for *write.* As Merrill Perlman has pointed out, however, acceptance of *author* as a verb is much higher in situations where it may not be entirely clear who did the actual writing. In a sentence such as *The Liberal government has authored new legislation on greenhouse gas emissions, authored* seems to be regarded as an acceptable alternative to verbs such as *introduced* or *unveiled.*

needs checking	Smith is a member of the Appeals Court, and has authored two books on the judicial system.
revised	Smith is a member of the Appeals Court, and has written two books on the judicial system.

• **bear/birth/give birth to**: For centuries standard English had no single word to describe the process of giving birth; one spoke of a woman *bearing children* or *giving birth to children.* In the late twentieth century, however, a usage that Walt Whitman had used in an 1855 poem entitled "There was a child went forth every day" (*She that conceived him in her womb and birthed him…*) started to become more and more common, and nowadays it is considered entirely acceptable to use *birth* as a transitive verb. The expression *birth a child* is certainly more concise than *give birth to a child*, and is widely felt as well to better reflect the active nature of the process.

• **breath/breathe**: *Breath* is the noun, *breathe* the verb.

needs checking	When you breath, your lungs take in oxygen.
revised	When you breathe, your lungs take in oxygen.

• **dependent/dependant**: *Dependent* is an adjective that describes someone or something that depends on someone or something else. In Canadian English, the noun is usually spelled *dependant*; your dependent children are your dependants.

needs checking	Emily is still dependant on her parents for financial support.
revised	Emily is still dependent on her parents for financial support.

• **dialogue**: As a verb, *talk* serves perfectly well, even after all these years.

awkward	The two department heads should dialogue with each other more frequently.
better	The two department heads should talk to each other more frequently.

• **enthuse/enthusiastic**: The verb *enthuse* is a relatively recent back formation from the adjective *enthusiastic*; *enthused* is its simple past tense form. Confusion between the two forms is now common.

needs checking	In 2014 millions were enthused about Norway's Olympic performance.
revised	In 2014 millions were enthusiastic about Norway's Olympic performance.
or	In 2014 millions enthused over Norway's Olympic performance.

• **first/firstly**: *Firstly* is now generally thought of as archaic, though it is not incorrect. Be sure to be consistent, though, in the use of *first, second,* etc., in lists.

needs checking	There were several reasons for France's reluctance to commit more resources to North America. First, she was consumed with the battle for supremacy in Europe. Secondly, the returns on previous investments had been minimal.

revised There were several reasons for France's reluctance to commit more resources to North America. First, she was consumed with the battle for supremacy in Europe. Second, the returns on previous investments had been minimal.

• **give/gift**: Until relatively recently it was universally understood that *give* is a verb and *gift* is a noun. The use of *gift* as a verb seems to have arisen in the context of institutional fundraising; in most cases, it is difficult to see any reason to say "thank you" for this *gift*.

needs checking Mr. Dench has generously gifted the university with funding for a new library.

revised Mr. Dench has generously given the university funding for a new library.

• **good/well**: The most common of the adjective-for-adverb mistakes.

needs checking As the manager put it, "He pitched good, but not real good."

fair He pitched well, but not really well.

better He did not pitch very well.

• **impact**: The use of *impact* as a verb has become widespread even in formal English, but *affect* remains an attractive option.

awkward The government's decision will impact upon wholesalers in all areas of the country.

better The government's decision will affect wholesalers in all areas of the country.

• **its/it's**: *Its* is an adjective meaning *belonging to it. It's* is a contraction of *it is*—a pronoun plus a verb. (Similarly, *whose* is an adjective meaning *belonging to whom*, whereas *who's* is a contraction of *who is*. See page 350.)

needs checking Its important to remember that the population of North America in this period was less than 10 million.

revised (less formal) It's important to remember that the population of North America in this period was less than 10 million.

revised (more formal) It is important to remember that the population of North America in this period was less than 10 million.

needs checking A coniferous tree continually sheds it's leaves.

revised A coniferous tree continually sheds its leaves.

• **lend/loan**: In Canadian English *loan* is used only as a noun; *lend* is the verb. (In American English, *loan* has long been used as a verb as well.)

needs checking	He was unwilling to loan his sister any money.
revised	He was unwilling to lend his sister any money.

• **like/as**: *Like* is a preposition, not a conjunction; it introduces a noun or pronoun in a phrase. If introducing a clause, which always includes a verb, use *as* in formal writing.

- He looks like his father.
  (*Like* introduces the noun *father*.)
- He looks as his father did at his age.
  (*As* introduces the clause *as his father did at his age*.)
- He is acting like a drunkard.
  (*Like* introduces the noun *drunkard*.)
- He is acting as if he were drunk.
  (*As* introduces the clause *as if he were drunk*.)

needs checking	Like I said before, smoking is forbidden.
revised	As I said before, smoking is forbidden.

needs checking	He runs like I do—with short, choppy strides.
revised	He runs as I do—with short, choppy strides.
or	He runs like me. We both take short, choppy strides.

needs checking	Duvalier ran Haiti like his father had done.
revised	Duvalier ran Haiti the way his father had.

The attempt is also sometimes made to use *like what* in place of *as*.

needs checking	Bush Sr. wanted to appear tough, like what Reagan had when he ordered the invasion of Grenada.
revised	Bush Sr. wanted to appear tough, as Reagan had when he ordered the invasion of Grenada.

On the Companion Website

Exercises on part-of-speech conversions may be found at **sites.broadviewpress.com/writingcdn**. Click on **Exercises** and go to **"Parts of Speech."**

• **loath/loathe**: *Loath* is the adjective; *loathe* is the verb.

needs checking	He told me he is beginning to loath his job.
revised	He told me he is beginning to loathe his job.
or	He is loath to return to his old job.

• **loose/lose**: *Loose* is normally used as an adjective meaning *not tight*; as a verb it means to *make loose* (e.g., *He loosed the reins*). *Lose* is, of course, always a verb.

needs checking	As soon as it became dark she began to loose control of herself.
revised	As soon as it became dark she began to lose control of herself.

needs checking	If this movie doesn't bring the song back to the hit parade, then you know it's flopped—and that Spielberg is loosing his touch.
revised	If this movie doesn't bring the song back to the hit parade, then you know it's flopped—and that Spielberg is losing his touch.

• **maybe/may be**: *Maybe* is an adverb that should be replaced by *perhaps* in formal writing. *May be* is a compound verb.

needs checking	May be he will come, but I doubt it.
revised	Maybe he will come, but I doubt it.
or	Perhaps he will come, but I doubt it.

needs checking	A prototype maybe ready by 2026.
revised	A prototype may be ready by 2026.

• **meantime/meanwhile**: *Meantime* is a noun, used most frequently in the phrase *in the meantime*. *Meanwhile* is an adverb.

needs checking	The Germans were preparing for an attack near Calais. Meantime, the Allies were readying themselves for the invasion of Normandy.
revised	The Germans were preparing for an attack near Calais. Meanwhile, the Allies were readying themselves for the invasion of Normandy.

• **medal/win a medal**: Until quite recently English lacked a one-word verb meaning *win a medal*. The verb *to medal* now fills that function, but many feel the new coinage has the feel of a counterfeit. In formal writing it is probably still best to use the more widely accepted currency.

less widely accepted	She medalled twice at the 2008 Olympics.
more widely accepted	She twice won medals at the 2008 Olympics.
or	She won two medals at the 2008 Olympics.

• **orgasm/have an orgasm**: For a long time the only one-word synonyms for *have an orgasm* or *achieve orgasm* were colloquial terms that clearly had no place in formal writing. In the late twentieth century people used *orgasm* as a verb as well as a noun. That usage is now becoming quite widely accepted.

less widely accepted	Twenty per cent of the respondents reported that on average they had orgasmed fewer than three times per month.
more widely accepted	Twenty per cent of the respondents reported that on average they had experienced orgasm fewer than three times per month.
or	Twenty per cent of the respondents reported that on average they had had fewer than three orgasms per month.

• **practice/practise**: In the US *practice* serves as both noun and verb. In Canada and Britain *practise* (verb) and *practice* (noun) should be distinguished.

US	The team will practice on Thursday.
UK/CDA	The team will practise on Thursday.

• **predominate/predominant**: *Predominate* is the verb, *predominant* the adjective. (Either *predominately* or *predominantly* may be used as adverbs.)

needs checking	The use of the word "hero" for a sandwich was predominate only in New York.
revised	The use of the word "hero" for a sandwich was predominant only in New York.
or	The use of the word "hero" for a sandwich predominated only in New York.

• **principal/principle**: *Principal* can be either a noun or an adjective. As a noun it means *the person in the highest position of authority in an organization* (e.g., *a school principal*) or *an amount of money*, as distinguished from the interest on it. As an adjective it means *first in rank or importance* (*The principal city of northern Nigeria is Kano*). *Principle* is always a noun, and is never used to describe a person; *a principle* is *a basic truth or doctrine, a code of conduct*, or *a law describing how something works.*

needs checking We feel this is a matter of principal.
revised We feel this is a matter of principle.

needs checking Up went the shares of the two principle companies in this emerging field.
revised Up went the shares of the two principal companies in this emerging field.

• **prophecy/prophesy**: *Prophecy* is the noun, *prophesy* the verb.

needs checking His comment should be regarded as a prediction, not a prophesy.
revised His comment should be regarded as a prediction, not a prophecy.

• **quality**: Although in colloquial English *quality* is frequently used as a replacement for *good* or *worthwhile*, in formal writing it should be used as a noun, not an adjective. It is useful to remember that something may as easily be of poor quality as of good quality.

needs checking The salesperson claims that this is a quality product.
revised The salesperson claims that this is a product of high quality.
or The salesperson claims that this is a good product.

• **quote/quotation**: In formal English *quote* is the verb, *quotation* the noun.

needs checking The following quote shows just how determined she is to change the constitution.
revised The following quotation shows just how determined she is to change the constitution.

• **real/really**: One of the most commonly made adjective-for-adverb mistakes.

needs checking Some of the fish we caught were real big.
fair Some of the fish we caught were really big.
better Some of the fish we caught were very big.

• **verb-noun confusion**: Where verbs and nouns have similar forms, be careful not to confuse them. Some of the most common examples are: *advice* (noun) and *advise* (verb); *extent* (noun) and *extend* (verb); *device* (noun) and *devise* (verb); *revenge* (noun) and *avenge* (verb).

needs checking	Gerald Ford, president from 1974 to 1976, has now to a large extend been forgotten.
revised	Gerald Ford, president from 1974 to 1976, has now to a large extent been forgotten.

needs checking	She wanted to revenge the harm he had caused her.
revised	She wanted to avenge the harm he had caused her.

• **whose/who's**: *Whose* means *belonging to whom*; *who's* is a contraction of *who is.*

needs checking	Kennedy is not normally remembered as the president who's policies embroiled the US in the Vietnam conflict, but several scholars have suggested that he was as much responsible as was Johnson.
revised	Kennedy is not normally remembered as the president whose policies embroiled the US in the Vietnam conflict, but several scholars have suggested that he was as much responsible as was Johnson.

M 2.7 Slang

• **slang/informal English**: The column to the left below lists words and expressions often used in conversation, but not in formal English. The corresponding formal words are listed to the right. The most frequently troublesome entries are treated separately.

anyways	anyway
anywheres, anyplace	anywhere
awful	***poor***, miserable, sick
awfully	very, extremely

Some authorities continue to hold that *awful* should retain its original meaning of *filled with or inspiring awe*. In any case, a better replacement can always be found. The same is even more true of the use of the adverb *awfully* as an intensifier to mean *very* (*awfully good*, *awfully small*, etc.).

boss	manager, supervisor
bunch	group
(except for grapes, bananas, etc.)	
buy	bargain
(as a noun—*a good buy*, etc.)	

go (to mean "say")	say
have got	have, own
kid	child, girl, boy
kind of, sort of	rather, in some respects
let's us	let us
lots of	a great deal of
mad	angry
(unless the meaning is *insane*)	

All contractions (*it's*, *he's*, *there's*, *we're*, etc.) should be avoided in formal writing, as should conversational markers such as *Well*, ...

• **attitude**: In colloquial English in recent years *attitude* has undergone a considerable transformation, becoming first a synonym for *bad attitude* and then a word that (depending on context) may denote an air of superiority or suggest the audacity and forceful irreverence of an "in-your-face" personality. In formal written English such colloquial usages as *she's got attitude* should be avoided.

• **could care less/couldn't care less**: In the early 1990s people started to say sarcastically *I could care less* to mean the opposite—that they couldn't care less. For some time *I could care less* seemed to be taking over, regardless of the tone of voice used, and the meaning of the words themselves seemed in danger of being lost. In recent years *couldn't care less* has made something of a comeback.

needs checking Most of the time most people could care less about what their elected representatives are doing.

revised Most of the time most people couldn't care less about what their elected representatives are doing.

• **get**: should not be used to mean *come*, *go*, *be*, or *become*. Such expressions as *get a hold of* are also inappropriate in formal writing.

needs checking Henry and Jane Seymour got married in 1536, only ten days after the death of Anne Boleyn.

revised Henry and Jane Seymour were married in 1536, only ten days after the death of Anne Boleyn.

• **go** (to mean *say*)

needs checking He goes, "What do you mean?"

revised He says, "What do you mean?"

M2 Usage

- **have got** (to mean *have*)

needs checking	He has got two houses and three cars.
revised	He has two houses and three cars.

In conversational English *got* has become widely used as an auxiliary verb, probably because of the awkwardness of pronouncing certain combinations involving common contractions. Thus we would never shorten *I have you covered* to *I've you covered*; instead we would say, *I've got you covered. Have got* is also an informal synonym for *have* in the sense of *possess*. Both these uses of *got* are usually to be avoided in formal writing.

- **let's say**: This expression should be omitted entirely from writing.

needs checking	Let's say for example a relative dies, a poor family will have to deal with financial worries as well as with grief.
revised	If, for example, a relative dies, a poor family will have to deal with financial worries as well as with grief.

- **like** (to mean *say* or *indicate through gesture*): An expressive idiom, but one to be avoided in writing.

conversational	She's like, "Why do we have to be here?" and I'm like, "Duh!"
formal	She wondered why we had to be there; to me it was obvious.

- **look to**: In formal writing one may speak of *looking to the future*, but the informal use of *look to* to mean *attempt* or *intend* should be avoided.

needs checking	From the moment he took power in France, Napoleon was looking to conquer Europe.
revised	From the moment he took power in France, Napoleon intended to conquer Europe.

- **off** (to mean *from*)

needs checking	I got it off him for two dollars.
revised	I bought it from him for two dollars.

- **put across, get across** (one's point): *Express, convince.*

needs checking	He could not get his point across.
revised	He could not persuade us he was right.

- **so** (as discourse marker): It is not incorrect to start various sorts of sentences using *so* as a conjunction—though if you do, the word should always be followed by a comma. Both of the following are correct:

- Sophie greatly enjoyed staying with her grandmother, so when the time came to leave, she was reluctant to say goodbye.
- Sophie greatly enjoyed staying with her grandmother. So, when the time came to leave, she was reluctant to say goodbye.

Here the word *so* indicates a connection between the two ideas; Sophie's reluctance to leave is explained by the degree to which she enjoyed staying with her grandmother.

In the following example, on the other hand, the word *so* does not indicate any connection between ideas. It is used simply as what linguists call a "discourse marker"—conversational filler, in other words:

Nice to see you again. So, did you watch the playoff game last night?

There can be no objection to using *so* in this way in conversation. Be careful not to do so in formal written work, however:

needs checking This essay has looked at the issue from both sides. So, what conclusions can be drawn?

revised This essay has looked at the issue from both sides. What conclusions can be drawn?

• **till/until**: In conversation or in literature *till* is a perfectly acceptable informal substitute for *until*. In formal written English, however, *until* should be used.

needs checking They waited till dawn to launch the attack.

revised They waited until dawn to launch the attack.

• **well**: In conversation *well* is often added to sentences while you are thinking of what to say. Do not do this in writing.

needs checking Well, at the end of the meeting there was some doubt within the cabinet as to which course to take.

revised At the end of the meeting there was some doubt within the cabinet as to which course to take.

• **when you get right down to it**: usually best omitted; use *otherwise*, *indeed*, or *in fact*.

M 2.8 Word Conventions

• **according to**: This expression normally is used only when one is referring to a person or to a group of people (e.g., *According to his lawyer, the accused was nowhere near the scene when the crime was committed*; *According to Shakespeare, Richard III was a murderer*).

needs checking According to geography, Congo is larger than all of Western Europe.

revised As we learn in geography, Congo is larger than all of Western Europe.

needs checking According to the story of *Cry, the Beloved Country*, Stephen Kumalo has a quick temper.

revised The events of the story show that Stephen Kumalo has a quick temper.

• **age/aged**: Do not use the noun *age* as a participle.

needs checking A woman age 35 was struck and killed by the car.

revised A woman aged 35 was struck and killed by the car.

• **all of**: Many authorities advise that the expression *all of* should be avoided in the interests of economy. Perhaps so, but there is certainly no error involved, and in many cases the addition of the word *of* improves the rhythm of the sentence; Lincoln's famous maxim "You can not fool all the people all of the time" would not be improved by dropping the *of*.

• **amount**: This word should be used only with things that are uncountable (sugar, goodwill, etc.).

needs checking A large amount of books were stolen from the library last night.

revised A large number of books were stolen from the library last night.

• **and**: In most cases *or* rather than *and* should be used as a connective if the statement is negative.

needs checking Moose are not found in South America, Africa, and Australia.

revised Moose are not found in South America, Africa, or Australia.

• **anyways/anywheres**: There is never a need for the *s*.

needs checking We were unable to find him anywheres.

revised We were unable to find him anywhere.

• **as**: When this word is used to relate the times at which two actions happened, the actions must have happened at the same time (e.g., *As I got out of bed, I heard the sound of gunfire*, where the hearing happens during the action of getting out; *As he was walking to work, he remembered that he had left the stove on*, where the remembering happens during the walking). *As* should not be used in this way if the two actions happened at different times. If one action is completed before the other begins, always use *when*.

needs checking As I had finished my geography assignment, I started my history essay.

revised When I had finished my geography assignment, I started my history essay.

(The finishing happens before the starting.)

needs checking As she discovered that the engine was overheating, she stopped the car immediately.

revised When she discovered that the engine was overheating, she stopped the car immediately.

(The discovering happens before the stopping.)

Note: Since *when* can be used both when actions happen simultaneously and when they happen at different times, anyone who is at all uncertain about this point is wise to avoid using *as* to refer to time, and always stick to *when*. This has the added advantage of avoiding the possible ambiguity as to whether *as* is being used to mean *because* or to mean *when*.

• **as/that/whether**: Do not use *as* to mean *that* or *whether*.

needs checking I don't know as how I can do the job in time.

revised I don't know whether I can do the job in time.

• **back formations**: A back formation is the formation of a word from what one would expect to be its derivative. The verb *laze*, for example, is a back formation from the adjective *lazy*; a more recent (and similar-sounding) back formation is the verb *liaise* from the noun *liaison*. Many back formations may be created from negatives that lack a positive form (*kempt*, *gruntled*, *ruthful*, *solent*, etc.). These may constitute amusing colloquialisms, but should be avoided in formal written English except where the writer is striving for a humorous effect.

informal Toronto is a pretty ruly place to watch a game. (Baseball manager Lou Piniella, as quoted by Robertson Cochrane in *The Globe and Mail*, 29 Oct. 1994)

more formal Toronto is a pretty civilized place to watch a game.

- **because of the following reasons/some reasons/many reasons**: The word *because* makes it clear that a cause or reason is being introduced. The addition of a phrase such as *of the following reasons* is redundant. Either use *because* on its own, or use *for the following reasons/many reasons*, etc.

needs checking During her first few years in Toronto, Susanna was unhappy because of several reasons.

revised During her first few years in Toronto, Susanna was unhappy for several reasons.

- **both**: The expressions *both alike*, *both equal*, and *both together* all tend to involve repetition.

needs checking Macdonald and Cartier both arrived together at about eight o'clock.

revised Macdonald and Cartier arrived together at about eight o'clock.

- **can be able**: *I can do it* and *I am able to do it* mean the same thing. Using the verbs together is redundant.

needs checking He thinks Minnesota can be able to win the Cup.

revised He thinks Minnesota can win the Cup.

or He thinks Minnesota will be able to win the Cup.

- **cannot help but**: One too many negatives; use *can but* or *cannot help*.

needs checking He couldn't help but think he had made a mistake.

revised He couldn't help thinking he had made a mistake.

or He could but think he had made a mistake.

- **change**: You *make a change* (not *do a change*).

needs checking The manager did several changes to the roster before the match with Russia.

revised The manager made several changes to the roster before the match with Russia.

- **comment**: We *make comments* (not *say* or *do them*).

needs checking Anyone who wishes to say any comments will have a chance to speak after the lecture.

revised Anyone who wishes to make any comments will have a chance to speak after the lecture.

- **compared to/than**: The use of *compared to* as a participial phrase often leads to ambiguity and error. Unless one is speaking of one person comparing something to something else, it is usually better to use *than*.

needs checking There were far fewer frogs in the area in 2021 compared to previous years.
revised There were far fewer frogs in the area in 2021 than there had been in previous years.

• **convince**: You *convince* people that they should do something, or *persuade* them to do it.

needs checking Reagan's advisers convinced him to approve the arms-for-hostages deal with Iran.
revised Reagan's advisers persuaded him to approve the arms-for-hostages deal with Iran.

• **elder/older**: *Elder* can act as an adjective (*my elder son*) or a noun (*the elder of the two*). *Older* can act only as an adjective. If using *than*, use *older*.

needs checking She is four years elder than her sister.
revised She is four years older than her sister.

• **for**: One use of this preposition is to show purpose. Normally, however, *for* can be used in this way only when the purpose can be expressed in one word (e.g., *for safety*, *for security*). It is not usually correct to try to express purpose by combining *for* with a pronoun and an infinitive: expressions such as *for him to be happy*, *for us to arrive safely* are awkward and should be avoided. Instead, one can express purpose either by beginning with *in order to* (e.g., *in order to make life easier, in order to increase yield per hectare*), or by using *so that* (e.g., *so that life will be made easier, so that yield per hectare will be increased*).

needs checking Please speak slowly for me to understand what you say.
revised Please speak slowly so that I can understand what you say.
needs checking The team must work hard for it to have a chance at the World Series.
revised The team must work hard if it is to have a chance at the World Series.

On the Companion Website

Exercises on the conventions of English usage may be found at **sites.broadviewpress.com/writingcdn**. Click on **Exercises** and **Writing Mechanics** and go to **"Usage."**

• **forget**: *To forget something* is *to fail to remember it*, not *to leave it somewhere*.

needs checking	I forgot my textbook at home.
revised	I left my textbook at home.
or	I forgot to bring my textbook from home.

• **had ought/hadn't ought**: Use *ought* or *ought not* instead.

needs checking	He hadn't ought to have risked everything at once.
revised	He ought not to have risked everything at once.
or	He should not have risked everything at once.

• **hardly**: *Hardly* acts as a negative; there is thus no need to add a second negative.

needs checking	The advertisers claim that you can't hardly tell the difference.
revised	The advertisers claim that you can hardly tell the difference.

• **how/what**: One may talk about *how something* (*or someone*) is, or *what something* (*or someone*) is like, but not *how they are like*.

needs checking	Tell me how it looks like from where you are.
revised	Tell me how it looks from where you are.
or	Tell me what it looks like from where you are.
needs checking	I do not know how the roads are like between St. John's and Corner Brook.
revised	I do not know what the roads are like between St. John's and Corner Brook.
or	I do not know how the roads are between St. John's and Corner Brook.

• **increase**: Numbers can be *increased* or *decreased*, as can such things as production and population (nouns which refer to certain types of numbers or quantities). Things such as houses, however, or books (nouns which do not refer to numbers or quantities) cannot be increased; only the number of houses, books, etc. can be increased or decreased, raised or lowered. (See also pages 327–28.)

needs checking	The government has greatly increased low-rent houses in the suburbs of Toronto.
revised	The government has greatly increased the number of low-rent houses in the suburbs of Toronto.

• **information**: One *gives information* (not *tells it*).

needs checking He told me all the information I wanted about how to apply.

revised He gave me all the information I wanted about how to apply.

• **investigation**: We *make*, *carry out*, or *hold an investigation* (not *do one*).

needs checking The manager did a thorough investigation into the disappearance of funds from his department.

revised The manager made a thorough investigation into the disappearance of funds from his department.

• **irregardless**: The result of confusion between *regardless* and *irrespective*. Use *regardless*.

needs checking She told us to come for a picnic, irregardless of whether it is rainy or sunny.

revised She told us to come for a picnic, regardless of whether it is rainy or sunny.

• **is when/is where**: Many people use these phrases when attempting to define something. There is always a better way.

needs checking Osmosis is when a fluid moves through a porous partition into another fluid.

revised Osmosis occurs when a fluid moves through a porous partition into another fluid.

or Osmosis is the movement of a fluid through a porous partition into another fluid.

• **journey**: You *make a journey* (not *do one*).

needs checking If we do not stop along the way, we can do the journey in an hour.

revised If we do not stop along the way, we can make the journey in an hour.

• **law**: A law is *passed*, *made*, or *put into effect* by the government, and *enforced* by the police. Laws are not *put* or *done*.

needs checking I think the government should put a law increasing the penalty for drunk driving.

revised I think the government should pass a law increasing the penalty for drunk driving.

• **less/fewer**: When something can be counted (e.g., people, books, trees), use *fewer*. Use *less* only with uncountable nouns (e.g., *sugar*, *meat*, *equipment*).

needs checking As the modern economy spreads through the countryside, less people will die of tropical diseases or infected wounds. (*The New York Times*, 12 May 1997)

revised As the modern economy spreads through the countryside, fewer people will die of tropical diseases or infected wounds.

needs checking There are less steps, and that means there is more room for error.

revised There are fewer steps, and that means there is more room for error.

• **lie** (meaning *speak falsely*): You *lie about something*, not *that something*.

needs checking He lied that he was eighteen years old.

revised He lied about his age, stating that he was eighteen.

or He lied when he said he was eighteen years old.

• **mistake**: Mistakes are *made* (not *done*).

needs checking He did seven mistakes in that short spelling exercise.

revised He made seven mistakes in that short spelling exercise.

• **more/most**: Most adjectives and adverbs have comparative and superlative forms; the comparative is used when comparing two things, the superlative when comparing three or more.

needs checking Smith was the most accomplished of the two.

revised Smith was the more accomplished of the two.

To use *more* with a comparative adjective, or *most* with a superlative adjective is to repeat oneself.

needs checking The bride looked like the most happiest person in the world.

revised The bride looked like the happiest person in the world.

or The bride looked like the most happy person in the world.

needs checking Gandalf is much more wiser than Frodo.

revised Gandalf is much wiser than Frodo.

• **nor**: This word is usually used with *neither*. Do not use it with *not*; when using *not*, use *or* instead of *nor*.

needs checking She does not drink nor smoke.

revised She does not drink or smoke.

or She neither drinks nor smokes.

needs checking Graham does not have the money nor the organizational skills to succeed in business.

revised Graham does not have the money or the organizational skills to succeed in business.

or Graham has neither the money nor the organizational skills to succeed in business.

• **nothing/nobody/nowhere**: These words should not be used with another negative word such as *not*. If one uses *not*, then one should use *anything* instead of *nothing*, *anybody* instead of *nobody*, *anywhere* instead of *nowhere*.

needs checking He could not do nothing while he was in prison.

revised He could not do anything while he was in prison.

• **old-fashioned**: Be sure not to leave off the *-ed* in this adjectival expression.

needs checking Let's do it the old-fashion way.

revised Let's do it the old-fashioned way.

• **opposed**: You are opposed *to* something or someone (not *with* or *against*).

needs checking Charles Darwin was opposed against the literal interpretation of the story of Creation, as found in Genesis.

revised Charles Darwin was opposed to the literal interpretation of the story of Creation, as found in Genesis.

• **per cent/percentage**: If you use *per cent*, you must give the number. Otherwise, use *percentage*.

needs checking The per cent of people surveyed who reported any change of opinion was very small.

revised The percentage of people surveyed who reported any change of opinion was very small.

or Only six per cent of the people surveyed reported any change of opinion.

Note: *Percentage* is always one word; authorities differ as to whether *per cent* should always be written as two words, or whether it also may be written as one word (*percent*).

• **preclude**: *To preclude something* is *to exclude any possibility of it happening*; people cannot be precluded.

needs checking Our cash flow problems preclude us from entering into any new commitments before 2026.
revised Our cash flow problems preclude any new commitments before 2026.
or We do not have enough money to make a commitment to you now.

• **position/theory**: Positions and theories *are held* or *are argued*; they do not hold or argue themselves.

needs checking Devlin's position holds that a shared public morality is essential to the existence of society.
revised Devlin's position is that a shared public morality is essential to the existence of society.
or Devlin holds that a shared public morality is essential to the existence of society.

• **reason**: The phrase *the reason is because* involves repetition; use *that* instead of *because*, or eliminate the phrase completely.

needs checking The reason ice floats is because it is lighter than water.
revised The reason ice floats is that it is lighter than water.
or Ice floats because it is lighter than water.
needs checking The reason I have come is because I want to apply for a job.
revised I have come to apply for a job.

• **short/scarce**: If a person is *short of something*, that thing is *scarce*.

needs checking Food is now desperately short throughout the country.
revised Food is now extremely scarce throughout the country.
or The country is now desperately short of food.

• **since/for**: Both these words can be used to indicate length (or duration) of time, but they are used in slightly different ways. *Since* is used to mention the point at which a period of time began (*since 6 o'clock, since the beginning of 2015, since last Christmas*, etc.). *For* is used to mention the amount of time that has passed (*for two years, for six months, for centuries*, etc.).

needs checking She has been staying with us since three weeks.
revised She has been staying with us for three weeks.
or She has been staying with us since three weeks ago.

• **so**: When used to show degree or extent, *so* is normally used with *that*: *so big that ... , so hungry that ...* , etc. In formal writing, *so* should not be used as an intensifier in the way that *very* is used.

needs checking Once the chemical reaction started, the container became so hot.

revised Once the chemical reaction started, the container became very hot.

• **some/any/someone/anyone**: With negatives (*not, never*, etc.) *any* is used in place of *some*.

needs checking He never gives me some help with my work.

revised He never gives me any help with my work.

• **speech**: You *make a speech* or *give a speech* (not *do a speech*).

needs checking The dean was asked to do a speech at the convocation.

revised The dean was asked to give a speech at the convocation.

• **start**: If both the time at which an event begins and the time that it finishes are mentioned, it is not enough to use only the verb *start*.

needs checking The dance started from 9 p.m. till midnight.

revised The dance started at 9 p.m. and finished at midnight.

or The dance continued from 9 p.m. until midnight.

or The dance lasted from 9 p.m. until midnight.

• **suppose/supposed**: Be sure to add the *d* in the expression *supposed to*.

needs checking We are suppose to be there by eight.

revised We are supposed to be there by eight.

• **supposed to/should**: These two are very similar in meaning, and may often be used interchangeably; if a person is *supposed to* do something, then that is what she *should* do. In the past tense, however, the question of when and when not to use *supposed to* is quite tricky. You may use it when you are clearly talking about a fixed plan that has not been carried out (e.g., *He was supposed to arrive before two o'clock, but he is still not here*). You should not use it to apply to any action that you think was wrong, or you feel should not have been carried out. The safe solution to this problem is always to use *should* instead of *supposed to*.

needs checking What she said was impolite, but he was not supposed to hit her for saying it.

revised What she said was impolite, but he should not have hit her for saying it.

needs checking The National Party government was not supposed to keep Nelson Mandela in jail for so many years.

revised The National Party government should not have kept Nelson Mandela in jail for so many years.

• **thankful/grateful**: We are *thankful* that something has happened, and *grateful* for something we have received.

needs checking	I am very thankful for the kind thoughts expressed in your letter.
revised	I am very grateful for the kind thoughts expressed in your letter.

• **too**: The word *too* suggests that something is *more than necessary*, or *more than desired*. Do not use it indiscriminately to lend emphasis.

needs checking	He looked too handsome in his new suit.
revised	He looked very handsome in his new suit.

• **try/sure**: Perhaps the most common error of all, in published books and articles as well as in less formal writing, is the use of *and* rather than *to* after *try* and *sure*.

needs checking	No one stepped in to try and save the poor animal.
revised	No one stepped in to try to save the poor animal.
needs checking	Burton had agreed with the Sultan not to try and convert the Africans to Christianity. (Alan Moorehead, *The White Nile*)
revised	Burton had agreed with the Sultan not to try to convert the Africans to Christianity.
needs checking	Be sure and take out the garbage before you go to bed.
revised	Be sure to take out the garbage before you go to bed.

• **use/used**: Be sure to add the *d* in the expression *used to*.

needs checking	He use to be much more reckless than he is now.
revised	He used to be much more reckless than he is now.

• **where**: Do not use *where* for *that*.

needs checking	I read in the paper where the parties are now tied in popularity.
revised	I read in the paper that the parties are now tied in popularity.

M 2.9 Joining Words

The art of combining correct clauses and sentences logically and coherently is as much dependent on taking the time to think through what we are writing—and how the reader will respond to what we write—as it is on knowledge of correct usage. It is all too easy for most of us to assume that the flow of our thoughts will be as clear to the reader as it is to us. In practical terms this leads to the omission of links in the argument or of joining words that help the reader to see those links. Almost as common is the tendency to give too many or contradictory cues to the reader—a tendency that is often an indication that ideas have not yet been thoroughly thought out. That in itself is nothing to be ashamed of; the key is to be willing to take the time to re-read and revise the work. Every good writer makes at least two and sometimes as many as five or six drafts of any piece of writing before considering it finished. Here are two examples, both taken from early drafts of books published by Broadview Press:

- At the end of World War II there was substantial optimism that the application of Keynesian analysis would lead to economic stability and security. Over the post-war period optimistic rationalism weakened in the face of reality.
- A short report in which you request an increase in your department's budget should be written in the persuasive mode. Most reports, however, do not have persuasion as their main objective. Persuasion, though, will often be one of their secondary objectives.

• **too few or too many cues** (see also "Non Sequitur"): The first of these passages gives the reader too few cues. What is the connection between the idea of the first sentence and that of the second? One can figure it out without too much difficulty, but the flow of the argument is briefly interrupted while one does so. The problem is easily solved by the addition of one word to the second sentence:

revised At the end of World War II there was substantial optimism that the application of Keynesian analysis would lead to economic stability and security. Over the post-war period, however, optimistic rationalism weakened in the face of reality.

The second passage suffers from the opposite problem; the use of *however* and *though* in consecutive sentences gives the reader the sense of twisting back on himself without any clear sense of direction. This sort of difficulty can be removed by rewording or rearranging the ideas:

revised A short report in which you request an increase in your department's budget should be written in the persuasive mode. Most reports, however, do not have persuasion as their main objective. Persuasion will thus be at most a secondary objective.

The following pages list the chief words and expressions used in English to join ideas together, and discuss problems that are often experienced with them.

Words to Connect Ideas Opposed to Each Other

All these words are used to indicate that the writer is saying two things which seem to go against each other, or are different from each other. For example, in the sentence, *He is very rich, but he is not very happy*, the fact that he is not happy is the reverse of what we might expect of a rich man. The word *but* indicates this opposition of ideas to the reader.

although
but
despite
even if
however
in spite of
nevertheless
though
whereas
while
yet

Although, though

These words are used to indicate that, within the same sentence, two things that seem to go against each other are being said. *Although* is usually used to introduce subordinate clauses, not phrases.

- Although he has short legs, he can run very quickly.
- Hume and Dr. Johnson, indeed, have a good deal in common, although Hume's attitude towards religion earned him Johnson's scorn.

• **although/but**: Be careful not to use both *although* and *but* in the same sentence; one is enough.

needs checking Although in many African countries the government is not elected by the people, but in Botswana the government is democratically elected.

revised Although in many African countries the government is not elected by the people, in Botswana the government is democratically elected.

or In most African countries the government is not elected by the people, but in Botswana the government is democratically elected.

But

This word is usually used in the middle of a sentence to show that the two ideas in the sentence oppose or seem to oppose each other. It is also quite correct, however, to use *but* at the beginning of a sentence, if what one is saying in the sentence forms a complete clause and if the idea of the sentence seems to oppose the idea of the previous sentence. Examples:

- The civilization of ancient Greece produced some of the world's greatest works of art and gave birth to the idea of democracy, but the Greeks also believed in slavery.
- The civilization of ancient Greece produced some of the world's greatest works of art and gave birth to the idea of democracy. But the Greeks also believed in slavery.

• **opposing or supporting ideas**: When one is dealing with complex combinations of ideas it is sometimes easy to forget which ideas are in fact in opposition and which in support.

needs checking Brandy and bourbon, with the most "congenors," have the highest hangover ratings. Red wine is a close second, followed by dark rum, sherry, scotch, rye, beer, white wine, gin, and vodka. Vintage red wines have 15 times as much histamine (it triggers allergic reactions) as white wine, but vintage whites have fewer congenors.

(The use of *but* is inappropriate here; that whites have both less histamine and fewer congenors is as one would expect; the two facts are both instances of white wines having fewer side effects than reds.)

revised Brandy and bourbon, with the most "congenors," have the highest hangover ratings. Red wine is a close second, followed by dark rum, sherry, scotch, rye, beer, white wine, gin, and vodka. Vintage red wines also have 15 times as much histamine (it triggers allergic reactions) as white wine does.

• **but**: Experienced writers are careful not to use *but* more than once in a single sentence, or in consecutive sentences; they realize that doing so tends to confuse the reader. (It is also unwise to use any combination of *but* and *however* in this way.)

needs checking Detective Smith said that Ryan had been legally in possession of three handguns and two rifles, but he thought it "incredible" that someone should be allowed to keep ammunition at his home. But he said any change in the firearms law was something which would not be discussed by him.

revised Detective Smith said that Ryan had been legally in possession of three handguns and two rifles. Smith said he thought it "incredible" that someone should be allowed to keep ammunition at his home, but he would not comment directly on whether there should be a change in the firearms law.

Despite

This word means the same as *although*, but it is used to introduce phrases, not clauses.

- Despite his old age, his mind is active and alert.
  (*Despite his old age* is a phrase; it has no verb.)
- Although he is very old, his mind is active and alert.
  (*Although he is very old* is a clause, with *he* as a subject and *is* as a verb.)
- Despite the rain, she wanted to go out to the park.
- Although it was raining, she wanted to go to the park.

• **despite**: Remember not to introduce clauses with *despite*.

needs checking Despite that the drink tasted very strong, there was very little alcohol in it.

revised Despite its strong taste, there was very little alcohol in the drink.

or Although the drink tasted very strong, there was very little alcohol in it.

Even if

This expression is used when one is introducing a clause giving a condition. The word *even* emphasizes that the condition is surprising or unusual. Examples:

- Even if I have to stay up all night, I am determined to finish the job.
  (Staying up all night would be very unusual.)
- Even if Bangladesh doubled its food production, some of its people would still be hungry.
  (Doubling its food production would be very surprising.)

However

When used as a joining word, *however* usually indicates that what one is saying seems to go against what one has said in the previous sentence. It should normally be set off by commas when used in this way:

- The country suffered greatly during the three-year drought. This year, however, the rains have been heavy.

• **however**: *However* should not be used to combine ideas within one sentence, unless a semicolon is used.

needs checking	Hitler attempted to conquer the Soviet Union however he was defeated.
revised	Hitler attempted to conquer the Soviet Union; however, he was defeated.
or	Hitler attempted to conquer the Soviet Union. However, he was defeated.
or	Hitler attempted to conquer the Soviet Union but he was defeated.
needs checking	There will not be regular mail pick-up from boxes this Friday, however regular mail pick-up will resume Monday.
revised	There will not be regular mail pick-up from boxes this Friday, but regular mail pick-up will resume Monday.
or	There will not be regular mail pick-up from boxes this Friday. However, regular mail pick-up will resume Monday.

(Note that *however* in the sense of *to whatever extent* is an adverb, and does not need to be set off by commas. *However tired we are, we must finish the job tonight.*)

Nevertheless

• Like *however*, *nevertheless* is normally used to show that the idea of one sentence seems to go against the idea of the previous sentence. It should not be used to join two clauses into one sentence. Example:

- According to the known laws of physics it is not possible to walk on water. Nevertheless, this is what the Bible claims Jesus did.

> **On the Companion Website**
>
> Exercises on joining words may be found at **sites.broadviewpress.com/writingcdn**. Click on **Exercises** and **Writing Mechanics** and go to **"Putting Ideas Together."**

M2 Usage

Whereas

This word is commonly used when one is comparing two things and showing how they differ. Like *although*, it must begin a subordinate clause, and may be used either at the beginning or in the middle of a sentence. Examples:

- Whereas the stereotypical New Yorker is usually thought of as being rude and unwelcoming, Californians are typically characterized as being friendly and relaxed.
- The stereotypical New Yorker is usually thought of as being rude and unwelcoming, whereas Californians are typically characterized as being friendly and relaxed.

• **whereas**: Any sentence that uses *whereas* must have at least two clauses—a subordinate clause beginning with *whereas* and a main clause.

needs checking In "The Rain Horse" a young person feels unhappy when he returns to his old home. Whereas in "The Ice Palace" a young person feels unhappy when she leaves home for the first time.

revised In "The Rain Horse" a young person feels unhappy when he returns to his old home, whereas in "The Ice Palace" a young person feels unhappy when she leaves home for the first time.

While

• **while**: *While* can be used in the same way as *although*. If there is any chance of confusion with the other meanings of *while*, however, it is better to use *although* in such circumstances.

needs checking While I support free trade in principle, I think it hurts this industry.

revised Although I support free trade in principle, I think it hurts this industry.

Yet

This word can be used either to refer to time (e.g., *He is not yet here*), or to connect ideas in opposition to each other. When used in this second way, it may introduce another word or a phrase, or a completely new sentence.

- His spear was firm, yet flexible.

- Jones positions himself as a critic of naturalism in art. Yet the aesthetic criteria he relies on are often founded on naturalistic principles.

• **yet**: *Yet*, like the other words in this group, should not be paired with another conjunction in such a way as to create too many twists and turns in the argument.

needs checking Varying the pace, altering the tone, director Joseph Rubens keeps us off balance. Ultimately, though, the pedestrian script catches up with him, yet not before *Sleeping with the Enemy* has made its point.

(The combination of *yet* and *though* is confusing for the reader.)

revised Varying the pace, altering the tone, director Joseph Rubens keeps us off balance. Ultimately, the pedestrian script catches up with him, yet not before *Sleeping with the Enemy* has made its point.

Words to Join Linked or Supporting Ideas

also	in fact
and	moreover
as well	not only ... but also
besides	plus
further	similarly
furthermore	so too
in addition	: [colon]
indeed	; [semicolon]

Also, and, as well

Also and *as well* are very similar both in meaning and in the way that they are used. Examples:

- He put forward his simplistic credo with enormous conviction. "To do well at school," he assured us, "you must be willing to study. It is also important to eat the right foods, exercise regularly, and get plenty of sleep." All the while, the one thing we all wanted, and none of us had managed to get, was plenty of sex.
- He put forward his simplistic credo with enormous conviction. "To do well at school," he assured us, "you must be willing to study. It is important as well to eat the right foods, exercise regularly, and get plenty of sleep." All the while, the one thing we all wanted, and none of us had managed to get, was plenty of sex.

• **also**: It is best not to use *also* to start sentences or paragraphs. Moreover, *also* should not be used in the way that we often use *and*—to join two clauses together into one sentence.

needs checking We performed the experiment with the beaker half full also we repeated it with the beaker empty.

revised We performed the experiment with the beaker half full, and we repeated it with the beaker empty.

or We performed the experiment with the beaker half full. We also repeated it with the beaker empty.

And

• **and**: If this word appears more than once in the same sentence, it's worth stopping to ask if it would not be better to start a new sentence. Usually the answer will be yes.

needs checking All my family attended the celebration and most of my friends were there and we enjoyed ourselves thoroughly.

revised All my family attended the celebration, and most of my friends were there, too. We enjoyed ourselves thoroughly.

• **as ... as**: When making comparisons one may use the *as ... as* combination or use a comparative adjective with *than*. But the two should not be combined.

needs checking Recent studies indicate that the average smoker is three times as likely to develop cancer than his non-smoking counterpart.

revised Recent studies indicate that the average smoker is three times more likely to develop cancer than is his non-smoking counterpart.

• **as well**: To avoid repetition, do not use *as well* in combination with *both*.

needs checking This method should be rejected, both because it is very expensive as well as because it is inefficient.

revised This method should be rejected, both because it is very expensive and because it is inefficient.

In addition, further, furthermore, moreover

All of these are commonly used to show that what the writer is saying gives additional support to an earlier statement she has made. An example:

- It was easy to see why many countries, despite their intense dislike of apartheid, still traded with South Africa. For one thing, it was the richest country in Africa. Many of its resources, moreover, were of strategic importance.

Notice that all four expressions are often used after sentences that begin with words such as *for one thing* or *first.*

Indeed, in fact

Both of these are used to indicate that what the writer is saying is a restatement or elaboration of the idea he has expressed in the previous sentence. Notice that a colon or semicolon may also be used to show this. Examples:

- Asia is the world's most populous continent. In fact, more people live there than on all the other continents combined.
- Asia is the world's most populous continent: more people live there than on all the other continents combined.

Not only ... but also

• **not only ... but also**: This combination is used to join two pieces of supporting evidence in an argument. The combination can help to create balanced, rhythmic writing, but if it is to do so it must be used carefully. Notice that it is not necessary to use *but also* in all cases, but that if the phrase is omitted a semicolon is normally required in order to avoid a run-on sentence.

needs checking Not only was Nirvana a commercial success, it was also among the first grunge bands to achieve musical respectability.

revised Not only was Nirvana a commercial success; it was also among the first grunge bands to achieve musical respectability.

or Nirvana was not only a commercial success, but also a critical one; it was among the first grunge bands to achieve musical respectability.

Plus

• **plus**: Do not use this word in the same way as *and* or *as well.*

needs checking For one thing, the council did not much like the design for the proposed new City Hall. Plus, there was not enough money available to build it that year.

revised For one thing, the council did not much like the design for the proposed new City Hall. As well, there was not enough money available to build it that year.

Words Used to Introduce Causes or Reasons

Relationships of cause and effect are at the heart of many arguments. It is common to experience some difficulty at first in understanding such relationships clearly. The discussion below of the word *because* may be helpful in this respect. To begin with, though, here is a list of words that are used to introduce causes or reasons:

as	for
as a result of	on account of
because	since
due to	

As

This word can be used either to show the relationship between two events in time, or to indicate that one event is the cause of another. This sometimes leaves room for confusion about meaning (ambiguity). The following sentence is a good example:

- As he was riding on the wrong side of the road, he was hit by a car.

This can mean either *When he was riding on the wrong side of the road ...* or *Because he was riding on the wrong side of the road....* Unless the writer is absolutely certain that the meaning is clear, it may be better to use *while* or *when* instead of *as* to indicate relationships in time, and *because* or *since* instead of *as* to indicate relationships of cause and effect.

Because

This word creates many problems for writers. The first thing to remember is that any group of words introduced with *because* must state a cause or reason. It must not state a result or an example.

- **because**: In the following sentences, *because* has been wrongly used:

needs checking The wind was blowing because the leaves were moving to and fro.

needs checking He had been struck by a car because he lay bleeding in the road.

A moment's reflection leads to the realization that both of these sentences are the wrong way round. The movement of the leaves is the result of the blowing of the wind, and the man's bleeding is the result of his having been hit. When the sentences are turned around, they become correct:

revised	The leaves were moving to and fro because the wind was blowing.
revised	He lay bleeding on the road because he had been struck by a car.

What leads many people to make mistakes like these is the sort of question that begins, *How do you know that...* or *Prove that...* or *Show that....* The person who is asked, "How do you know that the wind is blowing?" is likely to answer wrongly, "The wind is blowing because the leaves are moving to and fro." What he really means is, "I know the wind is blowing because I see the leaves moving to and fro." That answer is quite correct, since here the seeing is the cause of the knowing. Similarly, someone who is asked to show that the man in a newspaper story had been hit by a car might answer wrongly, "He had been struck by a car because he lay bleeding in the road." What he really means is, "I know that he had been struck by a car because I read that he lay bleeding in the road." It is of course awkward to use a lot of phrases such as *I know that* and *I see that.* Here are some easier and better ways of answering such questions:

- The movement of the trees shows that the wind is blowing.
- The fact that the leaves are moving proves that the wind is blowing.
- Since the man lay bleeding in the road, it seems likely that he had been hit by a car.

This problem is quite easily identified in the above sentences. In many formal writing contexts, the same problem can be much more difficult to spot. Look carefully at the following sentences:

needs checking	In the story "The Hero," Dora feels sorry for Julius because she sheds tears when he is expelled from school.
needs checking	A great many Republicans are not so concerned about the deficit as they claim to be, because they always call for increases in military spending.

In these sentences the source of the confusion may not be immediately clear. But if we ask whether or not Dora's tears are the *cause* of her feeling sorry for Julius, we realize the answer must be no. The tears, which presumably are the *result* of her feelings, are presented in this context as *evidence* that Dora feels sorry for Julius.

Is the fact that these Republicans always call for increases in military spending the *cause* of their being less concerned with the deficit than they claim? Again, the answer must be no. That fact is presumably being presented as an *example* of that lack of concern on the part of these Republicans, or as *evidence* in support of the claim that is being made regarding these Republicans.

In sentences such as this, in which the writer is trying to present evidence in support of an assertion, reversing the order of the ideas (as we did with the previous set of examples) is not the best solution to the problem. Can we in such circumstances use a word other than *because*? Unfortunately, English lacks any one word that conveys this idea concisely. The word *example* or the word *evidence* might serve this function well, if only the rules of English allowed nouns to be used as conjunctions. In informal conversation, this solution might be worth trying:

- In the story "The Hero," Dora feels sorry for Julius, *evidence*, she sheds tears when he is expelled from school.
- A great many Republicans are not so concerned about the deficit as they claim to be, *example*, they always call for increases in military spending.

In formal writing, of course, one cannot use the nouns *evidence* and *example* in this way. What you *can* do in formal writing, though, is use a semi-colon to indicate this sort of link between ideas:

revised In the story "The Hero," Dora feels sorry for Julius; she sheds tears when he is expelled from school.

revised A great many Republicans are not so concerned about the deficit as they claim to be; they always call for increases in military spending.

This is one of many situations in which the semi-colon can be extremely useful.

• **because**: It is best not to use *because* when listing several reasons for something; otherwise the writer gives the reader the impression that the first reason given is to be the only reason. The reader will then be surprised when others are mentioned.

needs checking He was happy because it was Friday. He was also happy because his team had won the game that morning and he had scored the winning goal. Finally, he was happy because he had done well on his exams.

revised He was happy for several reasons: it was Friday, he had scored the winning goal for his team that morning, and he had done well on his exams.

needs checking Frederick was able to enjoy such success because he was adroit at waiting for the right opportunity, and seizing it when it was handed him. He was also successful because he created a military machine that had no equal.

revised One reason Frederick was able to enjoy such success was that he was adroit at waiting for the right opportunity, and seizing it when it was handed him. But none of this would have been possible had he not also created a military machine that had no equal.

- **because**: Some people like to answer *How...?* questions by using *because*. Instead, the word *by* should be used.

needs checking How did she help him? She helped him because she lent him some money.

revised How did she help him? She helped him by lending him some money.

Due to

- **due to**: *Due* is an adjective and therefore should always modify a noun (as in the common phrase *with all due respect*). When followed by *to* it can suggest a causal relationship, but the word *due* must in that case refer to the previous noun:

  - The team's success is due to hard work.

    (*Due* refers to the noun *success*.)

It is not a good idea to begin a sentence with a phrase such as *Due to unexpected circumstances* ... or *Due to the fact that*.... To avoid such difficulties it is best to use *because*.

needs checking Due to the sudden resignation of our sales manager, the marketing director will take on additional responsibility for a short time.

revised Because our sales manager has resigned suddenly, the marketing director will take on additional responsibility for a short time.

Since

When used to introduce causes or reasons (rather than as a time word) *since* is used in essentially the same way as *because*.

Words Used to Introduce Results or Conclusions

accordingly	it follows that ...
as a result	so
consequently	therefore
hence	thus
in conclusion	to sum up
in consequence	to summarize
in sum	

As a result, hence

Both of these are used to show that the idea being talked about in one sentence follows from, or is the result of, what was spoken of in the previous sentence.

- His car ran out of gas. As a result, he was late for his appointment.
- His car ran out of gas. Hence, he was late for his appointment.

Notice the difference between these two and words such as *because* and *since*; we would say *Because* (or *since*) *his car ran out of gas, he was late for the appointment*.

• **hence**: Hence should not be used to join two clauses into one sentence, or to join words or phrases.

needs checking Her phone is out of order hence it will be impossible to contact her.

revised Her phone is out of order. Hence, it will be impossible to contact her.

needs checking It is not the film but the advertising that is exploitative, hence pornographic.

revised It is not the film but the advertising that is exploitative, and hence pornographic.

So

This word may be used to introduce results when one wants to mention both cause and result in the same sentence (e.g., *Her phone is out of order, so it will be impossible to contact her*). See page 209 above regarding beginning sentences with *so*.

• **so**: If *so* is used, *because* is not needed, and vice versa. One of the two is enough.

needs checking	Because he was tired, so he went to bed early.
revised	Because he was tired, he went to bed early.
or	He was tired, so he went to bed early.

Therefore

• **therefore**: *Therefore* should not be used to join two clauses into one sentence.

needs checking	Training is perceived as good, therefore the payment of a $30 million subsidy to McDonald's can be made to look like a benign act.
revised	Training is perceived as good; therefore, the payment of a $30 million subsidy to McDonald's can be made to look like a benign act.

M2
Usage

Words Used to Express Purpose

in order to	so that
in such a way as to	so as to

So that

• **so that**: When used beside each other (see also *so ... that* below) these two words show purpose; they indicate that we will be told why an action was taken. Examples:

- He sent the parcel early so that it would arrive before Christmas.
- She wants to see you so that she can ask you a question.

The words *such that* should never be used in this way to indicate purpose.

needs checking	The doctor will give you some medicine such that you will be cured.
revised	The doctor will give you some medicine so that you will be cured.
needs checking	Fold the paper such that it forms a triangle.
revised	Fold the paper so that it forms a triangle.
or	Fold the paper in such a way that it forms a triangle.

Words Used to Introduce Examples

for example	such as
for instance	: [colon]
in that	

For example, for instance, such as

The three expressions are used differently, even though they all introduce examples. *Such as* is used to introduce a single word or short phrase. It always relates to a plural noun that has appeared just before it.

- Crops such as tea and rice require a great deal of water.
  (Here *such as* relates to the noun *crops*.)
- Several African peoples, such as the Yoruba of Nigeria and the Makonde of Tanzania, attach a special ceremonial importance to masks.
  (*Such as* relates to *peoples*.)

For example and *for instance*, on the other hand, are complete phrases in themselves, and are normally set off by commas. Each is used to show that the entire sentence in which it appears gives an example of a statement made in the previous sentence. Examples:

- Some crops require a great deal of water. Tea, for example, requires an annual rainfall of at least 60 inches.
- Several African peoples attach a special ceremonial importance to masks. The Yoruba and the Makonde, for example, both believe that spirits enter the bodies of those who wear certain masks.
- Tornadoes are not only a Midwestern United States phenomenon. In 1983, for instance, more than 30 people were injured by a tornado in Los Angeles, California.

• **for example, for instance**: *For example* and *for instance* should not be used to introduce phrases that give examples. In such situations use *such as* instead.

needs checking In certain months of the year, for example July and August, El Paso, Texas, receives most of its rainfall.

revised In certain months of the year, such as July and August, El Paso, Texas, receives most of its rainfall.

or In certain months of the year El Paso, Texas, receives most of its rainfall.

In that

- **in that**: Do not confuse with *in the way that.*

needs checking	He is cruel in the way that he treats his wife harshly.
revised	He is cruel in that he treats his wife harshly.
or	He is cruel in the way that he treats his wife.

Such as

- **such as**: The addition of *and others* at the end of a phrase beginning with *such as* is redundant.

needs checking	In contrast to this perspective, sociological studies of ethnicity written from the "class" perspective (such as Benarez and Lee's 2014 paper, Chang's 2012 monograph, and others) have argued that ethnic inequality is only a special class of inequality in general.
revised	In contrast to this perspective, sociological studies of ethnicity written from the "class" perspective (such as Benarez and Lee's 2014 paper, and Chang's 2012 monograph) have argued that ethnic inequality is only a special class of inequality in general.

Words Used to Indicate Alternatives

either ... or	otherwise
if only	rather than
instead, instead of	unless
in that case	whether ... or
neither ... nor	

If only

This expression is normally used when we wish that something would happen, or were true, but it clearly will not happen, or is not true.

- If only he were here, he would know what to do.
  (This indicates that he is not here.)
- "If only there were thirty hours in a day ...," she kept saying.

In that case

This expression is used when we wish to explain what will happen if the thing spoken of in the previous sentence happens, or turns out to be true. Examples:

- He may arrive before six o'clock. In that case we can all go out to dinner.
- It is quite possible that many people will dislike the new law. In that case the government may decide to change it.

Do not confuse *in that case* with *otherwise*, which is used in the reverse situation (i.e., when one wishes to explain what will happen if the thing spoken of in the previous sentence does not happen, or turns out to be false).

Otherwise

This word has two meanings. The first is *in other ways* (e.g., *I have a slight toothache. Otherwise I am healthy*). The second meaning can sometimes cause confusion: *otherwise* used to mean *if not*. Here the word is used when we want to talk about what will or might happen if the thing spoken of in the previous sentence does not happen. Examples:

- I will have to start immediately. Otherwise, I will not finish in time.

  (This is the same as saying, *If I do not start now, I will not finish in time.*)
- The general decided to retreat. Otherwise, he believed, all his troops would be killed.

  (This is the same as saying, *The general believed that if he decided not to retreat, all his troops would be killed.*)
- You must pay me for the car before Friday. Otherwise, I will offer it to someone else.

  (i.e., *If you do not pay me for the car before Friday, I will offer it to someone else.*)

• **otherwise**: When used to mean *if not*, *otherwise* should normally be used to start a new sentence. It should not be used in the middle of a sentence to join two clauses.

needs checking	I may meet you at the party tonight, otherwise I will see you tomorrow.
revised	I may meet you at the party tonight. Otherwise, I will see you tomorrow.

Words Used to Show Degree or Extent

for the most part	to some extent
so ... that	too ... for ... to
such ... that	to some degree
to a certain extent	

So ... that

• **so ... that**: When separated from each other by an adjective or adverb, these two words express degree or extent, answering questions such as *How far...?*, *How big...?*, *How much...?* (Grammatically, *so* in these contexts introduces adjectives.) Examples:

- How sick is he? He is so sick that he may not last the night.
- How large is Texas? It is so large that you need several days to drive across it.

So ... that is the only combination of words that can be used in this way; it is wrong to say *very sick that* ... or *too large that*, just as it is wrong to leave out the word *so* and simply use *that* in such sentences.

needs checking	She was very late for dinner that there was no food left for her.
revised	She was so late for dinner that there was no food left for her.
needs checking	Dominic speaks quickly that it is often difficult to understand him.
revised	Dominic speaks so quickly that it is often difficult to understand him.

Such ... that

• **such ... that**: Like *so ... that*, the expression *such ... that* is used to express degree or extent, answering questions such as, *How big...?*, *How long...?*, *How fast...?* Grammatically, *such* in these contexts introduces noun phrases. Notice the difference in the way *so ... that* and *such ... that* are used.

- How far is it? It is such a long way that you would never be able to get there walking.
- It is so far that you would never be able to reach there walking.
- How large is he? He is such a large man that his trousers need to be made specially for him.
- He is so large that his trousers need to be made specially for him.

The difference between the two is of course that only one word is normally used between *so* and *that*, whereas two or three words (usually an article, an adjective, and a noun) are used between *such* and *that*. Be careful not to confuse the two, or to leave out *such*.

needs checking	It was a hot day that nobody could stay outside for long.
revised	It was such a hot day that nobody could stay outside for long.

That and Which

To understand when to use *that* and when to use *which* (according to traditional grammatical principles), one must first understand the difference between a restrictive clause and a non-restrictive clause (see also pages 398–99). A restrictive clause restricts the application of the noun it modifies. Here is an example:

- The horse that was injured yesterday should recover.

Here the clause *that was injured yesterday* restricts the meaning of the subject of the sentence—*horse*—to a particular horse. The clause helps to define the subject more narrowly. A non-restrictive clause does not restrict the application of the noun it modifies; instead it tells us more about the subject. Again, here is an example:

- The injured horse, which was the favourite to win today's race, should recover in time for the Derby.

Here the clause *which was the favourite to win today's race* tells us more about the horse but is not necessary to its definition. Notice that the non-restrictive clause is set off by commas, while the restrictive clause follows on directly after the noun it describes, with no intervening comma. As these examples illustrate, *that* is typically used with restrictive clauses, *which* with non-restrictive clauses.

• **that/which**: Students have long been taught that it is correct to use *that* in restrictive clauses and *which* in non-restrictive clauses.

needs checking	The only store which sells this brand is now closed.
revised	The only store that sells this brand is now closed.
needs checking	The position which Marx adopted owed much to the philosophy of Hegel.
revised	The position that Marx adopted owed much to the philosophy of Hegel.

Although the use of the word *which* in any restrictive clause provokes a strong reaction among some English instructors, there are clearly instances in which one is quite justified in using *which* in this way. Such is the case when the writer is already using at least one *that* in the sentence:

needs checking He told me that the radio that he had bought was defective.
revised He told me that the radio which he had bought was defective.

Better yet, in many cases, is to avoid the use of a second relative pronoun by rephrasing:

revised He told me that the radio he had bought was defective.

Indeed, instructors who object to *which* point out that rephrasing can often make the sentence shorter and crisper:

needs checking The ending, which comes as a surprise to most readers, is profoundly unsettling.
revised The ending is both surprising and unsettling.
needs checking The 2020 campaign, which had been carefully planned, was an enormous success.
revised The carefully planned 2020 campaign was an enormous success.

But *which* is not a special case in this regard. *That*, *who*, and *whose* can often be fruitfully removed in the same way:

needs checking The surplus that we now project for 2024 will probably be exceeded in 2025.
revised The projected 2024 surplus will probably be exceeded in 2025.
needs checking Eisenhower hired as his personal driver a woman who turned into a long-term friend.
revised Eisenhower and his driver became close friends.

The vice, then, is not *which* per se, but wordiness in general. Those who focus their attention on the one word and rail that "witches ride on broomsticks" might do better to treat the excessive use of *which* as a symptom of a much broader disease.

Interestingly, the rule about *that* and *which* seems to be a relatively recent invention, dreamt up by Henry and Francis Fowler and first propounded in their book *The King's English* in 1906. In the words of Joseph M. Williams, they felt

> the random variation between *that* and *which* in restrictive clauses [to be] messy, so they simply asserted that henceforth writers should (with some exceptions) limit *which* to non-restrictive clauses. (*Style: Ten Lessons in Clarity and Grace*, New York, Longman, 2000, 24–25)

Many instructors today are as anxious as were the Fowlers to limit the messiness in English. But, as Robert M. Martin fairly observes, it is "hard to imagine real contexts in which observation of the *that/which* distinction would result in better communication" (*Dalhousie Review*, Spring 2003, 19). Again, the better reason for observing the distinction is that doing so may help to reduce wordiness—not that the distinction itself rests on a particularly strong foundation.

Words Used to Make Comparisons

along the same lines
by comparison
in contrast
in the same way
likewise
on the one hand ...
... on the other hand
similarly

Other Joining Words and Expressions

as illustrated above/below
as mentioned above/below
as we can see/we can see that
assuming that
as shown in the diagram
in that
these findings indicate that
to begin with
whereby
in other words
in the event of
in light of
in this respect/in some respects
above/below
firstly/in the first place
secondly/in the second place
for one thing

M2.10 Wordiness

Wordiness is perhaps the most persistent disease afflicting modern writing; references to it permeate this book. Its opposite—the mistake of including too few words in a sentence—is also discussed in this section.

- **actual/actually**: Usually redundant.

needs checking Many people assume that Switzerland is made up entirely of bankers and watchmakers. In actual fact, the Swiss economy is very diversified.

revised Many people assume that Switzerland is made up entirely of bankers and watchmakers. In fact, the Swiss economy is very diversified.

• **as regards**: Use *about*, or rephrase.

needs checking As regards your request for additional funding, we have taken the matter under advisement.

revised We are considering your request for more money.

• **as stated earlier**: If so, why state it again?

needs checking The Venus flytrap, which as stated earlier is an insectivorous plant, grows only in a restricted area of New Jersey.

revised The Venus flytrap grows only in a restricted area of New Jersey.

• **as you know, as we all know**: Usually better omitted.

needs checking As we all know, Barack Obama won in convincing fashion over Mitt Romney in 2012.

revised Barack Obama won in convincing fashion over Mitt Romney in 2012.

• **aspect**: Often a pointer to an entire phrase or clause that can be cut.

needs checking The logging industry is a troubled one at the present time. One of the aspects of this industry that is a cause for concern is the increased production of cheaper timber in South America.

revised The logging industry is now a troubled one. Increased production of cheaper timber in South America has reduced the market for North American wood.

• **at a later date**: *Later.*

needs checking We can decide this at a later date.

revised We can decide this later.

• **at the present time**: *Now*, or nothing.

needs checking At the present time the company has ten employees.

revised The company has ten employees.

• **attention**: *It has come to my attention* that this expression is almost always unnecessarily wordy.

needs checking It has come to my attention that shipments last month were 15 per cent below targeted levels.

revised Shipments last month were 15 per cent below targeted levels.

• **basis/basically**: Both are often pointers to wordiness.

needs checking On the basis of the information we now possess it is possible to see that William Bligh was not the ogre he was once thought to be. Basically, he was no harsher than most captains of the time.

revised Recent research suggests that William Bligh was not the ogre he was once thought to be. He was no harsher than most captains of the time.

• **cause**: Sentences using *cause* as a verb can often be rephrased more concisely; try to think of other verbs.

needs checking The increased sales tax caused the people to react with fury.

revised The increase in sales tax infuriated the people.

needs checking The change in temperature caused the liquid to freeze within seventeen minutes.

revised The liquid froze within seventeen minutes of the temperature change.

• **close proximity to**: *Near.*

needs checking The office is situated in close proximity to shops and transportation facilities.

revised The office is near a shopping centre and a bus stop.

• **e.g. ... etc.**: If you begin by saying *for example*, it is redundant to add *and others* at the end of your list. See *also* and *such as* in "Joining Words."

needs checking In several African nations (e.g., Rwanda, Malawi, Democratic Republic of the Congo, etc.) tyrannical or murderous regimes were overthrown in the 1990s.

revised In several African nations (e.g., Rwanda, Malawi, Democratic Republic of the Congo) tyrannical or murderous regimes were overthrown in the 1990s.

• **etc.**: The Latin *et cetera*, or *etc.* for short, means *and the rest* or *and others*. To say *and etc.* is really to say *and and others*. Beware as well of combining *etc.* with expressions such as *such as*.

needs checking During recent years several countries (Greece, Argentina, and etc.) have amassed huge debts, which they are now unable to pay.

revised During recent years several countries (Greece, Argentina, etc.) have amassed huge debts, which they are now unable to pay.

needs checking Plants such as Venus flytraps, pitcher plants, etc. feed on insects.

revised Plants such as Venus flytraps and pitcher plants feed on insects.

or Some plants (Venus flytraps, pitcher plants, etc.) feed on insects.

• **exists**: Often a pointer to wordiness.

needs checking A situation now exists in which voters suspect the government's motives, regardless of whether or not they approve of its actions.

revised Voters now suspect the government's motives even if they approve of its actions.

• **fact**: Be wary of *the fact that* (as well as *in point of fact* and *actual fact*).

needs checking Due to the fact that we have discontinued this product, we are unable to provide spare parts.

revised Because we have discontinued this product, we are unable to provide spare parts.

needs checking The fact that every member nation has one vote in the General Assembly does not give each one equal influence.

revised Each member nation has one vote in the General Assembly, but some have more influence than others.

needs checking Despite the fact that virtually no one in those days could foresee the end of American surpluses, Jones could.

revised Jones was one of the few to foresee the end of American surpluses.

• **factor**: Heavily overused, and a frequent cause of wordiness.

needs checking An important factor contributing to the French Revolution was the poverty of the peasantry.

revised The poverty of the peasantry was a major cause of the French Revolution.

• **from my point of view, according to my point of view, in my opinion**: All three expressions are usually redundant.

needs checking From my point of view, basic health care is more important than esoteric and expensive machines or procedures that benefit few.

fair I think that basic health care is more important than esoteric and expensive machines or procedures that benefit few.

better Basic health care is more important than esoteric and expensive machines or procedures that benefit few.

- **I myself**: In almost all cases the addition of *myself* is needlessly repetitive.

needs checking	I myself believe in freedom of speech.
revised	I believe in freedom of speech.

(Note: For more on *myself* see page 292.)

- **in all probability**: *Probably*.

needs checking	In all probability we will be finished tomorrow.
revised	We will probably be finished tomorrow.

- **include**: Often a needed word or two is omitted after this verb. The best solution may be to rephrase or find another verb.

needs checking	The report includes both secondary and post-secondary education.
revised	The report includes material on both secondary and post-secondary education.
or	The report deals with both secondary and post-secondary education.
needs checking	The Thirty Years' War included most countries in Europe.
revised	The list of countries that fought in the Thirty Years' War includes almost every European nation.
revised	Almost every European country fought in the Thirty Years' War.

- **interesting**: In most cases the writer should not have to tell the reader that what he is saying is interesting.

needs checking	It is interesting to observe that illiteracy affects almost as high a proportion of native-born Americans as it does immigrants.
revised	Illiteracy affects almost as high a proportion of native-born Americans as it does immigrants.

- **mean for**: The preposition is unnecessary.

needs checking	I did not mean for him to do it all himself.
revised	I did not want him to do it all himself.

- **nature**: Often contributes to wordiness.

needs checking	The nature of the brain is to process information incredibly swiftly.
revised	The brain processes information extremely swiftly.

- **personally**: As a way of distinguishing views expressed by the same person acting in different capacities, *personally* serves a very useful function (e.g., *As a member of the cabinet he is obliged to support the measure, but personally he has doubts as to its appropriateness*). If you are not making this sort of distinction, though, it is safe to let your reader take it for granted that you are speaking for yourself rather than on behalf of others.

needs checking Personally, I feel that the Supreme Court has usually exercised its constitutional authority wisely in recent years.

revised I feel the Supreme Court has usually exercised its constitutional authority wisely in recent years.

• **point in time**: *Now* or *then*.

needs checking At that point in time central Africa was very sparsely populated.

revised Central Africa was then very sparsely populated.

• **really**: The adverb *really* has a place in formal writing when used to mean *in reality, truly* (*Vervoerd said he would change the regulations, but really he had no intention of doing so*). If you want to use an intensifier, however, *very* is preferable.

needs checking It is really important that this be done today.

revised It is very important that this be done today.

or This must be done today.

Often in such cases your point may be made more effectively without using intensifiers—and even without using adjectives:

needs checking Like any other animal raised in a modern factory farm, a factory-farmed pig leads a very appalling life. It spends its entire life in really hideous pens that do not permit it to turn around, let alone to walk or run. Such incredibly barbaric cruelty is justified on the grounds that without it, humans would be forced to pay somewhat more for bacon and ham.

revised Like any other animal raised in a modern factory farm, a factory-farmed pig leads an appalling life. It spends its entire life in pens that do not permit it to turn around, let alone to walk or run. Such cruelty is justified on the grounds that without it, humans would be forced to pay somewhat more for bacon and ham.

• **redundancy**: *Redundancies* are words or expressions that repeat in different words a meaning already expressed. Commonly used expressions that involve redundancy include *ATM machine, end result, plans for the future, general public, nod your head, optimistic about the future, a personal friend of mine*, and *mutual cooperation*. Sometimes a case may be made for using a phrase of this sort in order to emphasize a point. What is to be avoided is thoughtless and purposeless wordiness.

needs checking	This property will appreciate greatly in value.
revised	This property will appreciate greatly.
needs checking	The house is very large in size.
revised	The house is very large.
needs checking	It was decided it would be mutually beneficial to both of us if he left.
revised	It was decided it would be mutually beneficial if he left.
or	We agreed it would be better for both of us if he left.

• **regard, with regard to, as regards**: Try *about* or *over*, or rephrase.

needs checking	I am writing with regard to your proposal to centralize production.
revised	I am writing about your proposal to centralize production.
needs checking	As regards the trend in interest rates, it is likely to continue to be upward.
revised	Interest rates are likely to continue to increase.
needs checking	This Act gave the government powers with regard to the readjustment of industry.
revised	This Act gave the government powers over the readjustment of industry.

• **situation**: By avoiding this word you will usually make your sentence shorter and better.

needs checking	This treaty created a situation in which European countries gave up a degree of autonomy in return for greater security.
revised	Through this treaty European countries gave up a degree of autonomy in return for greater security.

• **there is/are/was/were**: These constructions often produce sentences that are needlessly long.

needs checking	There were many factors which undermined the government's popularity in this period.
revised	Many things undermined the government's popularity in this period.
needs checking	There are many historians who accept this thesis.
revised	Many historians accept this thesis.

• **too few words**: This mistake can happen anywhere in a sentence. One of the best tests of whether or not a writer has checked her work is whether or not there are missing words. In almost all cases, such omissions will be noticed through careful proofreading.

needs checking She rushed home to tell my family and about the accident.
revised She rushed home to tell my family and me about the accident.

needs checking Gandhi reminded the Conference that just one intercontinental ballistic missile could plant 200 million trees, irrigate one million hectares of land, or build 6,500 health care centres.
revised Gandhi reminded the Conference that the money spent on just one intercontinental ballistic missile could be used to plant 200 million trees, irrigate one million hectares of land, or build 6,500 health care centres.

• **too many words**: Many of the causes of this problem have been given separate entries.

needs checking So far as the purpose of this essay is concerned, it will concentrate on the expansion of Chinese influence.
revised This essay will concentrate on the expansion of Chinese influence.

needs checking Although the author does not claim to be writing a social study, the question arises whether the social implications of his analysis can be ignored.
revised Although the author does not claim to be writing a social study, his analysis does have social implications.

• **tragic/tragically**: Unnecessary use of either the adjective or the adverb constitutes overkill.

needs checking Her husband, her child, and more than one hundred others died in a tragic plane crash in March, 2019.
revised Her husband, her child, and more than one hundred others died in a plane crash in March, 2019.

• **would like to take this opportunity to**: *Would like.*

needs checking I would like to take this opportunity to thank my cousin in Peoria.
revised I am very grateful to my cousin in Peoria.
or I would like to thank my cousin in Peoria.

On the Companion Website

Exercises on wordiness may be found at **sites.broadviewpress.com/writingcdn**. Click on **Exercises** and go to **"Words and Usage."**

M2 Usage

M3 PUNCTUATION AND OTHER CONVENTIONS

M3.1 Punctuation Marks

The Period •

The most important mark of punctuation is the period, which is used to end sentences. The most common punctuation mistakes involve using (or failing to use) a period; for a full discussion of complete and incomplete sentences, comma splices, run-on sentences, and sentence fragments, see M1.3.

See below under "The Question Mark" for a discussion of statements concerning questions; like other statements, these should end with a period (not a question mark).

abbreviations: The period is also used to form abbreviations. Here are some examples:

Mr. Ms. Prof. e.g. etc. i.e. St. Ave. Feb.

With many abbreviations, whether periods are included or not has become a matter of convention. For abbreviations such as the following, most style guides now recommend omitting the periods:

academic degrees:	BA	MA	PhD	
directions	NW	SE	NNE	
eras	BCE	CE	(Before the Common Era; Common Era)	
institutions	UBC	CIBC	EU	UN
states and provinces	AB	ON	CA	NY

Some common abbreviations (*et al.*, for example) require a period in one position only. If you are in any doubt about whether or not to use a period in an abbreviation, or where to put it, look up the full form of what is being abbreviated.

needs checking Jones, Smithers et. al. will be there in person.
revised Jones, Smithers et al. will be there in person.

(*Et al.* is short for the Latin *et alia*, meaning *and others.*)

The Ellipsis . . .

Three dots are used to indicate the omission of one or more words needed to complete a sentence or other grammatical construction.

• **ellipsis:** Note that when used in quotation an ellipsis comes inside the quotation marks, and that when an ellipsis precedes a period the sentence should end with four dots (essentially the three-dot ellipsis followed by the period).

needs checking Harris shows more than a trace of paranoia in her book; she speaks, for example, of "the elements trying to subvert the essence of liberal society, of tolerance, of goodwill ... They are all around us."

revised Harris shows more than a trace of paranoia in her book; she speaks, for example, of "the elements trying to subvert the essence of liberal society, of tolerance, of goodwill.... They are all around us."

Ellipses may also be used to indicate the trailing off of speech: *Violet struggled for breath. "All my money," she gasped, "goes to...." Those were her last words.*

The Comma ,

(See M1.3 for a discussion of comma splices and run-on sentences.)

You may be familiar with this famous example of how important a comma can be:

It's time to eat, children. It's time to eat children.

If you're reading aloud, the comma indicates a good point to pause. But even more importantly, the comma shows the grammatical structure of the sentence; the comma indicates clearly that the noun "children" is not meant to be taken as the direct object of the verb "eat." This is the central function of the comma in modern English—to help the reader recognize the grammatical structure of the sentences being read. As a side benefit, commas also help those reading aloud to pause at places in a sentence where there are natural breaks in the grammatical structure. But commas should not be used simply to create pauses at any point in a long sentence where the writer thinks the reader might run out of breath.

It was not always thus. When commas began to appear in English prose (in the late sixteenth century), they were used simply as a way of suggesting pauses in speech. Given the extent to which people's natural speech patterns differ, it is no wonder that the placing of commas in seventeenth- and eighteenth-century usage seems to us haphazard. (In this respect eighteenth-century habits of punctuation resemble eighteenth-century habits of capitalization—see page 421.) A striking example is the Second Amendment to the American Constitution:

> A well regulated Militia, being necessary to the security of a free State, the right of the people to keep and bear Arms, shall not be infringed.

This is a sentence comprising two clauses, with a subordinate clause at the beginning providing context for the declaration made in the main clause. Though it is a long sentence, there is according to grammatical principles no good reason to include a comma anywhere except at the break between the two clauses:

> A well regulated Militia being necessary to the security of a free State, the right of the people to keep and bear Arms shall not be infringed.

In saying this sentence aloud some readers will undoubtedly pause slightly at points other than at the one marked by the comma. But it is at that point alone that there should be a comma (at least according to the conventions of modern English). The additional commas in early texts are in this case far more than a historical curiosity; they have fueled endless debate and more than one court case over the constitutionality of twentieth- and twenty-first-century gun control measures in America.

The above should not be taken to imply that there is no room for individuality when it comes to the inclusion of "structural" commas; far from it. Many writers, for example, like to use a comma to set off an opening phrase from the sentence that follows. And that is perfectly acceptable; both the versions below of the sentence that opened the previous paragraph are correct, as are both versions of the other sample sentence below:

> In saying this sentence aloud some readers will undoubtedly pause slightly at points other than at the one marked by the comma.

> In saying this sentence aloud, some readers will undoubtedly pause slightly at points other than at the one marked by the comma.

> In the spring of 2016 she left her family and moved to Rome.

> In the spring of 2016, she left her family and moved to Rome.

Again, the key point is that if structural commas are to be included, they must come at points in the sentence where there are natural breaks in the grammatical structure.

Although the omission or wrong use of a comma sounds like a small mistake, it can be very important. The following group of words, for example, forms a sentence only if a comma is included:

The Comma Worth a Million Dollars

In a 2006 case, a disagreement between two telecommunications companies over a comma was the subject of a million-dollar lawsuit. One company (Rogers Communications Inc.) argued that the contract between the two parties was valid for a minimum of five years, while the other (Bell Aliant Inc.) argued that it could be terminated at any time by either party, provided one year's notice was given.

Have a look at the relevant clause in the agreement and see what you think:

> This agreement shall be effective from the date it is made and shall continue in force for a period of five (5) years from the date it is made, and thereafter for successive five (5) year terms, unless and until terminated by one year prior notice in writing by either party.

How (if at all) would the meaning change if the last comma were removed?

> This agreement shall be effective from the date it is made and shall continue in force for a period of five (5) years from the date it is made, and thereafter for successive five (5) year terms unless and until terminated by one year prior notice in writing by either party.

The telecommunications regulator who decided the case ruled that that comma made all the difference. If the comma had been omitted, he ruled, the "unless and until terminated…" phrase would have applied only to the "thereafter" part of the agreement. With the inclusion of the comma, however, the "unless and until terminated…" phrase could reasonably be taken to apply to the initial five-year period as well as to the subsequent five-year terms that were contemplated. Bell Aliant was thus free to terminate the contract with one year's notice, even within the initial five-year period.

If the parties had used different punctuation, of course, they could have easily made the meaning plain:

> This agreement shall be effective from the date it is made and shall continue in force for a period of five (5) years from the date it is made. Thereafter it shall continue for successive five (5) year terms, unless and until terminated by one year prior notice in writing by either party.

What do you think? Was the regulator's ruling fair?

needs checking Because of the work that we had done before we were ready to hand in the assignment.

revised Because of the work that we had done before, we were ready to hand in the assignment.

Restrictive and non-restrictive modifiers: The omission or addition of commas can also completely alter the meaning of a sentence—as it did in the Queen's University Alumni letter that spoke of the warm emotions still felt by alumni for *our friends, who are dead* (rather than *our friends who are dead*). The second would have been merely a polite remembrance of those alumni who have died; the first suggests that all the friends are dead.

Such differences in meaning are not usually matters of life and death. In the following two sentences, the difference is a matter of how many stroganoffs are on the menu.

> The stroganoff, made with mushrooms and cashew cream, is the most popular item on our menu.
>
> The stroganoff made with mushrooms and cashew cream is the most popular item on our menu.

In the first sentence the implication is that there is only one stroganoff available; the one and only stroganoff is the most popular item on the menu, and in mentioning the mushrooms and cashew cream the server is simply providing some additional, incidental information. In the second sentence the omission of commas leaves open the possibility that there may be several stroganoffs on the menu; it's the one with the mushrooms and cashew cream that's the most popular. (Hint from the server: *don't order the beef stroganoff*.)

The grammatical distinction involved here is between restrictive and non-restrictive modifiers. Restrictive modifiers are essential to the full meaning of the word being modified; they restrict or limit the meaning of that word within the sentence. To indicate that they are essential to the meaning of the noun, they are not separated from it by commas. (The meaning of the second sentence is restricted to *the stroganoff made with mushrooms and cashew cream*.)

Non-restrictive modifiers, on the other hand, provide additional information that is not essential to the core meaning of the word being modified. As a way of indicating that the information provided by non-restrictive modifiers is incidental rather than essential to the word being modified, non-restrictive modifiers should be set off with commas.

(In the first stroganoff sentence, in which the information about the mushrooms and the cashew cream is not essential to the meaning of *stroganoff* within the sentence, *made with mushrooms and cashew cream* is set off by commas.)

needs checking Shoppers, who spend $100 or more, are eligible for the prize.

[The modifying clause *who spend $100 or more* is in this case essential to the meaning of *shoppers* in the context of this sentence; the group of people eligible is restricted to those who spend $100 or more.]

revised Shoppers who spend $100 or more are eligible for the prize.

The distinction between restrictive and non-restrictive modifiers may apply to adjective clauses (such as those above), adjective phrases, and also to appositives—nouns or noun phrases in apposition to another noun. Mistakes with appositives are common.

needs checking In Shakespeare's play, *The Tempest*, Gonzalo uses the same words that appear in Florio's translation of Montaigne's "Of Cannibals."

[This could be taken to imply that Shakespeare wrote only one play.]

revised In Shakespeare's play *The Tempest* Gonzalo echoes the language of John Florio's translation of Montaigne's "Of Cannibals."

(For more on restrictive and non-restrictive modifiers, see the discussion of *that* and *which* on pages 384–86.)

• **omission of commas**: Commas very commonly come in pairs, and it is wrong to omit the second comma in a pair. Be particularly careful when putting commas around a name, or around an adjectival subordinate clause.

needs checking My sister Caroline, has done very well this year in her studies.

revised My sister, Caroline, has done very well this year in her studies.

needs checking The snake which had been killed the day before, was already half-eaten by ants.

revised The snake, which had been killed the day before, was already half-eaten by ants.

• **extra comma:** Writers often add a comma when they feel a sentence is getting long, regardless of whether one is needed or is appropriate.

needs checking The ever-increasing gravitational pull of the global economy, is drawing almost every area of the earth into its orbit.

revised The ever-increasing gravitational pull of the global economy is drawing almost every area of the earth into its orbit.

• **serial comma:** An important use of commas is to separate the entries in lists. Many authorities feel that a comma need not appear between the last and second-last entries in a list, since these are usually separated already by the word *and*. Omitting the last comma in a series will occasionally lead to ambiguity, though; when in doubt, we recommend that you include the serial comma. And when the list includes items that have commas within them, use a semicolon to separate the items in the list.

needs checking This book is dedicated to my parents, Jane Goodall and God.

revised This book is dedicated to my parents, Jane Goodall, and God.

(The serial comma makes clear that Goodall and God are not the writer's parents.)

needs checking The three firms involved were McCarthy and Walters, Harris, Jones, and Engleby, and Cassells and Wirtz.

revised The three firms involved were McCarthy and Walters; Harris, Jones, and Engleby; and Cassells and Wirtz.

On the Companion Website

Exercises on comma splices, sentence fragments, and how to use punctuation may be found at **sites.broadviewpress.com/writingcdn**. Click on **Exercises** and go to **"Punctuation."**

The Question Mark ?

• **question mark:** Everyone knows that a question should be followed by a question mark, but it is easy to forget, particularly if one is writing quickly or if the question mark should appear within other punctuation.

needs checking Would Britain benefit from closer ties with Europe. The question continues to bedevil British political life.

revised Would Britain benefit from closer ties with Europe? The question continues to bedevil British political life.

It is easy to forget that sentences beginning with combinations such as *He asked if...* or *She wondered whether...* are statements, not questions. They may report a question in indirect speech, but they are not themselves questions, and should thus not end with a question mark.

needs checking Many scholars have asked whether Truman was justified in dropping the atomic bomb on Japan, or whether he should have relied on conventional weapons?

revised Many scholars have asked whether Truman was justified in dropping the atomic bomb on Japan, or whether he should have relied on conventional weapons.

or Many scholars have asked the following question: was Truman justified in dropping the atomic bomb on Japan, or should he have relied on conventional weapons?

The Exclamation Mark !

This mark is used to give extremely strong emphasis to a statement. It should be used very sparingly, if at all, in formal written work; most good writers avoid it completely, since they realize that it does not lend any additional impact to what they are saying.

The Semicolon ;

This mark is used to separate independent clauses where the ideas are closely related to each other. In most cases a period could be used instead; the semicolon simply signals to the reader the close relationship between the two ideas. In the following example the second sentence reinforces the statement of the first; a semicolon is thus appropriate, although a period is also correct:

- This book is both exciting and profound. It is one of the best books I have read.
- This book is both exciting and profound; it is one of the best books I have read.

Similarly in the following example the second sentence gives evidence supporting the statement made in the first sentence. Again, a semicolon is appropriate:

- The team is not as good as it used to be. It has lost four of its past five games.
- The team is not as good as it used to be; it has lost four of its last five games.

The semicolon is also used occasionally to divide items in a series that includes other punctuation:

A common notion is that the central distinction among punctuation marks such as the comma, semicolon, colon, and period is rooted simply in the length of the pause they ask the reader to make. Such indeed was the norm several centuries ago, when punctuation was designed less to indicate grammatical relationships than to mark pauses as an aid to the listener's understanding when the text was read aloud. Under that system, a period counted as four beats, a colon as three, a semicolon as two, and a comma as one. Ian Coutts, in an interesting article in *Quill and Quire* ("All about the Pause," February 2005, 7), uses a passage from the 1549 *Book of Common Prayer* as an example of how strangely such a system strikes the modern sensibility:

> Easter Day. The Collect.
>
> Almighty God, who through thine only begotten Son Jesus Christ hast overcome death, and opened unto us the gate of everlasting life; We humbly beseech thee, that, as by thy special grace preventing us thou dost put into our minds good desires, so by thy continual help we may bring the same to good effect; through Jesus Christ our Lord, who liveth and reigneth with thee and the Holy Ghost, ever one God, world without end.

Perhaps even stranger to modern eyes is the fashion in which the reading that follows is punctuated in sixteenth-century style:

> Mortify therefore your members which are upon the earth; fornication, uncleanness, inordinate affection, evil concupiscence, and covetousness, which is idolatry: For which things, sake the wrath of God cometh on the children of disobedience. In the which ye also walked some time, when ye lived in them.

- The following were told to report to the coach after practice: Jackson, a sophomore; Marshall, a junior; Nicola, a senior.

The semicolon, then, has a set of precise grammatical functions; it is not to be used simply to indicate a longer-than-usual pause, any more than the comma is to be used to join independent clauses.

needs checking The threat to the planet is constant and growing, it is to be found in the factories of Ohio; in the shrinking rain forests of Brazil; in the massive growth and massive pollution of China's cities; and in the coal-fired generation stations that still produce much of the world's electricity.

It is not only the practice of punctuation here that is at odds with today's practice; so too are the principles of capitalization and of grammar considerably different. Here are the two passages again, set down according to modern practice:

> Almighty God, who through thine only begotten Son Jesus Christ hast overcome death, and opened unto us the gate of everlasting life, we humbly beseech thee that, as by thy special grace preventing us thou dost put into our minds good desires, so by thy continual help we may bring the same to good effect; through Jesus Christ our Lord, who liveth and reigneth with thee and the Holy Ghost, ever one God, world without end.

> Mortify therefore your members which are upon the earth: fornication; uncleanness; inordinate affection; evil concupiscence; and covetousness, which is idolatry. For these things' sake the wrath of God cometh on the children of disobedience, in the which ye also walked some time, when ye lived in them.

Echoes of the ancient principles of punctuation are still to be found in surprising places. The section on punctuation in the fifteenth edition of *The Chicago Manual of Style* advises at one point that "the semicolon, stronger than a comma but weaker than a period, can assume either role." As Louis Menand fairly commented in discussing this passage in his review of the fifteenth edition, "What could the authors possibly have been thinking?" ("The End Matter," *The New Yorker*, 6 October 2003, 125). To retain elements of the old system of "pause punctuation" in the context of modern academic practice is simply to sow the seeds of confusion.

revised The threat to the planet is constant and growing. It is to be found in the factories of Ohio, in the shrinking rain forests of Brazil, in the massive growth and massive pollution of China's cities, and in the coal-fired generation stations that still produce much of the world's electricity.

or The threat to the planet is constant and growing; it is to be found in the factories of Ohio, in the shrinking rain forests of Brazil, in the massive growth and massive pollution of China's cities, and in the coal-fired generation stations that still produce much of the world's electricity.

(For more on the uses of the semi-colon, see Section M1.3.1.)

The Colon :

• **colon**: This mark is often believed to be virtually the same as the semicolon in the way it is used. In fact, there are some important differences. The most common uses of the colon are as follows:

- in headings, to announce that more is to follow, or that the writer is about to list a series of things.
- to introduce a quotation.
- between two clauses, to indicate that the second one provides an explanation of what was stated in the first.

This last (the least common way in which the colon is used) is very similar to the main use of the semicolon. The subtle differences are that the semicolon can be used in such situations when the ideas are not quite so closely related, and the colon asks the reader to pause for a slightly longer period. Some authorities, it should be noted, feel it is inappropriate to use a colon in this way; if in any doubt as to the appropriateness of using a colon to separate two independent clauses, the student is well advised to use a semicolon instead.

- Unquiet Union: A Study of the Federation of Rhodesia and Nyasaland.
- In the last four weeks he has visited five countries: Mexico, Venezuela, Panama, Haiti, and Belize.
- The theory of the Communists may be summed up in a single phrase: abolition of private property.

Be sure to use a colon (rather than a comma or a semicolon) to introduce a list.

needs checking The operation has supplied Mr. Bomersbach with four luxury cars, two Cadillacs, a Mercedes, and a Jaguar.

revised The operation has supplied Mr. Bomersbach with four luxury cars: two Cadillacs, a Mercedes, and a Jaguar.

The Hyphen -

• **hyphen:** This mark may be used to separate two parts of a compound word (e.g., *tax-free, hand-operated*). Notice that many such word combinations are hyphenated only if the combination acts as an adjective:

- No change is planned for the short term.
  (*Term* acts here as a noun, with the adjective *short* modifying it.)
- This is only a short-term plan.
  (Here the compound *short-term* acts as a single adjective, modifying the noun *plan*.)
- George Eliot is one of the major figures in the literature of the nineteenth century.
  (*Century* acts here as a noun, with the adjective *nineteenth* modifying it.)
- George Eliot is one of the major figures of nineteenth-century literature.
  (Here the compound *nineteenth-century* acts as a single adjective, modifying the noun *literature*.)

Hyphens are also used to break a word at the end of a line if there is not enough space. A hyphen should never be used to break up proper nouns, and should be used to break up other words only when it is placed between syllables. Any noun beginning with a capital letter (e.g., *Halifax*, *Blair*, *January*, *Harriet*) is a proper noun.

Whenever one is uncertain about whether or not to use a hyphen to break up a word, the easy solution is to put the entire word on the next line.

The Dash —

• **dash**: Dashes are often used in much the same way as parentheses, to set off an idea within a sentence. Dashes, however, call attention to the set-off idea in a way that parentheses do not:

- Peterborough (home of Broadview Press's distribution facility) is a pleasant city of 84,000.
- Peterborough—home of Broadview Press's distribution facility—is a pleasant city of 84,000.

A dash may also be used in place of a colon to set off a word or phrase at the end of a sentence:

- He fainted when he heard how much he had won: one million dollars.
- He fainted when he heard how much he had won—one million dollars.

• **em dashes and en dashes**: The above applies to what is known as the em dash—so-called because in most typefaces it is about the same length as the letter *m*. There is also a slightly shortened form of dash—known as the en dash—which fulfills a different function. Whereas an em dash is used to separate groups of words, an en dash is used to separate numbers, as in these examples:

- Paul Newman (1925–2008) was both a philanthropist and a noted actor.
- The street numbers are as follows: in the first block west of Main Street, 1–100; in the second block, 101–200; and so on.

Although it is standard to use the en dash in such circumstances in published work, the en dash does not appear on most keyboards, and the hyphen is usually used in its stead in everyday work. In most word processing programs an em dash may be formed by typing two hyphens (--). Note that no spaces should be left either before or after the dash. In some word processing programs a dash may be chosen from the menu symbols.

needs checking Taipei 101-at the time the tallest building in the world-was completed in 2004. Towers in Dubai and elsewhere have since surpassed it.

revised Taipei 101—at the time the tallest building in the world—was completed in 2004. Towers in Dubai and elsewhere have since surpassed it.

M3 Punctuation

Parentheses ( )

• **parentheses:** Parentheses are used to set off an interruption in the middle of a sentence, or to make a point which is not part of the main flow of the sentence. They are frequently used to give examples, or to express something in other words using the abbreviation i.e. Example:

- Several world leaders of the 1980s (Deng in China, Reagan in the US, etc.) were very old men.

Square Brackets [ ]

• **square brackets:** Square brackets are used for parentheses within parentheses, or to show that the words within the parentheses are added by another person.

- Lentricchia claims that "in reading James's Preface [to *What Maisie Knew*] one is struck as much by what is omitted as by what is revealed."
- Smith writes that as the end of the trial approached, "Sacco and Vanzetti had a good idea of what there [sic] fate would be."
  (Here the Latin *sic*, meaning *thus*, is used to indicate that the error is reproduced just as it appears in the original quotation.)

The Apostrophe '

• **apostrophe:** The two main uses of the apostrophe are to show possession (e.g., *Peter's book*) and to shorten certain common word combinations. The shortened forms (e.g., *can't*, *shouldn't*, *he's*) are known as contractions.

contractions: Contractions are used frequently in this book, which is relatively informal in its style. Contractions, however, should not be used in more formal written work. Use *cannot*, not *can't*; *do not*, not *don't*; and so on.

informal	The experiment wasn't a success because we'd heated the solution to too high a temperature.
more formal	The experiment was not a success because we had heated the solution to too high a temperature.

• **possession:** The correct placing of the apostrophe to show possession can be a tricky matter. When the noun is singular and does not already end with an *s*, an *s* at the end of the word, preceded by an apostrophe, shows possession (e.g., *Peter's*, *George's*, *Canada's*). When the noun is plural and ends in an *s* already, the apostrophe should be added after the *s*.

needs checking	We have been asked to dinner by Harriets mother.
revised	We have been asked to dinner by Harriet's mother.
needs checking	His parent's house is filled with antiques.
revised	His parents' house is filled with antiques.
needs checking	All three groups of parents attended their infant's one-month pediatric checkup, and observations were made of father's interactions with their infants.
revised	All three groups of parents attended their infants' one-month pediatric checkup, and observations were made of fathers' interactions with their infants.

Authorities differ on how one should show possession with singular nouns that already end in *s*. The MLA recommends that an *s* always be added at the end of such nouns, even where they are multi-syllabic and pronunciation with an additional *s* is ungainly:

- Dickens's next novel was *Bleak House*.
- Ulysses's voyage was a long one.
- Socrates's method of communicating his ideas has been as influential as the ideas themselves.

The Chicago Manual of Style, on the other hand, recommends adding just the apostrophe (with no additional *s*) where a singular noun ending in *s* is already more than one syllable. This approach has the great advantage of avoiding amusing but distracting tongue twisters:

- Dickens' next novel was *Bleak House*.
- Ulysses' voyage was a long one.
- Socrates' method of communicating his ideas has been as influential as the ideas themselves.

Whichever convention a writer chooses, he should be consistent. And be sure in such cases not to put an apostrophe before the first *s* in a noun ending with *s*.

needs checking Shield's novel is finely, yet delicately constructed. (concerning novelist Carol Shields)

revised Shields's novel is finely, yet delicately constructed.

Where possession is joint, an *s* should be added to the last mentioned noun:

- Bob and Carol's view is that this can be settled amicably.
- Woodward and Bernstein's persistence eventually paid off.

One important exception to the convention of using an apostrophe to show possession is the possessive *its*. In that case the form *it's* is used as a contraction of *it is*, and no apostrophe is included in the possessive *its*. If you are ever uncertain as to whether or not you are making the correct choice between *it's* and *its*, ask yourself if the sentence would make sense if you substituted *it is*. If it would, *it's* is the one you want; if not, you should be using *its*.

Apostrophes are used by some writers to form the plurals of letters and numbers:

- That sort of music was popular in the 1990's.
- She received straight A's in high school.

Since apostrophes are not otherwise used to show plurality, most authorities now prefer to omit the apostrophe:

- That sort of music was popular in the 1990s.
- She received straight As in high school.

Quotation Marks “ ”

The main use of quotation marks is to show that the words are repeated exactly as they were originally spoken or written. For a discussion of difficulties associated with this use see the discussion of direct and indirect speech in M3.2 below.

According to different conventions, words that are being mentioned in a grammatical sense, rather than used to convey meaning, may be set off by quotation marks, single quotation marks, or italics:

- The words “except” and “accept” are sometimes confused.
- The words ‘except’ and ‘accept’ are sometimes confused.
- The words *except* and *accept* are sometimes confused.

The use-mention distinction originated in analytic philosophy, but it has come to be recognized as a useful one in many contexts; see, for example, the discussion of 'the n-word' in "How to Be Good with Words," p. 144.)

- It was not until the Renaissance that 'meat' began to refer specifically to animal flesh; before that time the term could be used to refer to food of any sort.

  (In the above sentence, the word 'meat' is being mentioned, not used.)

- Though links between meat consumption and cancer have been observed since the 1960s, humans in many parts of the world continue to consume meat in large quantities.

  (In the above sentence the word 'meat' is being used, not mentioned.)

Quotation marks (or single quotation marks) are sometimes used to indicate that the writer does not endorse the quoted statement, claim, or description. Quotation marks are usually used in this way only with a word or a brief phrase. When they are so used they have the connotation of *supposed* or *so-called*; they suggest that the quoted word or phrase is either euphemistic or downright false:

- After a violent workout the weightlifters would each consume a "snack" of a steak sandwich, a half-dozen eggs, several pieces of bread and butter, and a quart of tomato juice.

In the following two versions of the same report, the more sparing use of quotation marks in the second version signals clearly to the reader the writer's scepticism as to the honesty of the quoted claim, and may be taken to imply that the former Russian president indulged his legendary fondness for alcohol during the flight.

- President Yeltsin appeared to stagger as he left the plane. "The president is feeling tired and emotional," his press secretary later reported.
- A "tired and emotional" President Yeltsin appeared to stagger as he left the plane.

• **misuse of quotation marks to indicate emphasis**: Quotation marks (unlike italics, bold letters, capital letters, or underlining) should never be used to try to lend emphasis to a particular word or phrase. Because quotation marks may be used to convey the sense *supposed* or *so-called* (see above), the common misuse of quotation marks to try to lend emphasis often creates ludicrous effects.

needs checking All our bagels are served "fresh" daily.
(The unintended suggestion here is that the claim of freshness is a dubious one.)
revised All our bagels are served fresh daily.
or All our bagels are served *fresh* daily.
(if emphasis is required in an advertisement)
needs checking Dogs must be "leashed." (BC Ferries sign)
revised Dogs must be leashed.

Single Quotation Marks ‘ ’

In North America the main use of single quotation marks is to mark quotations within quotations:

- According to Obama's press secretary, "When the president said, 'I will bring change to Washington,' he meant it."

Depending on convention, single quotation marks may also be used to show that a word or phrase is being mentioned rather than used (see above).

In the United Kingdom and some other countries, quotation marks and single quotation marks are used for direct speech in precisely the opposite way that North Americans use them; single quotation marks (or inverted commas, as they are sometimes called) are used for direct speech, and double quotation marks are used for quotations within quotations. Here is the correct British version of the above sentence:

- According to Obama's press secretary, 'When the president said, "I will bring change to Washington", he meant it.'

Note here that UK usage also places the comma outside the quotation mark.

M 3.2 Quotations

Direct Speech

Direct speech is a written record of the exact words used by the person speaking. The main rules for writing direct speech in English are as follows:

- The exact words spoken—and no other words—must be surrounded by quotation marks.

- A comma should precede a quotation, but according to American convention other punctuation should be placed inside the quotation marks. Examples:
  - He said, "I think I can help you."
    (The period after *you* comes before the quotation marks.)
  - "Drive slowly," she said, "and be very careful."
    (The comma after *slowly* and period after *careful* both come inside the quotation marks.)

On the Companion Website

Exercises on direct and indirect speech may be found at **sites.broadviewpress.com/writingcdn**. Click on **Exercises** and go to **"Punctuation."**

With each change in speaker a new paragraph should begin. Example:

> "Let's go fishing this weekend," Mary suggested. "It should be nice and cool by the water."
>
> "Good idea," agreed Faith. "I'll meet you by the store early Saturday morning."

British convention, however, places the punctuation outside the quotation marks:

- 'An iron curtain is descending across Europe', declared Winston Churchill in 1946.

Canadian usage demands that all punctuation go inside the quotation marks in quotations that are stand-alone sentences. At the same time, it allows writers either to follow the American convention or to make an exception when the punctuation clearly pertains only to the structure of the surrounding sentence and not to the quoted word or phrase:

- "An iron curtain is descending across Europe," declared Winston Churchill in 1946.
- Was it Churchill who described the post-war divide between newly Communist Eastern Europe and the West as "an iron curtain"?

The most common difficulties experienced when recording direct speech are as follows:

• **omission of quotation marks**: This happens particularly frequently at the end of a quotation.

needs checking She said, "I will try to come to see you tomorrow. Then she left.

revised She said, "I will try to come to see you tomorrow." Then she left.

• **placing punctuation outside the quotation marks**:

needs checking He shouted, "The house is on fire"!

revised He shouted, "The house is on fire!"

• **including the word *that* before direct speech**: *That* is used before passages of indirect speech, not before passages of direct speech.

needs checking My brother said that, "I think I have acted stupidly."

revised My brother said, "I think I have acted stupidly."

or My brother said that he thought he had acted stupidly.

needs checking The official indicated that, "we are not prepared to allow galloping inflation."

revised The official said, "We are not prepared to allow galloping inflation."

or The official indicated that his government was not prepared to allow galloping inflation.

• **when to indent**: In a formal essay, any quotation longer than four lines[1] should normally be indented to set it off from the body of the text. Any quotation of more than three lines from a poem should also be single-spaced and indented. Quotations set off from the body of the text in this way should not be preceded or followed by quotation marks.

needs checking Larkin's "Days" opens with childlike simplicity: "What are days for? / Days are where we live. / They come, they wake us / Time and time over." But with Larkin, the shadow of mortality is never far distant.

revised Larkin's "Days" opens with childlike simplicity:

> What are days for?
> Days are where we live.
> They come, they wake us
> Time and time over.

But with Larkin, the shadow of mortality is never far distant.

M3 Punctuation

1 This is what the MLA recommends; the APA specifies forty words.

Indirect Speech

Indirect speech reports what was said without using the same words that were used by the speaker. The rules for writing indirect speech are as follows:

- Do not use quotation marks.
- Introduce statements with the word *that*, and do not put a comma after *that*. Questions should be introduced with the appropriate question word (*what*, *why*, *whether*, *if*, *how*, *when*, etc.).
- First-person pronouns and adjectives (e.g., *I*, *me*, *we*, *us*, *my*, *our*) must often be changed to third person (*he*, *she*, *they*, *him*, *her*, *them*, etc.) if the subject of the main clause is in third person.

correct "I am not happy with our team's performance," said Paul.
also correct Paul said that he was not happy with his team's performance.

correct I said, "I want my money back."
also correct I said that I wanted my money back.
(Here the subject, *I*, is first person.)

- Second-person pronouns must also sometimes be changed.
- Change the tenses of the verbs to agree with the main verb of the sentence. Usually this involves moving the verbs one step back into the past from the tenses used by the speaker in direct speech. Notice in the first example above, for instance, that the present tense *am* has been changed to the past tense *was* in indirect speech. Here are other examples:

correct "We will do everything we can," he assured me.
correct He assured me that they would do everything they could.
(*Will* and *can* change to *would* and *could*.)
correct "You went to school near Brandon, didn't you?" he asked me.
correct He asked me if I had gone to school near Brandon.
(*Went* changes to *had gone*.)

- Change expressions having to do with time. This is made necessary by the changes in verbs discussed above. For example, *today* in direct speech normally becomes *on that day* in indirect speech, *yesterday* becomes *on the day before*, *tomorrow* becomes *the next day*, and so on.

The most common problems experienced when indirect speech is being used are as follows:

• **confusion of pronouns:** Many writers do not remember to change all the necessary pronouns when shifting from direct to indirect speech.

- When I met him he said, "You have cheated me." (direct)

needs checking When I met him he said that you had cheated me.
revised When I met him he said that I had cheated him.

- He will probably say to you, "I am poor. I need money."

needs checking He will probably tell you that he is poor and that I need money.
revised He will probably tell you that he is poor and that he needs money.

• **verb tenses:** Remember to shift the tenses of the verbs one step back into the past when changing something into indirect speech.

- She said, "I will check my tires tomorrow."

needs checking She said that she will check her tires the next day.
revised She said that she would check her tires the next day.

- "Can I go with you later this afternoon?" he asked.

needs checking He asked if he can go with us later that afternoon.
revised He asked if he could go with us later that afternoon.

Formatting Quotations

There are two ways to signal an exact borrowing: by enclosing it in double quotation marks and by indenting it as a block of text. Which you should choose depends on the length and genre of the quotation and the style guide you are following.

Short Prose Quotations

What counts as a short prose quotation differs among the various reference guides. In MLA style, "short" means up to four lines; in APA, up to forty words; and in Chicago Style, up to one hundred words. All the guides agree, however, that short quotations must be enclosed in double quotation marks, as in the examples below.

> *Short quotation, full sentence:*
> According to Terrence W. Deacon, linguists agree that a human child's capacity to acquire language is inborn: "Without question, children enter the world predisposed to learn human languages" (102).

Short quotation, partial sentence:

According to Terrence W. Deacon, linguists agree that human "children enter the world predisposed to learn human languages" (102).

Long Prose Quotations

Longer prose quotations should be double-spaced and indented, as a block, one tab space from the left margin. Do not include quotation marks; the indentation indicates that the words come exactly from the source. Note that indented quotations are often introduced with a full sentence followed by a colon.

> Terrence W. Deacon, like most other linguists, believes that human beings are born with a unique cognitive capacity:
>
> > Without question, children enter the world predisposed to learn human languages. All normal children, raised in normal social environments, inevitably learn their local language, whereas other species, even when raised and taught in this same environment, do not. This demonstrates that human brains come into the world specially equipped for this function. (102)

Verse Quotations

Quoting from verse is a special case. Poetry quotations of three or fewer lines (MLA) may be integrated into your paragraph and enclosed in double quotation marks, with lines separated by a forward slash with a space on either side of it, as in the example below.

> Pope's "Epistle II. To a Lady," in its vivid portrayal of wasted lives, sharply criticizes the social values that render older women superfluous objects of contempt: "Still round and round the Ghosts of Beauty glide, / And haunt the places where their Honor dy'd" (lines 241–42).

If your quotation of three or fewer lines includes a stanza break, MLA style requires you to mark the break by inserting two forward slashes (//), with spaces on either side of them.

> The speaker in "Ode to a Nightingale" seeks, in various ways, to free himself from human consciousness, leaving suffering behind. Keats uses alliteration and repetition to mimic the gradual dissolution of self, the process of intoxication or death: "That I might drink, and leave the world unseen, / And with thee fade away into the forest dim: // Fade far away, dissolve, and quite forget" (lines 19–21).

Poetry quotations of more than three lines in MLA, or two or more lines in Chicago Style, should be, like long prose quotations, indented and set off in a block from your main text. Arrange the lines just as they appear in the original.

> The ending of Margaret Avison's "September Street" moves from the decaying, discordant city toward a glimpse of an outer/inner infinitude:
>
> On the yellow porch
> one sits, not reading headlines; the old eyes
> read far out into the mild
> air, runes.
> See. There: a stray sea-gull. (lines 20–24)

Quotations within Quotations

You may sometimes find, within the original passage you wish to quote, words already enclosed in double quotation marks. If your quotation is short, enclose it all in double quotation marks, and use single quotation marks for the embedded quotation.

> Terrence W. Deacon is firm in maintaining that human language differs from other communication systems in kind rather than degree: "Of no other natural form of communication is it legitimate to say that 'language is a more complicated version of that'" (44).

If your quotation is long, keep the double quotation marks of the original.

> Terrence W. Deacon is firm in maintaining that human language differs from other communication systems in kind rather than degree:
>
> > Of no other natural form of communication is it legitimate to say that "language is a more complicated version of that." It is just as misleading to call other species' communication systems *simple* languages as it is to call them languages. In addition to asserting that a Procrustean mapping of one to the other is possible, the analogy ignores the sophistication and power of animals' non-linguistic communication, whose capabilities may also be without language parallels. (44)

Adding to or Deleting from a Quotation

While it is important to use the original's exact wording in a quotation, it is allowable to modify a quotation somewhat, as long as the changes are clearly indicated and do not distort the meaning of the original.

USING SQUARE BRACKETS TO ADD TO A QUOTATION

You may want to add to a quotation in order to clarify what would otherwise be puzzling or ambiguous to someone who does not know its context; in that case, put whatever you add in square brackets.

> Terrence W. Deacon writes that children are born "specially equipped for this [language] function" (102).

USING AN ELLIPSIS TO DELETE FROM A QUOTATION

If you would like to streamline a quotation by omitting anything unnecessary to your point, insert an ellipsis (three spaced dots) to show that you've left material out.

When the quotation looks like a complete sentence but is actually part of a longer sentence, you should provide an ellipsis to show that there is more to the original than you are using.

> As Terrence W. Deacon says, "... children enter the world predisposed to learn human languages" (102).

Note that if the quotation is clearly a partial sentence, ellipses aren't necessary.

> Terrence W. Deacon writes that children are born "specially equipped" to learn human language (102).

When the omitted material runs over a sentence boundary or constitutes a whole sentence or more, insert a period plus an ellipsis.

> Terrence W. Deacon, like most other linguists, believes that human children are born with a unique ability to acquire their native language: "Without question, children enter the world predisposed to learn human languages. . . . [H]uman brains come into the world specially equipped for this function" (102).

Be sparing in modifying quotations; it is all right to have one or two altered quotations in a paper, but if you find yourself changing quotations often, or adding to and omitting from one quotation more than once, reconsider quoting at all. A paraphrase or summary is very often a more effective choice.

Integrating Quotations

Quotations must be worked smoothly and grammatically into your sentences and paragraphs. Always, of course, mark quotations as such, but for the purpose of integrating them into your writing, treat them as if they were your own words. The boundary between what you say and what your source says should be grammatically seamless.

needs checking Terrence W. Deacon points out, "whereas other species, even when raised and taught in this same environment, do not" (102).

revised According to Terrence W. Deacon, while human children brought up under normal conditions acquire the language they are exposed to, "other species, even when raised and taught in this same environment, do not" (102).

AVOIDING "DUMPED" QUOTATIONS

Integrating quotations well also means providing a context for them. Don't merely drop them into your paper or string them together like beads on a necklace; make sure to introduce them by noting where the material comes from and how it connects to whatever point you are making.

needs checking For many years, linguists have studied how human children acquire language. "Without question, children enter the world predisposed to learn human language" (Deacon 102).

revised Most linguists studying how human children acquire language have come to share the conclusion articulated here by Terrence W. Deacon: "Without question, children enter the world predisposed to learn human language" (102).

needs checking "Without question, children enter the world predisposed to learn human language" (Deacon 102). "There is . . . something special about human brains that enables us to do with ease what no other species can do even minimally without intense effort and remarkably insightful training" (Deacon 103).

revised Terrence W. Deacon bases his claim that we "enter the world predisposed to learn human language" on the fact that very young humans can "do with ease what no other species can do even minimally without intense effort and remarkably insightful training" (102–03).

Signal Phrases

To leave no doubt in your readers' minds about which parts of your essay are yours and which come from elsewhere, identify the sources of your summaries, paraphrases, and quotations with signal phrases, as in the following examples.

- As Carter and Rosenthal have demonstrated, . . .
- In the words of one researcher, . . .
- In his most recent book McGann advances the view that, as he puts it, . . .
- As Nussbaum observes, . . .
- Kendal suggests that . . .
- Freschi and other scholars have rejected these claims, arguing that . . .
- Morgan has emphasized this point in her recent research: . . .
- As Sacks puts it, . . .
- To be sure, Mtele allows that . . .
- In his later novels Hardy takes a bleaker view, frequently suggesting that . . .

In order to help establish your paper's credibility, you may also find it useful at times to include in a signal phrase information that shows why readers should take the source seriously, as in the following example:

> In her landmark work, biologist and conservationist Rachel Carson warns that . . .

Here, the signal phrase mentions the author's professional credentials; it also points out the importance of her book, which is appropriate to do in the case of a work as famous as Carson's *Silent Spring*.

Below is a fuller list of words and expressions that may be useful in the crafting of signal phrases:

according to ________,
acknowledges
adds
admits
advances
agrees
allows
argues
asserts
attests
believes
claims
comments
compares
concludes
confirms
contends
declares
demonstrates
denies
disputes
emphasizes
endorses
finds
grants
illustrates
implies
in the view of ________,
in the words of ________,
insists
intimates
notes
observes
points out
puts it
reasons
refutes
rejects
reports
responds
suggests
takes issue with
thinks
writes

M3.3 Capitalization

• **capitalization:** Conventions concerning capitalization have been anything but fixed in the history of the English language. It was not until the late medieval period that capital letters began to be used consistently to begin sentences and proper names. From there the use of capitals became more and more common, until, during the eighteenth century, a great many common nouns were often capitalized. In particular, common nouns naming abstract qualities were capitalized frequently, but many writers would also capitalize without any great degree of consistency any noun or pronoun that they felt to be important. Here is a sample: ... *you may be Mine in the manner you now are for a much longer time, yet I at last may lose you, and one unlucky Moment destroy the Constancy of Ages.*

In the past ten years there has been a substantial resurgence of this eighteenth-century practice. Students and other writers—many of whom have not been taught at school the difference between a proper and a common noun—are reverting more and more frequently to the eighteenth-century practice of simply making a stab at what words should begin with a capital letter, without much sense of any rules governing the practice. The basis of those rules is very simple, but there are also a good many subtleties and grey areas.

needs checking In this Company we want to hire Managers who convey a strong sense of Authority.

revised In this company we want to hire managers who convey a strong sense of authority.

In English the fundamental principle on which the rules of capitalization are based is that proper nouns (naming specific persons, places, or things) should always be capitalized. Proper adjectives (adjectives formed from these proper nouns) are also always capitalized. Common nouns, however, are not normally capitalized. *Marx*, *California*, and *Spain*, are all proper nouns. *Marxist*, *Californian*, and *Spanish* are all proper adjectives. The nouns *sinker*, *state*, and *nation*, on the other hand, are all common nouns; they do not name *specific* persons, places, or things. Here are a number of other examples of proper and common nouns:

Proper	*Common*
June	summer
Parliament of Canada	in parliament
Mother (used as a name)	my mother
Memorial Day	as a memorial
National Gallery	a gallery
Director of Admissions	a director
Professor Smith	a professor
the Enlightenment	the eighteenth century
the Restoration (historical period in England)	the restoration (other uses of the word)
the Renaissance (historical period)	renaissance (a revival)
God	a god
Catholic (belonging to that particular church)	catholic (meaning *wide-ranging* or *universal*)
a Liberal (belonging to the Liberal Party)	a liberal (holding liberal ideals)

Some categories frequently cause difficulty over the issue of capitalization. When should one write *professor* and when *Professor*, for example? Following are some more detailed guidelines.

Names of People
Maya Angelou, Professor Smith, Samantha.

Names of Places
Cleveland, Asia, the North Pole, the White House. Note here that all nouns in a name should be capitalized (*Central Park, the Statue of Liberty*).

Names of Days of the Week, Months, and Holidays
Monday, January, Labour Day, Yom Kippur. Note that the names of seasons are not capitalized.

• **Academic names:** All nouns in a formal name should be capitalized: *the University of Chicago, Camosun College, Philosophy 150, Economics 205.* Note that, when not describing a specific course, the names of academic subjects are not capitalized unless they are names of languages. In formal use, capitalize *the Physics Department, the Department of History,* etc.

needs checking Most offices in the Philosophy department are located in the Arts Tower.

revised Most offices in the Philosophy Department are located in the Arts Tower.

needs checking She is studying Philosophy at the University of Michigan.

revised She is studying philosophy at the University of Michigan.

On the Companion Website

Exercises on capitalization may be found at **sites.broadviewpress.com/writingcdn**. Click on **Exercises** and **Writing Mechanics** and go to **"Punctuation."**

- **institutional names:** All nouns in these names should be capitalized (*the University of Toronto, the Audit Committee, the Board of Directors, the Golden Financial Corporation, the Department of Justice*). Note that where a specific body is not being named, capitals should not be used.

needs checking Every large company must have an Audit Committee.

revised Every large company must have an audit committee.

- **occupational names:** When a title is used before a person's name, it must be capitalized: *Reverend Philips*; *President Carter*; *Professor Said*. When the title appears as a substitute for the name, capitalizing the title is optional. As always in such cases, be sure to be consistent.

worth checking The Prime Minister will deliver a speech this afternoon, and the president of Shell Oil will be speaking this evening.

revised The Prime Minister will deliver a speech this afternoon, and the President of Shell Oil will be speaking this evening.

or The prime minister will deliver a speech this afternoon, and the president of Shell Oil will be speaking this evening.

When titles follow a name, capitalization of the title is optional.

Sandra Mbeki, professor of German
or Sandra Mbeki, Professor of German
Frank Gibbs, president of Acme Tools
or Frank Gibbs, President of Acme Tools

Names of Major Historical Events, Movements, or Periods

It is not surprising that students and other writers often become confused over whether or not to capitalize historical references of this sort, since the names of centuries, decades, and so on are not normally capitalized.

It is thus correct to refer to *the eighteenth century* in lower case, but *the Enlightenment* with a capital; to *the medieval period*, but to *the Middle Ages* with capitals; *the thirties*, to refer to the 1930s, but *the Depression* to refer to the economic condition that dominated the period. If we speak of the study of *Romantic literature* we are speaking of the study of the Romantic period (i.e., the late eighteenth and early nineteenth centuries), whereas if we speak of studying romantic literature we are referring to the study of any literary works with romantic themes. Here are a few more examples of major historical events, movements, or periods that are normally capitalized: *the Thirty Years' War*, *the Great Fire of London*, *World War II*, *the Big Bang*, *the Impressionists*.

Names of Religions, Deities, Religious Persons, Terms, or Texts
Nouns or adjectives of this sort are normally capitalized: *Buddhism*, *a Buddhist*, *Islam*, *a Muslim*, *Christian*, *Jewish*, *Holy Ghost*, *the Bible*, *the Qur'an*.

Names of Races, Groups, Nationalities, and Their Languages
Nouns or adjectives of this sort should be capitalized: *Mexican*, *Hispanic*, *the Yoruba*, *Nova Scotians*, *a Native American*, *Indigenous peoples of North America*, *European professor*, *Chinese*, *students learning Mandarin or French*. See pages 142–43 for a discussion of the special case of black/Black.

Names of Geographical Areas
Depending on context, certain geographical words may denote either a direction or an area—or, indeed, more than one area. If, for example, we say *keep travelling west, and you will reach the sea*, the word *west* is a direction and should not be capitalized. If, however, we write that *in the West, American voters tend to be fiscally conservative*, when referring to the western portion of the United States, it is normal to capitalize *West*. In a different context we might write *in the West, capitalism took root in the seventeenth and eighteenth centuries*. In that context *the West* is a synonym for *the Western World*. Similar multiple meanings may attach to the words *south*, *north*, and *east* and *South*, *North*, and *East*.

• **literary titles**: Major words in titles should be capitalized. Articles, short prepositions, and conjunctions are normally not capitalized in titles.

needs checking Robert Boardman discusses *The Bridge On The River Kwai* extensively in his book.

revised Robert Boardman discusses *The Bridge on the River Kwai* extensively in his book.

Names of Teams or Clubs

Where a specific name is given it should be capitalized (*the Vancouver Canucks, Team USA, Manchester United*). Where a specific team or club is mentioned but not given its formal name, no capitals should be used (*the national team, our bridge club*).

Names of Abstract Qualities

As in the eighteenth century, writers today are often inclined to capitalize the names of abstract qualities in order to signal their importance. These are common nouns, however, and should in almost all cases not be capitalized. An exception occurs if in the context the abstract quality is personified; in that case the noun may be regarded as a proper name (*if Chance is often blind, it is also often a powerful friend*).

needs checking Keats shared with writers of the Romantic period a strong interest in notions of Truth and Beauty.

revised Keats shared with writers of the Romantic period a strong interest in notions of truth and beauty.

Capitalization Following a Colon

Some style guides recommend capitalizing independent clauses that begin after a colon. Somewhat oddly, they do not similarly recommend capitalizing independent clauses that begin after a semicolon. In view of this inconsistency—and in view as well of the fact that the colon is often used for purposes other than separating independent clauses—it is probably wisest for students to refrain from any use of capitals following a colon.

M3.4 Abbreviations

Abbreviations are a convenient way of presenting information in a smaller amount of space. This section discusses conventions for using abbreviations in formal writing.

Titles

Titles are normally abbreviated when used immediately before or after a person's full name.

Mr. Isaiah Thomas — *Dr. Jane Phelps*
Sammy Davis Jr. — *Marcia Gibbs, MD*

When using a title together with the last name only, the full title should be written out.

Prof. Marc Ereshefsky — *Professor Ereshefsky*
Sen. Keith Davey — *Senator Davey*

Academic and Business Terms

Common abbreviations are acceptable in formal writing so long as they are likely to be readily understood. Otherwise, the full name should be written out when first used and the abbreviation given in parentheses. Thereafter, the abbreviation may be used on its own, as shown in these examples:

- The Atomic Energy Commission (AEC) has broad-ranging regulatory authority.
- The American Philosophical Association (APA) holds three large regional meetings annually.

Latin abbreviations

Several abbreviations of Latin terms are common in formal academic writing:

cf. *compare* (Latin *confer*)
e.g. *for example* (Latin *exempli gratia*)
et al. *and others* (Latin *et alia*)
etc. *and so on* (Latin *et cetera*: *and the rest*)
ibid. *in the same book or passage* (Latin *ibidem*: *in the same place*)
i.e. *that is to say* (Latin *id est*)
NB *note well* (Latin *nota bene*)

M3 Punctuation

Numbers

Numbers of one or two words should be written out. Use figures for all other numbers.

needs checking The building is 72 stories tall.
revised The building is seventy-two stories tall.

The same principle applies for dollar figures (or figures in other currencies).

needs checking She lent her brother 10 dollars.
revised She lent her brother ten dollars.

It is acceptable to combine figures and words for very large numbers:

- The government is projecting a $200 billion deficit.

In general, figures should be used in addresses, in dates, to give percentages, and to report scores or statistics.

needs checking In the third game of the tournament, Canada and the Czech Republic tied three three.

revised In the third game of the tournament, Canada and the Czech Republic tied 3–3.

Italics

Italics serve several different functions. While short stories, poems, and other works are set off by quotation marks, longer works and the names of newspapers, magazines, and so on should appear in italics:

"The Dead"	*Dubliners*
"Burnt Norton"	*Four Quartets*
"Budget Controversy Continues"	*The Economist*
"Smells Like Teen Spirit"	*Nevermind*

Italics are also used for the names of paintings and sculptures, television series, and software. In addition, italics are used for words or phrases from other languages in written English.

needs checking The play ends with an appearance of a deus ex machina.

revised The play ends with an appearance of a *deus ex machina.*

Either italics or quotation marks may be used to indicate that words are mentioned rather than used (see above, under "Quotation Marks"). Finally, italics are often used to provide special emphasis that is not otherwise clear from the context or the structure of the sentence.

M3.5 Spelling

Spelling and Sound

The wittiest example of the illogic of English spelling remains Bernard Shaw's famous spelling of *fish* as *ghoti*. The *gh* sounds like the *gh* in *enough*; the *o* sounds like the *o* in *women* (once spelled *wimmen*, incidentally); and the *ti* sounds like the *ti* in *nation* or *station*. Shaw passionately advocated a rationalization of English spelling; it still has not happened, and probably never will. Perhaps the best way to learn correct spelling is to be tested by someone else, or to test yourself every week or so on a different group of words. For example, you might learn the words from the list below beginning with *a* and *b* one week, the words beginning with *c* and *d* the next week, and so on.

• **spell-check**: No computer can be a substitute for careful proofreading. Spell-check is wonderful, but it cannot tell if it is your friend or your fiend, or if you have signed off a letter with best wishes or beast wishes.

• **spelling and sound—a/an**: Authorities agree that an *n* should be added to the indefinite article when the following word begins with a vowel sound. This is a "rule," it should be noted, that is based entirely on euphony; the reason that *a egg* is not "good English" is simply that it is awkward to say. Thus it is that we use *an* not only before words that begin with a vowel, but also before words that are pronounced as if they began with a vowel (*an hour*, *an f-word*).

Something of a grey area exists with a small group of words that have a *his-* sound at the beginning, and in which the second syllable is stressed. No one would think of writing *an hiccup* or *an hellish day*, and nor are most people ever tempted to write *an history* or *an hysterectomy*. Many people, though, think that *an hysterical outburst* sounds better than *a hysterical outburst*, and that *an historical introduction* sounds better than *a historical introduction*. As the first sound in an unstressed syllable, the *h* in such words is softer than the *h* in such words as *history*, where a strong stress is placed on the first syllable. Some authorities ridicule this common practice; we sound the *h* in such words, goes the argument, and therefore we should use *a* rather than *an*. But what is the rationale for this "rule" in the first place? Again, purely what sounds better. And the fact is that many people find it easier to say *an historical introduction* than *a historical introduction*. So why the fuss? We may reasonably disagree as to which sounds better, but there is surely no justification for terming one correct and the other incorrect.

• **spelling and sound**: Many spelling mistakes result from similarities in the pronunciation of words with very different meanings. These are covered in the list below. Other words that cause spelling difficulties are listed separately.

absent (adjective)	absence (noun)
absorb	absorption
accept	except
access (*entry*)	excess (*too much*)
advice (noun)	advise (verb)
affect (verb)	effect (noun)
allowed (*permitted*)	aloud

alter (*change*)	altar (*in a church*)
appraise (*value*)	apprise (*inform*)
base (*foundation*)	bass (*in music*)
bath (noun)	bathe (verb)
berry (*fruit*)	bury (*the dead*)
beside (*by the side of*)	besides (*as well as*)
birth	berth (*bed*)
bitten	beaten
bizarre (*strange*)	bazaar (*market*)
bloc (political grouping)	block
breath (noun)	breathe (verb)
buoy (*in the water*)	boy
buy (*purchase*)	by
cash	cache (*hiding place*)
casual (*informal*)	causal (*to do with causes*)
cause	case
ceased (*stopped*)	seized (*grabbed*)
ceiling (*above you*)	sealing
chick	cheek/chic (*stylish*; pronounced *sheek*)
chose (past tense)	choose (present tense)
cite (*make reference to*)	sight/site
climatic (*climate*)	climactic (*climax*)
cloths (*fabric*)	clothes
colonel (*officer*)	colonial (*of colonies*)
coma (*unconscious*)	comma (*punctuation*)
compliment (*praise*)	complement (*make complete*)
conscious (*aware*)	conscience (*sense of right*)
contract	construct
conventional (*usual*)	convectional (*transfer of heat*)
conversation	conservation/concentration
convinced	convicted (*of a crime*)
cord (*rope*)	chord (*music*)
council (*group*)	counsel (*advice*)
course	coarse (*rough*)
credible (*believable*)	creditable (*deserving credit*)
critic (*one who criticizes*)	critique (*piece of criticism*)
defer (*show respect*)	differ
deference (*respect*)	difference
deprecate (*criticize*)	depreciate (*reduce in value*)
desert (*dry place*; also *what is deserved*)	dessert (*sweet*)
device (*thing*)	devise (*to plan*)
died/had died	dead/was dead/dyed (*coloured*)
dissent (*protest*)	descent (*downward motion*)
distant (adjective)	distance (noun)
edition (*of a book*, etc.)	addition (*something added*)
emigrant	immigrant
entomology (*study of insects*)	etymology (*study of words*)
envelop (verb)	envelope (noun)
except	expect

exercise	exorcise (*remove*)
fear	fair/fare (*payment*)
feeling	filling
fell	feel/fill
flaunt (*display*)	flout (*disobey*)
formally	formerly (*previously*)
forth (*forward*)	fourth (*after third*)
forward	foreword (*in a book*)
foul	fowl (*birds*)
future	feature
genus (*biological type*)	genius (*creative intelligence*)
greet	great/grate (*scrape*)
guerrillas	gorillas
guided (*led*)	guarded (*protected*)
had	heard/head
heat	heart/hate
heir (*inheritor*)	air
human	humane (*kind*)
illicit (*not permitted*)	elicit (*bring forth*)
illusion (*unreal image*)	allusion (*reference*)
immigrate	emigrate
independent (adjective)	independence (noun)
inhabit (*live in*)	inhibit (*retard*)
instance (*occurrence*)	instants (*moments*)
intense (*concentrating*)	intents (*purposes*)
isle (*island*)	aisle (*to walk in*)
kernel	colonel
know	no/now
lack	lake
later	latter/letter
lath (*piece of wood*)	lathe (*machine*)
lead (*heavy element*)	led (*guided*)
leave	leaf
leave	live
leaving	living
lessen (*reduce*)	lesson
let	late
lightning (*from clouds*)	lightening (*becoming lighter*)
lose (*be unable to find*)	loose (*not tight*)
mad (*insane*)	maid (*servant*)
man	men
martial (*to do with fighting*)	marshal
mental	metal
merry	marry
met	meet/mate
minor (*underage*, or *lesser*)	miner (*underground*)
mist (*light fog*)	missed
moral (*ethical*)	morale (*spirit*)
mourning (*after death*)	morning
new	knew

of	off
on	own
ones	once
ordinance (*decree*)	ordnance (*guns*)
pain	pane (*of glass*)
patients (*sick people*)	patience (*ability to wait*)
peer (*look closely*)	pier (*wharf*)
perpetrate (*be guilty of*)	perpetuate (*cause to continue*)
perquisite (*privilege*)	prerequisite (*requirement*)
personal (*private*)	personnel (*employees*)
perspective (*vision*)	prospective (*anticipated*)
peruse (*study*)	pursue (*follow*)
poor	pour (*liquid*)/pore
precede (*go before*)	proceed (*continue*)
precedent	president
price (*cost*)	prize (*reward*)
prostate (*gland*)	prostrate (*lying down*)
quay (*wharf*; pronounced *key*)	key
quite	quiet (*not noisy*)
rein (*to control animals*)	rain/reign
release (*let go*)	realize (*discover*)
relieve (verb)	relief (noun)
residence (*place*)	residents (*people*)
response (noun)	responds (verb)
rid	ride
ridden	written
rise	rice
rite (*ritual*)	right/write
rod	rode/reared
rote (*repetition*)	wrote
saved	served
saw	seen
saw	so/sew
scene (*location*)	seen
seam (*in clothes*)	seem (*appear*)
secret	sacred (*holy*)
sell (verb)	sail (*boat*)/sale
senses	census (*population count*)
shed	shade
shone	shown
shot	short
sit	sat/set
smell	smile
snake	snack (*small meal*)
soar	sore (*hurt*)
sole (*single, a fish*, or *an undersurface*)	soul (*spirit*)
sort (*type or kind*)	sought (*looked for*)
steal (present tense)	stole (past tense)
straight (*not crooked*)	strait (*of water*)

striped (e.g., *a zebra*)	stripped (*uncovered*)
suite (*rooms* or *music*)	suit/sweet
super	supper (*meal*)
suppose	supposed to
sympathies (noun)	sympathize (verb)
tale (*story*)	tail
talk	took
tap	tape
than	then
they	there/their
thing	think
this	these
throw	threw (past tense)
tied	tired
urban (*in cities*)	urbane (*sophisticated*)
vanish (*disappear*)	varnish
vein (*to carry blood*)	vain
vicious (*brutal*)	viscous (*sticky*)
waist (*your middle*)	waste
wait	weight (*heaviness*)
waive (*give up*)	wave
wants	once
weak (*not strong*)	week
weather (*sunny*, *wet*, etc.)	whether (*or not*)
wedding	weeding
were	where
whole (*complete*)	hole (*empty space*)
wholly (*completely*)	holy (*sacred*)/holly
woman	women
won	worn
yoke (*for animals*)	yolk (*of an egg*)

• **English language spelling variations**: A number of words that cause spelling difficulties are spelled differently in different countries. In most cases Australians prefer British spellings. Either British or American is correct in Canada, so long as the writer is consistent.

American	**British**
behavior	behaviour
center	centre
color	colour
defense	defence
favor	favour
favorite	favourite
fiber	fibre
fulfill	fulfil
gray	grey
humor	humour
likable	likeable

maneuver	manoeuvre
marvelous	marvellous
meter (*measurement*)	metre
neighbor	neighbour
omelet	omelette
program	programme
Shakespearian	Shakespearean
skillful	skilful
skeptical	sceptical
theater	theatre
traveling	travelling

On the Companion Website

Exercises on spelling may be found at **sites.broadviewpress.com/writingcdn**. Click on **Exercises** and **Writing Mechanics** and go to **M3.**

Spelling: One Word or Two?

A number of very commonly used English words have over many years become accepted as one word because they are combined so often. Other similar combinations, however, should still be written as two words. In a few cases one can see English usage changing on this point right now. A generation ago, for example, *alright* as one word could not have been found in any dictionary. Now numerous authorities regard *alright* as acceptable, and perhaps in another generation or two it will have completely replaced *all right*. For the moment, though, it is best to stick with *all right* rather than the more colloquial *alright*.

One word preferred

What has been written as two words should be one. Here are some common examples:

already:	one word when used as an adverb (*He has finished already.*)
altogether:	one word when used as an adverb to mean *completely* or *entirely* (*He is not altogether happy with the result.*)
another	
anybody	
anyone:	one word unless it is followed by *of*
anytime:	one word when used as an adverb (*You can come over anytime.*)
awhile:	one word when used as an adverb

bathroom
bloodshed
businessman (but see "Bias-free Vocabulary" on pages 167–70)
cannot: *can not* is less common, but still acceptable
everybody
everyday: one word when used as an adjective (*Brushing your teeth should be part of your everyday routine*—here *everyday* is an adjective modifying the noun *routine*.)

needs checking Doctors perform procedures of this sort everyday.
revised Doctors perform procedures of this sort every day.

needs checking Doctors perform procedures of this sort as part of their every day routine.
revised Doctors perform procedures of this sort as part of their everyday routine.

everyone: one word unless it is followed by *of*
everything
forever
furthermore
indeed
intact
into: one word except in the relatively few cases where the senses of *in* and *to* are clearly separate (*She brought the craft in to land*.)
maybe: when used as an adverb meaning *perhaps* (*Maybe I will join you later*—here the verb is *will join* and *maybe* is an adverb.)
nearby
nobody
onto: see *into*
ourselves
somebody
someone
sometime: one word when used as an adverb (*I would love to see you sometime*.)
straightforward
themselves
wartime
whatever
whenever

Two words preferred

What has been written as one word should be two words. Here are some common examples:

a lot	
all ready:	two words when not used as an adverb (*We are all ready to go.*)
all right	
all together:	two words when not used as an adverb (*They were all together when I left them.*)
any time:	two words when used in a sentence as noun preceded by modifier (*Is there any time next week when we could meet?*)
every day:	two words when not used as an adjective (*We see each other every day.*)
every time	
in fact	
in front	
in order	
in spite of	
may be:	two words when used as a verb (*He may be here later tonight—may be* is the verb in the sentence.)
no one	
some time:	two words when used in a sentence as noun preceded by modifier (*Will you be able to take some time to study this?*)

Commonly Misspelled Words

Following is a list of some other commonly misspelled words:

abbreviation
absence
accelerator
accident
accidentally
accommodation
achieve
acknowledge
acquire
acquisition
acquit
acre
across
address
adjacent
advertisement
affidavit
aficionado
ambulance
ameba (also *amoeba*)
ammonia
among
amortize
amount
anachronism
analogous
analysis
anchor
androgynous
annihilate
antecedent
anti-Semitic
anxious
apocalypse
apparatus
apparently
appreciate
approach
architect
arguable
argument
arsonist
arteriosclerosis
artillery
asinine
atheist
author
auxiliary
awesome
awful
bacteria

basically
battery
beautiful
beginning
believe
boast
boastful
bouillon
breakfast
bulletin
burglar
burial
buried
business
candidate
capillary
cappuccino
Caribbean
carpentry
cautious
ceiling
chaise longue (or *chaise lounge*)
changeable
character
chilblain
chlorophyll
choir
cholesterol
chrome
chromosome
chronological
chrysalis
chrysanthemum
coincidence
colleague
colonel
colossal
column
commitment
committee
comparative
competition
competitor
complexion
conceive
condemn
conjunction
connoisseur
consensus
consistent
controller
convenience
cooperation
cooperative
courteous
courtesy
creator
creature
criticism
cyst
decisive
definite
delicious
description
desirable
despair
despise
destroy
develop
diesel
different
dilemma
dining
disappear
disappoint
disastrous
discrimination
disease
disintegrate
dissatisfied
dominate
dormitory
double
doubtful
drunkard
drunkenness
duchess
due
dyeing
dying
eclipse
eczema
effective
efficient
eighth
embarrass
employee
encourage
enemy
enmity
enormous
entertain
enthusiasm
entitle
entrepreneur
environment
enzyme
epidermis
epididymis
erroneous
esophagus
especially
espresso
essential
exaggerate
excessive
excite
exercise
exhilaration
existence
existent
experience
extraordinary
Fahrenheit
faithful
faithfully
farinaceous
fault
February
financial
foreigner
foretell
forty
fourth
gauge
gamete
germination
government
grammar
grateful
gruesome
guarantee
guerrillas
guilty
happened
happiest
harass
hatred
hectare
helpful
hyena
hypothesis
ichthyology
idiosyncratic
imaginary
imagine
immigration
immersible
impeccable
importance
impresario
inchoate
incomprehensible
indigenous
independent
indestructible
indispensable
ineffable
infinitesimal
inoculate
insufferable
intention
intentional
interrupt
irrelevant
irresponsible
isosceles
isthmus
itinerary
jealous
jeopardy
journalist
junction
kneel
knowledge
knowledgeable
laboratories
laboratory
language
lazy, laziness
ledger
leisure
liaise
liberation
library

license
lieutenant
liquid, liquefy
literature
lying
medicine
medieval
membrane
memento
merciful
mermaid
millennia
millennium
millionaire
mischief
mischievous
modern
naked
naughty
necessary
necessity
noticeable
nuclear
nucleus
obscene
obsolescent
obsolete
occasion
occasional
occupy
occur
occurred
occurrence
omit
ophthalmology
ourselves
paid
parallel
parliament
parliamentary
party
permissible
permission
perpendicular
perseverance
photosynthesis
playful
possess
possession
poultry
predictable
pregnancy
pregnant
prerogative
prescription
privilege
properly
psychiatric
psychological
punctuation
pursue
questionnaire
really
receipt
recommend
referee
reference
regret
repeat
repetition
replies
reply
residence (*place*)
residents (*people*)
restaurant
restaurateur
revolutionary
rheumatism
rhododendron
rhombus
rhubarb
rhyme
rhythm
saddest
sandals
scene
schedule
schizophrenic
science
scintillate
scissors
scream
scrumptious
search
seize
sense
separate
shining
shotgun
sigh
significant
simultaneous
sincerely
ski, skis, skied, skiing
slippery
slogan
smart
solemn
spaghetti
speech
spongy
sponsor
stale
stingy
stomach
stubborn
studious
studying
stupefy
stupid
subordinate
subpoena
substitute
subtle, subtlety
suburbs
succeed
success, successful
sue, suing
summary
supersede
surprised
surreptitious
surrounded
survive
symbol
synthesis
talkative
tarred
television
temperature
tendency
theoretical
theory
title
tough
tragedy
trophy
truly
unique
until
vacancy
vacillate
valuable
vegetable
vehicle
vicious
visitor
volume
voluntary
Wednesday
welcome
whisper
writer
writing
written
yield
zucchini

EAL: FOR THOSE WHOSE NATIVE LANGUAGE IS NOT ENGLISH

M4 EAL: For Those Whose Native Language Is Not English

The fact that different languages have different grammatical and syntactical conventions creates particular problems for anyone learning a new language. That is a point that may seem obvious, but a large percentage of the population of North America, Britain, and Australia (a majority of whom are unilingual) remain unaware of it as a felt reality. It is a measure of the degree to which English-speaking North Americans are unaccustomed to learning other languages that ESL—English as a Second Language—remains a widely-used umbrella term. We prefer EAL—English as an Additional Language—a term that allows for the possibility that someone learning English may already know several other languages.

This section of *The Broadview Guide to Writing* focuses on some of the peculiarities of English that are most likely to present difficulties to those learning the language. More often than not, multilingual students who are not yet fully fluent in English have at least as good a grasp of the formal grammatical principles of the language as do those for whom English is their first language. If you are not familiar with these principles, however, Section M1 (pages 171–230) may be helpful.

Because of the differences in the ways that the structure of a student's own language may compare with English, students from different linguistic backgrounds are likely to want to focus on different aspects of English; what is particularly challenging for someone whose first language is Vietnamese may seem straightforward to someone whose first language is Spanish, and vice versa. For that reason the following guide may be helpful:

> Many speakers of languages such as Chinese (in its various forms), Japanese, and Vietnamese are likely, as a result of the ways in which those languages differ structurally from English, to have particular difficulty with topics treated under the following headings in this book: articles (E1–2); plurals (E5); infinitives (E12); conjugation of verbs, especially in the simple present tense (M1.4); word order (M2.4, E17–18).

Many speakers of languages such as Russian, Polish, and Bulgarian are likely, as a result of the ways in which those languages differ structurally from English, to have particular difficulty with topics treated under the following headings in this book: articles (E1–2); omission of the predicate (E3); double negatives (E9); the present perfect tense (M1.4); word order (M2.4, E17–18); possessives (E7); relative pronouns such as *who* and *which* (E6); countable and uncountable nouns and words such as *much*, *many*, *little*, and *few* (E1).

Many speakers of languages such as French, Spanish, and Italian are likely, as a result of the ways in which those languages differ structurally from English, to have particular difficulty with topics treated under the following headings in this book: relative pronouns such as *who* and *which* (E6); double negatives (E9); comparatives and superlatives (E10); progressive (or continuous) verb tenses (M1.4, E14); word order (E17–18).

E1. **articles**: Articles are words used to introduce nouns. Unlike many other languages, English often requires the use of articles:

needs checking We are interested in house with garage.
revised We are interested in a house with a garage.

There are only three articles—*a*, *an*, and *the*. Articles show whether or not one is drawing attention to a particular person or thing. For example, we would say *I stood beside a house* if we did not want to draw attention to that particular house, but *I stood beside the house that the Taylors used to live in* if we wanted to draw attention to the particular house.

A (or *an* if the noun following begins with a vowel sound) is an indefinite article—used with singular nouns when you do not want to be definite or specific about which thing or person you are referring to. *The* is a definite article, used with singular or plural nouns when you *do* want to be definite or specific. Remember that, if you use *the*, you are suggesting that there can be only one or one group of what you are referring to.

In order to use articles properly in English it is important to understand the distinction English makes between nouns naming things that are countable (*houses*, *books*, *trees*, etc.) and nouns naming things that are not countable (*milk*, *confusion*, etc). *A* can be used with singular count nouns (*a radio*), *the* with singular and plural count nouns (*the carpet, the horses*). *The* should be used with a non-count noun when it is followed by a specifying phrase (*the furniture in my house*). Some non-count nouns name things that it does seem possible to count: *sugar, grass, furniture*, etc. In such cases counting must in English be done indirectly: *a grain of sugar, two grains of sugar, three blades of grass, four pieces of furniture*, and so on.

Distinguishing between count and non-count nouns is inevitably a challenge for those whose first language is not English. A dictionary such as *The Oxford Advanced Learner's Dictionary* can be very helpful; unlike most dictionaries it indicates whether or not each noun is a count noun.

needs checking They bought a nice furniture.
revised They bought a nice piece of furniture.

● *Frequently Used Non-count Nouns*

abstractions: advice, anger, beauty, confidence, courage, fun, happiness, hate, health, honesty, information, knowledge, love, poverty, truth, wealth, wisdom.

to eat and drink: bacon, beef, beer, bread, broccoli, butter, cabbage, candy, cauliflower, celery, cereal, cheese, chicken, chocolate, coffee, corn, cream, fish, flour, fruit, ice, ice cream, lettuce, margarine, meat, milk, oil, pasta, pepper, rice, salt, spinach, sugar, tea, water, wine, yogurt.

other substances: air, cement, clothing, coal, dirt, equipment, furniture, gas, gasoline, gold, grass, homework, jewellery, luggage, lumber, machinery, metal, mail, money, music, paper, petroleum, plastic, poetry, pollution, research, scenery, silver, snow, soap, steel, timber, traffic, transportation, violence, weather, wood, wool, work.

Note: The plural of many of these non-count nouns may be employed when you want to denote more than one type of the substance. *Breads*, for example, refers to different sorts of bread; *coffees* refers to different types of coffee, *grasses* to different types of grass, and so on.

E2. **dropping the article**: Articles are not used in English to the same extent that they are used in some other languages; nouns can frequently stand alone without their article, particularly when they are being used in a general, non-specific sense. When used in this way, non-count and plural-count nouns need no article.

needs checking If the English is to be spoken correctly, the good grammar is important.
revised If English is to be spoken correctly, good grammar is important.
needs checking The freedom is something everyone values.
revised Freedom is something everyone values.

In most cases no article is necessary before a noun that is capitalized:

needs checking They were strolling through the Stanley Park.
revised They were strolling through Stanley Park.

Unfortunately, there are many exceptions to this rule (e.g., *the Hebrides, the Netherlands, the Dominican Republic, the United Kingdom, the Soviet Union, the United States*). A dictionary such as *The Oxford Advanced Learner's Dictionary* should be consulted in any case where you are uncertain if an article is needed.

E3. **omission of the subject or predicate**: Many languages allow the subject or the predicate to be assumed in certain situations, whereas (with the exception of imperative formations such as [*you*] *come here this instant!*) English requires that sentences include explicit subjects and predicates.

needs checking Is very hot this afternoon.
revised It is very hot this afternoon.

needs checking She doctor and her husband carpenter. They both like their jobs.
revised She is a doctor and her husband is a carpenter. They both like their jobs.

needs checking Is not possible to finish the job this week.
revised It is not possible to finish the job this week.

needs checking Most authorities agree that malaria is a disease that could be targeted for eradication because would be feasible and relatively inexpensive to develop and distribute effective vaccines.

revised Most authorities agree that malaria is a disease that could be targeted for eradication because it would be feasible and relatively inexpensive to develop and distribute effective vaccines.

needs checking By the end of the century, were almost one million more people in Houston than there had been in 1980.

revised By the end of the century, there were almost one million more people in Houston than there had been in 1980.

Note: In this sort of sentence construction English requires a "dummy" subject (such as *it* or *there*) before the verb *to be*; by contrast, languages such as Spanish allow the subject to be assumed in similar circumstances.

E4. **repetition of the subject**: Unlike many other languages, English does not permit the repetition of either the subject or the object within a single clause.

needs checking The body of water outside the hotel it is called Chesapeake Bay.

revised The body of water outside the hotel is called Chesapeake Bay.

needs checking The members of the cast loved the play that they were acting in it.

revised The members of the cast loved the play that they were acting in.

E5: **plurals**: Since many languages do not form plural nouns differently from nouns in the singular, it is easy if your background is in one of those languages to omit the *s* in plural formations in English.

needs checking Many team play here every weekend.

revised Many teams play here every weekend.

E6. **gendered words/neutered words**: In Romance languages such as French all nouns are masculine or feminine; for that reason many speakers of these languages use a masculine or feminine pronoun in English where the neuter pronoun is required.

needs checking When I first saw the lake he was as smooth as glass.

revised When I first saw the lake it was as smooth as glass.

Most Romance languages and Slavic languages do not differentiate things from people in their relative pronouns. For that reason it is easy to forget to use *who* or *whom* rather than *that* or *which* in English.

needs checking	I spent the weekend visiting my grandparents, which are both in their eighties.
revised	I spent the weekend visiting my grandparents, who are both in their eighties.

E7. **possessives**: Some languages make no distinction between possessive pronouns and possessive adjectives; in others possessive adjectives agree with what is possessed, not the possessor. In both cases English's different approach can cause difficulty.

needs checking	I told him that the book was my.
revised	I told him that the book was mine.
or	I told him that it was my book.

needs checking	As he sat in his office he looked out of her window at the moon.
revised	As he sat in his office he looked out of his window at the moon.

Additional Material Online

Exercises specially designed for those whose native language is not English may be found at **sites.broadviewpress.com/writingcdn**. Click on **Exercises** and go to **"EAL."**

E8. **negatives**: Whereas English uses auxiliaries to form standard negatives, many languages use particles. As a result of this difference, the correct formation of negatives in English can present difficulties.

needs checking	In later life he not wanted to see his old friends.
revised	In later life he did not want to see his old friends.
or	In later life he never wanted to see his old friends.

E9. **double negatives**: Languages in both the Slavic and Romance groups permit double negatives, thus making it difficult for those whose first language is from one of those groups to become habituated to the English prohibition against double negatives—and to grasp that words such as *without* can function as negatives.

needs checking I never not like to be away from home very long.
revised I never like to be away from home for long.
or I do not like to be away from home for long.

needs checking No one can survive in this society without no money.
revised No one can survive in this society without money.
or No one can survive in this society with no money.
or No one can survive in this society without any money.

E10. **comparatives and superlatives**: In many languages comparatives and superlatives must always include a word equivalent to *more* or *most*; there are no parallels for English formations such as *better, best* or *larger, largest*. Not surprisingly, many whose first language is not English find it difficult to get used to the English system of alternative forms of the comparative and superlative.

needs checking I wanted to buy the more larger size.
revised I wanted to buy the larger size.

E11. **compound verb formations**: English has many verb tenses, and many compound verb forms, including compound negative forms; these cause particular difficulty for those who are used to a less heavily conjugated system of verb tenses.

needs checking I waited for some time, but he not come.
revised I waited for some time, but he did not come.

needs checking She always working hard to help her family.
revised She is always working hard to help her family.

E12. **infinitives**: The infinitive form (*to go, to be, to do*, etc.) is not native to many languages, particularly many Far Eastern languages. For that reason it is sometimes given tense or person markers. In English the infinitive must always keep the same form.

needs checking When she first met him she found it difficult to felt any sympathy for him.
revised When she first met him she found it difficult to feel any sympathy for him.

E13. **phrasal verbs**: A phrasal verb occurs when a word that would normally function as a preposition instead becomes part of a two-word verb. *Break in*, *take off*, *put on*, *pick up*, *give up*—these are all examples of phrasal verbs. In such combinations an adverb cannot intercede between the two.

needs checking	He put hurriedly on his clothes.
revised	He put on his clothes hurriedly.

E14. **continuous verb tenses** (see also under "Verbs and Verb Tense Difficulties" in "Writing Grammatically"): In English the continuous tenses are not normally used with many verbs having to do with feelings, emotions, or senses. Some of these verbs are *to see, to hear, to understand, to believe, to hope, to know, to think* (meaning *believe*), *to trust, to comprehend, to mean, to doubt, to suppose, to wish, to want, to love, to desire, to prefer, to dislike, to hate.*

needs checking	He is not understanding what I mean.
revised	He does not understand what I mean.
needs checking	At that time he was believing that everything on Earth was created within one week.
revised	At that time he believed that everything on Earth was created within one week.

E15. **infinitives and gerunds**: As discussed in the chapter on this topic earlier, there are no rules in English as to why some verbs must be followed by an infinitive and others by a gerund, while still others may take either. Some combinations are particularly odd from the point of view of anyone whose first language is not English. For example, *start to go* and *start going* may be used interchangeably in most circumstances, whereas *stop going* is the opposite of both; *stop to go* has a quite different meaning. Unfortunately, these combinations must be learned one by one. One helpful rule, however, is that an infinitive can never follow a preposition.

needs checking	They were planning for to go to New York for the holidays.
revised	They were planning to go to New York for the holidays.
or	They were planning on going to New York for the holidays.
or	They were planning a trip to New York for the holidays.

E16. **prepositions**: As discussed in the chapter on preposition problems earlier, there are no overarching logical principles governing the use of prepositions in English. We say *angry with someone* rather than *angry to someone* or *angry against someone* purely as a matter of convention. In some cases general guidelines may be offered, however. For example, where place and time are concerned, *in* is used for larger expanses of space and larger durations of time; *at* is used for specific times and specific addresses; and *on* is used for street names (without precise addresses) and days of the week or the month (without precise times). *She lives in England, she lives on Downing St., she lives at 10 Downing St; she will meet you at 1 p.m.; she will see you sometime in December; she will see you on December 15.*

needs checking	I live in 316 7th St. NW.
revised	I live at 316 7th St. NW.
or	I live on 7th St. NW.
or	I live in the house at 316 7th St. NW.

E17. **word order (subject/verb/object)**: The rules governing word order in English are much more rigid than those of many other languages. For one thing, the subject, verb, and object normally appear in that order. Many other languages permit far more freedom in the ordering of subject, object, and verb, and for that reason this basic structural element of English can be difficult to grasp.

needs checking	Yoshiki opportunities always welcomes.
revised	Yoshiki always welcomes opportunities.

(Note: Speakers of languages such as Japanese and Korean, in which the verb must always come last in a sentence, are particularly likely to experience this sort of difficulty with English.)

needs checking	Opportunities welcomes Yevgeny always.
revised	Yevgeny always welcomes opportunities.

(Note: Speakers of languages such as Russian, in which the object may appear before the subject, are particularly likely to experience this sort of difficulty with English.)

In most Romance languages object pronouns come before the verb. This often creates difficulties for native speakers of those languages with the word order required in English, where object pronouns normally follow the verb.

needs checking	When we these give him, he will be very grateful.
revised	When we give him these, he will be very grateful.

E18. **word order (adjectives and adverbs)**: In English, adjectives generally precede the noun to which they refer, while adverbs generally follow the verb to which they refer. Moreover, there are rules governing the order of adjectives and adverbs—rules which native English speakers have absorbed unconsciously, but which otherwise must be learnt. Since it is common to use two or more adjectives to describe something, problems often arise.

The proper order of adjectives: determiners (*my*, *his*, *this*, *that*, etc.); adjectives concerning number or quantity (*first*, *many*, *some*, etc.); adjectives expressing a subjective opinion (*beautiful*, *sad*, *fascinating*, etc.); adjectives concerning size or shape (*large*, *small*, *straight*, *flat*, etc.); adjectives describing age or condition (*old*, *clean*, *sharp*, *wet*, etc.); adjectives describing colour (*red*, *mauve*, *blue*, etc.); adjectives naming substances and adjectives that may also be used as nouns (*metal*, *woollen*, *English*, etc.); the noun.

needs checking	They lived in a white lovely house near the sea.
revised	They lived in a lovely white house near the sea.

Special Topic

SEEING AND MEANING

How to Read (and Write about) Visual Images

Special Topic

Seeing and Meaning

How to Read (and Write about) Visual Images

What does it mean to "read" a visual image? What is "visual literacy"? What should we be aware of when images interact with words?

Visual literacy is, at one level, a matter of not allowing oneself to be factually misled by what one sees. How dramatically has the stock of the Butterine Corporation risen? A cursory glance at the graph below seems to show pretty clearly that the value of Butterine shares has soared in recent months:

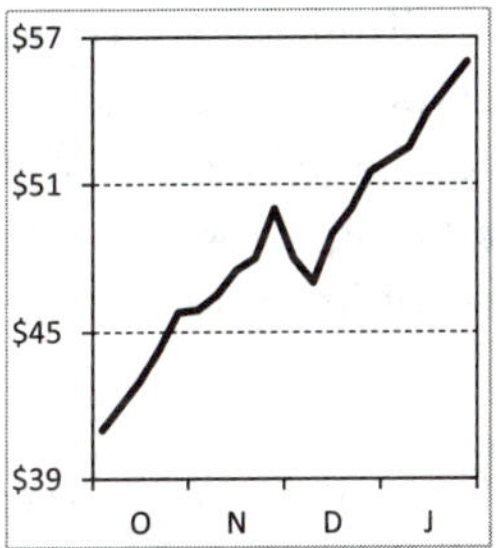

Look again, though, and we see the numbers on the left: the y axis begins not at 0 but at 39. From \$41 to \$56 within a few months is doing pretty well—but it's a far less dramatic increase than the immediate visual impression left by the graph suggests.

Another way to alter the visual impression conveyed by graphs is to increase or decrease the distance between the coordinates. Change the layout, and the very same facts convey a very different impression. Look at the graph below, for example—presenting Butterine's share price for the same four months, October through January:

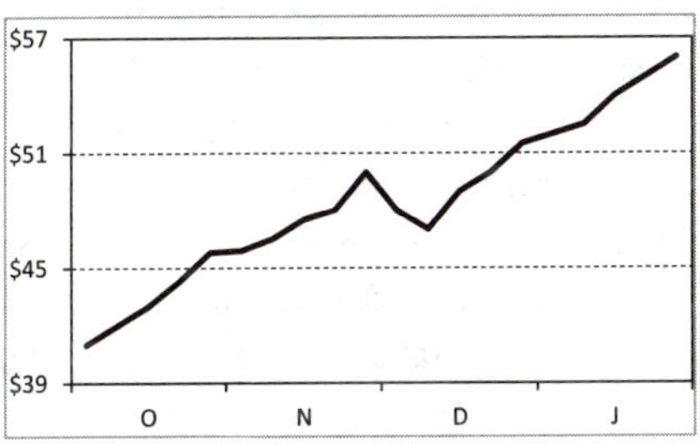

This graph presents exactly the same information for these months as does the one above it. Yet the impression it conveys is of a much more gradual increase; changing the spacing between each point on the x axis makes a considerable difference to the visual impression.

There is nothing inherently sinister in the existence of options such as these for presenting information. In many respected financial publications the accepted convention is, as a space-saving measure, to include only that portion of the full graph that shows the information; if the shares have fluctuated only between $40 and $60 over a given period, then there is no need to show the values below $40 or above $60. But it's important to be aware that the existence of a range of options for presenting information visually creates opportunities for the unscrupulous. As shady stock promoters and unprincipled advertisers have long known, a graph quickly flashed before our eyes can very easily create a misleading impression.

Once you are on the lookout, understanding visual conventions of this sort (and their potential to be misused) is a relatively straightforward matter. Understanding the visual language of paintings or photographs or other sorts of images can often be a good deal more challenging.

• **Focus**: When our eyes focus on something, we remain aware of the surrounding area, but as a blurred presence; nothing except what we are focusing on is sharply defined. The representational techniques of photography and painting can mimic that visual experience by showing one part of an image in much sharper detail than the rest of the image. They can also create two or more focal points in an image. A further possibility is to present everything in the image (even objects in the far distance) in sharp focus. (The latter can create an effect in the viewer's mind of everything in an image being at once real and unreal.) Such is the case in some of the landscape paintings of the Austrian painter Gustav Klimt. Notice how, in the image on page 451, we have little sense of distance: the hills that one part of our brains reads as "behind" the near hills are read by another part of our brain as "above" those hills.

Of course, representational techniques can also show everything out of focus; if, for example, one wants to create a sense of movement in an image, keeping everything out of focus is one way of doing so—as we see in the image on page 452, taken on the New York subway.

Gustav Klimt, *Litzlberg am Attersee* (c. 1915)

• **Perspective**: Blurred though it may be, the photograph below gives a clear sense of three dimensions; the converging lines of the subway riders to the left and the right (as well as their diminished size as they become more distant from the viewer) create the illusion of spatial depth. Whether in a painting, a drawing, a photograph, or a computer-generated image, objects represented according to the "laws of perspective" will appear smaller as they are more distant—just as they do when the human eye perceives them. Lines that would be parallel in three dimensions will converge towards a far-away "vanishing point"—again, as they seem to do as perceived by the human eye. (At the same time, of course, more distant objects will appear less distinct and fainter in colour.)

An image such as the Illinois Central travel poster (page 452) may not be entirely true-to-life in presenting Chicago in 1933, but

"Shake, Rattle, and Roll": New York Subway, February 2, 2015

it does appeal strongly to our sense of perspective—and thereby draws the viewer into the image.

This Ghirlandaio painting (on the same page) has a less obvious vanishing point, but nevertheless makes strong use of perspective in representing the distant world as a backdrop to the event that is the painting's primary focus, the birth of Christ.

Each of these images have a single vanishing point. A vanishing point may, as in these cases, be in the far distance of an image; alternatively, it may be beyond or "behind" what we are shown in the image, and need to be inferred from the information provided. There may also be more than one vanishing point in a single image. In Gustave Caillebotte's vast Paris street scene, for example (page 454), there is one vanishing point up the street to the left, another up the street behind the couple underneath the umbrella.[1]

---

1 It should perhaps also be noted here that many images in which objects are presented in perspective do not provide the viewer with any vanishing point. More distant objects are smaller in proportion to the degree they are more distant, but the viewer is given no sets of converging lines from which to infer one or more vanishing points.

Illinois Central travel poster (1933)

Ghirlandaio, *Adoration of the Magi* (1488)

Gustave Caillebotte, *Paris: Rainy Day* (1877)

On the following page is one more example of an image in which perspective plays a prominent part—this time a very different skyscraper picture, the historic Wainwright Building in St. Louis. The Wainwright Building is far less tall than the skyscrapers in the Illinois Central travel poster image above—but the use of perspective in the photograph makes the Wainwright Building *feel* taller than the buildings in the Chicago poster. Here, perspective operates primarily in terms of height; we are given little or no other sense of distance.

• **Viewpoint and Distance**: Looking up at something, of course, will make it seem more imposing, whereas looking down on it will make it seem less so. If a business wants its 70-storey headquarters to seem more impressive, it is likely to feature photographs from ground level, looking up; if a city filled with skyscrapers wants to make its canyon-like streets seem more friendly, one way is to make the viewer feel above it all.[1]

---

1 Interestingly, advertisements for luxury condominiums in tall buildings nowadays will often feature views looking straight out towards surrounding towers from a window on one of the highest floors.

Viewpoint makes a tremendous difference in shaping our visual perceptions of humans and other animals too; metaphors such as "I really look up to her" and "It felt like he was looking down on me" reflect an unfortunate reality about human perception. (Some studies have suggested that height is a greater predictor of future "earnings power" than level of education, or level of sociability, or anything else.)

When an image places the viewer on the same level as the subject of the image, any sense of superiority or inferiority tends to be minimized. Here again, we may sense how a frequently used metaphor—putting one person "on the same level" as someone else—reflects a powerful reality in our perceptual habits. Where the viewer is thus brought into direct visual connection with the eyes of the subject, particularly strong effects may be created; you may

Wainwright Building, St. Louis (2010)

notice that in advertisements that seem designed to convey sensual allure, the subject is often looking directly at the viewer. So too with appeals for funds from relief agencies; such appeals are often accompanied by visual images of children looking directly towards the viewer, shot either at eye level or looking slightly up. Direct eye contact can create a very direct appeal—even, according to the influential scholars Gunther Kress and Theo Van Leeuwen, a *visual demand*.

In the Manet painting below, the barmaid is depicted at the same level as the viewer; she is not quite looking directly at the viewer, however. What effect is created in this instance?

Edouard Manet, *Un Bar aux Folies-Bergère* (1881–82)

The barmaid is also separated from the viewer by the bar in the foreground. Visual distance (quite aside from the matter of perspective) is another key element in the construction of visual images. If the viewer is brought close to the subject, that facilitates the creation of a broader sense of closeness, or intimacy. Such closeness may be of a sort to encourage warmly sympathetic feelings in the viewer—but close-ups may also be powerful conveyors of other emotions.

Next is an example of an image—a nineteenth-century icon[1]—in which two sets of eyes are directed towards the viewer. In this case

1 Used in this context, *icon* refers to a sacred painting of Jesus, a saint, or another holy figure. In modern English, by contrast, the word *icon* and the phrase

Nineteenth-century icon of the Madonna and baby Jesus. ("TIKHVINSKI" is written on the back.) The original is painted on a piece of wood measuring 7.6 x 10 inches.

the invitation (or, perhaps it may be said, the demand) concerns religious belief. Images such as this, common throughout much of Christian history,[1] were created as an aid to prayer and contemplation; the spiritual attachment of a believer to the holy figures

iconic image are not typically used to imply that viewers will use the image in question to engage in prayer; the terms may refer to any easily recognized image that serves as a symbol for something larger—or they may simply refer to any image that is widely recognized.

1 In the medieval period, it was believed that icons were not created by an artist in the way that we think of an artist today painting an image on wood or paper or canvas; it was rather the Holy Spirit who created the image, acting through a human hand. The point was not that the icon would portray the figures in any naturalistically convincing way; what made them real was not verisimilitude but the direct contact of the Holy Spirit in their creation. *(continued on p. 458)*

was felt to be made more powerful if an image of those figures could always be viewed—and the direct gaze common to religious icons reflects this emphasis on the viewer's personal connection.

Even when the gaze of the subject(s) of an image is not turned towards the viewer, the sight lines within an image can be vitally important to the impression the image conveys. Look, for example, at the direction of gazes in the Giotto fresco on page 459 (another Christian image, this time depicting those mourning the death of Jesus Christ).

In every way the head of Christ is the focus of this image. Sight lines run towards it not only from the humans but also from the angels above. And interestingly, greater emotion is displayed on the faces of those closest to that centre than on the faces of those farthest away. (Giotto is thought to have been the first painter to use degrees of emotion in the expressions of the subjects in this way, to help create an emotional focus for a representational work.)

Let's look at a painting in which there are only two sight lines within the image—a late nineteenth-century work by the American painter Mary Cassatt (page 459). Cassatt has often been accused of sentimentalizing the connection between mother and child. Is that the case here? What emotions may we read into the mother's sidelong gaze? What might be implied here about parenting? Is the child or the mother the primary focus of the painting for the viewer?

• **Structural Lines**: Most representational images have a structure of lines formed by (or suggested by) the elements within them. In the Giotto fresco on the facing page, for example, the line of the wall forms a structural line in the image that provides further support to the "focusing" of the painting on the face of the dead Christ. In the Caillebotte painting above, the lamppost in the

---

Icons have continued to feature prominently in the Eastern Orthodox Church through to the modern era. Such images have been highly controversial, however. Various branches of Christianity have denounced their use as sinful (calling it "idolatry"), on the grounds that humans may too easily worship the image itself rather than that which it represents. Similarly, in Judaism it is forbidden to create or display a physical representation of Yahweh, and in Islam physical images of Allah and Muhammad are forbidden (and depictions of any people and animals are discouraged).

Giotto, *Lamentation* (c. 1305) (Scrovegni Chapel, Padua)

Mary Cassatt, *Breakfast in Bed* (1896)

centre forms a very strong structural line that boldly separates the painting into two halves. How are the halves connected? In part by the sight lines of the couple; both are looking to the "other half" of the painting. In part as well the two halves are connected by the diagonals leading towards the two vanishing points. And in part they are connected by other lines suggested by the elements of the painting—the line, for example, running across the painting from left to right from the couple on the extreme left along the cobblestones to the man in front of them, and on beyond to the right side of the painting.

What is the effect of the line of the lamppost being "broken" by the man's umbrella? By the collaboration between the man's coat and the shadow of the lamppost in continuing the central line through the lower part of the image?

Where do the structural lines run in the Illinois Central travel poster above? Or in the Cassatt painting above? How do they affect our interpretation of each work?

• **Relative Scale of Objects**: One other thing we may notice as we read the Cassatt painting is the relative size of child and mother. With the mother reclining and below the covers, it is the sitting child who takes up more of the painting. It would be too much to say that the mother is crowded out, but it is striking that the baby occupies more space. (The Russian icon above is in several respects an interesting point of comparison.)

A frequently cited image in discussions of relative scale is the painting on page 461(a detail from which is reproduced on the cover of this book), depicting the classical story of hubris and disobedience in which Icarus, flying with wings his father made him from feathers and wax, ignores his father's instructions and flies too close to the sun; the wax melts and he falls to his death in the sea.

In the original tale, Icarus is a heroic, tragic figure. How does Bruegel's picture provide a commentary on that tale? Why might the farmer be placed in the centre of the picture, and Icarus's legs on the lower right hand side? What are the sightlines in the image? What are the structural lines in the image? To what extent does the picture follow the "laws of perspective"? Is there a vanishing point? If so, how is it created? What part does the ox play in the image?

The legs of Icarus are a strikingly small part of the image as a whole, and yet, in relation to nearby objects (notably, the ship), they are depicted as substantially larger than life. How should that irony be interpreted?

What (if anything) is implied about life in the distant city on the shore to the left? In the 1560s Holland was beginning to develop into a great commercial and trading power; it was also becoming heavily urbanized, such that by the end of the century almost half the population was living in cities (the highest percentage in the world at the time). How and to what extent might this broader historical context be relevant to a reading of this image?

• **Colour, Contrast, Tone, Symbol, etc.**: A short overview such as this chapter attempts to provide can do no more than scratch the surface when it comes to covering the ways in which humans read visual images. The role of colour (bright colours / dull colours, level of saturation of colour, colour symbolism and suggestiveness, association of similarly coloured objects) is often of vital importance to the effect an image may have on viewers. So too

Pieter Bruegel, *Landscape with the Fall of Icarus* (c. 1560s)

is the role played by tone; sharp lines and high definition images create one sort of tone; soft lines and slightly blurred images a very different tone. And so too is the degree of contrast in an image; if bright, high definition areas abut very dark or low definition areas in an image, the impression created will be very different from that of an image featuring little contrast.

In addition, images may have powerful symbolic as well as literal value. A picture of a red maple leaf in a Canadian publication or of a bald eagle in an American publication will inevitably not simply be a leaf or a bird to viewers in those countries. A line or a wall or a shore may often function symbolically as well as literally in an image. Particular sorts of images may convey strongly gendered associations, or associations with youth or old age, or associations with a particular social status. The ways in which images may be read are numerous and varied; the point of this introduction is not to provide a full catalogue but rather to give some sense of where to start when trying to understand what a given image means—and how it conveys that meaning.

• **Words and Images**: W.H. Auden's 1938 poem "Musée des Beaux Arts" famously captures the central idea behind *Landscape with the Fall of Icarus*:

> In Breughel's *Icarus*, for instance: how everything turns away
> Quite leisurely from the disaster; the ploughman may
> Have heard the splash, the forsaken cry,
> But for him it was not an important failure ...

The painting, though, is not called *Icarus*. Precisely the point that Auden makes and that the painting itself makes visually is also made in the painting's title, *Landscape with the Fall of Icarus*—a title that foregrounds landscape in much the same way as the painting does. The words offer one clue to the painting's meaning, or at least to one of its most important meanings.[1]

1 Here again it is interesting to consider historical context. The sort of painting and drawing that has come to be known as *landscape art*—that is to say, art that portrays the land "by itself, for its own sake" (as the English writer Henry Peacham wrote in 1612, commenting on the development of *landtskip*

A similar function is performed by the titles of many other images. Think, for example, of the associations that come to mind with the phrase "breakfast in bed." The phrase suggests leisure: typically, an adult relaxing contentedly in bed while a servant or a family member brings breakfast. Look again at the Cassatt painting above and consider its title: *Breakfast in Bed.*

On page 464 is another example of the difference a title can make. The picture is in each case the same, but the impression created is very different. The title *House on Cameron Blvd., New Orleans* is very specific; it suggests little or nothing about the world outside the picture. The title *New Orleans, 2011*, on the other hand, could easily be taken to suggest that this derelict house is representative of the city as a whole in 2011. (That would be a false impression; by 2011 the city was well on the way to cleaning up the horrendous damage from Katrina, the August 2005 storm in which over 1,000 died and much of the city was submerged for many days.) Finally, the title *Everything Must Go* suggests that the image may be taken as representative of the transience of all things in this world; such a title extends the image's meaning beyond the context of any particular place.

In many images, of course, words are included within an image itself. A famous example of the powerful effect words in an image can have is the photograph on page 465, by Margaret Bourke-White.

Bourke-White, a well-known American photographer, was one of several photographers commissioned by the Farm Security Administration to document the lives of Americans during the 1930s. This particular image was taken in Louisville, Kentucky; it shows people who had been badly affected by a 1937 flood of the Ohio River waiting in line for relief. The image soon came to be taken as expressive of a much broader set of problems, though—the hardships suffered across the country during the Great Depression.[1]

---

in Dutch art), and not merely as ornament in images dominated by human subjects—developed in late sixteenth- and early seventeenth-century Holland. For the first time in human history, it was becoming common for paintings to bear titles beginning "Landscape with…."

1 Indeed, it is not uncommon to see this picture referred to as depicting people suffering the effects of drought rather than of flooding, *(continued on p. 465)*

Everything Must Go

New Orleans, 2011

House on Cameron Blvd., New Orleans

Margaret Bourke-White, *World's Highest Standard of Living* (1937)

Advertisement (1978), designed for the Conservative Party of Britain by Martyn Walsh of Saatchi and Saatchi. A follow-up, "Labour Still Isn't Working," was used in the 1979 British election campaign. The original ad was voted poster of the century in 1999 by a British advertising industry magazine.

What can be said of the contrast between the people portrayed in the poster and the people in the line-up beneath? To what extent does the line-up's spatial position below the poster help to make the photograph memorable? What does the contrast

as a result of the degree to which the "Dust Bowl" drought of the 1930s is associated with the economic hardship of the era.

between the implied movement of the automobile and the evident stasis of those in line contribute to the effect of the photograph? Does the photograph implicitly comment on contrasts in American life other than that between prosperity and economic hardship? Would the photograph be as memorable if it were in colour?

Let's look at how words interact with an image in a very different sort of context: the poster below, which has been called the most influential political advertisement of the twentieth century. In the 1970s, Britain's Labour Party, which (as its name suggests) maintained close ties to organized labour, was becoming highly unpopular—in large part because of high unemployment, together with a series of labour disruptions that the government seemed powerless to control. The poster preyed on voters' concerns about both those topics; one can read "not working" as "unemployed" (as the unemployment line on the poster suggests) but also as "on strike." More broadly, of course, the advertisement plays on the meanings of "not working"—the powerful suggestion being that the solutions to the nation's problems that were being tried by the Labour government weren't working. Finally, there is the implication that the Labour government hadn't been working hard enough—that it had been lazy in searching for solutions to Britain's problems.

Notice, too, how the advertisement presents the alternative; what do the words "better off" suggest? What does the relative size and position of words and images on the poster add to its meaning?

In 2012 the presidential campaign of Mitt Romney in the United States for a time employed a similar campaign, using the slogan "Obama isn't working"—sometimes in signs using text alone, sometimes with the slogan placed beside a picture of a smiling Barack Obama. Why do you think that combination of image and words turned out to be quite ineffective compared to the 1978–79 "Labour Isn't Working" campaign?

Think for a moment of Canadian politics. Which Canadian political party do you think would benefit most from a campaign that featured its leader's face in advertisements, accompanied by this slogan: NOT JUST A PRETTY FACE. A LEADER? What party or parties would benefit least from advertisements featuring its leader in this way? Why? If you were creating such an advertising campaign, what other words (if any) would you include with the image? From what angle would you show the face in question? Would you use an image that showed the leader looking directly at the viewer? Why?

Let's look at another advertisement, and try to bring together some of the perspectives discussed so far in this chapter. The advertisement below is one of a series; the Vancouver Humane Society has campaigned for years to ban rodeo competitions in calf-roping (often referred to by the rodeos themselves as "tie-down roping"). The subject is a controversial one, though there is surprisingly little argument over the central issue of whether or not calf-roping does involve cruelty; a clear majority of humane societies, veterinarians, and other authorities seem agreed that, at a minimum, it causes considerable fear and discomfort for the animal. (The Calgary Stampede itself does not argue directly that there is no suffering involved;

Vancouver Humane Society advertisement (2013)

they claim rather that they "care passionately" for the safety of the animals, and that serious injury is very rare.) A great deal could be said about the issues in the background[1]—but let's look at the advertisement itself.

Earlier advertisements in the campaign made explicit reference to the comparison between a human baby and a calf. The 2009 advertisement shows a picture of a cowboy roping the calf, seen from above, with the words *Bully* and *Baby* included and with lines connecting each word to the one it referred to. The 2010 advertisement shows a picture of a human baby beside a picture of a calf, made to look about the same size; both stare directly at the viewer. Underneath is this tag line: "Just three months old. Would you abuse a baby to entertain a crowd?"

The 2013 advertisement is considerably less forceful in its approach. It cannot be interpreted by the viewer as suggesting that a human baby and a baby cow are in some way equivalent. Nor does it use the word "baby" to name the calf. Rather the image shows a young human expressing affection towards a young non-human animal. Visually, though, it does suggest a parallel and a connection between the two. One is on the left, one on the right, with each occupying about the same amount of space in the frame. We can see the child's eyes directed towards the calf, and we can see the calf's eyes too—looking in her direction with evident contentment.

In the "Stampede blindness" image we see the eyes of a calf too—but clearly the animal is anything but contented. So far as the human figure is concerned, we see only his lower half, and his eyes are not shown—and we don't see any part of his body associated

1 The controversy has been largely over side issues. Arguments against the VHS campaign often suggest that those living elsewhere should not be putting forward their views on what happens in Calgary, and that the Vancouver Humane Society should pay attention to what happens in Vancouver, period. Further controversy has sometimes erupted over the refusal of some Calgary newspapers to publish the advertisements.

For its part, the Calgary Humane Society has tried to stake out a middle ground. The statement on its website reads as follows: "the CHS fundamentally opposes high risk rodeo events. While other organizations may wish to intervene to change rodeo and the Stampede through protest or other advocacy means, the CHS has found it can best protect the interests of the animals involved by working with organizations that put on such events."

with either thought or emotion. The loosely implied suggestion is of a human who is unseeing, unfeeling. (Here we may notice the tie-in with the sentence below: "have a heart for animals.")

The two images are visually linked: the child, like the calf-roper, is wearing denim, and both images show a white fence in the background. There is, however, a considerable contrast in colour between the images: the dull grey and grey/blue background of the rodeo image contrasts with the brightness of the white fence and green grass (suggestive of growth, and of life) in the image of the child and calf together. We may notice too that, although the frame of the top image is largely filled with a close-up of child and calf, the perspective of the receding fence lends a feeling of depth and spaciousness to the image; in an environment such as this, the image seems to suggest, non-human animals are given the space they need. The horizontal fence that blocks the top half of the second image, crowded by denim-clad legs, contributes to a very different atmosphere.

Notice the camera-angle in both images: low down, at almost the same level as the calf. Through the use of this viewpoint, the photographer is able to lend the image a more vivid sense of the experience as it is being lived by the calf.

The 2013 advertisement is a good deal more subtle than some of its predecessors, but it still targets viewers' emotions. Some would say that emotional appeals of this sort are inherently "manipulative"—that they are based on sentimentality and should have no part in advocacy advertisements concerning public issues (whether advertisements such as this one or equally "sentimentalized" appeals to help the victims of a drought or a tsunami). Others argue that it is entirely legitimate to appeal to our emotions as well as our intellect—indeed, that one important way in which advertisements should try to engage the viewer is through appeals to emotion.

What do you think? Try to analyze your own reaction to the advertisement; how persuasive do you find it? Is your response emotional, rational, or some of both? Where is the dividing line between legitimate appeals to emotion and efforts to "manipulate" the emotions? Or does any "difference" just boil down to choosing different words to describe the same thing?

The VHS has also run controversial advertisements on other subjects—this one perhaps the most memorable among them:

Vancouver Humane Society, transit advertisement (2013)

How would you compare this ad to the "Human kindness" Stampede advertisement? Which is more impactful or persuasive? What comments do you have about the way the image conveys its message?

One other point of comparison may be of interest here: a two-page "Meet the Faces of Farming and Ranching" advertisement that was published 28 December 2014 in *The New York Times Magazine*. The advertisement is not readable when reduced in size to fit the format of this book, but may be viewed online on *The Broadview Guide to Writing* website (where it is accompanied by questions and suggestions for discussion).[1]

On the Companion Website

Additional images and discussion questions may be found at **sites.broadviewpress.com/writingcdn**. Click on **"Seeing and Meaning."**

- **Images to Read, Consider, and Discuss**: To end the chapter and provide some opportunity to practice reading images, we will present below five images accompanied by questions but no direct commentary.

1 The Vancouver Humane Society Images are copyright © Vancouver Humane Society. The VHS made them available without restriction on their use in the book, and with no permission fee charged. (Similarly, the US Farmers & Ranchers Alliance made their "Meet the Faces of Farming and Ranching" advertisement available without restriction on its use for this project, and with no permission fee charged.)

The photograph below shows an observer considering two of the figures that comprise American sculptor George Segal's *Gay Liberation* (1980), one of the world's first pieces of public art created in honour of the struggle for LGBTQ+ rights. The park in which this copy of the sculpture has been on display since 1992 is adjacent to the Stonewall Inn, site of the events that set off the modern movement for gay rights in 1969. The history of those events rewards study—as does the history of Segal's sculpture. The questions below, however, relate primarily to the image itself and what we can read there.

Questions to consider:

- What can be read into the attitudes of the individuals who form the two couples? What may we infer about the connections between them?
- What are the sightlines of the figures in the sculpture? What can you say about their body language?
- What does the sculpture suggest about sexual orientation? About human relationships generally?
- Segal's sculptures are always coloured chalk white like this one. Comment on the effect this has on the viewer. Does the colour (or the absence thereof) have any racial connotations?

Looking at *Gay Liberation*, the Sculpture, Christopher Park, 2011 (2011)

- Thirty-one years separate the making of this sculpture and the taking of the photograph above. Comment on the attitudes of both the people in the photograph above. What may we infer from the photograph about the changes that occurred in those thirty-one years—or about anything that has *not* changed between the 1980s and the 2020s?
- What message do you think the sculpture might have conveyed in 1980 about stereotypes of gays and lesbians? To what extent (if at all) does it address stereotypes held today?
- What do you think the man on the bench in the centre of the photograph might be thinking? To what degree is the viewer led to share those thoughts? Is the viewer invited to adopt any particular point of view?
- What effect is created by the position of the bench on an angle within the photograph? How would the effect be different if the bench formed a straight line across the photograph?
- Until the second half of the twentieth century almost all sculptures of human figures were placed on pedestals that brought the figures off the ground. What effect is created when that is done? What effect is created by Segal's style of placing sculpted human figures directly on the ground?
- Comment on the viewpoint from which the photograph is taken. Does this viewpoint work against what you take to be the message of the sculpture, or in harmony with it? Why?

William Brymner, a painter who worked for some years in Paris in the 1880s, donated the large painting shown on page 473 to the Royal Academy of Arts when he was elected a fellow of the academy in 1886. The subject of the painting is a group of girls on a hillside, near a town on the coast of Yorkshire, England.

Questions to consider:

- What draws the viewer into this painting? Is there more than one area of the painting to which the viewer's eyes are particularly drawn by the structural lines of the image?
- How do you read the expressions of the girls? Does the painting suggest a thread of narrative? The girl to the right is knitting rather than participating in the making of the daisy chain. What comments might be made about the contrast between the two activities?
- What effect does the size of the central figures have in comparison to the size of the distant town? What effect does the presence of the sea have?

William Brymner, *A Wreath of Flowers* (1884)

- What effect does the placement of the sea within the overall composition have on the viewer's perception? Comment on the workings of perspective in the painting, and how they may connect to the meanings we may read into it.
- What (if anything) does the painting say about exclusion? About the ways in which children relate to one another? About jealousy and envy? About hierarchy? About social class? About the social construction of gender roles in nineteenth-century England?
- How would the impression given us by the painting be different if the viewpoint were from slightly above the children rather than slightly below them?
- What effect do the painting's bright but soft hues have on the viewer? How do they connect to the meaning(s) suggested by the image?
- What comment might you make about the placing of the path (a) in terms of the composition of the painting; and (b) in terms of the symbolism involved?
- How does the background scenery in the painting reinforce—or contrast with—the emotional content of the painting's narrative?

The advertisement shown above is one of the earliest in what has become a much-discussed advertising campaign. Oatly, a Swedish company founded in the early 1990s, launched the high-profile campaign in the second decade of this century, as interest in alternatives to dairy products was increasing throughout much of the world. In 2014 the Swedish Dairy Association launched a lawsuit against the company, alleging that the slogan "It's like milk but made for humans" was leading people to wrongly believe that drinking cow's milk was bad for them. The Dairy Association won the lawsuit, but Oatly's sales soared with the publicity (the company made the full transcript of the trial public).

Questions to consider:

- How would you characterize the tone of this advertisement?
- As with the Vancouver Humane Society advertisement discussed above, this advertisement has a clear viewpoint with respect to relationships between human and non-human animals. In what ways are the two advertisements similar? In what ways are they different?
- The image in the advertisement shows the carton on an angle. What effect does this placement of the product have?
- After reading the section on "Viewpoint and Distance" in this chapter, comment on these aspects of this photograph, and on the ways in which the photograph interacts with the surrounding text.
- Oatly advertisements stand in contrast to the advertisement for Louis Vuitton handbags that appears below; Oatly ads tend to be text-heavy,

and they try hard not to be sexy. (The text for one, displayed beside a very ordinary photo of a container of Oatly, reads as follows: "Taking super sexy photos of food can be exhausting, so we just used this pack shot instead.") Which approach do you think works better? Or does it depend on the product being advertised?

- The noun "milk" can refer to milk of many different sorts, since lactating females of many mammalian species—including the human species, of course—produce milk. The practice of using the noun in informal English to refer to *cow's milk*, specifically, is followed in this advertisement. Comment on this common linguistic habit.
- How would you describe the writing style of the text that appears at the right-hand side of the advertisement? Try adopting a similar style in writing a short paragraph about some other topic (rain suits and umbrellas, perhaps, or bicycles and cars).

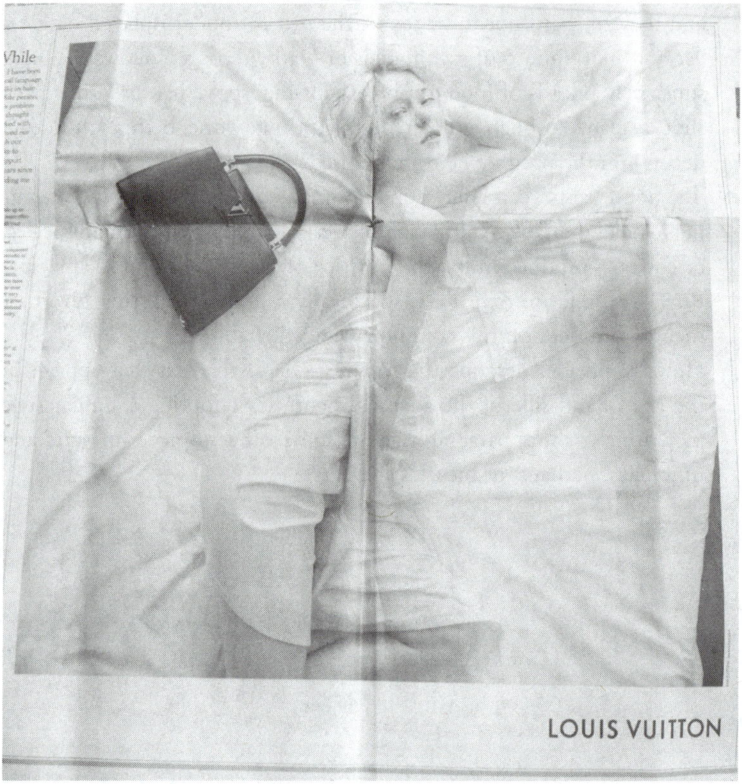

The photograph above shows a handbag advertisement as it was encountered by a reader of the 4 April 2021 issue of the *New York Times*. The original of the advertisement itself, together with other images featured in the same campaign (with Léa Seydoux posing with the handbag) may be found in many locations online.

Questions to consider:

- This image partakes of a long tradition of advertising that attempts to enlist sex appeal in selling products. Compare the approach of this example with at least one other example you are familiar with of an advertising campaign that relies heavily on sex appeal.
- After reading the section on "Viewpoint and Distance" in this chapter, comment on these aspects of the photograph used in this advertisement.
- Comment on the composition of the photograph; what effect does the placement of the handbag relative to the woman have?

- If you are able to access a colour version of this advertisement online, comment on the colours of the photograph and also on qualities such as level of colour saturation and contrast.
- There are no words in this photograph, but there are two letters. Comment on their significance and on their placement.
- Comment on the placing of the advertisement at the fold in the centre of the newspaper.
- In a newspaper article about this advertising campaign ("Léa Seydoux poses in nothing but crisp white bed sheets with a handbag in a sultry shoot for Louis Vuitton," *The Daily Mail*, 22 March 2021), Andrew Bullock asserts that the advertisement shown "portrays the intimate relationship between a woman and her bag and highlights the timeless elegance of the Capucines bag." Comment on this description, and on what it suggests about the values of modern society.
- What does the image suggest about the interconnections between money (or wealth) and sexuality?
- Comment on the gendered social convention of carrying a purse or handbag.
- In his 1899 book *The Theory of the Leisure Class*, American economist and sociologist Thorstein Veblen advanced the theory that in wealthy societies people value goods as much for the social signals they send as for the utility of the goods themselves. The term "conspicuous consumption" originates with Veblen; he hypothesized not only that the wealthy intentionally pay more for goods than their utility would suggest they are worth but also that those who are less wealthy are influenced to do the same. To what extent are Veblen's ideas applicable to an advertising campaign of this sort? To what extent are you and your friends influenced by advertising campaigns of this nature?
- The era when Veblen was writing (the 1890s) was a period of great wealth but also great inequality, with large corporations (whose bosses were often referred to as "robber barons") wielding tremendous influence. Can you draw parallels with today? How can you connect the messaging of an image such as this one with large ideas about society as a whole?
- Write two captions to accompany this ad—the first, a caption designed to reinforce the imagery and sell more handbags; and the second, a caption designed to undercut both the intended appeal of the visual image and the more general appeal of conspicuous consumption.

Restoring *Oppression Breeds Resistance,* Belfast (2010)

From the 1960s through to the signing of the "Good Friday Agreement" in 1998, the history of Northern Ireland was one of sectarian religious violence. That violence was part of a centuries-long conflict between Protestant and Catholic, English and Irish, and—for many of those centuries—rich and poor. From the 1970s onwards, murals were an important part of the struggle, for both the Catholic and the Protestant militants (the Irish Republican Army and the Ulster Volunteer Force, respectively). The twenty-first century has seen efforts both to create new murals (primarily on themes of peace and reconciliation) and to restore the historic ones from the 1970s and 1980s; both sorts of murals have become the subject of sightseeing tours.

- Comment on as many aspects of this image as you can.

WRITING CONTEXTS

WRITING CONTEXTS

C1 Writing Across the Disciplines

C1.1 Different Subjects, Different Styles

This unit introduces some of the conventions of writing in a number of the main academic disciplines. You may know that the conventions of writing vary between different disciplines, and that one should not expect that an approach to essay writing that works well in one discipline will work well in another. But even *within* each discipline there can be more than one set of accepted practices when it comes to academic writing. What is entirely appropriate to an essay in the continental tradition of philosophy is not likely to suit the requirements of a course in epistemology taught entirely in the analytic tradition; an essay in the interpretivist tradition in sociology will be inappropriate for a course taught from a positivist perspective; and so on. This section provides some sense of the divergent lines of approach in each discipline; additional information is provided in sections C1.2–C1.4, and on the companion website.

The list of subjects covered is weighted towards those that tend to place the greatest importance on writing (notably, the humanities and social sciences), though scientific writing is also covered. As this book is designed primarily for undergraduate use, some professional faculties (such as law) are not covered. Business and commerce are included, however, as are engineering and health sciences, since at many institutions courses in these subjects are offered beginning at the first-year undergraduate level. Inevitably, the picture provided here in such a short space is a greatly simplified one. We hope that the information provided will nevertheless provide some guidance to those beginning the effort of reading and writing in a new academic subject.

Included with the discussions of writing practices of the disciplines are brief discipline-specific lists of useful websites and respected journals. In the early years of this century a significant divide began to open up in the publishing of academic research. As the publishing of scholarly papers became more and more a digital enterprise, most journals went electronic, and made themselves available only through subscription, either to the journal directly or to one of the many aggregators that provide access to bundles of publications, primarily to university libraries. In the sciences and in some social sciences—most notably, Economics—many academics felt that these changes had resulted in a system that was too restrictive in the access it offered, too slow to publish new research, and too expensive. In response, scholars and scholarly associations began to found new open access journals and open access websites providing unrestricted free access to new research—including scholarly work in progress (drafts of journal articles, papers presented at conferences, etc.), as well as published academic papers that have already been peer-reviewed, edited, and so on. In Economics, most significant research now appears first in open access form through websites such as Research Papers in Economics and SSRN (the Social Science Research Network); in the sciences, PLOS (the Public Library of Science) and other open access publications have significantly altered the publishing landscape. The humanities have lagged behind the sciences and the social sciences in developing open access journals and websites—though SSRN now includes humanities networks in such subjects as Literature and Philosophy.

Students are also likely to benefit greatly from wide reading in general journals of news and opinion. Some of the most interesting, useful, and reliable general audience publications are *The Atlantic*, *The Economist*, *Harper's Magazine*, *The New Yorker*, and *The New York Review of Books*. Some articles from these publications are available online, as are some materials from leading newspapers such as *The New York Times*, *The Wall Street Journal*, the *Los Angeles Times*, *The Washington Post*, *The Guardian*, *The London Times*, *The Globe and Mail*, and *The Australian*. As well, websites such as the Arts and Letters site (www.aldaily.com) provide access to a selection of the most interesting pieces from many of these and other sources.

C1.2 English Studies

In no academic discipline has the question of writing style been so vexed in the past generation as it has in English Studies. For that reason—and because new styles of discourse that first took root in English studies have recently been spreading much more widely through other disciplines—more space will be devoted here to the writing conventions of this academic subject than to those of any other.

The study of English literature had by the late nineteenth century developed into a recognized academic subject, and for most of the twentieth century the discipline followed a broadly similar approach to writing about literature. While popular literary critics focused on evaluative judgements, academic critics moved substantially beyond the evaluative; the work of the scholar entailed pointing out aspects of a literary work that might not be obvious to the casual reader—whether they be points of style, of theme, of characterization, or of literary history—and clarifying those points for the reader. Irony, paradox, and contradiction were considered particularly fertile ground for the literary critic. In this sample, Toni Morrison (a literary scholar as well as a novelist) is analyzing a passage from one of Edgar Allan Poe's novels:

> They have been floating, Pym and Peters and the native, Nu-Nu, on a warm milk-white sea under a "white-ashy shower." The black man dies, and the boat rushes on through the white curtain behind which a white giant rises up. After that, there is nothing. There is no more narrative. Instead, there is a scholarly note, explanation, and an anxious, piled-up "conclusion." The latter states that it was *whiteness* that terrified the natives and killed Nu-Nu. The following inscription was carved into the walls of the chasms that travelers passed through: "I have graven it within the hills, and my vengeance upon the dust within the rock."
>
> No early American writer is more important to the concept of African Americanism than Poe. And no image is more telling than the one just described: the visualized but somehow closed and unknowable white form that rises from the mists at the end of the journey—or, at any rate, at the end of the narration proper. The images of the white curtain and the "shrouded human figure" with skin "the perfect whiteness of the human snow" both occur after the narrative has encountered blackness. The first white image seems related to the expiration and erasure of the serviceable and serving black figure, Nu-Nu. Both are figurations of impenetrable whiteness that surface in American literature whenever an Africanist presence is engaged....

These images of impenetrable whiteness need contextualizing to explain their extraordinary power, pattern, and consistency. Because they appear almost always in conjunction with representations of black or Africanist people who are dead, impotent, or under complete control, these images of blinding whiteness seem to function as both antidote for and meditation on the shadow that is companion to this whiteness—a dark and abiding presence that moves the hearts and texts of American literature with fear and longing. This haunting, a darkness from which our early literature seemed unable to extricate itself, suggests the complex and contradictory situation in which American writers found themselves during the formative years of the nation's literature.

(Toni Morrison, *Playing in the Dark: Whiteness and the Literary Imagination*, 1992 (32–33), analyzing Edgar Allan Poe's *The Narrative of Arthur Gordon Pym.*)

Notice here how Morrison combines a discussion of historical change in American literature, for which the past tense is used, with a reading of a particular text—for which the present tense is used (this convention is explained in more detail in section C2.3). Notice too the focus on an interesting paradox or contradiction.

The "evidence" employed in the arguments put forward by English Studies scholars is typically to be found in literary texts. But many English Studies scholars—particularly those with a strong background in theory—tend not to rely on a structure of "proof" buttressed by extensive quotation. The tendency of such scholars is rather to focus on small, suggestive details—to work elliptically, as it were. Here is an example:

The resonant details of the scene in which Brontë has Jane acquire her fortune mark Jane's financial and literary implication in colonialism as well. St. John announces Jane's accession to fortune by pulling the letter out of a "morocco pocket-book" (483), and he is able to identify Jane as the heiress because she has written her name, on a white sheet of paper, in "Indian ink" (486).

In this way the novel implicates in colonialism not only Jane's finances (the leather of the wallet has a colonial provenance) but the act of writing itself, for the pigment in which Jane has absently traced her name, with its startlingly colonial appellation, has such

> a provenance as well.... Like imperialist trade itself, bringing home the spoils of other countries to become commodities in England, such as Indian ink, the use of the racial "other" as a metaphor for class and gender struggles in England commodifies the dark-skinned people of the British empire as they exist in historical actuality and transforms them into East or West Indian ink with which to write a novel about ending injustices within England.
>
> The eruption of the words "Indian ink" into the novel at this telling moment hints at Brontë's uneasiness about the East Indian ventures to which England was turning in 1848, as well as about the West Indian colonies that were by then clearly becoming unprofitable after the abolition of slavery....
>
> (Susan Meyer, *Imperialism at Home: Race and Victorian Women's Fiction*, Ithaca, 1996, 93–94)

In some respects this passage may be likened to the passage by Toni Morrison that we looked at above; comment about the text is couched in the present tense, and the writer is clearly interested in drawing connections among the text, the author, and the wide sweep of historical and literary developments. In both passages quotation is minimal and one detail—the "white curtain" or the "Indian ink"—is made to serve a variety of purposes, suggest a range of connections.

That such a free-flowing approach to scholarly argument can forge interesting connections is now beyond doubt; scholars working through this sort of method have exerted an enduring impact on the discipline in the past generation. But in recent years many within the discipline have begun to feel that this more free-flowing approach to building arguments may bring its own set of difficulties—that it too often may run the risk of resting its conclusions on flimsy or unreliable foundations. In terms of writing style, the discipline as a whole tends now again to embrace the idea of clear and comprehensible expression, and advocates building arguments by marshaling a body of textual evidence, including extensive direct quotation.

A dominant activity of twenty-first-century English Studies is contextualizing; today's literary scholarship often involves placing literary works in the context of literary, cultural, and socio-economic developments, in order to show how literary works reflect the values (and contradictions) of the era from which they emerge. Here is an example, from an article discussing "eighteenth-century tragedy's peculiar yoking of a serious play to a lighthearted epilogue":

> *The Gamester: A Tragedy* animates these contradictions between the fear of tragic consequences and the pleasure of risk-taking.... The domestic prose tragedy literally wore down the actors with its wildly effusive emotion: it "demanded so much of the actors that after ten successive evenings they cried respite before continuing" (Van Lennep et al. 317). ...
>
> At tragedy's end Mrs. Beverley cleaves to an unshakable belief in poetic justice: "Yet Heav'n the guiltless Sufferer regards, / And whom it most afflicts, it most rewards" (246; act 3, sc. 7).... Beverley is ... transformed into a hysterical female: "At last he started up, look'd wild, and trembled; and like a Woman, seiz'd with her Sex's Fits, laugh'd out aloud, while the Tears trickled down his Face" (248; act 4, sc. 3). Misplaced reliance on speculation turns men into women, but not the sort of women represented by Mrs. Beverley.
>
> While the play attempts to mobilize the audience's passions toward creating national stability and prosperity, the epilogue disrupts that impulse. [The actress Hannah] Pritchard, like the actresses who later played Mrs. Beverley, leaves the stage dumbstruck with grief at the end of the fifth act, only to reappear promptly to deliver the comic epilogue "written by a friend."
>
> Speaking in her own person, she blithely asserts that gaming is the national addiction. Unlike the "Oriental" men with whom they are compared, Englishmen will not be swayed to abandon gambling... (272). The epilogue caps off the tragedy by seeming to license the very vices the play warns against.
>
> (Felicity Nussbaum, "The Unaccountable Pleasure of Eighteenth-Century Tragedy," *PMLA*, October 2014, 698–700)

We may notice here a transition between discussions of historical developments (in the past tense), and discussions of the text as a living literary entity, for which the present tense is used. The argument is built using extensive direct quotation from the text. As with the passage by Toni Morrison with which we began, clarity both of argument and of expression are here central goals of academic discourse.

CITATION AND DOCUMENTATION

MLA style is standard in the discipline. See section C3.1 for a full outline of MLA style, followed by a sample essay that makes use of the MLA system.

For further discussion of writing about literature, see sections **C2.1-2.4**.

C1.3 Humanities

History

Of the several styles of writing frequently practised by historians, the most established is much as one would expect—writing that tells a story. Even if one wished to question the prevailing academic orthodoxy, until relatively recently the accepted way of doing so was to tell the story again, from a different angle or with a different emphasis. One might pause periodically to analyze developments, discuss their causes, or address issues concerning the historical evidence, but the main mode of discussion would inevitably be narrative, using the simple past tense (or the past perfect tense when making reference in the course of a discussion of one set of historical events to something previous). Here is an example:

> Both Hitler and the Poles held rigid positions in the war of nerves. After 26 March, Hitler did not again formulate demands concerning Danzig until the day before war broke out. This was not surprising; it was his usual method. So he had waited for offers from Schuschnigg over Austria; so he had waited for offers from Benes, from Chamberlain, finally from the conference at Munich over Czechoslovakia. Then he did not wait in vain. Did he appreciate that this time no offer would come from the Poles? It seemed so from the record. On 3 April he issued instructions that preparations for an attack on Poland "must be made in such a way that the operation can be carried out at any time as from 1 September 1939."
>
> (A.J.P. Taylor, *The Origins of the Second World War*, London, 1961, 302–03)

Though the narrative style is the most established approach to the writing of history, it is by no means the most widely practised by academic historians today. For much of the twentieth century, the trend in the academic discipline of history was toward a more scientific approach that emphasized social and economic forces rather than narratives involving individuals. This sort of historical writing, which remains widespread, is more likely to focus on numbers than on historical incidents. Again, the writing is typically in the past tense, but the tone is very different from that of a traditional historical narrative. Here is an example:

> Was there any special character to these neighborhoods? Were they red-light districts or merely poor quarters? The most striking feature of these streets is how different they were from one another. Simnell Street contained common lodging houses inhabited by single dock laborers and families of hawkers. Koss Street, Southampton, while a "low" street and the scene of frequent drunken brawls, was the residence of skilled artisans living in nuclear families. 45 out of 70 households were nuclear (64.3 per cent); including subfamilies, 57 out of 77 (74.0 per cent) families were two-parent headed. Yet both Simnell and Koss streets had one or two houses characterized as brothels, where single women resided apart from their families. On the other hand, Plymouth's Granby and Central streets, which opened into the Octagon, the pub and entertainment center of Plymouth, had nuclear families living in single tenement rooms, yet almost two of every three adults were women.
>
> (J.R. Walkowitz and D.J. Walkowitz, "'We are not the beasts of the field': Prostitution and the Poor in Plymouth and Southampton under the Contagious Diseases Acts," in *Clio's Consciousness Raised: New Perspectives on the History of Women*, edited by M.S. Hartman and L. Banner, 1974, 192–225, 199)

Such historical writing as this aims to provide demonstrable proof (most of it empirical) of a particular line of argument; it is on this sort of approach that the claims of history to be as much one of the social sciences as one of the humanities rests.

Another broad approach to historical writing has been developed over the past generation. Influenced substantially by French cultural historians and theorists, this approach focuses largely on culture. Rather than attempt to prove a historical argument by assembling empirical evidence, cultural historians of recent generations have tended to operate as much by suggestion as by efforts to provide proof. Often sceptical of truth claims, they rely on suggestive anecdotes or pieces of information to provide insight into particular themes or aspects of historical reality. Often they approach topics from new and surprising angles—so, for example, Paul Edward Dutton inquires into what Charlemagne's mustache can tell us about eighth- and ninth-century Carolingian history and Robert Darnton explores various aspects of eighteenth-century life by discussing an attack in the 1730s by a group of printing apprentices on their masters' cats.

Some twenty-first-century historians have adopted the writing style pioneered by continental theorists. The extreme here may be represented by the following passage from David Lloyd's *Ireland After History* (on the need for a new approach to history):

> Constituted in simultaneity with, and different from, modern civil society, and representing in a certain sense the "constitutive other" of modernity, these spaces that are the objective of "new histories" are not, we have argued, to be conceived as alternative continuities, parallel to dominant narratives and only awaiting, in Gramsci's sense, to attain hegemony in order to be completed. On the contrary, and at the risk of deliberate hypostatization, the apparent discontinuity of popular or non-elite history furnishes indications of alternative social formations, difficult as these may be to document and decipher for the disciplined historian; the same discontinuity as well as the formal grounds for the persistence in assimilability of non-elite formations to the state.
>
> (As quoted by David A. Wilson in *The Globe and Mail*, 28 December 2004, A–12)

These two sentences—both nominated by David A. Wilson as candidates for a Worst Sentence in the World Award—are not typical of twenty-first-century historical writing, but this sort of style, with its contorted syntax, extraordinary density of abstraction, and verbal tics that resist precision ("in a certain sense"), is now not uncommon. Ironically, this began happening just as this sort of dense, opaque style was starting to go out of fashion in English Studies.

CITATION AND DOCUMENTATION

There is no universally accepted style of documentation for history. Many journals use some variety of Chicago Style; many use traditional footnotes or endnotes. For students the most important guideline is thus to follow whatever specifications each instructor may give you.

Philosophy

The academic discipline of philosophy as it has been practised in the English-speaking world in recent generations divides into two broad streams. By far the dominant stream is that of analytic philosophy. Perhaps above all, the tradition of analytic philosophy values clarity, and devotes very considerable effort to making fine distinctions that may help to clarify lines of thought. In doing so, it often employs hypothetical examples. Arguments are typically couched in the present tense, though the past tense is used if reference is being made to an argument from the past that is not being discussed as a live philosophical issue today. When analyzing or discussing an argument of the eighteenth-century philosopher David Hume, one would write "Hume *argues* ... "; when discussing Hume in the context of intellectual history, however, one would write "Hume *argued* ... " Analytic philosophers have a few verbal tics particular to their discipline (e.g., they tend to write "*on* Rawls's theory" where academics in other disciplines would write "*according to* Rawls's theory ... "), and they tend to employ a great many abstract nouns. Other than that, however, they prefer the clarity of sentences that are syntactically straightforward. Here is a sample:

> Deontological theories also capture our intuitions that certain things that have happened in the past are morally relevant. Consequentialist theories are strictly forward-looking moral theories. They look forward from the time of the decision at issue to see how we can bring about the best possible results in the future. Deontological theories allow that backward-looking considerations can have moral significance.
>
> (Heimir Geirsson and Margaret Holmgren, *Ethical Theory*, 3/e, Peterborough, 2018, 186–87)

The other stream of academic philosophy is commonly referred to as "continental philosophy." As the name suggests, it is heavily influenced by the writings of philosophers from continental Europe, from Nietzsche and Habermas to Heidegger and Foucault to Irigaray and Kristeva. Like analytic philosophers, those in the continental tradition tend to use a great many abstract nouns, but beyond that there are few similarities of style. Those in the continental tradition tend to be less interested in fine distinctions than in broad brushstrokes, and in many cases they embrace difficulty, even to the extent of cultivating a style that makes it difficult for the reader to decipher the meaning. Arguments are generally advanced in the present tense. Here is a sample:

> Notice that, unlike Barthes, Gadamer insists on the re-identification of one and the same text under plural, potentially infinite, interpretation and re-interpretation. The infinite openness of texts—in both an interpretive and historical sense (ultimately the same sense)—is ensured by the notion of reflexive application: the intentional import *of* a text essentially incorporates into *its* developing, endlessly reconstituted meaning but its recovery for our own historical experience and prejudice can make it out to be.
>
> (Joseph Margolis, "Reinterpreting Interpretation," *Journal of Aesthetics and of Criticism*, 43, Summer 1989, 249)

If the styles of philosophy may be broadly divided into the analytic and the continental, the content of philosophy is also divided into a variety of sub-disciplines, including aesthetics, ethics, epistemology, logic, and metaphysics. For the most part, conventions of writing do not vary widely among these; an analytic philosopher writing on a topic in aesthetics, for example, follows very much the same conventions of writing as an analytic philosopher writing on a topic in epistemology or ethics. The exception here is symbolic logic, which uses its own language—or rather, its own variety of symbolic languages.

CITATION AND DOCUMENTATION

There is no universally accepted style of documentation for philosophy. Many journals use some variety of Chicago Style; many use traditional footnotes or endnotes. For students the most important guideline is thus to follow whatever specifications each instructor may give you.

Art History

Scholarly writing in art history, like that in several other disciplines, alternates frequently between the past tense and the present tense, with the past tense used to discuss historical developments and the present tense employed when the appearance or present effect of a work is being discussed. Here is a sample:

> Most often, medieval image makers deployed usual iconographic means to present Christ as both earthly and divine. For example, a manuscript in Stuttgart (Landesbibliothek, Brev. 128, fol. 9v) assimilates numerous texts and pictorial sources ... to establish the Lord's majesty; it incorporates personifications of light and dark and winter and summer to position Him in relation to the world.
>
> (Herbert L. Kessler, *Seeing Medieval Art*, Peterborough, 2004, 74–75)

The style of the above passage (by a leading historian of medieval art, writing both for fellow scholars and for general readers and students) is somewhat challenging conceptually, but relatively straightforward in the structure of its sentences. It employs concrete nouns more frequently than it does abstract nouns, and the abstract nouns that are used (*majesty*, *personifications*) tend to be readily comprehensible.

If this passage represents one pole in art history writing, another, quite different style finds expression in the following passage:

> Thus perhaps at stake has always been the murderous capacity of images, murderers of the real, murderers of their own model, as the Byzantine icons could murder the divine identity. To this murderous capacity is opposed the dialectical capacity of representations as a visible and intelligible mediation of the Real. All of Western faith was engaged in this wager on representation: That a sign could refer to the depth of meaning, that a sign could exchange for meaning, and that something could guarantee this exchange—God, of course. But what if God himself can be simulated, that is to say, reduced to the signs which attest his existence? Then the whole system becomes weightless, it is no longer anything but a gigantic simulacrum—not unreal, but a simulacrum, never again exchanging for what is real, but exchanging in itself, in an uninterrupted circuit without reference or circumference.

(Jean Baudrillard, "The Evil Demon of Images and the Precession of Simulacra," in Thomas Docherty, ed., *Postmodernism: A Reader*, New York, 1993, 194)

This quotation (a translation from the French of a key passage by a leading postmodern theorist) is unlike the first passage in almost every respect. It aims to challenge the reader from every angle—in its style of writing as well as in the concepts themselves. It is extraordinarily dense, filled with abstract nouns (many of them specific to contemporary cultural theory), and lacking in concrete examples. It is syntactically complex, using devices such as the placing of phrases in apposition ("the murderous capacity of images, murderers of the real, murderers of their own model"), which have the effect of continually recasting the thoughts being presented—as well as of lengthening the sentences. Writing such as this, in the style of certain sorts of theoretical schools commonly styled "postmodernist," is frequently used in several of the humanities and social sciences. This style is frequently encountered in writing about art theory—contemporary theory in particular. The sorts of conventions that are followed in the Kessler passage, however, remain far more common in art history departments.

CITATION AND DOCUMENTATION

Art history and other disciplines in the fine arts generally use MLA Style.

C1.4 Natural and Applied Sciences

Biology

Academic writing about scientific subjects tends to be of two main sorts. The less common of these is the review article, in which the writer surveys and assesses evidence on a particular topic from various sources. Here is a passage from an abstract of a review article:

> Senescence is a complex, highly regulated, developmental phase in the life of a leaf that results in the co-ordinated degradation of macromolecules and the subsequent mobilization of components to other parts of the plant. The application of molecular biology techniques to the study of leaf senescence has, in the last few

> years, enabled the isolation and characterization of a large range of DNA clones representing genes that show increased expression in senescing leaves.... To date, genes encoding degradative enzymes such as proteases and nucleases, enzymes involved in lipid and carbohydrate metabolism, and enzymes involved in nitrogen mobilization, have all been identified as senescence-enhanced genes. A variety of other genes of no obvious senescence-related function have also been identified; their role in senescence may be less predictable and, possibly, more interesting.
>
> (V. Buchanan-Wollaston, "The Molecular Biology of Leaf Senescence," *Journal of Experimental Biology*, 1997, vol. 48, 181)

Notice here the variety of verb tenses used. When research is summarized the present perfect tense ("... *has enabled* the isolation ... ," "... enzymes involved ... *have all been identified* ") is used. The simple present tense is used when established scientific facts or ongoing realities are recounted ("Senescence *is* ... ," "... genes that *show* ..."). One other aspect of this passage worth noting is that it makes no reference to other research. Whereas abstracts in the social sciences (and in a behavioural science such as psychology) tend always to place an article in the context of previous research, the abstracts of many papers in the pure sciences make little or no reference to previous research. Even in the introduction to a paper in biology, chemistry, or physics, there tends to be less by way of direct reference to previous research than is common in scientific papers in the social sciences.

The more common sort of scientific writing is the research paper, in which the writer reports on original research. Such papers follow a standardized format, with a precise **title**; an **abstract** summarizing the paper; an **introduction** outlining the nature of, rationale for, and background to the research; a section describing the **method** or procedures followed; a section presenting the **results**; a section providing a **discussion** of the results, their significance, and their implications; and a list of **references**. Here is a typical passage from a section setting out the method followed in an experiment:

> Sperm samples were collected from adult males by penile electro-stimulation, and sperm capacitation and IVF were done as described previously [20], with a few minor modifications [17].

Briefly, 10x10² washed sperm/ml were re-suspended in 2 ml TALP medium and incubated at 37° in 5% CO_2 in air for 1–10 h. Sperm were treated for 30–35 min with 1 mW each of dibutyryl cyclic AMP (dbcAMP) and caffeine to induce hyper-activation. Hyper-activated sperm (300,000/ml) were then co-incubated with oocytes for 12–16 h in TALP medium containing 1mM each of dbcAMP and caffeine in micro-drops under mineral oil at 37° in a humidified atmosphere of 5% CO_2 in air. Sperm and remaining cumulus cells were then removed manually by pipetting through a finely pulled glass pipette, and oocytes were examined for evidence of fertilization.

(Ping Zheng et al., "The Primate Embryo Gene Expression Resource: A Novel Resource to Facilitate Rapid Analysis of Gene Expression in Non-Human Primate Oocytes and Pre-implantation Stage Embryos," *Biology of Reproduction*, January 2004)

As this passage well illustrates, the convention generally followed when describing methods employed and results obtained is to present the information in as clear and concise a fashion as possible, using the simple past tense.

While the equivalent of the review article in a university course is typically a term paper or research paper, the equivalent of the research paper is the lab report, in which the student writes up the results of an experiment performed in class.

For more discussions of the forms and conventions of writing in the sciences, see sections **C2.5–2.7**.

CITATION AND DOCUMENTATION

The Council of Science Editors (CSE) style is followed in biology. See the companion website for an overview of CSE style. Note that fields related to biomedicine often use the citation styles described under "Medicine and Health Sciences" below.

Chemistry

The conventions of writing followed in the pure sciences are broadly similar; see the discussion above under "Biology."

CITATION AND DOCUMENTATION

Writing in Chemistry often uses the style guide of the American Chemical Society: Coghill, Anne M., and Lorrin R. Garson, eds. *The ACS Style Guide: Effective Communication of Scientific Information.* 3rd ed., Amer. Chemical Soc., 2006.

Physics

The conventions of writing followed in the pure sciences are broadly similar; see the discussion above under "Biology."

CITATION AND DOCUMENTATION

In Physics, writers often use the style guide of the American Institute of Physics: *Style Manual: Instructions to Authors and Volume Editors for the Preparation of AIP Book Manuscripts.* 5th ed., AIP, 1995.

Engineering

CITATION AND DOCUMENTATION

For writing in Engineering, consult the style guide of the Institute of Electrical and Electronics Engineers: *IEEE Editorial Style Manual.* IEEE, V9.20.2021.

Medicine and Health Sciences

CITATION AND DOCUMENTATION

In biomedical publications, the two most common formats for preparing manuscripts are the American Medical Association (AMA) manual of style and *Citing Medicine, the NLM Style Guide for Authors, Editors, and Publishers. Citing Medicine* uses Vancouver style referencing as set out by the International Committee of Medical Journal Editors in Uniform Requirements for Manuscripts Submitted to Biomedical Journals.

In both AMA and Vancouver styles, citations are numbered in the order that they appear in the text using parentheses (1), square brackets [1], superscript[1], or a combination thereof [[1]]. A small number of journals use other in-text reference systems described by the Council of Science Editors, found in this book under Biology citations and references.

For more on AMA style, see Iverson et al., *AMA Manual of Style: A Guide for Authors and Editors*. 11th ed. New York, NY: Oxford University Press; 2020.

C1.5 Social Sciences

Anthropology

Anthropology is unique among academic disciplines in the way it is configured. At many universities the department of anthropology includes four fields or subdivisions: cultural anthropology (the study of other cultures, or the study of one's own culture with a fresh eye); physical anthropology (the study of the physical evolution of humans, and connections to other primates); archeology (the study of the past through physical artifacts); and linguistics (the scientific study of human languages). In other universities archeology and linguistics may be separate departments on their own, with the anthropology department focusing on the study of physical and cultural anthropology. At still other institutions, the department of anthropology focuses exclusively on cultural anthropology—and in some cases, it is combined with sociology as one academic department. To complicate the picture further, what is known as "cultural anthropology" in the United States is referred to as "social anthropology" in Britain. (Both terms are understood and accepted in Canada and Australia, though Canadians increasingly lean towards the American model.) Archeology, linguistics, and physical anthropology all tend towards a somewhat more scientific style of writing than does cultural anthropology. (For more on scientific styles of writing see the previous section.) This section will focus on the most prevalent field within the discipline, cultural anthropology.

Until relatively recently the feature that most clearly distinguished cultural anthropology from sociology was that anthropology dealt with other cultures, sociology with our own culture. Over the past two generations, that distinction has largely broken down, under both the pressure of a general realization among anthropologists of the degree to which perceptions of "otherness" were inherently problematic, and the practical pressures of greatly reduced funding for research in remote areas of the world. Cultural anthropologists are now at least as likely to focus on interesting and revealing aspects of cultures in the developed world as they are to focus on the kinship structures or belief systems of traditional societies in the Amazon basin or the forests of Papua New Guinea. But whereas the sociologist is likely to search for statistical information about aggregations of people, the anthropologist is far more likely to rely on observation and interviews to collect information on the basis of which are put forward "explanatory generalizations." (The early twentieth-century anthropologist Franz Boas, who was probably more influential than any other single figure in giving shape to the discipline, used this phrase to describe what anthropology, as a "human science," could offer; in contrast, he suggested that the natural sciences offer "particular descriptions.") Here are two passages of anthropological writing, one concerning the Yanomamo of southern Venezuela and northern Brazil, and the other discussing RVers in North America:

> The soul aspect of the *noreshi* [a sort of spirit or portion of the soul], however, can leave the human body at will and wander. Sickness results when the *noreshi* has left the body; unless it is brought back soon, the person will die.... When sickness is deemed to be the result of soul loss, the people who are closely related to the sick person hunt for his *noreshi*. I participated in one of these soul hunts. Kaobawa's group had set up a temporary camp across the river from its main village site, as they suspected raiders would attack them. While they were camped in their temporary village, one of the children became ill, and her malady was thought to be caused by soul loss....
>
> (Napoleon Chagnon, *Yanomamo: The Fierce People*, New York, 1968, 49)

> The people whose lifestyle we describe here challenge the stereotype of old age as a time of decline into senility, poverty, and illness. Their descriptions of their experiences, and their depictions of themselves and their fellow RVers defy the myths about elderly North Americans. They do not think of themselves as suffering the 'plight' of the elderly. The stereotype of seniors being lonely, isolated, ill, dependent, and suffering from the trauma of the 'empty nest' or meaningless retirement does not apply to them. They see themselves and their peers as adventurous, self-reliant, flexible, friendly, and 'gutsy.'...

(Dorothy and David Counts, *Over the Next Hill: An Ethnography of RVing Seniors in North America*, Peterborough, 2/e 2001, 50)

Much as the subject matter of these two passages may differ, we may notice that both advance generalizations about a culture or a subculture; that both couch these generalizations in the present tense; and that both support the generalizations they are making with evidence gleaned from personal interaction with members of the group being studied.

Not all cultural anthropology is characterized by an emphasis on the personal and the particular. As with other social sciences, postmodernist theory has exerted considerable influence within the discipline of cultural anthropology—and with it has come a writing style featuring long sentences, complex syntax, extremely high levels of abstraction, and a vocabulary quite different from that of traditional anthropology.

CITATION AND DOCUMENTATION

The American Anthropology Association publishes its own brief style guide. In almost all particulars it follows the Chicago Style of parenthetical citation. It does, however, make some exceptions, most notably in using a colon (rather than a comma) to separate date and page number in a parenthetical citation:

> Evidence now suggests that the kinship system of the Pacaa Nova is extraordinarily complex (Von Graeve 2003: 24–35).

The AAA Style Guide may be downloaded from the AAA website.

Economics

Writing on economics has its roots in the long but elegantly balanced sentences of Adam Smith in the eighteenth century. There was no such thing as a "discipline" of economics when Smith was writing, and it would be very much an anachronism to describe him as an economist. As passages such as the following illustrate, Smith came to the topic of "the wealth of nations" as a moral philosopher rather than as a social scientist:

> People of the same trade seldom meet together, even for merriment and diversion, [without] the conversation end[ing] in a

> conspiracy against the public, or in some contrivance to raise prices. It is impossible indeed to prevent such meetings, by any law which either could be executed, or would be consistent with liberty and justice. But though the law cannot hinder people of the same trade from sometimes assembling together, it ought to do nothing to facilitate such assemblies, much less to render them necessary.
>
> (Adam Smith, *The Wealth of Nations*, Book One, Chapter 10)

Ties with the traditions of philosophical and historical writing were not abandoned as the academic discipline of economics developed in the late nineteenth and earlier twentieth centuries, and even into the 1930s the arguments of economists were put forward more frequently with words than with numbers or equations. In 1933 the journal *Econometrica* was founded, with the intent of countering an anti-mathematical bias in the discipline.

No such bias against numbers and equations exists in the discipline of economics today. Most economists now rely very largely on mathematics and statistics, and largely as well on very specialized vocabulary. Even aside from obviously technical terms (*Pareto-neutral*, *Phillips curve*, and so on), a number of everyday English words (e.g., *optimal*, *equilibrium*) are also used by economists with precise technical meanings particular to the discipline. The following passage, taken from the introduction to a paper on measuring the well-being of populations, gives something of the flavour:

> The dominance criteria of Atkins (1970) and Shorrocks (1983) have become well known, and are now widely used for making welfare comparisons on the basis of income distribution data. These approaches, though, do not take into account the sort of non-income information—such as family size, age, type of housing—which is these days available in plenty in micro datasets, and may be of welfare relevance. Hence the old results have begun to be viewed as of limited usefulness. One could not, for example, use the generalized Lorenz dominance approach to recommend as welfare-improving the transfer of income from single persons to families with children, or to those with special needs such as old age or infirmity.

(Peter J. Lambert and Xavi Ramos, "Welfare Comparisons: Sequential Procedures for Heterogeneous Populations," *Economica*, vol. 69, no. 276, 2002, 549–62)

The above is typical not only in its highly technical vocabulary, but also in the way it positions itself in the context of an extensive literature. Here, as in most economic writing, the verb tenses are quite straightforward, with the simple present tense and the present perfect tense the most widely used.

Economics, as it is practised today, is probably more homogenous in its approach than any of the other social science disciplines. It is far from being all of a piece, however; writing in sub-disciplines such as economic history is often quite non-technical. The following passage, for example, could as easily have been written by a historian as an economist:

> Students of southern agriculture in the United States after the Civil War discovered a similar phenomenon. As the average size of farms began to shrink, small farmers had no choice but to grow cotton instead of corn. Although cotton production entailed much more risk, farmers could hope to survive only by adopting a strategy of buying corn in order to have more resources to devote to their cash crop (C. Wright 1978, 169). Consequently, higher corn prices would tend to work to the disadvantage of those farms that were too small to market grain.
>
> (Michael Perelman, *The Invention of Capitalism: Classical Political Economy and the Secret History of Primitive Accumulation*, Durham, NC, 2000, 298)

When one is dealing with economic history, of course, the past tense is the norm.

CITATION AND DOCUMENTATION

Although there is no universally accepted style of documentation for economics, APA (American Psychological Association) style is very widely used. See section C3.2 for a full outline of APA style.

Politics

The discipline that is variously styled "politics," "political studies," and "political science" borders on a considerable number of other academic disciplines. At one end, it looks at political theory historically (from Aristotle and Plato onwards), with interests not dissimilar to those of philosophers. What is the nature of the state? How may politics, morality, and the law best interact? And so on. The study of politics also inevitably overlaps with the study of history. And political science overlaps with sociology, too—in shared interests in social trends and ideology.

In most departments, the "science" in political science is a very real presence, and frequent reference is made to empirical studies as arguments are made concerning such things as the causes of electoral victories and defeats, and of changes in public opinion. Following are two examples:

> These results for the presidency also make it possible to return to a parallel analysis for the Senate, in ways that now seem substantively interpretable rather than statistically idiosyncratic. Indeed, the difference between the fortunes of local versus cosmopolitan Democratic candidates for Senate seats appears to reside largely in the way that the locals were following the pattern typical of local candidates for the House of Representatives, whereas cosmopolitans had already begun to follow the pattern of ... Northern Democratic candidates for the presidency. Figure 5.11 offers this parallel comparison.
>
> (Byron E. Shafer and Richard Johnston, *The End of Southern Exceptionalism: Class, Race, and Partisan Change in the Postwar South*, Cambridge, MA, 2009, 158)

> The CBS News/*New York Times* poll of March 21 to 25 [1984] covers the four days after the Illinois primary, the days during which news was disseminated about Hart's campaign controversies. There are enough interviews in this survey to divide it in half and treat each half of the survey independently. During the first half of this poll, the two days after the Illinois primary, when the commercials fracas was getting some publicity, Hart still led Mondale, 41 per cent to 38 per cent. In the second half of the survey, when the campaign news centered on Hart's embassy positions and his campaign management, Mondale jumped ahead 49 per cent to 29 per cent! This extraordinary turnaround is one more demonstration of how fragile the images and votes can be for candidates like Hart, or [George H.] Bush in 1980, or Carter

> in 1976, when voters are projecting future performance from campaign behavior.[35] It reemphasizes the discussion in Chapter 3 of the logic of incumbents' attacking their challenger(s) instead of trying to change opinions about themselves.
>
> (Samuel L. Popkin, *The Reasoning Voter: Communication and Persuasion in Presidential Campaigns*, 2/e, Chicago, 1994, 207)
>
> 35 Percentages from the March 5–8 CBS News/*New York Times* poll are based on 573 interviews: percentages from the second poll are based on 411 interviews, 235 on the first days and 176 on the last two days.

Notice in both of the above passages the shifts in verb tense. When Shafer and Johnston refer directly to events occurring in the past, the past verb tenses ("*were* following," "*had* already begun"), whereas when they comment on the meaning and relevance of the statistics they use the present tense ("These results *make* it possible" "the difference ... *appears* to reside"). Popkin also uses different verb tenses. When discussing the changes that occurred during the 1984 campaign, he uses the past tense ("Hart still *led*," "Mondale *jumped* ahead"), whereas when he comments on the ongoing relevance of these developments, he too switches to the present tense.

There are also interesting differences between the two passages. Shafer and Johnston use far more of the jargon that has been developed by the academic discipline of political science—including such phrases as *parallel analysis* and *substantively interpretable*. In contrast, Popkin adopts a less scholarly style, and for the most part relies on the vocabulary of everyday English.

CITATION AND DOCUMENTATION

There is no universally accepted citation and documentation system in this discipline, but the *Chicago Manual of Style* is probably the most widely used.

Psychology

Like others of the sciences and social sciences, psychology has many of its roots in philosophy; philosophers from Aristotle to John Locke and David Hume spent a good deal of time attempting to draw conclusions as to the workings of the human mind. It was not until the late nineteenth century that psychology began to be established as a scientific discipline—and even then writing on psychology tended more to resemble philosophical writing than the sort of writing we now associate with the academic discipline of psychology. William James, for example, whose classic work *The Principles of Psychology* helped to establish the discipline as a behavioural science, appeals in his writing to common experience in much the same way as Locke or Hume in earlier centuries:

> When we have been exposed to an unusual stimulus for many minutes or hours, a nervous process is set up which results in the haunting of consciousness by the impression for a long time afterwards. The tactile and the muscular feelings of a day of skating or riding, after long disuse of the exercise, will come back to us all through the night.
>
> (William James, *The Principles of Psychology*, 1890, Chapter 25)

At the same time as James was laying the foundations for the empirical study of psychology, another tradition of psychology was also beginning to take shape—psychoanalysis. Even more than James, this tradition adopted a writing style that had little in common with scientific writing as we know it today. The writings of Freud, Jung, and English-speaking followers such as Havelock Ellis and Ernest Jones, while often elegant, relied on personal observation, anecdote, and often bold assertion, rather than empirical measurements.

By the middle of the twentieth century, however, the influence of the psychoanalytic tradition was starting to wane, while the growth of psychology as a scientific discipline was quickening. The vast majority of writing in psychology came to rely on experimental evidence gathered according to standardized research methods. The typical article in psychology reports on an experiment, first summarizing the background of research against which the experiment has been conceived, then presenting method and results, before moving to a discussion of the results and a conclusion:

> Research on complex relational processes within families has revealed that parents' differential treatment of siblings is consistently linked with negative outcomes, such as children's poorer socio-emotional well-being (McGuire, Dunn, and Plomin, 1995; Stocker, 1995) and less positive sibling relationships (Brodie, Stoneman, and McCoy, 1992). However, what is not yet fully

> understood is how differential treatment relates to the quality of parent-child relationships. For example, do children or adolescents who feel they receive less-favored treatment than a sibling develop feelings of resentment toward this parent, setting the stage for poorer parent-child relationships? Or do children understand and perhaps "forgive" unequal treatment as warranted for particular reasons? ...
>
> Method.
>
> The sample included mothers, fathers, and two adolescents from 74 maritally intact families. Participating families lived in one of two small adjoining Mid-western cities (combined population 120,000) or a suburban or rural area proximal to the two cities. Participating families were recruited using newspaper ads and through flyers distributed at local schools.
>
> (Amanda K. Kowal, Jennifer L. Krull, and Laurie Kramer, "How the differential treatments of siblings is linked with parent-child relationship quality," *Journal of Family Psychology*, vol. 18, no. 4, 2004, 658–59)

Not all psychology writing is devoted to presenting the results of experiments, of course. But when writing for their fellow academics, psychologists tend to maintain the same vocabulary and writing style that characterizes reports on experiments. It may be interesting in this connection to compare the following two passages. In the first, psychologist Judith Rich Harris is writing for other psychologists in an academic journal; in the second, she is expressing very much the same idea in a book aimed at the general reader as well as the psychologist:

> When group identity is not salient, differentiation is likely to predominate over assimilation. If siblings see themselves as separate individuals rather than as part of the family group, status hierarchies and social comparisons may increase the differences among them. Dominance hierarchies would tend to make older siblings dominant over younger ones, which happens as a matter of course in most societies and which North American parents try very hard, and not very successfully, to prevent (Whiting and Edwards, 1988). However, there is little or no resemblance between children's relationships with their siblings and their rela-

> tionships with their peers (Abramovitch et al., 1986), which is consistent with the finding that birth order has no reliable effects on personality (Ernst and Angst, 1983; Reiss et al., 1994).
>
> (Judith Rich Harris, "Where is the child's environment? A group socialization theory of development," *Psychological Review*, vol. 102, no. 3, 1995, 332)

> Inevitably, children's relationships with their siblings are unequal. In most cases, the elder is the leader; the younger is the follower. The elder attempts to dominate, the younger to avoid domination. Peer relationships are different; peers are more equal, and often more compatible, than siblings. Among American children, conflict and hostility erupt far more frequently among siblings than among peers.
>
> (Judith Rich Harris, *The Nurture Assumption: Why Children Turn Out the Way They Do*, New York, 1998, 61)

Not only are the parenthetical references to scholarship absent from the second passage above; the vocabulary is also far less abstract, and the syntax is much simpler. Like all disciplines, psychology has developed a special vocabulary involving not only terms specific to the discipline (e.g., *dominance hierarchies*) but also habits of using particular words with great frequency (*salience* is a word that psychologists and social scientists generally find very useful, for example). Psychologists also often use variants of common English words in ways peculiar to the discipline; they tend, for example, to use the plural form *behaviours*, whereas people outside the discipline of psychology tend to use *behaviour* only in its singular form.

Psychologists tend to use the past tense when reporting on the methods they have followed and the results they have obtained in an experiment. They use the present tense, however, when discussing what the evidence shows about human behaviour. They also often use the present perfect tense when reporting on the findings of other research (e.g., *Barclay and Jones have found that ...*).

CITATION AND DOCUMENTATION

Not surprisingly, writing in psychology usually follows APA (American Psychological Association) Style. See section C3.2 for a full discussion of this citation style.

Sociology

The discipline of sociology is often said to divide into two broad streams. One of these, the positivist tradition (with roots going back to the classic work of Emile Durkheim) emphasizes empirical studies and employs methods that have much in common with those of the natural sciences. The writing style favoured by most sociologists writing in this tradition tends to be purposefully dry in tone (no matter how striking or provocative the information presented may be), and to be written in syntactically straightforward sentences. Such writing employs the present tense where an ongoing social situation or structure is being described, but shifts to the past tense frequently when referring to how specific studies were conducted. Here is a sample:

> In 1992, for parents with children under 19, with both spouses employed full-time, 95.9 per cent of women and 77.4 per cent of men participated in housework on a given day. In addition, for those who have children under 19, 63.7 per cent of women and 43.9 per cent of men participated in childcare (McFarlane, 1997: 73–77). Not only do employed men spend slightly less time in total productive activity than do employed women, but men's participation in unpaid work shows greater flexibility; they can more easily work around their paid work. This is probably a key factor underlying the higher stress experienced by women.
>
> (Rod Beaujot, *Earning and Caring*, Peterborough, 2000, 213)

The language of sociologists writing in this tradition is similar to that of those who employ empirical studies extensively in other social science disciplines; they often write of *controlling for various factors*, and of the *salience* of certain sorts of information. Particular to sociology is a frequent use of the noun *outcome*, including in the plural (e.g., *the study found several outcomes*).

In contrast, the interpretivist tradition of sociology, stemming largely from the classic works of Max Weber, tends to rely much less on empirical evidence—and, indeed, often to be sceptical of such evidence. It tends towards more free-flowing analyses, and makes reference far more frequently to theories and to broadly perceived social and cultural forces. In their writing style, interpretivist sociologists of the past generation have tended towards long sentences that are syntactically fairly complex, and towards abstract words that foreground their theoretical orientation. Here is a sample:

> Social theory, and more specifically post-colonial social theory, must be able to make sense of such events, which testify among other things to the cultural dynamism of peoples living in oppressive conditions. To make sense of this, it is necessary to get past a blanket notion of incommensurability between cultures. An imbalance in social power, favouring the white stream, was integral to the traditions that produced the merging of previously foreign cultural elements.
>
> (Claude Denis, *We Are Not You*, Peterborough, 1997, 157)

The author quoted above, like many (though by no means all) interpretivist sociologists, employs much of the vocabulary that theoretically oriented academic circles in the English-speaking world imported from France in the 1970s and 1980s—the style that may be loosely characterized as postmodern.

CITATION AND DOCUMENTATION

The most widely accepted style of citation and documentation is that of the American Sociological Association (ASA style). This is in many ways similar to other styles of parenthetical citation. Note, however, that page numbers may be given in the citation, in which case they are preceded by a colon:

> What Wright terms "idealized capitalism" (2000: 959) relates to the neoclassical economic model.

References are provided at the end of an essay, alphabetically by author:

> Pakulski, Jan and Malcolm Waters
> 1996 *The Death of Class*. London: Sage.
> Wright, Erik Olin
> 2000 "Working-class power, capitalist class interests, and class compromise." *American Journal of Sociology* 105: 957–1002.

C1.6 Business and Commerce

It is important, first of all, to be clear on the distinction between business writing—the writing of business letters, memos, and so on, which is covered in section C2.8—and academic writing about business and commerce. Academic styles of writing in departments or faculties of business or commerce fall into two broad categories. Much writing about business is highly technical, and resembles academic writing about economics. Here is a sample:

> A security market where the relative incidence of informed and uninformed trading determines liquidity may have more than one equilibrium. Equilibrium with high liquidity has a low bid-ask spread. This increases participation by traders who want to hedge risk exposure, as opposed to trading on private information, and justifies the small price impact of trades. Equilibrium with low liquidity has a high bid-ask spread. This deters some hedgers, increasing the relative incidence of informed trading, which justifies the larger spread. This analysis casts doubt on the relevance of comparative results in the existing literature relying on exogenous liquidity traders.
>
> (James Dow, "Is Liquidity Self-Fulfilling?" *Journal of Business*, 2004, vol. 77, no. 4, 78)

Notice that the discussion is largely couched in the present tense; the object of the study is to explore what *happens* as a general rule, not what happened in one particular case.

The other main style of academic writing about business is much less technical, and is in some respects unique to the study of business; this is the case study approach. Popularized by the Harvard Business School, this approach eschews abstract theoretical formulations and focuses instead on studies of real-world cases. Here is a sample:

> Early in its development Nestlé established production facilities outside of Switzerland. By 1986, Nestlé had plants in 60 countries. In determining whether to set up production facilities in a particular country, the company considered several factors, including the availability of raw materials, the overall economic climate, and consumer tastes and purchasing power.
>
> (W.D. Dobson and Andrew Wilcox, *How Leading International Dairy Companies Adjusted to Changes in World Markets*, Babcock Institute, University of Wisconsin, 2002, 7)

Notice here that the sentence structures are relatively simple, and that abstract language is avoided. Business case studies are often written with a view to being accessible to business people as well as to academics, and to that end often include such features as point-form "executive summaries." As one would expect, business case studies tend to be couched largely in the simple past tense—though the present perfect may be used if the writer refers to a business practice that is still current at a particular company.

CITATION AND DOCUMENTATION

Although there is no universally accepted style of citation and documentation for business and commerce, APA style is very widely used.

C2 Forms and Conventions

C2.1 The Meanings of Texts

In some respects the practice of writing about a text in the context of literary studies has a good deal in common with the practice of writing about a text in the context of other disciplines in which ideas are sometimes discussed in similar ways—philosophy, or intellectual history, or political theory, or interdisciplinary programs such as Humanities and Liberal Studies. In all these contexts, the primary focus of discussion is very frequently on what meaning(s) we draw from the text at hand. Often this is no easy task; very frequently texts have no single, clear, surface meaning, and may suggest quite different meanings to different readers.

Even many texts that convey a powerful sense of being meaningful are often resistant to efforts to pin that meaning down to anything precise and straightforward. The experience of reading *Adventures of Huckleberry Finn* is exciting, amusing, and emotionally engaging—and the book gives us a strong sense of saying something meaningful. But what is that meaning? Specifically, what does the book say to us about slavery, race, and racism? Does it, in effect, constitute a powerful argument against racism, as many have claimed? Or does it equivocate—sit on the fence, as it were, as some others have claimed, allowing or even encouraging privileged readers to feel good about themselves and their attitudes towards the injustices of the past without asking them to engage significantly with ongoing injustices?

Shakespeare's *The Merchant of Venice* is an enormously powerful story. But is it a story of a cruel and grasping moneylender receiving his comeuppance (as was presumed by Christian audiences for many centuries)? Should we read it rather as a story of anti-Semitism—of systemic cruelty against the moneylender? Or should we pay attention to those who remind us that Shylock the moneylender does not even appear in the play's final act, and read the play more for what it says about gender and about love—the love of one man for another as well as the love between a man and a woman?

W.H. Auden's poem "September 1, 1939," written just as World War II was breaking out in Europe (and now widely acknowledged to be among the most important poems in English of the twentieth century), appeals powerfully to readers in a variety of ways. Several of its lines ("a low, dishonest decade"; "those to whom evil is done / Do evil in return"; "We must love one another or die") have taken a permanent place in public discourse. But what should we take the poem to mean? Does it rate the sins of complacent democracies as poorly as the evils of psychopathic dictators such as Adolf Hitler, as some have suggested? Or is it a complex call to remain true to ideals of love as we struggle against evil?

Alongside all these questions may be questions of historical and biographical context. To what extent does it matter that *Adventures of Huckleberry Finn* is a historical novel? (When Twain wrote the book, slavery was already in the past—though many African Americans were being forced to live in conditions that approximated slavery.) To what extent does it matter that Shakespeare wrote *The Merchant of Venice* soon after the practice of lending money for interest had finally become legal in England—and in the middle of a period of more than three centuries during which Jews were banished from English soil? To what extent does it matter to the politics of "September 1, 1939" that Auden had left (some said "abandoned") Britain for America earlier in 1939?

We may often ask very similar questions about meaning, and also about historical and biographical context, when we are studying texts such as Plato's *Republic*, or Thomas More's *Utopia* or Niccolò Machiavelli's *The Prince* (texts that are more commonly taught as history or political theory than they are as literature). Are we to take the advice given to Machiavelli's Prince in a straightforward fashion? Are we to take More's Utopia to be the sort of society we should truly strive for? Or is it more appropriate to read such texts as being in whole or in part ironic?

The evidence as to how Machiavelli intended *The Prince* to be read or More intended *Utopia* to be read in the sixteenth century is no more conclusive than is the evidence as to how Twain intended *Huckleberry Finn* to be read in the nineteenth century. And there is no evidence whatsoever as to how Shakespeare intended *The Merchant of Venice* to be read or performed. We do have considerable evidence as to the effect W.H. Auden felt "September 1, 1939" would have or should have on readers—but he changed his mind on these questions repeatedly, significantly altering the poem more than once after its initial publication, and then for a period of many years not even allowing it to be reprinted. To sort out one clear view that the author had of the poem's meaning is, in the circumstances, quite impossible—and, even if we could, this would not preclude the possibility that the meanings best supported by the poem itself are not what Auden intended them to be.

Much as context may be important, then, we must also learn to look at the text of a literary work as something independent of its author—and as something open to interpretation. Moreover, we must often accept that there can never be any single interpretation of a text that can clearly be proven to be correct, and that will be accepted as correct by future eras as well as by our own.

Does that mean that any interpretation is equally valid? By no means. It would be absurd to suggest, for example, that *Adventures of Huckleberry Finn* constitutes a powerful argument for the United States to reinstitute slavery, or that "September 1, 1939" was written in support of Hitler and the Nazis. There are in every case limits to the range of reasonable arguments than can be made as to possible or plausible interpretations of a text.

Developing reasonable arguments as to how texts can or should be interpreted, then, is a central activity of literary studies. A related activity is to develop reasonable arguments as to how a text was interpreted when it was first published or performed—and to draw comparisons between the impact it had in its own time and the ways in which it is received today. Such arguments may be vitally relevant to our own situation. One might compare, for example, the reception to *Huckleberry Finn* in the America of the 1880s with the reaction to it in the same country in the twenty-first century; an essay exploring that issue might well reach the controversial conclusion that reading the novel as an anti-racist text today requires a level of historical knowledge and an understanding of the workings of irony that are beyond the reach of most teenagers—and that for those reasons the novel should not be taught at the high school level. One might argue for or against the decision of some recent editors to replace the offensive "n-word" in Twain's novel with the word "slave." Similarly, one might compare the way "September 1, 1939" was read during World War II with the way it was read in the early twenty-first century; the poem was widely reprinted in newspapers across North America following the September 11, 2001 attacks on

New York and Washington. To what extent is the poem a meaningful reference point when it comes to discussing the struggle against twenty-first-century terrorism?

Another activity within literary studies is developing arguments as to what should or should not be considered relevant to the interpretation of a literary text. If details about the author are known, when (if ever) should it be acceptable to take them into account in interpreting a text? Should it be considered relevant to how we interpret *Huckleberry Finn* that Twain as a young man briefly enlisted on the Confederate side in the Civil War, and then deserted? Should it be considered relevant that, later in life, he described the Civil War as "a blot on our history, but not as great a blot as the buying and selling of negro souls"? Should the fact that W.H. Auden was gay make a difference to how we read a line such as "We must love one another or die"?

Those questions may be interesting, but they will always be less important to how we interpret a text than the evidence within the text itself. To make a successful argument about a literary text you will need to be able to draw on evidence from within that text—which is something not a few students have difficulty figuring out how to do. Told to *refer to* the story of a work of fiction as they develop an argument in an essay, students all too easily find themselves *re-telling* the story of that work of fiction—summarizing it in their own words, while quoting selected phrases along the way. Summarizing is a useful and sometimes a necessary art, but summary can never take the place of argument. In the boxed insert below are three examples that should help to make clear the difference between summarizing part of the story of a work of literature and formulating an argument about that work of literature. All three examples are responses to the same assignment.

Framing Arguments about *Adventures of Huckleberry Finn*

> **Assignment**: Develop an argument concerning the treatment of racial issues in *Adventures of Huckleberry Finn*, and write a short essay putting forward your views. Pay particular attention to the ending of the novel (from Chapter XXXI onwards).

A) In Mark Twain's novel *Adventures of Huckleberry Finn* racial prejudice is expressed by many of the characters, among them Huck himself. After the dauphin manages to dupe Huck and sell Jim to a farmer named Silas Phelps, Huck reflects on what he should do and at first decides he should let Jim's "rightful owner" know where her runaway slave is now. Huck feels guilty for "stealing an old woman's [n-word] that hadn't ever done me no harm," and resolves to tell Miss Watson where she can find Jim. He drafts a letter to Miss Watson telling her of Jim's whereabouts, and feels "all washed clean of sin for the first time." But then he tears up the note and decides against betraying Jim. Huck recalls the good times he and Jim have shared together and thinks of how he is "the best friend old Jim ever had in the world, and the *only* one he's got now." Huck decides that he will go against what his conscience has told him, even if this means he will "go to hell." Instead, he walks to the Phelps plantation, where he meets a woman who, by coincidence, turns out to be the aunt of Huck's friend Tom Sawyer. The two have a conversation in which Tom's Aunt Sally makes it clear that she doesn't think of a Black person as a person. Pretending to be Tom, Huck is explaining why a trip on a Mississippi river steamer took longer than expected:

> "...We blowed out a cylinder-head."
> "Good gracious! anybody hurt?"
> "No'm. Killed a nigger."
> "Well, it's lucky; because sometimes people do get hurt...." (Ch. 32)

Comedy ensues when Aunt Sally goes off on a tangent, and before long the comedy becomes more complicated when Tom Sawyer appears on the scene and forms a plan to "steal" Jim; Huck is shocked that the seemingly righteous Tom could become "a *nigger stealer*." In the end the complicated plan goes wrong, but proves to have been unnecessary; Jim is freed anyway. Not much is said about the issue of race in the book's last chapter.

B) Much has been made of the frequent appearance of the "n-word" in *Adventures of Huckleberry Finn*—and of other expressions of racism, including by sympathetically portrayed characters such as Aunt Sally, who speaks with a complete lack of feeling as she directly implies that Black people are not to be classed as "people":

> "...We blowed out a cylinder-head."
> "Good gracious! anybody hurt?"
> "No'm. Killed a nigger."
> "Well, it's lucky; because sometimes people do get hurt...." (Ch. 32)

How is the reader to take such passages? To the enlightened twenty-first-century reader it may seem obvious that Aunt Sally's views are here being satirized. But is there anything in the text itself to support that reading? Is there any evidence in this case to suggest that the reader should fully reject Aunt Sally's view, and take black people and white people simply as people? Let us look at the passage immediately preceding that quoted. Before Huck catches a glimpse of Tom's Aunt Sally with her two children he sees a black woman with her two children. The two are presented in parallel fashion:

> A nigger woman come tearing out of the kitchen with a rolling-pin in her hand.... And behind the woman comes a little nigger girl and two little nigger boys, without anything on but tow-linen shirts, and they hung onto their mother's gown, and peeped out from behind her at me, bashful, the way they always do. And here comes the white woman running from the house, about forty-five or fifty year old, bareheaded, and her spinning-stick in her hand; and behind her comes her little white children, acting the same way the little niggers was doing. (Ch. 32)

The parallel is plain, and the implication should be clear; we should indeed see humans, whether black or white, simply as humans. The character of Huckleberry Finn may use the derogatory word that was universally used in his time to describe African Americans. But the sensibility behind Huck's words (and Twain's) is one that strongly encourages the reader to reject race prejudice.

C) Twain's novel *Adventures of Huckleberry Finn* is infected with racism at almost every turn. It's not only the much discussed matter of the word "nigger," which occurs over 220 times in the novel. Just as significant are conversations such as that between Huck and Tom's Aunt Sally, which make it explicit that African Americans are considered to be less than human, even by those white characters who are portrayed sympathetically in the novel. The context here is that Huck, pretending to be Tom, is explaining why a trip on a Mississippi river steamer took longer than expected:

> "... We blowed out a cylinder-head."
> "Good gracious! anybody hurt?"
> "No'm. Killed a nigger."
> "Well, it's lucky; because sometimes people do get hurt...." (Ch. 32)

Aunt Sally clearly does not regard "niggers" as equals—and there are no direct indications that we as readers should do any different. Even when Huck himself—the most sympathetically portrayed character of all—is praising Jim, he does so in racist terms; if Jim is good, he must to that extent be "white." So it is that when Tom has been wounded on the raft and Jim has said that he will refuse to leave him until a doctor is found, Huck comments approvingly of Jim: "I knowed he was white inside, and I reckoned he'd say what he did say" (Ch. 40).

No one could reasonably argue that *Adventures of Huckleberry Finn* wholeheartedly endorses all the racist views expressed by the novel's characters; it is clearly a novel of considerable complexity, and considerable irony. Indeed, various critics have argued that the text's ironic layering should lead us to read the novel as entirely discrediting the racist sentiments expressed by the novel's characters, and that the novel deserves to be read as a text that subverts racist attitudes. But such arguments presume an audience of enlightened and sophisticated readers sensitive to irony and to context. The fact is that Twain's novel has been read most frequently not by enlightened and sophisticated adults but by young children; it has been a staple of the school curriculum across North America. If we keep in mind that fact about the novel's audience, it is not unreasonable to suggest that *Adventures of Huckleberry Finn* may have done more to reinforce racist stereotypes than it has to undermine them.

The first of these is written competently enough so far as grammar and syntax are concerned. But it merely offers a recounting of various episodes from the book; it does not take a position, or develop an argument, as the assignment requires. The second and third passages, on the other hand, both put forward clear arguments relating to the novel and how it deals with the issue of race. The arguments point in very different directions, but both are well structured, and both are supported with evidence from the novel. Notice that the same quotation is used in all three passages. In the first, however, it is recounted as an incident in the story, not presented as evidence in an argument.

As was touched on above, the same sorts of textual material can in many cases count as evidence for the points you are making regardless of whether you are arguing for a particular interpretation of a novel or for a particular interpretation of a classic work of political theory. But there are also significant differences. For one thing, disciplines such as philosophy and history look to glean different sorts of meanings from classic texts. Most obviously, literary works do not always have to be discussed in the context of broad political and ethical issues in the sorts of ways we have discussed *Huckleberry Finn* (or, indeed, *The Merchant of Venice*, or "September 1, 1939"). We can read works of fiction, drama, and poetry with regard to poverty, social class, war, racial oppression, religious conflict—or any of the great ethical or social-political issues. But we can also consider what they have to say about the nature of love, or the experience of childhood, or the nuances of friendship, or the fear of death. In some cases those meanings may be quite plain to the reader—as they often are, for example, in the poems of Philip Larkin:

> They fuck you up, your mum and dad.
> They may not mean to, but they do. ("This Be the Verse")

> Life is first boredom, then fear.
> Whether or not we use it, it goes,
> And leaves what something hidden from us chose,
> And age, and then the only end of age. ("Dockery and Son")

More often than not, though, works of literature do not state meanings anything like so plainly as this. They deal very largely with those parts of our minds that we often find it difficult or impossible to neatly package meaning in this way. The meanings we experience may be hard to describe; we may experience time in ways that may have nothing to do with the clock or the calendar; our thoughts may flow one to the next in something of a jumble. Literature has the means to capture something of this experience, and to say something about it. But what it says to us in such circumstances will often be a matter of nuance. It will convey a sense of different sorts of meaning but not necessarily define them; it will suggest rather than explain.

C2.2 Meaning and Form in Literature

Literature is of course also capable of conveying various feelings that may have little or nothing to do with what we think of as "meaning." To experience literature may be to experience excitement, or joy, or fear, or amusement, or suspense, or sadness, or relief. And literature may also inspire feelings that—much as they may be connected to our experience of various emotions—are at a remove from the emotions. A sense of pleasure at how well the sounds of a poem seem to fit the sense; a pleasurable recognition of how skilfully a story has been constructed or at how vividly the characters in a play or a novel have been "brought to life." These are feelings that we refer to as aesthetic in nature. They may be closely connected to our emotional response; we may be brought to tears by a literary work while at the same time being struck by the aesthetic qualities that have helped to shape that emotional response (and to shape our sense of the work's meaning). But we nevertheless recognize the aesthetic as a distinct realm.

Can we make arguments about the emotional and the aesthetic responses that literature may prompt in the same way as we can make arguments about *Adventures of Huckleberry Finn* and race, or *The Merchant of Venice* and religion? Absolutely. Indeed, the formal qualities of a work—which might include its style, its structure, its vocabulary, its pacing, its rhythm, its realism or deliberate lack thereof—are sometimes so intertwined with its meanings that one cannot be discussed without the other. But some arguments about literature may focus on form more directly than others; literary studies is very much about being able to frame arguments on such topics as how the juxtaposition of incidental detail helps to suggest ironic meaning in *Adventures of Huckleberry Finn*, or how the narrative structure of *Heart of Darkness* affects the reader's response, or how the alternation of poetry and prose in *The Merchant of Venice* is a means both of reflecting and of resolving various tensions in the play, or how the rhythm of "September 1, 1939" (three stressed syllables per line, but no fixed pattern to the stresses, and no fixed number to the syllables) works in concert with the poem's themes.

Let us look at some other examples, and let us look at love. If we are to explore the ways in which the meanings of a literary work and the emotions it may arouse connect to its aesthetic qualities, it is hard to think of a better place to start than Alice Oswald's 1996 poem "Wedding":

> From time to time our love is like a sail
> and when the sail begins to alternate
> from tack to tack, it's like a swallowtail
> and when the swallow flies it's like a coat;
> and if the coat is yours, it has a tear
> like a wide mouth and when the mouth begins
> to draw the wind, it's like a trumpeter
> and when the trumpet blows, it blows like millions...
> and this, my love, when millions come and go
> beyond the need of us, is like a trick;
> and when the trick begins, it's like a toe
> tip-toeing on a rope, which is like luck;
> and when the luck begins, it's like a wedding,
> which is like love, which is like everything.

Is the essence of the poem to give expression to the feeling of pure joy that is so much a part of the human feeling of romantic love? Does the poem also offer an implicit endorsement of traditional marriage? Or does the poem, in its insistence that the joy of love is "like a trick," "like luck," imply a more melancholy undercurrent—that love of this sort is a matter of chance and illusion and will always be transitory? Is there perhaps a hint in the poem that the rushing whirlwind of love is inherently thoughtless, even self-centred and lover-centred to the point of irresponsibility; "millions come and go / beyond the need of us," the lover says, thereby setting to one side a whole world of hardship and need, in the self-centred way humans tend to do when consumed by romantic love. But does the poem's ending suggest a widening of love, an expansive exuberance that might include within itself all the different sorts of love, in addition to the romantic joy of two humans? It would be possible to devote an entire essay to arguing any one of these positions.

It would be possible too to devote an entire essay to arguing any one of a large number of things about the poem's form, and the ways in which form relates to content. How do the poem's rhythm and syntax work to suggest a rush of feeling? How do its images work to suggest a sense of spontaneity? The poem is a sonnet with more half-rhymes and "off-rhymes" than traditional full rhymes; in what ways is that structure of rhyme appropriate to the poem's meaning(s)? Those are just a few of the questions about this poem that might inspire essay-length answers.

Oswald's "Wedding" is an extraordinary example of a love poem; let us look briefly at an equally extraordinary poem that, on the face of it, could hardly be more different—Eavan Boland's "Against Love Poetry":

> We were married in summer, thirty years ago. I have loved you
> deeply from that moment to this. I have loved other things as well.
> Among them the idea of women's freedom. Why do I put these
> words side by side? Because I am a woman. Because marriage is not
> freedom. Therefore, every word here is written against love poetry.
> Love poetry can do no justice to this. Here, instead, is a remembered
> story from a faraway history: A great king lost a war and was paraded
> in chains through the city of his enemy. They taunted him. They
> brought his wife and children to him—he showed no emotion. They
> brought his former courtiers—he showed no emotion. They brought
> his old servant—only then did he break down and weep. I did not
> find my womanhood in the servitudes of custom. But I saw my
> humanity look back at me there. It is to mark the contradictions of
> a daily love that I have written this. Against love poetry.

Is the essence of the poem merely to reject the sorts of feelings that underlie love poetry? Does it implicitly reject the ideals of romantic love itself? To what extent and in what ways does it differentiate between romantic love and other forms of love—or between love at the moment of getting married and the love that is able to survive through a long marriage? What does the poem suggest about the struggle between love and freedom—and how does the "remembered story from a faraway history" connect to the poem's themes of love and freedom? What contradictions does the poem mark? What if anything does it suggest as to how they may be resolved in the living of our lives? The poem uses verbal structures of argument ("because…", "therefore…"); does it in fact make sense in terms of the conventions of logical argument? The poem starts off addressing another person ("We were married.... I have loved you…") but by the end seems to be addressed to a more general audience; why would this be? Again, it would be possible to devote an entire essay to answering any one of these questions.

It would be possible too to devote an entire essay to any one of a number of arguments concerning the form of the poem. Is it intrinsically a poem at all—or only a poem by extension, as it were, in that conventional love poetry is its necessary reference point? Why is it significant that the work is published as exactly fourteen lines of prose? Does the rhythm of the poem—if we may call it that—reflect in any way the content of what is being said? Does the syntax? (It is noteworthy, for example, that the piece includes numerous incomplete sentences.) The poem was originally published in a book that was also entitled *Against Love Poetry*, but within the book it was the second in a series entitled "Marriage"; what significance might there be in such nested titles? Those are just a few of the questions about this poem that might inspire essay-length answers. And we might add one more set of questions, if it were to be a long essay; to what extent are the meaning(s) suggested by Alice Oswald's "Wedding" and Eavan Boland's "Against Love Poetry" in conflict with each other? Might the ideas suggested by the two poems be to some extent complementary? How do the two poems mirror each other in their formal qualities?

How do the formal qualities of the work—the ways in which its meanings are expressed—harmonize with the meanings themselves?

Students often find it even more difficult to frame written arguments dealing with aesthetic questions—with *how* the meanings of a literary work are presented—than they do framing arguments about the meanings themselves. One fundamental question that it is always helpful to have in the back of one's mind is this: "How do the formal qualities of the work—the ways in which its meanings are expressed—harmonize with the meanings themselves?" In most literary works that reward study there will be interesting connections between the two—and these connections can often provide the subject matter for successful student essays. As in the two examples above, the ways in which the words of a poem are arranged on the page may be highly suggestive of what the poem is saying. Similarly in a work of drama or prose fiction: a layered plot or a complex narrative structure may mirror complexities of meaning in the text. The reliability or unreliability of a narrator or a shift in viewpoint may signal the underlying approach of the work towards reality itself. The style of narration may convey to us something of the nature of human consciousness. The ways in which different characters are presented may create a wide range of different reactions. In any genre, patterns of imagery or metaphor may be suggestive of broader ideas or themes—or of traits of the characters, or of character traits.

Sometimes the style of presentation may seem to go against the nature of the material being presented, or its apparent meaning; a poem about death may be written with a lively rhythm, or a character entering eagerly into a new relationship may be described in a flat and unemotional style. In a work of little literary merit dissonance of that sort between style and meaning may simply be a case of poor writing. But instances of dissonance of that sort can also occur in extraordinarily accomplished literary work; there may be tensions between form and content that lend complexity as well as vitality to literary works—and that themselves become key parts of the work's aesthetic.

One straightforward and often fruitful way to shape the "argument" of an essay about literature is simply to explain how some aspect of the form of a work expresses something of its meanings. Explain how the layered narrative structure of Mary Shelley's *Frankenstein* works to support the layers of meaning in the text. Explain how the half-rhymes and off rhymes of "Wedding" act in concert with the meanings suggested by the text. Explain what the use of verse and prose dialogue suggests about class and race dynamics in *The Merchant of Venice*. And so on. Beyond that, it may be helpful to run through the eight sets of questions that Ian Johnston provides as a prompt (see below).

Essay Ideas: How to Think about Literary Works

To organize an argumentative essay about a literary work, it's usually best to select something very particular about the work and focus your attention exclusively on that. Here is a partial list of possible choices:

1. What is the significance of a particular character or a particular moment in the career of a single character? Why is that moment important? What human possibility does that part of the fiction hold up to us? What does that moment reveal about something significant in the story? What would be missing if that moment or that character were not in the story? Often you can organize a useful interpretative essay around the contribution of an apparently minor character or event.
2. Does a particular character learn or fail to learn something important in the story? If the resolution of a narrative depends upon the education of a main character, then a major interpretative point in the story will undoubtedly be what that character has learned (or failed to learn). This question is often very fruitful if a major part of the narrative is a journey of some kind, as in *Huckleberry Finn* or *Gulliver's Travels* or *Heart of Darkness* or *The Odyssey*. Is the main character the same person at the end of the journey as at the start? If not, what has happened? Why is that significant? How does the character behave when he returns? Why?
3. What is the importance of the setting (the physical environment) or some aspect of it? How does this help to define for the readers the sense of nature presented in the text—or the sense of how the world operates, of the values of human life?
4. Is there an interesting recurring pattern in the fiction (e.g., in the treatment of women, the significance of food, the nature of work, the depiction of the gods, the images of nature, the attitude to money, the style of the clothes, and so on)? Is there one object in the story that is particularly significant?

5. Why does the story end the way it does? How does the conclusion affect our understanding of what has gone on? Is there any irony in the ending (i.e., any unresolved ambiguities)? Does that raise any questions and invite us to think about them?
6. Does the story call attention to any important ideas or themes? In what sense is there a conflict of ideas or attitudes being explored in the fiction?
7. What role does the narrator play in our response to the story? Is that voice reliable, playful, ironic? Does the narrator understand the significance of the story? How does that affect the interpretation?
8. Often a particular remark in a fiction (or the title itself) can make a useful focus for an essay (once again, a popular form of exam question or essay topic), as in, for example, one of the following:
   - What does Catherine in Brontë's *Wuthering Heights* mean by her famous remark, "Nelly, I am Heathcliff"? How does that help us to understand anything significant in the novel?
   - Discuss the significance of Conrad's title "Heart of Darkness."
   - What is significant, if anything, about Lily Briscoe's comment to herself in Woolf's *To the Lighthouse*: "Yes, she thought, laying down her brush in extreme fatigue, I have had my vision"?

And so on. Remember that in a relatively short essay you can deal only with one very particular aspect of the fiction, so select carefully, and confine the argument to the significance of that one feature you have selected. And make sure that you do not just describe what you have selected. Instead create an argumentative opinion about its significance. That will be your thesis, a statement or series of statements which says, in effect, "If we look closely at this single aspect of the fiction we can see ways in which it contributes something important to our understanding of the total story."

—excerpted from Ian Johnston, *Essays and Arguments: A Handbook for Writing Essays* (Broadview Press, 2015)

C2.3 The Text in the Present Tense

Learning to envision arguments about texts can be challenging; so too can learning how to phrase those arguments in ways that will be clear and persuasive to readers. The following two sections discuss common problems that arise in writing about literature at the level of sentence structure—and how to solve those problems. Students may also find it helpful to consult the first unit of this book ("Writing Processes") and section C1.2 above, which addresses "English Studies."

As we've seen in section C1, all academic subject areas have specialized vocabulary and conventions. One sort of convention that can take some getting used to is the way in which verb tenses are used. The past tense is, of course, normally used to name actions that happened in the past. But when one is writing about what happens in a work of literature (or, in some cases, about what is said in other sorts of texts), convention decrees that we use the simple present tense.

needs checking Romeo fell in love with Juliet as soon as he saw her.

revised Romeo falls in love with Juliet as soon as he sees her.

needs checking In her short stories, Alice Munro explored both the outer and the inner worlds of small town life.

revised In her short stories, Alice Munro explores both the outer and the inner worlds of small town life.

If literature in its historical context is being discussed, however, the simple past tense is usually the best choice:

needs checking Shakespeare writes *Romeo and Juliet* when he was about thirty years of age.

revised Shakespeare wrote *Romeo and Juliet* when he was about thirty years of age.

needs checking Alice Munro wins the 2013 Nobel Prize in Literature for mastery of the contemporary short story.

revised Alice Munro won the 2013 Nobel Prize in Literature for mastery of the contemporary short story.

In some circumstances either the past or the present tense may be possible in a sentence, depending on the context:

correct In her early work Munro often explored themes relating to adolescence.

[appropriate if the focus is on historical developments relating to the author]

also correct In her early work Munro often explores themes relating to adolescence.

[appropriate if the focus is on the work itself]

Often in an essay about literature the context may require shifting back and forth between past and present tenses. In the following passage, for example, the present tense is used except for the sentence that recounts the historical fact of Eliot refusing permission:

> T.S. Eliot's most notorious anti-Semitic remark is the opinion he expresses in *After Strange Gods* that in "the society that we desire," "any large number of free-thinking Jews" would be "undesirable" (64). Tellingly, Eliot never allowed *After Strange Gods* to be reprinted. But his anti-Semitism emerges repeatedly in his poetry as well. In "Gerontion," for example, he describes....

In such cases even experienced writers have to think carefully during the revision process about the most appropriate tense for each verb. Note in the following example the change in verb tense from *was* to *is*:

needs checking In *The Two Gentlemen of Verona* Shakespeare exhibited a degree and a variety of technical accomplishment unprecedented in the English drama. He still had much to learn as a dramatist and as a poet; in its wit or its power to move us emotionally *The Two Gentlemen of Verona* was at an enormous remove from the great works of a few years later. But already, in 1592, Shakespeare had mastered all the basic techniques of plot construction that were to sustain the structures of the great plays.

revised In *The Two Gentlemen of Verona* Shakespeare exhibits a degree and a variety of technical accomplishment unprecedented in the English drama. He still had much to learn as a dramatist and as a poet; in its wit or its power to move us emotionally *The Two Gentlemen of Verona* is at an enormous remove from the great works

> of a few years later. But already, in 1592, Shakespeare had mastered all the basic techniques of plot construction that were to sustain the structures of the great plays.

The same principles that are used in writing about literature also apply to writing about texts in many other disciplines. (Disciplines that follow APA style are the exception, preferring the past tense or the present perfect tense in such situations.) Generally, when you are treating the ideas you are discussing as "live" ideas, not just historical artifacts, it makes sense to use the present tense:

needs checking In an important recent book, Nelly Ferguson surveyed the history of the decline of empires, and predicted that during the course of the twenty-first century China will replace the United States as the world's leading power.

revised In an important recent book, Nelly Ferguson surveys the history of the decline of empires, and predicts that during the course of the twenty-first century China will replace the United States as the world's leading power.

needs checking In their 2009 paper Smith and Johnson suggested that parental influence is more important than that of peers, even for adolescents. This essay will examine these claims and assess their validity.

revised In their 2009 paper Smith and Johnson suggest that parental influence is more important than that of peers, even for adolescents. This essay will examine these claims and assess their validity.

In many disciplines, particularly in the sciences, it is also common to use the present perfect tense when discussing relevant recent research:

> Although research has often found the attitude-to-behavior connection to be quite weak, the behavior-to-attitude link has been shown to be quite strong. As Festinger (2008) and Kiesler, Nisbet, and Zanna (2006) have demonstrated, an asymmetry exists between the two possible directions. As Acheson (2009) has put it, "we are ... very good at finding reasons for what we do, but not very good at doing what we find reasons for" (25).

It is important to remember that the use of the present tense in such contexts is not dependent on how recently the ideas being discussed were first put forward; the key thing is whether or not you are discussing them as live ideas today. You may use the present tense when discussing a paper written six months ago—but you may also use the present tense when discussing a text dating from twenty-four centuries ago. Just as you may say when writing about literature that Shakespeare *explores* the potentially corrosive effects of ambition, so too you may say that Aristotle *approaches* ethical questions with an emphasis on individual virtue, and that Marx *values* highly the economic contribution of labour—even though Shakespeare and Aristotle and Marx are themselves long dead. As with the text of a story or poem, the writings of dead thinkers may be discussed as embodying live thoughts—ideas that may retain interest and relevance.

The writings of dead thinkers may be discussed as embodying live thoughts.

Conversely, if the ideas you are discussing are being considered historically, rather than as of current relevance, you should not use the present tense. A scientific theory that has been refuted is more likely to be written about as history than as a "live idea."

needs checking In several articles the renowned astronomer Fred Hoyle advances arguments against the big bang theory of the origin of the universe. Hoyle suggests that the universe perpetually regenerates itself.

[Hoyle's arguments have now been refuted.]

revised In several articles the renowned astronomer Fred Hoyle advanced arguments against the big bang theory of the origin of the universe. Hoyle suggested that the universe perpetually regenerates itself.

As is the case with writing about literature, academic writing in disciplines such as history or philosophy or political science may often look at a text *both* from a historical perspective *and* from the perspective of the live ideas that are put forward within it. In such circumstances the writer needs to be prepared to shift verb tenses depending on the context.

needs checking In *An Introduction to the Principles of Morals and Legislation*, Jeremy Bentham asked what question should be foremost in our minds as we considered how to treat non-human animals: "The question is not, Can they reason?, nor Can they talk? but, Can they suffer? Why should the law refuse its protection to any sensitive being?"

revised In *An Introduction to the Principles of Morals and Legislation*, Jeremy Bentham asks what question should be foremost in our minds as we consider how to treat non-human animals: "The question is not, Can they reason?, nor Can they talk? but, Can they suffer? Why should the law refuse its protection to any sensitive being?"

If one is writing about literature the writing will usually be in the *present* tense, but the quotations one wishes to use are likely to be in the *past* tense. Often it is thus necessary, if you are incorporating a quotation into a sentence, to rephrase and/or adjust the length of the quotation in order to preserve grammatical consistency. If a quotation is set apart from the body of your own writing, on the other hand, you do not need to (and should not) rephrase.

needs checking Emma Bovary lives largely through memory and fantasy. She daydreams frequently, and, as she reads, "the memory of the Vicomte kept her happy" (244).

[The past tense *kept* is inconsistent with the present tense *reads* and *daydreams*.]

revised Emma Bovary lives largely through memory and fantasy. She daydreams frequently, and, as she reads, the "memory of the Vicomte [keeps] her happy" (244).

or Emma Bovary lives largely through memory and fantasy. She daydreams frequently, and blends fact and fiction in her imaginings: "Always, as she read, the memory of the Vicomte kept her happy. She established a connection between him and the characters of her favorite fiction" (244).

Additional Material Online

Exercises on choosing the correct tense when writing about literature and about other academic subjects may be found at **sites.broadviewpress.com/writingcdn**. Click on **Exercises** and go to **"Verbs."**

C2.4 Authors and Speakers

A tangle of issues surrounding authorship can make it difficult to phrase sentences having to do with what an author says, or what a text says. Views expressed by a character or narrator must not be confused with those of the author, and—for works of drama, poetry, and fiction—it is important to use phrasing that focuses on what the text does rather than making assumptions about what the author might have intended. But we must also be careful of phrases such as "the book says..." that seem to grant authorial status to the text itself. Over time writers have developed a wide variety of strategies to deal with these sorts of awkwardness—to enable us to speak without obvious absurdity about the ways in which texts convey meanings. This is one area in which the passive voice often proves helpful.

needs checking In the book it says that Victor Frankenstein becomes "capable of bestowing animation upon lifeless matter" (Ch. 3).

revised Victor Frankenstein tells Robert Walton the story of how he became "capable of bestowing animation upon lifeless matter" (Ch. 3).

or In Shelley's novel the lead character, Victor Frankenstein, recounts his great scientific discovery: "I succeeded in discovering the cause of generation and life; [and] more, I became myself capable of bestowing animation upon lifeless matter" (Ch. 3).

needs checking In Genesis they give two quite different versions of the creation of Eve.

[The use of "they" when assigning responsibility where the actual people are unknown ("they should fix the potholes on this street," "they never used to do it this way," etc.) is colloquial and should be avoided in formal written work.]

revised Genesis offers us two quite different versions of the creation of Eve.

or Two quite different versions of the creation of Eve are given in Genesis.

[Notice how the passive voice ("are given") is used here.]

needs checking The poem says that the 1930s were "a low dishonest decade."

also needs checking In the poem it says that the 1930s were "a low dishonest decade."

revised In the poem's first stanza the 1930s are described as "a low dishonest decade."

[This construction, using the passive voice, can be used whether or not it is a character speaking, or the author speaking to us directly.]

or The speaker refers to the 1930s as "a low dishonest decade."

When referencing text that is not attributed to a specific character, it is conventional to use phrases such as *the speaker* (in the case of a poem) or *the narrator* (in the case of a novel) instead of saying *the poet* or *the author.* For some poems where the author does not seem to have adopted a persona—such as, arguably, "September 1, 1939"—it can be acceptable to refer to the author directly:

- Auden refers to the 1930s as "a low dishonest decade."

If you are at all in doubt it is safest to use a phrase such as "the speaker."

The next example shows the danger of equating statements in a book with the author's opinions:

needs checking In More's *Utopia* he says that landowners are "no longer content with leading an idle life and doing no harm to the country." In his view, they have now chosen to do real harm: "they leave no ground to be tilled, enclose every bit of land for pasture, pull down houses, and destroy towns."

[There are several problems here. The first is grammatical: *he* is a pronoun, and pronouns need to refer to nouns, whereas *More's* is a possessive adjective.]

still needs checking In his *Utopia* More declares that English landowners are "no longer content with leading an idle life and doing no harm to the country." In his view, they have now chosen to do real harm: "they leave no ground to be tilled, enclose every bit of land for pasture, pull down houses, and destroy towns."

[Thomas More's *Utopia* is a work of fiction in which various characters give their views; it cannot be assumed that any of the views put forward by the characters were also those of the author.]

revised In More's *Utopia* Raphael Hythloday declares that landowners are "no longer content with leading an idle life and doing no harm to the country." In Raphael's view, they have now chosen to do real harm: "they leave no ground to be tilled, enclose every bit of land for pasture, pull down houses, and destroy towns."

[Can we take this as More's own view? That question cannot be answered readily.]

needs checking The novel *The Jungle* tells us that the meatpacking industry is cruel to the workers in a wide variety of ways.

[We are not told this in so many words by the novel, as a non-fiction book or magazine article might tell us such things; rather we are shown the cruelties of the industry.]

revised The novel *The Jungle* depicts the cruel treatment of workers in the early twentieth-century meatpacking industry.

[Here the emphasis is on the novel as a work that may still speak to us today—as literature rather than a historical artifact.]

or Upton Sinclair's 1906 novel *The Jungle* depicted the cruel treatment of workers in the meatpacking industry; it had a powerful effect on public opinion.

[Here the emphasis is on the historical impact of the novel.]

Here are some other approaches to wording that may be useful as you write about texts—and try to negotiate the many issues involving what the characters have said, what the text has said, and what the author has said:

In the poem we are led to believe that …
Throughout the story we are led to sympathize with …
These lines in the poem suggest that …
The way this sentence is phrased implies that …
The fact that these deeds go unpunished at the end of the story suggests that …
The imagery in this stanza suggests that ….
Characters who make us laugh tend to be easy to relate to, and Falstaff … [*not* Characters who make us laugh tend to be easily relateable, …]

C2.5 The Scientific Research Paper

The many academic forms of writing about science include the review article (in which a writer surveys and assesses evidence on a particular topic from various sources); the research or experimental report, usually in the form of an article (in which a researcher writes up the results of an experiment of specific scope—lab reports are good practice for articles of this kind); the conference presentation or a poster board (in which scientists report in a limited or abbreviated fashion about specific research); the abstract (in which scientists provide a brief summary of the findings of a report or research paper); and the funding application, generally intended for a national or commercial grant or funding body (which usually includes an abstract and a statement of the importance of the research, along with a costing breakdown for the research).

The research paper is in many ways the paradigmatic type of scientific writing. Unlike articles in the humanities, research articles in the sciences are generally organized into specific sections that usually appear in a set order: introduction, methods, results, and discussion. The opening section of the article, the *Introduction,* tells the reader the purpose and nature of the study. How does it fit in with previous research? What has it been designed to show? What was the hypothesis? The norm is to keep the introduction fairly brief; normally, it explains a bit about the background to the paper and indicates why the research was undertaken. The paper's introduction may, in fact, include a background section or be called *Background.* While it is appropriate to position the paper in the larger context of previous research here, extended discussion of that larger picture is not normally included in the introduction.

The *Methods* section is often very detailed. An important principle is that the paper should provide enough information about how the research was set up and conducted that other researchers can replicate the results. The reader also needs enough information to be able to understand the rationale for each step in the process.

The Methods section in a scientific research paper is always written in the past tense. When you are conducting your own research, however, it can be helpful to set out the details of the process beforehand in the present and/or future tenses, and then read over your notes with a view to the larger picture. Is the research being set up in the most unbiased way possible? Can the proposed method truly be expected to provide evidence one way or the other as to whether the hypothesis is valid? Are the most useful statistical methods being used to assess the data?

The *Results* section, as its name suggests, details the results at length. It often includes tables, charts, and graphs as a way of visually presenting these results.[1] The *Discussion* section provides an analysis of the meaning of those results, both in terms of the particular experiment and in terms of past experiments in the same area. Do the results confirm or refute the original hypothesis? What questions are left unanswered? What significance does the data have in the context of other research in this area? In what ways is the research subject to drawbacks (e.g., small sample size, indeterminate findings, confounding elements, short timeframe)? Do the results prompt any recommendations for the future?

Finally, scientific papers are almost always accompanied by an abstract, which comes before the actual paper. The *Abstract* summarizes the entire paper in no more than one or two paragraphs (usually 250 words or less); it is meant to convey the essence of the research to those who may not have time to read the entire paper, or who may be trying to determine if the entire paper will be of interest to them. Abstracts are often included in searchable databases for this latter purpose.

1 *Results* and *Discussion* are usually treated as separate sections of a paper; some journals, however, will ask that they be combined into one section of the paper.

C2.6 Scientific Tone

Most contemporary natural sciences writers strive for objectivity of tone, while writers in the humanities and social sciences may foreground their own subject positions and sometimes adopt a less formal tone. Look, for example, at the way in which anthropologist Emily Martin opens her classic article on "The Egg and the Sperm":

> As an anthropologist, I am intrigued by the possibility that culture shapes how biological scientists describe what they discover about the natural world.... In the course of my research I realized that the picture of egg and sperm drawn in popular as well as scientific accounts of reproductive biology relies on stereotypes central to our cultural definitions of male and female. The stereotypes imply not only that female biological processes are less worthy than their male counterparts but also that women are less worthy than men. Part of my goal in writing this article is to shine a bright light on the gender stereotypes hidden within the scientific language of biology. Exposed in such a light, I hope they will lose their power to harm us.

Martin acknowledges at the outset that she occupies a specific position in relation to her research, and she uses the first person frequently ("I am intrigued," "I realized," "my goal"). Moreover, she acknowledges that her motive for conducting and publishing her research is not merely to expand objective knowledge about the world; she aims not only to shine a bright light on gender stereotypes, but also to reduce "their power to harm us." And yet, at its core, Martin's article is an example of careful scientific inquiry: she conducted a thorough survey of relevant scientific literature, her assessment of it follows scientific standards of objectivity, and she makes a strong argument based on clear and well-documented evidence.

Academics writing in natural science disciplines such as biology, chemistry, and physics, as well as those writing in the behavioural sciences (e.g., psychology, anthropology, sociology), all value scientific standards of objectivity and strive to make strong arguments based on strong evidence. However, differences in style and tone can be very noticeable, with the natural science disciplines tending towards a more formal and impersonal style than Martin adopts. But tone varies widely within the behavioural sciences as well; compare Martin's discussion of egg and sperm representations with the following behavioural science abstract for a 2012 scientific article that received a great deal of attention in general-interest media, "Facebook Use Predicts Declines in Subjective Well-Being in Young Adults":

> Over 500 million people interact daily with Facebook. Yet, whether Facebook use influences subjective well-being over time is unknown. We addressed this issue using experience-sampling, the most reliable method for measuring in-vivo behavior and psychological experience. We text-messaged people five times per day for two-weeks [sic] to examine how Facebook use influences the two components of subjective well-being: how people feel moment-to-moment and how satisfied they are with their lives. Our results indicate that Facebook use predicts negative shifts on both of these variables over time. The more people used Facebook at one time point, the worse they felt the next time we text-messaged them; the more they used Facebook over two-weeks, the more their life satisfaction levels declined over time. Interacting with other people "directly" did not predict these negative outcomes. They were also not moderated by the size of people's Facebook networks, their perceived supportiveness, motivation for using Facebook, gender, loneliness, self-esteem, or depression. On the surface, Facebook provides an invaluable resource for fulfilling the basic human need for social connection. Rather than enhancing well-being, however, these findings suggest that Facebook may undermine it.

There are obvious differences in tone between this passage and that by Martin quoted above. Most obviously, the writers employ terminology specific to the academic discipline in which they are writing: "subjective well-being," "predicts," "moderated by," and "negative outcomes." More generally, the abstract is much more impersonal in tone than the first paragraph of Martin's paper; the reader is not told of any moment of realization which led to these researchers' work, or of what effects they hope their research will have. Instead, the passage provides a summary of the reasons for the study, the nature of the study, the main results, and some sense of their significance—all in reasonably direct and specific prose.

But what makes it clear to a reader in its discipline? Notice first that the abstract succinctly sketches in the background and the gap in the research that it aims to fill: "Over 500 million people interact daily with Facebook. Yet, whether Facebook use influences subjective well-being over time is unknown."

We may imagine how the topic might be introduced much less succinctly:

> Facebook is used every day by people all round the world—overall, a total of more than 500 million people. There have been numerous studies that have examined Facebook use; a number of these have found correlations between high levels of Facebook use and low reported levels of subjective well-being. Those studies, however, have not tracked Facebook use and levels of subjective well-being together over time; doing so may provide a clearer picture of whether or not Facebook use does indeed negatively influence subjective well-being.

There is nothing grammatically wrong with these three sentences; they are simply long-winded, whereas in the abstract by Kross et al., everything except essential information is pared away.

Notice on the previous page, too, the relative brevity of the sentences used as the abstract opens—the first is only eight words long. Long sentences are certainly sometimes appropriate (and indeed necessary)—but in scientific writing as in other sorts, varying sentence length is a good way to help maintain reader interest.

Expressing ideas concisely and varying sentence length are two ways of making your writing clear and readable. Using parallel or balanced sentence structures is another. Notice how the parallel grammatical structures in the following sentence (*the more … the worse …; the more …, the more…*) emphasize the study's findings: "The more people used Facebook at one time point, the worse they felt the next time we text-messaged them; the more they used Facebook over two weeks, the more their life satisfaction levels declined over time."

Again, we may imagine how the same thoughts might be expressed in less readable fashion:

> Subjects who reported high levels of Facebook use at one time point also reported when we next text-messaged them that they felt worse, and this pattern was repeated over the full study, with subjects who used Facebook at high levels over the two-week

> period reporting declining levels of life satisfaction, a result that was strongest among those who reported the highest extended levels of Facebook use.

In this version the same ideas are expressed, but in far more words. Moreover, the sentence structure employed (successive subordinate clauses tacked onto a compound sentence) makes the reader work unnecessarily hard to understand what the writer is saying.

It is often imagined that complex and difficult-to-read sentence structures strike an appropriately academic tone—that direct sentences and rhetorical balance are for journalists or novelists, not students and scholars. If scientific research is important, however, then surely it's worthwhile to communicate that research in clear and readable prose.

C2.7 First Person and Active Voice

Students writing in disciplines such as biology, physics, psychology, or engineering are often advised to avoid grammatical structures associated with what might seem a subjective approach—most notably, the first person (*I* or *we*). Such advice is often also given to students writing English or history papers, and the reason is much the same: instructors want to discourage students from thinking of the writing of an academic paper as an exercise in expressing one's likes or dislikes. Unsubstantiated opinions are not appreciated in any of the academic disciplines. But how well one has supported one's argument bears no necessary relation to whether or not one has used the first person. In the Emily Martin example quoted above, Martin uses the first person extensively, but she doesn't just express an opinion; her study is supported using a lot of evidence, and the discussion itself is objective in nature.

Similarly, the abstract of the paper about Facebook by Ethan Kross et al. does not achieve its more formal and impersonal tone by avoiding the first person. Quite the contrary: Kross et al. use the first person twice in the first three sentences of the abstract: "We addressed," "We text-messaged."[1] Scientific objectivity, then, is not a matter of avoiding the first person; it is rather a matter

1 In the case of group authorship, which is very common in the sciences, the first person plural must, of course, be used.

of avoiding bias when framing one's research questions, of designing research projects intelligently and fairly, and of interpreting the results ethically.

Discussions of impersonality and objectivity in scientific writing have also often been framed in terms of the question of whether to use the active or the passive voice. For most of the twentieth century, many instructors in the natural sciences tried to train students to use the passive voice[1]—to write things like "*It* ***was decided*** *that the experiment* ***would be conducted*** *in three stages*" and "*These results* ***will be discussed*** *from several perspectives*" in order to convey a more impersonal and objective tone. However, statements in the active voice such as "*We* ***conducted*** *the experiment in three stages*" and "*We* ***will discuss*** *these results from several perspectives*" are not any more or less objective. The reader of an article knows the researchers did the experiment, so using the passive voice does not change the degree of objectivity—though it may add unnecessary words.

Indeed, while instructors in the natural sciences encouraged the passive voice, in the second half of the twentieth century many academics in English studies were reluctant to acknowledge that it had much of a part to play in academic writing—even scientific writing. In the 1990s, Andrea Lunsford and Robert Connors were playing something of a pioneering role in their discipline when they put forward the following advice in their influential handbook: "Much scientific and technical writing uses the passive voice effectively to highlight what is being studied rather than who is doing the studying." More than fifteen years later, a great many fellow writing studies scholars and composition teachers would give the same advice. Interestingly, just as handbook authors began to acknowledge that there could be a particular place for the passive voice in scientific writing, the scientific community began to swing around to the view that, much as the passive might sometimes have its place, the active voice should be the default writing choice. Here is Randy Moore, writing in *The American Biology Teacher* in 1991:

1 As Randy Moore and others have pointed out, nineteenth-century scientists used the active voice and the first person freely. The active voice and "first-person pronouns such as *I* and *we* began to disappear from scientific writing in the United States in the 1920s."

> The notion that passive voice ensures objectivity is ridiculous[; ...] objectivity has nothing to do with one's writing style or with personal pronouns. Objectivity in science results from the choice of subjects, facts that you choose to include or omit, sampling techniques, and how you state your conclusions. Scientific objectivity is a personal trait unrelated to writing.

The 1990s saw heated debates in the pages of certain scientific journals on the matter of whether the active or the passive should be the default. But in the end the decision was clear: the active voice was the best choice. Nearly every major scientific journal[1] now recommends that its authors use the active voice in most situations—and that they use the first person where appropriate as well. The various *Nature* journals, the *American Chemical Society Style Guide*, and the *American Society of Civil Engineers Style Guide* are representative. The following instructions are from their respective websites:

> *Nature* journals prefer authors to write in the active voice ("we performed the experiment ...") as experience has shown that readers find concepts and results to be conveyed more clearly if written directly. (*Nature*)

> Use the active voice when it is less wordy and more direct than the passive.... Use first person when it helps to keep your meaning clear and to express a purpose or a decision. (*ACS Style Guide*)

> Wherever possible, use active verbs that demonstrate what is being done and who is doing it....
>
> *Instead of:* Six possible causes of failure were identified in the forensic investigation.
>
> *Use:* The forensic investigation identified six possible causes of failure. (*ASCE Style Guide*)

Though the active voice is better as a default choice, in some circumstances it can still be better to use the passive. Especially in scientific writing, the passive voice is useful in many ways, including as a way of shifting attention away from the researcher to the experiment itself. Indeed, the following examples show clearly the types of statements that make effective use of the passive:

---

1 On his blog in 2012, Allen Downey conducted an informal survey and was able to identify only three exceptions: the *ICES Journal of Marine Science*, the *Journal of Animal Ecology*, and *Clinical Oncology and Cancer Research*.

- The cooling process was completed in approximately two hours.
- This compound is made up of three elements.
- Phenomena of this sort may be seen only during an eclipse.

Problems arise, however, when use of the passive reduces clarity or when the passive is used to disguise responsibility. Consider the following sentence in the passive voice, taken from the opening of a scientific article by Toby Knowles et al. from a 2007 PLOS ONE article entitled "Leg Disorders in Broiler Chickens": "Broiler chickens have been subjected to intense genetic selection." That is to say, they have been bred to grow so fast and become so heavy that they can barely walk. But this has not just happened; humans have done this to the birds, as part of a broad-based effort to generate more meat less expensively—too often, with little or no thought given to the birds themselves as sentient creatures. Here, the article's use of the passive voice de-emphasizes responsibility.

Yet the disguising or downplaying of agency—of just who is responsible for an action—is something that may be accomplished through a variety of verbal means. It need not be a matter of using the passive voice. Consider this example from another piece of scientific writing: Jeff Downing's "Non-invasive Assessment of Stress in Commercial Housing Systems": "hens need to deal with [challenges] in their environment.... In any flock there are likely to be some hens that perceive the challenges as more severe than others and have high corticosterone concentrations." In Downing's sentences, the hens are, in terms of grammatical voice, the active parties; they are the subjects of the verbs: "*hens* ***need***," "*hens* [...] ***perceive*** *the challenges*." But of course the controlling agents here in any sense other than a grammatical one are not the birds; it is humans who have subjected them to these "challenges"—if that euphemism is to be accepted. "Hardships," "privations," or "cruelties" are some of the other nouns that might be substituted for "challenges."

It would seem, then, that there is nothing pernicious in the passive voice itself. The passive voice is one means that *may* be used to disguise agency—and it is also a verbal construction that *may* involve unnecessary or inappropriate wordiness. If either is the case, if is often better to rephrase.

C2.8 Writing in the Workplace

Tone may be the most important aspect of business writing. The adjective *businesslike* conjures up images of efficiency and professional distance, and certainly it is appropriate to convey those qualities in most business reports, memos, and correspondence. In a great deal of business writing, however, it is also desirable to convey a warm personal tone; striking the right balance between the personal and the professionally distanced is at the heart of the art of business writing. A few guidelines are offered here.

Perhaps the best guard against significant errors in tone is to consult your colleagues whenever you are uncertain. Circulate a draft of any important document to others and ask their opinion. Is the tone too cold and formal? Is it too gushy and enthusiastic? Is it too direct? Or not direct enough?

needs checking Do you think it's fair to ask the accounts department to handle the extra work that would be entailed in moving to your new system? Get serious!

revised If we adopted the proposed new plan, there would be questions of fairness involved that I think would need to be addressed. The accounts staff is seriously concerned that the proposed new plan would entail significantly more work for them, while there appear to be no provisions for additional staff or compensation in the accounts area.

Perhaps because a direct and forceful style is often highly valued in business writing, it's easy to be *too* forceful. Bald statements are often not the most appropriate; it is better to qualify any generalizations you are making so as to be certain they are accurate. Be particularly careful about suggesting you are speaking for your entire organization; unless you are sure, you are well advised to qualify any extreme statements.

needs checking Our organization always underprices every competitor.

revised Our organization always tries to keep its prices lower than those of major competitors.

needs checking There is no way our organization would ever cut back on research and development.

revised As an organization we have a strong commitment to research and development.

Courtesy and Consideration

Given that business communication usually operates within a hierarchical power structure, it is particularly important to foreground consideration in business memos, letters, and e-mails. Avoid direct commands wherever possible; give credit to others when things go right; and take responsibility and apologize when things go wrong.

needs checking Here is the material we spoke of. Send the report in by the end of the month to my attention.

revised I enclose the material we spoke of. If you could send in the report by the end of the month to my attention, I'd be very grateful.

needs checking I am writing in response to your complaint. We carry a large number of products with similar titles, and sometimes errors in shipping occur. Please in future specify the ISBN of the item you are ordering, as that will help keep errors to a minimum.

revised Thank you for your letter—and my sincere apologies on behalf of our company for our mistake. As you may know, we carry a large number of products with similar titles, and (particularly in cases where our customer service department is not able to double-check against an ISBN) errors do sometimes occur. But that is an explanation rather than an excuse; I do apologize, and I have asked that the correct item be shipped to you immediately. Again, my sincere apologies—and my thanks to you for drawing this matter to my attention.

needs checking It has come to my attention that you have not been filling in your expense forms promptly. I would remind you that all employees are to submit expense forms within one week of the end of the month in which the expenses were incurred. Please comply from now on.

revised Harry, could you please make sure to submit your expense forms on time? I know it can be a pain to fill in these forms, but it really makes a difference to Carol and the others in accounts so that they can keep proper

> records month to month. If they have to go back into the records to make adjustments it can end up consuming an awful lot of their time. Thank you. I appreciate the effort—as I know Carol does too.

Memos

The memorandum or memo is a standard form of communication within an organization. In order to retain the attention of readers, memos are usually kept brief. (If a large volume of material is to be dealt with, it may be better to present the material in the form of a report, with a covering memo summarizing the key points or recommendations for action.)

Memos should follow a conventional format, whether on paper or in electronic form. See sites.broadviewpress.com/writingcdn for a sample memo.

Email

While there is general agreement that email is a relatively informal medium of communication, there is little consensus as to *how* informal it should be. In the workplace, it is always better to err on the side of being more rather than less formal in your emails whenever you are uncertain. As a general principle to follow, we would suggest that you always try to put yourself in the shoes of whoever will be receiving your email. That's a very different thing from acting according to the maxim *do unto others as you would have them do unto you*. You may well prefer to receive messages with only "Hey!" as a salutation (or with no salutation at all), but you will be well advised not to presume that others in the workplace feel the same. Try to think not only of the position but also of the temperament of the person you are emailing. If it's someone high up in the organization who you know to be always very busy and very formal in style, write your message accordingly. If it's an email to a young colleague who you know prefers that things be kept informal, then you can bring down the level of formality a bit. Even in this latter context, though, you should write in a style appropriate to your organization—a style that would not seem in any way embarrassing to you if your supervisor were to read what you had written.

These principles apply equally within your own workplace and when you are writing to people outside of your organization.

needs checking Hey, Barbara Lewis. My name is Harry Phelps and I am writing from Broadview Press. I'd really like to tell you about some new books that I'm hoping you'll choose as textbooks for your courses.

revised Dear Professor Smith

I gather you are scheduled to teach the Philosophy 200 "Knowledge and Reality" course next term. It's in that connection that I'm writing now; we at Broadview have just published a new anthology in this area that I thought might be of interest.

PROOFREADING

Before you hit *Send*, imagine yourself to be the person reading what you write.

It's too often assumed that, as an informal means of communication, emails or texts don't require proofreading. That may well be the case if you are dashing off a message of no more than a few words to a trusted colleague who is also a close friend. For anything beyond that, however, it's very important to read over your messages carefully before you send them—not only in order to catch and correct typos, but also to be sure that you are saying what you want to say clearly (and that you have not made any mistakes that might be embarrassing!).

SALUTATIONS

Opinions differ widely as to whether or not one should always include a salutation in an email. As a general rule, you should—though with internal workplace communications you may omit the salutation if you are confident your recipient is comfortable with that level of informality.

In writing someone outside your organization (or someone high up in your organization's hierarchy who you do not know well), it's advisable to use the same sort of formal salutation you would in a formal letter: Dear Ms. Jenkins; Dear Professor Ahmed; etc. In responding to an email you have received, it's good practice to follow the style of salutation that the writer has followed. If she has written *Hello Christine* and signed off as *Julia*, it is appropriate to respond *Hello Julia* and sign your message *Christine*.

LENGTH OF EMAILS

Understandably enough, many people don't like to receive very long emails; everyone is busy, and it can take a good deal of time even to skim through a very long message to pick out the main points. But it's sometimes important in any organization to communicate through longer documents, particularly when the matter at hand is complex. There is more than one way to resolve the resulting tension. One is to provide a summary of the contents of your email in the first paragraph, and then do everything possible (short paragraphs, bulleted points, etc.) to make things easier for your reader. Another (and in many ways preferable) approach is to include nothing beyond the short summary in your email and include a longer document with all the details as an attachment. (If you are taking this second approach, it is still advisable to do everything you can to make the document readable, of course.)

CC–ING

In any workplace, uncertainties may arise as to how many people you should send an email to—and, of these, who should be included in the main list of recipients, and who should be cc–ed. To a certain extent, the same core principle discussed above applies here: try to put yourself in the shoes of the recipient. If you know someone in your organization to be particularly concerned about being "kept in the loop," it's likely to be advisable to at least cc that person, even if any connection to their own responsibilities is minimal. If someone else, on the other hand, is always complaining about receiving too many emails and opining that everyone should be able to just get on with the work in their own area without telling everyone else about it, you are probably well advised to leave that person off the list of those cc–ed. But a person's responsibilities in an organization matter too—in this respect as in others. If you are sending an email about something that is directly relevant to another department in your organization, you should always copy in the appropriate people in that department, even if they have indicated a preference for receiving as few emails as possible.

In deciding who to cc and who to include among your addressees, you should try to think of the efficient use of everyone's time; if someone may be interested in what you are communicating but is not directly concerned, that person should be cc–ed rather than included among the addressees.

With multiple recipients and multiple senders, it's always good to pay close attention to which email addresses appear on which line. If, for example, you receive an email signed by two people, you should make sure when you reply that both those people are listed as recipients of your email. Similarly, when an email is sent by an individual to you and to another person in your organization, and you are the one to reply, you will need to cc the other addressee when you send your response. (Where others are cc–ed and you use *Reply All*, you will need to remove your colleague from the addressee line, and add him or her to the cc line.)

THE DANGERS OF *FORWARD* AND *REPLY ALL*

It's all too easy to make embarrassing mistakes with email by hitting *Reply All* when you meant to hit *Reply*, or by forwarding a message and forgetting that the thread you are forwarding may include confidential information which one or more recipients should not be privy to—or may include uncomplimentary remarks about one or more of the individuals involved. In order to avoid these sorts of embarrassments (and also in the interests of fostering a workplace environment of respect and goodwill) a good habit to cultivate is not to commit to writing anything you would be embarrassed to have a colleague or a client discover that you have said.

RESPONSE TIME

When electronic communication was in its infancy and people were still sending many formal communications by mail, it was common to expect that any email could and should be answered within a few hours. As the volume of email and the pressures on people's time have increased, such expectations have altered considerably. In many contexts it is now considered acceptable to take a week or more to reply to certain sorts of email. But again, context matters—as do the preferences of the people you are communicating with.

Here are two samples of the sort of response that it's quite appropriate to send a week or more after you receive certain sorts of email.

Hi Carlos

Many thanks for yours of last Wednesday. I wanted to be sure that I had thought through the implications of what you propose before I replied. I've done that now, and on balance I think your proposal is a good one. I have addressed some of the details point by point in the attached document (also pasted in below). I wonder if we could set up a meeting later this week to try to come to a decision. Perhaps via Zoom, this Thursday at 2 Eastern / 11 Pacific? Friday at the same time would also work for me. All the best,

Daphne

Dear Harriet

My apologies for having taken a good deal of time to respond to your very interesting email. I'm afraid it's been a very busy week, and I also wanted to take some time to think through your suggestions. I've had a chance to do that now, but it may still be some time before I can give you an absolutely definite answer; I'm going to have to meet with a few colleagues to be sure we are all on the same page before deciding to go ahead. My hope is that I can get back to you by the end of next week with confirmation that we will move forward; certainly I will try my best to do that. With my very best wishes,

Abigail

SUBJECT LINE

It may seem an obvious point that one should include a subject line appropriate to what you are writing in an email, but many organizational communications are derailed because people forget the obvious. If a new subject is introduced at the end of an email thread, and you want to communicate with the same people about this subject, take the extra ten seconds to change the subject line, or begin an entirely new thread for the discussion of the new subject. If you don't, there's a real possibility that a busy recipient, seeing yet another email apparently concerning a matter that has already been decided, may not even open the email.

Using an appropriate subject line is also a real help to everyone concerned when it comes to trying to locate the email weeks or months later; everyone relies from time to time on searches for a keyword relating to a subject dealt with in email correspondence.

EMAILS ABOUT SCHEDULING

Much as people often complain about time wasted in meetings, almost as much time can sometimes be wasted in setting up meetings. Here are some suggestions as to how to cut down on that wasted time.

If you are emailing several people to try to set up a meeting, suggest more than one possible time. And check people's schedules on your organization's shared calendar to make sure you suggest times when others are likely to be free.

If you are one of, say, eight recipients of a message asking what time(s) would work for a meeting, use *Reply*—not *Reply All.* There is no need for all the recipients to know that you can make it on the Tuesday but not the Wednesday; let the organizer of the meeting sort all that out, and you can reduce needless proliferation of emails.

Letters

It is now considered appropriate to send out almost all business communications electronically. In most jurisdictions, it is considered acceptable in most cases to send even signed contracts electronically. When formal letters are sent, it is also considered acceptable in most cases to send these as PDF attachments to a short email. In some contexts, however, it is still considered preferable to send such documents through the mail. And in almost any context it is appropriate to send a personal thank-you to a colleague or contact by mail.

Remember that all letters sent by mail—and all formal letters sent as PDF attachments—should be signed by hand above the sender's printed name.

Résumés and Application Letters

As suggested by the word *résumé* itself, which is French and means "summarized," most résumés should be kept short—one or two pages. They usually include categories of experience (Education, Employment, etc.) and/or skills (Research Skills; Management Skills; etc.) and are organized chronologically (in reverse order, so that the most recent accomplishments or occupations are listed first). Although it is sometimes used interchangeably with *résumé*, the initialism CV really means something different. It is short for the Latin *Curriculum Vitae*, or, roughly, *the course of life*—which suggests a comprehensive accounting of one's education, experience, and accomplishments. A CV may be as many pages as is required (and will likely grow longer through the course of one's life). In North America, a CV is most often requested of applicants to professional positions in academia or science or medicine; a résumé is usually expected otherwise, especially in the business world. In the UK, however, *CV* generally means a one or two page document, and the term *résumé* is less frequently used. Both are usually submitted accompanied by a cover letter, which should be kept brief, businesslike, and free of puffery (some fields, particularly in academia, have very specific templates for cover letters). See page 550 for a sample cover letter and page 551 for a sample résumé.

Business Reports, Plans, and Proposals

Documents such as these often begin with an *executive summary*—a concise summary prepared for the benefit of executives or others who do not have time to read the full document. In any business report, plan, or proposal, it is recommended practice to keep sentences and paragraphs brief, and to come directly to the point. Frequent headings are common—again, as a means of helping busy readers to navigate the document quickly and easily. For the same reason it is sometimes recommended practice to highlight the topic sentence in each paragraph, and it's common to present material in bulleted point form. The inclusion of visual material—charts, graphs, and diagrams that can often convey a point more quickly than words—is generally encouraged. Sometimes reports, plans, and proposals are presented in the form of memoranda (see above). See sites.broadviewpress.com/writingcdn for a sample opening of a business report.

Additional Material Online

Sample memos and business reports may be found at **sites.broadviewpress.com/writingcdn**. Click on **Writing Samples** and go to **"Writing in the Workplace."**

Joseph Alvarez
316 7th St. NW
Calgary, AB T2N 1N3
joseph.alvarez@hotmail.com

Ms. Dorothy Rosenberg
Personnel Dept.
Golden Mountain Resort
1212 James St.
Golden, BC V2R 4K5

April 3, 2022

Dear Ms. Rosenberg

I am writing to apply for employment at the Golden Mountain Resort this coming summer.

A résumé is enclosed; as you see, I have previous experience working outdoors as a guide, and I would certainly be interested in something similar this summer. I am also nearing completion of a university degree in English, and I would be particularly interested in any work there that might involve written communication.

My university classes are on Mondays, Wednesdays, and Fridays; I could come to Golden for an interview on any Tuesday or Thursday, and could probably make arrangements for another day if that were more convenient for you.

I can be reached either at the above address and e-mail address or by phone at (403) 283-8550; I will hope to hear from you. With best wishes,

Yours sincerely

Joseph Alvarez
encl.

Résumé
Joseph Alvarez • 316 7th St. NW
Calgary AB T2N 1N3 • (403) 283-8550
joseph.alvarez@hotmail.com

Education:

University of Calgary (2019–present)
- Two years completed towards a BA (Hons), English Literature
- Irene Stitt Scholarship, 2019–20

John A. Macdonald Secondary School
- Graduation Diploma, 2019

Employment:

Larry's Books (2019–2021)
Employer: Lawrence McPage
Position: Bookstore Clerk
- Maintained a well-stocked, organized book department
- Assisted customers with questions and special requests
- Used computer system to update inventory, place orders, and perform returns

Infinity Research (2017–2018)
Employer: Jane Rich
Position: Survey Assistant
- Conducted surveys by phone and email in a friendly and efficient manner
- Reorganized and updated office records

Other Activities:

- Sports Editor, UC News Campus Newspaper, 2018–19
- Captain, Senior Basketball Team, John A. Macdonald Secondary School, 2019
- Member, Debating Team, John A. Macdonald Secondary School, 2019

References available upon request.

Prof. Elizabeth Jones
Department of English
Faculty of Arts & Social Sciences
Loyola University
Ames, Iowa 64223

March 22, 2022

Dear Prof. Jones

Many thanks indeed for the proposal from you and Gary Collins for a new annotated edition of selected poems by Emily Dickinson.

As with all proposals for our Broadview Editions series, this one will go to outside reviewers before being brought to a meeting of our Humanities Editorial Board; the process typically takes two to three months before a formal decision is reached. I gather, however, that you are planning in the near future to apply for a grant to assist in research connected to this project. With that in mind I would like to say that we at Broadview have read through the proposal and find it extremely impressive. Certainly we are convinced that a market exists for a good edition of this sort, and I find it almost unimaginable that outside reviewers and Editorial Board members will not feel (as I do) that this is a very good proposal indeed. I fully expect as well as hope that it will move forward to publication with Broadview! With all best wishes,

Yours sincerely,

Don LePan
Director, Special Projects

C2.9 Informal and Personal Writing

Writing guides for undergraduates tend for the most part to focus (as this one does) on the processes involved in researching and writing academic essays—essays that engage in academic analysis and that make an academic argument. That's understandable, given that such a high percentage of undergraduate writing is indeed academic in character. But in the broader world most writing is not academic writing—and the processes of writing that are involved in non-scholarly contexts can be quite different from those that work best in writing academic papers.

How does one go about writing an essay—or a blog post—that is based on one's own experience? What about an informal essay that aims to provide a profile of another person's life and character, or of a particular place, or of a type of activity (bicycling, playing shortstop, praying)? Or a review, in which you try to convey your personal response to a film or book or play or television program, while at the same time giving a recommendation to others? Or a piece of writing that aims to say something in an informal, reflective way about a general topic (youth and age, life and death) or a particular cultural practice (painting murals in Lompoc, California; spending time on Instagram or TikTok, wearing make-up)?

An academic research paper presenting an argument must follow logical patterns. Logic certainly plays a part in structuring informal and personal writing as well—indeed, it's a vitally important element whenever informal writing attempts to persuade the reader. But logic is only a small part of the picture in most informal writing. A personal essay—even a personal essay that seeks to persuade the reader of something—is just as likely to employ anecdote and personal reflection as it is to employ step-by-step analysis. And whatever conclusions the writer draws are as likely to be based on personal experience, emotion, and intuition as they are on logical deduction or empirical evidence. If pieces of personal writing do try to persuade their readers of anything, they tend to do so through suggesting and evoking at least as much as they do through arguing; rather than being designed to demonstrate points conclusively, they are more often structured to raise questions, to spark interest, and to engage the reader imaginatively and emotionally.

C2.9.1 Purpose and Inquiry: Finding a Topic and Getting Started

How does a piece of writing happen? The final result may be a personal essay about something that happened between you and other members of your family, or a blog post about why you have grown to hate the New York Yankees, or a reflective piece about how watching *Wonder Woman* made you feel about women and men generally. But how do you get there? How do you get started?

To that question—frustratingly for many students—there is no one right answer. There is no more a single right process to follow in beginning to draft a good personal essay than there is one right process to follow in generating ideas for a research paper or argumentative essay. At one extreme is someone like Stephen Greenblatt, a literary scholar whose books and essays aimed at a general audience have been as widely praised as have been his scholarly monographs. Greenblatt has said that he works entirely without an outline:

> For the most part, I work sentence by sentence—that is, not with a list of key words, a set of phrases, or an outline and not, alas, in a great rush of feverish insight. If—as occasionally happens—I see my way forward, I scribble a list of places I hope to go, and sometimes that helps. But almost always for me it is one sentence at a time (often rewriting the same sentence over and over again). (Interview, *Writing Routines* website)

For this distinguished author, then, "the writing process" consists simply of working sentence by sentence and word by word, until a completed piece of writing emerges.

Needless to say, that's an approach to writing that wouldn't work well for most of us today. Most of us find it helpful to engage in some form of very rough writing when we start in on an assignment—perhaps writing very rough notes, perhaps beginning very rough drafts of different sections of the piece, without any thought as to how they might come together. Many find freewriting helpful as a first step—writing whatever comes into your head, without stopping, for a certain number of words or pages. At this stage, no idea is unworthy—the point is simply to write. (A variation of freewriting is "invisible writing": writing with one's eyes closed or the monitor switched off.) The result might be mostly unusable—or it might point in intriguing directions.

As you start to sense how a piece might be organized, it may be helpful to write a sketch—a very short rough draft that moves in the direction of what we think may form a complete piece. You may also find it helpful to write a very rough first draft on paper, freehand, leaving very wide margins, so that you can periodically jot down notes in the margin—phrases that may be useful at a future point in the piece, or points that you think you may want to include later. (Alternatively, you can take a similar approach with your computer, using the marginal comments function.) Until you've tried several different approaches, it may be hard for you to know what will work best for you. And you may well find that the process that works best for you will vary depending on the assignment. One approach may work wonderfully well for writing an essay of personal reminiscence, while another approach may turn out to suit you better if you are writing a review of a book or film, and yet another approach may seem right if you are trying to write a term paper for your history course.

The authors of this book, then, do not prescribe any one approach. We do encourage you, though, to follow the direction of your instructor; if your instructor recommends freewriting as an initial step for an assignment, or recommends writing a sketch as a first step, or recommends an outline, follow that approach; almost certainly she or he has a very good reason for recommending it!

But what if your instructor gives you an assignment that puts the onus on *you* to find a topic? What if you are asked to write a piece of 1,000 words, focusing on a personal experience of any sort? Or an essay of 750 words on any topic you care about deeply?

Caring about your topic, in fact, matters a great deal in the context of almost any piece of informal or personal writing. It's not easy to write something that the reader will find interesting if you're not much interested in the topic yourself. One way to begin the process of writing an informal piece, then, is simply to ask yourself what matters to you, or what you find interesting, and start there. It might be a relative or a friend or an acquaintance who means a great deal to you and who has expressed that in some remarkable fashion. It might be something remarkable you have witnessed—or have done yourself. It might be a movie or a television program or a book that has affected you deeply.

You might also try to frame a topic under the heading of something that you believe—that you believe to be true and important, or that you are in some way or another committed to. In the 1950s one of the most famous reporters of the Second World War, Edward Murrow, took to the peacetime airwaves as host of a radio program entitled *This I Believe*, on which a wide variety of individuals—famous and not-so-famous—tried to "distill into a few minutes the guiding principles by which they lived." In that tradition grew up the "This I Believe" Organization, which invites people to write 500 words on a subject that truly matters to them. As you might expect, many such essays focus on overarching religious or ethical principles. But people write as well on baseball and basketball, on their pets, on aspects of nature, on pieces of music that have made a difference to them—on thousands of different topics. The key is that they have a powerful motivation to write, because they care deeply about the subject matter. Nothing is more important to informal writing. If you don't much care about your subject, it will be immensely more difficult to give your writing the sort of focus that will lead the reader to care about your subject.

Often, though, that process turns out to be less straightforward than you might think. You might find yourself thinking after having written a few sentences *Wait! Do I really believe that any more?* Or you might ask yourself, *Do I believe all this without reservation?* You might start writing on your belief that playing team sports builds character and then start wondering if playing team sports might also sometimes foster an atmosphere of exclusion and elitism. Or you might start writing on the importance to you of the principle of free speech and find yourself wondering what limits there should be on what we say about one another.

If that turns out to be the case, the authors of this book would strongly advise against trying to squash your doubts in order to keep your writing going in the direction you had first intended. Instead, we suggest you ask *Why am I having these doubts?*—**and keep writing as you try to answer that question.** Through such processes, writing becomes a form of enquiry—in this case, a way of trying to understand our own doubts as well as our own beliefs. The sketch or first draft you end up with through this approach may be far less coherent or far less focused than the straightforward statement of belief you had expected to write. But it may also hold within it the germ of a piece of writing that could turn out to be far more interesting—to you as well as to your audience. You may well end up

"je suis moi-même la matière de mon livre."

The roots of many of today's various forms of informal, personal writing can be traced to the writings of sixteenth-century French writer Michel de Montaigne. Montaigne wrote short pieces on a wide variety of broad topics (marriage, education, sleep, conscience, sadness, books, cannibalism—to name but a few). More often than not, Montaigne's essays explore an idea rather than set out an argument in favour of a predetermined position. Montaigne saw writing of this sort less as a means of persuading the reader to adopt a certain conclusion than as a means of trying to grope one's way towards understanding. Hence the name he gave to these short pieces—*essais*, or, in English, *attempts*, *tries*. (The connection is a direct one; among its definitions of "essay" the *Oxford English Dictionary* offers the following: "the action or process of trying or testing.") And always, while attempting to understand some aspect of an idea or of the world, Montaigne was attempting to understand himself—reflecting on his own thoughts, impulses, and desires. In the preface to *Essais* (the book in which his collected essays were published), Montaigne famously declared, "lecteur, je suis moi-même la matière de mon livre" ("reader, I am myself the subject of my book"). In all these respects—the looseness of structure, the vision of writing as a means of groping towards understanding, the tendency to use writing to explore the outside world and the self simultaneously—Montaigne's writing continues to exert a powerful influence on literary non-fiction.

with enough raw material for two or more essays, and end up having to pare down your raw material in order to focus it in one direction or another. But you will be engaging in a process of exploration that is far more likely to be of interest to you (and to your reader) than if you take writing to be simply a process of putting thoughts that are already in your head onto a computer screen or a piece of paper. Writing can be many things, but one of the most important is surely a process of enquiry.

This last point touches on another point of importance about many forms of personal and informal writing: the writer themself may well be the primary or the only intended audience for the work. Whereas academic writing is almost always composed with an academic audience in mind (whether that audience be made up of researchers, students, or simply the course instructor), we often compose pieces of personal writing with no audience other than ourselves in mind. Perhaps we keep a diary or a journal; perhaps we recount our experiences on a special trip so that we'll be able to recall the trip vividly years from now; perhaps we make a regular practice of writing down our thoughts and reflections just to hone our appreciation of the world around us. The difference that such writing can make is highlighted in the student comments that this instructor received from students after giving them an unusual assignment:

> Teaching Virginia Woolf's *Mrs. Dalloway*, I asked my students to leave the class one day, walk around Manhattan for 30 minutes, pay attention to everything they observed, felt, and thought, and then write about it. Afterward, they told me they were surprised by how much seemed to happen during the interval: time stretched out, individual moments thickened, and they noticed things a block away that they had never seen before. Several commented that they generally spend too much time trying to get places and not enough time appreciating the world around them. (Timothy Aubry, Letter to *The Los Angeles Review of Books*, 20 December 2018)

It's a point worth emphasizing: much as personal and informal writing is a vitally important way in which humans communicate with one another, it can also be a wonderful way to communicate with yourself, and to expand the ways in which you appreciate the world.

C2.9.2 Informal and Personal Writing in a Digital World

Unlike academic writing, personal and informal writing need not conform to the conventions of an academic discipline. It can take many forms and have many different sorts of audience—nowadays perhaps more than ever before. Reflections that a generation ago might have remained in a writer's journal and have had an audience of one or two are now more likely to be posted on a blog or on a social networking site, and have an audience of entirely unpredictable size—perhaps a handful of friends, perhaps thousands or even millions of strangers.

The new technologies of reading and writing have brought with them enormous change. That they have revolutionized the process of revising written work (including revising in ways that entail a complete reorganization) is unquestionable; in the not-too-distant past "cut and paste" meant exactly that: cut up your written work into pieces, paste or tape it together again in whatever order you concluded was the best—and then re-type everything. Revolutionary as well is the degree to which today's informal and impersonal writing is *public*. It's vitally important for those writing personal reflections on a blog or in a Facebook post to be aware of their potential audience in certain cautionary ways. Someone a generation ago who wrote a diary entry about the behaviour of certain friends was not risking the loss of those friends, or a barrage of cyber-bullying, or the threat of legal action—all of which can happen to those in the modern world who hit *post* or *send* with a piece of personal writing that others may find offensive.

Various composition theorists have rightly noted that the Internet facilitates what are nowadays often called **multimodal** writing genres. The most obvious way in which writing can be multimodal is to incorporate visual images into the work—illustrations. Of course there's nothing new about books including pictures as well as words. Nor—as the box below highlights—is there anything revolutionary about combining words and pictures in informal and personal writing. But the range of possibilities today—and the ease with which different modes may be combined—is indeed revolutionary. Not surprisingly, the frequency with which words and images are combined in communications of all sorts has increased immeasurably. So too has multimodal writing that goes far beyond simply bringing words and pictures together; sound clips and video clips can now be pasted into a piece of electronic writing as easily as can any still image; many such combinations were not possible even in the early years of this century.

Multimodal Writing in Earlier Eras

In the age of the Kodak and the Polaroid, people would often paste photos into a journal of their travels. In the same way, in the era before photographs, the biologist Charles Darwin combined words with sketches in his *Voyage of the Beagle*. Long before the age of electronic communication, the artist Henri Matisse was among those who combined words with pictures in his personal correspondence. The beginning of his 12 January 1917 letter to his friend Paul Rosenberg is reproduced here; Matisse begins with thanks for the delicious mandarin oranges that Rosenberg had sent him—"delicieux mandarins que vous nous avez envoyées"—and by drawing a little sketch of the oranges themselves.

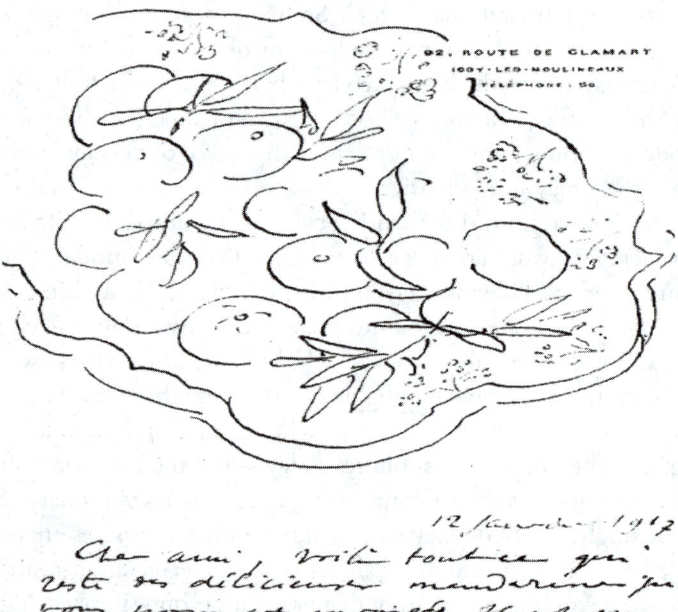

The ways in which all these things and more can be combined multi-modally is a fascinating area of study. In these pages we will touch only briefly on the interactions of words with still images, with video, and with sound; a much fuller discussion can be found in the "Seeing and Meaning" section of *The Broadview Guide to Writing*.

That the word *multimodal* is often used in this way can be confusing to students in first-year writing courses, since the same word is also sometimes used to refer to an entirely different aspect of writing: multimodal writing can also mean writing that, for example, simultaneously describes, narrates, and attempts to persuade the reader of something. The background here needs some filling in. For much of the twentieth century writing instructors were in the habit of referring to such things as description, narration, persuasion, and definition as "modes of writing"; indeed, many still are. But as theorists and teachers of writing began to realize in the latter decades of the twentieth century, this "modes of writing" approach can have the effect of encouraging students to think in terms of rigid categories. If essays had to be categorized as descriptive in nature, or narrative in nature, it was easy to lose sight of a vitally important reality: almost all personal writing is, in this respect, a hybrid. Descriptive material can be intertwined with narrative, persuasive, and other sorts of material in myriad ways.

That's not to say that there is nothing to be gained from exploring how something may best be described, or how a story may best be recounted. We will have a good deal to say in these pages about descriptive, narrative, reflective, and persuasive elements in writing (which we will refer to as "elements" or "patterns" of writing rather than as "modes," so as to avoid confusion with the newer use of "modes"); understanding these elements can be an important step in the development of a writer. In exploring these elements, however, it is crucial to understand that no single element is likely to predominate an entire piece of writing. When we deal with narrative, descriptive, persuasive, and reflective elements in informal and personal writing, our focus will be not merely on understanding such elements in isolation within particular passages of prose; we will focus far more on how these elements can be intertwined—how they can work together in the context of a complete piece of writing.

The main focus of *The Broadview Guide* is on crafting pieces of essay-length writing—regardless of whether these be written for submitting to a newspaper or literary magazine, for posting on a blog, for fulfilling an academic assignment, for creating a personal journal, or simply for experiencing the pleasure of writing them. But no section on informal and personal writing would be complete without some acknowledgement of the influence today of pieces of writing that are much shorter than essay-length.

Is it really possible to write anything truly meaningful or memorable using 280 characters or fewer? Or 140 characters or fewer? You be the judge:

> We cease loving ourselves if no one loves us.
>
> The search for the truth is the noblest of occupations, and its publication a duty.
>
> Nowadays people know the price of everything and the value of nothing.
>
> Children begin by loving their parents; as they grow older they judge them; sometimes they forgive them.
>
> Without self-confidence we are as babes in the cradle.
>
> If we had no faults, we would not take so much pleasure in noting those of others.
>
> A refusal of praise is a desire to be praised twice.
>
> Hypocrisy is a tribute paid by vice to virtue.
>
> Pick-up artists and garbage men should switch names.

It's interesting that many such memorable comments follow certain well-worn formats. One of these is the "X is…" format, where X typically is an abstract quality—"Love is…," "Freedom is …," "The search for truth is…," "Hypocrisy is …," etc. Another is the "if" format: "If we had no faults…," "If the Internet wasn't so addictive…," "If we all had everything we desired…, etc. (An interesting exercise is to try writing a handful of general maxims using each of these formulae.)

In any case, the small sampling above should be sufficient to convince any doubters that the art of concision—of crafting an insightful or witty thought that can be expressed in few words—is a valuable one. And arguably, the more concise the better. Margaret

Atwood, for example—often lauded for the quality of her tweets—was quoted in a 2019 interview lamenting Twitter's decision to allow tweets of up to 280 characters: "I take advantage of the 280. But it's made me sloppier, I have to say. You don't have the discipline of 140. ... It's like a haiku—you really have to pay attention."

In a way, this is simply to reinforce a point made about writing in general: the more you can pare away unnecessary verbiage, the better you will communicate what you want to say. Compare, for example, the impact of these 165 characters—

> What goes on in factory farms and slaughterhouses is horrific, but we are shielded from the horror; it's hidden away from us, behind high fences and windowless walls—

with the impact of the 65 characters of Paul and Linda McCartney's famous comment—

> If slaughterhouses had glass walls, everyone would be vegetarian.

It hardly needs saying that the shorter comment has the greater impact.

There's no necessary connection, though, between the pithiness of a memorable comment and the medium through which it is delivered. Of the reflections quoted above, indeed, only the last (sent 29 May 2013 by @ceejoyner) is a tweet. The three preceding it are among the hundreds of "reflections; or sentences and moral maxims" penned by François, Duc De La Rochefoucauld. Rochefoucauld's comments—almost all of them fewer than 140 characters long—were published in the late seventeenth century. And the first five of the comments above are quotations that were originally published in full-length essays or books, taken out of their original context. The pithy comment, in other words, has a long, long history predating the arrival of Twitter.

François, Duc De La Rochefoucauld, master of 140-characters-or-fewer comments

Not all tweets, of course, come in the form of pithy comments that may lead us to see some aspect of the world in a new light. Some aim to inspire:

> Thank you for everything. My last ask is the same as my first. I'm asking you to believe—not in my ability to create change, but in yours. (Barack Obama, @POTUS44, 1 January 2017)

A great many more are intended simply to pass on information, or to entertain. Of these, a majority include links to visual material; the spirit of this tweet from @yeehaw_meg (accompanied, as one might imagine, by a video) is the spirit of a great deal of the material on Twitter: "I hate going to weddings because I always wake up to a video someone took of me drunk dancing."

When tweets combine text and visual material, it's often the case that the text adds little. Sometimes, though, the two together have an impact greater than either would have on its own. In the tweet below, the error of the headline writer becomes much more entertaining when preceded by the Twitter writer's few lines of imagined dialogue. The dialogue makes no sense on its own, but dialogue plus image make for a delightful combination:

ABE SWEATPANTS
@carltonhimself

"You're sure that's the right word?"

"Like, 80% sure, yeah."

"Print it."

MLB

Amphibious pitcher makes debut

Vendite becomes first pitcher in 20 years to pitch with both arms in MLB game

Many, of course, feel strongly that the medium does matter—that, however closely a seventeenth-century maxim may seem to resemble a tweet, the world of social media creates entirely different conditions for the dissemination of thoughts that can be expressed in 140 written characters or fewer. Many have argued that the degree to which social media in general are often emotionally charged makes them problematic. Zadie Smith, the acclaimed British/American essayist and novelist is resoundingly of that view. In a 2017 interview Smith expressed her view quite crisply (in 109 characters): "Because I'm not on Twitter, I'm not on Instagram, I'm not on the internet, I never hear people shouting at me."

What do you think of a 280-character world—or of a 140-character world? Perhaps you could express your views on the topic in a comment of 140 characters or fewer—and/or in an essay of 1,400 words or fewer.

C2.9.3 Openings

Whereas academic essays typically signal to the reader in the first paragraph where the essay is headed—most commonly with a thesis statement that makes plain what the writer will argue—most essays of an informal or personal sort open quite differently. They may open with story material; they may open with description; they may open with material that is initially quite puzzling to the reader. In a great many cases, the informal essay's overall purpose and theme may not be immediately evident; many successful openings to literary essays lead the reader to feel curious.

It's a truism that writers of informal or personal essays should strive to capture—and hold—the interest of the reader. But how is that actually done? One sure way to pull the reader in immediately is through a striking opening:

> When my mother was pregnant with me, she told me later, a party of Ku Klux Klan riders galloped up to our home in Omaha, Nebraska, one night. (opening to "Nightmare," the first chapter of Malcolm X and Alex Haley's *The Autobiography of Malcolm X*)

> The hardest substance in the human body is the white enamel of the teeth. (opening sentence of Atul Gawande's essay "The Way We Age Now")

> I remember the very day that I became colored. (beginning of the second paragraph of Zora Neale Hurston's "How It Feels to Be Colored Me")

> My favorite definition of a "feminist" is one offered by Su, an Australian woman who, when interviewed for Kathy Bail's 1996 anthology *DIY Feminism*, said feminists are "just women who

> don't want to be treated like shit." (opening sentence of Roxanne Gay's essay "Bad Feminist: Take One")

> Climate change is global-scale violence against places and species, as well as against human beings. (opening sentence of Rebecca Solnit's essay "Climate Change Is Violence")

> You know a Steve McCurry picture when you see one. His portrait of an Afghan girl with vivid green eyes, printed on the cover of *National Geographic* in June 1985, is one of the iconic images of the twentieth century. (opening two sentences of Teju Cole's essay, "A Too-Perfect Picture")

> Contrary to popular belief, the past was not more eventful than the present. (opening sentence of George Orwell's essay, "My Country Right or Left")

Notice that there is no one formula to a striking opening. It can be an allusion to a dramatic incident (Malcolm X); a small but striking fact (Gawande); a sentence that turns the normal way of looking at things inside out (Hurston); a blunt, funny quotation (Gay); an assertion that surprises us by its boldness (Solnit) or that surprises us in some other way (Cole, whose opening sentence surely leads most readers to ask themselves, "I do? Really?"); or a statement as striking for its succinct expression as for its insight (Orwell). And this list of possible approaches, of course, comes nowhere close to exhausting the possibilities. There are many, many ways, to arrest readers' attention with an opening sentence or opening paragraph.

You should not be made to feel, though, that any good piece of personal or informal writing *must* have a striking opening; a great many quite brilliant essays do not. Miriam Toews's "A Father's Faith," for example, which is overall a strikingly memorable personal essay, begins in the most ordinary of ways:

> On the morning of May 13, 1998, my father woke up, had breakfast, got dressed, and walked away from the Steinbach Bethesda Hospital, where he had been a patient for two and a half weeks.

The first four paragraphs continue to recount the father's walk on that day. It is not until the end of the fourth paragraph that we are told that the walk ended with his death—and not until near the end of the essay that it becomes entirely clear that he died by suicide.

The essay explores from the daughter's point of view what it must have been like to live as her father did, a devout believer, but also a man suffering from serious mental illness in a religious community where depression or despair tended to be regarded as evidence of a failure of faith. It's an essay that begins in simple fashion and progressively becomes more and more involving, both intellectually and emotionally.

Desmond Cole's superb essay "The Skin I'm In" also begins in unremarkable fashion. The first paragraph, while mildly interesting, is certainly not intensely gripping:

> The summer I was nine, my teenage cousin Sana came from England to visit my family in Oshawa. He was tall, handsome, and obnoxious, the kind of guy who could palm a basketball like Michael Jordan. I was in his shadow during his visit, totally in awe of his confidence—he was always saying something clever to knock me off balance.

It's not until the second paragraph that the core subject of the essay (the way in which dark-skinned people tend to be treated by the police) begins to emerge:

> One day, we took Sana and his parents on a road trip to Niagara Falls. Just past St. Catharines, Sana tossed a dirty tissue out the window. Within seconds, we heard a siren: a cop had been driving behind us, and he immediately pulled us onto the shoulder.

From there the essay becomes a fascinating exploration of racism, both on the part of law enforcement officers and in society at large—an essay that moves smoothly from personal anecdote to broad generalizations backed by statistical evidence and reflections on the psychological mechanisms of racism before moving back into narration, offering further personal anecdotes.

An essay's opening, then, need not be extraordinarily striking. It's worth giving some thought to attracting the reader's attention through an arresting first sentence or two. But it's worth remembering too that any reader who is willing to turn their attention to an essay in the first place will surely not stop reading if the first sentence—or the first few paragraphs—do not grip them intensely. If readers find themselves bored after reading two or three pages they may well stop reading, but almost any reader will give almost any essay a bit of time. Essays that do little in their opening sentences to draw attention to themselves but build reader interest in one way or another over several pages can be of just as high a quality as essays that grip the reader from the first sentence onwards.

C2.9.4 Descriptive Elements

When we think of description, we tend to think first of adjectives and adverbs. If we are asked what a person looks like, we think first of adjectives such as *tall, short, long-haired, balding, young, old.* If we're asked to describe how something should be done, we might think of adverbs such as *quickly, slowly, cautiously, carefully, thoroughly.* And it's true that adjectives and adverbs can play an important role in descriptions. But effective description as an element of effective writing involves a good deal more than choosing adjectives and adverbs. Let's look at some of the ways in which a writer can describe a scene in ways that bring it alive for the reader, using the opening to N. Scott Momaday's acclaimed essay "The Way to Rainy Mountain" as an example:

> A single knoll rises out of the plain in Oklahoma, north and east of the Wichita range. For my people, the Kiowas, it is an old landmark and they gave it the name Rainy Mountain. The hardest weather in the world is there. Winter brings blizzards, hot tornadic winds arise in the spring, and in summer the prairie is an anvil's edge. The grass turns brittle and brown, and it cracks beneath your feet. There are green belts along the rivers and creeks, linear groves of hickory and pecan, willow and witch hazel. At a distance in July or August the steaming foliage seems almost to writhe in fire. Great green and yellow grasshoppers are everywhere in the tall grass, popping up like corn to sting the flesh, and tortoises crawl about on the red earth, going nowhere in plenty of time. Loneliness is an aspect of the land.

Momaday surely uses adjectives to great effect here. Here and there he uses adjectives in somewhat unusual ways (referring to *brittle* grass and *steaming* foliage, for example). But many of the adjectives he uses are quite ordinary (a *single* knoll, an *old* landmark, the *hardest* weather). He makes verbs do a certain amount of the work of describing; the grass *cracks* beneath your feet, the grasshoppers are *popping* up. He uses metaphor (the prairie *is an anvil's edge*) and simile (the foliage *seems almost to writhe in fire*) to good effect. And the rhythms of the prose also help to lend it descriptive power; the slow rhythm of *the hardest weather in the world is there* evokes the prolonged nature of what must be endured—and of course the slow rhythm of *going nowhere in plenty of time* evokes the movement of the tortoises he is describing.

No matter how accomplished, though, descriptive passages count for little unless they are placed in a memorable context. Momaday's opening would not be much remarked on if the essay it begins were not memorable for a good deal more than descriptions of landscape. By the end of the paragraph, the essay has already begun to broaden, with a powerful element of reflection entering in:

> To look upon that landscape with the sun at your back is to lose the sense of proportion. Your imagination comes to life, and this, you think, is where Creation was begun.

The next paragraph introduces the reader to the topic of the author's grandmother:

> I returned to Rainy Mountain in July. My grandmother had died in the spring, and I wanted to be at her grave. She had lived to be very old, and at last infirm. Her only living daughter was with her when she died, and I was told that in death her face was that of a child.

In language much simpler than that of the first paragraph (no striking adjectives here) the author brings in a narrative element, looking back at her life and death—and also forward, expressing his own desire now to be at her grave. From here the essay by turns employs narrative, descriptive, and reflective elements in a way that manages, within a mere 16 paragraphs, to give a vivid sense not just of the landscape but also of Kiowa traditions, of Momaday's grandmother, and of Momaday himself. The opening description turns out to have been in the service of much larger ends.

Context can make a world of difference, even when descriptive elements are employed only very briefly. Here, for example, is a well written little description of an afternoon baseball game at Dodger Stadium:

> It is late afternoon. The sun lights up the San Gabriel Mountains. The pastel ballpark fills with fans. (George Vecsey, "My Field of Memories: I See the New Dodgers and Summon the Old," *The New York Times*, 23 October 2017)

The adjective *pastel* is a particularly nice touch here; with one word the writer conjures up for us an atmosphere of soft pinks and blues and greens. And using *lights up* as a verb (rather than the more ordinary *The sun shines on*) intensifies the brightness of this little bit of description. But for all that, the description would not be particularly memorable without its context. The writer is reminiscing about his years watching the Dodgers, going back to the 1950s when the team still played in Brooklyn. When their owner suddenly moved the team to Los Angeles in 1956, this writer was, like millions of other fans, angry and uncomprehending. Here, then, is the description with a bit more context:

> One season later, the Dodgers move to Los Angeles.... I believe the Dodger owner Walter O'Malley is the worst person in the world....
>
> In 1964 I am sent to Dodger Stadium with the Mets. It is late afternoon. The sun lights up the San Gabriel Mountains. The pastel ballpark fills with fans.... I finally understand O'Malley's move to L.A.

Why would anyone want to move to Los Angeles? Those eighteen words of description provide at least a partial answer.

Let's look now at an extended example of how a descriptive element can function in a piece of informal or personal writing. The passage below, from Mark Twain's *Life on the Mississippi*, is one of the most oft-cited examples of memorable descriptive writing in American literature. Mark Twain is describing a sunset on the river:

> I still keep in mind a certain wonderful sunset which I witnessed when steamboating was new to me. A broad expanse of the river was turned to blood; in the middle distance the red hue brightened into gold, through which a solitary log came floating, black and conspicuous; in one place a long, slanting mark lay sparkling upon the water; in another the surface was broken by boiling, tumbling rings, that were as many-tinted as an opal; where the ruddy flush was faintest, was a smooth spot that was covered with

> graceful circles and radiating lines, ever so delicately traced; the shore on our left was densely wooded, and the somber shadow that fell from this forest was broken in one place by a long, ruffled trail that shone like silver; and high above the forest wall a clean-stemmed dead tree waved a single leafy bough that glowed like a flame in the unobstructed splendor that was flowing from the sun. There were graceful curves, reflected images, woody heights, soft distances; and over the whole scene, far and near, the dissolving lights drifted steadily, enriching it, every passing moment, with new marvels of coloring.

An interesting exercise: Write a passage of descriptive prose that answers the question "What is TikTok?" or "What is Instagram?" for someone wholly unfamiliar with social media.

What makes this passage memorable? The image of a "broad expanse of the river" turning "to blood" is surely striking—much more striking than it would be if Twain had used the adjective "blood-red" or written that it *seemed as if* the river were turning to blood. And the rest of the passage certainly makes it possible for the reader to visualize the scene. But what truly makes this section of *Life on the Mississippi* memorable is the context surrounding the description of this remembered scene:

> … [W]hen I had mastered the language of this water and had come to know every trifling feature that bordered the great river as familiarly as I knew the letters of the alphabet, I had made a valuable acquisition. But I had lost something, too. I had lost something which could never be restored to me while I lived. All the grace, the beauty, the poetry had gone out of the majestic river! **I still keep in mind a certain wonderful sunset which I witnessed when steamboating was new to me. A broad expanse of the river was turned to blood; in the middle distance the red hue brightened into gold, through which a solitary log came floating, black and conspicuous; in one place a long, slanting mark**

lay sparkling upon the water; in another the surface was broken by boiling, tumbling rings, that were as many-tinted as an opal; where the ruddy flush was faintest, was a smooth spot that was covered with graceful circles and radiating lines, ever so delicately traced; the shore on our left was densely wooded, and the somber shadow that fell from this forest was broken in one place by a long, ruffled trail that shone like silver; and high above the forest wall a clean-stemmed dead tree waved a single leafy bough that glowed like a flame in the unobstructed splendor that was flowing from the sun. There were graceful curves, reflected images, woody heights, soft distances; and over the whole scene, far and near, the dissolving lights drifted steadily, enriching it, every passing moment, with new marvels of coloring.

I stood like one bewitched. I drank it in, in a speechless rapture. The world was new to me, and I had never seen anything like this at home.

But as I have said, a day came when I began to cease from noting the glories and the charms which the moon and the sun and the twilight wrought upon the river's face; another day came when I ceased altogether to note them. Then, if that sunset scene had been repeated, I should have looked upon it without rapture, and should have commented upon it, inwardly, in this fashion: "This sun means that we are going to have wind to-morrow; that floating log means that the river is rising, small thanks to it; that slanting mark on the water refers to a bluff reef which is going to kill somebody's steamboat one of these nights, if it keeps on stretching out like that; those tumbling 'boils' show a dissolving bar and a changing channel there; the lines and circles in the slick water over yonder are a warning that that troublesome place is shoaling up dangerously; that silver streak in the shadow of the forest is the 'break' from a new snag, and he has located himself in the very best place he could have found to fish for steamboats; that tall dead tree, with a single living branch, is not going to last long, and then how is a body ever going to get through this blind place at night without the friendly old landmark?"

No, the romance and the beauty were all gone from the river. All the value any feature of it had for me now was the amount of usefulness it could furnish toward compassing the safe piloting of a steamboat....

In the overall context in which Twain sets the description, the sunset is memorable not for itself, but as an example of a broader psychological truth—the way in which beauty can be dimmed and even extinguished by familiarity, and of how our aesthetic sense can be overwritten by the habits of the workaday world. The writing that surrounds the oft-quoted passage of description, we should note, is not itself descriptive in character. In the surrounding text Twain is reflecting, not describing—reflecting on the passage of time, and on how it changes our perceptions.

We have already seen how easily attempts to label an entire piece of writing as an example of one element or another (*narrative* or *descriptive* or *reflective* or *persuasive*) tend to break down; we see it again here. A famous piece of memorable descriptive writing turns out to be memorable primarily because of the reflective writing that surrounds it.

C2.9.5 Narrative Elements

At its simplest, a narrative is simply a sequence, in which one thing happens, and then another thing happens, and then another thing happens. Anyone who has read a fair bit of medieval literature will be familiar with narrative passages of this sort:

> Then upon this day a lord of that castle, Sir Bliaunt, took his arms on horseback with a spear to seek adventures. And, as he rode in a forest, there met him two knights..., Sir Breunis Sans Pité, and his brother, Sir Bartelot. And these two ran both at once on Sir Bliaunt and brake their spears upon his body. And then they drew their swords and made great battle, and fought long togethers. But at the last Sir Bliaunt was sore wounded and felt himself faint, and anon he fled on horseback toward his castle...
> (Sir Thomas Malory, *Le Morte Darthur*, from the tale "Sir Tristram de Lyones")

Narrative sequences of this sort are deeply rooted in oral history—in chronicles that preserved for posterity a record of important events in the order that they occurred. That's not likely to be your aim when you introduce narrative elements into a piece of informal or personal writing. It's much more likely that you'll introduce narrative elements for other reasons. The story material may simply be interesting in itself, and have to it a built-in arc of beginning, middle and end that you sense will engage readers. Or you might want to employ narrative in order to make a vivid point about an idea, or to provide an example of a general point, or to illuminate something about someone's character. Let's say you want to describe someone you knew slightly years before—Vern, we'll call him. You might try doing it first with adjectives:

> Vern was a truly unusual person; he would do odd, eccentric things, and say odd, eccentric things, but without any evident awareness that they *were* eccentric.

But that sort of description doesn't convey any vivid sense of anything to the reader. Introducing a narrative element will convey much more:

> In the spring of my sixteenth year, my great friend Kenny and I spent eight weeks in a Driver's Ed class in Chatham, Ontario. Spring can be a warm time in Chatham, but back then the folks at Young Drivers didn't believe in air-conditioned rooms. In the classrooms where we met, humming fluorescent lights—their bulbs shaped like light sabers—would light the whole, windowless room; air circulation was nonexistent. One guy, though—a quiet guy who always sat in the first row—would show up every time wearing a ski jacket over top of one of those heavyweight lumberjack-style shirts. Vern always left those layers of clothing on for the duration of class. (I remember that Kenny once passed me a scrap of paper during one of those classes; it said only, "Vern's gotta be a bit warm.")
>
> Vern spoke infrequently, and when he did speak, it was in a voice that sounded far too gravelly for any 16-year-old. When the instructor asked him questions, he almost always answered correctly—but, as with all of us, the wrong answers are always the memorable ones. In Vern's case the memorable moment came when he was asked "What's a blind spot?" Vern rearranged himself a little inside the ski-jacket and hunched forward a little, peering at the instructor as if he was having a little trouble seeing himself. Finally he came up with an answer: "It's when you can't see…" There was a pregnant pause, and then more gravel as he clarified "AT ALL!"
>
> It would be great to be able to report that Kenny and I eventually struck up a warm friendship with Vern and found out what

> he was really like and why he wore all those layers—or to be able to report that Vern found fame and fortune years later as a sports star, or a successful business owner, or a stand-up comedian. I never saw or heard of Vern after those classes ended, but I think of him every year when warm weather comes round.

In any piece of writing in which the narrative element dominates for more than a few lines, holding the reader's interest is very often a matter of arousing a sense of expectation, or in some other way a sense of active curiosity as to what will happen in the narrative. Sometimes that will happen as a matter of course, simply because of the nature of the story material. If you tell your readers of something important having been lost, they will instinctively wonder if it will be found, and will be inclined to read on in order to find out. Similarly, if you start a narrative with an account of someone accosting you and demanding your wallet, or an account of a hurricane making landfall near the town in which you live, the story material will in itself ensure that your reader feels some interest in finding out what happened. But what if your narrative material is taken from everyday life? Much as you intend to take the reader somewhere interesting, the story material itself may not be so immediately engaging as the opening sentences of an account of a robbery or a hurricane might be. Your narrative might begin, for example, with a visit to the grocery store, or with taking the dog out for a walk. Or—as does one of the most famous American essays of the last century—it might focus on thoughts of a family trip to a vacation spot you haven't visited in many years:

> A few weeks ago … I bought myself a couple of bass hooks and a spinner and returned to the lake where we used to go, for a week's fishing and to revisit old haunts. On the journey over to the lake I began to wonder what it would be like. I wondered how time would have marred this unique, this holy spot—the coves and streams, the hills that the sun set behind, the camps and the paths behind the camps. I was sure that the tarred road would have found it out and I wondered in what other ways it would be desolated.

E.B. White's "Once More to the Lake" is usually thought of as an essay that focuses on description and personal reflection. But as the above passage suggests, it's also a good example of narration—of the ways in which a writer can build forward-looking interest in the mind of the reader, simply by making his or her own forward-looking thoughts part of the narrative.

Another way in which a writer can hold our interest—and this applies as much to descriptive or reflective writing as it does to narration—is to appeal directly to fellow feeling in the reader. In "Once More to the Lake" that's exactly what White does just after the passage quoted above:

> It is strange how much you can remember about places like that once you allow your mind to return into the grooves which lead back. You remember one thing, and that suddenly reminds you of another thing. I guess I remembered clearest of all the early mornings, when the lake was cool and motionless, remembered how the bedroom smelled of the lumber it was made of and of the wet woods whose scent entered through the screen.

The "you" here, of course, is a *you* that is more or less equivalent to the third person "one"; White could as easily have written "It is strange how much one can remember...." The feel of this *you*, though, is more inviting to the reader than is a third person *one*.

Sometimes it can be hard to distinguish this sort of "third person" *you* that, in its bare meaning, is virtually interchangeable with *one*, from the conventional second person *you* with which one person addresses another—or with which a writer may directly address the reader. Let's look, for example, at a passage from the second paragraph of the George Orwell essay "My Country Right or Left":

> [I]f you were alive during the war of 1914–18, and if you disentangle your real memories from their later accretions, you find that it was not usually the big events that stirred you at the time. ... I was eleven when the war started. If I honestly sort out my memories and disregard what I have learned since, I must admit that nothing in the whole war moved me so deeply as the loss of the Titanic had done a few years earlier.

The use of *you* in these sorts of ways can lead the reader to feel an experiential connection—even when it's impossible to have had the experience that is being appealed to. Orwell was writing in 1940; no one alive today, of course, can remember the events of the First

World War—or remember hearing the news of the *Titanic* having been lost. Yet the passage still manages to appeal to our fellow feeling—to our awareness that the most important things that have happened during our lives are not always the ones that we remember most vividly.

Like the White essay, this Orwell piece not infrequently employs narration—not so much the narration of historical events as the narration of the author's memories of his reactions to those events, over roughly three decades of the early twentieth century. And like White, Orwell also builds interest by incorporating forward-looking thoughts into the narrative:

> I do not know for certain in what year I first knew war was coming.... For several years the coming war was a nightmare to me....

Towards the end Orwell's essay turns—as does White's—to reflection. The points Orwell has made along the way about memory turn out to have been made in the service of larger points having to do with the ways in which memory can be collectively shaped in a society—and in particular how a "long drilling in patriotism" is bound to have a great effect on shaping attitudes towards war, regardless of the dictates of reason.

These observations about two famous twentieth-century essays point to a larger truth about pattern in personal and informal writing: moving from one pattern to another in a piece of writing will often improve the structure of that piece of writing and make it more engaging to the reader.

Interestingly, this can be just as true of pieces of writing that, to greater or lesser degree, engage in argument or persuasion as it is of those that spend more time on description or narration (or reflection, or definition, or any other rhetorical category). Whereas persuasive essays in many scholarly disciplines may be expected to "stick to the script" as the writer puts forward an argument, essays of a more informal, personal sort in which a persuasive element is prominent tend to benefit from rhetorical and stylistic variety. Indeed, essays that are, to some extent at least, descriptive *and* narrative *and* reflective *and* argumentative are often among the most interesting and effective pieces of writing. Roxanne Gay's "Bad Feminist, Take One," for example, is very largely concerned with arguing that feminism can and should take many forms, and that feminists should not have to "be everything to everyone." But "Bad Feminist, Take One" is in large part also a book review of Sheryl Sandberg's *Lean In*; it's an essay that includes amusing personal anecdotes, an essay that includes various reflections on class and on race, and an essay that includes discussions of several other books, as well as various magazine articles. It keeps our interest by ranging widely not just in subject matter but also in rhetorical style.

To recognize and appreciate rhetorical variety in this sort of way is to go against much of the advice students were usually given not too long ago, when the norm was to try to force students to think of narrative essays, descriptive essays, persuasive essays, and so on as discrete categories. Here, for example, is what Thomas S. Kane and Leonard J. Peters advised in their introduction to the section of their then-popular textbook anthology, *Writing Prose*: "The essence of good narration is organizing the story into beginning, middle, and end.... The writer's task, especially in brief narration, is to concentrate upon the story itself." Yet strikingly, four of the five essays that Kane and Peters include as examples of the narrative essay do nothing of the sort. Rather than tell a story from beginning to middle to end, they are continually shifting from mode to mode.[1] Even during the height of the era in which writing authorities were classifying essays into such rhetorical categories, the classification system bore little relation to reality; then, as now, when it comes to a consideration of almost any actual essay in its full form, the categories almost inevitably break down.

---

1 An essay on the great electrical blackout of 1965, for example, begins with a paragraph of reflection that focuses on material from Jonathan Swift's *Gulliver's Travels*. The second paragraph makes the relevance of those reflections clear, noting how modern society may be "tied down by its electric grid" in much the same way as Swift's Gulliver was tied down by the Lilliputians. The following three paragraphs describe the effects of the blackout ("Instead of panic, quiet camaraderie filled the air"), but tell no sequential story. The final two paragraphs turn in different directions—one reflecting on human nature ("in Hobbes's 'state of nature' people had turned out to be lambs rather than wolves") and one reflecting on practicalities and their policy implications in a technological age. Nowhere in this supposedly "narrative" essay is there a "story," in the sense of a narrative with a beginning, middle, and end.

A cautionary note here, however: If you are thinking of adding a story about your own experience to, for example, a book or movie review or an op-ed piece in which you are putting forward an argument, it's important that what you recount of your own experience be both relevant and interesting. The personal anecdotes Roxanne Gay includes in her book review really are amusing, and they are relevant, too. In similar fashion, Orwell's personal recollections in "My Country Right or Left" are both interesting and relevant to the general points he is making. If, on the other hand, you simply tack on to a discussion of the ideas put forward in a film you have seen information about how you were feeling on the night you saw it, or information on who you went with and what food and drink the two of you may have consumed at the theatre, that sort of personal material will likely detract from the points you want to make about the film, not enhance them.

C2.9.6 Persuasive Elements

A great deal of informal and personal prose focuses in one way or another on putting forward an argument—on trying to persuade the reader of something. But the sorts of argument put forward are usually of a rather different character than the sorts of arguments that are made in academic writing. For one thing, the "evidence" on which they are based may often be anecdotal or conjectural, and where statistical or other hard evidence is provided, or authorities quoted, it is considered acceptable to do so without formal citation. One can refer to "a recent study by University of California researchers" without providing the name of the study, its date of publication, or indeed the name of the scholarly journal in which it appeared; arguments made in a piece of informal writing are normally not buttressed by any formal system of citation and documentation.

Arguments put forward in informal writing can vary widely in length. They are often "op-ed" length—the typical length of an opinion piece in a newspaper, or somewhere between 650 and 900 words. But they are sometimes shorter, and they can be considerably longer. Sometimes they can be book-length—as is, for example, Jonathan Safran Foer's *Eating Animals*. Whatever their length, they tend to be much less tightly structured than arguments made in academic writing. Look, for example, at how Foer structures this part of his argument:

> Thanksgiving is the meal we aspire for other meals to resemble. Of course, most of us can't (and wouldn't want to) cook all day every day, and of course such food would be fatal if consumed with regularity, and how many of us really want to be surrounded by our extended families every single night? (It can be challenge enough to have to eat with myself.) But it's nice to imagine all meals being so deliberate. Of the thousand-or-so meals we eat every year, Thanksgiving dinner is the one that we try most earnestly to get right. It holds the hope of being a good meal, whose ingredients, efforts, setting, and consuming are expressions of the best in us. More than any other meal, it is about good eating and good thinking.
>
> And, more than any other food, the Thanksgiving turkey embodies the paradoxes of eating animals: what we do to living turkeys is just about as bad as anything humans have ever done to any animal in the history of the world.…
>
> This will be the first year [my family celebrates] Thanksgiving in my home, the first time I will prepare the food, and the first Thanksgiving meal at which my son will be old enough to eat the food the rest of us eat. If this entire book could be decanted into a single question … it might be this: should we serve turkey at Thanksgiving? (Jonathan Safran Foer, *Eating Animals*, 2009)

Foer proceeds elliptically, moving from personal reflection on the meaning of Thanksgiving to a discussion of the way in which turkeys are treated to a discussion of his own family's Thanksgiving dinner. That looseness of structure is maintained throughout most of the book, as Foer brings in American history, information about factory farming, narratives of the first Thanksgiving of his childhood, and reflections on his special relationship with his grandmother. The sum total is an effective argument against eating the products of factory farming (and, indeed, against eating animal products), but Foer nowhere follows the sort of argumentative progression that you'd expect to find in an academic essay—or, for that matter, in an op-ed piece in a newspaper or on a website.

How, then, do such "arguments" manage to persuade the reader? To understand how informal writing can be persuasive even when it has little apparent logical structure, it may be helpful to be aware of the three categories of appeal that were set out by the classical rhetoricians of ancient Greece more than 2,300 years ago. As codified by

Aristotle, rhetorical appeals could be based on any combination of *pathos*, *ethos*, and *logos*. Those three concepts remain widely and usefully employed in many discussions of literary writing today.

The word *pathos* is sometimes thought to hold pejorative connotations—to describe an appeal to the emotions that is too contrived, too blatant, or too superficial. Appeals to the emotions may surely be all of those things. But they need not be any of them—and certainly the term *pathos*, properly used, carries very much the same meaning today as it did for the ancients, referring to any appeal to the emotions. Such appeals have a legitimate place in many forms of argumentation, given that our responses to experiences inevitably involve both heart and head; indeed, many would argue that the direction our reason takes is always informed at some level by our initial emotional responses. Such appeals may take many forms; Foer makes a variety of different appeals to the emotions in *Eating Animals*—not least of all when he describes how "what we do to living turkeys is just about as bad as anything humans have ever done to any animal in the history of the world."

For Aristotle and other ancient Greek authorities, an appeal to *ethos* was one based on the character of the person presenting the argument, whether that had to do with the speaker's position of authority, his or her perceived honesty, or other ethical virtues. In modern usage, appeals to ethos often rest on the position of authority of the speaker or writer—or the people that the speaker or writer cites. Someone who supports their argument by writing of "a recent study by University of California researchers" or "a recent book by a Nobel Prize winning scientist," is typically looking for the prestige of that highly respected university or that highly respected award to lend credibility to their argument. Appeals to ethos may also rest, though, on the perceived character of the writer. In the excerpt above, the appeal made in the first and third paragraphs is in part based on ethos; we sense from what he writes that the author is someone who cares deeply about family values—and about "good eating and good thinking."

Logos is often translated as logic, and to a large extent appeals based on logos may indeed be appeals that are logical in nature. But in the world of rhetoric such appeals are not always made according to the principles of inductive or deductive logic that apply to most academic essays. The meaning of logos in the ancient world was multi-faceted. It could mean *reason* or *logic*, but it could also simply mean *word*; in the context of literary non-fiction, an appeal based on logos may perhaps best be understood as an appeal based on the ideas that the words hold. But often that appeal is indeed based on the underlying logic of the ideas. Embedded in the paragraphs excerpted above from Foer's book, for example, is the suggestion of a powerful logical argument:

- We want Thanksgiving to be an expression of "the best in us," ethically as well as in other ways.
- Turkeys raised for sale as Thanksgiving food are treated with horrific cruelty.
- Eating these birds cannot therefore be an expression of our highest ethical standards; we should refrain from doing so.

Experienced writers such as Foer are highly adept at embedding such arguments within prose that includes passages of reflection, of description, and of personal narrative. When students first begin to draft pieces of informal prose that are intended to advance an argument, though, they may be well advised to focus more narrowly on points of argument that do *not* bring personal narrative into play. Instead, it may be helpful to begin with a rigorous paragraphing structure such as is suggested in the first part of this text, where arguments for and against the legalization of marijuana are used as an extended example. (See especially sections P2.1 and P2.5.)

Much as the structure of arguments put forward in informal and personal writing may be loose, and much as such arguments need not be buttressed by the same rigorous systems of citation and documentation that are the norm in academic writing, it is still crucial that the fundamentals of an argument be sound. Getting one's logic—and one's facts—right may not be so frequently the focus of informal writing as it is of academic writing, but it is still vitally important. And it's something that a surprising number of writers who compose pieces of informal writing for a living don't much bother about. Take, for example, the 2022 controversy over the teaching of sonnets at the University of Salford in Britain. Here's what Rex Murphy of the *National Post* newspaper had to say on the topic:

> Within the strict and limited form of the literary sonnet may be found some of the most exquisite and artistic creations of the poetic mind. They are the exhalations of literary genius.... To

> take these triumphs of the creative poetic mind out of consideration, and to lay on them the brand that they are "products of white western culture" and as such need to be "decolonized" (whatever that murk of a verb can possibly mean) is to commit a sacrilege against poetry and art. But such are elements in the idiot days we live in, that there is a university—at least that's what it's called, but names mean nothing in many cases—Salford, in England, where Shakespeare flourished and where Milton birthed his imperishable genius, which is doing just that. (Rex Murphy, "How Ridiculous Is It for Universities to Sideline Sonnets? Let Me Count the Ways," 21 May 2022)

Murphy was one of several commentators who deplored the supposed "sacrilege" of the "cancelling" of the sonnet by this university. The problem with these commentators' claims? They were deploring something that had not in fact occurred. What had happened was that a single course at the University of Salford—a second-year course in creative writing entitled Writing Poetry in the Twenty-First Century, not a survey of English literature—had decided to place less emphasis on the sonnet. Yes, this single course had indeed noted that such forms "tend to be the products of white western culture." But the sonnet had not been banished—not even from this one course. Previously, students enrolled in the course had been required to compose sonnets in both of the course's two assessments. After the change in the curriculum, they would still be required to compose sonnets (as well as sestinas and tankas), and one of the two assessments would

Some interesting possible subjects for an informal persuasive essay: Should addiction to social media (or to the Internet generally) be regarded in much the same fashion as society regards alcohol or drug addiction? At what age (if at all) should young children be allowed to have their own tablets or smartphones? To what extent should the screen time of young children be limited? (image: Wikipedia Commons Images / Intel Free Press: Child with an Apple iPad)

still require students to submit both a sonnet and a tanka for assessment (with students having the option of submitting a third poem in a form of their own design). As Scott Thurston of the English and Creative Writing Department made clear, the only difference was that there would be slightly less emphasis in the *assessments* on the sonnet and especially on the sestina, though even in the case of the sestina students would still be required to compose in that form as part of their exercises. Far from taking the sonnet "out of consideration" across the entire university, Salford had not even banished it from this single creative-writing course.

Getting your facts right, then—and putting them together in a logical fashion—is arguably just as important in informal writing as it is in formal academic prose.

C2.9.7 Reflective Elements

A good deal of what Michel de Montaigne writes in his *Essais* (see the boxed highlight) does not fit into any of the categories we have discussed so far. It is not descriptive, it does not narrate a story, and it is not structured as persuasive writing. What Montaigne offers us in much of these pieces are simply his reflections—his thoughts about himself and humans in general, and about the world. Famously, many of his reflections concern his own thoughts and his own writing:

> When I am attacked by gloomy thoughts, nothing helps me so much as running to my books. They quickly absorb me and banish the clouds from my mind.
>
> If I speak of myself in different ways, that is because I look at myself in different ways.
>
> I speak the truth, not so much as I would, but as much as I dare; and I dare a little more as I grow older.

That tendency—to reflect largely on our selves when we engage in reflective writing—has persisted through to our own time. From Francis Bacon and Margaret Cavendish in the seventeenth century to Mary Wortley Montagu and Samuel Johnson in the eighteenth, Samuel Taylor Coleridge and Mark Twain in the nineteenth, Virginia Woolf and George Orwell in the twentieth, to Zadie Smith, Ta-Nehisi Coates, Rebecca Solnit and innumerable others in the twenty-first century, writers of reflective prose have reflected largely on themselves:

> "I had rather die in the adventure of noble achievements, than live in obscure and sluggish security." (Margaret Cavendish, *The Blazing World*)

> "I give myself sometimes admirable advice, but I am incapable of taking it." (Mary Wortley Montagu, *Letters*)

> "For many years, I have been moved by the blue at the far edge of what can be seen, that color of horizons, of remote mountain ranges, of anything far away. The color of that distance is the color of an emotion, the color of solitude and of desire, the color of there seen from here, the color of where you are not. And the color of where you can never go." (Rebecca Solnit, *A Field Guide to Getting Lost*)

As the quotation from Solnit illustrates, nature, too, is frequently the subject of reflective writing—as is human nature:

> I find it wholesome to be alone the greater part of the time. To be in company, even with the best, is soon wearisome and dissipating. I love to be alone. I never found the companion that was so companionable as solitude. (Henry David Thoreau, *Walden*)

> Now I see the secret of making the best person, it is to grow in the open air and to eat and sleep with the earth. (Walt Whitman, "Song of the Open Road")

But notice how, with much reflective writing, the writer's reflections on themselves and their own thoughts and feelings slide into generalizations about humanity in general. Solnit begins by writing of how she personally has been moved by certain shades of blue; by the end of her next sentence, she has slipped into the second person, suggesting through the repeated use of "you" that at some level we all share these feelings.

For many writers of reflective prose, this tendency towards generalization—towards universalizing what one thinks or feels oneself—is a continual habit. Here is Thoreau again—but this time writing not as "I" but as "we":

> We need the tonic of wildness—to wade sometimes in marshes where the bittern and the meadow-hen lurk, and hear the boom-

> ing of the snipe; to smell the whispering sedge where only some wilder and more solitary fowl builds her nest, and the mink crawls with its belly close to the ground. At the same time that we are earnest to explore and learn all things, we require that all things be mysterious and unexplorable, that land and sea be infinitely wild, unsurveyed and unfathomed by us because unfathomable. We can never have enough of nature." (Henry David Thoreau, *Walden*)

This sort of generalizing can enliven one's writing and help engage the reader's attention. If you write "I can never have enough of nature," the attention of many readers may not be fully engaged; lots of people feel that they can never have enough of nature, and there may not be a reason to think of this writer's reflections on the topic as being of any particular interest. But if you write "*we* can never have enough of nature," the reader will be pressed to ask a series of questions: Is that true? Is it true for all humans? Is it true for all humans all the time? Is it perhaps a generalization that may not be literally true, but that has to it a kernel of truth? The reader's attention is suddenly and powerfully engaged.

When writers generalize in this way, though, they are walking a fine line. Take things just a little further than Thoreau does and, rather than engaging the reader with a provocative idea, you run the risk of seeming self-centred and out of touch—as in the second of these passages:

> Though it took me a long time to realize this, I can only feel fully human if I've spent some time in the wild. Really in the wild—not just somewhere in a local park where I'm out of sight of other humans for a few moments, but in the wilderness, where the call of the loon is the loudest sound I can hear.

> Humans can only feel fully human if they have spent some time in the wild. Really in the wild—not just somewhere in a local park where you're out of sight of other humans for a few moments, but in the true wilderness, where the call of the loon is the loudest sound you can hear.

The first is an interesting expression of a deep personal preference; the second has to it a distinct whiff of arrogance. By using extreme language ("can *only* feel fully human") in converting a personal reflection into a generalization about humanity as a whole, the writer runs the risk of leading readers to dismiss the generalization out of hand. Is it really true that *all* humans can *only* feel fully human if these conditions are met? Of course not. If that were the case, no one who lives in London or Lagos or Mumbai all their life could be classed as fully human. What does this writer really know of all humans?

One can also, of course, simply take care to qualify one's generalizations. They may not be quite so provocative, but that may often be all to the good. George Orwell often wrote informal prose of a reflective nature, and often put forward provocative generalizations, but he was also very good at qualifying those generalizations as appropriate:

> On the whole, human beings want to be good, but not too good and not quite all the time. ("All Art Is Propaganda")

As we touched on briefly above, generalizing one's own impressions is not always done by shifting from the first-person singular to the first-person plural. It can also be done by using the second person (as we saw in the above quotation from Rebecca Solnit) or the third person. If we recast the above quotation above from Mary Wortley Montagu in the third person, for example, a piece of humorous self-deprecation becomes a pointed comment on humanity as a whole:

> People often give themselves admirable advice, but are rarely capable of taking it.

A very common pattern in informal writing is for the prose to slide from reflection into attempted persuasion. At some level, it may perhaps fairly be said that any generalization which presents an assertion constitutes an attempt to persuade the reader. If what you are writing is to any extent on a contested topic, though, readers are unlikely to be persuaded by bald, unsupported assertions. (The fundamental error of many blowhard op-ed columnists is to imagine that a series of unsupported assertions constitutes a valid argument.) But good reflective prose may shade into persuasive prose in a variety of subtle ways. Look, for example, at this passage from a review article by Zadie Smith:

> I must be in Mark Zuckerberg's generation—there are only nine years between us—but somehow it doesn't feel that way. This despite the fact that I can say (like everyone else on Harvard's

> campus in the fall of 2003) that "I was there" at Facebook's inception, and remember Facemash and the fuss it caused.... At the time, though, I felt distant from Zuckerberg and all the kids at Harvard. I still feel distant from them now.... The more time I spend with the tail end of Generation Facebook (in the shape of my students) the more convinced I become that some of the software currently shaping their generation is unworthy of them. They are more interesting than it is. They deserve better. ("Generation Why?")

Smith slides from personal reflection (and recollection) into the beginnings of an argument that young people "deserve better" than Facebook by way of social media.

Here's another example; in the passage below, Annie Dillard moves from anodyne reflections on how humans spend time towards an argument in favour of keeping to a schedule:

> How we spend our days is, of course, how we spend our lives. What we do with this hour, and that one, is what we are doing. A schedule defends from chaos and whim. It is a net for catching days. It is a scaffolding on which a worker can stand and labor with both hands at sections of time. A schedule is a mock-up of reason and order—willed, faked, and so brought into being; it is a peace and a haven set into the wreck of time; it is a lifeboat on which you find yourself, decades later, still living. (*The Writing Life*)

With a bit of effort, it is possible to recast the core ideas that Dillard is expressing here as a logical progression—a clear structure of argument:

- There is a tendency towards "chaos and whim" in all our lives.
- If we do nothing to impose structure on our lives, we are in danger of frittering away whole days, which will turn into whole lives.
- It therefore makes sense for us to make schedules, and to do our best to stick to them.

Expressed in the way that Dillard has done, though—in prose that is more reflective than persuasive in form, and that works by poetic suggestion as much as it does through logic—the ideas take on a richness that is entirely lacking in their stripped-down "logical progression" form.

• • •

We have seen from more than one angle how generalizing can play a central role in writing that presents the writer's reflections. It's worth noting that the rejection of commonly made generalizations can also be an excellent jumping-off point for reflective writing. Here, for example, is a reflection that Rebecca Solnit puts forward in *Recollections of My Non-Existence*:

> It's often assumed that anger drives [the work of activism], but most activism is driven by love; a life among activists has convinced me.

And here are two other examples:

> Most people in North America seem to believe it to be inevitable that teenagers will go through a stage of rebellion against their parents. But is that true? Did teenagers in medieval Europe all go through a stage of rebellion against their parents? Do teenagers in rural Zambia all go through a stage of rebellion against their parents?

> A surprising number of people clearly think that the place where they live is, quite simply, the best place on earth. Even a moment's reflection is enough to cast doubt on such assumptions.

From a beginning such as the first of these, one could develop a fuller argument by providing examples—or flesh out one's thoughts with personal recollections concerning one's own teenage years and those of one's friends. Similarly with the second example, one could move on to a discussion of some of the world's most beautiful places—or turn to personal reflection on the degree to which the place in which you live deserves consideration as one of the world's best places.

• • •

A great many writers have offered the world their reflections on writing itself, and what it means to be "a writer." In some cases, those reflections are purely personal; when Carol Ann Duffy said that she had found a piece of advice offered by Pablo Picasso very useful—"Inspiration will come, but it must find you working"—she did not suggest that all other writers should feel the same. Similarly, when George Orwell wrote the following comment about his own orientation towards writing, he did not suggest that all writers have (or should have) the same orientation:

> When I sit down to write a book, I do not say to myself, 'I am going to produce a work of art.' I write it because there is some lie that I want to expose, some fact to which I want to draw attention, and my initial concern is to get a hearing. ("Why I Write")

But surprisingly few writers stick to their own experience when they reflect on the process of writing—and nor do many of them qualify the generalizations they make with phrases such as "for me at least" or "for many writers" or "much of the time." In many cases, though, a consideration of the comments writers have made about writing can make for lively discussion—and perhaps provide a taking off point for a piece of reflective writing of your own. Here is a sampling:

> So long as you write what you wish to write, that is all that matters; and whether it matters for the ages or only for hours, nobody can say. (Virginia Woolf, *A Room of One's Own*, 1929)

> As a [person], you know who is right and who is wrong. You have to make decisions and enforce them. As a writer you should not judge. You should understand. (Ernest Hemingway, "Monologue to the Maestro," 1935)

> Writing is a very silly business at best.... And the greatest foolishness of all lies in the fact that to do it all, the writer must believe that what he is doing is the most important thing in the world. And he must hold to this illusion even when he knows it is not true. (John Steinbeck, diary entry, 3 September 1951)

> In the way that musicians have to play a lot of chords, writers have to write a lot. The short review is like a very short essay. You have to set the scene, you have to lay out the facts and somehow negotiate the relationship between them and your opinions and ideas and interpretations, and you have to come up with some kind of conclusion, and a lot of times you have to do that in eight hundred words. (Rebecca Solnit, "Room to Roam," Interview, 2007)

> The difference [between writing for an academic and writing for a general audience] is that with ... a general audience, no one is being compelled to read the damn thing; that someone is going to have to want to turn the page, and therefore I try to use whatever narrative skills I have to motivate a reader through what is

> often quite difficult, complex material. (Stephen Greenblatt, "The Sense of Life in What Humans Create," Interview, *Los Angeles Review of Books*, 2017)

> There's no point in having a healthy word-count, unless they're the right words. Writing's not an industrial process.... Compression is the first grace of style and takes hard labour. (Hilary Mantel, Interview, *Literary Hub*, 2020)

> You don't start out writing good stuff. You start out writing crap and thinking it's good stuff, and then gradually you get better at it. That's why I say one of the most valuable traits is persistence. It's just so easy to give up! (Octavia E. Butler, *Locus Magazine* interview, 2000)

C2.9.8 Closings

The final paragraphs of many pieces of personal and informal writing follow a pattern not unlike that of most pieces of academic writing; in one way or another they remind the reader of the essay's main points, summarizing or restating what is most important so as to convey a sense of finality. That's something that can be accomplished in different ways in different sorts of personal and informal writing. Here are a couple of examples:

> All in all, then, there are strong arguments for governments to exert far more control over today's media giants. If our governments do not move in that direction, we risk having our democratic values increasingly undermined, and our children's minds increasingly warped by the addictive power of social media. (concluding sentences to an essay offering an informal, "op-ed" style argument for tightening regulation of social media)

> The plane gathered speed as it moved down the runway, and then I could see that the wheels had left the ground; within a few moments we were banking over the Hudson, and the fantastic skyscrapers that had so awed me during our time in New York were shrinking to tiny silver slivers, glinting in the sun. But if anything truly seemed smaller after that first week in the big city, it was me. And maybe that wasn't a bad thing. I was at any rate determined to act less like a big shot once we were home again in Smithers. (concluding sentences to an essay recounting how the

> writer—who had developed a swelled head as a senior in his home town high school—had reacted to and been changed by his first week in a truly large city)

Many of the finest endings find ways to reference the essay's main points while also in one way or another going beyond them—striking a different note, or giving the ideas a slightly different turn, or suggesting a broader relevance to what has been said. Let's return to three of the essays whose openings we discussed earlier, and look at how they close.

Teju Cole's "A Too-Perfect Picture" criticizes the photography of Steve McCurry—with its "strong colors, clear emotional appeal, and crisp composition"—as photography that indulges in fantasy and crowds out real life. In his final paragraph the writer re-frames those criticisms while at the same time broadening his theme, referring not just to McCurry's work but to all photography that "delivers a quick message—sweetness, pathos, humour—and fails to do more," and making a more general point about the relationship between art and the human realities art tries to depict:

> Art is always difficult, but it is especially difficult when it comes to telling other people's stories.... What honors those we look at, those whose stories we try to tell, is work that acknowledges their complex sense of their own reality. Good photography, regardless of its style, is always generous in this way. For this reason, it outlives the moment that occasions it. Weaker photography delivers a quick message—sweetness, pathos, humor—and fails to do more. But more is who we are.

The turn that the last, short sentence gives to the word "more," and to the entire essay, gives the reader a good deal to think through.

Miriam Toews ends the extraordinary essay discussed above ("A Father's Faith") by shifting from recollection and reflection on her father's life and death to an imagined scene. It is a scene that returns to the theme of religion (and how differently father and daughter react to religion), but gives it a different emphasis. Midway through the essay Toews has written bitterly about the role that religion played in the town of Steinbach:

> I know about brain chemistry and depression, but there's still a part of me that blames my dad's death on being Mennonite and

> living in that freaky, austere place where this world isn't good enough, and admission into the next one, the perfect one, means everything, where every word and deed gets you closer or farther away from eternal life. If you don't believe that, then nothing Steinbach stands for will make sense. And if life doesn't make sense you lose yourself in it, your spirit decays. That's what I believed had happened to my dad, and that's why I hated my town.

In the essay's final paragraph, the writer looks at the same subject again, but from a different angle, and through an imaginative lens. Whereas before she has recounted why she hated her town, now she turns to what she has decided she loves about her town—and again, her father's faith is at the centre of it:

> What I love about my town is that it gave my dad the faith that stopped him from being afraid in those last, violent seconds he spent on earth. And the place in my mind where we meet is on the front steps of my dad's church, the big one on Main Street across from Don's Bakery and the Goodwill store. We smile and talk for a few minutes outside, basking in the warmth of the summer sun he loved so much. Then he goes in and I stay outside, and we're both happy where we are.

One of the many notable things about this conclusion is the shift in verb tenses. Throughout the essay Toews has used the simple past tense and the past perfect tense in recounting the events of her father's life and her father's death ("My dad smiled and thanked her, and mentioned that he could hear the [train] whistle. Moments later, he was dead," "I learned my dad had been depressed all his life," "That's what I believed had happened to my dad, and that's why I hated my town"). But in this final paragraph, she shifts to the present tense—the perpetual present—as she creates a place in her mind where the two meet, converse, and, by going their separate ways, can both find happiness.

Finally, let's look at the closing of Desmond Cole's "The Skin I'm In." As we have seen, the essay is an exploration of the issue of racist behaviour in Canadian society—particularly on the part of the police. The essay closes with Cole recounting his attempt to see whatever file the police have on him. The only way he can access that file, he discovers, is through making a Freedom of Information request—a process that typically takes months.

> I have no idea what I'll find in my file. Does it classify me as Black West African or Brown Caribbean? Are there notes about my attitude? Do any of the cops give a reason as to why they stopped me? All I can say for certain is that over the years I've become known to police. That shorthand has always troubled me—too many black men are "known" through a foggy lens of suspicion we've done nothing to earn. Maybe if they really got to know us, they'd treat us differently.

By referencing two of the ways in which the word "know" is commonly used, the writer neatly summarizes the contrast between the way things should be and the way they have remained for too long. The paragraph neatly ties together the essay's themes, while leaving the reader with much to reflect on.

C2.9.9 Informal and Personal Writing: Samples for Discussion

A recurring theme in these discussions of informal and personal writing has been the degree to which different elements—descriptive, narrative, persuasive, and reflective—interact in most sorts of informal and personal writing. For that reason, we have tagged each of the samples that appear here as expressive of various elements and genres.

View from a Park Bench

(DESCRIPTION / NARRATION)

A hundred feet away, a middle aged woman does knee bends and dance moves at the edge of the sun on the grass. There is the smell of cut grass, and of the wood chips they spread beneath the shrubs. A man on a bike drifts lazily by, black T-shirt, black shorts, a little cap with devil's horns on it tight to his head. A man in rags shuffles around the perimeter, a plastic bag over his shoulder; he must be no more than 45. Across the green a man on a bench plays guitar—faint sounds drift over from the other side of the park. A grandfather in sunglasses frowns, pushing a baby in an orange stroller. There's another baby stroller, the man behind it young, striding, smiling; the sounds of hip hop are coming from somewhere at the back of the stroller. The baby is under cover. An older man with short legs wags his hips as he walks. He holds on a leash two retrievers, one black, one golden brown, all three of them old and slow. The sounds of the cars on the street nearby drift in and out of the music as the lights change and the intersection clears. Then there's quiet again. An old jogger makes his way along the fence, and two back-packers. The brakes of a truck squeal as it brakes for the red light. Thick trees line the square. The breeze picks up a little, and brings with it a faint smell of dog droppings. There's the song of a starling.

A young man sits one bench over, hunched over, silent. He is still for a long time and then he coughs—a dry hack, a nasty cough.

A young woman sleeps through it all, head on her pillow, sleeping bag beside her. Middle class, by the look of her. Fifteen feet away two older souls sit on a blanket, their belongings around them in bags. One of them has a large jug of water. "Spring water," I can hear him saying. He leans over and kisses the woman, smiling. They kiss again, lightly, affectionately, like any couple that's come a long way together, and the two find that there is love still between them. She roots about in a bag and pulls out a mickey of whiskey, takes a long swig.

QUESTIONS

1. This piece includes nothing by way of reflection on the part of the author. What effect does that approach have on the reader?
2. Comment on the degree to which senses other than the sense of sight are brought in to the piece.
3. The piece is written entirely in the present tense. Try rewriting a paragraph or two in the past tense. Then try rewriting the same paragraph or two in incomplete sentences, replacing the verbs with present participles (e.g., replace *shuffle* with *shuffling*, *sleeps* with *sleeping*, etc.). What effect do these changes have on the reader?
4. What can you infer about the author of this piece?
5. Comment on the degree to which adjectives and adverbs are used.
6. Try writing a "slice of life going by" piece yourself. How easy or difficult is it to make the piece interesting without including any of your own reflections on what you experience.
7. Comment on the paragraphing in this piece of writing. Could it be written as one, long paragraph?

[The following two writing samples should be read and discussed together.]

Untitled

(NARRATION)

The town I live in now has just acquired a baseball franchise. The Night Owls, one of several new teams in the West Coast League, played their first-ever game May 31st. (For the record, they lost 5–1 to the Portland Pickles, in Portland.) We have a fine little stadium in Nanaimo, opened by Mickey Mantle in 1976. When the league awarded Jim Swanson's group a franchise for Nanaimo, the city agreed to put in proper modern lighting and upgrade the stadium in various other ways, and the team made a number of further improvements.

It was a mad scramble to put the finishing touches on everything, but the stadium was ready for the home opener in early June. The line-ups for everything were way too long, and the chalk line from first base to the foul pole wasn't quite straight, and of course the Night Owls didn't win (for the record, it was Edmonton 7, Night Owls 5). But the Night Owls still had a chance in the ninth, there were some fine hits, there was some hooting and hollering, and a thousand or more fans went home happy.

That evening was overcast and cool, and there was an occasional bit of drizzle during the game. Yesterday, on the other hand, was exactly how baseball should be. The long weekend was beginning, and it was sunny and warm, with a light breeze. The hometown Night Owls were hosting the Pilots from nearby Ladysmith in a holiday weekend exhibition game. And the hometown side got off to a perfect "small ball" start. Get a man on first, have him steal second, and then drive him home with a single. 1–0 Night Owls. Small ball seemed likely to work in the third, too, when runners on first and second were clearly distracting the Pilots' pitcher, who finally balked; the umpire waved the runners to second and third. But the next two batters couldn't connect, and those runners were stranded; it was still 1–0 at the end of four. For those four innings the Pilots had been stymied by good pitching and great defence—especially by the hard-charging, smooth-throwing Night Owls third baseman, an ever-smiling young Hawaiian by the name of Xander Sielken.

I had to leave at the end of five innings; I was meeting someone for dinner at 8. Just as I was leaving the park there was a strong sign that small ball might not win out. The Pilots had gotten a runner on first to start the sixth—that's when I had to leave. As I was walking out behind the right-field fence I heard a cheer go up, and then a small boy raced past me. He was the first to get to the home run ball, which dropped about thirty feet ahead of me. Pilots 2, Night Owls 1.

After dinner I checked in on the game again from home, and watched the ninth, live-streamed. By then it was 5–3 Pilots. The Night Owls looked to be going down without a fight in the bottom of the ninth; two strikeouts were followed by an easy pop-up. But then, amazingly, the Pilots' third baseman couldn't squeeze the ball; it somehow popped out of his glove and squirted onto the grass behind him. The Night Owls had a man on first, bringing the potential tying run to the plate.

Didn't happen; a ground-out ended the game, and the Pilots went back to Ladysmith happy.

Wahoos, Space Cowboys, and Pickles: The Joys of Baseball

(NARRATION / DESCRIPTION / REFLECTION)

The names of the teams give you some idea of how seriously minor league baseball takes itself—and is taken by its fans. The Portland Pickles. The Wenatchee AppleSox. The Sugarland Space Cowboys. The Albuquerque Isotopes. The Akron Rubber Ducks. The Pensacola Blue Wahoos. And, of course, the Savannah Bananas. Sure, you can find a few Dodgers and Tigers and Cardinals too. And yes, the local fans can go a bit wild when their team wins something on home field. But that's about as far as it goes. I remember when I lived in Calgary and the Cannons (the old Triple A team that relocated to Albuquerque in 2003) beat the Fresno Grizzlies to win their conference championship how excited everyone at the ballpark was. But how many paid attention to what happened after that in the league championship series and Triple A World Series? Hardly anyone. (For the record, the Cannons lost the PCL Championship to the New Orleans Zephyrs, three games to two.)

The town I live in now has just acquired a baseball franchise. The Night Owls, one of several new teams in the West Coast League, played their first-ever game May 31st. (For the record, they lost 5–1 to the Pickles, in Portland.) Here in Nanaimo we have a fine little stadium that was opened by Mickey Mantle in 1976. When the league awarded Jim Swanson's group a franchise for Nanaimo, the city agreed to put in proper modern lighting and upgrade the stadium in various other ways, and the team made a number of further improvements.

It really is a beautiful park, with great views from almost everywhere. The little grandstand is a bit cramped but it has character, and it's covered, so you're protected against the rain, and you're very close to home plate. The outfield beer garden and the viewing area mounted on scaffolding above the center field fence offer lovely long-range views, and the low bleachers on the third base side give you a down-low sense of the action, without any mesh to obstruct your view.

It was a mad scramble to put the finishing touches on everything, but the stadium was ready for the home opener in early June. The line-ups for everything were way too long, and the chalk line from first base to the foul pole wasn't quite straight, and of course the Night Owls didn't win. (For the record, it was Edmonton 7, Night Owls 5.) But the Night Owls still had a chance in the ninth, there were some fine hits, there was some hooting and hollering, and a thousand or more fans went home happy.

That evening was overcast and cool, and there was an occasional bit of drizzle during the game. Yesterday, on the other hand, was exactly how baseball should be. The long weekend was beginning, and it was sunny and warm, with a light breeze. The hometown Night Owls were hosting the Pilots from nearby Ladysmith in a holiday weekend exhibition game. And the hometown side got off to a perfect "small ball" start. Get a man on first, have him steal second, and then drive him home with a single. 1–0 Night Owls. Small ball seemed likely to work in the third, too, when runners on first and second were clearly distracting the Pilots' pitcher, who finally balked; the umpire waved the runners to second and third. But the next two batters couldn't connect, and those runners were stranded; it was still 1–0 at the end of four. For those four innings the Pilots had been stymied by good pitching and great defence—especially by the hard-charging, smooth-throwing Night Owls third baseman, an ever-smiling young Hawaiian by the name of Xander Sielken.

The Night Owls' home opener, 3 June 2022

I had to leave at the end of five innings; I was meeting someone for dinner at 8. Just as I was leaving the park there was a strong sign that small ball might not win out. The Pilots had gotten a runner on first to start the sixth—that's when I had to leave. As I was walking out behind the right-field fence I heard a cheer go up, and then a small boy raced past me. He was the first to get to the home run ball, which dropped about thirty feet ahead of me. Pilots 2, Night Owls 1.

In low-level baseball, no one cares that much about the score, especially in an exhibition match. You live in the present; you go for the play, on a play-by-play basis, and for the play of the sun on the deep green of the grass in the lengthening shadows, and for the pleasure of a cold beer or two on a warm evening. When your favorite player comes to the plate you holler, "Come on, Josh!" and when there's a speedster on first you holler, "Take second!"

But who doesn't pay at least a little bit of attention to the score? Who doesn't at some level want their team to win? After dinner I checked in on the game again from home, and watched the ninth, live-streamed. By then it was 5–3 Pilots. The Night Owls looked to be going down without a fight in the bottom of the ninth; two strikeouts were followed by an easy pop-up. But then, amazingly, the Pilots' third baseman couldn't squeeze the ball; it somehow popped out of his glove and squirted onto the grass behind him. The Night Owls had a man on first, bringing the potential tying run to the plate.

Didn't happen; a ground-out ended the game, and the Pilots went back to Ladysmith happy. But the hometown fans had to be happy too; what's not to like about small town baseball in the summer?

For about as long as there has been baseball there have been complaints that the game is too slow. And in recent years it *has* been too slow; the length of the average major league game has crept inexorably upwards, to well over three hours. In the minor leagues, things have been changing; intercollegiate leagues have recently instituted a twenty-second time limit between pitches, and the professional minor leagues a thirty second limit. That's cut the length of games by close to half an hour in many cases.

If it's true that baseball needs to get faster, it's also true that it does us all good to be comfortable with some things in life having a slow pace to them. No, we shouldn't have to wait the better part of a minute between each pitch. But we should be OK with a sport in which, for long stretches, nothing much happens. We chat, we take in the atmosphere—and we're ready for those moments when things really do get exciting. A base gets stolen, somebody hits a triple, there's a play at the plate, the game is tied and then the pitcher walks the next batter. "Take second!" you holler. Maybe that will happen, maybe it won't. Life's like that; often things take time, and often they don't turn out as you'd hoped. But the grass is still green, and there's always tomorrow.

QUESTIONS

1. The first of the above two pieces is almost entirely narration. Of the material added in the second of the two pieces, how much is narration, how much description? What does the descriptive material add to the piece? What does the reflective material add?
2. As an exercise, write a brief piece of narrative prose telling a story of attending some event (perhaps a sports event, or a play, or a music festival, or a meeting, or a political rally). Try to make it *only* a narrative (i.e., include as little descriptive or reflective material as possible). Save that version, and then write additional passages providing more description, and also reflecting on what you saw. Has the piece been improved? If so, in what ways?
3. Discuss how narration, description, and reflection are blended in the second of the above pieces.
4. How would you describe the tone of this piece of writing?
5. Are the team names listed in the first paragraph humourous? Why?
6. What is the effect of the inclusion of the parenthetical sentences beginning "For the record…"?
7. What is the effect of the personal quirks in the narrative (leaving after the fifth inning, tuning in at home for the ninth inning, etc.)?
8. Does the photograph add anything to this piece? Would it be better to include more photographs? Would it be better to include video clips? How would the effect of the piece be changed if that were done?
9. Is it in fact true that "it does us all good to be comfortable with some things in life having a slow pace to them"?
10. Look up the recent history of the Savannah Bananas. Would you say that their approach makes a mockery of a sport that deserves to be treated with respect? Or is it an example of harmless fun?
11. What verb tenses predominate in this piece of writing? How would the tone of the piece be changed if the present tense were used for the narrative passages?
12. Comment on the paragraphing in this piece of writing.

Ashes

(MEMOIR / DESCRIPTION / NARRATION / REFLECTION)

For the last year of her life my mother had, as they say, lost it. Anything she picked up, she would lose in a minute. Any thought that she had, she would lose in a second. She was in the nursing home's double-doored lock ward, so the one thing she couldn't lose was herself.

She'd been dead for several years before I managed to lose her.

No, not "lose." Misplace.

My mother's ashes came in a lacquered box, about 10 inches long, 6 inches wide, and a couple of inches deep. Inside, what was left of her was in a plastic bag. Thick plastic, the open end folded over twice. There was no twist-tie—no extra precautionary measure to prevent her escaping.

Anyone who has ever seen the ashes of a loved one—but why do I write "seen"? We are all so conditioned to think that what we see is what is most important, when what we hear and taste and smell and feel can matter just as much. What we *feel*, in this case. The seeing is ordinary, unremarkable. But the feel of a human's ashes? Anyone who has ever experienced that feeling will tell you that they're heavy—a lot heavier than you'd expect. For their volume, they must weigh three or four times more than the ashes from a wood fire. And they are gritty, with little chunks all through—not soft like wood ashes. The bones, I guess.

My mother could never decide what she wanted done with her after she died. She knew she wanted to be cremated—that much was clear. But after that?

She'd said at one point that maybe she'd like to have her ashes buried next to her own mother's grave. But that was in Pennsylvania, nowhere near where any of the family lived now—and besides, she'd said that, for herself, she didn't feel any strong connection to the place.

Perhaps I should bury the ashes in Calgary, the city I was living in—or in Ottawa, the city my brother lived in, where our mother had lived herself for more than twenty years. But it was so cold there, and she'd never been very fond of anywhere in Ontario.

Maybe scatter the ashes? That would be fine—but where? A few of her favorite places, I supposed; I could think of two or three spots that might qualify. I equivocated. More than once I wished that mother had been more definite as to what she wanted to happen, after she died.

So it was that, for years, I kept the box that held her ashes, not sure what to do with it. With *them*. With *her*? For a while they were on the top shelf of a cupboard, for a while in a bureau drawer. But at least I knew where they were—and some day I would decide what to do with them.

Then I moved. Then I moved again a year later. And then that place was turned upside down by renovations, and everything had to be moved from one room to another and back again.

So it was that early last year, when for some reason I started to think seriously about doing something about my mother's ashes, I couldn't find them. I looked in the bureau drawer where I was sure they had been for a while at one point. I looked on the top shelf of the renovated cupboards. The basement? A lot of things had ended up in a jumble in the basement during that renovation. I looked in each place more than once. She was nowhere to be found. A few days later I looked again, and a few weeks after that I looked once more. She had not reappeared.

My mother had died of Alzheimer's, and now I couldn't remember where I had put her.

I tried to laugh, as we so often do about things that have to do with death. If it hadn't been me who was responsible, maybe I would have found it funny. I tried to tell myself it didn't matter, that she really hadn't cared about what would happen to her after she died. And she hadn't. She hadn't been religious in any way—other than having liked the sound of a choir. She had believed that we die, and that's it; what lives on is whatever we have done in the world, and our children.

At odd moments over the course of almost a year I found myself looking for her again. Might I have put her in that forgotten space behind the furnace? Might I have stored her in that closet upstairs that's never used? I looked behind everything. Twice.

To be reminded of the death of a loved one is to be reminded of one's own mortality—many people will tell you that. But it's not true for everyone; certainly it's not true for me. I may sometimes be reminded of my own mortality by the death of someone I've known much more distantly—an acquaintance from high school days, for example, who I was never close to then and have rarely seen since. But if I'm reminded of the death of a loved one, I'm reminded of the loved one—nothing and no one else. This was about my mother, and I had lost her.

She always had a tendency to make her children feel guilty about one thing or another. She was doing it still.

I found her last week. The box that held her ashes was in a dark corner of the basement, behind four things and underneath two others; somehow I had missed her all those times when I thought I'd looked everywhere.

What to do now? Finding my mother means I no longer have to tussle with that twinge of guilt that no one who loses their mother can avoid. But it also means coming up hard against the fact of her never coming back.

I'll be travelling to Pennsylvania for a conference in the spring. Maybe I'll take her with me.

QUESTIONS

1. Much of this essay is devoted to telling a story. But several paragraphs are taken up primarily with description or reflection. Identify those paragraphs, and then comment on how the essay would read without them.
2. Comment on the paragraphing in this piece of writing.
3. Comment on the first sentence of the fifth paragraph. What is the effect of this interruption in the train of thought?
4. At several other points the writer also poses questions. Who is being addressed with these questions? Rewrite at least one of the relevant passages so that it no longer includes any question. How is the effect altered?
5. In the third-last paragraph, there is little or no description provided of the area of the basement where the writer finds the container of ashes. Do you think the paragraph would be improved by the addition of more detail? Why or why not?
6. In at least three instances, a paragraph in this essay ends with a sentence fragment—in one case, with a fragment of a single word. Comment on the appropriateness (or inappropriateness) of breaking the rules of grammar in cases such as these.
7. Find examples of the following in this essay:
   a. repetition of phrasing or of sentence structure
   b. reader-inclusive language, and/or passages that in some way appeal to fellow-feeling in the reader
   c. passages expressing plans, expectations, or other forward-looking thoughts
8. The essay carries a fairly nondescript title. What would be the effect if one of the following titles were used instead:
   a. The Year I Lost My Mother
   b. Losing a Parent
   c. Ashes to Ashes
   d. Lost and Found

Chicago Style and "The Chicago of the North"

(MEMOIR / DESCRIPTION / REFLECTION / PERSUASION)

As most people in Winnipeg are aware, during the early decades of the twentieth century the city was often referred to as "the Chicago of the North." I confess I had thought of this historical moniker as being uncontroversial, but I recently came across a Brent Bellamy column in the August 25, 2014 *Winnipeg Free Press* that took issue with the whole concept. As Bellamy points out, Winnipeg skyscrapers in the early twentieth century arose through a good many connections to architects from New York and elsewhere, as well as from connections to Chicago architects. Winnipeg's Exchange District is often today characterized in its entirety as being "Chicago Style" or "Chicago School," and Bellamy is I think right that such a description is problematic. (I think it's also worth noting the degree to which Chicago and New York architects from the period are not discrete categories; before Frederick Dinkelberg designed the Jewelers' Building in Chicago he had designed the Flatiron [aka the "Fuller Building"] in New York. After Raymond Hood designed the faux Gothic Chicago Tribune Tower in Chicago he went on to design Art deco and modernist towers in New York. And so on.)

It still seems to me, though, that the *best* of the towers in Winnipeg's Exchange District are in fact strongly influenced by the Chicago style. If the terms "Chicago School" or "Chicago Style" architecture from the early twentieth century are to mean anything, it is surely that, in addition to a steel frame and a cornice, a skyscraper will have large windows to let in the light (this made possible by the walls not needing to support the building's weight); and the windows will be in groups, with vertical elements between the window groupings that emphasize the building's height. A skyscraper such as the Union Bank Building on Winnipeg's Main Street, by this definition, is not Chicago Style; though it does have a cornice, there is no strong vertical element to the design, and the windows are small and evenly spaced. Nor does the Grain Exchange fit the description of a Chicago Style tower.

Union Bank Building

C2.9 Informal and Personal Writing

Lindsay Building (above)
Confederation Life Building (right)

The Lindsay Building, on the other hand, or the Confederation Life Building, or the Union Trust Building—all, to my eye, more attractive skyscrapers than the Union Bank Building—do indeed fit the "Chicago Style" description.

More important than the buildings themselves, of course, was the spirit of the city. People called Winnipeg the Chicago of the North not just because some of its skyscrapers resembled some of the skyscrapers in Chicago, but because they felt the bustling spirit of the railway town that was the Canadian gateway to the west resembled that of the railway town that filled the same role in America. The comparison certainly would not be apt today—and I guess that was a large part of Bellamy's point in his *Free Press* piece. But in the 1910s or 1920s or 1930s? My guess is that the expression "Chicago of the North" captured something real; both were growing up in similar ways, and growing up fast.

QUESTIONS

1. This essay could be re-written as a conventional essay in an academic style—with everything phrased so as to remove any "I" or "me." What would be the effect if the essay were rewritten in that way?
2. To what extent would this essay suffer if the photographs were not included?
3. To what extent would the essay be enhanced if video clips rather than still photographs were included?

4. Using Google Street View, write a description of a busy block or two near where you live. Then go to the same area in person and, without looking at the first description you wrote, write a new description of the same stretch. Compare the two descriptions and comment on the differences.
5. Write a brief piece reflecting on one or more architectural styles that are prevalent in a neighbourhood in your town or city.

In Remembrance: Dennis McKerlie

(MEMOIR / DESCRIPTION / NARRATION / REFLECTION)

One day in the fall of 2011 Dennis McKerlie checked himself into a Calgary hospital. A philosophy professor, McKerlie had been telling colleagues and friends for many months that he was having trouble remembering things, and that he thought it might be serious. He was barely into his sixties; no one really believed him, and on some days he wasn't sure he believed himself. But on this day he found he couldn't remember the way home.

McKerlie spent the rest of his life in institutions, as a rare form of Alzheimer's destroyed his mind. From the Foothills Hospital he moved to a foul-smelling seniors' home in Bowness, then to a luxuriously bland seniors' home near the river in central Calgary, then to a succession of homes in and around Saskatoon (home of his brother Kent—his closest relative).

McKerlie was possessed of one of the brightest minds in a department filled with very bright minds. He was unfailingly modest about his abilities—and it was a modesty honestly felt; he genuinely believed that he was nothing special. But until those last years he possessed extraordinary powers of reasoning, a vast body of general knowledge, and remarkable powers of recall. Even when he had lost the ability to find his way home he could follow complex philosophical arguments—and recall the names, positions, and strengths and weaknesses of virtually every major league baseball player of the 1950s.

Dennis was also possessed of one of the kindest and gentlest hearts I have ever known. He grew up in small town Manitoba and never developed the presumption or the sense of entitlement that so many extraordinarily gifted people acquire on their way to success. He was in many ways an Eeyore. Living alone and without the sort of love that most of us think of first when we think of love, he was often sad, but never bitter. He loved golf and jazz and baseball and philosophical discussion and wry humor and the poems of Philip Larkin, and the process of thinking things through. And he loved his brother and his nephew and his friends—though in that sort of context he would never use the word "love."

Dennis would gently smile or laugh when other people said or did funny things but never when he was funny himself, which was often. One day his friend and colleague Ann Levey wondered why he was looking down all the time. "Are you depressed, or what?" she asked.

"I don't know," said Dennis. "I guess I like my shoes."

As the disease ate away at his mind Dennis could no longer be very funny, or find much of the world funny, or put thoughts together very well. "Is the food any good here?" I asked him when I visited him this past spring, only a few weeks before he died; by then he had been moved into a friendly little seniors' home in Langham, Saskatchewan.

"I don't know. But that might be because I'm not very interesting."

In the last year or two of his life Dennis was subject to terrible rages, directed always against himself. He would bang his head against the wall, telling the world that he was a terrible person and that they mustn't pretend otherwise, that he was someone who had behaved horribly to others, that he was someone who had never lived up to his potential, that he was someone who did not deserve to live.

Dennis' great work was a groundbreaking philosophical monograph, *Justice Between the Young and the Old*, described by Rutgers philosopher Jeff McMahan as "the most sophisticated, imaginative, rigorous and comprehensive—in short, the best—discussion to date of the problem of intergenerational justice." The product of three decades of work, it was published late in 2013 by Oxford University Press. The book's final chapter is "Alzheimer's Disease." After that comes "Conclusion," which ends with this sentence: "When the people we have loved reach the boundary of coherence, we can understand the bitterness of Philip Larkin's poem 'The Old Fools.'"

By the time *Justice Between the Young and the Old* had reached the proof stage, Dennis could no longer read. When the book was published, I took my copy along when I visited him in Langham, and asked if he could sign it. He scribbled on a page as a child scribbles. "Is that all right?" he asked.

They tried to move Dennis one last time, in early May, to a seniors' home somewhere in Saskatoon—a home I never found out the name of. A few days later he was gone.

Dennis was 65 when his life ended—an age that many today would not call old. Dennis was not among them. "The Old Fools," of course, ends like this:

Can they never tell
What is dragging them back, or how it will end? Not at night?
Not when the strangers come? Never, throughout
The whole hideous inverted childhood? Well,
We shall find out.

QUESTIONS

1. Essays that attempt to sum up a human life usually contain a mix of generalizations about the person and specific facts. What sort of specifics make a person "come alive" in a piece such as this?
2. At what points do you find this piece emotionally affecting? Why do you think that those passages have such an effect?
3. Explain the reference "an Eeyore."
4. Comment on the use of adjectives and adverbs in this piece.
5. Ann Wroe, who writes a weekly obituary column that appears on the last page of *The Economist* magazine, has penned many of the most evocative such pieces of this century. Look up two or three of these and compare them with the conventional obituaries that appeared elsewhere at the same time. What is different about the style in which Wroe writes? (Among those that you might consider in particular: Esther Bejarano, Chadwick Boseman, Leonard Cohen, George Floyd, Chester Nez, Nancy Reagan, Amjad Sabriar, Asfaw Yemiru.)
6. Wroe has said that, to her, "there's no life that's more important than another." She added that she often thinks "that the lives we think of as 'little lives' are the most interesting." What do you think?

(Spare) Change for the Better

(REFLECTION / PERSUASION)

"Everyone always pays with plastic now"—you hear it constantly. But of course it's not true. For one thing, there are still a good many Luddite oldsters like me who still use cash for the odd purchase. But there are also a lot of people who don't carry plastic—people who are very poor, people who are homeless, people who don't even have a bank account. It's largely for that reason that we should make a point of always carrying some cash—all of us, that is, who don't always say no to those asking for "spare change," or to those who entertain us by busking on our streets. Imagine New Orleans's French Quarter or Vancouver's Granville Island without street musicians; that vision could well become a reality if we give up carrying cash.

But it's not just homeless people and street musicians who need us to be able to offer them small amounts of cash; it's also a great many people who have traditionally depended on tips for a significant part of their income. Our tendency has long been to think of tips mainly in connection with dining out—and especially, in connection with dining out in sit-down restaurants. Over the course of the pandemic that perception shifted somewhat, as take-out and home delivery from restaurants became more and more popular. We grew much more used to adding 10% or 15% or 20% as a tip to the bill when paying with plastic in those situations. But there's often no option to add a percentage when we buy fast food; the only way to tip those low-paid workers is usually with cash. And the same is true of the low-paid workers who clean your hotel room, or who do a range of other low-paid jobs. In an ideal world those people would simply be paid a living wage, and tips wouldn't be needed. Sadly, we're a long way from that sort of transformation; without the few dollars left with a hastily scrawled "thank you" on the bedside table for the hotel housekeeping worker, and without the fifty cents or dollar thrown in the tip jar for the fast-food worker who just served us, those people will struggle even more.

Let's make their lives a little easier instead of a little harder. And let's save street music in our cities. Let's always keep a few coins in our pockets, and a few small bills in our wallets and purses. Change for the better.

QUESTIONS

1. This little essay is made up of reflections on a particular societal change and of material designed to persuade readers to adopt a particular course of action. How persuasive is it? Why?
2. What rhetorical effect does the emphasis on street musicians and hotel housekeeping staff have? To what extent would the argument be less persuasive if the emphasis (in the context of giving money away) were more on being able to give to homeless people more readily?
3. Do you think many people reading this piece would say to themselves, "Yes, that makes sense," but then continue to not carry any form of payment with them other than plastic? Discuss the psychological mechanisms involved in this sort of behaviour—and try to think of other examples of it.
4. What audience is being addressed in this short essay? How can you tell?
5. Discuss the use of the first person in this piece. To what extent is the use of the first person plural helpful rhetorically; would the piece be less effective if the writer had concluded by saying that "people should always keep a few coins in their pockets…"?
6. Discuss the impact of some of the terms used to describe people's levels of wealth or poverty—terms such as *poor*, *low-income*, *wealthy*, *rich*, *well-off*, *high net worth*. What about the verbs; does it make a difference if we speak of what people *are paid* for certain sorts of work vs. what they *earn* for those sorts of work? What about expressions such as *making good money*, *having a good income*?

[The following two writing samples should be read and discussed together.]

Untitled

(DESCRIPTION / NARRATION)

There's just a straggle of customers at the bar, and the dance floor's all empty, so you can see the music, not just hear it. Up on the little stage by the front door two players make notes in the air. One's long-haired and muscled, shouldering tattoos and a guitar. He's low volume but taut with energy, his voice a falsetto, reedy like Skip James. The other is slight and sun-glassed with a quiet smile, all shirted, his fingers curling into the deep strings of the bass. Both of them are late twenties—old enough to be worldly wise with wry smiles, young enough to be young. One is black, one white. They play slow songs from a place somewhere between jazz and the blues, slow songs for a slow afternoon. A neon sign above the door spells "Blue Moon" in yellow. Squares of sun angle through the squares of the panes of the huge windows into bright squares on the floor. Above the stage a wide mirror angles more light into the room, more warmth. People listen, people clap. The shadows of strumming flit back and forth in the brightness on the floor. The gentle music sways, and the shadows lengthen so slowly that you won't notice time until the muscled, bare-shouldered one asks it of the slight, shirted one. The slight one says it's 4:15, and they decide to play one more.

And they do play one more, and the world and its people drift by in the sun outside those great windows. A tall, thin man in dreadlocks. A carrot-haired boy, singing. A child walking determined, independent, clutching a sweet, two steps ahead of a gently smiling mother. An elegantly dressed couple, one black, one white. A leather-faced couple, one with a backpack, one with a guitar in a case slung over his shoulder; they look like they've been sleeping rough. Voices talking idly somewhere in the shadows by the bar:

—*You remember this place when they used to have sagging armchairs and a wicker couch?*

—*Oh yeah. Down where the piano is now, and the stage was on the other side.*

—*It's a long time ago. That was just after the storm.*

—*You miss that couch?*

—*Sure I miss that couch. But it's better now.*

Look out the panes of those large windows, and watch the world. There's a young man in a cloth cap, winding slowly down the street on a bicycle with absurdly high handlebars, sipping a drink as his feet turn the pedals. Two women look back at something on the sidewalk behind them, laughing, holding hands. A man in a cloth cap with a trumpet. A teenager in a pork pie hat, deep in thought. Another couple holding hands—one in a blue skirt rippling in the breeze, white; her partner younger, Asian. On the street a uniformed brass band walks by—six of them in uniform, no one playing yet, a police car behind them, lights flashing but making no sound. Off to a parade, somewhere.

A short woman with purple hair and nose rings passes by, walking purposefully. An old man with long white hair pokes his face in at the door, waves to the band, walks on. A squat couple in shorts comes in the door, taking short steps, breathing hard in the heat. They lower themselves onto a bench by the far wall. This is the quiet set, and there are still places to sit. By 8:00 or 9:00 it will be jammed; there will hardly be anywhere to stand, let alone sit. The whole street will be swarming.

Twelve Years after the Storm

(DESCRIPTION / NARRATION / REFLECTION)

Blue sky, and it only feels humid to the tourists. This is New Orleans, twelve years after the storm. Mid-October, mid afternoon. Frenchmen Street, home of the music, is sleepy. But there's music and there's joy and there's peace at the Spotted Cat.

You can join the straggle of customers at the bar. The dance floor's all empty, so you can see the music, not just hear it. Up on the little stage by the front door two players make notes in the air. One's long-haired and muscled, shouldering tattoos and a guitar. He's low volume but taut with energy, his voice a falsetto, reedy like Skip James. The other is slight and sun-glassed with a quiet smile, all shirted, his fingers curling into the deep strings of the bass. Both of them are late twenties—old enough to be worldly wise with wry smiles, young enough to be young. One is black, one white. They play slow songs from a place somewhere between jazz and the blues, slow songs for a slow afternoon. A neon sign above the door spells "Blue Moon" in yellow. Squares of sun angle through the squares of the panes of the huge windows into bright squares on the floor. Above the stage a wide mirror angles more light into the room, more warmth. People listen, people clap. The shadows of strumming flit back and forth in the brightness on the floor. The gentle music sways, and the shadows lengthen so slowly that you won't notice time until the muscled, bare-shouldered one asks it of the slight, shirted one.

—*What's the time?*

—*It's four fifteen.*

—*We'll play one more?*

—*Let's play one more.*

And they play one more, and the world and its people drift by in the sun outside those great windows. A tall, thin man in dreadlocks. A carrot-haired boy, singing. A child walking determined, independent, clutching a sweet, two steps ahead of a gently smiling mother. An elegantly dressed couple, one black, one white. A leather-faced couple, one with a backpack, one with a guitar in a case slung over his shoulder; they look like they've been sleeping rough. Voices talking idly somewhere in the shadows by the bar:

—You remember this place when they used to have sagging armchairs and a wicker couch?

—Oh yeah. Down where the piano is now, and the stage was on the other side.

—It's a long time ago. That was just after the storm.

—You miss that couch?

—Sure I miss that couch. But it's better now.

Look out the panes of those large windows, and watch the world. There's a young man in a cloth cap, winding slowly down the street on a bicycle with absurdly high handlebars, sipping a drink as his feet turn the pedals. Two women look back at something on the sidewalk behind them, laughing, holding hands. A man in a cloth cap with a trumpet. A teenager in a pork pie hat, deep in thought. Another couple holding hands—one white; her partner younger, Asian. On the street a uniformed brass band walks by—six of them in uniform, no one playing yet, a police car behind them, lights flashing but making no sound. Off to a parade, somewhere.

A short woman with purple hair and nose rings passes by, walking purposefully. An old man with long white hair pokes his face in at the door, waves to the band, walks on. A squat couple in shorts comes in the door, taking short steps, breathing hard in the heat. They lower themselves onto a bench by the far wall. This is the quiet set, and there are still places to sit. By 8:00 or 9:00 it will be jammed; there will hardly be anywhere to stand, let alone sit. The whole street will be swarming.

—Were going to take a little break now. A fifteen minute break. I'm Salvatore, and this is Robin on the bass. That's the tip jar. We're called "Up, Up, We Go," and we'll be back real soon. Really. Stick around. We'll be back.

I think back—back to the storm, and to the years right before the storm, and the years right after the storm. The race hatred, the poverty, the injustice, the corruption, the desperation, the despair. Has all that disappeared? No, of course not. But has it gotten better? Has life become more livable? Is there less injustice, less corruption, less desperation and despair? Unquestionably, yes. The music has come back; the tourists have come back; the city has come back. Will it take a lot more hard work and a lot more money and a lot more good will before things are truly well in the Crescent City? Unquestionably, yes. Don't forget the tip jar as you leave.

QUESTIONS

1. How different does the piece as a whole seem without the material added in the second version? In what ways does it seem different?
2. How does the title affect how you read the piece?
3. Imagine how the central portion of this piece of writing could be framed differently—with an entirely different first and last paragraph that would point the piece in another direction entirely. What might that direction be? Try drafting a different first and last paragraph.
4. Discuss how description and narration are blended in the central portion of the piece (i.e., the part first presented on its own above).
5. What verb tenses predominate in this piece of writing? How would the tone of the piece be changed if different verb tenses were used?
6. The writer of this piece not infrequently writes in sentence fragments rather than complete sentences. With particular reference to paragraph 7 (the paragraph that begins "And they play one more"), comment on the appropriateness (or inappropriateness) of breaking the rules of grammar in this way in a piece such as this.
7. Say something about the effect created by the following words and phrases, in each case comparing them to other words or phrases that could be substituted: *sleepy* in paragraph 1; *deep strings* in paragraph 3; *lower themselves* in paragraph 14.
8. The word *straggle* in paragraph 2 is normally used as a verb; here it is used as a noun. What effect does it create? What other noun might be used in its place?
9. Comment on the paragraphing in this piece of writing.
10. Find examples of the following in this essay:
    a. repetition of phrasing or of sentence structure
    b. reader-inclusive language, and/or passages that in some way appeal to fellow-feeling in the reader
    c. passages expressing forward-looking thoughts

Why Eggs and Ham Are Not Green

(BLOG POST / PERSUASION / REFLECTION)

What does it mean to be green? At it simplest, being green surely means to support policies—and, at a personal level, to adopt habits of behaviour—that are good for the planet.

It seems that researchers are increasingly coming to the conclusion that the biggest single thing human animals can do for the planet is, at a personal level, to stop eating other animals. And, at a government level, we can stop providing billions in subsidies to those sectors of the food industry that turn non-human animals (and their milk and eggs) into human food. Results of the most broadly-based study to date were published earlier this year in the prestigious journal *Science*. The study, led by Joseph Poore of the Department of Zoology at Oxford University, has the unappetizing title of "Reducing food's environmental impacts through producers and consumers." Its conclusion? "Moving from current diets to a diet that excludes animal products has transformative potential, reducing food's GHG emissions by 49%...." For a developed nation, "dietary change has the potential for a far greater effect on food's different emissions," reducing them by as much as 73%. Poore used more direct language when interviewed by *The Guardian* (a leading British newspaper): "A vegan diet is probably the single biggest way to reduce your impact on planet Earth—not just greenhouse gases, but global acidification, eutrophication, land use, and water use. It is far bigger than cutting down on your flights or buying an electric car."

It's no secret that the byproducts of large-scale agribusiness include large-scale pollution of the traditional sort. In recent years researchers have begun to appreciate as well the extent to which large-scale agriculture contributes to climate change. That's not only—or even mainly—the result of methane emissions from the obvious sources (emissions from the rear ends of cows and pigs, emissions from slaughterhouse effluent, etc.). It's also the result of deforestation; to the extent that we choose to eat animal products, far more forest needs to be turned into farmland than would be the case if we adopted a whole-foods, plant-based diet. Animal agriculture is fundamentally inefficient: rather than grow crops to feed humans directly, we devote massive amounts of land and of energy to growing crops to feed animals that will later be killed and fed to humans. "Meat, aquaculture, eggs, and dairy use 83% of the world's farmland and contribute 56–58% of food's different emissions, despite providing only 37% of our protein and 18% of our calories," the Oxford study reports.

But aren't eating local, and eating meat or cheese from organically certified farms just as good for the environment as going vegan? No, is the short answer. To be sure, obtaining our nourishment from organic meat or dairy is better than obtaining it from factory-farmed meat or dairy—but the Oxford study confirms that it's far worse than obtaining our nourishment from beans, greens, nuts, and fruit; in the long run, even organic animal agriculture is simply not sustainable. Poore provided a personal perspective in his interview with *The Guardian*: "The reason I started this project was to understand if there were sustainable animal producers out there. But I have stopped consuming animal products over the last four years of this project." Given all the evidence, you'd think that every Green Party would have made eliminating subsidies to animal agriculture a central plank of its platform. You'd expect too a suite of measures designed to encourage us all to adopt a whole foods, plant-based diet—or, at the very least, to greatly reduce our consumption of non-human animals.

If you thought that, you'd be dead wrong. Again and again when it comes to agriculture and food policies, Green Party platforms such as those of Green Party US, the Green Party of Canada, and the UK Green Party tout their support of organic farming and of eating local—and say nothing about discouraging the consumption by humans of animal products. Even Germany's powerful Green Party—which calls for an end to "industrial livestock farming within the next 20 years"—does not put forward any set of policies designed to reduce the consumption by humans of non-humans.

Greens, in other words, are not truly green—and conventional mainstream parties that claim to be "green" are no better. Arguably, the only parties with platforms that qualify as truly green are parties such as the tiny Animal Protection Party in Canada, and the Party for the Animals in the Netherlands. That name may sound laughable to some, but the Party for the Animals has several seats in the Dutch Parliament, and it's largely as a result of their pressure that the Dutch government has become one of the few in the world to make the reduction of meat consumption a goal.

None of this should be taken to suggest that it's wrong to tax carbon emissions and encourage renewable sources of power generation. But for parties to say they are green and not propose any measures to reduce the human consumption of non-human animals is to ignore—excuse the metaphor—the elephant in the room.

QUESTIONS

1. What is the writer endeavouring to convince readers to do in this piece? How can you tell?
2. Consider the title of this piece. How does it work to capture the reader's attention? What role can allusions play to engage a reader's interest?
3. What evidence does this writer use to bolster their argument? List three examples.

4. The writer of this piece delves into the cultural meaning of "green." What meanings of "green" does this piece explore? How does this symbol help structure the argument of the essay?
5. Although this is an informal piece of writing, it does present an argument: What do you think is the main thesis? Write down the thesis and sketch out an outline of the main arguments that are used to support it.
6. Consider the ending of this essay. How is this use of what is known as a "dead metaphor"—a metaphor used so often it has lost its power—effective in this context?
7. How does the writer use *pathos* (an appeal to the emotions) to help make their argument? What about *ethos* (an appeal to respected authorities) and *logos* (logical argument)?

The Strategy Behind Tonight's Walk-Off Win by Dee Gordon and the Marlins

(BLOG POST / NARRATION / REFLECTION)

Baseball is a game of strategy, but if you always stick with the same strategy you become predictable—and your team loses. A textbook example of the importance of flexibility in forming strategy occurred today in extra innings in Miami. With the game tied in the bottom of the ninth the Marlins had had the bases loaded, and couldn't score. In the top of the tenth the Phillies had had the bases loaded, and couldn't score. Now, in the bottom of the tenth, and with two out, the Marlins again had the bases loaded. My baseball hero, Dee Gordon, was coming to the plate. Dee is a poster boy of small ball; his game is beating out the throw to first, and then stealing a base, and then when the throw from the catcher or the pitcher goes astray, taking another base on the error.* But infield hits are harder to come by when the bases are loaded with two out and the defense is playing five infielders.

That's where you need strategy—and, if I may be immodest for a moment, that's where I come into the picture. For weeks I've been fine-tuning strategy with my two Miami Marlins hats; I wore the beige hat with the bright red and yellow and blue logo when I saw the Marlins play two games in Milwaukee a couple of weeks ago; they lost, so for a few days I switched to the dark grey/light grey hat. When that strategy backfired I went back to the beige hat—and the Marlins responded with a string of wins going into the All-Star break. I had to switch again when the Dodgers beat the Marlins last Friday—but the switch proved ineffective. I switched to the beige again on Sunday; that wasn't working either.

Back to tonight. I had put the grey hat on as the game went to the bottom of the ninth. But that hadn't done the trick in the ninth; how best to deal with this crucially important opportunity now, in the bottom of the tenth? Dee was down a strike after the first pitch—and that's when it came to me. I grabbed the beige Marlins hat and put it on—right on top of my double grey Marlins hat. And presto—on the very next pitch Dee lined a run-scoring single to right. Walk-off win for the Fish!

Now I don't want to take all the credit for this; many events have more than one cause, and I have to believe this was one of them. The quality of the pitch, the placement of the Phillies outfielders, the strategy of Don Mattingly and of the Marlins' coaching staff—all these probably played a part. Dee's own skill may have had something to do with it. But it would be absurd to claim that the hat strategy wasn't also in this case a contributing cause. I'm waiting now for Don and for Dee to be in touch—to say thanks, of course, but also to advise me on how often I should resort to the two-hat strategy in the future. Should it be reserved for these sorts of game-on-the line crisis moments? Or should there be a place for it in everyday strategy?

• • •

As a nine-year old I'm sure something close to one half of my mind was persuaded that I really could influence the outcome of far-away hockey games by putting on a Montreal Canadiens jersey. The equivalent percentage now is down to—what? Perhaps an eighth or a tenth of my mind? But like so many humans, I'm loath to give up that 1/8th or 1/10th. It would be like letting go completely of the child within. And who wants to do that—even at the ripe old age of 63? Go Fish Go! I'll do what I can to help.

* Fans love stolen bases (and bunt singles, and going first to third on a another player's single, and scoring from first on another player's double, and all the other manifestations of speed on the base-paths), but for many years now baseball's conventional wisdom has underrated the value of speed—in large part, I would suggest, because it's difficult for statistics to capture its disruptive impact; when a Dee Gordon or a Billy Hamilton is on base, pitchers are distracted, fielders tense up—and the defense makes mistakes (many of which are not egregious enough to show up in the box score as errors, but can still cost a base or a run).

QUESTIONS

1. How does the writer use the elements of narration and reflection in this piece? Mark out the sections of the piece that are narrative, and those that you think are reflective. Do you find them effective? Do they work together?

2. Consider the lengths of sentences in this piece. Are most of them compound or complex (and thus long), or are they simple, short sentences? Is a rhythm established between them? What effect do the short sentences have?
3. What would be the effect on this piece if the last section were removed? Would your opinion about the narrator change? If so, how?
4. What expectations does the tone of this piece of writing establish initially? How are those expectations upended?
5. Compare the ways in which humour is generated in this essay with the way(s) in which humour is generated in one or more other essays of your choosing (perhaps a piece by Mark Twain, or Jonathan Swift, or David Sedaris, or Sophia Benoit).
6. Do we tend to not take humourous writing seriously enough when we discuss the different sorts of essay writing?

What Life Is Like When You're Poor

(BOOK REVIEW / DESCRIPTION / PERSUASION / REFLECTION)

[Review of *This Has Always Been a War: The Radicalization of a Working-Class Queer* by Lori Fox (Arsenal Pulp Press, 2022, 320 pages)]

What is life like when you're poor? The closest I've ever come to going hungry was when, for two brief periods when I was young, I was without funds. At one point I ran out of money when I was a student in Britain, had to take a job as a hospital cleaner, and lived on rice and macaroni with margarine for a couple of weeks while I was waiting for my first pay cheque. At another point I miscalculated how much money I would need when I was travelling for a couple of months, and I ended up going hungry for 24 hours as I was hitchhiking from New York to Toronto. But these were temporary inconveniences. Even during the period just after my first child was born when our little family was almost certainly living for a time below the poverty line, I always knew that, if I really had to, I could contact my parents or my brother and they would have wired me enough money to see us through. What is life like when you're genuinely, permanently poor?

Over the past hundred years, that question has been the starting point for several now-classic books. Two that particularly stand out—George Orwell's 1933 *Down and Out in Paris and London* and Barbara Ehrenreich's 2001 *Nickel and Dimed*—were reissued in 2021. The authors of both were not themselves poor; they "lived poor" for periods of time in order to find out (as Ehrenreich put it) how anyone lives "on the wages available to the unskilled. How, in particular, were the roughly four million women about to be booted into the labor market by welfare reform going to make it on \$6 or \$7 an hour?" Now, with Lori Fox's *This Has Always Been a War*, we have the book-length testimony of someone who has been poor not as part of a journalistic project, but for life. Like those of Orwell and Ehrenreich, Fox's book is both a memoir and a work of societal analysis; like them too, it deserves the widest possible readership.

Fox describes scraping by as a server in countless restaurants and bars, from Belleville to Whitehorse, as well as at various jobs in forestry and in agriculture, mostly in western and northern Canada. They (Fox's preferred pronoun) display a fine eye, and a fine ear, and a flair for pungent language in describing those experiences in searing detail:

> Earlier that day, while the house was buzzing with the hum of full seats, or diners ordering, eating, talking, the owner of the restaurant—an elderly, bottom-heavy man with a white Yosemite Sam moustache and a well-documented proclivity for eye-f***ing the servers while they worked, the younger the better—had been in for lunch.

Fox's book is not all about work; it's also about living in our society as a queer, non-binary person. As with the book's stories of the workplace, the accounts here of relationships gone wrong are raw and often wrenching; it's hard not to feel moved by Fox's experiences with love gone wrong. What makes this a truly important book, though, are the stories Fox tells of how so much of our economy functions—driven by greed, and status-seeking, and unthinking cruelty on the part of those with wealth and power towards those who work at some of the toughest jobs for the lowest pay. Fox brings it all viscerally to life, making us feel something of what it's like to be constantly worrying if you can make the rent, or living out of your vehicle as you move from one crappy job to another.

Fox is very good at analysis too. Here, for example, is part of a section on the practice of tipping in restaurants: "By fostering income inequality, tips create an artificial class division; both front and back of house are underpaid working-class groups, but neither feels much solidarity with the other because the tip system allows servers to feel superior to back of house, while at the same time giving the back of house a genuine grievance that is, rather conveniently, not directed at the business itself."

After reading Fox's account of what life is really like for low-income workers, I find it hard to disagree with the book's conclusions concerning the oppression of those workers by those with money and power. Even many who treat their workers relatively well contribute to the massive inequality: "I am not saying that [a particular orchard owner in Naramata] was a bad person. I don't think that's true at all. I just want to know why one man should have two houses and an orchard full of fruit when other people in his village don't even have a bed and a place to keep their beer cold."

Four chapters in particular (on the economics of life as a server, on the sexist pressuring of servers by management, on how impossibly difficult ever-increasing rents have made it for low-income people to get by, and on how low-income workers are treated in the upscale community of Naramata in BC's wine district) make for utterly compelling reading. Those four chapters, at least, deserve to be read by all workers, all employers—indeed, by all Canadians.

I have only two caveats about the book's arguments. One is that it repeatedly suggests that the oppression of workers at the lower end of the scale is a practice peculiar to capitalism. The sad fact is that workers at the lower end of the scale have been horrifically treated under a very wide range of economic systems, including feudalism, mercantilism, a wide variety of oligarchies, today's Chinese-style "communism"—the list is a long one. But this is in essence a mere quibble. If for every time Fox attacks "capitalism" we substitute "an economic system in which a small minority have a hugely disproportionate share of the wealth and the power," what Fox writes makes perfect sense.

The other caveat concerns the book's final chapter, which paints a picture of Fox in nature, fishing in a canoe on a northern lake, and catching a pike. "We take a breath together," Fox writes of themself and the fish. "I say thank you and I take the knife in my right hand." Fox is at pains to describe the way in which the fish is killed—with a knife, not bludgeoning it over the head—and to suggest that killing it in this way demonstrates an understanding that fish "do feel pain, and they do feel fear. … I think it's important to do everything—even killing—with thoughtfulness and compassion." A full dose of thoughtfulness and compassion, I have to think, would have entailed letting the pike go free.

But *This Has Always Been a War* is not a book about the relationship between human and non-human animals; it's a book about what is, to Fox, an ongoing, undeclared war between economic classes. How, we should ask, can the conditions that breed hostility be brought to an end? What can we do to better the lives of low-income workers? Part of the answer to that question is of course economic and political, in the narrow sense of the word; we can insist that they be paid more. We can and should pass living wage legislation. But realistically, will this ever happen without changes in our social and political psychology? If we are ever to build the political will to create a fair Canada, we need to stop focusing so relentlessly on "the middle class." And those of us who are not in poverty need to stop looking all the time at those who are even better off than we are; we need to start paying attention to the situation of those who are less fortunate. As a society, we need to decide that it should not be ethically or socially acceptable for the highest paid in any organization to be paid any more than four to five times what those at the bottom of the scale are paid. Not 40 to 50 times more, as it was a century ago, and not 400 to 500 times more, as it has become in some companies today. Four to five times more. That's the level that's been recommended by fair-minded thinkers from Plato to Ed Schreyer. But don't take it from a Greek philosopher, or a former Governor-General, or from me; we need to hear much more frequently from voices such as that of Lori Fox—the voices of working-class people who speak clearly, bluntly, powerfully, and persuasively.

QUESTIONS

1. Consider the first two paragraphs of this piece. How does the writer introduce the central themes and contexts of the book being reviewed? What rhetorical strategies does the writer employ to connect to their reader (*ethos*, *pathos*, *logos*)?
2. Argue for or against the inclusion of the personal material in the first paragraph of this piece. Would the piece be improved if it began with the question that ends the first paragraph?
3. A good book review considers both the achievements and problems presented by any given book. What does this writer like about this book? What issues do they have with it? Does the reviewer recommend the book to their readers?
4. How does the writer use the element of reflection in this piece? Does it add to the effectiveness of the argument?
5. The writer cites direct quotations from Fox's book four times in this review. Do these quotations contribute to the persuasiveness of this piece? If so, how?
6. Argue for or against the inclusion of the second-last paragraph. Is this material simply not relevant to the main point(s) being made in the review? Or is it an interesting aside that makes an important point?
7. Highlight all the adverbs in the last paragraph. What effect do they have on the prose in this concluding section of the review?
8. How does the writer use rhetorical questions in the first paragraph of the review (a rhetorical question doesn't require a direct answer). Is this an effective strategy?
9. A shorter version of this piece was published 6 July 2022 in *The Globe and Mail.* Compare that version with this; which do you think is better?

STYLE GUIDES

C3.1 MLA STYLE

C3 Style Guides

C3.1 MLA Style

"MLA style" refers to the referencing guidelines of the Modern Language Association, which are favoured by many disciplines in the humanities. The main components of the MLA system are in-text author-page number citations for the body of an essay, and a bibliography giving publication details—the list of "Works Cited"—at the end of it.

This section outlines the key points of MLA style. Two full-length sample essays appear at the end of the section, which should be read in conjunction with P2.9 (Incorporating Sources) and P2.10 (Plagiarism). Consult the *MLA Handbook* (9th edition, 2021) if you have questions not answered here; you may also find answers at the website of the MLA, www.mla.org.

C3.1.1 About In-text Citations

• **in-text citations**: Under the MLA system a quotation or specific reference to another work is followed by a parenthetical page reference:

- Bonnycastle refers to "the true and lively spirit of opposition" with which Marxist literary criticism invigorates the discipline (204).

The work is then listed under "Works Cited" at the end of the essay:

- Bonnycastle, Stephen. *In Search of Authority: An Introductory Guide to Literary Theory.* 3rd ed., Broadview Press, 2007.

(See below for information about the "Works Cited" list.)

• **no signal phrase** (or author not named in signal phrase): If the context does not make it clear who the author is, that information must be added to the in-text citation. Note that no comma separates the name of the author from the page number.

- Even in recent years some have continued to believe that Marxist literary criticism invigorates the discipline with a "true and lively spirit of opposition" (Bonnycastle 204).

• **placing of in-text citations**: Place in-text citations at the ends of clauses or sentences in order to keep disruption of your writing to a minimum. The citation comes before the period or comma in the surrounding sentence. (If the quotation ends with punctuation other than a period or comma, include it in the quotation, and place a period or comma after the in-text citation.)

- Ricks refuted this point early on (16), but the claim has continued to be made in recent years.
- In "The Windhover," on the other hand, Hopkins bubbles over; "the mastery of the thing!" (8), he enthuses when he thinks of a bird, exclaiming shortly thereafter, "O my chevalier!" (10).

When a cited quotation is set off from the text, however, the in-text citation should be placed after the concluding punctuation.

- Muriel Jaeger draws on the following anecdote in discussing the resistance of many wealthy Victorians to the idea of widespread education for the poor:

> In a mischievous mood, Henry Brougham once told [some well-off acquaintances who were] showing perturbation about the likely results of educating the "lower orders" that they could maintain their superiority by working harder themselves. (105)

• **in-text citation when text is in parentheses**: If an in-text citation occurs within text in parentheses, square brackets are used for the reference.

- The development of a mass literary culture (or a "print culture," to use Williams's expression [88]) took several hundred years in Britain.

• **page number unavailable**: Many web sources lack page numbers. If your source has no page or section numbers, no number should be given in your citation. Do not count paragraphs yourself, as the version you are using may differ from others.

- In a recent web posting a leading critic has clearly implied that he finds such an approach objectionable (Bhabha).

If the source gives explicit paragraph or section numbers, as many websites do, use the appropriate abbreviation, followed by the number.

- Early in the novel, Austen makes it clear that the "business" of Mrs. Bennet's life is "to get her daughters married" (ch. 1).
- In "The American Scholar" Emerson asserts that America's "long apprenticeship to the learning of other lands" is drawing to a close (par. 7).

Note that (as is not the case with page numbers) MLA style requires a comma between author and paragraph or section numbers in a citation.

- Early in the novel, Mrs. Bennet makes it clear that her sole business in life is "to get her daughters married" (Austen, ch. 1).

• **one page or less**: If a source is one page long or less, it is advisable to still provide the page number (though MLA does not require this).

- In his *Chicago Tribune* review, Bosley calls the novel's prose "excruciating" (1).

• **multiple authors**: If there are two authors, both authors should be named either in the signal phrase or in the in-text citation, connected by *and*.

- Chambliss and Best argue that the importance of this novel is primarily historical (233).
- Two distinguished scholars have recently argued that the importance of this novel is primarily historical (Chambliss and Best 233).

If there are three or more authors, include only the first author's name in the in-text citation, followed by *et al.*, short for the Latin *et alia*, meaning *and others*.

- Meaning is not simply there in the text, but in the complex relationships between the text, the reader, and the Medieval world (Black et al. xxxvi).

• **corporate author**: The relevant organization or the title of the piece should be included in the in-text citation if neither is included in the body of your text; make sure enough information is provided for readers to find the correct entry in your Works Cited list. Shorten a long title to avoid awkwardness, but take care that the shortened version begins with the same word as the corresponding entry in the "Works Cited" list, so that readers can move easily from the citation to the bibliographic information. For example, *Comparative Indo-European Linguistics: An Introduction* should be shortened to *Comparative Indo-European* rather than *Indo-European Linguistics*. The first two examples below cite unsigned newspaper and encyclopedia articles; the last is a corporate author in-text citation.

- As *The New York Times* reported in May 2021, many of the new voting laws being enacted were driven by disinformation about election integrity ("Perpetual Motion Machine").
- In the 1990s Sao Paulo began to rapidly overtake Mexico City as the world's most polluted city ("Air Pollution" 21).
- There are a number of organizations mandated "to foster the production and enjoyment of the arts in Canada" (Canada Council for the Arts 2).

• **more than one work by the same author cited**: If you include more than one work by the same author in your list of Works Cited, you must make clear which work is being cited each time. This may be done either by mentioning the work in a signal phrase or by including in the citation a short version of the title.

- In *The House of Mirth*, for example, Wharton writes of love as keeping Lily and Selden "from atrophy and extinction" (282).
- Wharton sees love as possessing the power to keep humans "from atrophy and extinction" (*House of Mirth* 282).
- Love, as we learn from the experience of Lily and Selden, possesses the power to keep humans "from atrophy and extinction" (Wharton, *House of Mirth* 282).

• **multi-volume works**: Note, by number, the volume you are referring to, followed by a colon and a space, before noting the page number. Use the abbreviation "vol." when citing an entire volume.

- Towards the end of *In Darkest Africa* Stanley refers to the Victoria Falls (2: 387).
- In contrast with those of the medieval period, Renaissance artworks show an increasing concern with depicting the material world and less and less of an interest in metaphysical symbolism (Hauser, vol. 2).

• **two or more authors with the same last name**: If the Works Cited list includes two or more authors with the same last name, the in-text citation should supply both first initials and last names, or, if the first initials are also the same, the full first and last names:

- One of the leading economists of the time advocated wage and price controls (Harry Johnston 197).

- One of the leading economists of the time advocated wage and price controls (H. Johnston 197).

• **indirect quotations**: When an original source is not available but is referred to by another source, the in-text citation includes *qtd. in* (an abbreviation of *quoted in*) and a reference to the second source. In the example below, Casewell is quoted by Bouvier; the in-text citation directs readers to an entry in the Works Cited list for the Bouvier work.

- Casewell considers Lambert's position to be "outrageously arrogant" (qtd. in Bouvier 59).

• **short poems**: For short poems, cite line numbers rather than page numbers.

- In "wont you celebrate with me," Clifton describes a speaker who forges her identity "here on this bridge between / starshine and clay" (lines 8–9).

If you are citing the same poem repeatedly, use just the numbers for subsequent references.

- Clifton asks the reader to celebrate that "everyday / something has tried to kill me / and has failed" (12–14).

• **longer poems**: For longer poems with parts, cite the part (or section, or "book") as well as the line (where available). Use Arabic numerals, and use a period for separation.

- In "Ode: Intimations of Immortality" Wordsworth calls human birth "but a sleep and a forgetting" (5.1).

• **novels or short stories**: When a work of prose fiction has chapters or numbered divisions the citation should include first the page number, and then book, chapter, and section numbers as applicable. (These can be very useful in helping readers of a different edition to locate the passage you are citing.) Arabic numerals should be used. A semicolon should be used to separate the page number from the other information.

- When Joseph and Fanny are by themselves, they immediately express their affection for each other, or, as Fielding puts it, "solace themselves" with "amorous discourse" (151; ch. 26).

- In *Tender Is the Night* Dick's ambition does not quite crowd out the desire for love: "He wanted to be loved too, if he could fit it in" (133; bk. 2, ch. 4).

- **plays**: Almost all plays are divided into acts and/or scenes. For plays that do not include line numbering throughout, cite the page number in the edition you have been using, followed by act and/or scene numbers as applicable:
  - As Angie and Joyce begin drinking together Angie pronounces the occasion "better than Christmas" (72; act 3).
  - Near the conclusion of Inchbald's *Wives as They Were* Bronzely declares that he has been "made to think with reverence on the matrimonial compact" (62; act 5, sc. 4).

For plays written entirely or largely in verse, where line numbers are typically provided throughout, you should omit the reference to the page number in the citation. Instead, cite the act, scene, and line numbers, using Arabic numerals. For a Shakespeare play, if the title isn't clear from the introduction to a quotation, an abbreviation of the title may also be used. The in-text citation below is for Shakespeare's *The Merchant of Venice*, Act 2, Scene 3, lines 2–4:

- Jessica clearly has some fondness for Launcelot: "Our house is hell, and thou, a merry devil, / Dost rob it of some taste of tediousness. / But fare thee well; there is a ducat for thee" (*MV* 2.3.2–4).

- **works without page numbers**: If you are citing literary texts where you have consulted editions from other sources (on the web or in an ebook, for instance), the principles are exactly the same, except that you need not cite page numbers. For example, if the online Gutenberg edition of Fielding's *Joseph Andrews* were being cited, the citation would be as follows:
  - When Joseph and Fanny are by themselves, they immediately express their affection for each other, or, as Fielding puts it, "solace themselves" with "amorous discourse" (ch. 26).

Students should be cautioned that online editions of literary texts are often unreliable. Typically there are far more typos and other errors in online versions of literary texts than there are in print versions, and such things as the layout of poems are also frequently incorrect. It is often possible to exercise judgement about such matters, however. If, for example, you are not required to base your essay on a particular copy of a Thomas Hardy poem but may find your own, you will be far better off using the text you will find on the Representative Poetry Online site run out of the University of Toronto than you will using a text you might find on a "World's Finest Love Poems" site.

• **sacred texts**: The Bible and other sacred texts that are available in many editions should be cited in a way that enables the reader to check the reference in any edition. For the Bible, book, chapter, and verse should all be cited, using periods for separation. The reference below is to Genesis, chapter 2, verse 1.

- According to the Judeo-Christian story of creation, at the end of the sixth day "the heavens and the earth were finished" (Gen. 2.1).

• **works in an anthology or book of readings**: In the in-text citation for a work in an anthology, use the name of the author of the work, not that of the editor of the anthology. The page number, however, should be that found in the anthology. The following citation refers to an article by Frederic W. Gleach in an anthology edited by Jennifer Brown and Elizabeth Vibert.

- One of the essays in Brown and Vibert's collection argues that we should rethink the Pocahontas myth (Gleach 48).

In your list of Works Cited, this work should be alphabetized under Gleach, the author of the piece you have consulted, not under Brown. If you cite another work by a different author from the same anthology or book of readings, that should appear as a separate entry in your list of Works Cited—again, alphabetized under the author's name.

• **tweets**: Cite tweets by giving the author's name in your text rather than in an in-text citation.

- Stephen King has written about the elusive nature of artistic inspiration, tweeting for example in May 2021 that "[g]ood writing is a delight to those who read it and a mystery to those who write it."

C3.1.2 About Works Cited; MLA Core Elements

The Works Cited list in MLA style is an alphabetized list at the end of the essay (or article or book). The entire list, like the main part of the essay, should be double-spaced throughout, and each entry should be given a hanging indent: the first line is flush with the left-hand margin, and each subsequent line is indented one tab space.

The Works Cited list should include information about all the sources you have cited. Do not include works that you consulted but did not cite in the body of your text.

MLA style provides a set of citation guidelines that the writer follows and adapts, regardless of whether the source being cited is print, digital, audio, visual, or any other form of media. All sources share what the MLA calls "Core Elements," and these, listed in order, create the citation for each entry: Author, Title of Source, Title of Container (larger whole), Contributor, Version, Number, Publisher, Publication Date, and Location. Each element is followed by the punctuation marks shown in the table below, unless it is the last element, which should always close with a period. (There are a few exceptions to this rule, which are outlined below.) Most sources don't have all the elements (some don't have an author, for example, or a version, or a location); if you find that this is the case, omit the element and move on to the next.

The table can function as a guide when creating citations. Once you have found all the publication details for your source, place them in order and punctuate according to the table, leaving out any elements for which you don't have information. It is common for a source to have more than one "container"—such as an article printed in a journal and found on an online database. For sources like these, the table below can be filled out a second time, beginning with item 3 for the second container. Please see the section below on "Title of Container" for details and examples.

1. Author.
2. Title of source.
3. Title of container,
4. Contributor,
5. Version,
6. Number,
7. Publisher,
8. Publication Date,
9. Location.

In the sections below, you will discover how to identify the core elements of MLA style and how to use them across media. For a list of examples, please see pages 647–57.

Author

This element begins your citation. For a **single author**, list the author's last name first, followed by a comma, and then the author's first name or initials (use whatever appears on the work's title page or copyright page), followed by a period.

Graham, Jorie. *From the New World*. Ecco, 2015.

Johnson, George M. *All Boys Aren't Blue*. Farrar, Straus and Giroux, 2020.

If a source has **two authors**, the first author's name should appear with the last name first, followed by a comma and *and*. Note also that the authors' names should appear in the order they are listed; sometimes this is not alphabetical.

Rectenwald, Michael, and Lisa Carl. *Academic Writing, Real World Topics*. Broadview Press, 2015.

If there are **three or more authors**, include only the first author's name, reversed, followed by a comma and *et al.* (the abbreviation of the Latin *et alia*, meaning *and others*).

Waldron, Janice L., et al. *The Oxford Handbook of Social Media and Music Learning*. Oxford UP, 2020.

Sources that are **edited** rather than authored are usually cited in a similar way; add "editor" or "editors" after the name(s) and before the title.

Renker, Elizabeth, editor. *Poems: A Concise Anthology*. Broadview Press, 2016.

When referring to an edited version of a work written by another author or authors, list the editor(s) after the title, in the Contributor element.

Trollope, Anthony. *The Eustace Diamonds*. 1873. Edited by Stephen Gill and John Sutherland, Penguin, 1986.

Authors can be organizations, institutions, associations, or government agencies ("corporate authors"). If a work has been issued by a **corporate author** and no author is identified, the entry should be listed by the name of the organization that produced it, using the name of the organization as recorded by the source.

Ontario, Ministry of Natural Resources. *Achieving Balance: Ontario's Long-Term Energy Plan*. Queen's Printer for Ontario, 2016, www.energy.gov.on.ca/en/ltep/achieving-balance-ontarios-long-term-energy-plan. Accessed 10 June 2021.

If the work is published by the same organization that is the corporate author, skip the author element and list only the publisher. The citation will begin with the source title.

2020 Annual Report. Broadview Press, 2021.

"History of the Arms and Great Seal of the Commonwealth of Massachusetts." Commonwealth of Massachusetts, www.sec/state.ma.us/pre/presea/sealhis/htm. Accessed 5 May 2021.

"Our Mandate." Art Gallery of Ontario, www.ago.net/mandate. Accessed 10 May 2021.

Works with an **anonymous author** should be alphabetized by title, omitting the author element.

Sir Gawain and the Green Knight. Edited by Paul Battles, Broadview Press, 2012.

Works under a **pseudonym**, or **works that are by an author that has published under more than one name**, can be treated in several ways. The pseudonym or name that your source records as author may simply be used as-is in the author element. If you are citing an older work by someone who has since changed their name, you may substitute in the current name the person is using. For trans authors, for example, use an author's chosen name—do not mention former names in either your citations or your prose, regardless of the name that is listed by your source. MLA calls this "consolidating"—this way, all works by one person can be cited under one name. For example, if you are citing the novelist Agatha Christie (who also wrote under the name Mary Westmacott), it is fine to consolidate the titles under "Agatha Christie" (unless the pseudonym is relevant to your writing, in which case see other options below):

Christie, Agatha. *Absent in the Spring.* 1944. HarperCollins, 1997.

---. *Murder on the Orient Express.* 1934. HarperCollins, 2011.

If a writer uses more than one pseudonym, it may be useful to cite their works using the writer's better-known name. In this case, you may use the better-known name in the author element, followed by the lesser-known name in square brackets and preceded by *published as* (in italics).

Oates, Joyce Carol [*published as* Lauren Kelly]. *Take Me, Take Me with You.* HarperCollins, 2005.

You may also simply place the author's more well-known name in square brackets and omit the lesser-known pseudonym, indicating that the name has been supplied by you and was originally published under another name.

[Oates, Joyce Carol]. *Take Me, Take Me with You.* HarperCollins, 2005.

Online usernames are copied out exactly as they appear on the screen.

@newyorker. "With the resignation of Turkey's Prime Minister, the country's President now stands alone and unchallenged." *Twitter*, 6 May 2016, www.twitter.com/NewYorker/status/728676985254379520.

Note that the author element is flexible. If you are discussing the work of a film director, for example, the director's name should be placed in the author element, with a descriptor.

Hitchcock, Alfred, director. *The Lady Vanishes*. United Artists, 1938.

If, on the other hand, you are discussing film editing, you would place the film editor in the author element. In this case, you might also include Hitchcock's name in the "Contributor" element.

Dearing, R.E., film editor. *The Lady Vanishes*. Directed by Alfred Hitchcock, United Artists, 1938.

If no single contributor's work is of particular importance in your discussion of a film or television source, omit the author element altogether.

"The Buys." *The Wire*. Created by David Simon and Ed Burns, directed by Peter Medak, season 1, episode 3, HBO, 16 June 2002.

If you are citing a **translated source** and the translation itself is the focus of your work, the translator or translators can be placed in the author element.

Lodge, Kirsten, translator. *Notes from the Underground*. By Fyodor Dostoevsky, edited by Kirsten Lodge, Broadview Press, 2014.

When the work itself is the focus, as is usually the case, the author should remain in the author element, and the translator moved to the "Contributor" element:

Dostoevsky, Fyodor. *Notes from the Underground*. Translated and edited by Kirsten Lodge, Broadview Press, 2014.

This principle holds true across media and elements. Adapt the MLA structure to create citations that are clear, relevant to your work, and useful to your reader.

• Title of Source

The title of your source follows the author element. Copy the title as you find it in the source, but with MLA-standard capitalization and punctuation. Capitalize the first word, the last word, and all key words, but not articles, prepositions, coordinating conjunctions, or the *to* in infinitives.

Carson, Anne. *The Albertine Workout*. New Directions, 2014.

If there is a **subtitle**, include it after the main title, following a colon.

Bök, Christian. *The Xenotext: Book 1*. Coach House Books, 2015.

Your title gives the reader information about the source. Italicized titles indicate that the source is a complete, independent whole. A title enclosed in quotation marks tells the reader that the source is part of a larger work.

A **book** is an independent whole, so the title is italicized.

Sowerby, Githa. *Three Plays*. Edited by J. Ellen Gainor, Broadview Press, 2021.

Other examples include **long poems** (*In Memoriam*), **magazines** (*The New Yorker*), **newspapers** (*The Guardian*), **journals** (*The American Poetry Review*), **websites** (*The Camelot Project*), **films** (*Memento*), **television shows** (*The X-Files*), and **compact discs** or **record albums** (*Dark Side of the Moon*).

A **poem, short story**, or **essay** within a larger collection is placed in quotation marks.

Wordsworth, William. "The Solitary Reaper." *Poems, in Two Volumes*, edited by Richard Matlak, Broadview Press, 2016, p. 153.

Other examples include **chapters in books** ("The Autist Artist" in *The Man Who Mistook His Wife for a Hat and Other Clinical Tales*), **encyclopedia articles** ("Existentialism"), **essays in books or journals** ("Salvation in the Garden: Daoism and Ecology" in *Daoism and Ecology: Ways within a Cosmic Landscape*), **short stories** ("Young Goodman Brown"), **short poems** ("Daddy"), **pages on websites** ("The Fisher King" from *The Camelot Project*), **episodes of television shows** ("Small Potatoes" from *The X-Files*), and **songs** ("Eclipse" from *Dark Side of the Moon*). Put the titles of **public lectures** in quotation marks as well ("Walls in *The Epic of Gilgamesh*").

These formatting rules apply across media forms. A website is placed in italics; a posting on the website is placed in quotation marks.

Stein, Sadie. "Casting the Runes." *The Daily: The Paris Review Blog*, 9 Oct. 2015, www.theparisreview.org/blog/2015/10/09/casting-the-runes/.

If the title of a stand-alone work contains the title of a work that is not independent, the latter is put in double quotation marks, and the entire title is put in italics (*"Self-Reliance" and Other Essays*). If the title of a stand-alone work appears within the title of another independent work, MLA recommends that the latter be put in italics and the former not (*Chaucer's* House of Fame*: The Poetics of Skeptical Fideism*). If the title of a non-independent work is embedded in another title of the same kind, put the inner title in single quotation marks and the outer title in double quotation marks ("The Drama of Donne's 'The Indifferent'").

When a stand-alone work appears in a **collection**, the work's title remains in italics.

> James, Henry. *The American. Henry James: Novels 1871–1880*, edited by William T. Stafford, Library of America, 1983.

● Title of Container

Very often your source is found within a larger context, such as an **anthology**, **periodical**, **newspaper**, **digital platform**, or **website**. When this is the case, the larger whole is called the "container." For an article in a newspaper, for example, the article is the "source" and the newspaper is the "container." For a song on an **album**, the song is the "source" and the album is the "container."

The title of the container is usually italicized and followed by a comma.

> Russell, Anna. "The Beguiling Legacy of *Alice in Wonderland*." *The New Yorker*, 11 July 2021, www.newyorker.com/culture/culture-desk/the-beguiling-legacy-of-alice-in-wonderland.

The container is anything that contains another work: a website; a book that is a collection of stories, poems, plays, or essays; a magazine; a journal; an album; or a database.

When doing research, particularly online, one often comes across nested containers, in which, for example, an article is found in a periodical, which is itself found on a database. All containers are recorded in the citation, so your reader knows exactly how to find your source. Add more container elements as needed. Additional containers should follow the period at the end of the information given for the first container (usually after the date or location element).

It can be helpful to see this process charted out. Notice that the publication information for the containers follows that of the source.

Here is an example of an **article from a periodical**, accessed from an online database.

1. Author.	Lamothe, Daphne.
2. Title of source.	"The City-Child's Quest: Spatiality and Sociality in Paule Marshall's *The Fisher King*."
CONTAINER 1:	
3. Title of container,	*Meridians*,
4. Contributor,	
5. Version,	
6. Number,	vol. 15, no. 2,
7. Publisher,	
8. Publication Date,	2017,
9. Location.	pp. 491–506.
CONTAINER 2:	
3. Title of container,	*JSTOR*,
4. Contributor,	
5. Version,	
6. Number,	
7. Publisher,	
8. Publication Date,	
9. Location.	www.jstor.org/stable/10.2979/meridians.15.2.10.

Citation as It Would Appear in the Works Cited List:

Lamothe, Daphne. "The City-Child's Quest: Spatiality and Sociality in Paule Marshall's *The Fisher King*." *Meridians*, vol. 15, no. 2, 2017, pp. 491–506. *JSTOR*, www.jstor.org/stable/10.2979/meridians.15.2.10.

The next example is an **e-book** accessed from a digital platform.

1. Author.	Copeland, Edward, and Juliet McMaster, editors.
2. Title of source.	*The Cambridge Companion to Jane Austen.*
CONTAINER 1:	
3. Title of container,	
4. Contributor,	
5. Version,	2nd ed.,
6. Number,	
7. Publisher,	Cambridge UP,
8. Publication Date,	2010.
9. Location.	
CONTAINER 2:	
3. Title of container,	*Cambridge Core,*
4. Contributor,	
5. Version,	
6. Number,	
7. Publisher,	
8. Publication Date,	2011,
9. Location.	https://doi.org/10.1017/CCO9780521763080.

Citation as It Would Appear in the Works Cited List:

Copeland, Edward, and Juliet McMaster, editors. *The Cambridge Companion to Jane Austen.* 2nd ed., Cambridge UP, 2010. *Cambridge Core*, 2011, https://doi.org/10.1017/CCO9780521763080.

The elements are recorded sequentially to create your citation. Notice that any elements that don't apply to this source are left out. Note that for a **self-contained e-book** that you access on an e-reader or in a proprietary web app, you may treat the citation as you would a print book, adding "e-book ed." in the Version element.

1. Author.	Austen, Jane.
2. Title of source.	*Pride and Prejudice.*
CONTAINER 1:	
3. Title of container,	
4. Contributor,	Edited by Robert P. Irvine,
5. Version,	2nd ed., e-book ed.,
6. Number,	
7. Publisher,	Broadview Press,
8. Publication Date,	2020.
9. Location.	

Citation as It Would Appear in the Works Cited List:

Austen, Jane. *Pride and Prejudice*. Edited by Robert P. Irvine, 2nd ed., e-book ed., Broadview Press, 2020.

Here is an example citation of a **performance in a television series**, accessed on Hulu.

1. Author.	Washington, Kerry, performer.
2. Title of source.	"The Spark."
CONTAINER 1:	
3. Title of container,	*Little Fires Everywhere,*
4. Contributor,	directed by Lynn Shelton,
5. Version,	
6. Number,	season 1, episode 1,
7. Publisher,	Best Day Ever Productions et al.,
8. Publication Date,	2020.
9. Location.	
CONTAINER 2:	
3. Title of container,	*Hulu,*

4. Contributor,	
5. Version,	
6. Number,	
7. Publisher,	
8. Publication Date,	
9. Location.	www.hulu.com/series/little-fires-everywhere-bce24897-1a74-48a3-95e8-6cdd530dde4c.

Citation as It Would Appear in the Works Cited List:

Washington, Kerry, performer. "The Spark." *Little Fires Everywhere*, directed by Lynn Shelton, season 1, episode 1, Best Day Ever Productions et al., 2020. *Hulu*, www.hulu.com/series/little-fires-everywhere-bce24897-1a74-48a3-95e8-6cdd530dde4c.

● Contributor

There may be other key people who should be credited in your citation as contributors. This element follows the title of the source and the container (if there is one). The MLA recommends that you include the names of contributors who are important to your research, or if they help your reader to identify the source. Before each name, place a description of the role (do not abbreviate):

adapted by
directed by
edited by
illustrated by
introduction by
narrated by
performance by
translated by

If your listing of a contributor follows the source title, it is capitalized (following a period). If the contributor follows a container, it will be lower-case (following a comma).

Mechain, Gwerful. *The Works of Gwerful Mechain*. Translated by Katie Gramich, Broadview Press, 2018.

James, Henry. *The American. Henry James: Novels 1871–1880*, edited by William T. Stafford, Library of America, 1983.

In the Contributor element, include the most relevant contributors not already mentioned in the author element. If you are writing about a television episode and a certain performance is one of the elements you discuss, for example, include the performer's name in the Contributor element, along with any other contributors you wish to include.

> Medak, Peter, director. "The Buys." *The Wire*, created by David Simon and Ed Burns, performance by Dominic West, season 1, episode 3, HBO, 16 June 2002.

Note that the MLA guidelines are flexible; for this part of the citation especially, consider what your readers most need to know about your source and include that information. Note also that there is some flexibility in the author element; if a particular performance or other contribution is the major focus in your discussion of the source, it can be cited in the author element instead.

• Version

If your source is **one of several editions**, an **e-book edition**, or a **revised version**, record those details in this element of your citation, followed by a comma. The word "edition" is abbreviated in your citation (ed.).

> Edgeworth, Maria, et al. *Moral Tales: A Selection*. Edited by Robin Runia, e-book ed., Broadview Press, 2021.

> Fowles, John. *The Magus*. Rev. ed., Jonathan Cape, 1977.

> Shelley, Mary. *Frankenstein*. Edited by D.L. Macdonald and Kathleen Scherf, 3rd ed., Broadview Press, 2012.

You may also come across **expanded editions**, **revised editions**, and **updated editions**, all of which may be noted in this element of your citation. Different media might use different terminology. For example in film you may find a **director's cut**, or in music an **abridged version** of a concerto: use the same principles as above, providing the relevant information in the Version element of your citation.

> Coen, Ethan, and Joel Coen, directors. *Blood Simple*. Director's cut, Universal, 2001.

• Number

If your source is part of a **multi-volumed work**, or if it is part of a journal that is issued in numbers and/or volumes, include the volume information in this Number element of your citation.

If you are citing **two or more volumes** of a multi-volume work, the entry may note the total number of volumes. If you cite only one of the volumes, list it after the title.

Jeeves, Julie, editor. *A Reference Guide to Spanish Architecture*. 3 vols., Hackett, 2005.

Mercer, Bobby, editor. *A Reference Guide to French Architecture*. Vol. 1, Hackett, 2002.

Include the **volume and issue numbers** for journals. Use the abbreviations *vol.* for volume and *no.* for issue number.

Gregory, Elizabeth. "Marianne Moore's 'Blue Bug': A Dialogic Ode on Celebrity, Race, Gender, and Age." *Modernism/Modernity*, vol. 22, no. 4, 2015, pp. 759–86.

Some journals do not use volume numbers and give only an issue number.

Sanger, Richard. "Goodbye, Seamus." *Brick*, no. 93, summer 2014, pp. 153–57.

The Number element is also where you record issue numbers for comic books, or the season and episode numbers for a television series.

Washington, Kerry, performer. "The Spark." *Little Fires Everywhere*, directed by Lynn Shelton, season 1, episode 1, Best Day Ever Productions et al., 2020. *Hulu*, www.hulu.com/series/little-fires-everywhere-bce24897-1a74-48a3-95e8-6cdd530dde4c.

● Publisher

In this element of your citation, record the organization that produced the source, whether it be the publisher of a book, the organization running a website, or the studio producing a film. (In the case of a secondary container, include the organization that produced the container.) Do not abbreviate, except in the case of university presses, which may be abbreviated as *UP*.

To find the publisher of a **book**, look on the title page or on the copyright page.

Joyce, James. *Exiles*. Edited by Keri Walsh, Oxford UP, 2021.

Rush, Rebecca. *Kelroy*. Edited by Betsy Klimasmith, Broadview Press, 2016.

For a **film** or **television series**, the studio or company that produced the show is recorded in the information on the back of a DVD or in the opening and closing credits.

Simon, David, creator. *The Wire*. HBO, 2002–2008.

For **websites**, the publisher's information can often be found in the copyright notice at the bottom of the page.

Bogan, Louise. "Women." 1922. *Representative Poetry Online*, edited by Ian Lancashire, University of Toronto, 2000.

You may omit a publisher's name in the following kinds of publications:

- A periodical (journal, magazine, newspaper).
- A work published by its author or editor.
- A website whose title is essentially the same as the name of the publisher.
- A website not involved in producing the works it is making available (YouTube, JSTOR, ProQuest). These are listed as containers, but not as publishers.

If **two or more publishers** are listed for your source, cite them both and separate them with a forward slash (/).

Banting, Keith G., editor. *Thinking Outside the Box: Innovation in Policy Ideas*. School of Policy Studies, Queen's University / McGill–Queen's University Press, 2015.

• Publication Date

In this element of your citation, record the date of publication for your source. For **books**, this date is found on the copyright page (and sometimes on the title page). If several editions are listed, use the date for the edition you have consulted.

Stevenson, Robert Louis. *Strange Case of Dr. Jekyll and Mr. Hyde*. Edited by Martin A. Danahay, 3rd ed., Broadview Press, 2015.

Online sources almost always have a date posted, and this is the date you should record in this element.

Heller, Nathan. "The Big Uneasy: What's Roiling the Liberal-Arts Campus?" *The New Yorker*, 30 May 2016, www.newyorker.com/magazine/2016/05/30/the-new-activism-of-liberal-arts-colleges.

A source may be associated with **more than one publication date**. An article online may have been previously published in print, or an article printed in a book may have been published previously in a periodical. In this case, the MLA recommends that you record the date that is most relevant to your use of the source. If you consulted the online version of an article, for example, ignore the date of print publication and cite the online publication date.

For books, we record the year of publication. For other sources, whether to include a year, month, and day depends on your source and the context in which you are using it. If you are citing an **episode from a television series**, for example, it is usually enough to record the year it aired.

> Medak, Peter, director. "The Buys." *The Wire*, created by David Simon and Ed Burns, season 1, episode 3, HBO, 2002.

If, however, the context surrounding the episode is being discussed in your work, you should be more specific about the date:

> Medak, Peter, director. "The Buys." *The Wire*, created by David Simon and Ed Burns, season 1, episode 3, HBO, 16 June 2002.

For a **video posted on a website**, include the date on which the video was posted. In the example below, the posting date should be included in the second container, which records the details for the digital platform. The date the video was released is included in the publication details for the source.

> McDonald, Emily, director. *Looking Back with Pride*. Forever Pictures, 2021. *Vimeo*, uploaded by Emily McDonald, 21 June 2021, www.vimeo.com/565585933.

If you are citing a **comment posted on a web page**, and the time the content was posted is indicated, include the time in your entry.

> Evan. Comment on "Another Impasse on Gun Bills, Another Win for Hyperpolitics." *The New York Times*, 21 June 2016, 9:02 a.m., www.nytimes.com/2016/06/22/us/politics/washington-congress-gun-control.html.

Larger projects are created over a longer span of time. If you are documenting a web project as a whole, include the full range of years during which it was developed.

> Secord, James A., et al., editors. *Darwin Correspondence Project*. 1974–2016, www.darwinproject.ac.uk/.

The dates of publication for **periodicals** vary. Include in full the information provided by the copyright page, whether it be indicated by season, year, month, week, or day.

> Gander, Forrest. "A Most Ingenious Work of Literature." *Brick*, no. 107, summer 2021, pp. 11–18.

> Salenius, Sirpa. "Transatlantic Interracial Sisterhoods: Sarah Remond, Ellen Craft, and Harriet Jacobs in England." *Frontiers: A Journal of Women Studies*, vol. 38, no. 1, 2017, pp. 166–96. *JSTOR*, www.jstor.org/stable/10.5250/fronjwomestud.38.1.0166.

● Location

The content of the Location element varies considerably between print, digital, and other sources.

For **print sources** within a periodical or anthology, record a page number (preceded by p.) or a range of page numbers (preceded by pp.).

> Gregory, Elizabeth. "Marianne Moore's 'Blue Bug': A Dialogic Ode on Celebrity, Race, Gender, and Age." *Modernism/Modernity*, vol. 22, no. 4, 2015, pp. 759–86.

An **online work** is located by its DOI or URL. If a DOI (Digital Object Identifier) is available, it is a more reliable and preferred option, as DOIs do not change when the source moves (whereas URLs do). If your source has no DOI but offers a "stable" URL, choose that one to include in your citation. The publisher in this case has agreed not to change the URL. Note that the MLA considers the inclusion of URLs to be optional, as there are downsides to including them (such as their instability and their tendency to create messier citations). In general, however, it is advisable to include them, unless your instructor advises otherwise. When copying a URL into your citation, remove the *http://*; this means that usually the URL will begin with *www*. For excessively long URLs, the MLA recommends truncating them, leaving readers enough of the address to find the source but avoiding an unruly citation. If you need to break a URL or DOI over two or more lines, do not insert any hyphens at the break point; instead, when possible, break after a colon or slash or before other marks of punctuation.

> Jesse, Tom. "John Ashbery's Unexceptional Politics." *Pacific Coast Philology*, vol. 55, no. 2, 2021, pp. 171–90. *JSTOR*, www.jstor.org/stable/10.5325/pacicoaspHil.55.2.0171.

Yearling, R. "*Hamlet* and the Limits of Narrative." *Essays in Criticism: A Quarterly Journal of Literary Criticism,* vol. 65, no. 4, 2015, pp. 368–82. *ProQuest,* https://doi.org/10.1093/escrit/cgv022.

We find a **television episode** on a DVD by its disc number. Place the disc number in the Location element.

"The Buys." *The Wire,* created by David Simon and Ed Burns, directed by Peter Medak, season 1, episode 3, HBO, 2002, disc 1.

For a **work of art** that you have seen in person, cite the name of the institution and city where you saw it in the Location element. Leave out the name of the city if the city name is part of the institution name (e.g., The Art Institute of Chicago).

Sargent, John Singer. *Henry James.* 1913, National Portrait Gallery, London.

Some **archived sources** have a different system for locating objects in the archive. Where this is the case, include the code or number in the Location element.

Blake, William. *The Marriage of Heaven and Hell.* 1790–1793, The Fitzwilliam Museum, Cambridge, 123-1950. Illuminated printed book.

If you are citing a **live performance** or **lecture**, name the location and the city. Omit the city name if it is part of the location name.

Royal Winnipeg Ballet. *The Princess and the Goblin.* Directed and choreographed by Twyla Tharp, performances by Paloma Herrera and Dmitri Dovgoselets, 17 Oct. 2012, Centennial Concert Hall, Winnipeg.

• Supplemental Elements

You may include any of the following elements in your citation if you think they are necessary or helpful to your reader. Supplemental elements are typically inserted into two possible places in your citation—after the title of your source, if it applies primarily to the source (such as an original publication date), or at the end of the citation, if it applies to the citation as a whole (such as a date of access). Add a period at the end of a supplemental element, regardless of its placement.

Date of Original Publication

If your source has been republished, it may give your reader some important context if you include the date of original publication. If you do so, place the date immediately after the source title and close with a period.

> Trollope, Anthony. *The Eustace Diamonds.* 1873. Edited by Stephen Gill and John Sutherland, Penguin, 1986.

City of Publication

Including the city of publication is not very useful these days, so the MLA has decided to remove this element from citations. There are two situations, however, where you may wish to include the city. If the book was published before 1900, the city of publication is associated more closely with the source than the publisher. For these books, you may substitute the city of publication for the publisher.

> Dickens, Charles. *Our Mutual Friend.* Vol. 1, New York, 1865.

Some publishers release more than one version of a text in different countries (a British and an American edition, for example). If you are reading an unexpected version of a text, or the version you are reading has historical significance, place the name of the city in front of the publisher.

> Lawrence, D.H. *Lady Chatterley's Lover.* London, Penguin, 1960.

Books in a Series

If your source is a book in a series, you may add the series name in roman (i.e., without italics) at the end of your citation, preceded by a period.

> Klooster, Wim, editor. *Spanish American Independence Movements: A History in Documents.* Broadview Press, 2021. Broadview Sources Series.

Unexpected Type of Work

If your source needs further explanation, place a descriptive term (e-mail, transcript, broadcast, street performance, talk, address) at the end of the citation, preceded by a period.

> Rosenheim, Jeff. "Diane Arbus." Art Gallery of Ontario, 6 May 2016, Toronto. Lecture.

Date of Access

It is optional to include a date of access for your online citations, and the MLA recommends you do so when the work lacks a publication date or if the website has ceased to exist.

> Crawford, Isabella Valancy. "The Canoe." *Representative Poetry Online*, edited by Ian Lancashire, University of Toronto, www.tspace.library.utoronto.ca/html/1807/4350/poem596.html. Accessed 10 Dec. 2020.

Examples

The following are examples of MLA-style citations for sources across various media. While these examples can offer useful guidance, remember that the MLA guidelines may be adapted to suit the details of the sources you are documenting, as well as the context in which you are using them.

- **single author**:

> Graham, Jorie. *From the New World.* Ecco, 2015.
>
> Ingalls, Rachel. *Mrs Caliban.* 1982. Faber & Faber, 2021.

- **two authors**:

> Davis, Lydia, and Eliot Weinberger. *Two American Scenes.* New Directions, 2013. Pamphlets Series.
>
> Rectenwald, Michael, and Lisa Carl. *Academic Writing, Real World Topics.* Broadview Press, 2015.

- **three or more authors**:

> Fantuzzi, Marco, et al., editors. *Reception in the Greco-Roman World: Literary Studies in Theory and Practice.* Cambridge UP, 2021.
>
> Fromkin, Victoria, et al. *An Introduction to Language.* 4th Canadian ed., Nelson, 2010.

- **corporate author**:

> *2020 Annual Report.* Broadview Press, 2021.
>
> "History of the Arms and Great Seal of the Commonwealth of Massachusetts." Commonwealth of Massachusetts, www.sec/state.ma.us/pre/presea/sealhis/htm. Accessed 15 June 2021.
>
> Ontario, Ministry of Natural Resources. *Achieving Balance: Ontario's Long-Term Energy Plan.* Queen's Printer for Ontario, 2016,

www.energy.gov.on.ca/en/ltep/achieving-balance-ontarios-long-term-energy-plan.

- **works with an anonymous author**: Works with an anonymous author should be alphabetized by title.

Pearl. Edited and translated by Jane Beal, Broadview Press, 2020.

- **two or more works by the same author**: The author's name should appear for the first entry only; for subsequent entries substitute three hyphens for the name of the author.

Menand, Louis. "Bad Comma: Lynne Truss's Strange Grammar." Review of *Eats, Shoots and Leaves*, by Lynne Truss. *The New Yorker*, 28 June 2004, www.newyorker.com/magazine/2004/06/28/bad-comma.

---. *The Metaphysical Club: A Story of Ideas in America.* Farrar, Straus and Giroux, 2001.

- **works under a pseudonym**: These are given using the same formatting as author's names. Online usernames are given as they appear.

@TheAtlantic. "The president is loath to acknowledge that many Americans support the recent attacks on democracy, 'and those who don't face a system stacked against them,' @GrahamDavidA writes." *Twitter*, 14 July 2021, www.twitter.com/TheAtlantic/status/1415363709950701572.

- **edited works**:

Renker, Elizabeth, editor. *Poems: A Concise Anthology*. Broadview Press, 2016.

When referring to an edited version of a work written by another author or authors, list the editor(s) after the title.

Trollope, Anthony. *The Eustace Diamonds.* 1873. Edited by Stephen Gill and John Sutherland, Penguin, 1986.

- **works in translation**: The translator is normally listed in the Contributor element of the citation.

Bolaño, Roberto. *By Night in Chile.* Translated by Chris Andrews, New Directions, 2003.

If your work focuses on the translation itself, you may list the translator in the author element, moving the author to the Contributor element.

Andrews, Chris, translator. *By Night in Chile*. By Roberto Bolaño, New Directions, 2003.

• **selections from anthologies or collections of readings**: A selection from a collection of readings or an anthology should begin with the name of the author of the selection. If they are available, be sure to add the selection's inclusive page numbers after the anthology's publication date.

Crawford, Isabella Valancy. "The Canoe." *Representative Poetry Online*, edited by Ian Lancashire, University of Toronto, 1997, www.rpo.library.utoronto.ca/poems/canoe.

Skelton, John. *Magnificence*. *The Broadview Anthology of Tudor Drama*, edited by Alan Stewart, Broadview Press, 2021, pp. 125–80.

Whitman, Walt. "Song of the Redwood-Tree." *Leaves of Grass*, Boston: James R Osgood and Co, 1881–82. *The Walt Whitman Archive*, edited by Matt Cohen et al., www.whitmanarchive.org/published/LG/1891/poems/93.

• **cross-references for works from the same collection or anthology**: It can be more efficient to create a full entry for the collection or anthology, and then to list each cited item in its own entry. Position the entries in the Works Cited list alphabetically, as you normally would, and use a short form for the collection or anthology, as in the following example:

Brown, Jennifer S.H., and Elizabeth Vibert, editors. *Reading Beyond Words: Contexts for Native History*. Broadview Press, 1996.

Cruikshank, Julie. "Discovery of Gold on the Klondike: Perspectives from Oral Tradition." Brown and Vibert, pp. 433–59.

Gleach, Frederic W. "Controlled Speculation: Interpreting the Saga of Pocahontas and Captain John Smith." Brown and Vibert, pp. 21–42.

• **multi-volume works**: If you are citing one or more of the volumes, list them after the title. The entry may note the total number of volumes at the end of the citation (this is optional).

Jeeves, Julie, editor. *A Reference Guide to Spanish Architecture*. 3 vols., Hackett, 2005.

Mercer, Bobby, editor. *A Reference Guide to French Architecture*. Vol. 1, Hackett, 2002. 3 vols.

• **different editions**: The edition should be specified whenever it is not the first edition. Include whatever the title page indicates about the particular edition, and use abbreviations (e.g., *rev. ed.* for *revised edition*, *2nd ed.* for *second edition*, and so on).

Acheson, Katherine O. *Writing Essays about Literature: A Guide for University and College Students*. 2nd ed., Broadview Press, 2021.
Fowles, John. *The Magus*. Rev. ed., Jonathan Cape, 1977.
The Bible. Authorized King James Version, Oxford UP, 2008.

• **republished sources**: When a source was previously published in a different form, you may include information about the prior publication. This is a supplemental element; include this information at your discretion, if you feel it would give your reader important context for the source.

MacMillan, Margaret. "Hubris." *History's People: Personalities and the Past*, Massey Lectures, CBC Radio, 3 Nov. 2015, www.cbc.ca/radio/ideas/history-s-people-personalities-the-past-lecture-2-1.3301571. Podcast. Originally delivered at the Arts and Culture Centre, St. John's, NL, 25 Sept. 2015, 7:00 p.m. Lecture.

• **reference work entries**: List by the author of the entry, if known; otherwise, list by the entry itself. The citation of a well-known reference work (because such works are frequently updated) should not have full publication details; provide the edition number, date, and location only. Don't include page numbers for works that arrange their entries alphabetically.

"Artificial." *Oxford English Dictionary*. 2nd ed., 1989.
"Baldwin, James, 1924–1987." *ProQuest Biographies*, 2006. *Literature Online*, www-proquest-com./encyclopedias-reference-works/baldwin-james-1924-1987.
Fowler, H.W. "Unique." *The King's English*, 2nd ed., 1908. *Bartleby.com*, www.bartleby.com/116/108.html#2. Accessed 20 May 2021.

• **works with a title in the title**: A title that is usually italicized should remain italicized when it appears within quotation marks:

Yearling, R. "*Hamlet* and the Limits of Narrative." *Essays in Criticism: A Quarterly Journal of Literary Criticism*, vol. 65, no. 4, 2015, pp. 368–82. *ProQuest*, https://doi.org/10.1093/escrit/cgv022.

Titles that are in quotation marks that appear within other titles in quotation marks are enclosed by single quotation marks:

> Berndt, Katrin. "Trapped in Class? Material Manifestations of Poverty and Prosperity in Alice Munro's 'Royal Beatings' and 'The Beggar Maid.'" *Neohelicon*, vol. 47, 18 Aug. 2020, pp. 521–35. *SpringerLink Journals*, https://doi.org/10.1007/s11059-020-00550-1.

An italicized title that is included within another italicized title is neither italicized nor placed in quotation marks. It appears in roman:

> Morelli, Stefan. *Stoppard's* Arcadia *and Modern Drama*. Ashgate, 2004.

If a title normally enclosed in quotation marks appears in an italicized title, keep the quotation marks:

> Runzo, Sandra. *"Theatricals of Day": Emily Dickinson and Nineteenth-Century American Popular Culture*. U of Massachusetts P, 2019.

• **material from prefaces, introductions, etc.**: If you refer to something from a work's preface, introduction, or foreword, the reference under Works Cited should begin with the name of the author of that preface, introduction, or foreword. Add inclusive page numbers after the date of publication.

> Stage, Kelly. Introduction. *The Roaring Girl*, by Thomas Middleton and Thomas Dekker, Broadview Press, 2019, pp. 7–17.

• **magazine articles**: The title of the article should appear in quotation marks, the title of the magazine in italics. If no author is identified, the title of the article should appear first. If the magazine is published monthly or every two months, give the date as month and year. For magazines published weekly or every two weeks, give the date as day, month, and year. Abbreviate the names of months (except for *May*, *June*, and *July*).

> Enright, Robert. "Ways of Looking, Ways of Not Seeing: An Interview with Shaan Syed." *Border Crossings*, no. 156, May 2021, www.bordercrossingsmag.com/article/ways-of-looking-ways-of-not-seeing.
>
> "Greens in Pinstriped Suits." *The Economist*, 21 May 2016, www.economist.com/news/business/21699141-climate-conscious-shareholders-are-putting-big-oil-spot-greens-pinstriped-suits.

If you accessed the article online, you may include the date of access, though it is a supplemental element. If the website is hosted by a body other than the magazine itself, include it as a second container with its accompanying publication details.

> Gladwell, Malcolm. "The Art of Failure: Why Some People Choke and Others Panic." *The New Yorker,* 21 Aug. 2000, www.newyorker.com/magazine/2000/08/21/the-art-of-failure. Accessed 10 Feb. 2021.
>
> Kreimer, Julian. "Mernet Larsen." *Art in America,* vol. 104, no. 4, 2016, pp. 115–16. *Academic Search Complete,* www.search.ebscohost.com/login.aspx?direct=true&db=114088897&site=ehost-live. Accessed 9 Feb. 2021.

• **newspaper articles**: The basic principles to follow with newspaper articles or editorials are the same as with magazine articles (see above). Note, however, that when the newspaper's sections are paginated separately, section as well as page numbers are often required. If an article is not printed on consecutive pages, include only the first page number followed by a plus sign. In the following reference the article begins on page 3 of the first section:

> Yakabuski, Konrad. "Many Looking for Meaning in Vice-Presidential Debate." *The Globe and Mail,* 12 Oct. 2012, p. A3+.

If you are citing an online version of a newspaper article you should include the date you accessed the site. The site name, if it is different from the container title, should also be included.

> Friedman, Lisa. "Democrats Call for a Tax on Imports from Polluting Countries." *The New York Times,* 14 July 2021, www.nytimes.com/2021/07/14/climate/border-carbon-tax-united-states.html. Accessed 2 May 2021.

• **journal articles**: The basic principles are the same as with magazine articles, but entries for journal articles include the volume and issue numbers.

> Belcourt, Billy-Ray. "Meditations on Reserve Life, Biosociality, and the Taste of Non-Sovereignty." *Settler Colonial Studies,* vol. 8, no. 1, Jan. 2018, pp. 1–15, https://doi.org/10.1080/2201473X.2017.1279830.

If you are citing an online version of a journal article you should include any additional containers and their publication details (databases, for example).

Sohmer, Steve. "12 June 1599: Opening Day at Shakespeare's Globe." *Early Modern Literary Studies: A Journal of Sixteenth- and Seventeenth-Century English Literature*, vol. 3, no. 1, 1997. *ProQuest*, www.extra.shu.ac.uk/emls/emlshome.html.

• **book reviews**: The name of the reviewer (if it has been provided) should come first, followed by the title of the review (if there is one), and then by the information on the book itself.

Leiter, Brian, and Michael Weisberg. "Do You Only Have a Brain? On Thomas Nagel." Review of *Why the Materialist Neo-Darwinian Conception of Nature Is Almost Certainly False*, by Thomas Nagel, *The Nation*, 22 Oct. 2012, www.thenation.com/article/do-you-only-have-brain-thomas-nagel/.

Lennon, J. Robert. "I Was Trying to Find the Edge." Review of *Second Place*, by Rachel Cusk, *London Review of Books*, vol. 43, no. 11, 3 June 2021, www.lrb.co.uk/the-paper/v43/n11/j.-robert-lennon/i-was-trying-to-find-the-edge.

• **periodical publications in online databases**:

Moy, Olivia Loksing. "Reading in the Aftermath: An Asian American *Jane Eyre*." *Victorian Studies*, vol. 62 no. 3, 2020, pp. 406–20. *Project MUSE*, muse.jhu.edu/article/771238.

• **illustrated books**: Include the illustrator's name as well as the author's name.

Juster, Norman. *The Phantom Tollbooth*. Illustrated by Jules Feiffer, Yearling-Random House, 1961.

• **graphic narratives**: In many graphic narratives, both the illustrations and the text are created by one person; these kinds of works should be documented as in the first example below. Use the second example's format for works whose text is by one person and illustrations are by another.

Leavitt, Sarah. *Tangles: A Story about Alzheimer's, My Mother, and Me*. Freehand Books, 2010.

Butler, Octavia E. *Kindred: A Graphic Novel Adaptation*. Art by John Jennings, adapted by Damian Duffy, Abrams Books, 2017.

• **films or television episodes**: These entries may be tailored to the context in which you are citing the work. If you are discussing the work of a director, for example, place the director's name in the Author element:

Medak, Peter, director. "The Buys." *The Wire*, created by David Simon and Ed Burns, season 1, episode 3, HBO, 16 June 2002.

Zhao, Chloé, director. *Nomadland*. Performances by Frances McDormand, Gay DeForest, Patricia Grier, and Linda May, Searchlight Pictures, 2020. *Hulu*, www.hulu.com/nomadland-movie.

If you are discussing a particular performance, place the actor's name in the Author element.

Moss, Elizabeth, performer. "A Little Kiss." *Mad Men*, directed by Jennifer Getzinger, AMC, 25 Mar. 2012.

Washington, Kerry, performer. "The Spark." *Little Fires Everywhere*, directed by Lynn Shelton, season 1, episode 1, Best Day Ever Productions et al., 2020. *Hulu*, www.hulu.com/series/little-fires-everywhere-bce24897-1a74-48a3-95e8-6cdd530dde4c.

- **online videos**: If your source is a video on a website, cite, if you can, who uploaded the video, and the date on which the video was posted.

McDonald, Emily, director. *Looking Back with Pride*. Forever Pictures, 2021. *Vimeo*, uploaded by Emily McDonald, 21 June 2021, www.vimeo.com/565585933.

- **radio broadcasts**:

"Glenn Gould Special." *The Sunday Edition*, narrated by Robert Harris and Michael Enright, CBC Radio One, 23 Sept. 2012.

- **podcasts**:

"Are Young People Losing Faith in Democracy?" *Talking Politics*, hosted by David Runciman, 2 Nov. 2020, www.talkingpoliticspodcast.com/blog/2020/285-are-young-people-losing-faith-in-democracy.

- **recorded music**:

Bridgers, Phoebe. "Motion Sickness." *Stranger in the Alps*, Dead Oceans, 2017.

- **live performances**: If you are citing a live performance or lecture, include the physical location and the city where the performance or lecture was delivered, as well as the date. Omit the city name if it is part of the location name. Include other information about the performance—the names of the director, the conductor, and/or lead performers, for instance—where such information is relevant. If your work focuses on the contribution of a performance's director, for example, cite that person in the Author element. Other important contributors follow the title in the Contributor element.

> Bedford, Brian, director. *The Importance of Being Earnest.* By Oscar Wilde, performances by Brian Bedford, Santino Fontana, David Furr, Charlotte Parry, and Sarah Topham, Roundabout Theatre Company, 3 July 2011, American Airlines Theatre, New York.
>
> MacMillan, Margaret. "Hubris." *History's People: Personalities and the Past*, 25 Sept. 2015, 7:00 p.m., Arts and Culture Centre, St. John's, NL. Massey Lecture.

• **works of visual art**: When citing a physical object you have experienced, such as a work of art, provide in the Location element the name of the institution and city where you experienced it. Leave out the name of the city if the city name is part of the institution name (e.g., Art Institute of Chicago).

> Belmore, Rebecca. *Fringe.* 2008, National Gallery of Canada, Ottawa.
>
> Sargent, John Singer. *Henry James.* 1913, National Portrait Gallery, London.

If you access a work of art online or in a book, you should include full information about the website or volume you consulted.

> Colquhoun, Ithell. *Scylla.* 1938, Tate Gallery, London. *Tate Women Artists*, by Alicia Foster, Tate, 2004, p. 85.
>
> Giotto di Bondone. *Lamentation.* 1304–06, Capella Scrovegni, Padua. *Web Gallery of Art*, www.wga.hu/frames-e.html?/html/g/giotto/. Accessed 29 Jan. 2021.

• **interviews**: Begin all entries for interviews with the name of the person being interviewed, and if there is a title for the interview, include it (in quotation marks if it is part of another work, or in italics if it has been published by itself). If there is no title, or if the title does not make clear that the work is an interview, write *Interview*, and give the name of the interviewer, if known. Finish with whatever publication information is appropriate. If you conducted the interview yourself, give the name of the person you interviewed, the medium (*Personal interview*, *Telephone interview*), and the date.

> Lockwood, Patricia. "Patricia Lockwood Is a Good Reason to Never Log Off." Interview by Gabriella Paiella, *GQ*, 15 Feb. 2021, www.gq.com/story/patricia-lockwood-book-interview.

Rankine, Claudia. "The Art of Poetry No. 102." Interview by David L. Ulin, *Paris Review*, no. 219, winter 2016, www.theparisreview.org/interviews/6905/the-art-of-poetry-no-102-claudia-rankine.

Rosengarten, Herbert. Personal interview, 21 Jan. 2013.

• **online projects**: In the case of large projects, cite the full range of years during which the project has been developed:

Secord, James A., et al., editors. *Darwin Correspondence Project.* 1974–2016, www.darwinproject.ac.uk/.

Willett, Perry, editor. *Victorian Women Writers Project.* Indiana University Digital Library Program, 1995–2016, webapp1/dlib.indiana.edu/vwwp/welcome.do. Accessed 26 Nov. 2021.

• **e-books**: E-book citations should follow the basic pattern for physical books, with the format recorded in the Version element.

Edgeworth, Maria, et al. *Moral Tales: A Selection.* Edited by Robin Runia, e-book ed., Broadview Press, 2021.

Note that the above formatting applies to publications formatted for e-book web readers or e-readers. If you have accessed or downloaded an e-book from a website, digital platform, or database, format your citation as you would any other source found online, by adding a Container element and by citing a DOI or stable URL in the Location element.

Austen, Jane. *Pride and Prejudice.* 1813. *Project Gutenberg*, 2008, www.gutenberg.org/files/1342/1342-h/1342-h.htm. Accessed 20 Feb. 2021.

• **information databases**:

Morissette, René, et al. "Working from Home: Potential Implications for Public Transit and Greenhouse Gas Emissions." *Statistics Canada*, 22 Apr. 2021, https://doi.org/10.25318/36280001202100400005-eng.

• **entry in a wiki**: Wikis are online sites that can be added to and edited by any site user; as such, they may be subject to frequent changes made by any number of authors and editors. Do not, therefore, provide any authors' names. Start with the entry's title; then give the name of the wiki, the site publisher, the date of the entry's last update, the location, and the date you accessed the site.

"William Caxton." *Wikipedia*. Wikimedia Foundation, 27 May 2021, www.en.wikipedia.org/wiki/William_Caxton. Accessed 16 July 2021.

• **blog post**: Include the title of the posting as your source title, the blog title as the first container, and the name of the blog host as a publisher.

Gluck, Heather. "Brontë Society Fights to Keep 'Lost' Emily Brontë Poems Available for the Public." *MobyLives*, Melville House, 14 June 2021, www.mhpbooks.com/bronte-society-fights-to-keep-lost-emily-bronte-poems-available-for-the-public/.

• **e-mail message**: Use the subject as the title and place it within quotation marks.

Milton, Frank. "Thoughts on Animal Rights." Received by the author, 15 Jan. 2013.

If it is not clear from the context of your work that the source being cited is an e-mail, you may wish to add a supplemental element to the end of your citation that indicates the type of work.

Stuart, Jennifer. "My Experience of the Attack." Received by the author, 17 May 2016. E-mail.

• **tweet**: Copy the full, unchanged text of the tweet in the title element and enclose it in quotation marks. The username is included as the Author element.

@TheAtlantic. "The president is loath to acknowledge that many Americans support the recent attacks on democracy, 'and those who don't face a system stacked against them,' @GrahamDavidA writes." *Twitter*, 14 July 2021, www.twitter.com/TheAtlantic/status/1415363709950701572.

• **comment posted on a web page**: Usernames are given in full, unchanged. If the comment is anonymous, skip the author element. If the comment does not have its own title, provide instead a description of the comment that includes the title of the work being commented on (e.g., Comment on "Clinton Aims for Decisive Victory"). If it is available, include the exact time of posting in the Publication Date element.

Evan. Comment on "Another Impasse on Gun Bills, Another Win for Hyperpolitics." *The New York Times*, 21 June 2016, 9:02 a.m., www.nytimes.com/2016/06/22/us/politics/washington-congress-gun-control.html.

MLA Style Sample Essays

Following are two sample essays written in MLA style. Note that further sample essays, some of which also employ MLA style, are available on the companion website associated with this book.

cover page (not required in MLA style, but may be required by some instructors)

Monumental Problems:

Setting the Criteria for Decisions in Political Aesthetics

By Robin Lee

all text centred

Prof. K. D. Smith

Humanities 205

20 October 2021

Robin Lee

Lee 1

Professor Smith

Humanities 205

20 October 2021

name and page number in top right corner

Monumental Problems:

Setting the Criteria for Decisions in Political Aesthetics

In recent years the level of political controversy over public monuments has greatly increased. Heated disagreements have arisen in America (over monuments honouring Confederate leaders and supporters of slavery); in Canada (over monuments honouring John A. Macdonald and other leaders of the past who were complicit in the ill-treatment of Indigenous Canadians); in Britain (over monuments honouring James Colston and other leaders of the past who were involved in the slave trade); and elsewhere around the world. Should these controversial monuments be removed? Should they be preserved but locked away, accessible only to historians and art historians? Should they be accessible to all, but be displayed in low-key fashion in museums or art galleries (with full contextualization provided) rather than be raised on pedestals in public places? Should they simply be destroyed as relics of a past we have moved beyond? Or should hard choices be made in individual cases, with some works preserved, some not? In the heat of claims and counterclaims it can be difficult to sort out what criteria are truly relevant for such decisions. This essay will

first line of all paragraphs indented

text left-justified and ragged right

Lee 2

first paragraph ends with a statement of the essay's thesis

examine issues of relevance from several angles and will argue that one criterion in particular deserves to be considered more frequently—the aesthetic value of a work of art. Debates on these issues rightly include considerable discussion of historical, political, and ethical issues, but too often entirely neglect aesthetic considerations.

2 It is important at the outset to recognize that cities, nations, and cultures have been removing public monuments for almost as long as they have been erecting them. In ancient Rome, for example, it was common to remove and destroy monuments honouring one leader as soon as the next one came to power; the Romans termed this process *damnatio memoriae* or "condemnation of memory/legacy" (Byrne). The notion that societies can and should periodically re-assess the leaders of the past and revise their assessment of who deserves to be honoured with public monuments is not an idea dreamed up in the disrespectful twenty-first century; it has been with us for millennia.

if your source has no numbered pages or sections, no number is given

3 Nor is it an idea that should be associated with any particular part of the political spectrum. Some have suggested that it is predominantly those on the political left who want to remove public monuments honouring figures they feel do not deserve to be honoured.[1] But the left has no monopoly on such practices—far from it. Anti-communists joyously took down thousands of statues of Soviet leaders after the fall of the Soviet Union in 1990. The Communist government of East Germany tore down statues of Wilhelm I (the first

endnote inserted to give additional information

Lee 3

German Emperor) in 1950. Militaristic Canadians tore down a statue of the Kaiser in 1914, as Canada was going to war with Germany. Countries throughout Africa have removed public memorials to European colonial and imperialist figures. Back in 1912 the Kentucky chapter of the Daughters of the Confederacy was keen not only to erect a statue honouring Confederate leader Jefferson Davis but also to remove a statue of Abraham Lincoln in order to make way for Davis ("Objectionable"). And so it has gone; the idea of removing public monuments of discredited leaders is decidedly not something the radical left has dreamed up in our own era.

for a source listed by title, use a shortened title for parenthetical citation

Nor is it a "freedom of speech" or "freedom of expression" issue, 4
much as some have suggested that to be the case.[2] In Canada and the United States, as in democracies around the world, any individual remains free to commission and display in their front yard a statue of Robert E. Lee, of Joseph Stalin, or of whomever they like; the issue is whom governments decide (on behalf of the people as a whole) to honour with public monuments in civic squares, in public parks, or in front of legislatures and courthouses. Inevitably, views as to who deserves or does not deserve to be so honoured change over time, and are often highly charged politically; consensus is often elusive.

text double-spaced throughout

One of the greatest mistakes of the debate over public monu- 5
ments is to suppose that such monuments are intended primarily in order to preserve the historical record. On the contrary, statues placed

Lee 4

on pedestals in prominent public places are placed there in order to honour those represented—and to invite the public to look up to them, both literally and figuratively.[3] The controversial Robert E. Lee monument in New Orleans, for example, "rose 109 feet. The bronze figure of Lee alone stood 16 feet tall and was hailed at the time as 'the largest bronze statue ever cast in New York'" (Cox 43).[4] Outsized statues of figures raised and presented in this fashion, then, are not *merely* statues of historical figures; they have become public monuments as well as statues. Such a statue is inevitably, as Benedito Machava of Yale University puts it, "a political statement" (Machava 00:03).

for audio and visual media works, use a time-stamp to locate the citation

6 Conversely, the act of removing a public monument in itself says nothing about history; there is no claim more absurd in the ongoing debate over public monuments than the frequently-made suggestion that removing a statue from a public place is tantamount to "erasing history."[5] The ways in which Jefferson Davis and Robert E. Lee shaped American history, and in which John A. Macdonald shaped Canadian history, are entirely unaffected by whether or not their statues are displayed in places of honour in our cities; their actions continue to be remembered, written about, and extensively discussed in schools and universities.

7 The reality is that arguments over the degree to which we may want to honour leaders of the past with public monuments today are first and foremost arguments about our political and ethical views and

Lee 5

values today—not arguments about what happened decades or centuries ago. To be sure, those seeking to defend Macdonald downplay the policies that were designed to "do away with the tribal system and assimilate the Indian people in all respects" (qtd. in Beazley), just as those seeking to defend Lee and Davis downplay the extent to which these leaders were defenders of enslaving what Davis called "the servile race." But unrepentant racists aside (and it should be admitted that their numbers are not negligible), everyone acknowledges *both* that Macdonald played a central role in Canada's Confederation, *and* that his policies towards the Indigenous people in Canada were oppressive. The substantial disagreement is as to which values should be accorded more emphasis in our own time. Do we value the knitting together of a nation more than we deplore the oppression of its native peoples? Similarly, it is broadly agreed *both* that Robert E. Lee and Jefferson Davis were defenders of slavery who were themselves enslavers *and* that they were well-mannered and behaved graciously in defeat. The substantial disagreement is again as to what values should be accorded more emphasis in our own time. Do we value graciousness in defeat more than we deplore the slavery and subsequent oppression of a substantial portion of a nation's people?

for indirect sources, use the abbreviation "qtd. in" ("quoted in")

Other values too are at stake in these controversies. In fighting for slavery (and "states' rights"),[6] for example, Davis and Lee were also fighting against federal interference in an economic system according 8

Lee 6

to the principles of which those with vast amounts of capital should be allowed to do what they wish with it.[7] That fight too has a powerful echo in debates in America today (and, indeed, around the world); to what degree should a belief in the desirability of all humans being treated equitably outweigh a belief that capitalism should be allowed free rein?

9 Not everything, of course, can or should be seen only through the lens of today. Those who say we should not assess historical figures entirely by the standards of today make a fair point; we need to understand the ways in which earlier eras differed from our own. It would be obviously absurd to argue that John A. Macdonald or Woodrow Wilson should be disparaged because they did not support gay rights, when no one in late nineteenth- or early twentieth-century North America contemplated equal rights on the basis of sexual orientation. We need to understand too that "the standards of the past" are never uniform. During the same decade that Woodrow Wilson was doing everything in his power while President of Princeton to keep African Americans from attending that university, the presidents of Columbia and Yale were for the first time welcoming African Americans into those institutions. On the matter of Macdonald's Conservative government setting up the oppressive system of Indigenous residential schools, it seems fair to point out that very few in mainstream white society at the time opposed his action; when Wilfrid Laurier's Liberals

Lee 7

came to power, indeed, they greatly expanded the system (and it was under Laurier's successor, Robert Borden, that it was made compulsory under the Indian Act for all Indigenous children to attend either industrial or residential schools). It seems fair to point out too that the attitudes adopted by Macdonald and other Canadian politicians of the 1870s were in many respects considerably less oppressive than those adopted by their American counterparts at the time; no one in Macdonald's government was making statements as extreme as American Congressman James Michael Cavanaugh's 1868 assertion: "I have never in my life seen a good Indian except when I have seen a dead Indian" (Mieder 42). When it comes to the matter of public monuments, discussion will inevitably focus less on achieving entirely balanced assessments of how individuals behaved in the context of their own time than on questions of who (and of what sorts of behaviour) we wish to *honour* in the present. But our answers to those questions may sometimes be appropriately shaded in one direction or the other to the extent that they are informed by an awareness of history's nuances.

parenthetical references at end of short quotations followed by punctuation

10 Even more important is that our judgements on such matters should be informed by an awareness of social psychology. When Indigenous Canadians such as Marie Knockwood (a member of the Abegweit First Nation who was taken from her home in Prince Edward Island and forced to attend the Shubenacadie Residential School in Nova Scotia when she was 10 years old) testify that they feel

Lee 8

"full of anger and bitterness" when they see Macdonald honoured with public monuments, it matters (MacLeod). When African Americans such as Nicole Moliere of New Orleans testify that walking or driving past statues of the likes of Lee and Davis feels like "a daily assault" (qtd. in O'Neal), it matters.

11 Such concerns were very much on the minds of the New Orleans City Council and Mayor Mitch Landrieu when they decided in 2017 to remove the Lee and Davis monuments—along with a number of other Confederate monuments.[8] At the moment they remain in storage, awaiting a final decision as to where or if they should again be displayed.

12 How should the fate of such statues be decided? And what considerations should be given most weight in reaching those decisions? Sathnam Sanghera is among those who have suggested that, in the case of many British colonial monuments, at least, it may be better to leave monuments where they are and to "level the playing field" not by destroying old monuments but by erecting new monuments alongside them to present the other side of the story (167). As a purely practical matter, however, it would surely take many decades to "level the playing field" in this way. Moreover, the approach Sanghera recommends would continue to invite the public to revere many figures who, most people now agree, do not deserve to be so honoured.

13 Many have suggested that all such monuments should still be

Lee 9

displayed publicly, but in a venue such as a museum where they can be accompanied by full contextualization, and where their placement does not suggest that they are to be regarded with veneration. That indeed seems an attractive solution—until one considers all the implications. Consider for one thing the financial implications. Art historian Erin L. Thompson is one scholar who has done exactly that—and she argues persuasively against preservation. She references an investigation that concluded "that in the previous ten years, taxpayers had spent at least 40 million dollars preserving Confederate monuments," and she draws attention as well to the added cost of displaying them in museums rather than in public as monuments:

> [At the University of North Carolina], when protesters in 2018 tore down the "Silent Sam" Confederate statue [see fig. 7], U.N.C. proposed building a new museum to house it that would cost over five million dollars and almost a million dollars a year in ongoing maintenance and security. So I look at these statues as money sinks. And I think about all of the amazing sites of African-American history or Native American history that are disintegrating from lack of funding and think those dollars could be better spent elsewhere. (Qtd. in Bromwich)

long quotations indented—no quotations marks used except for quotations within a quotation

in-text citation following block quotation comes after final punctuation and no punctuation follows

Thompson makes an important point; re-deploying all the problematic monuments within museums would be extraordinarily expensive. But

Lee 10

it would surely be an extreme measure not to preserve *any* of them. How, then, should societies choose?

14 At this point it seems to me important to consider one more truth about these public monuments. We have noted the importance of acknowledging that such monuments make political statements. We have noted too the need for decisions regarding such monuments to be informed not only by today's values and today's politics but also by an awareness of history and an awareness of social psychology. We need further to remember that when statues acquire the status of public monuments, they do not cease to be statues. They do not cease, that is to say, to be *aesthetic* objects. This aesthetic side is more often than not entirely forgotten, as politically charged discussions about them become more and more heated.[9] But it is vitally important to keep it in mind when societies take statues off their pedestals and try to decide the fate of what were *formerly* public monuments.

15 To open discussion of the aesthetic element, I would like to consider a case over which debate has been rather less heated than have been many of the arguments over statues of Confederate leaders—or, indeed, over statues of Macdonald. The largest monument issue in the continent's largest city has involved a president often praised for his aggressive "trust busting" and for other progressive policies—Theodore Roosevelt. On racial issues, Roosevelt's record is mixed; undeniably racist in some respects, he was arguably rather less so than most white

Americans of his era—and certainly quite considerably less so than was his successor, Woodrow Wilson. But a mixed record on such issues by the standards of a hundred years ago is not likely to lead to a twenty-first-century consensus that one deserves to be put on a pedestal.

Roosevelt was an important benefactor of the Museum of Natural 16
History, and when he died the Memorial Association created by the New York State Legislature recommended that the museum would be the most appropriate location for a memorial honouring him.[10] Eventually the nature of the monument itself was decided on, and the various parties—the Memorial Association, the New York State legislature, and the American Museum of Natural History Board of Trustees (which included representatives of the Roosevelt family)—together specified that the monument should be made up of "an equestrian statue of Roosevelt with two accompanying figures on foot, one an American Indian and the other a native African, representing his gun bearers and suggestive of Roosevelt's interest in the original peoples of these widely separated countries" (qtd. in Marber 93). In a sentence quoted much less frequently, they specified as well the imposing height of the monument: "this group [of figures] will rise to a height of 30 feet above the sidewalk" (Freundlich 123). They commissioned James Earle Fraser—at the time acclaimed as one of the nation's finest sculptors—to create the work. When the statue (see fig. 1 and fig. 2) was finally unveiled, Fraser provided his own description of the group of

Lee 12

figures and their significance: "The two figures at [Roosevelt's] side are guides symbolizing the continents of Africa and America, and if you choose may stand for Roosevelt's friendliness to all races" (American Museum of Natural History, "What Did").

when citing two or more works by the same author, add a title to the in-text citation, shortened if necessary

Fig. 1. James Earle Fraser, *Equestrian Statue of Theodore Roosevelt* (front view detail), 1939.

Lee 13

Fig. 2. James Earle Fraser, *Equestrian Statue of Theodore Roosevelt* (side view detail), 1939.

partial bibliographic details for figures and tables can be included in the caption, with full details in the Works Cited list (as here)

That is not, of course, how many perceive the relationship among the three figures today. The positioning of the figures, as the statement issued by the museum when they decided in 2020 to remove the statue put it, "communicates a racial hierarchy that the museum and members of the public have long found disturbing" (American Museum of Natural History, "Addressing the Statue"). That judgement is surely correct; regardless of Fraser's original intent or the intent of those who commissioned him to create the work, there can be no doubt the arrangement of the figures suggests to many minds—certainly including many African American and Indigenous American minds—a relationship in which the white man is regarded as inher-

17

ently superior, the other two inherently inferior. In removing the statue from its prominent place on a triple pedestal outside the front of the museum, they did nothing to "erase history." What they did was to change the status of the object. Removed from its place of honour as a public monument, it loses that status; it becomes simply a statue. For the moment that statue—like the New Orleans statues of Lee and Davis—is in storage, awaiting a final decision as to its long-term fate. Is it a statue that deserves to be preserved? Let us set ethics and politics to one side for a moment, and pay some attention to aesthetics.

18 To begin with, we should acknowledge that the fashion in which the three humans and the horse are arranged—much as it portrays a hierarchy that we now rightly understand to be inappropriate—is quite striking visually. All three figures are rendered in entirely lifelike fashion; the positioning of the limbs, the musculature, the facial expressions—in every respect these figures feel human. But more than that, they feel—to me at least—like interesting humans. Clearly heroism is intended to be celebrated here in the presentation of all three figures, but that is surely not all that is conveyed. Along with the heroic determination of the conqueror, is there not in Roosevelt's expression something of arrogance, and of ruthlessness? The expressions of the two other figures are more difficult to read. Strength and determination, certainly. Stoicism? Perhaps. And pride—especially in the face of the Native American figure. Can hints of sorrow

Lee 15

be detected behind the surface of these faces? And is there a hint, especially in the face of the African, of a strength and determination that could readily be refocused into resistance against the conqueror? In short, all three faces have to them a good deal of complexity—an extraordinary amount of complexity, given that the heroic genre necessitates a substantial degree of idealization in the presentation. All three offer the viewer a good deal to reflect on, and are capable of sparking thoughts that go against the grain of a statue that may seem at first to be a straightforward idealization of an historical figure. The entire work, indeed, is capable of sparking such thoughts. Look, for example, at the way in which Roosevelt is pulling hard on the horse's double reins—here too we can sense a hint more of cruelty than of heroism. In the words of Art History professor Harriet F. Senie of The City College of New York, "the Fraser sculpture is a good work of art by any artistic standards" (American Museum of Natural History, "Perspectives").[11] It surely deserves to be preserved—and, in some appropriate venue, at some point in the future, made available to the public again.

As it happens, Fraser's spouse, Laura Gardin Fraser, was also 19
among the leading sculptors of the era—and her work too has been embroiled in controversy. Here again it is worth considering the aesthetic side of the argument. Perhaps her best-known work is her 1946 statue (figs. 3–6) depicting Robert E. Lee and Stonewall Jackson on their way to the battle of Chancellorsville. The first double equestrian

statue to be completed in America, it stood for many decades as a monument in Wyman Park in Baltimore, mounted on a large pedestal. At its base were various inscriptions celebrating Lee and Jackson as "Christian soldiers" who "waged war like gentlemen" ("Lee Jackson Monument"). In 2017, following the recommendation of a special commission appointed by the city, the statue was removed and placed in storage.

Fig. 3. Laura Gardin Fraser, *Stonewall Jackson and Robert E. Lee Monument* (front view detail), 1948.

Lee 17

Fig. 4. Laura Gardin Fraser, *Stonewall Jackson and Robert E. Lee Monument* (close up detail of Jackson), 1948.

Fig. 5. Laura Gardin Fraser, *Stonewall Jackson and Robert E. Lee Monument* (close up detail of Lee), 1948.

Lee 18

Fig. 6. *Laura Gardin Fraser in Her Studio at Work on Model for "Lee-Jackson Monument,"* c. 1947.

20 Again, let us set ethics and politics aside for a moment and consider aesthetics. It is difficult not to be struck immediately by the lifelike quality of Fraser's sculpting. The figures feel as if they are in motion, and every detail—the feet in the stirrups, the hands on the binoculars—feels convincing. Many equestrian statues have a static quality to them; this one feels entirely dynamic. And the expressions of the figures have considerable depth and complexity to them—Lee has a calm, almost impassive façade on his features, while Jackson's expression conveys a rougher sort of determination that perhaps hints as well at the ferocity of his religious devotion and his devotion to

military discipline. The sculpting has the power to suggest a wide range of thoughts as to how these men would be inclined to act as generals—and, indeed, as husbands, fathers, and enslavers. Perhaps even more striking, though, is the overall composition of the work. The way in which the figures—equine as well as human—are placed together is highly artistic, even as it feels entirely natural; the lines and the curves of the figures convey an extraordinary sense of peacefulness and harmony. That the relationship between the two generals was extremely close is well-known—Lee is said to have remarked that he lost his right arm when Jackson died. And yet there is a powerful tension underlying this harmony; however strong the relationship between them, these are generals who are about to lead their troops into a battle in which thousands will die.

Fraser spent twelve years working on the statue; it shows. On 21
aesthetic grounds alone, I would argue that this is a work worth preserving, worth contextualizing, and worth making available to the public.

Spending some time on the aesthetics of statues such as these sets 22
the aesthetic qualities of a number of other statues that have been the subject of controversy into bold relief. Illustrated below are the "Silent Sam" UNC monument (fig. 7) of an anonymous Confederate soldier that Erin L. Thompson references; the New Orleans monument in honour of Jefferson Davis (fig. 8) that was removed in 2017; and a

Lee 20

Regina, Saskatchewan monument in honour of John A. Macdonald (fig. 9) that was removed in April 2021. The figure in the UNC monument is not an obviously poor work, but nor is it strikingly accomplished; the face is blandly inexpressive and the figure has a static, posed feeling to it. The New Orleans Davis statue seems to me to have little to recommend it aesthetically either. Arching backwards but with one arm thrown forward, Davis is presumably meant to look heroic, but his pose seems awkward and ungainly. Awkward arm extension is an aesthetic issue too with the Regina monument to Macdonald. That monument, which dates from 1967, was controversial at that time for aesthetic rather than political reasons; one local gallery curator called it "commonplace," a "caricature" that "tells us absolutely nothing about the character of the man," while another (Ronald Bloore, who would soon become a nationally-known artist) described it as a work that "totally lacks artistic merit" (qtd. in Martin). What's more—as a comparison with photographs of Macdonald makes very clear—the work bears very little resemblance to the person being portrayed.

sentence structured so that it flows grammatically into quotation

Lee 21

Fig. 7. John A. Wilson, *Silent Sam*, 1913.

Fig. 8. Edward Virginius Valentine, *Jefferson Davis Monument*, 1911.

Lee 22

Fig. 9. Sonia de Grandmaison, *John A. Macdonald Memorial* (detail), 1967.

23 Whereas the aesthetic case is extremely strong for the preservation in perpetuity of works such as James Earle Fraser's equestrian statue of Roosevelt and Laura Gardin Fraser's double equestrian statue of Lee and Jackson, the aesthetic case for the preservation in perpetuity of these other works is surely much weaker. The case is particularly weak for its preservation in perpetuity *at public expense*. Resources for such things are always in short supply, and (as Thompson suggests) there is a strong argument for giving priority when distributing those scarce resources to those who have been disadvantaged in the past—to providing funds to support Indigenous and Black sculptors today, and

Lee 23

to providing funds to support the creation of work honouring heroic figures from the past who were never in earlier eras considered fit subjects for public monuments. Before we commit—at very considerable expense—to preserving all of the many hundreds of monuments erected in honour of Lee and Davis, and all of the dozens of monuments erected in honour of Macdonald, we should surely commit to balancing the scales. Before we commit to funding the placing of a contextualized Lee and a contextualized Davis in every American museum and of a contextualized Macdonald in every Canadian one, we should surely look to commission more monuments honouring Frederick Douglass and Harriet Tubman, Mary Shadd and Ida Wells, Tecumseh and Sitting Bull.[12]

In the current climate it may well be needlessly divisive to destroy any statues—even those statues that have little or no interest or historical importance, and little claim to aesthetic merit. To store them away at the lowest possible expense for another generation or two may well be the most advisable solution for the present. But let us not commit to the preservation of all these monuments in perpetuity; when it comes time to display some of these pieces in contextualized fashion in museum settings, let us be selective in choosing for preservation only the most interesting, the most important, and the most valuable aesthetically. 24

final paragraph restates and broadens the essay's main argument

Lee 24

Notes

1 Limbaugh, for example, links the movement to remove monuments to "the American and the worldwide left."

notes numbered as in text

2 Donald Trump is a notable example. As Macaya et al. report, he made the following statement about the removal of Confederate monuments during a speech he delivered in Tulsa: "This cruel campaign of censorship and exclusion violates everything we hold dear as Americans." When Virginia's governor announced the state's intention to take down a prominent public memorial to Robert E. Lee, state senator Amanda Chase argued that, because such monuments are a form of artistic expression, removing them raises "First Amendment concerns" (Carrington and Strother). In Canada, former journalist Robert Roth is among those who contend that taking down public monuments honouring former prime ministers is "to suppress free speech" (Llana).

each note indented

3 An exception is John Dann's statue of Sir John A. Macdonald, which was removed from its place in front of Victoria's City Hall in 2017. Dann has drawn attention to the fact that in this case the statue was not raised high above the street level but rather placed at eye level with passers-by: "It's not a sculpture on a pedestal, it's not a monument. It's a portrait of a man and that man is accessible to the people who go in and out of the building" (Canadian Press).

4 Also relevant is the location of such monuments. As

Rebecca Shehan and Jennifer Speights-Binet point out, "The monuments held prominent locations in highly traveled areas—their adjacency to quotidian traffic underpinned the taken-for-grantedness of white supremacy" (351).

5 See, for example, Constantine, "Ignoring American History," and Caplan, "Huckabee."

6 It seems appropriate to put the term "states' rights" in quotation marks here; the vast majority of reputable historians now see the argument that was long put forward by Southern whites—that the central issue in the Civil War was "states' rights" (rather than slavery)—is at best a smokescreen, and at worst an outright lie.

7 Jefferson Davis made the matter clear in his 29 April 1861 speech to the Confederate Congress: "The South were willing purchasers of property suitable to their wants, and paid the price of the acquisition without harboring a suspicion that their quiet possession was to be disturbed" (Ainsworth and Kirkley 258).

8 Landrieu's speech explaining how he had become convinced that removing the monuments was the right thing to do received national coverage. The explanation touched extensively on the personal: "Another friend asked me to consider these four monuments from the perspective of an African American mother or father trying to explain to their fifth-grade daughter who Robert E. Lee is and why he stands atop of our beautiful city. Can you do it? Can you look into

Lee 26

that young girl's eyes and convince her that Robert E. Lee is there to encourage her? Do you think she will feel inspired and hopeful by that story? Do these monuments help her see a future with limitless potential? Have you ever thought that if her potential is limited, yours and mine are too? We all know the answer to these very simple questions. When you look into this child's eyes is the moment when the searing truth comes into focus for us. This is the moment when we know what is right and what we must do. We can't walk away from this truth. We must always remember our history and learn from it. But that doesn't mean we must valorize the ugliest chapters, as we do when we put the Confederacy on a pedestal—literally—in our most prominent public places" (Landrieu).

9 If the aesthetic aspect is touched on at all, it tends to be in an aside in which the aesthetic value (or lack thereof) of a work is merely asserted, rather than discussed in any extended fashion. Such is the case, for example, with the offhand reference in an *Economist* column concerning a statue of Cecil Rhodes outside of Oxford University's Oriel College, in which the columnist asserts the statue to be "ugly" (Bagehot).

10 The original plan was not, however, to locate the memorial on the steps of the museum; it was rather to include it adjacent to the museum, as part of a promenade through Central Park that would have linked the American Museum of Natural History with the

Metropolitan Museum of Art (Reynolds).

11 Marber is one other scholar who has expressed a view on the aesthetics of the issue: "Additionally, it is undeniable that the Equestrian Statue has inherent artistic and art-historical merit" (95).

12 It is striking that Gabriel Koren, one of the very few sculptors to have made statues of prominent African Americans a specialty (her statue of Frederick Douglass stands in New York's Central Park), has experienced considerable financial difficulty; in 2015 she was forced out of her Brooklyn studio, no longer able to afford the rent (Swarns).

Lee 28

Works Cited

each entry begins at left margin; subsequent lines are indented

MLA recommends truncating excessively long URLs after host location

works cited are listed alphabetically by author

Ainsworth, Fred C., and Joseph W. Kirkley, eds. *The War of the Rebellion: A Compilation of the Official Records of the Union and Confederate Armies.* Series 4, vol. 1, Government Printing Office, 1900, www.books.google.ca/books. Accessed 14 July 2021.

American Museum of Natural History. "Addressing the Statue." Statement. *American Museum of Natural History*, June 2020, www.amnh.org/exhibitions/addressing-the-theodore-roosevelt-statue#statement. Accessed 19 May 2021.

——. "Perspectives on the Statue." *American Museum of Natural History*, www.amnh.org/exhibitions/addressing-the-theodore-roosevelt-statue/perspectives-today. Accessed 18 July 2021.

——. "What Did the Artists and Planners Intend?" *American Museum of Natural History*, www.amnh.org/exhibitions/addressing-the-theodore-roosevelt-statue/making-the-statue. Accessed 18 July 2021.

Bagehot [Adrian Woolridge]. "Britain's Academic Split: Problem-solving v Problem-wallowing." *The Economist,* 19 June 2021, www.economist.com/britain/2021/06/19/britains-academic-split-problem-solving-v-problem-wallowing.

Beazley, Doug. "Decolonizing the Indian Act." *National Magazine*, Canadian Bar Association, 18 Dec. 2017, www.nationalmagazine

Lee 29

.ca/en-ca/articles/law/in-depth/2017/decolonizing-the-indian-act. Accessed 13 July 2021.

Bromwich, Jonah Engel. "What Does It Take to Tear Down a Statue?" Interview with Erin L. Thompson, *New York Times*, 11 June 2020, www.nytimes.com/2020/06/11/style/confederate-statue-columbus-analysis.html.

Byrne, Patrick. "Americans Channel Ancient Rome in Condemning Confederate Statues." *The Hill*, 23 Aug. 2017, www.thehill.com/blogs/pundits-blog/state-local-politics/347562-americans-channel-ancient-rome-in-erecting-statues. Accessed 10 March 2021.

Canadian Press. "Vancouver Artist of Removed Macdonald Statue Says It Was Never Intended as a Monument." 15 Aug. 2018, www.lethbridgenewsnow.com/2018/08/15/artist-behind-macdonald-statue-says-it-was-never-intended-as-a-monument/. Accessed 13 July 2021.

Caplan, Talia. "Huckabee: Erasing American History Is 'Dangerous,' Can Lead to a Lost Civilization." *Fox News*, 23 June 2021, www.foxnews.com/media/huckabee-erasing-history-dangerous-can-lead-lost-civilization. Accessed 14 July 2021.

Carrington, Nathan T., and Logan Strother. "Legally, Confederate Statues in Public Spaces Aren't a Form of Free Speech." *Newsday*, 20 June 2020, www.newsday.com/opinion/commentary/confederate-statues-free-speech-black-lives-matter-protests

double spacing used throughout

italics used for titles of books, journals, magazines, etc.

Lee 30

-racism-1.45750735. Accessed 10 July 2021.

Constantine, Tim. "Ignoring American History Is Dangerous." *Washington Times*, 12 June 2021, www.washingtontimes.com/news/2020/jun/12/ignoring-american-history-is-dangerous/. Accessed 12 July 2021.

Cox, Karen L. *No Common Ground: Confederate Monuments and the Ongoing Fight for Racial Justice.* U of North Carolina P, 2021.

Fraser, James Earle. *Equestrian Statue of Theodore Roosevelt* (front view detail). 1939, New York City. Photograph by Roberto Machado Noa, 2020, www.medium.com/the-polis/statues-arent-about-preserving-history.

—. *Equestrian Statue of Theodore Roosevelt* (side view detail). 1939, New York City. Photograph by LunchboxLarry, 2013, www.commons.wikimedia.org/wiki/File:Equestrian_statue_of_Theodore_Roosevelt.jpg.

Fraser, Laura Gardin. *Stonewall Jackson and Robert E. Lee Monument.* 1948, Baltimore. Photograph by Jerry Jackson, *Baltimore Sun*, 2015, www.baltimoresun.com/opinion/op-ed/bs-ed-confederate-lessons-20151027-story.html.

—. *Stonewall Jackson and Robert E. Lee Monument* (close up detail of Jackson), 1948, Baltimore. Photograph by C. Ryan Patterson, in *Special Commission to Review Baltimore's Public Confederate Monuments*, 2016, www.baltimoreplanning.wixsite.com/

Lee 31

monumentcommission/.

——. *Stonewall Jackson and Robert E. Lee Monument* (close up detail of Lee), 1948, Baltimore. Photograph by C. Ryan Patterson, in *Special Commission to Review Baltimore's Public Confederate Monuments*, 2016, www.baltimoreplanning.wixsite.com/monumentcommission/.

Freundlich, A.L. *The Sculpture of James Earle Fraser.* Universal Publishers, 2001.

Grandmaison, Sonia de. *John A. Macdonald Memorial.* 1967, Regina, Saskatchewan. Photograph by Scotwood 72, Wikimedia Commons, 2006, www.commons.wikimedia.org/wiki/File:Macdonaldstat.jpg.

Landrieu, Mitch. "Speech on the Removal of Confederate Monuments in New Orleans." Transcript. *New York Times*, 23 May 2017, www.nytimes.com/2017/05/23/opinion/mitch-landrieus-speech-transcript.html.

"Laura Gardin Fraser in Her Studio at Work on Model for 'Lee-Jackson Monument.'" c. 1947, www.nationalcowboymuseum.org/explore/art-sculpture/.

"Lee Jackson Monument, 1948." *Special Commission to Review Baltimore's Public Confederate Monuments*. www.baltimoreplanning.wixsite.com/monumentcommission/leeandjacksonmonument. Accessed 18 July 2021.

Lee 32

Limbaugh, Rush. "Limbaugh to Activists Targeting Historical Monuments." *Washington Times*, 15 Aug. 2017, www.washingtontimes.com/news/2017/aug/15/rush-limbaugh-to-activists-targeting-historical-mo/.

Llana, Sara Miller. "Canada's Founder Oppressed Indigenous Peoples. Should His Statues Stand?" *Christian Science Monitor*, 19 Oct. 2020, www.csmonitor.com/World/Americas/2020/1019/.

Macaya, Melissa, et al. "Trump Holds Rally in Tulsa, Oklahoma." *CNN*, 21 June 2020, www.cnn.com/politics/live-news/trump-rally-tulsa-oklahoma/. Accessed 20 May 2021.

Machava, Benedito. "The Fate of Africa's Colonial Statues." *YouTube*, n.d., https://www.youtube.com/watch?v=GO6qduD3hd4. Accessed 14 July 2021.

MacLeod, Nicola. "Residential School Survivor Says P.E.I. John A. Macdonald Statue Should Be Removed." *CBC News*, 11 Sept. 2020, www.cbc.ca/news/canada/prince-edward-island/pei-marie-knockwood-john-a-macdonald-statue-1.5719669. Accessed 30 June 2021. Video.

Marber, Sinclaire Devereux. "Bloody Foundation? Ethical and Legal Foundations of (Not) Removing the Equestrian Statue of Theodore Roosevelt at the American Museum of Natural History." *Columbia Journal of Law and the Arts*, vol. 43, no. 1, Dec. 2019, www.journals.library.columbia.edu/index.php/lawandarts/article/view/4126.

Lee 33

Martin, Ashley. "Regina's John A. Macdonald Statue: Looking Back, Looking Forward." *Regina Leader Post*, 18 Sept. 2020, www.leaderpost.com/news/local-news/reginas-john-a-macdonald-statue-looking-back-looking-forward. Accessed 15 July 2021.

Mieder, Wolfgang. "'The Only Good Indian Is a Dead Indian': History and Meaning of a Proverbial Stereotype." *The Journal of American Folklore*, vol. 106, no. 419, winter 1993, pp. 38–60. *JSTOR*, www.jstor.org/stable/541345?read-now=1&seq=4#page_scan_tab_contents.

"Objectionable to Kentucky Confederate Daughters." *Kentucky Messenger-Inquirer*, 15 Nov. 1912, www.newspapers.com/image/375908902/.

O'Neal, Lonnae. "New Orleans, Robert E. Lee, and the South's Treasonous History of Alternative Facts." *The Undefeated*, 22 May 2017, www.theundefeated.com/features/new-orleans-robert-e-lee-highway/. Accessed 18 June 2021.

Reynolds, Donald Martin. "The Original Plan for the Theodore Roosevelt Monument." *Sculpture Review*, 8 Oct. 2020, https://doi.org/10.1177/0747528420967271.

Sanghera, Sathnam. *Empireland: How Imperialism Has Shaped Modern Britain.* Viking, 2021.

Shehan, Rebecca, and Jennifer Speights-Binet. "Negotiating Strategies in New Orleans's Memory-work: White Fragility in the Politics

Lee 34

of Removing Four Confederate-inspired Monuments." *Journal of Cultural Geography*, vol. 36, no. 3, 2019, pp. 346–67. https://doi:10.1080/08873631.2019.1641996.

Swarns, Rachel L."Priced Out of Brooklyn, a Sculptor Seeks a New Studio to Rent." *New York Times*, 16 Aug. 2015, www.nytimes.com/2015/08/17/nyregion/priced-out-of-brooklyn-a-sculptor-seeks-a-new-studio-to-rent.html.

Valentine, Edward Virginius. *Jefferson Davis Monument*. 1911, New Orleans. Photograph by Ashley Merlin for the New Orleans Monumental Task Committee, 2015.

Wilson, John A. *Silent Sam*. 1913, Chapel Hill, North Carolina. Photograph, 2012, www.commons.wikimedia.org/wiki/File:SilentSambyJohnAWilson.tif.

Snopek 1

name and page number in top right corner

Helena Snopek

Professor T. Chinara

English 232

18 April 2021

Motherhood, Wicked Witches, and Obsession:
Uncovering Feminist Meaning in the Rapunzel Narrative

Canonical fairy tales such as those of the Grimm Brothers are generally told in the voice of an omniscient narrator who recalls the story's plot without giving interpretive attention to characters or their actions. Frequently, this lack of complexity stems from a reliance on character archetypes, especially archetypes emerging from gendered, patriarchal traditions of the societies from which the stories arise. The wicked stepmother, the passively beautiful daughter, and the heroic prince who rescues the latter from the former are some of these archetypes. All are certainly present in the Grimms' "Rapunzel"; however, this story seems to be more conducive than many to feminist reinterpretations because of its complex themes of longing, isolation, possessiveness, and the nature of motherhood. Donna Jo Napoli uncovers these themes from the traditional tale and forefronts them in her novelization, *Zel*, by offering multiple character perspectives that

first line of all paragraphs indented

first paragraph ends with a statement of the essay's thesis

Snopek 2

dispute omniscient narratives and reject simplistic value judgements on those characters, whether villainous or heroic.

2 Napoli reinterprets "Rapunzel" not by drastically altering its characters or plot, but by delving into the psychological motivations that may lie behind, but are not revealed by, the model tale. Her novel tells the story of a mother and daughter living on an isolated farm, apparently self-sufficient and happy together until the child's thirteenth birthday. Upon that occasion, motivated by her daughter's encounter with a strange noble named Konrad, the mother proceeds to confine her in a tower as a safeguard against such perceived external threats. In most of its narrative plot points, the novel differs little from its source material, yet it functions as a postmodern reading because of the depth of personality its main characters are allowed. The most significant reinterpretation Napoli demonstrates is her use of multiple narrative perspectives: a third of the novel each is allowed for the daughter Rapunzel, or Zel; her love Konrad; and the Mother figure, and these are routinely switched throughout the novel.

text left-justified and ragged right

3 Mother, significantly, is the only character given the privilege of a first-person perspective. Such an emphasis gives her an increased sense of agency and considerably changes the reader's relationship to a character traditionally conceived of as a villain. The fairy tale is therefore transformed from a straightforward narrative interpreted and reported through the voice of an omniscient narrator to a vehicle for discussion

Snopek 3

between characters and their readers, where the thoughts of both the character and the reader come together to create meaning.

According to Hilary S. Crew, in Napoli's tale, in "contradistinction to the Brothers Grimms' different versions of the tale, readers are potentially positioned to, at least, understand the motives of a woman who makes a bargain with devils to procure the daughter she so needed" (82). The emphasis, then, is not to transform any of the story's traditional characters, but to allow them a voice and therefore agency. Christy Williams describes this as the creation of "a tension between the prescribed roles of popularized, conventional fairy-tale characters like the wicked stepmother and a postmodern rescripting of those roles" (257). Such a narrative technique "shifts the focalization and the motivations for these actions . . . to allow for meaning that is not possible" (Williams 258). It is therefore not the alteration of the tale but of its telling that, for Napoli, creates and uncovers new meanings.

4 — parenthetical references at end of quotations are followed by punctuation — when author's name is included in parenthetical reference, the page number follows the name

One of these meanings stems from an examination of what motherhood and childhood mean both to individuals and to the society of which those individuals are part. Our first glimpse inside Mother's story occurs in town with Zel; Mother's first words to the reader tell of her "enjoying the unity of Mother and Daughter, weaving through the crowds like a single strand of yarn" (Napoli 13). This surprisingly mystical image instantly reveals Mother's intense,

5 — sentence structured so that it flows grammatically into quotation

Snopek 4

almost unnatural attachment to her daughter, which becomes both the instigator of the novel's conflict and its thematic centre. The novel's willingness to portray genuine—if still ultimately destructive—affection between the archetypally wicked stepmother and her supposedly victimized stepdaughter itself runs counter to the tendency of fairy tales to, in Kendra Reynolds' words, "[instigate] and [maintain] generational tensions between young and old women as an attempt to eradicate the possibility of intergenerational cooperation" (179).

6 Linnea Hendrickson, in her exploration of Paul Zelinsky's version of the tale, asserts that "Rapunzel" tells the story of "the successive roles of virgin, mother, and crone" (220). Napoli's reimagining retains this theme as these roles intertwine in its characters: Zel moves from virginity to motherhood, while Mother embraces all three roles at different points from her desperate, childless past to her abasement and death at the end of the novel. We can additionally note that not only do individual characters move through these linear roles, but that the relationship between characters in these roles changes through the story as well. The roles must be separated from one another. Namely, the virgin must be allowed to separate from the mother in order to mature. For Allan G. Hunter, the "theme [of 'Rapunzel'] seems to be that of longing" (60). I would add to this that, in *Zel,* mere longing is, in the case of motherly love, pushed to the boundaries of obsession, blocking such maturation from taking place.

Snopek 5

This obsession is prompted, however, by the characters' societal context: in a culture where women are defined by their capacity to bear children, Mother clings desperately to the object who allows her to fill that role. Sylvia López comments on the role of motherhood in societies such as that of the Grimms, where the archetypal version of "Rapunzel" originated, stating that "women, according to bourgeois, patriarchal ideology of the nineteenth century, existed to be mothers. Until they married and had a child they were made to feel invisible" (785). Understanding this conflict makes it easier to understand and sympathize with the desperation childlessness would inspire in a woman such as Mother, if not necessarily to support the actions undertaken to remedy that childlessness. 7

The subsequent part of Mother's narrative is told in a flashback, relatively late in the novel, where she temporarily becomes a third-person narrator of her own life. Having been abandoned by her husband for her inability to conceive, the desperate woman is approached by a devil who offers her an avenue to motherhood in exchange for her services. Discovering within herself a lack of emotion and of faith, she decides to make the choice "on the basis of a personal judgement: How much was a daughter worth? . . . 'Anything and everything.' The answer was absolute" (125–30). The story that follows this crisis of faith is familiar; the woman, now with powers of witchcraft, tempts her pregnant neighbour to steal from her rapunzel plant and, as retali- 8 ation, demands possession of the baby girl when she is born. Throughout this segment of the narrative Mother differentiates between the two women by simply calling herself the "barren woman" and the other the "pregnant woman," respectively (134). These depersonalizing terms exemplify the way women are, in such a culture, defined by their potential for motherhood.

9 By telling this particular part of the story, Mother lets the reader know not only how she came to obtain her prized daughter, but also how she became infamous as the fairy tale witch. Are we, by the information given here, meant to judge Mother for these actions, or to forgive her completely? It seems neither is possible. Certainly, her actions are not laudable, as the reader can easily discover when comparing her section of the narrative to the sections of Zel and Konrad. When Mother's unity with Zel is threatened by the affection of a young nobleman, prompting her realization of Zel's impending sexual maturity, Mother imprisons the girl in the story's famed tower (64–70). Until this imprisonment, the girl's attitude towards her mother has ostensibly been one of genuine affection, but after this climactic event Zel becomes less trusting and increasingly bitter towards her. She lives in squalor—as exemplified by the frank description of the "bucket of feces and urine against the [tower's] rounded wall" (Napoli 150)—and only bothers to dress herself when Mother comes to see her: "Zel keeps her dress clean for Mother's sake. . . .

She is dressed, clean, and well behaved for Mother. . . . Mother has never guessed that Zel goes naked. Mother doesn't know what Mother doesn't want to know" (151).

That haunting last thought points to a newly obvious divide 10
between the mother and daughter that has been aggravated, ironically, by Mother's very insistence on protecting their intimate relationship. This situation contrasts strongly with that earlier image of two women "weaving through the crowds like a single strand of yarn" (Napoli 13). In that part of the story Mother had felt a "sharp loss" as she'd left Zel to run an errand, as though she were "sacrificing [their] wholeness. . . . The only consolation is that the separation is temporary." It becomes evident, however, that even this initial sense of wholeness was only illusory; in fact, when we speak of parent–child relationships, it is wholeness that is temporary, not separation.

This is true because peoples' personalities themselves, especially 11
those of children, are infinitely susceptible to change. The theme of sexual maturation is thus extremely important to *Zel.* Allan G. Hunter's book *Princes, Frogs and Ugly Sisters* has a chapter on the Grimms' "Rapunzel" in which he addresses this theme and thereby casts light on the way this theme is played up by Napoli. Hunter compares Rapunzel's imprisonment and subsequent liaison with the prince to the way "the convent-reared child is likely to be very easily led astray by others who are more sexually adventurous" (61). "The king's son,"

italics used for titles of books, journals, etc.

he argues, "is certainly sexually adventurous." This remains true in *Zel*, where Count Konrad searches obsessively for the young girl he met in town, apparently willing to risk his family's political future dependant on an arranged marriage and wed this peasant stranger. This is not only a love story but a coming-of-age story where it is natural for the girl to want to separate from her mother, and therefore unnatural for the mother to want to prevent this occurrence. When faced with the thought of this separation, Mother "blanch[es]. Zel will not be wed within the year. No. She must not leave me" (Napoli 18). This becomes an important facet of the theme of longing, when not only does a mother long for a child but a boy longs for a girl. Ultimately, in *Zel*, the daughter becomes a victim of both of these desires; even her name, taken from the plant which sealed her fate, cements her position as an object of longing: "Everyone wants to possess Rapunzel, a passive flower and a caged bird that longs to be free" (Hendrickson 215).

12 To Hunter, "Rapunzel" is partly about "the way parents and parentlike figures can change when they're worried about their daughters' chastity" (60). Thus, one could argue that Mother herself undergoes an important character journey in *Zel*, though we might be hard-pressed to call it maturation. While Hunter considers the witch of the Grimms' tale to represent "the spirit of self-love that the young couple find themselves rebelling against" (62), this is not the case in *Zel*; Mother's love for Zel is perhaps irresponsible, but not selfish or

narcissistic. The roots of her overprotectiveness of Zel and her disdain for Konrad more likely lie in a profound misunderstanding, possibly a willed ignorance, of the personalities and desires of both those youths. Disturbingly, the years in which Zel had been happiest become the years that Mother most regrets: "Oh, what a terrible twist. I had raised a child in the best way I knew how, and it was that mistake that kept her from me now" (142). Mother regrets raising her child in a way that allowed the child to develop her own natural desires, as though this were an occurrence over which she'd ever had control.

This is why perspective plays such a significant role in Napoli's 13
tale. On the one hand, reserving one third of the narrative for each character's separate voice and thoughts allows the reader more understanding of their complexity and, in Mother's case, allows for "identification with a traditional villain through shifting focalization" (Williams 257). In Crew's words, "[r]eaders are invited to empathize with the apparently unmediated subjectivity of a character who has not only been objectified and vilified in the traditional tales but whose representation has, more generally, been symbolic of misogynist attitudes toward women" (79). The narrative strategy of having multiple perspectives is democratic in that it allows for equal representation among characters, both heroes and villains, and abandons the connotation that the voice of any one character could be more or less valid than others. On the other hand, while first-person perspective

Snopek 10

liberates the character in question, it also restricts the overarching narrative. Crew, for instance, has argued that Napoli "foregrounds the limitations of the first-person narrative by drawing attention to her protagonist's restricted point of view and the limitations of her knowledge" (80).

14 Multiple perspectives as presented in *Zel* therefore urge inquiry into the role of villains in fairy tales. In canonical tales, "the witch metaphor is effective, since, from a man's point of view, 'liberated' women are a danger to society" (Donlan 609). To an extent, Mother represents such a liberated woman in that she takes the agency to rebel against her religion, to obtain a daughter against all natural laws, and to keep herself and that daughter isolated against a society that would anticipate their separation: "'I fear no forces of the Lord,'" Mother says of herself, "'I take no part in the petty struggles of society'" (Napoli 101). While Mother's ultimate actions are certainly not laudable, it can easily be seen how they become fodder for destructive myths about wicked women in fairy tales. According to Hunter, "[the witch's] major role in this tale is to stop people getting what they desire strongly . . . *and she does this for no understandable reason*" (62, emphasis mine). When her reason is made understandable, the status of the villain becomes less definite.

15 Donlan argues that in "Rapunzel," both the witch's theft of the baby girl and her later imprisonment of her are acts of mere sad-

Snopek 11

ism (608–09). While the extent to which we are able to sympathize with Mother in Napoli's version is arguable, it is surely impossible to understand any of her actions as stemming from mere sadism. She experiences no joy in the unhappiness of those around her; her acts are acts of desperation, not of cruelty. Donlan feels that witch characters "seem determined to destroy innocence and beauty" (609), and while this may apply to some other of the tales his article discusses, it does not necessarily apply to the Rapunzel narrative, neither in the Grimms' interpretation nor in Napoli's. Crew notes how this shift is foregrounded in *Zel* where, "[i]n contradistinction to the Brothers Grimms' versions . . . in which the love and relationship between mothers and daughters are absented and devalued, the relationship between mothers and daughters is made central to Napoli's stories" (90). Both Mother in Napoli's novel and perhaps even the Enchantress from the Grimms are more like guardians of innocence and beauty who have taken this guardianship too far: near the beginning of *Zel*, Mother says, "I am filled with elation at the thought of Zel's beauty in this dress and dread at the thought that anyone other than me should appreciate that beauty" (18).

The extent to which we forgive Mother may lie in the extent to 16
which we understand Zel's feelings about her. Donlan has accused the Grimms' Rapunzel of being a passive character, "[submitting] to being Mother Gothel's tower prisoner, obediently lowering her

braids on command" (607), but, while these factual events remain the same in *Zel*, the use of perspective once again makes readers forgive a character for the actions that may originally have placed her, superficially, within the limits of a fairy tale trope. Zel is, at least at the beginning, destructively obedient to Mother, but she is also a thirteen-year-old girl who knows next to nothing of the world outside her relationship to that woman; she cannot be expected to abandon that relationship easily. Napoli illustrates the couple's relationship not as an impersonal relationship between a captor and a prisoner, but as a close union between a girl and the woman who has for years acted as her loving parent. Even this emphasis is not really a grand step away from the Grimms' narrative, for, though its readers are not given insight into the nature of their affection for one another, one could hypothetically imagine that a relationship wherein the witch regularly climbs the tower to groom her captive is not necessarily an antagonistic relationship.

17 López remarks that "in many fairy tales, the death of the wicked witch restore[s] the normal order" (788). To some extent, this remains true both in "Rapunzel" and *Zel*. When Zel is finally able to separate from Mother and move to a new town to raise her children, Mother dies and becomes part of the landscape, "watch[ing] the world" (Napoli 220); this seems like a completion of the cycle of virgin, mother, and crone. Zel, now matured and initiated into parenthood

Snopek 13

herself, is able to reflect on the impressions Mother left on her life:

> She looks into these faces and she believes there isn't a one of them who wouldn't sell his soul for the right price. She has to believe this. She loved Mother. When she murmurs tender words in her daughters' ears, when she caresses them and combs their hair . . . Her heart opens. Even to the woman who traded away her child, the unknown woman . . . [Zel] owes her life to the unknown woman. She owes her soul to the witch woman. (219–20)

long quotations indented—no quotation marks used except for quotations within a quotation

She simultaneously acknowledges Mother's role in her suffering and understands why that suffering had to happen.

18

Though criticisms such as Donlan's highlight many of the flaws in these patriarchal narratives, they fail to acknowledge that narrative techniques can be at least as much to blame as the characters themselves. Napoli sees "Rapunzel" as a story rooted in a truth that has been violently misrepresented by popular narratives. Hendrickson calls "Rapunzel" "a story about family, motherhood, love, longing, about holding on and letting go" (212), and these terms can evidently be applied both to the canonical tale and the present rewrite of it. It is a story both of the way longing can itself be destructive, but also of how a relationship can be destroyed by attempts to restrict longing, as in the longing of the two young lovers. Moreover, *Zel* turns "Rapunzel" into a story about the understanding and empathy essential to

final paragraph restates and broadens the essay's main argument

Snopek 14

these relationships; when Zel is asked by her mother what kind of magical powers she would like to possess, the girl replies, "The gift of understanding and being understood, now that would be a real gift" (Napoli 141). That simple line well summarizes the primary theme of Napoli's revision. It seeks not to change traditional fairy tale characters and exert control over them, but to understand and respect the actions they originally performed.

Snopek 15

Works Cited

Crew, Hilary S. "Spinning New Tales from Traditional Texts: Donna Jo Napoli and the Rewriting of Fairy Tale." *Children's Literature in Education,* vol. 33, no. 2, 2002, pp. 77–95. *Springer*, https://doi.10.1023/A:1015292532368.

Donlan, Dan. "The Negative Image of Women in Children's Literature." *Elementary English,* vol. 49, no. 4, 1972, pp. 604–11. *JSTOR*, www.jstor.org/stable/41387825.

Grimm, Jacob, and Wilhelm Grimm. "Rapunzel." *Folk and Fairy Tales: Concise Edition*, edited by Martin Hallett and Barbara Karasek, Broadview Press, 2011, pp. 123–25.

Hendrickson, Linnea. "The View from Rapunzel's Tower." *Children's Literature in Education,* vol. 31, no. 4, 2002, pp. 209–23. *Springer,* https://doi.10.1023/A:1026458318053.

Hunter, Allan G. *Princes, Frogs, and Ugly Sisters: The Healing Power of the Grimm Brothers' Tales*. Ebook, Findhorn, 2010.

López, Sylvia. "From Monstrous to Mythical: The Mother Figure in Galdós's *Casandra* and *El caballero encantado*." *Hispania,* vol. 85, no. 4, 2002, pp. 784–94. *JSTOR*, https://doi.10.2307/4141217.

Napoli, Donna Jo. *Zel*. Puffin, 1996.

Reynolds, Kendra. *The Feminist Architecture of Postmodern Anti-Tales: Space, Time, and Bodies*. Ebook, Taylor & Francis, 2020.

double spacing used throughout

each entry begins at left margin; subsequent lines are indented

italics used for titles of books, journals, magazines, etc.

works cited are listed alphabetically by author

Snopek 16

MLA recommends truncating excessively long URLs after host location

Williams, Christy. "Who's Wicked Now? The Stepmother as Fairy-Tale Heroine." *Marvels & Tales,* vol. 24, no. 2, 2010, pp. 255–71. *JSTOR*, www.jstor.org/stable/41388955.

C3.2 APA STYLE

C3.2 APA Style

The American Psychological Association (APA) style is used in many scientific, health, behavioural science, and social science disciplines. APA style calls for parenthetical references in the body of a paper; the main components in these are author, date, and (possibly) page or paragraph number. APA also requires that full bibliographical information about the sources be provided in a list called "References" at the end of the essay.

This section outlines the key features of APA style and includes, at the end, a full sample essay using APA citation. Additional full sample essays in APA style are available on the Broadview website. Go to http://sites.broadviewpress.com/writingcdn. If you have more detailed questions, consult *The Publication Manual of the American Psychological Association* (7th edition, 2020). You may also find answers at www.apastyle.org.

C3.2.1 Incorporating Sources in APA Style

The following material should be read in conjunction with the introductory discussion of citation, documentation, and plagiarism (see sections M2.9 and P2.10).

There are three main ways of working source material into a paper: summaries, paraphrases, and direct quotations. In order to avoid plagiarism, care must be taken with all three kinds of borrowing, both in the way they are handled and in their referencing. In what follows, a passage from page 102 of a book by Terrence W. Deacon (*The Symbolic Species: The Co-Evolution of Language and the Brain*, published by Norton in 1997) serves as the source for a sample summary, paraphrase, and quotation. The examples feature the APA style of in-text parenthetical citations, but the requirements for presenting the source material are the same for all academic referencing systems.

original source

Over the last few decades language researchers seem to have reached a consensus that language is an innate ability, and that only a significant contribution from innate knowledge can explain our ability to learn such a complex communication system. Without question, children enter the world predisposed to learn human languages. All normal children, raised in normal social

> environments, inevitably learn their local language, whereas other species, even when raised and taught in this same environment, do not. This demonstrates that human brains come into the world specially equipped for this function.

Summarizing

An honest and competent summary, whether of a passage or an entire book, must not only represent the source accurately but also use original wording and include a citation. It is a common misconception that only quotations need to be acknowledged as borrowings in the body of an essay, but without a citation, even a fairly worded summary or paraphrase is an act of plagiarism. The first example below is faulty on two counts: it borrows wording (underlined) from the source, and it has no parenthetical reference.

needs checking Researchers agree that language learning is innate, and that only innate knowledge can explain how we are able to learn a system of communication that is so complex. Normal children raised in normal ways will always learn their local language, whereas other species do not, even when taught human language and exposed to the same environment.

The next example avoids the wording of the source passage, and a parenthetical citation notes the author and date. APA does not require that page or paragraph numbers be provided in summarized material, but you may wish to include them so that readers can more easily find the original passage.

revised There is now wide agreement among linguists that the ease with which human children acquire their native tongues, under the conditions of a normal childhood, demonstrates an inborn capacity for language that is not shared by any other animals, not even those who are reared in comparable ways and given human language training (Deacon, 1997).

Paraphrasing

Whereas a summary is a shorter version of its original, a paraphrase tends to be about the same length. However, paraphrases, like summaries, must reflect their sources accurately while using changed wording, and must include a citation. The original material's page number (or paragraph number for a nonpaginated online source) is not absolutely essential for a paraphrase, but APA suggests it be added as an aid to any reader who would like to refer to the original text. What follows is a paraphrase of the first sentence of the Deacon passage, which despite having a proper citation, falls short by being too close to the wording of the original (underlined).

needs checking Researchers in language have come to a consensus in the past few decades that the acquisition of language is innate; such contributions from knowledge contribute significantly to our ability to master such a complex system of communication (Deacon, 1997, p. 102).

Simply substituting synonyms for the words and phrases of the source, however, is not enough to avoid plagiarism. Even with its original wording, the next example also fails but for a very different reason: it follows the original's sentence structure, as illustrated in the interpolated copy below it.

needs checking Recently, linguists appear to have come to an agreement that speaking is an inborn skill, and that nothing but a substantial input from inborn cognition can account for the human capacity to acquire such a complicated means of expression (Deacon, 1997, p. 102).

Recently (*over the last few decades*), linguists (*language researchers*) appear to have come to an agreement (*seem to have reached a consensus*) that speaking is an inborn skill (*that language is an innate ability*), and that nothing but a substantial input (*and that only a significant contribution*) from inborn cognition (*from innate knowledge*) can account for the human capacity (*can explain our ability*) to acquire such a complicated means of expression (*to learn such a complex communication system*) (Deacon, 1997, p. 102).

What follows is a good paraphrase of the passage's opening sentence; this paraphrase captures the sense of the original without echoing the details and shape of its language.

revised Linguists now broadly agree that children are born with the ability to learn language; in fact, the human capacity to acquire such a difficult skill cannot easily be accounted for in any other way (Deacon, 1997, p. 102).

Quoting Directly

Unlike paraphrases and summaries, direct quotations must use the exact wording of the original. Because they involve importing outside words, quotations pose unique challenges. Quote too frequently, and you risk making your readers wonder why they are not reading your sources instead of your paper. Your essay should present something you want to say—informed and supported by properly documented sources, but forming a contribution that is yours alone. To that end, use secondary material to help you build a strong framework for your work, not to replace it. Quote sparingly, therefore; use your sources' exact wording only when it is important or particularly memorable.

To avoid misrepresenting your sources, be sure to quote accurately, and to avoid plagiarism, take care to indicate quotations as quotations, and cite them properly. If you use the author's name in a signal phrase, follow it with the date in parentheses, and be sure the verb of the phrase is in the past tense (*demonstrated*) or present perfect tense (*has demonstrated*). For all direct quotations, you must also include the page number (or paragraph number for a nonpaginated online source) of the original in your citation, as in the following examples.

Below are two problematic quotations. The first does not show which words come directly from the source.

needs checking Deacon (1997) maintained that children enter the world predisposed to learn human languages (p. 102).

The second quotation fails to identify the source at all.

needs checking Many linguists have argued that "children enter the world predisposed to learn human languages."

The next example corrects both problems by naming the source and indicating clearly which words come directly from it.

revised Deacon (1997) maintained that "children enter the world predisposed to learn human languages" (p. 102).

Formatting Quotations

There are two ways to signal an exact borrowing: by enclosing it in double quotation marks and by indenting it as a block of text. Which you should choose depends on the length and genre of the quotation and the style guide you are following.

SHORT QUOTATIONS

What counts as a short quotation differs among the various reference guides. In MLA style, "short" means up to four lines; in APA, up to forty words; and in Chicago Style, up to one hundred words. All the guides agree, however, that short quotations must be enclosed in double quotation marks, as in the examples below.

Short quotation, full sentence: According to Deacon (1997), linguists agree that a human child's capacity to acquire language is inborn: "Without question, children enter the world predisposed to learn human languages" (p. 102).

Short quotation, partial sentence: According to Deacon (1997), linguists agree that human "children enter the world predisposed to learn human languages" (p. 102).

LONG QUOTATIONS

In APA style, longer quotations of forty words or more should be double-spaced and indented, as a block, one-half inch from the left margin. Do not include quotation marks; the indentation indicates that the words come exactly from the source. Note that indented quotations are often introduced with a full sentence followed by a colon.

> Deacon (1997) maintained that human beings are born with a unique cognitive capacity:
>
> > Without question, children enter the world predisposed to learn human languages. All normal children, raised in normal social environments, inevitably learn their local language, whereas other species, even when raised and taught in this same environment, do not. This demonstrates that human brains come into the world specially equipped for this function. (p. 102)

QUOTATIONS WITHIN QUOTATIONS

You may sometimes find, within the original passage you wish to quote, words already enclosed in double quotation marks. If your quotation is short, enclose it all in double quotation marks, and use single quotation marks for the embedded quotation.

> Deacon (1997) was firm in maintaining that human language differs from other communication systems in kind rather than

> degree: "Of no other natural form of communication is it legitimate to say that 'language is a more complicated version of that'" (p. 44).

If your quotation is long, keep the double quotation marks of the original. Note as well that in the example below, the source's use of italics (*simple*) is also faithfully reproduced.

> Deacon (1997) was firm in maintaining that human language differs from other communication systems in kind rather than degree:
>
> > Of no other natural form of communication is it legitimate to say that "language is a more complicated version of that." It is just as misleading to call other species' communication systems *simple* languages as it is to call them languages. In addition to asserting that a Procrustean mapping of one to the other is possible, the analogy ignores the sophistication and power of animals' non-linguistic communication, whose capabilities may also be without language parallels. (p. 44)

Adding to or Deleting from a Quotation

While it is important to use the original's exact wording in a quotation, it is allowable to modify a quotation somewhat, as long as the changes are clearly indicated and do not distort the meaning of the original. You may want to add to a quotation in order to clarify what would otherwise be puzzling or ambiguous to someone who does not know its context; put whatever you add in square brackets.

USING SQUARE BRACKETS TO ADD TO A QUOTATION

> Deacon (1997) concluded that children are born "specially equipped for this [language] function" (p. 102).

If you would like to streamline a quotation by omitting anything unnecessary to your point, insert an ellipsis (three spaced dots) to show that you've left material out.

USING AN ELLIPSIS TO DELETE FROM A QUOTATION

When the quotation looks like a complete sentence but is actually part of a longer sentence, you should provide an ellipsis to show that there is more to the original than you are using.

> Deacon (1997) concluded that "... children enter the world predisposed to learn human languages" (p. 102).

Note the square brackets example above; if the quotation is clearly a partial sentence, ellipses aren't necessary.

When the omitted material runs over a sentence boundary or constitutes a whole sentence or more, insert a period plus an ellipsis.

> Deacon (1997) claimed that human children are born with a unique ability to acquire their native language: "Without question, children enter the world predisposed to learn human languages.... [H]uman brains come into the world specially equipped for this function" (p. 102).

Be sparing in modifying quotations; it is all right to have one or two altered quotations in a paper, but if you find yourself changing quotations often, or adding to and omitting from one quotation more than once, reconsider quoting at all. A paraphrase or summary is very often a more effective choice.

INTEGRATING QUOTATIONS

Quotations must be worked smoothly and grammatically into your sentences and paragraphs. Always, of course, mark quotations as such, but for the purpose of integrating them into your writing, treat them otherwise as if they were your own words. The boundary between what you say and what your source says should be grammatically seamless.

needs checking Deacon (1997) pointed out, "whereas other species, even when raised and taught in this same environment, do not" (p. 102).

revised According to Deacon (1997), while human children brought up under normal conditions acquire the language they are exposed to, "other species, even when raised and taught in this same environment, do not" (p. 102).

Avoiding "dumped" quotations

Integrating quotations well also means providing a context for them. Don't merely drop them into your paper or string them together like beads on a necklace; make sure to introduce them by noting where the material comes from and how it connects to whatever point you are making.

needs checking For many years, linguists have studied how human children acquire language. "Without question, children enter the world predisposed to learn human language" (Deacon, 1997, p. 102).

revised Most linguists studying how human children acquire language have come to share the conclusion articulated by Deacon (1997): "Without question, children enter the world predisposed to learn human language" (p. 102).

needs checking "Without question, children enter the world predisposed to learn human language" (Deacon, 1997, p. 102). "There is … something special about human brains that enables us to do with ease what no other species can do even minimally without intense effort and remarkably insightful training" (Deacon, 1997, p. 103).

revised Deacon (1997) based his claim that we "enter the world predisposed to learn human language" on the fact that very young humans can "do with ease what no other species can do even minimally without intense effort and remarkably insightful training" (pp. 102–103).

Signal Phrases

To leave no doubt in your readers' minds about which parts of your essay are yours and which come from elsewhere, identify the sources of your summaries, paraphrases, and quotations with signal phrases, as in the following examples.

- As Carter and Rosenthal (2011) demonstrated, …
- According to Ming et al. (2014), …
- In his latest article McGann (2015) advanced the view that …
- As Vieira (2020) observed, …
- Bonilla and Tillery (2020) have suggested that …
- Freschi (2004) was not alone in rejecting these claims, arguing that …
- Cabral et al. (2015) emphasized this point in their recent research: …
- Sayeed (2003) has maintained that …
- In a compelling article, Caxaj (2019) concluded that …
- In her later work, however, Hardy (2005) overturned previous results, suggesting that …

In order to help establish your paper's credibility, you may also find it useful at times to include in a signal phrase information that shows why readers should take the source seriously, as in the following example:

> In this lucid and groundbreaking work, psychologist and economist Daniel Kahneman (2011) described ...

Here, the signal phrase mentions the author's professional credentials; it also points out the importance of his book, which is appropriate to do in the case of a work as famous as Kahneman's *Thinking Fast and Slow*.

Below is a fuller list of words and expressions that may be useful in the crafting of signal phrases:

according to ________	endorsed
acknowledged	found
added	granted
admitted	illustrated
advanced	implied
agreed	in the view of ________,
allowed	in the words of ________,
argued	insisted
asserted	intimated
attested	noted
believed	observed
claimed	pointed out
commented	put it
compared	reasoned
concluded	refuted
confirmed	rejected
contended	reported
declared	responded
demonstrated	suggested
denied	thought
disputed	took issue with
emphasized	wrote

C3.2.2 About In-text Citations

• **in-text citation**: The APA system emphasizes the date of publication, which must appear within an in-text citation. Whenever a quotation is given, the page number, preceded by the abbreviation *p.*, must also be provided. Note that when two authors are mentioned in the body of the text, it is necessary to spell out the word "and":

- Rahman and Gilman (2020) argue that democratic participation needs to be "understood as a constant, sustained practice that outlives election cycles and stretches beyond voting or other formal, governmental channels for citizen imput" (p. 107).

It is common to mention in the body of your text the surnames of authors that you are citing, as is done in the example above. If author names are not mentioned in the body of the text, however, they must be provided within the in-text citation. In the example below, note the comma between the names and date of publication.

- One analysis of democratic participation (Rahman & Gilman, 2020) emphasizes that civic engagement needs to be an ongoing process that "stretches beyond voting or other formal, governmental channels for citizen input" (p. 107).

If the reference does not involve a quotation (as it commonly does not in social science papers), only the date need be given as an in-text citation, provided that the author's name appears in the signal phrase. For paraphrases, APA encourages, though does not require, a page number reference as well. The in-text citation in this case must immediately follow the author's name:

- Rahman and Gilman (2020) argue that true democratic participation needs to be an ongoing process that extends beyond the process of formal voting (p. 107).

A citation such as this connects to a list of references at the end of the paper. In this case the entry under "References" at the end of the paper would be as follows:

- Rahman, K. S., & Gilman, H. R. (2020). *Civic power: Rebuilding American democracy in an era of crisis.* Cambridge University Press.

Notice here that the date of publication is again foregrounded, appearing immediately after the authors' names. Notice that the formatting of titles must follow APA style; details follow below.

- **no signal phrase (or author not named in signal phrase)**: If the context does not make it clear who the author is, that information must be added to the in-text citation. Note that commas separate the author, the date, and the page number elements:

  - Some political scientists are urging that democratic participation needs to be seen as an ongoing process that "stretches beyond voting or other formal, governmental channels for citizen input" (Rahman & Gilman, 2020, p. 107).

• **titles of stand-alone works**: Stand-alone works are those that are published on their own rather than as part of another work. The titles of stand-alone works (e.g., journals, magazines, newspapers, books, and reports) should be in italics. Writers in the social and behavioural sciences do not normally put the titles of works in the bodies of their papers, but if you do include the title of a stand-alone work, all major words and all words of four letters or more should be capitalized. For book and report titles in the References list, however, capitalize only the first word of the title and subtitle (if any), plus any proper nouns. Journal, magazine, and newspaper titles in the list of References are exceptions; for these, capitalize all major words.

In-text: Such issues are treated at length in *Ethical and Legal Issues in Nursing* (DeMarco et al., 2019).

References list: DeMarco, J. P., Jones, G. E., & Daly, B. J. (2019). *Ethical and legal issues in nursing*. Broadview Press.

• **titles of articles and chapters of books**: The titles of these works, and anything else that is published as part of another work, are also not usually mentioned in the body of an essay, though if they are, they should be put in quotation marks, with all major words capitalized. In the References, however, titles of these works should *not* be put in quotation marks or italicized, and no words should be capitalized, with the exception of any proper nouns, and the first word in the title and the first in the subtitle, if any.

In-text: In "End of Life and the Refusal of Treatment," the role of nurses in end-of-life care is analyzed in depth (DeMarco et al., 2019, pp. 139–191).

References list: DeMarco, J. P., Jones, G. E., & Daly, B. J. (2019). End of life and the refusal of treatment. *Ethical and legal issues in nursing* (pp. 139–191). Broadview Press.

• **placing of in-text citations**: When the author's name appears in a signal phrase, the in-text citation comes directly after the name. Otherwise, the citation follows the paraphrased or quoted material. If a quotation ends with punctuation other than a period or comma, then this should precede the end of the quotation, and a period or comma should still follow the parenthetical reference, if this is grammatically appropriate.

- The claim has been convincingly refuted by Ricks (2010), but it nevertheless continues to be put forward (Dendel, 2013).
- One of Berra's favourite coaching tips was that "ninety per cent of the game is half mental" (Adelman, 2007, p. 98).
- Adelman (2007) notes that Berra at one point said to his players, "You can observe a lot by watching!" (p. 98).
- Vieira (2020) considers the legitimacy of politicians claiming to represent silent constituencies.

• **citations when text is in parentheses:** If a parenthetical reference occurs within text in parentheses, commas are used to set off elements of the reference.

- (See Figure 6.1 of Harrison, 2012, for data on transplant waiting lists.)

• **electronic source—page number unavailable:** If online material is in PDF format, the page numbers are stable and may be cited as one would the pages of a printed source. Most online sources, however, lack page numbers altogether. In such cases you should provide a section or paragraph number if a reference is needed. For paragraphs, use the abbreviation "para."

- In a recent web posting a leading theorist has clearly stated that he finds such an approach "thoroughly objectionable" (Bhabha, 2012, para. 7).
- Carter and Zhaba (2009) describe this approach as "more reliable than that adopted by Perkins" (Method section, para. 2).

For ebooks, do not include location numbers, but provide the chapter, section, and/or paragraph numbers instead. If you are citing longer texts from electronic versions, chapter references may be more appropriate. For example, if the online Gutenberg edition of Darwin's *On the Origin of Species* were being cited, the citation would be as follows:

- Darwin refers to the core of his theory as an "ineluctable principle" (1859, Chapter 26).

Notice that *chapter* is capitalized and not abbreviated.

Students should be cautioned that online editions of older or classic works are often unreliable; typically there are far more typos and other errors in such versions than there are in print versions. It is often possible to exercise judgement about such matters, however. If, for example, you are not required to base your essay on a particular edition of Darwin's *Origin of Species* but may find your own, you will be far better off using the text you will find on the reputable Project Gutenberg site than you will using a text you might find on a site such as "Manybooks.com."

• **audiovisual works:** Audio books, online lectures, YouTube videos, TV shows, or movies should include a time stamp marking the relevant quotation instead of a page number.

- Adichie believes that people can and should act to create deep cultural change: "Culture does not make people; people make culture" (2012, 27.06–27.09).

• **two or more dates for a work:** If you have consulted a re-issue of a work (whether in printed or electronic form), you should provide both the original date of publication and the date of the re-issue (the date of the version you are using).

- Emerson (1837/1909) asserted that America's "long apprenticeship to the learning of other lands" was "drawing to a close" (para. 1).

The relevant entry in the list of references would look like this:

- Emerson, R. W. (1909). *Essays and English traits*. P. F. Collier & Son. (Original work published 1837)

If you are citing work in a form that has been revised by the author, however, you should cite the date of the revised publication, not the original.

- In a preface to the latest edition of his classic work (2004), Watson discusses its genesis.

• **two authors:** If there are two authors, both should be named either in the signal phrase or in the in-text citation. Use *and* in the signal phrase but *&* in parentheses.

- Chambliss and Best (2010) have argued that the nature of this research is practical as well as theoretical.
- Two distinguished scholars have argued that the nature of this research is practical as well as theoretical (Chambliss & Best, 2010).

• **three or more authors:** In the body of the text and in the in-text citation, list the first author's name followed by "et al." (short for the Latin *et alia*: *and others*).

- Chambliss et al. (2011) have argued that the nature of this research is practical as well as theoretical.

- Four distinguished scholars have argued that the nature of this research is practical as well as theoretical (Chambliss et al., 2011).

If you are citing more than one work with similar groups of authors, you will need to write out more names to avoid confusion. If for example you are citing works with these two sets of authors:

> Haley, Caxaj, George, Hennebry (2020)
> Haley, Caxaj, Diaz, Cohen (2020)

You would cite them in-text as follows:

> (Haley, Caxaj, George, et al., 2020)
> (Haley, Caxaj, Diaz, et al., 2020)

• **organization as author:** As you would with an individual human author, provide the name of an organization either in the body of your text or in a parenthetical citation. Recommended practice is to provide the full name of an organization on the first occasion, followed by an abbreviation, and then to use the abbreviation for subsequent references:

- Blindness has decreased markedly but at an uneven pace since the late 1800s (National Institute for the Blind [NIB], 2002).

• **author not given:** If the author of the source is not given, it may be identified in the parenthetical reference by the title, which may be represented by a short form if the title is long.

- Confusion over voting reform is widespread ("Results of National Study," 2018).

• **date not given:** Some sources, particularly electronic ones, do not provide a date of publication. Where this is the case, use the abbreviation *n.d.* for *no date*.

- Some still claim that evidence of global climate change is difficult to come by (Sanders, n.d.; Zimmerman, 2018).
- Sanders (n.d.) and Zimmerman (2018) still claim that evidence of global climate change is difficult to come by.

• **two or more works in the same citation:** In this case, the works should appear in in-text citations in the same order they do in the list of references. If the works are by different authors, arrange the sources alphabetically by author's last name and separate the citations with a semicolon. If the works are by the same authors, arrange the sources by publication date. Add *a*, *b*, *c*, etc. after the year to distinguish works written by the same authors in the same year.

- Various studies have established a psychological link between fear and sexual arousal (Aikens et al., 1998; Looby & Cairns, 2008).
- Various studies appear to have established a psychological link between fear and sexual arousal (Looby & Cairns, 1999, 2002, 2005).
- Looby and Cairns (1999a, 1999b, 2002, 2005a, 2005b) have investigated extensively the link between fear and sexual arousal.

• **two or more authors with the same last name**: If the References list includes two or more authors with the same last name, the in-text citation should supply an initial:

- One of the leading economists of the time advocated wage and price controls (H. Johnston, 1977).

• **works in a collection of readings or anthology**: In the in-text citation for a work in an anthology or collection of readings, use the name of the author of the work, not that of the editor of the anthology. If the work was first published in the collection you have consulted, there is only the one date to cite. But if the work is reprinted in that collection after having first been published elsewhere, cite the date of the original publication and the date of the collection you have consulted, separating these dates with a slash. The following citation refers to an article by Ana S. Iltis that was reprinted in a collection of readings edited by Elisabeth Gedge and Wilfrid Waluchow.

- One of the essays in Gedge and Waluchow's collection argues that we should restrict, but not prohibit, placebo-controlled trials (Iltis, 2004/2012).

In your list of references, this work should be alphabetized under Iltis, the author of the piece you have consulted, not under Gedge.

The next example is a lecture by Georg Simmel first published in 1903, which a student consulted in an edited collection by Roberta Garner that was published in 2001.

- Simmel (1903/2001) argues that the "deepest problems of modern life derive from the claim of the individual to preserve the autonomy and individuality of his existence" (p. 141).

The reference list entry would look like this:

> Simmel, G. (2001). The metropolis and mental life. In R. Garner (Ed.), *Social theory–Continuity and confrontation: A reader* (pp. 141–153). Broadview Press. (Original work published in 1903)

As you can see, in your reference list these works are listed under the authors of the pieces (Iltis or Simmel), not under the compilers, editors, or translators of the collection (Gedge & Waluchow or Garner). If you cite another work by a different author from the same anthology or book of readings, that should appear as a separate entry in your list of references—again, alphabetized under the author's name.

• **indirect source:** If you are citing a source from a reference other than the source itself, you should use the phrase "as cited in" in your in-text citation.

- In de Beauvoir's famous phrase, "one is not born a woman, one becomes one" (as cited in Levey, 2001, para. 3).

In this case, the entry in your reference list would be for Levey, not de Beauvoir.

• **personal communications:** These are any communications that cannot be found by your reader, such as emails, classroom lectures, messages on online discussion groups, text messages, unrecorded speeches, personal interviews, and conversations (among others). This type of communication should not be added to your list of references but documented only as an in-text citation. Provide the initials and surname of the person you communicated with as well as the date of communication.

- K. Montegna (personal communication, January 21, 2019) has expressed scepticism over this method's usefulness.

• **Indigenous traditional knowledge and oral traditions:** APA guidelines suggest that before including Indigenous traditional knowledge in your paper, it should be confirmed to be both accurate and permitted—some Indigenous stories, for example, are to be told only at certain times and by certain people, and some are only to be told orally and are not meant to be printed. If the material you are citing can be found in a source discoverable by your readers, add it to your reference list following the formatting for the source type and cite in-text accordingly. If you spoke with an Indigenous person yourself or are citing materials that cannot be found by your readers, you can tailor the format for personal communications (see above) to create an in-text citation. In this case, give the person's full name and the Indigenous group to which they belong, as well as any other details that you think are important, followed by "personal communication" and the date or range of dates. It is also vital to communicate with the Indigenous person being cited, so they can confirm both that your citation is accurate and that they have agreed to be included in your work. Here is an example of how to format an in-text citation of a personal communication with an Indigenous writer:

- We spoke with Jeannette Armstrong (Sylix Nation, lives on the Penticton Indian Band Reserve, British Columbia, Canada, personal communication, June 1991) about her work as director of the En'owkin Centre …

C3.2.3 About References

The list of references in APA style is an alphabetized listing of sources that appears at the end of an essay, article, or book. This list, entitled *References*, includes all the information necessary to identify and retrieve each of the sources you have cited, and only the works you have cited. Lists that include all the sources you have consulted are called *Bibliographies*, but these are not required by APA. The list of references should include only sources that can be accessed by your readers, and so it should not include personal communication, such as private letters, memos, e-mail messages, and telephone or personal conversations. Those should be cited only in your text (see the section above).

Entries should be ordered alphabetically by author surname, or, if there is no known author, by title. The first line of each entry should be flush with the left-hand margin, with all subsequent lines indented about one half inch. Double-space throughout the list of references.

The basic format for all entries consists of four major elements, all of which are somewhat flexible and can be customized to suit your source. The four elements (in the order they appear in your reference entry) are author, date, title, and source. Remember that one function of the list of references is to provide the information your readers need if they wish to locate your sources for themselves; APA allows any "non-routine" information that could assist in identifying the sources to be added in square brackets to any entry (e.g., [Sunday business section], [Film], [Interview with O. Sacks]).

In the References examples that follow, information about entries for electronic sources has been presented in an integrated fashion alongside information about referencing sources in other media, such as print, audiovisual, and so on. Note that the DOI (Digital Object Identifier) or URL is the last element of your reference entry for digital sources, and a crucial one for readers when they want to use your reference to find the source. Include the DOI or URL as a hyperlink in your document, beginning "http://" or "https://". DOIs must be formatted "https://doi.org/xxxxx" (the "xxxxx" being the DOI number). Any articles with older DOI formatting should be reformatted to this new standard. This means that the label "DOI" is no longer needed before the link; it is also unnecessary to include the words "Accessed from" or "Retrieved from" before DOI and URL links. The only exception to this rule is if the material is unarchived and frequently updated—in this case you may want to add a retrieval date, as the content could differ if your reader seeks access at a later time. Copy and paste the DOI or URL directly into your References list; do not add line breaks, even if the hyperlink is moved onto its own line by your word-processing software. Do not add any other punctuation, including periods, as it may interfere with link functionality.

- **work with single author:** For a work with one author the entry should begin with the last name, followed by a comma, and then the author's initials as applicable, followed by the date of publication in parentheses. Note that initials are generally used rather than first names, even when authors are identified by first name in the work itself. After the title of the work, add the publisher's name, leaving out abbreviations such as *Inc.* and *Co.* (but keeping *Press* and *Books*). If a DOI is available, APA requires that it be included, whether you are using the print or digital version.

> Hueglin, T. O. (2021). *Federalism in Canada: Contested concepts and uneasy balances.* University of Toronto Press.

- **two authors:** List both authors by their last names and initials, separated by a comma and ampersand:

> Caxaj, S., & Diaz, L. (2018). Migrant workers' (non)belonging in rural British Columbia, Canada: Storied experiences of marginal living. *International Journal of Migration, Health and Social Care, 14*(2), 208–220. https://doi.org/10.1108/ijmhsc-05-2017-0018

- **three to twenty authors**: Last names should in all cases come first, followed by initials. Use commas to separate the authors' names, and use an ampersand rather than *and* before the last author. Note that the authors' names should appear in the order they are listed; sometimes this is not alphabetical.

  Warne, R. T., Astle, M. C., & Hill, J. C. (2018). What do undergraduates learn about human intelligence? An analysis of introductory psychology textbooks. *Archives of Scientific Psychology, 6*(1), 32–50. https://doi.org/10.1037/arc0000038

- **more than twenty authors**: List the names of the first nineteen authors, add an ellipsis, and then give the last author's name.

  Akerboom, J., Chen, T., Wardill, T. J., Tian, L., Marvin, J. S., Mutlu, S., Calderón, N. C., Esposti, F., Borghuls, B. G., Sun, X. R., Gordus, A., Orger, M. B., Portugues, R., Engert, F., Macklin, J. J., Filosa, A., Aggarwal, A., Kerr, R. A., Takagi, R., ... Looger, L. L. (2012). Optimization of a GCaMP calcium indicator for neural activity imaging. *Journal of Neuroscience, 32*(40), 13819–13840. https://doi.org/10.1523/JNEUROSCI.2601-12.2012

- **works with an organization as author**: If a work has been issued by a government body, a corporation, or some other organization and no author is identified, the entry should be listed by the name of the group. If this group is also the work's publisher, do not include the publisher in the source element of the citation.

  Broadview Press. (2019). *Annual report.* https://sec.report/Document/0001398344-19-016555/

  Environment and Climate Change Canada. (2016). *Pan-Canadian framework on clean growth and climate change: Canada's plan to address climate change and grow the economy.* http://publications.gc.ca/pub?id=9.828774&sl=0

  Canadian Nurses Association. (2017). *Code of ethics.* https://cna-aiic.ca/nursing-practice/nursing-ethics

- **works with unknown author**: When a work does not have an author, move the title to the author position in your citation. Only if the work is signed "Anonymous" do you begin the citation with "Anonymous" in the author position. Alphabetize the entry in your References list according to "Anonymous" (if applicable), or to the first important word in the title (ignoring articles such as "The," "A," and "An").

For in-text citations, once the title has been stated in full either in the narrative or in a parenthetical citation, you may from then on use an abbreviated version, italicized or in quotation marks, as appropriate. For example, the Oxford English Dictionary could be abbreviated as OED, and italicized in your in-text citation as (*OED*, 2019). The reference list entry would be as follows:

> *Oxford English Dictionary*. (2020). https://www.oed.com

- **two or more works by the same author:** The author's name should appear for all entries. Entries should be ordered by year of publication, beginning with the earliest.

> Mouffe, C. (2019). *For a left populism*. Verso.
> Mouffe, C. (2020). *The return of the political*. Verso.

- **two or more works by the same author in the same year:** If two or more cited works by the same author or group of authors have been published in the same year, see if they have more specific dates: if they do, list the works chronologically. If works are listed only by year, list them before the ones with a specific date. If two of the works have the same date, arrange these alphabetically according to the title and use letters to distinguish them: (2020a), (2020b), and so on.

> Employment and Social Development Canada. (2019a). *Temporary Foreign Worker Program 2012–2019*. https://open.canada.ca/data/en/dataset/76defa14-473e-41e2-abfa-60021c4d934b
> Employment and Social Development Canada. (2019b). *What we heard: Primary agriculture review*. https://www.canada.ca/en/employment-social-development/services/foreign-workers/reports/primary-agriculture.html

- **prefaces, introductions, forewords, afterwords:** Cite these sections of a work as you would a chapter title:

> DeMarco, J. P., Jones, G. E., & Daly, B. J. (2019). Introduction. *Ethical and legal issues in nursing*. Broadview Press.

- **edited works:** Entries for edited works include the abbreviation *Ed.* or *Eds.* The second example below is for a book with both an author and an editor; since the original work in this entry was published earlier than the present edition, that information is given in parentheses at the end.

> Armstrong, C. L., & Morrow, L. A. (Eds.). (2019). *Handbook of medical neuropsychology: Applications of cognitive neuroscience* (2nd ed.). Springer.

Sapir, E. (1981). *Selected writings in language, culture, and personality.* D. G. Mandelbaum (Ed.). University of California Press. (Original work published 1949)

• **works with an author and a translator:** The translator's name, along with the designation *Trans.*, is included in parentheses after the title; the original publication date is given in parentheses following the present edition's publication information.

Jung, C. G. (2006). *The undiscovered self* (R. F. C. Hull, Trans.). Signet. (Original work published 1959)

• **selections from edited books and collections of readings:** An article reprinted in an edited collection of readings should be listed as follows:

Holmes, S., & Buchbinder, L. (2020). In a defunded health system, doctors and nurses suffer near-impossible conditions. In M. C. Schwartz (Ed.), *The ethics of pandemics* (pp. 25–27). Broadview Press.

• **selections from multivolume works:**

Truth, S. (2008). Speech delivered at the Akron, Ohio convention on women's rights, 1851. In A. Bailey, S. Brennan, W. Kymlicka, J. T. Levy, A. Sager, & C. Wolf (Eds.), *The Broadview anthology of social and political thought: Vol. 1. From Plato to Nietzsche* (pp. 964–965). Broadview Press. (Original work published 1851)

• **ebooks and audiobooks:** If the ebook content is the same as an existing physical book, you do not need to specify which version you cited (APA style states that if a DOI is available, that information should be included whether you use the print or the electronic version). If the electronic version is different from the print, then you should specify that you are using the ebook version. Similarly, you do not need to state that you are using an audiobook version, unless it differs from the print version or you want to add narrator information.

Atkins, J. W. (2013). *Cicero on politics and the limits of reason: The* Republic *and* Laws. Cambridge University Press. https://doi.org/10.1017/CBO9781107338722

Herman, E. S., & Chomsky, N. (2017). *Manufacturing consent* (J. Pruden, Narr.) [Audiobook]. Random House. https://www.audible.ca/pd/Manufacturing-Consent-Audiobook/B072BSNQ9K (Original work published 1988)

- **periodical articles (with and without DOIs):** Articles from journals, magazines, online platforms, and newspapers follow the same pattern of citation. Notice that article titles are not enclosed in quotation marks, and that both the periodical title and the volume number (if applicable) are in italics. If all issues of a given volume of a periodical begin with page 1, include the issue number as well, directly after the volume number, in parentheses and not italicized. Page ranges for periodicals should follow after a comma, be separated by an en dash, and close with a period. If there are discontinuous page numbers (in a print newspaper, for example), separate the page numbers with commas (for example 25–34, 45). The citation should finish with a period, unless it ends with a DOI or URL, in which case no period should be added. Include the DOI or URL as a hyperlink, beginning "http://" or "https://". DOIs must be formatted "https://doi.org/xxxxx" (the "xxxxx" being the DOI number). Note that if a DOI is available, APA asks that you add it to the citation, even if you consulted the print version.

Li, J., Osher, D. E., Hansen, H. A., & Saygin, Z. M. (2020). Innate connectivity patterns drive the development of the visual word form area. *Scientific Reports, 10*, Article 18039. https://doi.org/10.1038/s41598-020-75015-7

Luque, J. S., & Castañeda, H. (2012). Delivery of mobile clinic services to migrant and seasonal farmworkers: A review of practice models for community-academic partnerships. *Journal of Community Health, 38*(2), 397–407. https://doi.org/10.1007/s10900-012-9622-4

Pinquart, M., & Kauser, R. (2018). Do the associations of parenting styles with behavior problems and academic achievement vary by culture? Results from a meta-analysis. *Cultural Diversity and Ethnic Minority Psychology, 24*(1), 75–100. https://doi.org/10.1037/cdp0000149

Example from a periodical only available in print form (no DOI or URL):

Bowlin, B. (2019). Still alive, mostly. *The Fiddlehead, 281*, 47–48.

- **abstract of a periodical article:** Cite as you would the journal article itself, adding *Abstract* in square brackets.

Yang, C., Sharkey, J. D., Reed, L. A., Chen, C., & Dowdy, E. (2018). Bullying victimization and student engagement in elementary, middle, and high schools: Moderating role of school climate [Abstract]. *School Psychology Quarterly, 33*(1), 54–64. https://doi.org/10.1037/spq0000250

• **magazine articles:** The basic principles are the same as for journal articles. Note that neither quotation marks nor italics are used for the titles of articles. If no author is identified, the title of the article should appear first. For monthly magazines, provide the month as well as the year; for magazines issued more frequently, give the day, month, and year.

Aziza, S. (2020, October 30). For Persian Gulf migrant workers, the pandemic has amplified systemic discrimination. *The Nation*. https://www.thenation.com/article/world/migrants-coronavirus-persian-gulf/

Dyer, A. (2012, November/December). The end of the world … again. *SkyNews, 18*(4), 38–39.

The rise of the yuan: Turning from green to red. (2012, October 20). *The Economist, 405*(42), 67–68.

• **newspaper articles:** The basic principles to follow with newspaper articles or editorials are the same as with magazine articles (see above). Notice that if there is no letter assigned to a newspaper section, you should give the section's title in square brackets.

Bennett, J. (2012, December 16). How to attack the gender pay gap? *The New York Times* [Sunday business section], 1, 6.

Waldbieser, J. (2020, November 3). Escape the boredom trap. *New York Times*. https://www.nytimes.com/2020/11/03/parenting/boredom-kids-pandemic.html?searchResultPosition=7

• **reviews:** Reviews of any type of media—books, TV shows, podcasts, films, albums—can be found in many different publications, including websites, newspapers, blogs, and magazines. Your reference should be formatted according to the citation format of the publication in which the review is found, with the name of the reviewer (if it has been provided) listed first, followed by the date and title of the review, and the information on the source itself, as follows:

Semuels, A. (2020, January 14). Soon a robot will be writing this headline [Review of the book *A world without work: Technology, automation, and how we should respond*, by D. Susskind]. *New York Times*. https://www.nytimes.com/2020/01/14/books/review/a-world-without-work-daniel-susskind.html

• **reference work entries with an individual author:** List by the author of the entry, if known; otherwise, list by the entry itself.

Toole, B. A. (2017). Byron, (Augusta) Ada King, countess of Lovelace (1815–1852). In D. Cannadine (Ed.), *Oxford dictionary of national biography* (September 1, 2017 ed.). Oxford University Press. https://doi.org.10.1093/ref:odnb/37253

• **reference work entries with an organization as author:** List the organization name in the author element of your citation. Note that if a reference work accessed online is continuously updated, you should use "n.d." as the publication year ("no date"). In this case, you should add a retrieval date in your citation.

American Psychological Association. (n.d.). Sample standard deviation. In *APA dictionary of psychology*. Retrieved November 12, 2020, from https://dictionary.apa.org/sample-standard-deviation

• **diagnostic manuals (*DSM* and *ICD*):** If the publisher and author are the same, you do not need to include the publisher in your reference list citation.

American Psychiatric Association. (2013). *Diagnostic and statistical manual of mental disorders* (5th ed.). https://doi-org.10.1176/appi.books.9780890425596

World Health Organization. (2019). *International statistical classification of diseases and related health problems* (11th ed.). https://icd.who.int/browse11/l-m/en

Note that when citing these manuals in your text, they may be abbreviated; it is also customary to create an in-text citation for a manual on the first mention of it:

- *Diagnostic and Statistical Manual of Mental Disorders* (5th ed.; DSM-5; American Psychiatric Association, 2013)

After this first instance, it is not necessary to repeat citations of these manuals in your paper (they can be referred to by their abbreviations), unless you are quoting or paraphrasing, in which case you should provide further in-text citations.

• **articles from databases:** Some databases—such as the Cochrane Database of Systematic Reviews and UpToDate—make their articles available only within the databases. Format these citations as you would an article from a periodical (see above).

Martin-McGill, K. J., Bresnahan, R., Levy, R. G., & Cooper, P. N. (2020). Ketogenic diets for drug-resistant epilepsy. *Cochrane Database of Systematic Reviews*. https://doi.org/10.1002/14651858.CD001903.pub5

For the UpToDate database, include a retrieval date, because these articles are continually edited, and the different versions are not archived:

Kim, Y., & Gandhi, R. T. (2020). Coronavirus disease 2019 (COVID-19): Management in hospitalized adults. *UpToDate*. Retrieved November 17, 2020, from https://www.uptodate.com/contents/coronavirus-disease-2019-covid-19-management-in-hospitalized-adults?search=covid%2019%20treatment&source=covid19_landing&graphicRef=128045#graphicRef128045

• **dissertations from a database, published and unpublished**: Published theses and dissertations can be found on databases such as ProQuest. For these references, the title of the thesis or dissertation should be followed by a description ("Doctoral dissertation" or "Master's thesis," for example) and name of the institution that granted the degree in square brackets.

Porteny, T. (2019). *Improving migrant health policies and programs: From the normative to the positive* [Doctoral dissertation, Harvard University]. DASH: Digital Access to Scholarship at Harvard. http://nrs.harvard.edu/urn-3:HUL.InstRepos:42029506

If you are citing an unpublished thesis or dissertation, the university granting the degree appears as the source element rather than in square brackets after the title:

Arthur, K. (2017). *We are having all kinds of fun: Fluidity in shoebox project* [Unpublished doctoral dissertation]. University of Waterloo.

• **data sets**: Entries for data sets in your references list should include the date of publication or of collection, as well as the version number. A retrieval date should only be included if the data is still being gathered. As with many of the APA bracketed descriptions, the one following the title is flexible, and you can use it to specify the kind of data you are citing (data set, code book, etc.).

Statistics Canada. (2019). *Life expectancy, at birth and at age 65, by sex, three-year average, Canada, provinces, territories, health regions and peer groups* (Table 13100389) [Dataset]. https://open.canada.ca/data/en/dataset/00c99f50-4f07-4e8c-b61d-9e188a51ed82

• **software and reference apps**: References to commonly used software and apps do not need to be cited in your paper unless you quote directly or paraphrase information from such a source. Below is an example of a reference list entry for information found on a reference app:

Unbound Medicine, Inc. (2020). Anemia, in *Nursing Central* (Version 1.44) [Mobile app]. Apple App Store, https://apps.apple.com/ca/app/nursing-central/id300420397

• **films and video recordings:** Begin entries for motion pictures with the name of the director, followed by the date of release, the film's title, the medium in square brackets, and the name of the studio. In most cases, the director of the film is stated in the author position of the citation; this element is flexible, however, and you can list the name of a host, producer, or composer if more appropriate.

Attenborough, D. (Narrator). (2017). *Blue Planet II* [Nature Documentary Series]. BBC.

Nolan, C. (Director). (2020). *Tenet* [Film]. Warner Bros; Syncopy.

• **episodes from television series:** Entries for television show episodes should begin with the names of the writer and director, followed by the date, episode title, medium, series title, and production company's name. Identify the role, in parentheses, of each person listed. While the writer's and director's names are given in the example below, this element is flexible and you can include other relevant names if needed, along with their role descriptions.

Lindelof, D., (Writer), Jefferson, C. (Writer), & Williams, S. (Director). (2019, November 24). This extraordinary being (Season1, Episode 6) [Television series episode]. In D. Lindelof (Executive Producer), *The Watchmen*. HBO; WarnerMedia.

• **TED Talks:** If you are citing a TED Talk from the TED website, the author should be the speaker of the talk. If you are citing a version from YouTube, list the account owner as the author for ease of retrieval:

Jauhar, S. (2019, July). How your emotions change the shape of your heart [Video]. TEDSummit. https://www.ted.com/talks/sandeep_jauhar_how_your_emotions_change_the_shape_of_your_heart?

TED. (2019, October 5). Sandeep Jauhar: How emotions change the shape of your heart [Video]. YouTube. https://www.youtube.com/watch?v=mwoLhdHRt_0

• **YouTube and other streaming videos:** As mentioned above, videos accessed on streaming services such as YouTube or Vimeo should have the person who uploaded the video listed as author. If that person is simply a username, place the username in the author position; if the person's real name is known, place the name (inverted as usual) in the author position, followed by the username in square brackets.

Blank, D. (2009). Timelapse: Los Angeles wildfire [Video]. Vimeo. https://vimeo.com/6356422

University of Oxford. (2010, October 21). An introduction to general philosophy [Video lecture by Peter Millican]. YouTube. https://www.youtube.com/watch?v=hdCBGWcd4qw

• **podcasts:** The host of the podcast should be listed as author, along with the role description in parentheses. The podcast should be specified as audio or visual in square brackets after the title. Add the URL when available—if you have accessed the podcast through an app, you may omit adding the URL.

Runciman, D. (Host). (2020, November 2). Are young people losing faith in democracy? (No. 285) [Audio podcast episode]. In *Talking Politics*. https://www.talkingpoliticspodcast.com/blog/2020/285-are-young-people-losing-faith-in-democracy

• **music recordings**: Arrange an entry for a music recording as follows: give the writer's name, the copyright date of the piece of music, its title, the album title, the medium in square brackets, and the label name. If the piece is recorded by someone other than the writer, note that in square brackets after the piece's title. Add the recording date at the end of the entry if it differs from the copyright date. If the music is available only online, include a URL for ease of retrieval.

Pass, J. (1988, February 3). Cheek to cheek [Song]. On *Blues for Fred* [Album; CD]. Pablo Records. (Original song by Irving Berlin published 1935)

Cardi B. (2017). Bodak yellow [Song]. On *Invasion of Privacy* [Album]. Atlantic Records.

Chopin, F. (1996). *Nocturnes* [Recorded by Maria João Pires]. Deutsche Grammophon. (Original works written between 1827–1846)

• **recorded webinars:** The following format should only be used for retrievable webinars; to cite unrecorded webinars, follow the formatting listed above for personal communications.

Chodos, H., & Caron, L. (Guest speakers). (2019, January 31). *Best advice; Recovery-oriented mental health and addiction care in the patient's medical home* [Webinar]. Mental Health Commission of Canada. https://www.mentalhealthcommission.ca/English/media/4240

- **interviews:** How you format an entry for an interview will depend on where it is located. If you watched or listened to a recording of the interview, use the format appropriate to the medium. The second example below is for an interview of Jane Goodall posted on YouTube. The first example is for an interview with Willie Nelson printed in a periodical. Here, the entry follows the format for a newspaper article, with the interviewer in the author position, and information about the interviewee in square brackets. Notice as well that, although the periodical is called a magazine, this publication goes by date only, not volume and issue number, and so the newspaper article format is the appropriate choice. These guidelines apply only to published interviews; unpublished interviews you have conducted yourself are considered private correspondence and should not be included in your References list.

> Goldman, A. (2012, December 16). The silver-headed stranger [Interview with W. Nelson]. *New York Times Magazine*, 12.
>
> CBC News: The National. (2016, April 22). *Jane Goodall interview* [Video]. YouTube. https://www.youtube.com/watch?v=3h1UbYZV-IU

- **blog posts:** Start with the writer's name; then give the full date, entry title, blog title, and URL.

> Accetti, C. I., & Oskian, G. (2020, November 17). What is a consultative referendum? The democratic legitimacy of popular consultations. *Political Science Now.* https://politicalsciencenow.com/what-is-a-consultative-referendum-the-democratic-legitimacy-of-popular-consultations/

- **Wikipedia article:** Because Wikipedia pages can be revised by anyone, their content tends to change over time. In order for your readers to be able to access the same version of the article you are citing, use the archived version for your citation. To do this, go to the "View History" tab on the Wikipedia page and click on the date you accessed the article. The URL for that archived version is a permanent link that you can cite as the location in your reference. If the link is not labelled as permanent, include the retrieval date.

> Behaviorism. (2020, August 4). In *Wikipedia.* https://en.wikipedia.org/w/index.php?title=Behaviorism&oldid=971230907

- **social media:** When you use social media to discover content located elsewhere, cite the location of the original posting (for example if you find a news article via Twitter, cite the article itself, not the Tweet). Only create references for social media posts when you cite the content directly. If the author's real name is known, place the name (inverted as usual) in the author position, followed by the username in square brackets. If you only have the username, place it in the author position (including the symbol @, if applicable). Your reference should include all the non-standard spelling, capitalization, acronyms, and emojis that can be found in social media posts. If you cannot recreate an emoji in your word-processing software, include square bracketed descriptions "[smiling face with heart-eyes]" for example. A complete list of descriptions for the various emojis can be found at https://unicode.org/emoji/charts/emoji-list.html. The title of a social media post should be the text of the first 20 words. If there are any audiovisuals, include a square bracketed note to that effect after the title.

The following format for a Facebook post reference can be used for most social media platforms; further examples for Instagram and Twitter are included below.

- **Facebook posts**:

College of Nurses of Ontario. (2020, November 13). *What is "reflective practice"? Why do I need an action plan? Reflection should be part of a nurse's everyday routine* [Video]. Facebook. https://www.facebook.com/collegeofnurses/posts/2773432936208758

Peltier, A. (2020, September 4). *For everyone who does work protecting the waters and the lands and to everyone we cross paths with, keep doing* [Link attached to notice of documentary screening featuring Peltier]. Facebook. https://www.facebook.com/Waterwarrior1/posts/901124333712126

- **Instagram photos or videos**:

Art Gallery of Ontario [@agotoronto]. (2020, August 23). *In the late 1950s and '60s, when artists felt pressure to live and work in the metropolitan centres of the world* [Photograph]. Instagram. https://www.instagram.com/p/CEPtIubAUmS/?utm_source=ig_web_copy_link

- **tweets:** If the author's real name is known, provide it first, followed by the author's screen name in square brackets. If the author's real name cannot be determined, provide only the screen name, without the square brackets. Include only the date, not the time. Include the entire tweet.

Johnson Space Center [@NASA_Johnson]. (2020, November 17). Let the science begin! [Test tube emoji]. *Astronaut Kate Rubins has been conducting science experiments on the @Space_Station, and with NASA's SpaceX Crew-1* [Gif and link attached]. https://twitter.com/NASA_Johnson/status/1328751028242587649?s=20

• **other webpages and websites:** In the case of websites and webpages that are not part of an overarching publication, create a reference for each page that you cite. If you are not quoting or paraphrasing the website in your text, but are discussing it generally, you do not need to create a reference for it—simply place the URL in parentheses as an in-text citation. If you are quoting or paraphrasing material from a webpage, and an author or editor is indicated, list by author; otherwise, list by title. If the source is undated or its content is likely to change, you should include the date on which you accessed the material. Use square brackets to include information that will help identify the source.

Fox, L. (2020, November 17). *Fate of the stimulus looks bleak as lawmakers turn attention to spending deadline.* CNN. https://www.cnn.com/2020/11/17/politics/stimulus-negotiations-latest-congress/index.html

World Health Organization. (2020, November 13). *WHO establishes council on the economics of health for all.* https://www.who.int/news/item/13-11-2020-who-establishes-council-on-the-economics-of-health-for-all

• **visual works:** When creating references for visual works such as paintings, maps, infographics, and photographs, include the medium in square brackets after the title.

• **work of art in a gallery or gallery website:** Note that in this case the name of the gallery or museum, as well as the city, province, and country where it is located, are listed in the source element, in addition to the URL. If the work is not available on a website, omit the URL.

Belmore, R. (1987–1991). *Rising to the occasion* [Sculpture]. Art Gallery of Ontario, Toronto, Ontario, Canada. https://ago.ca/collection/object/95/173

• **stock images or clip art:**

oksmith. (2020). *Doctor with mask #4* [Clip art]. Openclipart. https://openclipart.org/detail/325362/doctor-with-mask-4

• **infographics:**

The Economist. (2020, November 13). *Against the clock: Performance of world chess champions and their opponents* [Infographic]. https://www.economist.com/graphic-detail/2020/11/13/the-queens-gambit-is-right-young-chess-stars-always-usurp-the-old

• **maps:**

Pew Research Center. (2019, April 11). *Immigrant share in U.S. is lower than in many other countries* [Map]. https://www.pewresearch.org/fact-tank/2019/04/11/6-demographic-trends-shaping-the-u-s-and-the-world-in-2019/ft_19-01-31_foreignbornshare_immigrantshareinus_2-2/

• **photographs:**

Adams, A. (1943). *Manzanar from Guard Tower, view west (Sierra Nevada in background), Manzanar Relocation Center, California* [Photograph]. Library of Congress. https://www.loc.gov/pictures/collection/manz/item/2002695970/

• **PowerPoint slides, lecture notes, recorded Zoom lectures:** If the slides, lecture notes, or recorded Zoom lectures you are citing are available online, create a reference such as the first example listed below. If the material is on a closed learning management system or intranet and your readers have access, include the name of the site and the URL for the login page in your reference (see the second example below). If your audience does *not* have access to the materials, cite these resources as personal communications (see above).

University of British Columbia. (2011, November 24). *The social side of mobile health* [PowerPoint slides by D. Hooker]. SlideShare. https://www.slideshare.net/ubc/the-social-side-of-mobile-health-10314829

The following is a reference citation for a recorded Zoom class posted on an internal university learning management system:

Ruddock, J. (2020, June 3). *Lecture 5: ENGL 234* [Archived recording of Zoom class]. Moodle. https://moodle.concordia.ca/moodle/course/view.php?id=125464

• **conference presentations:** To cite a conference session that you attended in person, include the names of presenters in the author element, the date and title, and the name of the conference and location. If you accessed the discussion online, add the URL or DOI in the location element.

Felher, B. (Chair), Cook, J., Johnson, P., & Lentschke, L. (Speakers). (2019, March 13–16). *Performing protest: Resistance rhetorics and the minoritarian response* [Panel]. Conference on College Composition and Communication, Pittsburgh, PA, United States.

Among the details to notice in this reference system:

- Where two or more works by the same author are included in References, they are ordered by date of publication.
- APA style prefers author initials rather than first names.
- Only the first words of titles and subtitles are capitalized, except for proper nouns.
- The date appears in parentheses near the beginning of each entry in References.
- The in-text citation comes directly after the name of the author or after the end quotation mark. Often, these citations fall just before the period or comma in the surrounding sentence.
- If an in-text citation occurs within text in parentheses, commas are used to set off elements of the reference.
- When a work has appeared in an edited collection, information on the editors must be included in the reference.
- Authors' first and last names are reversed; note the use of the ampersand (&) in place of *and* between author names.
- Translators should be included where appropriate in the References list.
- Publisher should be listed in References entries for print works.
- Months and publisher names are not abbreviated; the day of the month follows the name of the month.
- Online references include the date of publication or of last revision in parentheses immediately after the author's name. Note that, if a DOI or URL ends a reference entry, there is no period at the end of the entry.

APA Style Sample Essay

Following is a full sample of text with citations in APA style. The sample essay included here follows the APA guidelines for student papers, including the title page formatting that is recommended for students; your instructor may, of course, have specific requirements that you should also follow. Professional papers have different requirements under APA style. If you are submitting your paper for publication, consult with the publisher for formatting specifics, and see information on professional formatting on the APA website (https://apastyle.apa.org).

For student papers, include a title page, page numbers, your text, and a "References" page. Depending on the content of your paper, you may also include tables, figures, and appendices. APA guidelines suggest that student papers may omit a running head, author note, and abstract, unless your instructor requests that you include such elements.

top right-hand corner pagination begins with title page

1

Resistance to Vaccination: A Review of the Literature

Jeremy P. Yap

Psychology Department, Wagner College

PS 252: Health Psychology

Dr. J.B. Martin

February 25, 2021

include your course number and title, your instructor's name, and the due date for your paper on separate lines

2

Resistance to Vaccination: A Review of the Literature

title should be centred and bolded

Since the late 1990s, vaccination has become highly controversial. This paper will review the literature on the subject, with a particular focus on the vaccination of children, by posing and responding to three key questions:

1. How effective is the practice of vaccination—and how safe?
2. Why have vaccination rates declined?
3. What are the best ways to increase rates of vaccination?

This is an area in which medical science must engage with the research findings of social psychologists; there is an urgent need to find effective solutions. The problems are sufficiently complex, however, that it seems unlikely that any single approach will be sufficient to resolve them.

How Effective Is the Practice of Vaccination—and How Safe?

There is overwhelming evidence on a variety of fronts that vaccination is one of the great triumphs of modern medical science. Thanks to the spread of vaccination, smallpox and polio have been eliminated in most of the world. The Centers for Disease Control and Prevention (2020) reports that diseases such as measles, mumps, and rubella, for which a combined vaccine has for generations been routinely given to children, are almost unknown in areas where vaccination is near-universal. The example of measles is an instructive

3

one. Before the practice of vaccination was introduced, measles infected several million children every year in the United States alone, and killed more than 500 annually. After vaccination became common practice, measles almost entirely disappeared in North America—until recently. Now it is a threat once again in the United States and Canada—and not a threat to be taken lightly. According to the World Health Organization (2020), measles still kills over 100,000 worldwide each year; for 2018 the figure was 142,300.

Evidence for the effectiveness of vaccination is very strong in the case of polio and smallpox, and in the case of "childhood diseases" such as measles and rubella. There is also strong evidence that vaccination against influenza has been successful in bringing about significantly reduced rates of infection (Atwell et al., 2019). Importantly, though, the success of vaccination depends in large part on so-called "herd immunity." So long as approximately 95% or thereabouts of a population have been vaccinated, the incidence of a disease catching on in that population is negligible. When vaccination rates dip below that level, however, the risk for those who have not been vaccinated increases dramatically. Despite this, some communities where vaccination is readily available nonetheless have vaccination rates dramatically below the percentage required for herd immunity. In California, for example, where a 2015 outbreak

for citation of work with three or more authors use "et al."

of measles has received wide attention, Maimuna et al. (2015) have estimated that in the relevant population clusters vaccination rates have dropped below 50%.

What about the other side of the ledger? Have there been cases of patients suffering adverse effects after taking a vaccine? And if so, do the benefits of vaccination outweigh the risks? Here too the answers seem clear. Yes, there have been cases of adverse effects (notably, fever and allergic reactions for some individuals). But as Schmid et al. (2017) and others have concluded, these are rare, and on balance vastly outweighed by the benefits of mass vaccination. Perhaps the broadest study of vaccines, their effectiveness, and their occasional side effects was that conducted by the Institute of Medicine (2011), which reviewed vaccines used against chickenpox, influenza, hepatitis B, human papillomavirus, measles, mumps, rubella, meningitis, and tetanus. Their conclusion was clear:

> Vaccines offer the promise of protection against a variety of infectious diseases ... [and] remain one of the greatest tools in the public health arsenal. Certainly, some vaccines result in adverse effects that must be acknowledged. But the latest evidence shows that few adverse effects are caused by the vaccines reviewed in this report. (p. 4)

square brackets used for a word not in the original quotation

centred headings for sections

5

Except in rare cases, then (as with certain individuals susceptible to severe allergic reactions), the benefits of vaccines clearly far outweigh the risks.

Why Have Vaccination Rates Declined?

Near the end of the last century, British medical researcher Andrew Wakefield and his colleagues (1998) published a study linking the vaccination of children against diseases such as measles, mumps, and rubella to increased incidence of gastrointestinal disease, and also to increased incidence of "developmental regression"—notably, autism. The study appeared in *The Lancet*, one of the world's leading medical journals, and had a major impact—but an entirely unfortunate one. News of the study's findings spread widely, with thousands of articles in the popular press in 2001 and 2002 questioning the safety of vaccination. Parents whose children suffered from autism started to blame vaccination, and many of them launched lawsuits.

It was not until six years later that serious doubts were publicly raised. Investigative journalist Brian Deer (2004) revealed that Wakefield's study was compromised by a serious conflict of interest; he had received financial compensation from parties intending to sue vaccine manufacturers before he embarked on the research. And, as was gradually discovered, the research itself had been fabricated.

6

In 2010 *The Lancet* finally retracted the 1998 article, and Wakefield himself was censured. By that time, a very great deal of damage had been done; public confidence in vaccines had dropped precipitously.

Fabricated research results are not the sole cause of the lack of confidence in vaccination that many continue to express. To some extent, confidence in vaccination among the general public has always been shaky. The very nature of vaccination—giving the patient a very small, modified dose of an illness in order to prevent further harm—seems counterintuitive to many. As Brendan Nyhan observed in an interview with Julia Belluz (2015), "people have always been suspicious of vaccines. There has always been an instinctive response to the idea of using a disease to protect yourself against the disease. It gives people the heebie jeebies" (para. 8). In a meta-analysis, Atwell et al. (2019) report that humans are far more likely to get vaccinated when they believe the disease in question to pose a serious threat—a finding which should not come as surprising, and which explains why doubts about vaccines have found fertile ground in places where the vaccines themselves have largely or entirely succeeded. As Jerome Groopman (2015) has observed, "we no longer see children stricken with polio in wheelchairs, or hear of those suffocating from diphtheria, of babies born to mothers with rubella whose eyes are clouded by cataracts and hearts deformed" (p. 30). If one continually

provide paragraph number when page numbers are unavailable

7

sees people suffering from such diseases, one is likely to be far more aware of their dangers than is the case in nations where vaccination has succeeded in reducing their incidence to zero or near-zero.

When doubts have been raised and scandals have arisen, the media have too often not been as responsible as one would wish. On the one hand, as discussed by Nelson (2014), Jennings and Russell (2019) and others, some media outlets have tacitly encouraged scientifically irresponsible statements by taking an "impartial" approach to the facts, reporting the claims of anti-vaccination activists with no scientific credentials and of reputable scientific authorities as if they had equal authority. Other media outlets, however, have sometimes swung too far in the other direction, adopting a supercilious or contemptuous tone towards those who have doubts about vaccination. Much as it is important to spread factual information as to the dangers of allowing one's children to remain unvaccinated, it is counterproductive to present information in a tone that is disrespectful of the audience one is hoping to persuade. As Angelina Chapin (2015) has pointed out, when

acceptable to include first name in a signal phrase

> people's beliefs contradict science, there's an obvious temptation to cut them down. But we should be more careful with how we deliver our arguments. On a policy level, messaging should come from people that communities trust,

> such as doctors or religious leaders. At the dinner table or on Facebook, try a little empathy. It will help the medicine go down and the immunization rates go up. (para. 12)

The attitudes with which we approach these discussions, in short, can make a world of difference.

Interestingly, studies such as that of Maimuna et al. (2015) suggest that those with high levels of education are at least as likely as those with less education to be anti-vaccination. One important factor in the social psychology of attitudes towards vaccination that does seem to have had an impact (albeit a negative one), has been the degree to which the issue has become charged with ideological content. Those who are generally suspicious of government and/or of modern science have been slow to accept the overwhelming weight of evidence in support of vaccination. That should perhaps not be surprising; as Kraft et al. (2015) and others have reported, to the extent that beliefs about factual matters are intertwined with ideology, our minds become immunized against information in the other direction, even when that information is of a purely factual nature. Moreover, this is a "tendency that appears to be evident among liberals and conservatives alike" (p. 121). When they are coloured by ideology—and by emotion—our beliefs as to the facts of the matter are highly resistant to change.

What Are the Best Ways to Increase the Rates of Vaccination?

Clearly it is important for health care workers, educators, and those in the media to inform themselves of the facts and to spread this information. But simply informing the public of the facts is evidently insufficient to change behaviour. Several studies have found that parents who have been fully informed of the scientific background are no more likely to vaccinate their children—and in some cases are *less* likely (Callaghan et al., 2019; Nyhan et al., 2014).

Just as important as the facts themselves, it seems, is the way they are reported to patients. The attitudes expressed by health care workers to patients play a key role. Though the vast majority of health care workers accept the evidence regarding vaccination, they have become aware that it is a hot-button issue and—not wanting to be insensitive to patients' concerns—have sometimes not been clear and emphatic about the dangers of not vaccinating. If health care workers ask parents if they "believe in" vaccinating their children, their phrasing is likely to provide support to the views of those patients who think the science about vaccinations to be uncertain. Conversely, an attitude that remains friendly while taking the facts as a given may be more helpful. There have been numerous studies on the degree to which it may help to frame information positively to patients (Anderson et al., 2020; Thomson et al., 2018;

10

and Wegwartha et al., 2014). Though these have not been entirely conclusive, it is hard to imagine that it is not preferable to present facts in a tone that will encourage others to appreciate them, and to act accordingly. Angelina Chapin's common-sense advice on this point (quoted above) rings true.

It may well be, however, that adopting the right tone with patients and in media reports will not be enough; regulatory and/or legislative changes may be required as well in some jurisdictions. It is important to note that the United States as a whole has not suffered any steep decline in vaccination rates; to a large extent the problem is associated with jurisdictions that make it easy for parents to opt out of vaccinations for their children. In contrast, where vaccination is the strong "default position"—mandatory for children with few possible exemptions—vaccination rates in recent years have tended to remain at well over 90%. As Margaret Talbot (2015) has observed of the United States,

> the highest vaccination rate in the country is in Mississippi, a state with an otherwise dismal set of health statistics. It allows people to opt out of vaccines only for medical reasons—not for religious or personal ones. States that make it easier not to vaccinate have higher rates of infectious diseases. (pp. 19–20)

quotation of more than 40 words is indented 0.5 inches from left margin

Is the answer, then, simply to pass stricter laws in jurisdictions that currently have loose ones? Much as such action may be desirable, given current levels of resistance to vaccination of children, it is questionable whether efforts to make the practice mandatory would be successful in many areas—and they would be sure to inflame passions on all sides.

The experience of the European Union suggests that it may not always be necessary to make vaccination mandatory. Vaccination rates are high throughout Europe, even though only 14 of the 29 countries in the EU have any mandatory vaccinations (Haverkate et al., 2012). In the remainder, vaccination is recommended rather than required. There is some evidence that in North America, too, non-compulsory strategies can in certain circumstances be as effective as compulsion in raising vaccination rates (El-Amin et al., 2012). Again, the strength with which a recommendation is put forward can make a world of difference to the degree to which that recommendation is followed. If parents are simply informed that vaccination is recommended and that they may vaccinate their children against measles if they wish at such and such a time and place, the uptake rate is likely to be low. If parents are informed that a medical ordinance specifies that children should be vaccinated against measles, and that low vaccination rates put all children at risk, the uptake rate will surely be much higher.

12

There is a widespread tendency to presume that Americans will be more likely to resist government "intrusions" into citizens' lives than will Canadians. In the case of attitudes towards vaccination, however, it is not at all clear that the presumption is correct. Whereas every American state has at least some requirement (albeit often weakened by "personal belief" exemptions) that children be vaccinated before attending school, only a minority of Canadian provinces have such regulations (Walkinshaw, 2011).

Whatever approaches are taken in each jurisdiction, it will be essential that attention be paid not only to the medical and biological facts, but also to laws and regulations—and to social psychology.

list of references begins on a new page

13

list of references alphabetized by author's last name

author initials used—not first names

References

Anderson, M. G., Ballinger, E. A., Benjamin, D., Frenkel, L. D., Hinnant Jr., C. W., & Zucker, K. W. (2020). A clinical perspective of the U.S. anti-vaccination epidemic: Considering marginal costs and benefits, CDC best practices guidelines, free riders, and herd immunity. *Vaccine, 38*(50), 7877–7879. https://doi.org/10.1016/j.vaccine.2020.10.068

Atwell, K., Dube, E., Gagneur, A., Omer, S. B., & Suggs, L. S. (2019). Vaccine acceptance: Science, policy, and practice in a "post-fact" world. *Vaccine, 37*(5), 677–682. https://doi.org/10.1016/j.vaccine.2018.12.014

Belluz, J. (2015, February 7). Debunking vaccine junk science won't change people's minds. Here's what will [Interview with B. Nyhan]. *Vox.* http://www.vox.com/2015/2/7/7993289/vaccine-beliefs

Callaghan, T., Motta, M., Sylvester, S., Trujillo, K., & Blackburn, C. C. (2019). Parent psychology and the decision to delay childhood vaccination. *Social Science & Medicine, 238*(112407). https://doi.org/10.1016/j.socscimed.2019.112407

Centers for Disease Control and Prevention. (2020, November 5). *Measles History.* https://www.cdc.gov/measles/about/history.html

14

Chapin, A. (2015, February 13). How to talk to anti-vaxxers. *Ottawa Citizen*. http://ottawacitizen.com/opinion/columnists/how-to-talk-to-anti-vaxxers

Deer, B. (2004, February 22). Revealed: MMR research scandal. *The Sunday Times* (London). http://www.thesundaytimes.co.uk/sto/

El-Amin, A. N., Parra, M. T., Kim-Farley, R., & Fielding, J. E. (2012). Ethical issues concerning vaccination requirements. *Public Health Reviews, 34*(1), 1–20. http://www.publichealthreviews.eu/upload/pdf_files/11/00_El_Amin.pdf

Groopman, J. (2015, March 5). There's no way out of it [Review of the book *On immunity: An introduction*]. *The New York Review of Books*, 29–31.

Haverkate, M., D'Ancona, F., Giambi, C., Johansen, K., Lopalco, P. L., Cozza, V., & Appelgren, E. (2012, May). Mandatory and recommended vaccination in the EU, Iceland and Norway: Results of the VENICE 2010 survey on the ways of implementing national vaccination programmes. *Eurosurveillance, 17*(22), 31. http://www.eurosurveillance.org/ViewArticle.aspx?ArticleId=20183

Institute of Medicine. (2011, August 25). Adverse effects of vaccines: Evidence and causality [Report brief]. http://www.iom.edu/Reports/2011/Adverse-Effects-of-Vaccines-Evidence-and-Causality.aspx

provide URL for web-sourced material when DOI not available

15

Jennings, F. J., & Russell, F. M. (2019). Civility, credibility, and health information: The impact of uncivil comments and source credibility on attitudes about vaccines. *Public Understanding of Science, 28*(4), 417–432. https://doi.org/10.1177/0963662519837901

Kraft, P. W., Lodge, M., & Taber, C. S. (2015, March). Why people "don't trust the evidence": Motivated reasoning and scientific beliefs. *Annals of the American Academy of Political and Social Science, 658*(1), 121–133. https://doi.org/10.1177/0002716214554758

Maimuna, S., Majumder, M. P. H., Cohn, E. L., Sumiko, R., Mekaru, D. V. M., Huston, J. E., & Brownstein, J. S. (2015, March 16). Substandard vaccination compliance and the 2015 measles outbreak [Research Letter]. *JAMA Pediatrics, 169*(5), 494–495. https://doi.org/10.1001/jamapediatrics.2015.0384

Nelson, R. (2014, October). The reporting of health information in the media. *American Journal of Nursing, 114*(10), 19–20. https://doi.org/10.1097/01.NAJ.0000454842.04985.c6

Nyhan, B., Reifler, J., Richey, S., & Freed, G. L. (2014, April 1). Effective messages in vaccine promotion: A randomized trial. *Pediatrics, 133*(4), e835–e842. https://doi.org/10.1542/peds.2013-2365

all materials that have a DOI available must include the DOI in the reference entry, even if you accessed a print version

16

Schmid, P., Rauber, D., Betsch, C., Lidolt, G., & Denker, M. (2017). Barriers of influenza vaccination intention and behavior: A systematic review of influenza vaccine hesitancy, 2005–2016. *PLoS ONE, 12*(1). https://doi.org/10.1371/journal.pone.0170550

Talbot, M. (2015, February 16). Not immune. *The New Yorker, 91*(1), 19–20.

Thomson, A., Vallée-Tourangeau, G., & Suggs, L. S. (2018). Strategies to increase vaccine acceptance and uptake: From behavioral insights to context-specific, culturally-appropriate, evidence-based communications and interventions. *Vaccine, 36*(44), 6457–6458. https://doi.org/10.1016/j.vaccine.2018.08.031

Wakefield, A. J., Murch, S. H., Anthony, A., Linnel, J., Casson, D. M., Malik, M., Berelowitz, M., Dhillon, A. P., Thomson, M. A., Harvey, P., Valentine, A., Davies, S. E., & Walker Smith, J. A. (1998). Ileal-lymphoidnodular hyperplasia, non-specific colitis, and pervasive developmental disorder in children. *Lancet, 351*, 637–641. https://doi.org/10.1016/S0140-6736(97)11096-0 (Retraction published 2010, *Lancet, 375*, p. 445)

Walkinshaw, E. (2011, November 8). Mandatory vaccinations: The international landscape. *Canadian Medical Association Journal, 183*(16), e1167–e1168. https://doi.org/10.1503/cmaj.109-3993

paste DOIs or URLs into your citation; do not break the link up or punctuate

17

Wegwartha, O., Kurzenhäuser-Carstens, S., & Gigerenzera, G. (2014, March 10). Overcoming the knowledge–behaviour gap: The effect of evidence-based HPV vaccination leaflets on understanding, intention, and actual vaccination decision. *Science Direct: Vaccine, 32*(12), 1388–1393. https://doi.org/10.1016/j.vaccine.2013.12.038

World Health Organization. (2020, October 27). *Measles (Immunization, Vaccines and Biologicals).* http://www.who.int/immunization/monitoring_surveillance/burden/vpd/surveillance_type/active/measles/en/

C3.3 CHICAGO STYLE

C3.3 Chicago Style

C3.3.1 About Chicago Style

The University of Chicago's massively comprehensive *Chicago Manual of Style* (17th edition, 2017) provides full information on two documentation systems: an author-date system of citation that is similar to APA style, and a traditional foot- or endnoting system. The latter, which this book refers to as Chicago Style, and which is often used in the history and philosophy disciplines, is outlined below. This chapter also includes, at the end, a short essay excerpt using Chicago Style documentation. Full sample essays in Chicago Style are available on the Broadview website. Go to sites.broadviewpress.com/writingcdn. You can also find additional information at Chicago Style's online site (www.chicagomanualofstyle.org).

In the pages that follow, information about electronic sources has been presented in an integrated fashion, with information about referencing hard copies of print sources presented alongside information about referencing online versions. General guidelines covering entries for online sources are as follows. Begin each note and bibliography entry for an electronic source as you would for a non-electronic source, including all relevant publication information that the source makes available. Then provide either the website's URL, followed by the usual end punctuation for the note or entry, or, if available, the source's digital object identifier (DOI): a string of numbers, letters, and punctuation, beginning with *10*, usually located on the first or copyright page. If both a URL and DOI are available, provide only the latter; DOIs are preferred because they are stable links to sources, whereas URLs are often not permanent. If you need to break a URL or DOI over two or more lines, do not insert any hyphens at the break point; instead, break after a colon or double slash or before other marks of punctuation. Note that Chicago Style does not put angle brackets around URLs. Except when there is no publication or modification date available, Chicago Style does not require the addition of access dates for online material, but your instructors may wish you to include them. If so, put them before the URL or DOI, after the word *accessed*.

• **notes**: The basic principle of Chicago Style is to create a note each time one cites a source. The note can appear at the foot of the page on which the citation is made, or it can be part of a separate list, titled

Notes, situated at the end of the essay and before the bibliography. For both foot- and endnotes, a superscript number at the end of the clause in which the reference appears points to the relevant note:

- Levy and Mole suggest that the emotional attachment some people feel for print books is "historically and culturally constructed, and it could be constructed differently in the future."[1]

The superscript number [1] here is linked to the information provided where the same number appears at either the foot of the page or in the list of notes at the end of the main text of the paper:

1. Michelle Levy and Tom Mole, *The Broadview Introduction to Book History* (Peterborough, ON: Broadview Press, 2017), 138.

Notice that the author's name is in the normal order, elements of the note are separated by commas, publication information is in parentheses, and the first line of the note is indented. The note ends with a page number for the citation.

In addition, all works cited, as well as works that have been consulted but are not cited in the body of your essay, must be included in an alphabetically arranged list, titled *Bibliography*, that appears at the end of the essay. The entry there would in this case be as follows:

Levy, Michelle, and Tom Mole. *The Broadview Introduction to Book History*. Peterborough, ON: Broadview Press, 2017.

In the entry in the bibliography, notice that the first author's name is inverted, elements of the entry are separated by periods, and no parentheses are placed around the publication information. Also, the entry is given a hanging indent: the first line is flush with the left-hand margin, and subsequent lines are indented. Notice as well that the province or state of publication is included in both notes and bibliography entries if the city of publication is not widely known.

In the various examples that follow, formats for notes and bibliography entries for each kind of source are shown together.

• **titles: italics/quotation marks**: Notice in the above example that the title is in italics. Titles of short works (such as articles, poems, and short stories) should be put in quotation marks. In all titles key words should be capitalized. For more details, see the Title of Source section in the chapter on MLA documentation above (pages 633–35).

• **multiple references to the same work**: For later notes referencing an already-cited source, use the author's last name, title (in shortened form if it is over four words long), and page number only.

1. Levy and Mole, *Broadview Introduction to Book History*, 154.

If successive references are to the same work, you may omit the title of the work just cited, in order to avoid repetition.[1]

1. Sean Carver, "The Economic Foundations for Unrest in East Timor, 1970–1995," *Journal of Economic History* 21, no. 2 (2011): 103.
2. Carver, 109.
3. Carver, 111.
4. Jennifer Riley, "East Timor in the Pre-Independence Years," *Asian History Online* 11, no. 4 (2012): par. 18, http://www.aho.ubc.edu/prs/text-only/issue.45/16.3jr.txt.
5. Riley, par. 24.

Carver, Sean. "The Economic Foundations for Unrest in East Timor, 1970–1995." *Journal of Economic History* 21, no. 2 (2011): 100–21.

Riley, Jennifer. "East Timor in the Pre-Independence Years." *Asian History Online* 11, no. 4 (2012). http://www.aho.ubc.edu/prs/text-only/issue.45/16.3jr.txt.

• **page number or date unavailable**: If an Internet document is in PDF format, the page numbers are stable and may be cited in the same way that one would the pages of a printed book or journal article. Many Internet pages are unstable, however, and many more lack page numbers. Instead, provide a section number, paragraph number, or other identifier if available.

2. Hanif Bhabha, "Family Life in 1840s Virginia," *Southern History Web Archives* 45, no. 3 (2013): par. 14, accessed March 3, 2021, http://shweb.ut.edu/history/american.nineteenthc/bhabha.html.

Bhabha, Hanif. "Family Life in 1840s Virginia." *Southern History Web Archives* 45, no. 3 (2013). Accessed March 3, 2021. http://shweb.ut.edu/history/american.nineteenthc/bhabha.html.

If you are citing longer texts from electronic versions, and counting paragraph numbers is impracticable, chapter references may be more appropriate. For example, if the online Gutenberg edition of Darwin's

1 This recommendation represents a change from previous editions, which had recommended using *ibid.* (an abbreviation of the Latin *ibidem*, meaning *in the same place*) for successive references. The 17th edition discourages the use of *ibid.*

On the Origin of Species were being cited, the citation would be as follows:

- Darwin refers to the core of his theory as an "ineluctable principle."[1]

1. Charles Darwin, *On the Origin of Species* (1859; Project Gutenberg, 2001), chap. 26, http://www.gutenberg.darwin.origin.frrp.ch26.html.

Darwin, Charles. *On the Origin of Species*. 1859. Project Gutenberg, 2001. http://www.gutenberg.darwin.origin.frrp.ch26.html.

Students should be cautioned that online editions of older or classic works are often unreliable; typically there are far more typos and other errors in online versions of literary texts than there are in print versions. It is often possible to exercise judgement about such matters, however. If, for example, you are not required to base your essay on a particular edition of Darwin's *Origin of Species* but may find your own, you will be far better off using the text you will find on the reputable Project Gutenberg site than you will using a text you might find on a site such as "Manybooks.com."

When there is no date for a source, include *n.d.*, as in the first example below. When there is no date for an online source, include your access date.

1. Thomas Gray, *Gray's Letters*, vol. 1 (London: John Sharpe, n.d.), 60.
2. Don LePan, *Skyscraper Art*, accessed February 10, 2020, http://www.donlepan.com/Skyscraper_Art.html.

Gray, Thomas. *Gray's Letters*. Vol. 1. London: John Sharpe, n.d.
LePan, Don. *Skyscraper Art*. Accessed February 10, 2020. http://www.donlepan.com/Skyscraper_Art.html.

C3.3 Chicago Style

- **two or more dates for a work**: Note that in the Darwin example above both the date of the original publication and the date of the modern edition are provided. If you are citing work in a form that has been revised by the author, however, you should cite the date of the revised publication, not the original, and use the abbreviation *rev. ed.* to indicate that the work has been revised.

1. Robert Mutti, *Making Up Your Mind*, rev. ed. (Peterborough, ON: Broadview Press, 2014), 150.

Mutti, Robert. *Making Up Your Mind*. Rev. ed. Peterborough, ON: Broadview Press, 2014.

• **two or three authors**: If there are two or three authors, they should be identified as follows in the footnote and in the bibliography. Pay attention to where commas do and do not appear, and note that in the bibliography entry, only the first author's name is inverted. Put the names of the authors in the order in which they appear in the work itself.

1. Joerg Fingerhut and Jesse J. Prinz, "Aesthetic Emotions Reconsidered," *The Monist* 103, no. 2 (April 2020): 223, https://doi.org/10.1093/monist/onz037.

Fingerhut, Joerg, and Jesse J. Prinz. "Aesthetic Emotions Reconsidered." *The Monist* 103, no. 2 (April 2020): 223–29. https://doi.org/10.1093/monist/onz037.

• **four or more authors**: In the footnote name only the first author, and use the phrase *et al.*, an abbreviation of the Latin *et alia*, meaning *and others*. In the bibliography name all authors, as below:

11. Victoria Fromkin et al., *An Introduction to Language*, 4th Canadian ed. (Toronto: Nelson, 2010), 113.

Fromkin, Victoria, Robert Rodman, Nina Hyams, and Kirsten M. Hummel. *An Introduction to Language*. 4th Canadian ed. Toronto: Nelson, 2010.

• **organization as author/reference work/government document**: Identify by the organization if known, and otherwise by the title of the work. Unsigned newspaper articles or dictionary and encyclopedia entries are usually not listed in the bibliography. In notes, unsigned dictionary or encyclopedia entries are identified by the title of the reference work, e.g., Wikipedia, and unsigned newspaper articles are listed by the title of the article.

6. Major League Baseball, *2021 Regular Season Standings*, accessed June 9, 2021, https://www.mlb.com/standings.

7. "Argentina's President Calls on UK Prime Minister to Relinquish Control of Falkland Islands," *Vancouver Sun*, January 3, 2013, A9.

8. Broadview Press, "Broadview's 2020 Recycled Paper Usage and Charitable Donations," accessed May 3, 2021, https://broadviewpress.com/broadviews-2020-recycled-paper-usage-and-charitable-donations/.

9. Commonwealth Corporation of Massachusetts, *Resources for Individuals & Communities in Response to Coronavirus (COVID-19)*, 2020, accessed January 12, 2021, https://archives.lib.state.ma.us/bitstream/handle/2452/831037/on1178881472.pdf?sequence=1&isAllowed=y.

10. Wikipedia, s.v. "Mary Wollstonecraft," last modified May 19, 2021, 11:46, https://en.wikipedia.org/w/index.php?title=Mary_Wollstonecraft&oldid=1023975388.

11. *OED Online*, s.v. "aesthetic, n.1," last modified March 2021, accessed May 25, 2021, https://www-oed-com./view/Entry/3237?rskey=49BHJn&result=1&isAdvanced=false.

The following are the bibliography entries for the preceding notes (notice that, because unsigned newspaper articles and articles from well-known reference works are not usually included in Chicago Style bibliographies, the Wikipedia, *Oxford English Dictionary*, and *Vancouver Sun* articles are not included). Ignore initial articles (*the*, *a*, *an*) when alphabetizing.

Broadview Press. "Broadview's 2020 Recycled Paper Usage and Charitable Donations." Accessed May 3, 2021. https://broadviewpress.com/broadviews-2020-recycled-paper-usage-and-charitable-donations/.

Commonwealth Corporation of Massachusetts. *Resources for Individuals & Communities in Response to Coronavirus (COVID-19)*. 2020. Accessed January 12, 2021. https://archives.lib.state.ma.us/bitstream/handle/2452/831037/on1178881472.pdf?sequence=1&isAllowed=y.

Major League Baseball. *2021 Regular Season Standings*. Accessed June 9, 2021. https://www.mlb.com/standings.

• **works from a collection of readings or anthology**: In the citation for a work in an anthology or collection of essays, use the name of the author of the work you are citing. If the work is reprinted in one source but was first published elsewhere, include the details of the original publication in the bibliography.

6. Eric Hobsbawm, "Peasant Land Occupations," in *Uncommon People: Resistance and Rebellion* (London: Weidenfeld & Nicolson, 1998), 167.

7. Daniel Heath Justice, "The Necessity of Nationhood: Affirming the Sovereignty of Indigenous National Literatures," in *Introduction to Indigenous Literary Criticism in Canada*, ed. Heather Macfarlane and Armand Garnet Ruffo (Peterborough, ON: Broadview Press, 2015), 245.

Hobsbawm, Eric. "Peasant Land Occupations." In *Uncommon People: Resistance and Rebellion*, 166–90. London: Weidenfeld & Nicolson, 1998. Originally published in *Past and Present* 62 (1974): 120–52.

Justice, Daniel Heath. "The Necessity of Nationhood: Affirming the Sovereignty of Indigenous National Literatures." In *Introduction to Indigenous Literary Criticism in Canada*, edited by Heather Macfarlane and

Armand Garnet Ruffo, 241–55. Peterborough, ON: Broadview Press, 2015. Originally published in *Moveable Margins*, edited by Chelva Kanaganayakam. Toronto: TSAR Publications, 2005.

• **indirect source**: If you are citing a source from a reference other than the original source itself, you should include information about both sources, supplying as much information as you are able to about the original source.

- In de Beauvoir's famous phrase, "one is not born a woman, one becomes one."[1]

1. Simone de Beauvoir, *The Second Sex* (London: Heinemann, 1966), 44, quoted in Ann Levey, "Feminist Philosophy Today," *Philosophy Now*, par. 8, accessed October 8, 2020, http://www.ucalgary.ca.philosophy.nowsite675 .html.

de Beauvoir, Simone. *The Second Sex.* London: Heinemann, 1966. Quoted in Ann Levey, "Feminist Philosophy Today," *Philosophy Now*. Accessed October 8, 2020. http://www.ucalgary.ca.philosophy. nowsite675.html.

• **two or more works by the same author**: After the first entry in the bibliography, use three hyphens to begin subsequent entries of works by the same author (rather than repeat the author's name). Entries for multiple works by the same author are normally arranged alphabetically by title.

Menand, Louis. "Bad Comma: Lynne Truss's Strange Grammar." *The New Yorker,* June 28, 2004. http://www.newyorker.com/critics /books/?040628crbo_books1.

---. *The Metaphysical Club: A Story of Ideas in America.* New York: Knopf, 2002.

• **edited works**: Entries for edited works include the abbreviation *ed.* or *eds.* Note that when *ed.* appears after a title, it means "edited by."

5. Roberto Frega and Steven Levine, eds., *John Dewey's Ethical Theory: The 1932 Ethics* (London: Routledge, 2021), 256.

6. Mary Shelley, *Frankenstein*, 3rd ed., ed. Lorne Macdonald and Kathleen Scherf, Broadview Editions (Peterborough, ON: Broadview Press, 2012), 89.

Frega, Roberto, and Steven Levine, eds. *John Dewey's Ethical Theory: The 1932 Ethics*. London: Routledge, 2021.

Shelley, Mary. *Frankenstein*. 3rd ed. Edited by Lorne Macdonald and Kathleen Scherf. Broadview Editions. Peterborough, ON: Broadview Press, 2012.

• **translated works**: The name of the translator follows the work's title. Notice that, in the first example below, the work's author is unknown; begin with the author's name if it is known.

1. *Beowulf*, trans. R.M. Liuzza, 2nd ed. (Peterborough, ON: Broadview Press, 2012), 91.

2. Franz Kafka, "A Hunger Artist," *The Metamorphosis and Other Stories*, trans. Ian Johnston (Peterborough, ON: Broadview Press, 2015), 112.

Beowulf. Translated by R. M. Liuzza. 2nd ed. Peterborough, ON: Broadview Press, 2012.

Kafka, Franz. "A Hunger Artist." *The Metamorphosis and Other Stories*. Translated by Ian Johnston. Peterborough, ON: Broadview Press, 2015.

• **e-books**: Electronic books come in several formats. The first of the two sample citations below is for a book found online; the second is for a book downloaded onto an e-reader.

4. Mary Roberts Rinehart, *Tish* (1916; Project Gutenberg, 2005), chap. 2, http://www.gutenberg.org/catalog/world/readfile?fk_files=1452441.

5. Lao Tzu, *Tao Te Ching: A Book about the Way and the Power of the Way*, trans. Ursula K. Le Guin (Boston: Shambhala, 2011), verse 12, iBooks.

Lao Tzu. *Tao Te Ching: A Book about the Way and the Power of the Way*. Translated by Ursula K. Le Guin. Boston: Shambhala, 2011. iBooks.

Rinehart, Mary Roberts. *Tish*. 1916. Project Gutenberg, 2005. http://www.gutenberg.org/catalog/world/readfile?fk_files=1452441.

• **magazine articles**: The titles of articles appear in quotation marks. If no authorship is attributed, list the title of the article as the "author" in the footnote, and, if a bibliography entry is deemed necessary, the magazine title may be listed there as "author." Specific page references should be included in notes, but page ranges for magazine articles may be omitted from the bibliography.

2. Ferdinand Mount, "Ruthless and Truthless," *London Review of Books*, May 6, 2021, 7.

3. "The Impact of Green Investors," *Economist*, March 27, 2021, https://www.economist.com/finance-and-economics/2021/03/27/the-impact-of-green-investors.

4. Alec MacGillis, "The Union Battle at Amazon Is Far from Over," *New Yorker*, April 13, 2021, https://www.newyorker.com/news/news-desk/the-union-battle-at-amazon-is-far-from-over.

Economist. "The Impact of Green Investors." March 27, 2021. https://www.economist.com/finance-and-economics/2021/03/27/the-impact-of-green-investors.

MacGillis, Alec. "The Union Battle at Amazon Is Far from Over." *New Yorker*, April 13, 2021. https://www.newyorker.com/news/news-desk/the-union-battle-at-amazon-is-far-from-over.

Mount, Ferdinand. "Ruthless and Truthless." *London Review of Books*, May 6, 2021.

• **newspaper articles**: The basic principles to follow with newspaper articles or editorials are the same as with magazine articles (see above). Give page numbers in the note if your source is a hard copy rather than an electronic version, but indicate section designation alone in the bibliography entry.

1. Konrad Yakabuski, "Many Looking for Meaning in Vice-Presidential Debate," *The Globe and Mail*, October 12, 2012, A3.

2. Emma Graney and Jeffrey Jones, "Big Oil Loses Carbon Emissions Showdown in Landmark Case," *Globe and Mail*, May 26, 2021, https://www.theglobeandmail.com/business/article-canadas-oil-industry-on-watch-after-dutch-court-orders-shell-to-cut/.

Graney, Emma, and Jeffrey Jones. "Big Oil Loses Carbon Emissions Showdown in Landmark Case." *Globe and Mail*, May 26, 2021. https://www.theglobeandmail.com/business/article-canadas-oil-industry-on-watch-after-dutch-court-orders-shell-to-cut/.

Yakabuski, Konrad. "Many Looking for Meaning in Vice-Presidential Debate." *The Globe and Mail*, October 12, 2012, sec. A.

• **journal articles**: The basic principles are the same as with magazine articles, but volume number, and issue number (if the journal is published more than once a year), should be included as well as the date. Give page numbers or e-locator numbers where available. For online journal articles, provide the DOI, if available, rather than the URL.

1. Amy Y. Li, "The Weight of the Metric: Performance Funding and the Retention of Historically Underserved Students," *The Journal of Higher Education* 90, no. 6 (April 2019): 970–71, https://doi.org/10.1080/00221546.2019.1602391.

2. Amanda L. Griffith and Veronica Sovero, "Under Pressure: How Faculty Gender and Contract Uncertainty Impact Students' Grades," *Economics of Education Review* 83 (May 2021): 6, e102126, https://doi.org/10.1016/j.econedurev.2021.102126.

3. Esteban M. Aucejo et al., "The Impact of COVID-19 on Student Experiences and Expectations: Evidence from a Survey," *Journal of Public Economics* 191 (November 2020): 2–3, e104271, https://doi.org/10.1016/j.jpubeco.2020.104271.

Aucejo, Esteban M., Jacob French, Maria Paola Ugalde Araya, and Basil Zafar. "The Impact of COVID-19 On Student Experiences and Expectations: Evidence from a Survey." *Journal of Public Economics* 191 (November 2020): e104271. https://doi.org/10.1016/j.jpubeco.2020.104271.

Griffith, Amanda L., and Veronica Sovero. "Under Pressure: How Faculty Gender and Contract Uncertainty Impact Students' Grades." *Economics of Education Review* 83 (May 2021): e102126. https://doi.org/10.1016/j.econedurev.2021.102126.

Li, Amy Y. "The Weight of the Metric: Performance Funding and the Retention of Historically Underserved Students." *The Journal of Higher Education* 90, no. 6 (April 2019): 965–91. https://doi.org/10.1080/00221546.2019.1602391.

• **films and video recordings**: Include the director's name, the city of production, the production company, and date. Depending on the context, you may wish to add further details (actors, writers, producers) to the author section of the citation. Add the medium of publication if the film is recorded on DVD or videocassette; if it is streamed online, add the air date and URL.

1. *The Birds,* directed by Alfred Hitchcock (1963; Los Angeles: Universal Studios Home Entertainment, 2005), DVD.

2. *Nomadland,* directed by Chloé Zhao, featuring Frances McDormand (Los Angeles: Searchlight Pictures, 2020), on Hulu, https://www.hulu.com/nomadland-movie.

Hitchcock, Alfred, dir. *The Birds.* 1963; Los Angeles: Universal Studios Home Entertainment, 2005. DVD.

Zhao, Chloé, dir. *Nomadland*. Featuring Frances McDormand. Los Angeles: Searchlight Pictures, 2020, on Hulu. https://www.hulu.com/nomadland-movie.

• **television broadcasts**: To cite an episode, start with the title of the show; then give the episode number, broadcast date, and network. Include the names of the relevant contributors. The bibliography entry should be listed under the director's name.

1. *Little Fires Everywhere*, season 1, episode 1, "The Spark," directed by Lynn Shelton, written by Liz Tigelaar, aired March 18, 2020, on Hulu, https://www.hulu.com/series/little-fires-everywhere-bce24897-1a74-48a3-95e8-6cdd530dde4c.

Shelton, Lynn, dir. *Little Fires Everywhere*. Season 1, episode 1, "The Spark." Written by Liz Tigelaar. Aired March 18, 2020, on Hulu. https://www.hulu.com/series/little-fires-everywhere-bce24897-1a74-48a3-95e8-6cdd530dde4c.

• **sound recordings**: Include the original date of recording if it is different from the recording release date, as well as the recording number and medium.

1. Glenn Gould, performance of *Goldberg Variations*, by Johann Sebastian Bach, recorded 1981, CBS MK 37779, 1982, compact disc.

Gould, Glenn. Performance of *Goldberg Variations*. By Johann Sebastian Bach. Recorded 1981. CBS MK 37779, 1982, compact disc.

• **interviews and personal communications**: Notes and bibliography entries begin with the name of the person interviewed. Only interviews that are broadcast, published, or available online appear in the bibliography.

7. Claudia Rankine, "The Art of Poetry No. 102," interview by David L. Ulin, *Paris Review*, no. 219 (Winter 2016), accessed February 20, 2021, https://www.theparisreview.org/interviews/6905/the-art-of-poetry-no-102-claudia-rankine.

8. Patricia Lockwood, "Patricia Lockwood Is a Good Reason to Never Log Off," interview by Gabriella Paiella, *GQ*, February 15, 2021, accessed April 2, 2021, https://www.gq.com/story/patricia-lockwood-book-interview.

9. Willie Nelson, "The Silver-Headed Stranger," interview by Andrew Goldman, *New York Times Magazine*, December 16, 2012, 12.

10. Herbert Rosengarten, telephone interview by author, January 17, 2020.

Lockwood, Patricia. "Patricia Lockwood Is a Good Reason to Never Log Off." Interview by Gabriella Paiella. *GQ*, February 15, 2021. Accessed April 2, 2021. https://www.gq.com/story/patricia-lockwood-book-interview.

Nelson, Willie. "The Silver-Headed Stranger." Interview by Andrew Goldman. *New York Times Magazine*, December 16, 2012, 12.

Rankine, Claudia. "The Art of Poetry No. 102." Interview by David L. Ulin. *Paris Review*, no. 219 (Winter 2016). Accessed February 20, 2021. https://www.theparisreview.org/interviews/6905/the-art-of-poetry-no-102-claudia-rankine.

• **book reviews**: The name of the reviewer (if it has been provided) should come first, as shown below:

1. Brian Leiter and Michael Weisberg, "Do You Only Have a Brain? On Thomas Nagel," review of *Why the Materialist Neo-Darwinian Conception of Nature Is Almost Certainly False*, by Thomas Nagel, *The Nation*, October 22, 2012, http://www.thenation.com/article/170334/do-you-only-have-brain-thomas-nagel.

Leiter, Brian, and Michael Weisberg. "Do You Only Have a Brain? On Thomas Nagel." Review of *Why the Materialist Neo-Darwinian Conception of Nature Is Almost Certainly False*, by Thomas Nagel. *The Nation*, October 22, 2012. http://www.thenation.com/article/170334/do-you-only-have-brain-thomas-nagel.

• **blog posts**: Begin with the author's name, if there is one.

1. Tom Clayton, "York School Crowdfunds for 'Magical' Reading Cottage," *MobyLives* (blog), May 18, 2021, https://www.mhpbooks.com/york-school-crowdfunds-for-magical-reading-cottage/.

Clayton, Tom. "York School Crowdfunds for 'Magical' Reading Cottage." *MobyLives* (blog), May 18, 2021. https://www.mhpbooks.com/york-school-crowdfunds-for-magical-reading-cottage/.

• **websites**: Unless the website title is also that of a book or periodical, do not put the site's title in italics. If possible, indicate when the site was last updated; otherwise, include your date of access.

1. The Camelot Project, University of Rochester, last modified December 21, 2012, http://www.lib.rochester.edu/camelot/cphome.stm.

The Camelot Project. University of Rochester. Last modified December 21, 2012. http://www.lib.rochester.edu/camelot/cphome.stm.

• **online videos**: Include the author or principal performer, length of the video, and date of posting, if available, as well as the medium and its source.

1. Anindya Kundu, "The 'Opportunity Gap' in US Public Education," TED video, January 23, 2020, 5:33, https://www.youtube.com/watch?v=wRG5_-9eE4w.

Kundu, Anindya. "The 'Opportunity Gap' in US Public Education." TED video. January 23, 2020. https://www.youtube.com/watch?v=wRG5_-9eE4w.

• **tweets**: Chicago Style recommends that a tweet be fully transcribed (up to 160 characters). This can happen in your note or in the text of your essay (see the examples below). If you include the tweet and citation information in the body of your essay, you may omit a note. In most cases, you need not include a bibliography entry for a tweet, but if you are citing the tweet more than once, or if it is an extended thread, then you may wish to create an entry. Note that, like all websites that don't have a print counterpart, Twitter is not italicized; note also that time stamps should be included in both the note and bibliography entry.

- On May 17, 2021, Stephen King tweeted about the elusive nature of artistic inspiration: "Good writing is a delight to those who read it and a mystery to those who write it."

1. Stephen King (@StephenKing), "Good writing is a delight to those who read it and a mystery to those who write it," Twitter, May 17, 2021, 9:10 p.m., https://twitter.com/StephenKing/status/1394460364549627906.

King, Stephen (@StephenKing). "Good writing is a delight to those who read it and a mystery to those who write it." Twitter, May 17, 2021, 9:10 p.m. https://twitter.com/StephenKing/status/1394460364549627906.

Chicago Style Sample

A sample of text with citations in Chicago Style appears below. Note that a full sample essay in Chicago Style appears on the adjunct website associated with this book.

Urban renewal is as much a matter of psychology as it is of bricks and mortar. As Paul Goldberger has described, there have been many plans to revitalize Havana.[1] But both that city and the community of Cuban exiles in Florida remain haunted by a sense of absence and separation. As Lourdes Casal reminds us,

> Exile
> is living where there is no house whatever in
> which we were ever children ...[2]

The psychology of outsiders also makes a difference. Part of the reason Americans have not much noticed the dire plight of their fifth-largest city is that it does not "stir the national imagination."[3] Conversely, there has been far more concern over the state of cities such as New Orleans and Quebec City, whose history and architecture excite the romantic imagination. As Nora Phelps has discussed, the past is in itself a key trigger for romantic notions, and it is no doubt inevitable that cities whose history is particularly visible will engender passionate attachments.[4] And as Stephanie Wright and Carole King have detailed

---

1. Paul Goldberger, "Annals of Preservation: Bringing Back Havana," *The New Republic*, January 2004, 54, accessed March 4, 2020, http://www.findarticles.comgoldberg.p65.jn.htm.

2. Lourdes Casal, "Definition," trans. Elizabeth Macklin, *The New Yorker*, January 26, 1998, 79.

3. Witold Rybczynski, "The Fifth City," review of *A Prayer for the City*, by Buzz Bissinger, *New York Review of Books*, February 5, 1998, 13.

4. Nora Phelps, "Pastness and the Foundations of Romanticism," *Romanticism on the Net* 11 (May 2001): par. 14, accessed March 4, 2020, http://users.ox.ac.uk/~scato385/phelpsmws.htm.

in an important case study,[1] almost all French-speaking Quebecers feel their heritage to be bound up with that of Quebec City. (Richard Ford's character Frank Bascombe has suggested that "New Orleans defeats itself" by longing "for a mystery it doesn't have and never will, if it ever did,"[2] but this remains a minority view.)

In addition to the roles history and memory play in shaping our approach to urban renewal, new research also points to the crucial impact of nature experience on psychological health. This has prompted urban designers, city planners, and psychologists to prioritize access to green and blue spaces in their design plans for cities. One important dimension of this emergent research is environmental justice; as one study of Los Angeles's San Fernando Valley concludes, "We find that low-income neighborhoods … have higher traffic volumes, fewer shade trees, and street environments that are less clean and well maintained compared to high-income areas and that similar disparities exist between ethnic minority and white communities."[3] A just vision of urban revitalization would include prioritizing access to natural environments for all members of the community.

---

1. Stephanie Wright and Carole King, *Quebec: A History*, 2 vols. (Montreal: McGill-Queen's University Press, 2012).

2. Richard Ford, *The Sportswriter*, 2nd ed. (New York: Random House, 1995), 48.

3. Alessandro Rigolon, Zeynep Toker, and Nara Gasparian, "Who Has More Walkable Routes to Parks? An Environmental Justice Study of Safe Routes to Parks in Neighborhoods of Los Angeles," *Journal of Urban Affairs* 40, no. 4 (2018): 576, https://doi.org/10.1080/07352166.2017.1360740.

The bibliography relating to the above text would be as follows:

Bibliography

Casal, Lourdes. "Definition." Translated by Elizabeth Macklin. *The New Yorker*, January 26, 1998, 79.

Ford, Richard. *The Sportswriter*. 2nd ed. New York: Random House, 1995.

Goldberger, Paul. "Annals of Preservation: Bringing Back Havana." *The New Republic*, January 2004, 50–62. Accessed March 4, 2020. http://www.findarticles.com.goldberg.p65.jn.htm.

Phelps, Nora. "Pastness and the Foundations of Romanticism." *Romanticism on the Net* 11 (May 2001). Accessed March 4, 2020. http://users.ox.ac.uk/~scat0385/phelpsmws.htm.

Rigolon, Alessandro, Zeynep Toker, and Nara Gasparian. "Who Has More Walkable Routes to Parks? An Environmental Justice Study of Safe Routes to Parks in Neighborhoods of Los Angeles." *Journal of Urban Affairs* 40, no. 4 (2018): 576–91. https://doi.org/10.1080/07352166.2017.1360740.

Rybczynski, Witold. "The Fifth City." Review of *A Prayer for the City*, by Buzz Bissinger. *New York Review of Books*, February 5, 1998, 12–14.

Wright, Stephanie, and Carole King. *Quebec: A History*. 2 vols. Montreal: McGill-Queen's University Press, 2012.

Among the details to notice in this reference system:

- Where two or more works by the same author are included in the bibliography, they are normally arranged alphabetically by title.
- All major words in titles and subtitles are capitalized.
- Date of publication must appear, where known. Provision of access dates for electronic materials is recommended for sources that are likely to change over time.
- Commas are used to separate elements within a footnote, and, in many circumstances, periods separate these same elements in the bibliographic entry.
- When a work has appeared in an edited collection, information on the editors must be included in both the first note and the bibliographic reference.
- First author's first and last names are reversed in the bibliography.
- Translators must be noted both in footnotes and in the bibliography.
- Publisher as well as city of publication should be given.
- Months and publisher names are not abbreviated.
- The day of the month comes after the name of the month.
- Online references should include a publication date, if available, and/or a revision date. You may also include both: "Published June 10, 2019; last modified February 3, 2021." If neither date is available, you may include the date of access: "Accessed March 2, 2022."

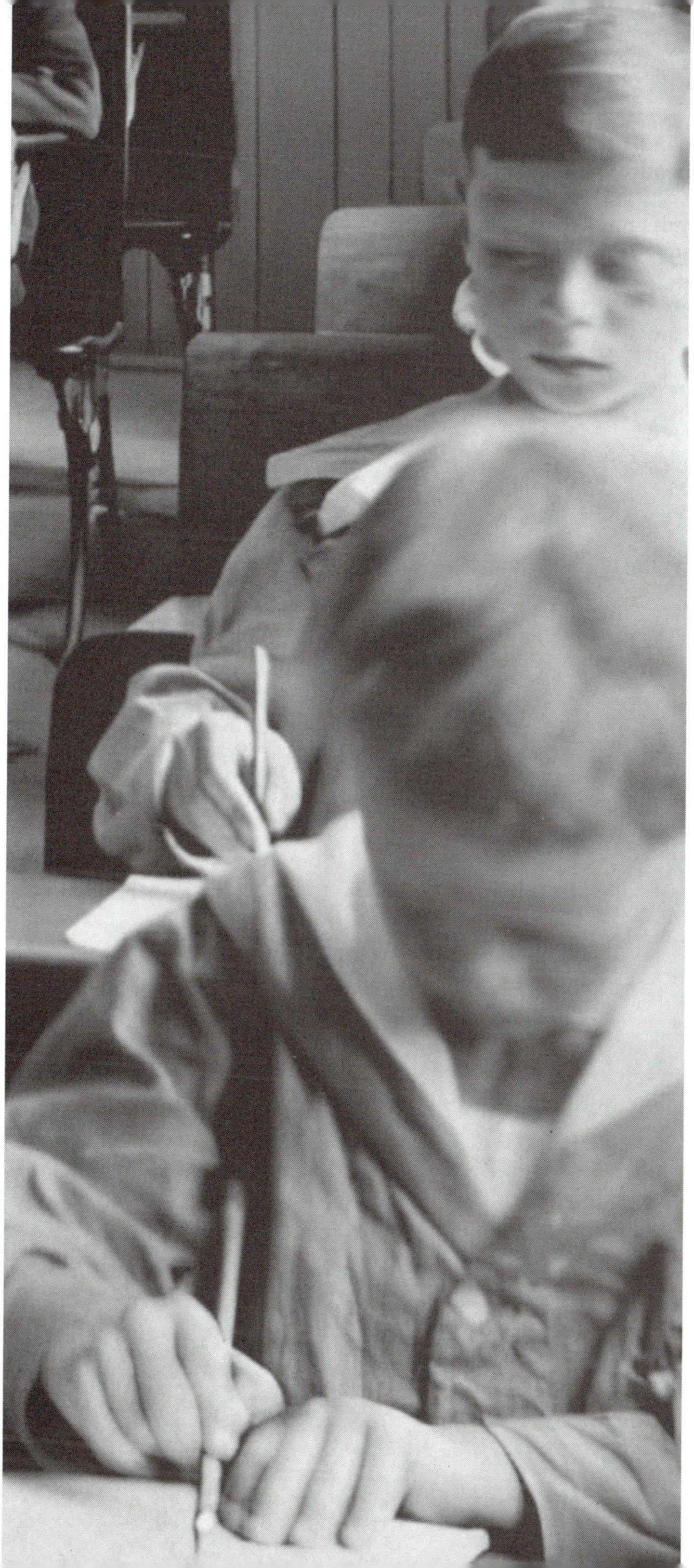

Appendices / Index

APPENDIX 1: *Essay Checklist*

____ Does this piece of writing have a clear purpose? Have I made that purpose clear to the reader? Particularly, have I made this purpose completely clear near the beginning (whether in a formal thesis statement or otherwise)?

____ Is that purpose again made clear near the conclusion?

____ Does the opening paragraph engage the reader's interest?

____ Does the concluding paragraph do more than just reiterate the opening?

____ What audience is this written for? Is the tone suited to the intended audience?

____ If this is an academic paper, have I avoided excessively informal language?

____ If this is an academic or argumentative paper, have I avoided using the first person singular unless it serves a good purpose?

____ If the essay is meant to be argumentative or persuasive, of what am I trying to persuade my audience? Have I made this purpose clear throughout the essay?

____ Does the essay follow a clear path? Are there too many digressions? Is there extraneous material that should be cut, or transferred out of the body of the text and into a note?

____ Is the structure of the argument signalled by the paragraphing? Does the paragraph remain the unit of composition throughout?

____ Does the point I am making remain clear in every paragraph? In every sentence?

____ Does every sentence and paragraph contribute to the point I am making? Does my writing ever tend toward distracting tangents?

____ Is there some variety in sentence structure and length? Have I avoided awkward sentence constructions? And run-on sentences?

____ Are most verbs in the active voice?

____ Do the verbs always agree with the subjects?

____ Have I avoided dangling modifiers (or other dangling constructions)?

____ Do I use concrete and specific language wherever possible?

____ Do I avoid excessive use of jargon or unnecessarily obscure language?

____ Am I careful in my use of qualifiers, avoiding statements that are too bald or extreme, but not qualifying all the strength or interest out of my argument?

____ Is my writing ever wordy? Where could I still trim?

____ Did I revise (from hard copy) and rewrite the essay thoroughly?

____ Did I proofread after I had revised?

____ Have I checked the punctuation carefully throughout?

____ Are conventions in spelling and punctuation (e.g., Canadian spelling, use of the serial comma) used consistently throughout?

____ Have I proofread as well as used a computer spell-check?

____ Have I used the correct system of documentation? Do the references follow this system consistently throughout?

____ Have I given appropriate acknowledgement to all the sources I used? Is there any point at which I might have been guilty of plagiarism by paraphrasing without acknowledgement?

____ Have I double-checked all quotations I've used against their source for accuracy? Am I confident that the quotations and paraphrases used do not misrepresent their authors' views?

____ Does the format (line spacing, margins, notes, etc.) follow the specifications of the style I am using (and/or any format specifications provided by my instructor)?

____ Have I answered all the above questions honestly?

APPENDIX 2: *Correction Key*

abbr	Abbreviation error (425–26)
adj	Adjective used improperly (180–81, 342)
adv	Adverb used improperly (181–82, 342)
agr	Agreement issue with subject & verb (214–16)
amb	Ambiguity (254–59, 293–95)
appr	Appropriateness of language issue (121–70)
awk	Awkward expression or construction (90–107)
cap	Capitalization faulty (421–25)
	Close up
dang	Dangling construction, dangling modifier (254–59)
	Delete
dict	Diction faulty (91–95)
frag	Fragment (incomplete sentence) (196–97, 205–08)
^	Insert
ital	Italics
lc	Lowercase should be used (421–25)
¶	Paragraph: begin a new paragraph here (44–49)
no ¶	Paragraph: do not begin a new paragraph here (44–49)
//	Parallelism faulty or lacking (96–97, 100–01, 297–300)
pass	Passive voice (104–05, 229–31, 538–40)

- **p** Punctuation error (394–411)
  - Apostrophe (or single quotation mark) needed (351–52, 407–09, 417)
  - Comma needed (395–99)
  - Period needed (196–212, 394)
  - Quotation marks needed (409–11)
- **pron** Pronoun reference error (182–84, 285–95)
- **rep** Repetition
- **run-on** Run-on sentence (fused sentence or comma splice) (196–204)
- **ss** Sentence structure faulty
- **sl** Slang or overly informal language (350–53)
- **#** Space should be added
- **sp** Spelling error (427–37)
- **t** Tense of verb wrong (213–27, 259–60, 525–28)
- **tr** Transition faulty or insufficient (210–11, 364–86)
- Transposed elements
- **v** Verb form wrong (213–27)
- **w** Wordiness (230–31, 386–93)

PERMISSIONS ACKNOWLEDGEMENTS

TEXT

Boland, Eavan. "Against Love Poetry," from *Against Love Poetry: Poems* by Eavan Boland. Copyright © 2001 by Eavan Boland. Used by permission of W.W. Norton & Company, Inc.

Oswald, Alice. "Wedding," from *Spacecraft Voyager 1: New and Selected Poems*. Copyright © 1996 by Alice Oswald. Reprinted with the permission of The Permissions Company, Inc., on behalf of Graywolf Press, Minneapolis, MN: www.graywolfpress.org.

IMAGES

Billboard, "The American Way"
Margaret Bourke-White / Masters Collection / © Getty Images

Conservative Party campaign poster. Copyright © the Conservative Party UK. Reprinted with permission.

IMAGES REPRODUCED ON THE DIVIDERS

WRITING PROCESSES

Photographer unknown, *Interior of Bates Hall Library, Boston* (detail), c. 1891. (Library of Congress Photo: LC-USZ62-90719)

WRITING MECHANICS

Fernand Léger, *Discs* (detail), 1918–19. (Los Angeles County Museum of Art)

EAL: FOR THOSE WHOSE NATIVE LANGUAGE IS NOT ENGLISH

Edvard Munch, *Girls on the Bridge* (detail), 1902.

SPECIAL TOPIC: HOW TO BE GOOD WITH WORDS

Andrea del Sarto, *Portrait of a Woman with a Volume of Petrarch* (detail), c. 1528. (Uffizi Gallery)

SPECIAL TOPIC: SEEING AND MEANING

William Brymner, *A Wreath of Flowers* (detail), 1894. (National Gallery of Canada)

WRITING CONTEXTS

Jacopo da Pontormo, *Two Young Scholars* (detail), 1524. (Collezione Vittorio Cini, Venice)

STYLE GUIDES

Irving Ramsey Wiles, *Woman Reading on a Bench / Sunshine and Shadow*, (detail) 1895. (Thyssen-Bornemisza Collection)

APPENDICES AND INDEX

Photographer unknown, Students, Model School, Ottawa, late 1800s (detail). (Library and Archives Canada)

INDEX

Entries in **bold** are to words, not topics.

Appendices / Index

The Authors

Doug Babington was for many years Director of the Writing Centre at Queen's University; he is co-author of *Writing Analytically with Readings* (2012) and also author of a book of bilingual poems, *News from the Recent Quake* (2015).

Corey Frost, an Associate Professor in the English Department at The City University of New Jersey, has published widely on poetry and poetics, orality, and digital pedagogy; his *A Prescription for Zombies: A Critical Approach to English Grammar and Usage* is forthcoming from Broadview Press.

Don LePan's other books include *The Broadview Pocket Glossary of Literary Terms* (2013), *Animals: A Novel* (2010), and *Lucy and Bonbon: A Novel* (2022); he is a general editor of *The Broadview Anthology of British Literature* and Co-Managing Editor of *The Broadview Anthology of American Literature*.

Maureen Okun, for many years a professor in both the English and the Liberal Studies Departments at Vancouver Island University, is the author, co-author, or editor of several books, among them Sir Thomas Malory's *Le Morte Darthur: Selections* (2014).

Nora Ruddock is co-author of *The Broadview Pocket Guide to Citation and Documentation* and co-editor of *The Broadview Anthology of Expository Prose* and of *Popular Culture: A Broadview Topics Reader*.

Karen Weingarten, Associate Chair of the English Department at Queens College, CUNY, is the author of *Abortion in the American Imagination: Before Life and Choice, 1880–1940* (2014); her book *Pregnancy Test* is scheduled for 2023 publication in Bloomsbury's Object Lessons series.

This book is made of paper from well-managed FSC® - certified forests, recycled materials, and other controlled sources.

MIX
Paper from responsible sources
FSC® C103567

PERMANENT

For the seventh edition, *The Broadview Guide to Writing* has been reorganize into three broad sections (writing processes, writing mechanics, and writin contexts). The material on argument has been expanded and revised; two ne sample essays in MLA style have been added; and the material on researchin and writing academic essays has been fully rewritten. Coverage of informal an personal writing is included for the first time.

Comments on the sixth edition:

"*The Broadview Guide* remains the most readable writing guide available—at an price. It's the only writing guide I've ever read for fun. Moreover, it's sensible, and it's complete. The authors assume nothing, but they don't condescend.... The chapter on visual literacy [provides] an interesting group of paintings and photographs along with a set of clear, concrete ways to 'read' them."
Jacky Bolding, University of the Fraser Valley

"The chapter on 'How to Be Good with Words' braves every thorny patch of ethic usage imaginable with clear-eyed candor, a serious and generous sensibility, an refreshing wit.... [Overall,] *The Broadview Guide to Writing* is not only informativ and impressive; it is smart—smartly written and smartly designed."
Dennis Paoli, Co-coordinator, Writing Across the Curriculum, Hunter College, CUNY

"... an excellent choice—a comprehensive writing guide, but also a valuable introduction to communication and critical thinking in today's academic world I will be recommending this text to students at all levels."
Maria DiCenzo, Wilfrid Laurier University

"Even the most useful reference guides are not always, well, shall we say, riveting. A refreshing exception is *The Broadview Guide to Writing*, which is smart, helpful, and even fun to read."
Gerald Graff and Cathy Birkenstein, authors of *They Say / I Say: The Moves That Matter in Academic Writing*

"In a market replete with writing guides, this practical book stands out.... *The Broadview Guide* re-energizes this pedagogical field by providing clear and concise explanations supported by examples."
Anne Quéma, Acadia University

• Extensive treatment of research methods, and of argument • In-depth coverage of ML and other citation styles • Wide-ranging treatment of writing styles in different academ disciplines • Focused coverage of issues specific to thos whose native language is not English • A full chapter o language issues relating to gender, race, class, religio sexual orientation, disability, etc. • Companion websi featuring a wide range of interactive exercises

ISBN 978-1-55481-540-1

9 781554 815401

broadview press
www.broadviewpress.com